Dictionary of Literary Biography

Documentary Series

edited by Matthew J. Bruccoli and Richard Layman (1989)

7 *Modern American Poets: James Dickey, Robert Frost, Marianne Moore,* edited by Karen L. Rood (1989)

8 *The Black Aesthetic Movement,* edited by Jeffrey Louis Decker (1991)

9 *American Writers of the Vietnam War: W. D. Ehrhart, Larry Heinemann, Tim O'Brien, Walter McDonald, John M. Del Vecchio,* edited by Ronald Baughman (1991)

10 *The Bloomsbury Group,* edited by Edward L. Bishop (1992)

11 *American Proletarian Culture: The Twenties and The Thirties,* edited by Jon Christian Suggs (1993)

12 *Southern Women Writers: Flannery O'Connor, Katherine Anne Porter, Eudora Welty,* edited by Mary Ann Wimsatt and Karen L. Rood (1994)

13 *The House of Scribner, 1846-1904,* edited by John Delaney (1996)

14 *Four Women Writers for Children, 1868-1918,* edited by Caroline C. Hunt (1996)

15 *American Expatriate Writers: Paris in the Twenties,* edited by Matthew J. Bruccoli and Robert W. Trogdon (1997)

16 *The House of Scribner, 1905-1930,* edited by John Delaney (1997)

17 *The House of Scribner, 1931-1984,* edited by John Delaney (1998)

18 *British Poets of The Great War: Sassoon, Graves, Owen,* edited by Patrick Quinn (1999)

19 *James Dickey,* edited by Judith S. Baughman (1999)

See also DLB 210, 216, 219, 222

Yearbooks

1980 edited by Karen L. Rood, Jean W. Ross, and Richard Ziegfeld (1981)

1981 edited by Karen L. Rood, Jean W. Ross, and Richard Ziegfeld (1982)

1982 edited by Richard Ziegfeld; associate editors: Jean W. Ross and Lynne C. Zeigler (1983)

1983 edited by Mary Bruccoli and Jean W. Ross; associate editor Richard Ziegfeld (1984)

1984 edited by Jean W. Ross (1985)

1985 edited by Jean W. Ross (1986)

1986 edited by J. M. Brook (1987)
1987 edited by J. M. Brook (1988)
1988 edited by J. M. Brook (1989)
1989 edited by J. M. Brook (1990)
1990 edited by James W. Hipp (1991)
1991 edited by James W. Hipp (1992)
1992 edited by James W. Hipp (1993)
1993 edited by James W. Hipp, contributing editor George Garrett (1994)
1994 edited by James W. Hipp, contributing editor George Garrett (1995)

1995 edited by James W. Hipp, contributing editor George Garrett (1996)

1996 edited by Samuel W. Bruce and L. Kay Webster, contributing editor George Garrett (1997)

1997 edited by Matthew J. Bruccoli and George Garrett, with the assistance of L. Kay Webster (1998)

1998 edited by Matthew J. Bruccoli, contributing editor George Garrett, with the assistance of D. W. Thomas (1999)

Concise Series

Concise Dictionary of American Literary Biography, 7 volumes (1988-1999): *The New Consciousness, 1941-1968; Colonization to the American Renaissance, 1640-1865; Realism, Naturalism, and Local Color, 1865-1917; The Twenties, 1917-1929; The Age of Maturity, 1929-1941; Broadening Views, 1968-1988; Supplement: Modern Writers, 1900-1998.*

Concise Dictionary of British Literary Biography, 8 volumes (1991-1992): *Writers of the Middle Ages and Renaissance Before 1660; Writers of the Restoration and Eighteenth Century, 1660-1789; Writers of the Romantic Period, 1789-1832; Victorian Writers, 1832-1890; Late-Victorian and Edwardian Writers, 1890-1914; Modern Writers, 1914-1945; Writers After World War II, 1945-1960; Contemporary Writers, 1960 to Present.*

Concise Dictionary of World Literary Biography, 20 volumes projected (1999-): *Ancient Greek and Roman Writers; German Writers; African, Carribbean, and Latin-American Writers.*

Dictionary of Literary Biography® • Volume Two Hundred Twenty-Two

H. L. Mencken
A Documentary Volume

Dictionary of Literary Biography® • Volume Two Hundred Twenty-Two

H. L. Mencken
A Documentary Volume

Edited by
Richard J. Schrader
Boston College

A Bruccoli Clark Layman Book
The Gale Group
Detroit • San Francisco • London • Boston • Woodbridge, Conn.

Advisory Board for
DICTIONARY OF LITERARY BIOGRAPHY

Printed in the United States of America

The paper used in this publication meets the minimum requirements
of American National Standard for Information Sciences–Permanence
Paper for Printed Library Materials, ANSI Z39.48-1984. ∞™

ISBN 0-7876-3131-0

10 9 8 7 6 5 4 3 2 1

For Betty Adler and Vincent Fitzpatrick

Contents

Plan of the Series

... Almost the most prodigious asset of a country, and perhaps its most precious possession, is its native literary product—when that product is fine and noble and enduring.

Mark Twain*

The advisory board, the editors, and the publisher of the *Dictionary of Literary Biography* are joined in endorsing Mark Twain's declaration. The literature of a nation provides an inexhaustible resource of permanent worth. We intend to make literature and its creators better understood and more accessible to students and the reading public, while satisfying the standards of teachers and scholars.

To meet these requirements, *literary biography* has been construed in terms of the author's achievement. The most important thing about a writer is his writing. Accordingly, the entries in *DLB* are career biographies, tracing the development of the author's canon and the evolution of his reputation.

The purpose of *DLB* is not only to provide reliable information in a convenient format but also to place the figures in the larger perspective of literary history and to offer appraisals of their accomplishments by qualified scholars.

The publication plan for *DLB* resulted from two years of preparation. The project was proposed to Bruccoli Clark by Frederick G. Ruffner, president of the Gale Research Company, in November 1975. After specimen entries were prepared and typeset, an advisory board was formed to refine the entry format and develop the series rationale. In meetings held during 1976, the publisher, series editors, and advisory board approved the scheme for a comprehensive biographical dictionary of persons who contributed to North American literature. Editorial work on the first volume began in January 1977, and it was published in 1978. In order to make *DLB* more than a reference tool and to compile volumes that individually have claim to status as literary history, it was decided to organize volumes by

From an unpublished section of Mark Twain's autobiography, copyright by the Mark Twain Company

topic, period, or genre. Each of these freestanding volumes provides a biographical-bibliographical guide and overview for a particular area of literature. We are convinced that this organization—as opposed to a single alphabet method—constitutes a valuable innovation in the presentation of reference material. The volume plan necessarily requires many decisions for the placement and treatment of authors who might properly be included in two or three volumes. In some instances a major figure will be included in separate volumes, but with different entries emphasizing the aspect of his career appropriate to each volume. Ernest Hemingway, for example, is represented in *American Writers in Paris, 1920–1939* by an entry focusing on his expatriate apprenticeship; he is also in *American Novelists, 1910–1945* with an entry surveying his entire career, as well as in *American Short-Story Writers, 1910–1945, Second Series* with an entry concentrating on his short stories. Each volume includes a cumulative index of the subject authors and articles. Comprehensive indexes to the entire series are planned.

Since 1981 the series has been further augmented by the *DLB Yearbooks*, which update published entries and add new entries to keep the *DLB* current with contemporary activity. There have also been *DLB Documentary Series* volumes which provide biographical and critical source materials for figures whose work is judged to have particular interest for students. One of these companion volumes is devoted entirely to Tennessee Williams.

We define literature as the *intellectual commerce of a nation:* not merely as belles lettres but as that ample and complex process by which ideas are generated, shaped, and transmitted. *DLB* entries are not limited to "creative writers" but extend to other figures who in their time and in their way influenced the mind of a people. Thus the series encompasses historians, journalists, publishers, book collectors, and screenwriters. By this means readers of *DLB* may be aided to perceive literature not as cult scripture in the keeping of intellectual high priests but firmly positioned at the center of a nation's life.

DLB includes the major writers appropriate to each volume and those standing in the ranks behind them. Scholarly and critical counsel has been sought in deciding which minor figures to include and how full their entries should be. Wherever possible, useful references are made to figures who do not warrant separate entries.

Each *DLB* volume has an expert volume editor responsible for planning the volume, selecting the figures for inclusion, and assigning the entries. Volume editors are also responsible for preparing, where appropriate, appendices surveying the major periodicals and literary and intellectual movements for their volumes, as well as lists of further readings. Work on the series as a whole is coordinated at the Bruccoli Clark Layman editorial center in Columbia, South Carolina, where the editorial staff is responsible for accuracy and utility of the published volumes.

One feature that distinguishes *DLB* is the illustration policy–its concern with the iconography of literature. Just as an author is influenced by his surroundings, so is the reader's understanding of the author enhanced by a knowledge of his environment. Therefore *DLB* volumes include not only drawings, paintings, and photographs of authors, often depicting them at various stages in their careers, but also illustrations of their families and places where they lived. Title pages are regularly reproduced in facsimile along with dust jackets for modern authors. The dust jackets are a special feature of *DLB* because they often document better than anything else the way in which an author's work was perceived in its own time. Specimens of the writers' manuscripts and letters are included when feasible.

Samuel Johnson rightly decreed that "The chief glory of every people arises from its authors." The purpose of the *Dictionary of Literary Biography* is to compile literary history in the surest way available to us–by accurate and comprehensive treatment of the lives and work of those who contributed to it.

The *DLB* Advisory Board

Introduction

The *Dictionary of Literary Biography Documentary Volumes* series is a reference source with a twofold purpose: it makes significant literary documents accessible to students and scholars, as well as to nonacademic readers; and it supplements the regular *DLB* volumes. The *Documentary Volumes* were conceived to provide access to a range of material that many students never have the opportunity to see. By themselves, they serve as a compact archive; used in conjunction with the regular *DLB* volumes, they expand the biographical and critical documents on which the *DLB* essays are based. The *DLB* places authors' lives and works in the perspective of literary history; the *Documentary Volumes* chronicle literary history in the making.

H. L. Mencken, one of America's greatest men of letters, has entries in four regular *DLB* volumes—*DLB 11: American Humorists, 1800–1950; DLB 29: American Newspaper Journalists, 1926–1950; DLB 63: Modern American Critics, 1920–1955;* and *DLB 137: American Magazine Journalists, 1900–1960, Second Series*—because he had several careers. Like his hero Mark Twain, he left a huge body of writings filled with quotable opinions on almost every subject. During the impeachment proceedings of January 1999, for example, former Senator Dale Bumpers of Arkansas, defending President William Jefferson Clinton, said: "It was a breach of his family trust. It is a sex scandal. H. L. Mencken said one time, 'When you hear somebody say, "This is not about money," it's about money.' And when you hear somebody say, 'This is not about sex,' it's about sex." Mencken always gets a laugh.

In his lifetime, when books canvassing the opinions of the famous were popular, Mencken was quoted many dozens of times in areas ranging from political credos to favorite sandwiches. His columns were syndicated nationally, amusing or horrifying the country during a world war and a series of what he considered appalling presidencies. The magazines he edited had the attention of flappers and philosophers. And his books and essays—social, literary, and music criticism; reportage; humor; plays; philological studies; hoaxes; translations and analyses of Friedrich Nietzsche and Henrik Ibsen; memoirs of his youth; a defense of women; treatises on the gods and on right and wrong; and a dictionary of quotations (in which, according to legend, some of the quotations were invented by Mencken)—have made the Sage of Baltimore one of the commanding literary presences of the twentieth century.

In the modern age, only Twain might be considered Mencken's superior as a humorist and satirist. These two careers are treated in this volume as aspects of the many others in which Mencken engaged. He was, perhaps, the best journalist the United States ever produced, and he wrote the most enduring book on American English. As a result, he appears on two of the "top 100" lists for the twentieth century: the reports from the 1925 Scopes "Monkey Trial" came in eighth among the best works of journalism selected in February 1999 by a panel of experts assembled by the New York University School of Journalism, and his *The American Language* (1919; revised and enlarged, 1921 and 1923; corrected, enlarged, and rewritten, 1936; supplemented, 1945, 1948) was ninth among nonfiction books announced in April 1999 by the Modern Library.

Mencken was also a major voice for German Americans in an age when his mother country was being demonized; a local voice, whose journalism dealt with Baltimore's sanitation problems as effectively as it skewered Washington politicians; and a libertarian voice that made him a culture hero in the Jazz Age. These achievements were of a piece with his literary criticism. His editor at the *Baltimore Sun* remarked in a reminiscence that Mencken's primary interest "was not literary expression for its own sake but rather the use of that expression for social criticism. In Europe, where his writings were almost always available in translation, his role was accepted as that of social philosopher, which was precisely what Baltimoreans had known him to be all the time."

Mencken edited two of the most significant magazines of the 1910s and 1920s: *The Smart Set* and *The American Mercury*. His voice dominated in them, but he made sure that those previously undervalued by the literary establishment were also heard. He was the leading promoter of the new writing that came out of the ferment of the previous century as he cleared the way for the realism and naturalism that are taken for granted today. He encouraged women writers and gave unprecedented space to minority authors in an effort to challenge the complacency of the national letters and the national conscience.

Mencken wrote the first book on George Bernard Shaw and the first book in English on Nietzsche. But as a literary critic he is best remembered for championing such writers as Theodore Dreiser and Sinclair Lewis in hundreds of articles, reviews, and dust-jacket blurbs. If he can be said to have a mission, it was to destroy the vestiges of puritanism; to this end he went so far as to arrange his own arrest for vending "obscene" literature so that the matter might be settled in court. He expected that a "civilized minority"–people secure enough in their beliefs to tolerate and even promote dissent–would always support him.

The final chapter of Mencken's multifaceted career is not yet finished. He left behind several works with orders that they be released at various intervals following his death, which occurred in 1956. Other writings of his have been mined from the voluminous papers he bequeathed to the Enoch Pratt Free Library in Baltimore. He is, thus, responsible for a series of posthumous uproars that almost match the fury that greeted what he published during his lifetime. Charges of bigotry have been leveled by a generation that cannot understand how a man born in 1880 could think differently than they and that regards satire as mean-spirited. But Walter Lippmann said in 1926, "He calls you a swine, and an imbecile, and he increases your will to live." Almost thirty years later, on Mencken's seventy-fifth birthday, U.S. Supreme Court justice Felix Frankfurter wrote Mencken: "From that first meeting of ours, at the Ritz in Boston, through those happy parties of ours in Baltimore and the messages since and to this day, you have replenished life for me, by confirming my zest for it and adding yours. I hail thee!" If Mencken has a problem today, it is that many of his detractors have not been educated well enough to understand his comic persona.

Seeking to place Mencken in a tradition, four writers have independently compared him, not to other great journalists, critics, and humorists, but to Walt Whitman. Edmund Wilson tells how, in his comic lists, Mencken "makes his poetry of the democratic life which absorbs and infuriates him," creating a sardonic panorama that is as much a symptom of the times as Whitman's enumerations were typical of the more optimistic early republic. Carl Van Doren, making a similar point, notes that Mencken sees what Whitman often overlooks, such as the "herd-like conventionality" that to the poet meant "noble cohesiveness." Robert E. Spiller finds the lone wolf howling in Mencken's great *Prejudices* series (1919–1927) equal in "historical picturesqueness" to Whitman's lone eagle. Spiller compares

The American Language (1919), with its three revised and enlarged editions (1921, 1923, 1936) and two supplements (1945, 1948) to Whitman's *Leaves of Grass* (1855; revised and enlarged, 1856, 1860–1861, 1867, 1871, 1881–1882, 1891–1892) in that it "grew by accretion and revision more in the manner of a living organism than of a card index." And Mencken's friend, the humorist H. Allen Smith, excused the contradictions in Mencken's life and work by quoting the great-souled poet: "Do I contradict myself? Very well, then, I contradict myself; (I am large–I contain multitudes)." Whitman, like Mencken, had several careers (including journalism), a similarity that made both men penetrating observers of the American scene. Mencken's lifework may be the best *summa critica* of the first half of the twentieth century, and its reception in the second half and beyond is writing another kind of commentary on the times.

H. L. Mencken: A Documentary Volume assembles, in separate chapters, documents related to Mencken's most notable careers: man of letters, journalist, historian of language, libertarian pundit, magazine editor, and antipuritan literary critic. His lengthy posthumous career, in which he is still "stirring up the animals," is dealt with in the final chapter. Various kinds of materials have been gathered, some of them previously unpublished and most not easily accessible to the general reader. Writings by Mencken both exemplify and chronicle his interests; special effort was made to incorporate as many theoretical statements, such as interviews and manifestos, as possible. Writings by others throw additional light on his work and document its reception and influence. Handwritten and typed documents are printed verbatim, including errors; in previously published documents silent corrections have been made of obvious typographical errors. Ellipses within brackets indicate excisions made by the editor of this volume; ellipses not enclosed in brackets are reproduced from the original documents. Similarly, insertions by the editor of this volume are in brackets and italics (such insertions have been kept to the barest minimum needed for understanding the texts); bracketed material not in italics is reproduced from the originals. Some of the illustrations are typescripts in which one can see Mencken at work; others illuminate or extend the text; many show the commercial side of his publishing endeavors, particularly in connection with Alfred A. Knopf; and not a few give a visual impression of the "carnival of buncombe" he satirized: war hysteria, the Scopes "Monkey Trial," political conventions, book banning, and the Ku Klux Klan. The list could be extended almost indefinitely, and no one but Mencken was up to the task.

–Richard J. Schrader

Acknowledgments

This book was produced by Bruccoli Clark Layman, Inc. Karen L. Rood is senior editor for the *Dictionary of Literary Biography* series. Philip B. Dematteis was the in-house editor.

Production manager is Philip B. Dematteis.

Administrative support was provided by Ann M. Cheschi, Dawnca T. Williams, and Mary A. Womble.

Accountant is Kathy Weston. Accounting assistant is Angi Pleasant.

Copyediting supervisor is Phyllis A. Avant. Senior copyeditor is Thom Harman. The copyediting staff includes Brenda Carol Blanton, James Denton, Worthy B. Evans, Melissa D. Hinton, William Tobias Mathes, and Jennifer S. Reid. Freelance copyeditor is Rebecca Mayo.

Editorial associates are Margo Dowling and Richard K. Galloway.

Layout and graphics supervisor is Janet E. Hill. Graphics staff includes Karla Corley Brown and Zoe R. Cook.

Office manager is Kathy Lawler Merlette.

Photography editors are Charles Mims, Scott Nemzek, and Paul Talbot. Digital photographic copy work was performed by Joseph M. Bruccoli and Zoe R. Cook.

SGML supervisor is Cory McNair. The SGML staff includes Tim Bedford, Linda Drake, Frank Graham, and Alex Snead.

Systems manager is Marie L. Parker.

Typesetting supervisor is Kathleen M. Flanagan. The typesetting staff includes Kimberly Kelly, Mark J. McEwan, Patricia Flanagan Salisbury, and Alison Smith. Freelance typesetter is Delores Plastow.

Walter W. Ross did library research. He was assisted by Steven Gross and the following librarians at the Thomas Cooper Library of the University of South Carolina: circulation department head Tucker Taylor; reference department head Virginia W. Weathers; Brette Barclay, Marilee Birchfield, Paul Cammarata, Gary Geer, Michael Macan, Tom Marcil, and Sharon Verba, reference librarians; interlibrary loan department head John Brunswick; and Robert Arndt, Jo Cottingham, Hayden Battle, Marna Hostetler, Nelson Rivera, Marieum McClary, and Erika Peake, interlibrary loan staff.

The editor is, once more, indebted to George H. Thompson and Jack R. Sanders, who generously shared their knowledge and their collections. His debts at Boston College are primarily to two technical wizards, Stephen Vedder of the Audiovisual Department and Professor Michael J. Connolly, Coordinator of the Faculty Microcomputer Resource Center.

In Baltimore he was granted access to the incomparable Mencken Room at the Enoch Pratt Free Library. Thanks are owed first of all to Averil J. Kadis, who handles rights and permissions for the Pratt. And he also gladly acknowledges the help of the persons to whom this book is dedicated. The works that the late Betty Adler created in the library may fairly be considered the basis of all Mencken scholarship. The works of the present curator of the H. L. Mencken Collection, Vincent Fitzpatrick, are equally distinguished. His unparalleled knowledge of the archive, not to mention his unfailing kindness and patience, have been recognized time and again by Mencken scholars.

The most recent presidents of the Mencken Society, Arthur J. Gutman and Ray Stevens, represent an ideal audience. The editor is grateful for their help and encouragement.

Judith S. Baughman, a veteran of this series, advised the editor at crucial times in the making of the book. The editor incurred a special debt to three men at Bruccoli Clark Layman: Philip B. Dematteis and Paul Talbot provided expert care in the editorial process, and Matthew J. Bruccoli oversaw the editor's labors from beginning to end.

Permissions

Previously unpublished H. L. Mencken material in the Enoch Pratt Free Library and the collections of George H. Thompson and Richard J. Schrader, together with Mencken's letters, *American Mercury* and *Smart Set* articles, an inscription and broadside at The Harry Ransom Humanities Research Center at the University of Texas at Austin, the speech on editorials of 16 April 1937, and the 1948 Library of Congress interview are published by permission of the Enoch Pratt Free Library in accordance with the terms of the will of H. L. Mencken.

The following have granted permissions to publish texts whose copyright they control:

Trustees of the Joseph Conrad Estate: Conrad letter of 11 November 1917.

The Dreiser Trust and the Trustees of the University of Pennsylvania: Theodore Dreiser letters of 24 August 1925 and 16 June 1939.

Harold Matson Co., Inc.: excerpts from *Life in a Putty Knife Factory,* © 1943, 1971 by the Estate of H. Allen Smith; excerpts from *A Short History of Fingers,* © 1963 by H. Allen Smith, 1991 by the Estate of H. Allen Smith.

The following property-rights holders have granted permission to quote from material in their possession: F. Scott Fitzgerald Papers and H. L. Mencken Collection, Princeton University Library; Theodore Dreiser Papers, Rare Book and Manuscript Library, University of Pennsylvania; H. L. Mencken Collection (#6253), Clifton Waller Barrett Library, Special Collections Department, University of Virginia Library; H. L. Mencken Papers, Manuscripts and Archives Division, The New York Public Library, Astor, Lenox and Tilden Foundations; The Lilly Library, Indiana University, Bloomington, Indiana; The Enoch Pratt Free Library, Baltimore.

The following publisher has granted permission to publish material by H. L. Mencken: Alfred A. Knopf, a Division of Random House, Inc.: excerpts from *Prejudices: Fifth Series* (© 1926 by Alfred A. Knopf Inc., renewed 1954 by H. L. Mencken); excerpts from *Prejudices: Sixth Series* (© 1927 by Alfred A. Knopf Inc., renewed 1955 by H. L. Mencken); excerpts from *Newspaper Days* (© 1941, renewed 1969 by August Mencken and Mercantile Safe Deposit and Trust Co.); excerpts from *My Life as Author and Editor* (© 1993 by Alfred A. Knopf Inc.).

The following periodicals have granted permission to publish material by H. L. Mencken: *Baltimore Sun:* "Darrow's Eloquent Appeal"; "Law and Freedom"; "Al and the Pastors"; "Sound and Fury"; "The More Abundant Dialectic"; "Three Long Years"; "Help for the Jews"; "Mencken Calls Tennis Order Silly." *Chicago Tribune:* "Two Wasted Lives" (© by Chicago Tribune Company. All rights reserved. Used with permission).

The following publishers have granted permissions to publish material about H. L. Mencken: HarperCollins Publishers, Inc.: excerpts from Richard Wright, *Black Boy,* Chapter XIII (© 1937, 1942, 1944, 1945 by Richard Wright; renewed 1973 by Ellen Wright). Simon & Schuster: letter of Harrison Hale Schaff, in Isaac Goldberg, *The Man Mencken: A Biographical and Critical Survey* (© 1925 by Isaac Goldberg).

The following material about H. L. Mencken is reprinted in whole or in part by permission of the authors (*) or the periodicals in which it first appeared: *Baltimore Sun:* Hamilton Owens, "H. L.'s Pungent Pen a Challenge to Orthodoxy"; John C. Schmidt, "The Library's Mencken Room"; Marjorie Mathis, "With Rites 'Rich in Irony,' Pratt Opens Mencken Room." *Bulletin of the New York Public Library:* Anonymous, "A Scout for the Scholars: H. L. Mencken." *Catholic World* (Paulist Press): Theodore Maynard, "Mencken Leaves 'The American Mercury'" (© 1934). *Christian Century:* Anonymous, "Mr. Mencken Leaves the Mercury" (© 1933 Christian Century Foundation. Reprinted by permission from the 18 October 1933 issue of *The Christian Century*). *Christian Science Monitor:* *Merle Rubin, "Baltimore's Complacent Iconoclast."

Chronicles: *Chilton Williamson Jr., review of *Thirty-five Years of Newspaper Work,* by H. L. Mencken. *Current History* (successor to *Forum*): Irving Babbitt, "The Critic and American Life." *Editor & Publisher:* Stephen J. Monchak, "H. L. Mencken Rides Again" (© 1938 ASM Communications, Inc.). *Esquire:* Bynum Shaw, "Scopes Reviews the Monkey Trial" (© Hearst Communications, Inc. *Esquire* is a trademark of Hearst Magazines Property, Inc. All rights reserved). *Menckeniana: A Quarterly Review:* Alistair Cooke, Mencken Centennial Banquet Speech; Alf Landon, "HLM and AML: The 1936 Campaign"; Raven I. McDavid Jr., "The Impact of Mencken on American Linguistics"; Theodore R. McKeldin, "Baltimore, My Baltimore"; William D. Schaefer, Proclamation Designating September 7–13,

1980, as "H. L. Mencken Week" in Baltimore. *The New Republic:* Edmund Wilson, "Talking United States"; *Baron Wormser, "A Satirist." *New York:* Linda Hall, "Mencken Unearthed." *The New York Times:* Julian P. Boyd, "Prejudices According to Mencken" (© 1956 by The New York Times Co.); George Gent, "Mencken's Letters Displayed Today" (© 1971 by The New York Times Co.); Russell Baker, "Prejudices Without the Mask" (© 1989 by The New York Times Co.); Terry Teachout, "Mencken Unsealed" (© 1993 by The New York Times Co.) *The New York Times Book Review:* *William Manchester, Letter to the Editor. *Southwest Review* (successor to *The Reviewer*): Gerald Johnson, "The Congo, Mr. Mencken." *The Washington Post:* *Jonathan Yardley, "Mencken's Unsurprising Prejudices."

Dictionary of Literary Biography® • Volume Two Hundred Twenty-Two

H. L. Mencken
A Documentary Volume

H. L. Mencken (photograph by Bachrach)

Dictionary of Literary Biography:
A Documentary Volume

Chronology

1880

12 September   Henry Louis Mencken is born at 380 West Lexington Street, Baltimore, the first child of August and Anna Abhau Mencken.

1881   The Mencken family moves to another rented house, on Russell Street in Baltimore.

1883

October   August Mencken purchases a house at 1524 Hollins Street, Baltimore.

1896

23 June   Mencken graduates valedictorian from the Baltimore Polytechnic Institute (a high school) and enters the family cigar business.

Summer   Mencken's first publication, "Ode to the Pennant on the Centerfield Pole," appears in the *Baltimore American.*

1899

13 January   Mencken's father dies, after which Mencken begins his journalistic career as a reporter with the *Baltimore Morning Herald.*

1903

6 June   Mencken's first book, *Ventures into Verse,* is published.

October   Mencken becomes city editor of the *Morning Herald.*

1904

    The Saturday Night Club is founded.

February   Mencken covers the Baltimore Fire.

June–July   Mencken reports on his first political conventions.

1905

December   Mencken's *George Bernard Shaw: His Plays* is published.

1906

June   Mencken joins the *Baltimore Evening News*.

July   Mencken joins the *Baltimore Sunday Sun*.

1908

January   Mencken's *The Philosophy of Friedrich Nietzsche* is published.

May   Mencken meets George Jean Nathan.

Spring
or Summer   Mencken meets Theodore Dreiser.

November   Mencken begins reviewing books for *The Smart Set*.

1909

February
or March   Mencken's translations of Henrik Ibsen's *A Doll's House* and *Little Eyolf* are published.

1910

7 February   Mencken's *The Gist of Nietzsche* is published.

19 March   *Men versus the Man: A Correspondence between Robert Rives La Monte, Socialist, and H. L. Mencken, Individualist,* is published.

April   Mencken helps found the *Baltimore Evening Sun* and becomes associate editor.

29 April   Dr. Leonard K. Hirshberg's *What You Ought to Know about Your Baby,* largely ghostwritten by Mencken, is published.

1911

8 May   Mencken's first "Free Lance" column appears in the *Evening Sun*.

1912

December?   Mencken's *The Artist: A Drama without Words* is published.

1914

29 May   *Europe after 8:15,* by Mencken, Nathan, and Willard Huntington Wright, is published.

September   Mencken becomes co-editor of *The Smart Set* with Nathan.

1915

23 October   The final "Free Lance" column appears.

1916

Summer   Mencken organizes the defense of Theodore Dreiser's *The "Genius."*

22 September   Mencken's *A Little Book in C Major* is published.

17 November   Mencken's *A Book of Burlesques* is published.

December   Mencken travels to Germany as a war correspondent.

1917

March   Mencken returns to Baltimore and ceases writing for the *Sunpapers*.

June   Mencken begins writing for the *New York Evening Mail*, continuing to do so until July 1918.

September   *Pistols for Two,* by Mencken and Nathan, is published.

8 October   *A Book of Prefaces,* the first of Mencken's books published by Alfred A. Knopf, appears.

1918

1 April   Mencken's *Damn! A Book of Calumny* is published by Philip Goodman.

17 September   Goodman publishes Mencken's *In Defense of Women.*

1919

14 March   Knopf publishes the first edition of Mencken's *The American Language.*

20 September   Knopf publishes Mencken's *Prejudices: First Series.*

1920

25 January   Knopf publishes *Heliogabalus: A Buffoonery in Three Acts,* by Mencken and Nathan.

6 February   Knopf publishes *The American Credo,* by Mencken and Nathan.

9 February   Mencken resumes work for the *Sunpapers* with his first "Monday Article" in the *Evening Sun.*

18 February   Knopf publishes Mencken's translation of Nietzsche's *The Antichrist.*

27 October   Knopf publishes *Prejudices: Second Series.*

1921

March   Mencken becomes a contributing editor of *The Nation.*

December   Knopf publishes the second edition of *The American Language.*

1922

6 October   Knopf publishes *Prejudices: Third Series.*

1923

February   Knopf publishes the third edition of *The American Language.*

December   The last issue of *The Smart Set* edited by Mencken and Nathan appears.

1924

January   The first issue of *The American Mercury,* co-edited by Mencken and Nathan, is published by Knopf.

24 October   Knopf publishes *Prejudices: Fourth Series.*

9 November   Mencken begins writing columns for the *Chicago Tribune.*

1925

July	Mencken covers the Scopes "Monkey Trial" in Dayton, Tennessee.
August	Mencken becomes sole editor of *The American Mercury*.
October	Knopf publishes *Americana 1925*, edited by Mencken.
13 December	Mencken's mother dies.

1926

5 April	Mencken is arrested on the Boston Common for selling copies of a banned issue of *The American Mercury*.
1 October	Knopf publishes *Americana 1926*, edited by Mencken.
20 October	Knopf publishes Mencken's *Notes on Democracy*.
12 November	Knopf publishes *Prejudices: Fifth Series*.

1927

21 October	Knopf publishes *Prejudices: Sixth Series*.

1928

20 January	Knopf publishes *Menckeniana: A Schimpflexikon*, edited by Mencken and Sara Powell Haardt.
29 January	Mencken's final *Chicago Tribune* article appears.

1930

14 March	Knopf publishes Mencken's *Treatise on the Gods*.
27 August	Mencken and Haardt are married and take up residence at 704 Cathedral Street, Baltimore.

1932

1 September	Knopf publishes Mencken's *Making a President: A Footnote to the Saga of Democracy*.

1933

December	The last issue of *The American Mercury* edited by Mencken appears.

1934

5 April	Knopf publishes Mencken's *Treatise on Right and Wrong*.
12 December	Mencken's final article for *The Nation* appears.

1935

31 May	Sara Haardt Mencken dies.

1936

March	Mencken returns to 1524 Hollins Street, where he resides for the rest of his life.
April	Knopf publishes the fourth edition of *The American Language*.

1937

3 May	Knopf publishes *The Sunpapers of Baltimore, 1837–1937,* by Mencken, Gerald W. Johnson, Frank R. Kent, and Hamilton Owens.

1938

31 January	Mencken's final "Monday Article" appears; he edits the *Evening Sun* from January to May.

1940

22 January	Knopf publishes Mencken's *Happy Days, 1880–1892.*

1941

February	Mencken ends his writing career in the *Sunpapers* but remains on the payroll.
20 October	Knopf publishes Mencken's *Newspaper Days, 1899–1906.*

1942

20 April	Knopf publishes *A New Dictionary of Quotations on Historical Principles from Ancient and Modern Sources,* edited by Mencken.

1943

1 March	Knopf publishes Mencken's *Heathen Days, 1890–1936.*

1945

20 August	Knopf publishes *Supplement I* to *The American Language.*

1946

18 October	Knopf publishes Mencken's *Christmas Story.*

1948

12 March	Knopf publishes *Supplement II* to *The American Language.*
June–July	Mencken resumes writing for the *Sunpapers,* covering the national political-party conventions.
1 August–9 November	Mencken writes occasional articles for the *Sun.*
23 November	A stroke leaves Mencken permanently unable to read or write.

1949

1 June	Knopf publishes *A Mencken Chrestomathy.*

1950

December	The Saturday Night Club is disbanded.

1956

29 January   Mencken dies of a heart attack at his home.

17 April   The Mencken Room is opened at the Enoch Pratt Free Library, Baltimore.

18 April   Knopf publishes *Minority Report: H. L. Mencken's Notebooks.*

1971

29 January   Mencken's correspondence held by the New York Public Library is unsealed.

1976

March   The Mencken Society is founded.

1988

25 March   *The Editor, the Bluenose, and the Prostitute: H. L. Mencken's History of the "Hatrack" Censorship Case,* edited by Carl Bode, is published.

1989

29 November   Knopf publishes *The Diary of H. L. Mencken,* edited by Charles A. Fecher.

1993

4 January   Knopf publishes Mencken's *My Life as Author and Editor,* edited by Jonathan Yardley.

1994

22 August   *Thirty-five Years of Newspaper Work: A Memoir by H. L. Mencken,* edited by Fred Hobson, Vincent Fitzpatrick, and Bradford Jacobs, is published.

1995

30 January   Knopf publishes *A Second Mencken Chrestomathy, Selected, Revised, and Annotated by the Author,* edited by Terry Teachout.

1996

21 September   *Do You Remember? The Whimsical Letters of H. L. Mencken and Philip Goodman,* edited by Jack Sanders, is published.

Prologue: Man of Letters

In Prejudices: Fifth Series *(1926) H. L. Mencken notes that there is still a vacancy in the position of national man of letters, at least according to a tradition whose representatives he generally attacked. Though not likely to "go down the bay on a revenue-cutter" to serve as official greeter, he had by then assumed the role of our leading critic and commentator. Like William Dean Howells's friend Mark Twain, he also partly filled the role of national funny man (a "national misfortune," according to Matthew Arnold), whose opinion on practically anything was sought because it made good copy. The writings of Mencken and Twain still serve that purpose (excerpt from "Want Ad," in* Prejudices: Fifth Series, *pp. 190–192).*

The death of William Dean Howells in 1920 brought to an end a decorous and orderly era in American letters, and issued in a sort of anarchy. One may best describe the change, perhaps, by throwing it into dramatic form. Suppose Joseph Conrad and Anatole France were still alive and on their way to the United States on a lecture tour, or to study Prohibition or sex hygiene, or to pay their respects to Henry Ford. Suppose they were to arrive in New York at 2 P. M. to-day. Who would go down the bay on a revenue-cutter to meet them—that is, who in addition to the newspaper reporters and baggage-searchers—who to represent American Literature? I can't think of a single fit candidate. So long as Howells kept to his legs he was chosen almost automatically for all such jobs, for he was the dean of the national letters, and acknowledged to be such by everyone. Moreover, he had experience at the work and a natural gift for it. He looked well in funeral garments. He had a noble and ancient head. He made a neat and caressing speech. He understood etiquette. And before he came to his growth, stretching back into the past, there was a long line precisely like him—Mark Twain, General Lew Wallace, James Russell Lowell, Edmund Clarence Stedman, Richard Watson Gilder, Bryant, Emerson, Irving, Cooper, and so on back to the dark abysm of time.

Such men performed a useful and highly onerous function. They represented letters in all public and official ways. When there was a grand celebration at one of the older universities they were present in their robes, freely visible to the lowliest sophomore. When there

was a great banquet, they sat between generals in the Army and members of the firm of J. P. Morgan & Company. When there was a solemn petition or protest to sign—against fiat money, the massacres in Armenia, municipal corruption, or the lack of international copyright—they signed in fine round hands, not for themselves alone, but for the whole fraternity of American literati. Most important of all, when a literary whale from foreign parts was sighted off Fire Island, they jumped into their frock coats, clapped on their plug-hats and made the damp, windy trip through the Narrows on the revenue-cutter, to give the visitor welcome in the name of the eminent living and the illustrious dead. It was by such men that Dickens was greeted, and Thackeray, and Herbert Spencer, and Max O'Rell, and Blasco Ibáñez, and Matthew Arnold, and James M. Barrie, and Kipling, and (until they found his bootleg wife under his bed) Maxim Gorky. I name the names at random. No worthy visitor was overlooked. Always there was the stately committee on the revenue-cutter, always there was the series of polite speeches, and always there was the general feeling that the right thing had been done in the right way—that American literature had been represented in a tasteful and resounding manner.

Who is to represent it to-day? [. . .]

As his review of Howells's book on Twain reveals, Mencken looked on Howells as a representative of the old order, while he saw Twain as perennial (review of William Dean Howells, My Mark Twain, *Smart Set [January 1911]: 166–167).*

The name of "MY MARK TWAIN," by William Dean Howells (*Harper's,* $1.40), is well chosen, for the book is less a record of events than an attempt at a personal interpretation. The Mark Twain that we see in it is a Mark Twain whose gaunt Himalayan outlines are discerned but hazily through a pink fog of Howells. There is an evident effort to palliate, to tone down, to apologize. The poor fellow, of course, was charming, and there was a lot of merit in some of the things he wrote—but what a weakness he had for thinking aloud! What oaths in his speech! What awful cigars he smoked! How barbarous his contempt for the strict sonata form! It seems incredible,

9

William Dean Howells and Samuel L. Clemens (Mark Twain) in 1909. Mencken reviewed Howells's My Mark Twain *in* The Smart Set *in 1911.*

Edmund Wilson wrote an essay on Mencken for The New Republic *during Mencken's ascendancy as a literary and social critic. A representative of the new generation of intellectuals and on his way to becoming one of the nation's leading men of letters, Wilson perceptively defined Mencken's public role as "the civilized consciousness of modern America" and heard in his voice a counterpart to that of Walt Whitman ("H. L. Mencken," New Republic [1 June 1921]: 10–13).*

I

A man has withdrawn from the tumult of American life into the seclusion of a house in Baltimore. He is unmarried and has surrounded himself with three thousand books. From this point of vantage he watches the twentieth century with detached and ironic dismay. A not ungenial materialist, he reflects that all human activities are, after all, mainly physical in origin: inspiration is a function of metabolism; death is an acidosis; love is a biological phenomenon; idealism is insanity. But the body is capable of much enjoyment; why worry about its obvious supremacy? As long as there is Chicken à la Maryland and plenty of liquor from the boot-leggers, as long as it is possible to read Conrad and hear Bach and Beethoven occasionally, why should a man of aristocratic temperament be particularly disturbed about anything? Let the capitalist exploit the wage-slave and the wage-slave blow up the capitalist; let political charlatans and scoundrels pick the pockets of the Republic; let the women run the men to ground and the men break their hearts for the women; let the people go off to the wars and destroy each other by the billion. They can never rob Mencken of his sleep nor spoil a single dinner for him. Outside, it is all a question of Christianity and democracy, but Mencken does not believe in either, so why should he take part in the brawl? What has he to do with the mob except to be diverted by its idiocy? He may occasionally attend a political convention to gratify a "taste for the obscene" or entertain his speculative mind by predicting the next catastrophe, but, on the whole, the prodigious din and activity and confusion of the nation roars along without touching him particularly; it is all to him "but as the sound of lyres and flutes." . . .

Something like this is the comic portrait which Mencken has painted of himself; he has even pretended that it is the character in which he prefers to be accepted. But there is, behind this comic mask, a critic, an evangelist and an artist; there is a mind of extraordinary vigor and a temperament of extraordinary interest, and neither of these has ever yet been examined as seriously as it should have been. Mencken has been left far too much to the rhapsodies of his disciples and the haughty sneers of his opponents. Indeed, he has

indeed, that two men so unlike as Clemens and Howells should have found common material for a friendship lasting forty-four years. The one derived from Rabelais, Chaucer, the Elizabethans and Benvenuto Cellini—buccaneers of the literary high seas, loud laughers, law breakers, giants of an elder day; the other came down from Jane Austen, Washington Irving and Hannah More. The one wrote English as Michelangelo hacked marble, broadly, brutally, magnificently; the other was a maker of pretty waxen groups. The one was utterly unconscious of the means whereby he achieved his staggering effects; the other was the most toilsome, fastidious and self-conscious of craftsmen. Read the book. It will amuse you; better still, it will instruct you. If you get nothing else out of it, you will at least get some notion of the abyssmal difference between the straightforward, clangorous English of Clemens and the simpering, coquettish, overcorseted English of the later Howells. [. . .]

assumed such importance as an influence in American thought that it is high time some one subjected him to a drastic full-length analysis. The present writer has only space for the briefest of suggestions.

II

The striking things about Mencken's mind are its ruthlessness and its rigidity. It has all the courage in the world in a country where courage is rare. He has even had the fearlessness to avoid the respectable and the wholesome, those two devils which so often betray in the end even the most intelligent of Americans. He fought outspokenly against optimism, Puritanism and democratic ineptitude, at a time when they had but few foes. It is well to remember, now that these qualities have become stock reproaches among the intelligentsia, that it was Mencken who began the crusade against them at a lonely and disregarded post and that we owe to him much of the disfavor into which they have recently fallen,–and also that it was Mencken who first championed the kind of American literary activity of which we have now become proudest. But the activity of his mind is curiously cramped by its extreme inflexibility. In the first place, as a critic, he is not what is called "sympathetic." His criticisms deal but little with people from their own point of view: he simply brings the other man's statements and reactions to the bar of his own dogma and, having judged them by that measure, proceeds to accept or reject them. Though one of the fairest of critics, he is one of the least pliant.

In the second place, in spite of his scepticism and his frequent exhortations to hold one's opinions lightly, he himself has been conspicuous for seizing upon simple dogmas and sticking to them with fierce tenacity. When he is arguing his case against democracy or Christianity, he reminds one rather of Bishop Manning or Dr. Straton than of Renan or Anatole France. The true sceptics like Renan or France see both the truth and weakness of every case; they put themselves in the place of people who believe differently from themselves and finally come to sympathize with them,–almost, to accept their point of view. But Mencken, once having got his teeth into an idea, can never be induced to drop it, and will only shake his head and growl when somebody tries to tempt him with something else.

Thus, in 1908, when he published his admirable book on Nietzsche, he had reached a certain set of conclusions upon society and ethics. Humanity, he had come to believe, is divided into two classes: the masters and the slaves. The masters are able and courageous men who do whatever they like and are not restrained by any scruples save those that promote their own interest; the slaves are a race of wretched underlings, stupid,

"The Baltimore Anti-Christ": caricature of Mencken by Stephen Longstreet (Arlyn Bruccoli Collection)

superstitious and untrustworthy, who have no rights and no raison d'être except to be exploited by the masters. To talk of equality and fraternity is the most fatuous of nonsense: there is as much difference in kind between the masters and the slaves as there is between men and animals.

Therefore, Christianity is false because it asserts that all souls are worth saving and democracy is a mistake because it emancipates the slaves and tries to make them the masters. It is absurd to try to correct the evolutionary process which would allow the fittest to survive and the weaklings and fools to go under. "I am," Mr. Mencken has said, "against the under dog every time." But things are getting more and more democratic and consequently worse and worse. What we need is an enlightened aristocracy to take charge of society. But there has never been any such aristocracy and we are certainly not going to produce one. In the meantime, one can but curse the mob and die at one's post.

I have not space here to criticize these views—to ask, for instance, when he says he thinks the strong should be allowed to survive at the expense of the weak, whether he means the strong like Jack Johnson or the strong like Nietzsche and Beethoven. I must assume

Mencken wearing suspenders given to him by the actor Rudolph Valentino; painting by Nikol Schattenstein, 1927 (courtesy of the Enoch Pratt Free Library)

He has taken up a position in which it is impossible that any development should please him. He detests the present state of affairs, but he disbelieves in liberalism and radicalism, and any change in their directions would presumably only make him detest the world more. He really hates repression and injustice, but he has long ago repudiated the idea of human rights to freedom and justice and he consequently cannot come out as their champion.

There have, however, been a few signs of late that he feels his old house too small: in his recent discussion of Mr. Chafee's book on free speech, he reached a pitch of righteous indignation at which he has scarcely been seen before. "In those two years," he cried, "all the laborious work of a century and a half—toward the free and honest administration of fair laws, the dealing of plain justice between man and man, the protection of the weak and helpless, the safeguarding of free assemblage and free speech—was ruthlessly undone." This is obviously in direct contradiction to the faith he has previously professed. What has one who is "against the under dog every time" to do with "the protection of the weak and helpless"? He has told us again and again that we should let the weak and helpless perish.

The truth is that in the last few years Mencken has entered so far into the national intellectual life that it has become impossible for him to maintain his old opinions quite intact: he has begun to worry and hope with the American people in the throes of their democratic experiment. I know that this is a terrible statement; it is as if one should say that the Pope had begun to worry and hope with the western world in its attempt to shake off creed; but I honestly believe it is true. This phenomenon seemed to make its appearance toward the last page of The American Language; and if it does not come to bulk yet larger we shall have one of our strongest men still fighting with one arm tied behind his back.

III

So much for the critic; but what of the evangelist and artist? For Mencken, in spite of all his professions of realistic resignation, is actually a militant idealist. Most Americans—even of fine standards—have long ago resigned themselves to the cheapness and ugliness of America, but Mencken has never resigned himself. He has never ceased to regard his native country with wounded and outraged eyes. The shabby politics, the childish books, the factories turning out wooden nut-megs have never lost their power to offend him. At this late date, he is, I suppose, almost the only man in the country who still expects American novelists to be artists and American politicians gentlemen.

that the confusion of thought is apparent to the reader and go on to point out that Mencken has been upholding these theories without modification since 1908 at least. He has cherished them through the European war and through the industrial war that has followed it. (Quite recently they have led him into the absurdity of asserting that it would have been a good thing for America if the war had continued longer, because this would have stamped out "hundreds of thousands of the relatively unfit." The men who were left at the end of the war in the French and German armies, were, he adds "very superior men.") And, in consequence, it seems to me that he has cut himself off in an intellectual cul-de-sac.

He has much to say to America that is of the first usefulness and importance: he has no peer in the brilliance and effectiveness of his onslaught upon political ignorance and corruption, upon Y. M. C. A.'ism and popular morality, upon the cheapness and sordidness of current ideals. But, though the moral strength which gives him courage is drawn partly from his Nietzschean principles, these principles so close his horizon as to render his social criticism rather sterile. In the matters of politics and society he can do nothing but denounce.

And his expression of his resentment is by no means temperate or aloof. It is righteous indignation of the most violent sort. His denunciations are as ferocious as those of Tertullian or Billy Sunday. It is in purpose rather than in method that he differs from these great divines. (See especially his excommunication of the professors in the essay on The National Letters.) In his exhortations to disobey the rules of the current American morality he has shown himself as noisy and as bitter as any other Puritan preacher.

And this brings us to what is perhaps, after all, the most important thing about Mencken, the thing which gives him his enormous importance in American literature today: it is the fact that here we have a genuine artist and man of first-rate education and intelligence who is thoroughly familiar with, even thoroughly saturated with, the common life. The rule has been heretofore for men of superior intelligence, like Henry Adams and Henry James, to shrink so far from the common life that, in a country where there was practically nothing else, they had almost no material to work on, and for men who were part of the general society, like Mark Twain, to be handicapped by Philistinism and illiteracy; but in the case of Mencken we have Puritanism and American manners in a position to criticize itself. For in his attitude toward all the things with which Puritanism is supposed to deal Mencken is thoroughly American and thoroughly Puritan. If he were what he exhorts us to be in regard to the amenities and the pleasures he would never rage so much about them. His sermons would be unintelligible, I should think, to a Frenchman or an Italian. Nobody but a man steeped in Puritanism could have so much to say about love and yet never convey any idea of its beauties or delights; poor Aphrodite, usually identified in his pages with the whore and the bawdy-house, wears as unalluring a face as she does in the utterances of any Y. M. C. A. lecturer: no one else would confine himself to a harsh abuse, on principle, of the people who have outlawed love. Nobody else would express his enthusiasm for the innocent pleasures of alcohol in such a way that it sounded less like a eulogy than like an angry defiance. He is an unmistakable product of Puritan training and environment. Horace or Anatole France, who really represent the sort of civilization which Mencken admires, would never be so acutely conscious of the problems of love and art and wine; they would take them easily for granted and enjoy them as a matter of course. But Mencken, who was born an American, with the truculent argumentative mind of the Puritan, can never enjoy them as a matter of course, as even some Americans can do, but must call down all the dark thunders of logic to defend them, like any Milton or Luther.

And he is saturated with the thought and aspect of modern commercial America. He is, we feel, in spite of everything, in the long run most at home there; are we not told that once, when walking in Paris in the spring, he was annoyed by the absence of a first-class drug-store? Instead of taking refuge among remote literatures, like Mr. Cabell and Mr. Pound, he makes his poetry of the democratic life which absorbs and infuriates him. He takes the slang of the common man and makes fine prose of it. He has studied the habits and ideas and language of the common run of his countrymen with a close first-hand observation and an unflagging interest. And he has succeeded in doing with the common life what nobody else has done,—(at least with any authentic stamp of literary distinction): he has taken it in all its coarseness and angularity and compelled it to dance a ballet, in which the Odd Fellow, the stock-broker, the Y. M. C. A. Secretary, the Knight of Pythias, the academic critic, the Methodist evangelical, the lecturer at Chautauquas, the charlatan politician, the Vice Crusader, the Department of Justice, the star-spangled army officer,—and the man who reveres all these, with all his properties and settings: the derby hat, the cheap cigar, the shaving soap advertisement, the popular novel, the cuspidor, the stein of prohibition beer, the drug store, the patent medicine, the American Legion button,—join hands and perform, to the strains of a sombre but ribald music, which ranges from genial boisterousness to morose and cynical brooding.

Take the following passage, for example, from a sort of prose poem:

> Pale druggists in remote towns of the hog and cotton belt, endlessly wrapping up Peruna. . . . Women hidden away in the damp kitchens of unpainted houses along the railroad tracks, frying tough beefsteaks. . . . Lime and cement dealers being initiated into the Knights of Pythias, the Redmen or the Woodmen of the World. . . . Watchmen at lonely railroad crossings in Iowa, hoping that they'll be able to get off to hear the United Brethren evangelist preach. . . . Ticket-choppers in the Subway, breathing sweat in its gaseous form. . . . Family doctors in poor neighborhoods, faithfully relying upon the therapeutics taught in their Eclectic Medical College in 1884. . . . Farmers plowing sterile fields behind sad meditative horses, both suffering from the bites of insects. . . . Greeks tending all-night coffee-joints in the suburban wildernesses where the trolley-cars stop. . . . Grocery clerks stealing prunes and gingersnaps and trying to make assignations with soapy servant-girls. . . . Women confined for the ninth or tenth time, wondering hopelessly what it is all about. . . . Methodist preachers retired after forty years of service in the trenches of God, upon pensions of $600 a year. . . . Wives and daughters of Middle Western country bankers, marooned in Los Angeles, going tremblingly to swami seances in dark smelly rooms. . . . Chauffeurs in

The critic Edmund Wilson (left), who heard in Mencken's voice a counterpart to that of the poet Walt Whitman (right)

huge fur coats waiting outside theatres filled with folks applauding Robert Edeson and Jane Cowl. . . . Decayed and hopeless men writing editorials at midnight for leading papers in Mississippi, Arkansas and Alabama. . . .

One recalls the enumeration of another set of visions:

The pure contralto sings in the organ loft,
The carpenter dresses his plank, the tongue of his fore-
    plane whistles its wild ascending lisp,
The married and unmarried children ride home to their
    Thanksgiving dinner,
The pilot seizes the king-pin, he heaves down with a strong
    arm,
The mate stands braced in the whale-boat, lance and har-
    poon are ready,
The duck-shooter walks by silent and cautious stretches,
The deacons are ordain'd with cross'd hands at the altar,
The spinning girl retreats and advances to the hum of the
    big wheel,
The farmer stops by the bars as he walks on a First-day
    loaf and looks at the oats and rye, . . .
The young fellow drives the express-wagon (I love him,
    though I do not know him),

The half-breed straps on his light boots to compete in the
    race,
The Wolverine sets traps on the creek that helps fill the
    Huron,
The clean-hair'd Yankee girl works with her sewing
    machine or in the factory or mill,
The Missourian crosses the plains toting his wares and his
    cattle. . . .

This was the day before yesterday, and Mencken is today. Is not Mencken's gloomy catalogue as much the poetry of modern America as Walt Whitman's was of the early Republic? When the States were fresh and new and their people were hardy pioneers, we had a great poet, from whose pages the youth and wonder of that world can reach us forever; and now that that air is soured with industry and those pioneers have become respectable citizens dwelling in hideously ugly towns and devoted to sordid ideals, we have had a great satirist to arouse us against the tragic spectacle we have become. For Mencken is the civilized consciousness of modern America, its learning, its intelligence and its taste, realizing the grossness of its manners and mind and crying out in horror and chagrin.

Journalist: The National Stage

In a kind of parody of the naturalistic writing he promoted, Mencken uses Dreiserian specificity to record in Happy Days, 1880–1892 *(1940) the seminal event of his youth. Like many of the* Days *essays, this one first appeared in* The New Yorker *(excerpt from "In the Footsteps of Gutenberg," pp. 202–203).*

On November 26, 1888, my father sent his bookkeeper, Mr. Maass, to the establishment of J. F. W. Dorman, at 217 East German street, Baltimore, and there and then, by the said Maass's authorized agency, took title to a Baltimore No. 10 Self-Inker Printing Press

and a font of No. 214 type. The press cost $7.50 and the font of type $1.10. These details, which I recover from the receipted bill in my father's file, are of no conceivable interest to anyone else on earth, but to me they are of a degree of concern bordering upon the super-colossal, for that press determined the whole course of my future life. If it had been a stethoscope or a copy of Dr. Ayers' Almanac I might have gone in for medicine; if it had been a Greek New Testament or a set of baptismal grappling-irons I might have pursued divinity. As it was, I got the smell of printer's ink up my nose at the tender age of eight, and it has been swirling through my

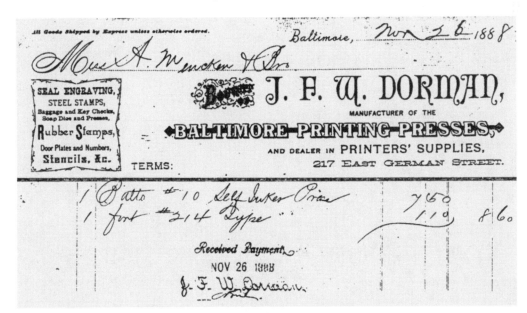

Receipt, made out to Mencken's father, for the toy printing press that, Mencken said, "determined the whole course of my future life" (courtesy of the Enoch Pratt Free Library)

sinuses ever since. [. . .]

One of Mencken's earliest printing efforts: a business card for his father, with hand-drawn Masonic emblems (courtesy of the Enoch Pratt Free Library)

15

WITH
KITCHENER TO KHARTUM

BY

G. W. STEEVENS

AUTHOR OF
'EGYPT IN 1898,' 'THE LAND OF THE DOLLAR,' 'WITH THE
CONQUERING TURK,' ETC.

WITH MAPS AND PLANS

NEW YORK
DODD, MEAD & COMPANY
1899

Title page for one of the books that inspired Mencken to take up journalism. Mencken regarded Steevens as "the greatest newspaper reporter who ever lived."

In his teens Mencken became a reporter for the Baltimore Morning Herald, *and in 1903 he rose to city editor. In* Newspaper Days, 1899–1906 *(1941) he records how he found his job and learned his trade (excerpt from "Allegro con Brio," pp. 3–16).*

My father died on Friday, January 13, 1899, and was buried on the ensuing Sunday. On the Monday evening immediately following, having shaved with care and put on my best suit of clothes, I presented myself in the city-room of the old Baltimore *Morning Herald,* and applied to Max Ways, the city editor, for a job on his staff. I was eighteen years, four months and four days old, wore my hair longish and parted in the middle, had on a high stiff collar and an Ascot cravat, and weighed something on the minus side of 120 pounds. I was thus hardly a spectacle to exhilarate a city editor, but Max was an amiable fellow and that night he was in an extra-amiable mood, for (as he told me afterward) there was a good dinner under his belt, with a couple of globes of malt to wash it down, and all of his reporters, so far as he was aware, were transiently sober. So he received me very politely, and even cordially. Had I any newspaper experience? The reply, alas, had to be no. What was my education? I was a graduate of the Baltimore Polytechnic. What considerations had turned my fancy toward the newspaper business? All that I could say was that it seemed to be a sort of celestial call: I was busting with literary ardors and

A MONOGRAPH OF THE NEW

BALTIMORE COURT HOUSE.

One of the Greatest Examples of
American Architecture, and the Foremost Court House of
the United States, Including an Historical Sketch of the Early Courts of Maryland.

Title page for Mencken's first appearance in a book, an unsigned essay in a work published in the year he began his journalistic career (1899)

Max Ways, city editor of the Baltimore Morning Herald, *who gave Mencken his first newspaper job (drawing by Irving Ward; from Paul Winchester and Frank D. Webb,* Newspapers and Newspaper Men of Maryland Past and Present *[1905])*

had been writing furiously for what, at eighteen, was almost an age—maybe four, or even five years. Writing what—prose or verse? Both. Anything published? I had to play dead here, for my bibliography, to date, was confined to a couple of anonymous poems in the Baltimore *American*—a rival paper, and hence probably not admired.

Max looked me over ruminatively—I had been standing all the while—and made the reply that city editors had been making to young aspirants since the days of the first Washington hand-press. There was, unhappily, no vacancy on the staff. He would take my name, and send for me in case some catastrophe unforeseen—and, as I gathered, almost unimaginable—made one. I must have drooped visibly, for the kindly Max at once thought of something better. Did I have a job? Yes, I was working for my Uncle Henry, now the sole heir and assign of my father's old tobacco firm of Aug. Mencken & Bro. Well, I had better keep that job, but

maybe it might be an idea for me to drop in now and then of an evening, say between seven thirty and seven forty-five. Nothing, of course, could be promised; in fact, the odds against anything turning up were appalling. But if I would present myself at appropriate intervals there might be a chance, if it were God's will, to try me out, soon or late, on something commensurate with my undemonstrated talents. Such trial flights, it was unnecessary to mention, carried no emolument. They added a lot to a city editor's already heavy cargo of cares and anxieties, and out of the many that were called only a few were ever chosen.

I retired nursing a mixture of disappointment and elation, but with the elation quickly besting the disappointment—and the next night, precisely at seven thirty-one, I was back. Max waved me away without parley: he was busy jawing an office-boy. The third night he simply shook his head, and so on the fourth, fifth, sixth and seventh. On the eighth—or maybe it was the ninth or tenth—he motioned me to wait while he finished thumbing through a pile of copy, and then asked suddenly: "Do you ever read the *Herald*?" When I answered yes, he followed with "What do you think of it?" This one had all the appearance of a trap, and my heart missed a couple of beats, but the holy saints were with me. "I think," I said, "that it is much better written than the *Sunpaper*." I was to learn later that Max smelled something artful here, but, as always, he held himself well, and all I could observe was the faint flutter of a smile across his face. At length he spoke. "Come back," he said, "tomorrow night."

I came back, you may be sure—and found him missing, for he had forgotten that it was his night off. The next night I was there again—and found him too busy to notice me. And so the night following, and the next, and the next. To make an end, this went on for four weeks, night in and night out, Mondays, Tuesdays, Wednesdays, Thursdays, Fridays, Saturdays and Sundays. A tremendous blizzard came down upon Baltimore, and for a couple of days the trolley-cars were stalled, but I hoofed it ever hopefully to the *Herald* office, and then hoofed it sadly home. There arrived eventually, after what seemed a geological epoch by my calendar, the evening of Thursday, February 23, 1899. I found Max reading copy, and for a few minutes he did not see me. Then his eyes lifted, and he said casually: "Go out to Govanstown, and see if anything is happening there. We are supposed to have a Govanstown correspondent, but he hasn't been heard from for six days."

The percussion must have been tremendous, for I remember nothing about getting to Govanstown. It is now a part of Baltimore, but in 1899 it was only a country village, with its own life and tribulations. No cop was in sight when I arrived, but I found the volunteer firemen playing pinochle in their engine-house. The blizzard had blockaded their front door with a drift fifteen feet high, but they had dug themselves out, and were now lathering for a fire, though all the water-plugs in the place were still frozen. They had no news save their hopes. Across the glacier of a street I saw two lights—a bright one in a drugstore and a dim one in a funeral parlor. The undertaker, like nearly all the rest of Govanstown, was preparing to go to bed, and when I routed him out and he came downstairs in his pants and undershirt it was only to say that he had no professional business in hand. The druggist, hugging a red-hot egg-stove behind his colored bottles, was more productive. The town cop, he said, had just left in a two-horse buggy to assist in a horse-stealing case at Kingsville, a long drive out the Belair pike, and the Improved Order of Red Men had postponed their oyster-supper until March 6. When I got back to the *Herald* office, along toward eleven o'clock, Max instructed me to forget the Red Men and write the horse-stealing. There was a vacant desk in a far corner, and at it, for ten minutes, I wrote and tore up, wrote and tore up. Finally there emerged the following:

> A horse, a buggy and several sets of harness, valued in all at about $250, were stolen last night from the stable of Howard Quinlan, near Kingsville. The county police are at work on the case, but so far no trace of either thieves or booty has been found.

Max gave only a grunt to my copy, but as I was leaving the office, exhausted but exultant, he called me back, and handed me a letter to the editor demanding full and friendly publicity, on penalty of a boycott, for an exhibition of what was then called a kinetoscope or cineograph. "A couple of lines," he said, "will be enough. Nearly everybody has seen a cineograph by now." I wrote:

> At Otterbein Memorial U.B. Church, Roland and Fifth avenues, Hampden, Charles H. Stanley and J. Albert Loose entertained a large audience last night with an exhibition of war scenes by the cineograph.

I was up with the milkman the next morning to search the paper, and when I found both of my pieces, exactly as written, there ran such thrills through my system as a barrel of brandy and 100,000 volts of electricity could not have matched. Somehow or other I must have done my duty by Aug. Mencken & Bro., for my uncle apparently noticed nothing, but certainly my higher cerebral centers were not focussed on them. That night I got to the *Herald* office so early that Max had not come back from dinner. When he appeared he

looked me over thoughtfully, and suggested that it might be a good plan to try my talents on a village adjacent to Govanstown, Waverly by name. It was, he observed, a poor place, full of Methodists and Baptists who seldom cut up, but now and then a horse ran away or a pastor got fired. Reaching it after a long search in the snow, and raking it from end to end, I turned up two items—one an Epworth League entertainment, and the other a lecture for nearby farmers, by title (I have the clipping before me), "Considering the Present Low Price of Hay, Would It Not Be Advisable to Lessen the Acreage of Hay for Market?" Max showed no enthusiasm for either, but after I had finished writing them he handed me an amateur press-agent's handout about a new Quaker school and directed me to rewrite it. It made twenty-eight lines in the paper next morning, and lifted me beyond the moon to Orion. On the night following Max introduced me to two or three reporters, and told them that I was a youngster trying for a job. My name, he said, was Macon. They greeted me with considerable reserve.

Of the weeks following I recall definitely but one thing—that I never seemed to get enough sleep. I was expected to report at the cigar factory of Aug. Mencken & Bro. at eight o'clock every morning, which meant that I had to turn out at seven. My day there ran officially to five thirty, but not infrequently my uncle detained me to talk about family affairs, for my father had died intestate and his estate was in process of administration, with two sets of lawyers discovering mare's nests from time to time. Thus it was often six o'clock before I escaped, and in the course of the next hour or so I had to get home, change my clothes, bolt my dinner, and return downtown to the *Herald* office. For a couple of weeks Max kept me at my harrying of the remoter suburbs—a job, as I afterward learned, as distasteful to ripe reporters as covering a fashionable church-wedding or a convention of the W.C.T.U. I ranged from Catonsville in the far west to Back River in the east, and from Tuxedo Park in the north to Mt. Winans in the south. Hour after hour I rode the suburban trolleys, and one night, as I recall uncomfortably over all these years, my fares at a nickel a throw came to sixty cents, which was more than half my day's pay from Aug. Mencken & Bro. Max had said nothing about an expense account, and I was afraid to ask. Once, returning from a dismal village called Gardenville, a mile or two northeast of the last electric light, I ventured to ask him how far my diocese ran in that direction. "You are supposed to keep on out the road," he said, "until you meet the Philadelphia reporters coming in." This was an ancient Baltimore newspaper wheeze, but it was new to me, and I was to enjoy it a great deal better when I heard it worked off on my successors.

But my exploration of the fringes of Baltimore, though it came near being exhaustive, was really not long drawn out, for in a little while Max began to hand me city assignments of the kind that no one else wanted—installations of new evangelical pastors, meetings of wheelmen, interviews with bores just back from Europe, the Klondike or Oklahoma, orgies of one sort or another at the Y.M.C.A., minor political rallies, concerts, funerals, and so on. Most of my early clippings perished in the great Baltimore fire of 1904, but a few survived, and I find from them that I covered a number of stories that would seem as antediluvian today as a fight between two brontosauri—for example, the showing of a picture-play by Alexander Black (a series of lantern-slides with a thin thread of banal recitative), and a chalk-talk by Frank Beard. When it appeared that I knew something of music, I was assigned to a long series of organ recitals in obscure churches, vocal and instrumental recitals in even more obscure halls, and miscellaneous disturbances of the peace in lodge-rooms and among the German singing societies. Within the space of two weeks I heard one violinist, then very popular in Baltimore, play Raff's Cavatina no less than eight times. The *Herald's* music critic in those days, an Englishman named W. G. Owst, was a very indolent fellow, and when he discovered that I could cover such uproars without making any noticeable bulls, he saw to it that I got more and more of them. Finally, I was entrusted with an assault upon Mendelssohn's "Elijah" by the Baltimore Oratorio Society—and suffered a spasm of stage fright that was cured by dropping into the Pratt Library before the performance, and doing a little precautionary reading.

Thus the Winter ran into Spring, and I began to think of myself as almost a journalist. So far, to be sure, I had been entrusted with no spot news, and Max had never sent me out to help a regular member of the staff, but he was generous with his own advice, and I quickly picked up the jargon and ways of thought of the city-room. In this acclimatization I was aided by the device that had helped me to fathom Mendelssohn's "Elijah" and has always been my recourse in time of difficulty: what I couldn't learn otherwise I tried to learn by reading. Unhappily, the almost innumerable texts on journalism that now serve aspirants were then still unwritten, and I could find, in fact, only one formal treatise on the subject at the Pratt Library. It was "Steps Into Journalism," by E. L. Shuman of the Chicago *Tribune,* and though it was a primitive in its class it was very clearly and sensibly written, and I got a great deal of useful information out of it. Also, I read all of the newspaper fiction then on paper—for example, Richard

Mencken's first newspaper article, from the Baltimore Morning Herald *for 24 February 1899 (courtesy of the Enoch Pratt Free Library)*

Harding Davis's "Gallegher and Other Stories," Jesse Lynch Williams's "The Stolen Story and Other Stories," and Elizabeth G. Jordan's "Tales of the City-Room," the last two of which had but lately come out. [*(Footnote)* It must have been a little later that I read "With Kitchener to Khartoum," "From Capetown to Ladysmith" and the other books of George W. Steevens, of the London *Mail.* They made a powerful impression on me, and I still believe that Steevens was the greatest newspaper reporter who ever lived.]

How I found time for this reading I can't tell you, for I was kept jumping by my two jobs, but find it I did. One night, sitting in the city-room waiting for an assignment, I fell asleep, and the thoughtful Max suggested that I take one night off a week, and mentioned Sunday. The next Sunday I stayed in bed until noon, and returned to it at 8 p.m., and thereafter I was ready for anything. As the Spring drifted on my assignments grew better and better, and when the time came for high-school commencements I covered all of them. There were five in those days, beginning with that of the City College and ending with that of the Colored High-school, and I heard the Mayor of Baltimore unload precisely the same speech at each. Max, who knew the man, complimented me on making his observations sound different every time, and even more or less intelligent, and I gathered the happy impression that my days as an unpaid volunteer were nearing their end. But a city editor of that costive era, at least in Baltimore, could take on a new man only by getting rid of an old one, and for a month or so longer I had to wait. Finally, some old-timer or other dropped out, and my time had come. Max made a little ceremony of my annunciation, though no one else was present. My salary, he said, would be $7 a

The city staff of the Baltimore Morning Herald *in 1900. Mencken is in the top row, third from right (courtesy of the Enoch Pratt Free Library).*

week, with the hope of an early lift to $8 if I made good. I would have the use of a book of passes on the trolley-cars, and might turn in expense-accounts to cover any actual outlays. There was, at the moment, no typewriter available for me, but he had hopes of extracting one from Nachman, the business manager, in the near future. This was followed by some good advice. *Imprimis,* never trust a cop: whenever possible, verify his report. *Item,* always try to get in early copy: the first story to reach the city-desk has a much better chance of being printed in full than the last. *Item,* be careful about dates, names, ages, addresses, figures of every sort. *Item,* keep in mind at all times the dangers of libel. Finally, don't be surprised if you go to a house for information, and are invited to lift it from the *Sun* of the next morning. "The *Sun* is the Bible of Baltimore, and has almost a monopoly on many kinds of news. But don't let that fact discourage you. You can get it too if you dig hard enough, and always remember this: any *Herald* reporter who is worth a damn can write rings around a *Sun* reporter."

This last was very far from literally true, as I was to discover when I came to cover stories in competition with such *Sun* reporters as Dorsey Guy and Harry West, but there was nevertheless a certain plausibility in it, for the

Sun laid immense stress upon accuracy, and thus fostered a sober, matter-of-fact style in its men. The best of them burst through those trammels, but the rank and file tended to write like bookkeepers. As for Max, he greatly favored a more imaginative and colorful manner. He had been a very good reporter himself, with not only a hand for humor but also a trick of pathos, and he tried to inspire his slaves to the same. Not many of them were equal to the business, but all of them save a few poor old automata tried, and as a result the *Herald* was rather briskly written, and its general direction was toward the New York *Sun,* then still scintillating under the impulse of Charles A. Dana, rather than toward the Baltimore *Sun* and the *Congressional Record.* It was my good fortune, during my first week on the staff, to turn up the sort of story that Max liked especially—the sudden death of a colored street preacher on the street, in the midst of a hymn. I was not present at the ringside, and had to rely on the cops for the facts, but I must have got a touch of drama into my report, for Max was much pleased, and gave me, as a reward, a pass to a performance of Rose Sydell's London Blondes.

I had gathered from the newspaper fiction mentioned a few pages back that the typical American city editor was a sort of cross between an ice-wagon driver

Mencken at his desk in the city room of the Herald, *November 1901 (courtesy of the Enoch Pratt Free Library)*

and a fire-alarm, "full of strange oaths" and imprecations, and given to firing whole files of men at the drop of a hat. But if that monster actually existed in the Republic, it was surely not in the Baltimore *Herald* office. Max, of course, was decently equipped for this art and mystery: he could swear loudly enough on occasion and had a pretty hand for shattering invective, but most of the time, even when he was sorely tried, he kept to good humor and was polite to one and all. Whenever I made a mess of a story, which was certainly often enough, he summoned me to his desk and pointed out my blunders. When I came in with a difficult story, confused and puzzled, he gave me quick and clear directions, and they always straightened me out. Observing his operations with the sharp eyes of youth, I began to understand the curious equipment required of a city editor. He had to be an incredible amalgam of army officer and literary critic, diplomat and jail warden, psychologist and fortune-teller. If he could not see around corners and through four or five feet of brick he was virtually blind, and if he could not hear overtones audible normally only to dogs and children he was almost deaf. His knowledge of his town, as he gathered experience, combined that of a police captain, an all-night hackman, and a priest in a rowdy parish. He was supposed to know the truth about everyone and everything, even though he seldom printed it, and one of his most useful knowledges—in fact, he used it every day—was his knowledge of the most probable

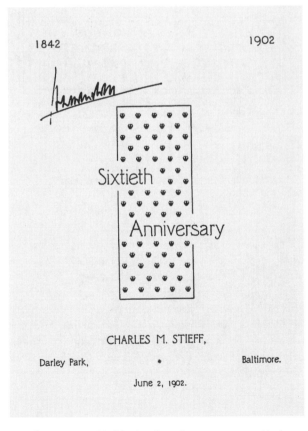

Title page signed by Mencken for a piano-company pamphlet he produced (courtesy of the Enoch Pratt Free Library)

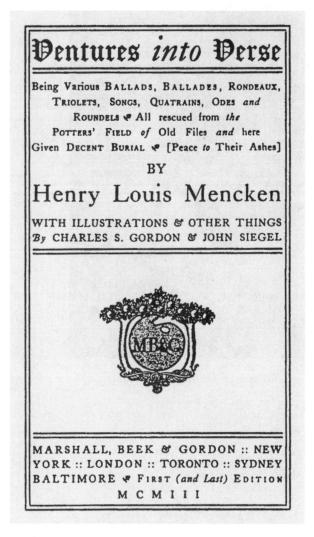

Ventures into Verse

Being Various BALLADS, BALLADES, RONDEAUX,
TRIOLETS, SONGS, QUATRAINS, ODES and
ROUNDELS ❧ All rescued from the
POTTERS' FIELD of Old Files and here
Given DECENT BURIAL ❧ [Peace to Their Ashes]

BY

Henry Louis Mencken

WITH ILLUSTRATIONS & OTHER THINGS
By CHARLES S. GORDON & JOHN SIEGEL

MARSHALL, BEEK & GORDON :: NEW
YORK :: LONDON :: TORONTO :: SYDNEY
BALTIMORE ❧ FIRST (and Last) EDITION
MCMIII

*Title page for Mencken's first book, a collection of his newspaper
and magazine verse*

whereabouts of every person affected with a public interest, day or night. [. . .]

*In the same year in which he became city editor Mencken pub-
lished his first book,* Ventures into Verse *(1903). Two years
later a sketch in* Newspapers and Newspaper Men of
Maryland Past and Present *was the first mention of Mencken
in a book. The same volume includes a poem that is the first work
of Mencken's ever reprinted in a book (excerpt from Paul Winchester and Frank D. Webb,* Newspapers and Newspaper
Men of Maryland Past and Present *[Baltimore: Sibley,
1905], p. 73).*

Henry L. Mencken, assistant managing editor of
the *Herald,* was born in Baltimore and has never
worked on any other paper than the one whose staff he
now helps to direct. Starting as a reporter on the street

when a half-grown boy, he worked his way up from
position to position, through all the different outside
posts, to dramatic editor, then Sunday editor, and
finally city editor. Today, when the managing editor of
the *Herald* is absent, it is Mencken who takes charge
until his return, and this condition has existed for a
year or two, although the promotion to his present
office was only recently made.

He is a good manager and a man of excellent
newspaper judgment. He is one of the cleverest feature
writers in Baltimore and the *Herald's* best dramatic
critic.

Mr. Mencken has done well in other lines than
straight newspaper work. "Ventures Into Verse," a volume of poems which he published a year or more ago,
was received with complimentary notice in nearly
every newspaper office in the country. His short stories
and poems have been published in many of the magazines.

*During Mencken's career nearly every town, large or small, had
a newspaper. Big cities had several, and many papers had more
than one daily edition. Ethnic and linguistic groups were served
by papers written in their languages and catering to their interests. Before radio and television, famous reporters, such as Henry
Stanley, who "discovered" Dr. David Livingstone in Africa, and
Nellie Bly, who went around the world in seventy-two days, were
the media superstars. This romantic allure was among the factors
that drew in the teenaged Mencken. The public's dependence on
the press for information in an era that lacked other forms of mass
communication accounts for the urgency and guildlike camaraderie
in his reminiscences of the Baltimore Fire of 1904. This was the
defining event of his early career, the one that tempered his profes-
sionalism and, in his corner of the world, placed him among the
heroes of journalism (excerpt from "Fire Alarm," in* Newspaper
Days, 1899–1906 *pp. 276–286).*

At midnight or thereabout on Saturday, February
6, 1904, I did my share as city editor to put the *Sunday
Herald* to bed, and then proceeded to Junker's saloon to
join in the exercises of the Stevedores' Club. Its members, having already got down a good many schooners,
were in a frolicsome mood, and I was so pleasantly edified that I stayed until 3:30. Then I caught a
night-hawk trolley-car, and by four o'clock was snoring
on my celibate couch in Hollins street, with every hope
and prospect of continuing there until noon of the next
day. But at 11 a.m. there was a telephone call from the
Herald office, saying that a big fire had broken out in
Hopkins Place, the heart of downtown Baltimore, and
fifteen minutes later a reporter dashed up to the house
behind a sweating hack horse, and rushed in with the
news that the fire looked to be a humdinger, and prom-

ised swell pickings for a dull Winter Sunday. So I hoisted my still malty bones from my couch and got into my clothes, and ten minutes later I was on my way to the office with the reporter. That was at about 11:30 a.m. of Sunday, February 7. It was not until 4 a.m. of Wednesday, February 10, that my pants and shoes, or even my collar, came off again. And it was not until 11:30 a.m. of Sunday, February 14—precisely a week to the hour since I set off—that I got home for a bath and a change of linen.

For what I had walked into was the great Baltimore fire of 1904, which burned a square mile out of the heart of the town and went howling and spluttering on for ten days. I give the exact schedule of my movements simply because it delights me, in my autumnal years, to dwell upon it, for it reminds me how full of steam and malicious animal magnetism I was when I was young. During the week following the outbreak of the fire the *Herald* was printed in three different cities, and I was present at all its accouchements, herding dispersed and bewildered reporters at long distance and cavorting gloriously in strange composing-rooms. My opening burst of work without a stop ran to sixty-four and a half hours, and then I got only six hours of nightmare sleep, and resumed on a working schedule of from twelve to fourteen hours a day, with no days off and no time for meals until work was over. It was brain-fagging and back-breaking, but it was grand beyond compare—an adventure of the first chop, a razzle-dazzle superb and elegant, a circus in forty rings. When I came out of it at last I was a settled and indeed almost a middle-aged man, spavined by responsibility and aching in every sinew, but I went into it a boy, and it was the hot gas of youth that kept me going. The uproar over, and the *Herald* on an even keel again, I picked up one day a volume of stories by a new writer named Joseph Conrad, and therein found a tale of a young sailor that struck home to me as the history of Judas must strike home to many a bloated bishop, though the sailor naturally made his odyssey in a ship, not on a newspaper, and its scene was not a provincial town in America, but the South Seas. Today, so long afterward, I too "remember my youth and the feeling that will never come back any more—the feeling that I could last forever, outlast the sea, the earth, and all men . . . Youth! All youth! The silly, charming, beautiful youth!"

Herald reporters, like all other reporters of the last generation, were usually late in coming to work on Sundays, but *that* Sunday they had begun to drift in even before I got to the office, and by one o'clock we were in full blast. The fire was then raging through a whole block, and from our fifth-floor city-room windows it made a gaudy show, full of catnip for a young city edi-

Mencken as city editor in the temporary Herald *office on South Charles Street in 1904 (courtesy of the Enoch Pratt Free Library)*

tor. But the Baltimore firemen had a hundred streams on it, and their chief, an old man named Horton, reported that they would knock it off presently. They might have done so, in fact, if the wind had not changed suddenly at three o'clock, and begun to roar from the West. In ten minutes the fire had routed Horton and his men and leaped to a second block, and in half an hour to a third and a fourth, and by dark the whole of downtown Baltimore was under a hail of sparks and flying brands, and a dozen outlying fires had started to eastward. We had a story, I am here to tell you! There have been bigger ones, of course, and plenty of them, but when and where, between the Chicago fire of 1871 and the San Francisco earthquake of 1906, was there ever one that was fatter, juicier, more exhilarating to the journalists on the actual ground? Every newspaper in Baltimore save one was burned out, and every considerable hotel save three, and every office building without exception. The fire raged for a full week, helped by that bitter Winter wind, and when it fizzled out at last the burned area looked like Pompeii, and up from its ashes rose the pathetic skele-

The Baltimore Fire, February 1904 (photograph by the Baltimore Sun)

tons of no less than twenty overtaken and cremated fire-engines—some of them from Washington, Philadelphia, Pittsburgh and New York. Old Horton, the Baltimore fire chief, was in hospital, and so were several hundred of his men.

My labors as city editor during that electric week were onerous and various, but for once they did not include urging lethargic reporters to step into it. The whole staff went to work with the enthusiasm of crusaders shinning up the walls of Antioch, and all sorts of volunteers swarmed in, including three or four forgotten veterans who had been fired years before, and were thought to have long since reached the dissecting-room. Also, there were as many young aspirants from the waiting-list, each hoping for his chance at last, and one of these, John Lee Blecker by name, I remember brilliantly, for when I told him to his delight that he had a job and invited him to prove it he leaped out with exultant gloats—and did not show up again for five days. But getting lost in so vast a story did not wreck his career, for he lived to become, in fact, an excellent reporter, and not a few old-timers were lost, too. One of the best of them, sometime that afternoon, was caught in a blast when the firemen began dynamiting buildings, and got so coagulated that it was three days before he was fit for

anything save writing editorials. The rest not only attacked the fire in a fine frenzy, but also returned promptly and safely, and by four o'clock thirty type-writers were going in the city-room, and my desk was beginning to pile high with red-hot copy.

Lynn Meekins, the managing editor, decided against wasting time and energy on extras: the story, in truth, was too big for such banalities; they would have seemed like toy balloons in a hurricane. "Let us close the first city edition," he said, "at nine o'clock. Make it as complete as you can. If you need twenty pages, take them. If you need fifty, take them." So we began heaving copy to the composing-room, and by seven o'clock there were columns and columns of type on the stones, and picture after picture was coming up from the engraving department. Alas, not much of that quivering stuff ever got into the *Herald,* for a little before nine o'clock, just as the front page was being made up, a couple of excited cops rushed in, howling that the buildings across the street were to be blown up in ten minutes, and ordering us to clear out at once. By this time there was a fire on the roof of the *Herald* Building itself, and another was starting in the press-room, which had plate-glass windows reaching above the street level, all of them long

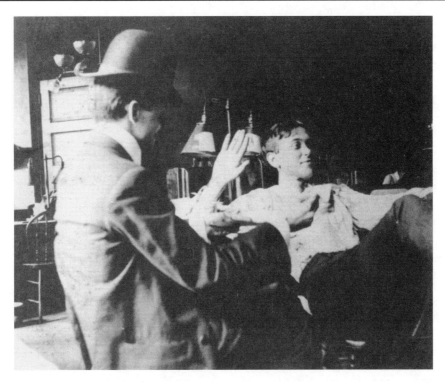

Wells Hawks, press agent of the Baltimore Academy of Music, supposedly offering a bribe to Herald *drama critic Mencken (courtesy of the Enoch Pratt Free Library)*

ago smashed by flying brands. We tried to parley with the cops, but they were too eager to be on their way to listen to us, and when a terrific blast went off up the street Meekins ordered that the building be abandoned.

There was a hotel three or four blocks away, out of the apparent path of the fire, and there we went in a dismal procession—editors, reporters, printers and pressmen. Our lovely first edition was adjourned for the moment, but every man-jack in the outfit believed that we'd be back anon, once the proposed dynamiting had been done—every man-jack, that is, save two. One was Joe Bamberger, the foreman of the composing-room, and the other was Joe Callahan, my assistant as city editor. The first Joe was carrying page-proofs of all the pages already made up, and galley-proofs of all the remaining type-matter, and all the copy not yet set. In his left overcoat pocket was the front-page logo-type of the paper, and in his left pocket were ten or twelve halftones. The other Joe had on him what copy had remained in the city-room, a wad of Associated Press flimsy about the Russian-Japanese war, a copy-hook, a pot of paste, two boxes of copy-readers' pencils—and the assignment-book!

But Meekins and I refused to believe that we were shipwrecked, and in a little while he sent me back to the *Herald* Building to have a look, leaving Joe No. 2 to round up such reporters as were missing. I got there

safely enough, but did not stay long. The proposed dynamiting, for some reason unknown, had apparently been abandoned, but the fire on our roof was blazing violently, and the press-room was vomiting smoke. As I stood gaping at this dispiriting spectacle a couple of large plate-glass windows cracked in the composing-room under the roof, and a flying brand—some of them seemed to be six feet long!—fetched a window on the editorial floor just below it. Nearly opposite, in Fayette street, a sixteen-story office building had caught fire, and I paused a moment more to watch it. The flames leaped through it as if it had been made of matchwood and drenched with gasoline, and in half a minute they were roaring in the air at least 500 feet. It was, I suppose, the most melodramatic detail of the whole fire, but I was too busy to enjoy it, and as I made off hastily I fully expected the whole structure to come crashing down behind me. But when I returned a week later I found that the steel frame and brick skin had both held out, though all the interior was gone, and during the following Summer the burned parts were replaced, and the building remains in service to this day, as solid as the Himalayas.

At the hotel Meekins was trying to telephone to Washington, but long-distance calls still took time in 1904, and it was fifteen minutes before he raised Scott C. Bone, managing editor of the Washington *Post.* Bone was having a busy and crowded night

Account of the event that "made" Mencken as a journalist. He was still working for the Morning Herald *at this time (from Harold A. Williams,* Baltimore Afire *[Baltimore: Schneidereith, 1954]; reproduced by permission).*

himself, for the story was worth pages to the *Post,* but he promised to do what he could for us, and presently we were hoofing for Camden Station, a good mile away–Meekins and I, Joe Bamberger with his salvage, a copy-reader with the salvage of the other Joe, half a dozen other desk men, fifteen or twenty printers, and small squads of pressmen and circulation men. We were off to Washington to print the paper there–that is, if the gods were kind. They frowned at the start, for the only Baltimore & Ohio train for an hour was an accommodation, but we poured into it, and by midnight we were in the *Post* office, and the hospitable Bone and his men were clearing a place for us in their frenzied composing-room, and ordering the press-room to be ready for us. [*(Footnote)* Bone was an Indianan, and had a long and honorable career in journalism, stretching from 1881 to 1918. In 1919 he became publicity chief of the Republican National Committee, and in 1921 he was appointed Governor of Alaska. He died in 1936.]

Just how we managed to get out the *Herald* that night I can't tell you, for I remember only trifling details. One was that I was the principal financier of the expedition, for when we pooled our money at Camden Station it turned out that I had $40 in my pocket, whereas Meekins had only $5, and the rest of the editorial boys not more than $20 among them. Another is that the moon broke out of the Winter sky just as we reached the old B. & O. Station in Washington, and shined down sentimentally on the dome of the Capitol. The Capitol was nothing new to Baltimore journalists, but we had with us a new copy-reader who had lately come in from Pittsburgh, and as he saw the matronly dome for the first time, bathed in spooky moonlight, he was so overcome by patriotic and aesthetic sentiments that he took off his hat and exclaimed, "My God, how beautiful!" And a third is that we all paused a second to look at the red glow over Baltimore, thirty-five miles away as the crow flies. The fire had really got going by now, and for four nights afterward the people of Washington could see its glare from their streets.

Bone was a highly competent managing editor, and contrived somehow to squeeze us into the tumultuous *Post* office. All of his linotypes were already working to capacity, so our operators were useless, but they lent a hand with the make-up, and our pressmen went to the cellar to reinforce their *Post* colleagues. It was a sheer impossibility to set up all the copy we had with us, or even the half of it, or a third of it, but we nevertheless got eight or ten columns

H.L.Mencken,
        1524 Hollins street
        Baltimore, Md.

About 6500 words.

Fire Alarm.   Finished Nov 19/41   Mencken

At midnight or thereabout on Saturday, February 6, 1904, I did my

share as city editor to put the old Baltimore Sunday Herald to bed, and

then proceeded to Frank Junker's saloon opposite the City Hall, to join

in the exercises of the Stevedores' Club.   Its members, having already got

down a good many schooners, were in a frolicksome mood, and I was so

pleasantly edified that I stayed until 3.30.   Then I caught a night-hawk

trolley-car, and by four o'clock was snoring on my celibate couch in Hollins

street, with every hope and prospect of continuing there until noon of the

next day.   But at 11 A.M. there was a telephone call from the Herald

office, saying that a big fire had broken out in Hopkins Place, the heart

of downtown Baltimore, and fifteen minutes later a reporter dashed up to

the house behind a sweating hack horse, and burst in to say that the fire

looked to be a humdinger, and promised swell pickings for a dull Winter

Sunday.   So I hoisted my still malty carcass from my couch and

got into my clothes, and ten minutes later I was on my way to the office

with the reporter.   That was at about 11.30 A.M. of Sunday, February

7.   It was not until 4 A.M. of Wednesday, February 10, that my pants and

shoes, and even my collar, came off again.   And it was

not until 11.30 A.M. of Sunday, February 14 — precisely a week to the hour

since I set off — that I got home for a bath and a change of linen.

For what I had walked into was the great Baltimore fire of 1904, which

burned a square mile out of the heart of the town and went howling and splattering

spluttering on for ten days.   I give the exact schedule of my movements

simply because it delights me, in my antumnal years, to dwell upon it, for

it reminds me how full of steam and malicious animal magnetism I was

when I was young.   During the week following the outbreak of the fire

the Herald was printed in three different cities, and I was present at all its

accouchements, herding dispersed and bewildered reporters at long distance and cavorting gloriously

in strange composing-rooms.   My opening burst of work without a step ran to

Page from the typescript for the chapter in Mencken's Newspaper Days, 1899–1906 *(1941) describing the Baltimore Fire (courtesy of the Enoch Pratt Free Library)*

-267-

XIX

Fire Alarm

At midnight or thereabout on Saturday, February 6, 1904,
I did my share as city editor to put the Sunday Herald to bed,
and then proceeded to Junker's saloon to join in the exercises
of the Stevedores' Club.   Its members, having already got down
a good many schooners, were in a frolicksome mood, and I was so
pleasantly edified that I stayed until 3:30.   Then I caught a
night-hawk trolley-car, and by four o'clock was snoring on my
celibate couch in Hollins street, with every hope and prospect
of continuing there until noon of the next day.   But at 11 A.M.
there was a telephone call from the Herald office, saying that
a big fire had broken out in Hopkins Place, the heart of downtown
Baltimore, and fifteen minutes later a reporter dashed up to
the house behind a sweating hack horse, and rushed in with the
news that the fire looked to be a humdinger, and promised swell
pickings for a dull Winter Sunday.   So I hoisted my still malty
bones from my couch and got into my clothes, and ten minutes
later I was on my way to the office with the reporter.   That
was at about 11.30 A.M. of Sunday, February 7.   It was not until
4 A.M. of Wednesday, February 10, that my pants and shoes, or
even my collar, came off again.   And it was not until 11:30 A.M.

Page from the typescript for Mencken's final revision of the chapter (courtesy of the Enoch Pratt Free Library)

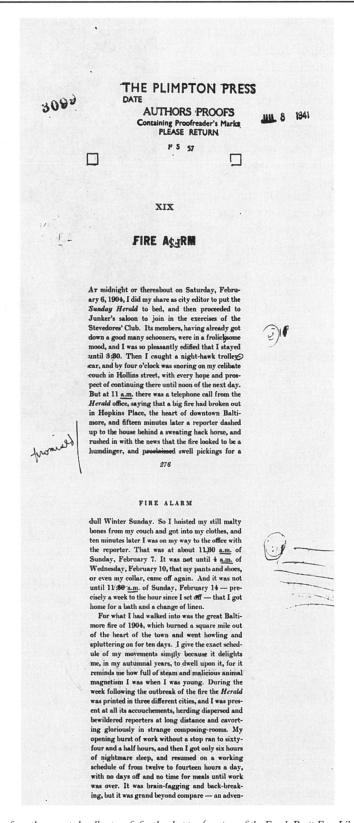

XIX

FIRE ALARM

At midnight or thereabout on Saturday, February 6, 1904, I did my share as city editor to put the *Sunday Herald* to bed, and then proceeded to Junker's saloon to join in the exercises of the Stevedores' Club. Its members, having already got down a good many schooners, were in a frolicsome mood, and I was so pleasantly edified that I stayed until 3:30. Then I caught a night-hawk trolley car, and by four o'clock was snoring on my celibate couch in Hollins street, with every hope and prospect of continuing there until noon of the next day. But at 11 a.m. there was a telephone call from the *Herald* office, saying that a big fire had broken out in Hopkins Place, the heart of downtown Baltimore, and fifteen minutes later a reporter dashed up to the house behind a sweating hack horse, and rushed in with the news that the fire looked to be a humdinger, and proclaimed swell pickings for a

276

FIRE ALARM

dull Winter Sunday. So I hoisted my still malty bones from my couch and got into my clothes, and ten minutes later I was on my way to the office with the reporter. That was at about 11.30 a.m. of Sunday, February 7. It was not until 4 a.m. of Wednesday, February 10, that my pants and shoes, or even my collar, came off again. And it was not until 11:30 a.m. of Sunday, February 14 — precisely a week to the hour since I set off — that I got home for a bath and a change of linen.

For what I had walked into was the great Baltimore fire of 1904, which burned a square mile out of the heart of the town and went howling and spluttering on for ten days. I give the exact schedule of my movements simply because it delights me, in my autumnal years, to dwell upon it, for it reminds me how full of steam and malicious animal magnetism I was when I was young. During the week following the outbreak of the fire the *Herald* was printed in three different cities, and I was present at all its accouchements, herding dispersed and bewildered reporters at long distance and cavorting gloriously in strange composing-rooms. My opening burst of work without a stop ran to sixty-four and a half hours, and then I got only six hours of nightmare sleep, and resumed on a working schedule of from twelve to fourteen hours a day, with no days off and no time for meals until work was over. It was brain-fagging and back-breaking, but it was grand beyond compare — an adven-

Page from the corrected galley proofs for the chapter (courtesy of the Enoch Pratt Free Library)

into type, and the *Post* lent us enough of its own matter to piece out a four-page paper. In return we lent the hospitable *Post* our halftones, and they adorned its first city edition next morning. Unhappily, the night was half gone before Bone could spare us any press time, but when we got it at last the presses did prodigies, and at precisely 6.30 the next morning we reached Camden Station, Baltimore, on a milk-train, with 30,000 four-page *Heralds* in the baggage-car. By 8 o'clock they were all sold. Our circulation hustlers had no difficulty in getting rid of them. We had scarcely arrived before the news of our coming began to circulate around the periphery of the fire, and in a few minutes newsboys swarmed in, some of them regulars but the majority volunteers. Very few boys in Baltimore had been to bed that night: the show was altogether too gaudy. And now there was a chance to make some easy money out of it.

Some time ago I unearthed one of these orphan *Heralds* from the catacombs of the Pratt Library in Baltimore, and gave it a looking-over. It turned out to be far from bad, all things considered. The story of the fire was certainly not complete, but it was at least coherent, and three of our halftones adorned Page 1. The eight-column streamer-head that ran across its top was as follows:

HEART OF BALTIMORE WRECKED BY
GREATEST FIRE IN CITY'S HISTORY

Well, brethren, what was wrong about that? [. . .]

Later that same year Mencken reported on his first political convention. He would be a fixture at these affairs until 1948, turning them into "carnivals of buncombe" for his readers at a time when they were far more important than the cut-and-dried one-ballot sessions of today. The article on William Jennings Bryan at the 1904 Democratic Convention is closer to factual—even favorable—reporting than the demonization of the Great Commoner that Mencken would develop over the next twenty years (excerpt from "Hon. Henry G. Davis for Vice-President," Baltimore Morning and Sunday Herald, 10 July 1904, p. 1).

St. Louis, Mo., July 9.—With the soft red glow of the dawn paling the harsh glare of arc and incandescent light, and 20,000 heavy-eyed men and women rousing themselves to hear what he had to say, William Jennings Bryan, of Nebraska, fought his last fight in the big convention hall here this morning and went down to defeat with the yells of his enemies ringing in his ears.

For fifty hours he had been tireless and sleepless, struggling in committee room and on the floor, by

William Jennings Bryan in 1896 (courtesy of Townsend Studio, Lincoln, Nebraska)

word and deed, for the things that seemed to him sacred. Now, with his voice a mere whisper, his collar a rag, his hair disheveled, his eyes sunken and his face pallid and deep-lined, the old leader arose before his old retainers and his victorious foes, an imperial and a mighty figure, and said good-by.

It was the tragic climax of what many an observer says has been the most melodramatic national convention in years. When he stumbled out, half an hour later, Bryan was half carried to his hotel by his brother, and sank upon his bed limp and unconscious.

"A Bit of a Bore," Said Belmont.

"It's a bit of a bore," said the dilettante millionaire Belmont upon the platform, rubbing his eyes.

For eight years Bryan had battled against men of Belmont's breed, and now Belmont was smiling upon him patronizingly and saying that his eloquence was a bore.

None who sweltered in that foul-smelling, steaming hall during those exciting ten hours will ever forget the sight. Thirty thousand men and women were there—delegates, alternates, native Bryanites of Missouri, and a Hearst clique that earned its wages to the last cent.

On the platform Chairman Champ Clark wore out his voice in three hours, and in the galleries the shouters had to work in relays. Coats and collars were shed, and an ocean of ice water was gulped down, but the physical discomforts of the place increased hour by hour and before long everyone was perspiration-soaked and impatient and out of humor.

Scarcely a corporal's guard deserted, and at midnight there were still 25,000 in the hall. Men grew weak and red-eyed in that sickening heat as the hours dragged on and women grew ghastly pale. Still men and women remained, and when the dawn came and Bryan arose to fight his last fight, 20,000 were there to cheer him.

It was broad daylight when the crowd left—broad daylight of a hot summer morning—and the thousands filed out slowly. They had seen a drama more stirring than all the tragedies that Shakespeare ever wrote and it was not make-believe, either. So they dragged along to their homes and hotels in silence and went to sleep.

This afternoon when the convention reassembled not 8000 persons were in the hall. The Vice-President had still to be named, but who would arise heavy-eyed to see a sham battle when he had watched the clash of arms at Appomattox or Waterloo? One who judged the strength of men merely by the cheers they brought forth would have said, before the roll call of states, that Bryan had won his fight and that Hearst was the democracy's choice for the presidency. But all of this was the work of the galleries.

The Hearst Outburst.

When the great Hearst outburst came it was the galleries more than the few loud-yelling delegates from Hearst states that made the tumult. Hearst men were everywhere, with handkerchief signals to other and lesser Hearst men. They had planned this riot of ear-splitting noise months ahead and they carried it through their program without a hitch.

On the floor they waved standards. From their leaders on the platform they took their cues. In the galleries they yelled, calmly and steadily and with the business-like air of men receiving fixed wages for performing certain well-defined work.

The majority of the delegates—the men whose votes were to count for more than the loudest of cheers—sat in silence throughout this turmoil. It was a show worth seeing and hearing, and they enjoyed it, but it did not make their blood course through their veins a bit faster than usual, and it did not lift them to their feet as did Bryan's speech at Chicago in 1896.

Mencken's press badge (reproduced by permission from Betty Adler's H. L. M.: The Mencken Bibliography [Baltimore: Johns Hopkins University Press, 1961])

So, too, it was again when the great Nebraskan himself arose before them, after the night had been spent and the dawn had come. The galleries had been calling for him since midnight, and once, when he had arisen in his place to make a commonplace announcement, there had been a mighty cheer. But when he struggled to the platform at last, in his familiar alpaca coat and his old white string tie, scarcely a delegate gave him greeting.

Bryan Weak and Haggard.

Bryan looked weak and haggard as he faced the huge crowd and his voice was hoarse and scarcely audible. But as soon as he began to speak a hush fell that was eloquent in itself, and nearly every word he said was heard and understood.

"Eight years ago," he began, "the democratic party gave me its standard to bear. Four years ago that commission was renewed. Tonight I come to you to give it back. You say that I have run my course, and some of you may say that I have not fought a good fight, but none of you"—and the Nebraskan's shattered voice rose to a height that reminded his hearers of the old days—" none of you can deny that I have kept the faith!"

There was more eloquence in this than can ever be set down in black and white. It was a surrender and a

Mencken (second row, fifth from left, smoking cigar) covering the 1936 Republican National Convention (courtesy of the Enoch Pratt Free Library)

defiance, and as Bryan paused and stepped back, with head erect and eyes flashing fire, there arose a whoop that made the formal cheering for Parker and the machine-made "enthusiasm" for Hearst seem puny. [. . .]

By the time of the 1936 Republican Convention Mencken's satiric style was fully formed, carrying him even further beyond mere reportage, and he was a world-famous writer for the Sun *("'Three Long Years' Usurps Honor Given 'Oh, Susanna' As G. O. P. Campaign Song," Baltimore Sun, 11 June 1936, p. 1).*

Convention Hall, Cleveland, June 10. The campaign song of the Republicans, it appears, is not to be "Oh, Susanna" after all, but a parody of "Three Blind Mice."

It was born last night of the fortunate conjunction of a phrase in the speech of the Hon. Frederick Steiwer and a happy thought in the head of Louis Rich, bandmaster of the convention. By noon today it was all over town, and when the Hon. Bertrand H. Snell, the permanent chairman of the convention, let go with his inaugural address this afternoon it actually broke into his remarks.

Bandmaster's Happy Thought

The Hon. Mr. Steiwer's phrase, as readers of these dispatches will recall, was "three long years." It was his answer to a series of rhetorical questions, and after he had intoned it *andante lamentoso* two or three times the crowd began to join in.

This gave Mr. Rich his idea. Turning to his artists he shouted "F sharp, E and D, all in unison," and the last time "three long years" was chanted the band supported the crowd with the notes. They constituted the opening measure of "Three Blind Mice."

Woman Sends Words

All this went out by radio, and in a little while Mr. Rich began to receive telegrams from fans. One of them was a Mrs. Wilder Tileston, of New Haven, Conn. It was as follows:

Three long years (repeated)
Full of grief and tears (repeated)
They've all added on to the farmers' debt,
They've put all the taxpayers into a sweat,
They're the worst the country has ever seen yet.
Three long years.

This seemed swell stuff to Mr. Rich, and he was soon in communication with the convention press agent, the Hon. Theodore G. Huntley. Mr. Huntley saw the point at once, and in half an hour he had a staff of six poets at work, writing parodies. Six of these parodies were mimeographed by noon, and when the convention reassembled for today's first session Mr. Rich had the melody scored for his band.

Twice, as I have said, it broke into the Hon. Mr. Snell's speech, and this evening, as the crowd assembled for the Hoover session, the band played it over and over, and the crowd made efforts to sing it. Tonight Mr. Rich is still bombarded by telegrams, many of them containing suggestions for additional stanzas. He is the musical director of Station WHK, Cleveland, and a very up-and-coming professor.

Snell Effective in Speech

The Hon. Mr. Snell had less to say than the Hon. Mr. Steiwer, but he said it rather more effectively. Instead of banging away at machine-gun speed, as Steiwer did, he permitted himself a more leisurely tempo, with plenty of room for gestures.

He was done out in a swell new Palm Beach suit and a neat haircut, and altogether made a pretty good job of his harangue, though what he had to say was hardly more than a repetition of what Steiwer had said last night. The first burst of really hearty clapper-clawing came when he shoved his fists into the air, threw back his head, rolled his eyes, and had at the delegates and alternates with this one:

"Thank God no Republican President has ever violated his constitutional oath by calling upon the members of his party in Congress to violate theirs!"

Greeted By Demonstration

It was dreadfully hot down on the floor, but the hearts of the delegates and alternates were still full of veneration for the Constitution, and when Dr. Snell staggered back from the microphone to give them a chance they leaped to their feet and gave a loud holler—in fact, the loudest to be heard in this somewhat gummy convention until Hoover tackled them tonight.

The rest of Dr. Snell's speech was largely made up of echoes from Revolutionary times.

"Can this be America," he roared, "where citizens live and breathe only by the gracious consent of an ambitious ruler?"

Other Extracts Given

The nays plainly had it, and the hon. gentleman went on:

"Against this demoralizing reign of irresponsible incompetence I hear today America's earnest prayer for deliverance."

A fine stage pause followed, and one could almost hear the minute men marching down the road, praying for deliverance from both New Deal professors and hit-and-run automobilists.

"The voice of the people," continued Dr. Snell, "calls us not merely to oppose another political party as in the past, but rather to resist the encroachments of an alien system of capricious personal government. Shall we measure up to this patriotic duty?"

Respects to Washington, Lincoln

This time the ayes prevailed, and the learned speaker proceeded to quote George Washington and Abraham Lincoln, both of whom he spoke of in the highest terms. He ended with a polite reference to God, who, by orthodox Republican theory, has been an *ex officio* member of the Republican National Committee since Civil War days.

The speech, intellectually speaking, seldom got above the level of a high school commencement address, but it served its purpose very well, and its success with the delegates and alternates was considerably above that of Dr. Steiwer's hour of high-speed gargling last night. But it was Steiwer who launched the campaign song, and for that great service to his country he will probably get some notice in the school books. The reward of Dr. Snell will be only the happy memory of a hot and useless duty gallantly done.

In the centennial issue of Menckeniana *ninety-three-year-old Alf Landon recalled Mencken's part in Landon's 1936 presidential campaign ("HLM and AML: The 1936 Campaign,"* Menckeniana, *75 [Fall 1980]: 47–49).*

More and more, the historical meaning of the 1936 presidential campaign, in which Henry L. Mencken took such an active part, is being analyzed and appreciated in the light of current events by those who know their history.

To start with, it was most unusual. For the first time, two great previous Democrat presidential nominees—Al Smith, in 1928, and Ambassador John W. Davis from West Virginia, in 1924—publicly supported a Republican presidential candidate.

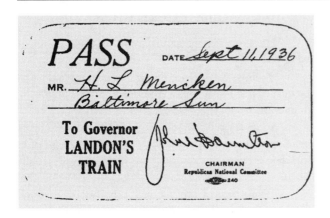

Mencken's press pass for Alfred M. Landon's campaign train, September 1936 (courtesy of the Enoch Pratt Free Library)

Wilson's Secretary of War, Newton D. Baker, said to me after the election, "I didn't vote for you, Governor, but all my family did."

Before a Gridiron dinner in 1938, Mr. Justice Felix Frankfurter said, "Mr. Justice Brandeis is limited to an hour a day for visits with outsiders. I know he would like to have a visit with you because he liked your presentation of the issues." I said I would be honored if that could be arranged.

Mr. Justice Brandeis was complimentary and made plain his concern over the lasting effect on our political system of the changes in government that were taking place. Of course, we did not discuss constitutional questions at all.

It was a nice Sunday morning and Justice Frankfurter and I were walking back to my hotel. I asked him, "How do you reconcile your position with Mr. Justice Brandeis?" He said, "It's very difficult."

Henry Mencken, of equally high rank in the arts and letters with these distinguished political and judicial figures, also took a most unusual, active personal interest in this 1936 presidential campaign. With his knowledge of history, he foresaw, with them, the weakening and inevitable destruction of our democratic processes in the course of time by President Franklin Roosevelt's incipient interventionist policies.

I had never met Mr. Mencken. He joined my campaign train to have some discussions with me. I had finished my last back-platform talk and had thrown myself on the long seat in my car. I heard Mr. Mencken asking one of my staff, "Will he be able to finish the campaign?" "Oh, yes," he replied, "give him fifteen minutes and he'll be ready to finish off the evening with a long visit with you."

From then on, whenever I was in Washington, we had many discussions of the new and far-reaching New

Mencken (right) with the guest of honor at a dinner for Landon at the Southern Hotel, Baltimore, 20 December 1936 (courtesy of the Enoch Pratt Free Library)

Mencken covering the Republican National Convention in 1948, his last year as a journalist

Deal political conditions. He gave a nice dinner for me in Baltimore.

The *American Mercury,* started by Mr. Mencken, was a well-known magazine at the time covering public issues. In the October, 1936, edition, he had his own piece, "The Case for Dr. Landon." It covered both candidates with his usual sparkling wit.

Now where are we in public affairs today relative to those fears in this unusual 1936 presidential campaign?

My No. 1 issue was inflation, which—once started on a false theory of public financing—would steadily weaken the economy of our country. It has been recognized and stated in most of the campaigns since. This is the prime issue today, according to the statements of both President Carter and the Republican presidential candidate, Ronald Reagan.

President Franklin Roosevelt assured the American people that it did not make any difference how much money we owed, because we owed it to ourselves. In 1935, President Roosevelt said he was going to manage the economy of the country; that the anti-trust laws belonged to the horse-and-buggy days.

I took the position that that meant a huge federal bureaucracy. We have that today.

How is it working? As Mencken foresaw, it has become large and powerful and is growing more pow-

erful all the time, because power feeds on power. It interprets and expands the intent of the Congress and the policies of a president in all legislation to fit its own intent, which is to expand constantly in size and power. President John F. Kennedy said some few months early in his office that he found the federal bureaucracy paid no attention to his presidential policies. That has been the record of every succeeding president.

I'm not talking about legislative acts and presidential policies like banking acts and the Home Loan, although they are forced to fight off constant interference by the federal bureaucracy. The sweeping federal bureaucracy I am talking about covers all public activities and is now entering educational institutions—even their athletic departments.

This federal bureaucracy moves the congressional legislation around to suit itself. For instance, it took education out of HEW and instituted a new Department of Education under its management.

The congressional and presidential control of government affairs, state and national, is consistently shifting to this sweeping federal bureaucracy by its administrative decisions. President Carter said early in his campaign that he was going to change this. President Ford was trying to do that also. Neither succeeded.

Congress has the control, if it wants to exercise it, by cutting the appropriations.

Mencken as "The Free Lance"; caricature by W. F. Pensch, November 1915 (courtesy of the Enoch Pratt Free Library)

By our constitutional provisions, we have three branches of the federal government—executive, legislative and judicial. So the federal bureaucracy, that is really a fourth branch, has no constitutional authority.

It was these monumental changes in our system of government and their results which Mencken and I foresaw and feared in 1936.

I treasure the memory of the years when we carefully considered the future of our nation in the light of current major public events.

Mencken's regular columns had, in the meantime, brought him national renown. Already a notable book reviewer for The Smart Set *magazine, he helped to establish the* Baltimore Evening Sun *in 1910 and published a series of columns headed "The Free Lance" from 1911 until 1915. They dealt with a variety of parochial and general concerns and provoked considerable outrage across the country. By the time the series ended, he was co-editor of* The Smart Set *and had everyone's attention. In the heyday of the series he laid out his journalistic philosophy ("to give a good show") in an Establishment periodical. Though he always denied being a crusader, he shows here how his*

favored method actually betters society ("Newspaper Morals," Atlantic Monthly, *113 [March 1914]: 289–297).*

Aspiring, toward the end of my nonage, to the black robes of a dramatic critic, I took counsel with an ancient whose service went back to the days of *Our American Cousin,* asking him what qualities were chiefly demanded by the craft.

"The main idea," he told me frankly, "is to be interesting, to write a good story. All else is dross. Of course, I am not against accuracy, fairness, information, learning. If you want to read Lessing and Freytag, Hazlitt and Brunetière, go read them: they will do you no harm. It is also useful to know something about Shakespeare. But unless you can make people *read* your criticisms, you may as well shut up your shop. And the only way to make them read you is to give them something exciting."

"You suggest, then," I ventured, "a certain—ferocity?"

"I do," replied my venerable friend. "Read George Henry Lewes, and see how *he* did it—sometimes with a bladder on a string, usually with a meat-axe. Knock somebody in the head every day—if not an actor, then the author, and if not the author, then the manager. And if the play and the performance are perfect, then excoriate someone who does n't think so—a fellow critic, a rival manager, the unappreciative public. But make it hearty; make it hot! The public would rather be the butt itself than have no butt in the ring. That is Rule No. 1 of American psychology—and of English, too, but more especially of American. You must give a good show to get a crowd, and a good show means one with slaughter in it."

Destiny soon robbed me of my critical shroud, and I fell into a long succession of less æsthetic newspaper berths, from that of police reporter to that of managing editor, but always the advice of my ancient counselor kept turning over and over in my memory, and as chance offered I began to act upon it, and whenever I acted upon it I found that it worked. What is more, I found that other newspaper men acted upon it too, some of them quite consciously and frankly, and others through a veil of self-deception, more or less diaphanous. The primary aim of all of them, no less when they played the secular Iokanaan than when they played the mere newsmonger, was to please the crowd, to give a good show; and the way they set about giving that good show was by first selecting a deserving victim, and then putting him magnificently to the torture. This was their method when they were performing for their own profit only, when their one motive was to make the public read their paper; but it was still their method when they were battling bravely and unself-

THE FREE LANCE

PROPOSED design for a face for a volunteer snouter and sabbatical Peeping Tom of the plupious Lord's Day Alliance:

EXPERIMENT to show the "awful effects of cigarette-smoking," from the current issue of the Baltimore *Southern Methodist*:

Take a number of live flies and confine them in a glass case. Burn the substance of a cigarette in a small dish, and with breath or bellows blow the smoke into the case. The flies will die in a few minutes, so deadly poisonous does the atmosphere become.

AND how long will they live if the smoke of burning hay is blown in, or of scorched coffee, or of incinerated deacon whiskers?

CASH balances in municipal depositories at the opening of business last Wednesday, as reported in to-day's *Municipal Journal*:

National Marine Bank........$316,108.02
National Bank of Commerce.. 198,492.04
Calvert Bank............... 88,377.41
Next highest bank.......... 50,368.83

THE city's money is dished out to the banks by Commissioners of Finance. The present Commissioners are the following:

The Hon. John M. Littig, president of the National Marine Bank.
The Hon. Harry Fahnestock, director of the National Bank of Commerce.
The Hon. James Harry Preston, vice-president of the Calvert Bank.
The Hon. Richard Gwinn, vice-president of the Calvert Bank.
The Hon. James F. Thrift.

A BAND of pious brothers. One for all and all for one. Égalité! Fraternité! The Hon. Mr. Littig is Athos, the Hon. Mr. Fahnestock is Porthos and the Hon. MM. Preston and Gwinn are Aramis. But who is D'Artagnan? The Hon. Jim Thrift? Not at all. D'Artagnan is the Hon. Eugene Levering, guardian of other folks' morals —and president of the National Bank of Commerce. The Hon. Mr. Levering is the busiest of all our local moralists. Scarcely a week goes by that he doesn't give the tail of the devil a

virtuous yank. He is hot against Pilsener and "Alma, wo wohnst du?" Sunday concerts and the deadly cigarette, cocktails and "September Morn," the white slave traffic and the mint julep, Back River and Havre de Grace, the "turkey trot" and Gaby des Lys, the cabaret and draw poker, opium and "coke," chewing tobacco and the highball, snuff and the betel nut. But no one has ever heard the hon. gent. say a word against caffeine, and no one has ever heard him say a word against the old-fashioned and brotherly doings in the City Hall.

BY insisting that the slum babies had better die than be saved by tainted money, the Hon. Young Cochran scores one on Dr. Donald R. Hooker, whose late attack upon the Hon. Eugene O'Dunne thus pales into puerility. Which suggests the plan of offering a silver-gilt halo to that local moralist who achieves the greatest feat of pious derringdo each year. We have in Baltimore a number of very eminent performers, and some of them show a lot of originality. If an annual prize were hung up it would inspire them to further and perhaps unparalleled effort. Such a professor as Young Cochran, for example, is almost a genius, and with a little encouragement he might put over something so astonishing that the attention of the whole world would be attracted to Baltimore. And the chance to pull down an 18-carat halo should also improve the form of Dr. Hooker, Old Doc Davis, the Hon. William H. Anderson, the Hon. Sunday-School Field, the Hon. McCay McCoy and the Hon. Eugene Levering. Who will be the first to subscribe?

FROM an editorial on the Penitentiary in the learned *Evening News*:

A year ago not one item of the day's routine but was punitive in its intention and effect.

A SHINING example of that exuberant overstatement, which is one of the most characteristic symptoms of moral inflammation. Was there anything "punitive" in the system which allowed the prisoners to earn $25,000 a year for themselves? Was there anything "punitive" about the rule allowing convicts to decorate and furnish their cells as they chose, and to array themselves in lingerie designed and embroidered to their liking, and to anoint themselves with musk and frankincense to their taste? These last forms of "punishment" were actually denounced by the O'Dunne Commission as luxurious, Persian and corrupting! (Page 68.) Let the estimable *News* not forget the testimony of its own witnesses. Even that cheerful and accomplished liar, the Hon. Charles S. Henry, was forced to admit that the Hon. John F. Weyler *sometimes* treated him well.

IT is interesting to note, by the way, how quickly the common sense of

the people of Maryland reacted against the ludicrous extravagance of the O'Dunne report. According to the advance notices, it was going to knock out the contract system, blow up the Penitentiary Board, send Warden Leonard down for the count and bring the Terrible Weyler before the bar of the Criminal Court. But nothing of the sort, of course, has actually happened. The contract system is still in full blast, the Penitentiary Board is still on the job, Warden Leonard has been formally re-elected—and all of the "evidence" against the Terrible Weyler has gone to pieces. *Sic semper bunk!*

TYPHOID rate per 1,000 of men in the regular army, as reported by the War Department:

1906	5.66	1910	2.32
1907	3.35	1911	.80
1908	2.94	1912	.18
1909	3.03		

NOTE the dramatic drop in 1911 and the still more remarkable drop in 1912. In 1911 the use of anti-typhoid vaccine was introduced in the army, and in 1912 it was made compulsory. The effect of that use has been to reduce typhoid, once the worst plague of the soldier, both in war and in peace, to the triviality of measles. During the last 10 months of 1912 there were but 12 cases of typhoid in the whole army, and but two deaths. Neither of the men who died had been vaccinated. One was a recent recruit and the other was an officer who had been away from quarters when the inoculations were made.

H. L. MENCKEN.

Mencken's Baltimore Sun *column for 7 June 1913, dealing with a variety of topics (courtesy of the Enoch Pratt Free Library)*

THE FREE LANCE

RISING to a question of personal privilege, I beg to assure those gentlemen of the Letter Column who mistake my defense of the slandered and hard-pressed Germans for a laudable (or heinous) manifestation of patriotism that I am not a German and am not bound to Germany by sentimental ties. I was born in Baltimore of Baltimore-born parents; I have no relatives, near or remote, in Germany, nor even any friends (save one Englishman!); very few of my personal associates in this town are native Germans; I read the German language very imperfectly, and do not speak it or write it at all; I never saw Germany until I was 25 years old; I have been there since but twice; I am of English and Irish blood as well as German.

WHAT is more, the most massive influences of my life have all been unmistakably English. I know Kinglake's "Crimea" and Steevens' "With Kitchener to Khartoum" a great deal better than I know any history of the American Revolution or Civil War; I make a living writing the language of Thackeray and Huxley, and devote a good deal of time to studying it; I believe thoroughly in that imperialism for which England has always stood; I read English newspapers and magazines constantly, and have done so for 15 years; I regard the net English contribution to civilization as enormously greater than the German contribution; I am on good terms with many Englishmen, always get along well with them, and don't know a single one that I dislike.

ALL this by way of necessary explanation. But the Englishman upon whom the glory and greatness of England rests is not the Englishman who slanders and blubbers over Germany in this war. The England of Drake and Nelson, of Shakespeare and Marlow, of Darwin and Huxley, of Clive and Rhodes is not the England of Churchill and Lloyd-George, of Asquith and McKenna, of mongrel allies and bawling suffragettes, of "limehousing" and "mafficking," of press-censors and platitudinarians, of puerile moralizing and silly pettifogging. The England that the world yet admires and respects was a country ruled by proud and forthright men. The England that today poses as the uplifter of Europe is a country ruled by cheap demagogues and professional pharisees. The slimy "morality" of the unleashed rabble has conquered the clean and masculine ideals of the old ruling caste. A great nation has succumbed to mobocracy, and to the intellectual dishonesty that goes with it.

WHAT is the war really about? Why are the nations fighting one another? In so far as Germany and England are concerned, the cause is as plain as a pike-staff. Germany, of late years, has suddenly become England's rival as the boss of Europe, and with Europe, of the world. German trade has begun to prevail over English trade; German influence has begun to undermine English influence; even upon the sea, the new might and consequence of Germany have begun to challenge England's old lordship. The natural result is that the English have grown angry and alarmed, and the second result is that they yearn to crush and dispose of Germany before it is too late—i.e., before the Germans actually become their superiors in power, and so beyond their reach.

SUCH a yearning needs no defense. It is natural, it is virtuous, it is laudable. National jealousies make for the security, the prosperity and the greatness of the more virile nations, and hence for the progress of civilization. But did England, filled with this yearning, openly admit it, and then proceed in a frank and courageous manner to obtain its satisfaction in a fair fight? England did not. On the contrary, she artfully dissembled, her mouth full of pieties, until Germany was beset by enemies in front and behind, and then she suddenly threw her gigantic strength into the unequal contest. And did she, even then, announce her cause, state her motive, tell the truth? She did not. She went into battle with a false cry upon her lips, seeking to make her rage against a rival appear as a frenzy for righteousness, shedding crocodile tears over Germany's sins, wearing the tin halo and flapping chemise of a militant moralist.

I DO not like militant moralists, whether they be nations or individuals. I distrust the man who is concerned about his neighbor's sins, and who calls in the police (or the Turcos, or the Sikhs, or the Russians) to put them down. I have never known such a man who was honest with himself, nor is there any record of such a one in all history. They were a nuisance in the days of Christ, and His most bitter denunciations were leveled against them. They are still a nuisance today, though they impudently call themselves Christians, and even seek to excommunicate all persons who object to their excesses. That their shallow sophistries appeal to the mob, that they are especially numerous and powerful under a mobocracy, is but one more proof that mobocracy is the foe of civilization, and not only of civilization, but also of the truth.

FOR the manly, stand-up, ruthless, truth-telling, clean-minded England of another day I have the highest respect and reverence. It was an England of sound ideals and great men. But for the smug, moralizing, disingenuous England of Churchill and Lloyd-George, of hollow pieties and saccharine protestations, of Japanese alliances and the nonconformist conscience—for this new and oleaginous England, by Gladstone out of Pecksniff, I have no respect whatever. Its victory over Germany in this war would be a victory for all the ideas and ideals that I most ardently detest, and upon which, in my remote mud-puddle, I wage a battle with all the strength that I can muster, and to which I pledge my unceasing enmity until that day when the ultimate embalmer casts his sinister eye upon my fallen beauty.

WHEN I think of this new, this saponaceous, this superbrummagem England, so smug and slick without and so full of corruption and excess within, I am beset by emotions of the utmost unpleasantness. I snort; I swear; I leak large globulous tears. It is my hope and belief that this sick and bogus England will be given a good licking by the Deutsch, to the end that truth and health may prevail upon the earth. If the Mailed Fist cracks it, I shall rejoice unashamed. The Mailed Fist is dedicated to the eternal facts of life, to the thing behind the mere word, to the truth that is above all petty quibbling over theoretical rights and wrongs. I am for the Mailed Fist, gents, until the last galoot's ashore.

MEANWHILE, the Hon. William Jennings Bryan continues to make sheep's eyes at the Nobel prize. Like all uplifters, a thrifty fellow!

READ the Towsontown *New Era*, and escape the Sunday drought.—
Adv.   H. L. MENCKEN.

Mencken's column for 29 September 1914, attacking England's actions in World War I

ishly for the public good, and so discharging the highest duty of their profession. They lightened the dull days of midsummer by pursuing recreant aldermen with bloodhounds and artillery, by muckraking unsanitary milk-dealers, or by denouncing Sunday liquor-selling in suburban parks—and they fought constructive campaigns for good government in exactly the same gothic, melodramatic way. Always their first aim was to find a concrete target, to visualize their cause in some definite and defiant opponent. And always their second aim was to shell that opponent until he dropped his arms and took to ignominious flight. It was not enough to maintain and to prove; it was necessary also to pursue and overcome, to lay a specific somebody low, to give the good show aforesaid.

Does this confession of newspaper practice involve a libel upon the American people? Perhaps it does—on the theory, let us say, that the greater the truth, the greater the libel. But I doubt if any reflective newspaper man, however lofty his professional ideals, will ever deny any essential part of that truth. He knows very well that a definite limit is set, not only upon the people's capacity for grasping intellectual concepts, but also upon their capacity for grasping moral concepts. He knows that it is necessary, if he would catch and inflame them, to state his ethical syllogism in the homely terms of their habitual ethical thinking. And he knows that this is best done by dramatizing and vulgarizing it, by filling it with dynamic and emotional significance, by translating all argument for a principle into rage against a man.

In brief, he knows that it is hard for the plain people to *think* about a thing, but easy for them to *feel*. Error, to hold their attention, must be visualized as a villain, and the villain must proceed swiftly to his inevitable retribution. They can understand that process; it is simple, usual, satisfying; it squares with their primitive conception of justice as a form of revenge. The hero fires them too, but less certainly, less violently than the villain. His defect is that he offers thrills at second-hand. It is the merit of the villain, pursued publicly by a *posse comitatus,* that he makes the public breast the primary seat of heroism, that he makes every citizen a personal participant in a glorious act of justice. Wherefore it is ever the aim of the sagacious journalist to foster that sense of personal participation. The wars that he wages are always described as the people's wars, and he affects to be no more than their strategist and *claque.* When the victory has once been gained, true enough, he may take all the credit without a blush; but while the fight is going on he always pretends that every honest yeoman is enlisted, and he is even eager to make it appear that the yeomanry began it on their own motion, and out of the excess of their natural virtue.

I assume here, as an axiom too obvious to be argued, that the chief appeal of a newspaper, in all such holy causes, is not at all to the educated and reflective minority of citizens, but frankly to the ignorant and unreflective majority. The truth is that it would usually get a newspaper nowhere to address its exhortations to the former, for in the first place they are too few in number to make their support of much value in general engagements, and in the second place it is almost always impossible to convert them into disciplined and useful soldiers. They are too cantankerous for that, too ready with embarrassing strategy of their own. One of the principal marks of an educated man, indeed, is the fact that he does *not* take his opinions from newspapers—not, at any rate, from the militant, crusading newspapers. On the contrary, his attitude toward them is almost always one of frank cynicism, with indifference as its mildest form and contempt as its commonest. He knows that they are constantly falling into false reasoning about the things within his personal knowledge,—that is, within the narrow circle of his special education,—and so he assumes that they make the same, or even worse errors about other things, whether intellectual or moral. This assumption, it may be said at once, is quite justified by the facts.

I know of no subject, in truth, save perhaps baseball, on which the average American newspaper, even in the larger cities, discourses with unfailing sense and understanding. Whenever the public journals presume to illuminate such a matter as municipal taxation, for example, or the extension of local transportation facilities, or the punishment of public or private criminals, or the control of public-service corporations, or the revision of city charters, the chief effect of their effort is to introduce into it a host of extraneous issues, most of them wholly emotional, and so they contrive to make it unintelligible to all earnest seekers after the truth.

But it does not follow thereby that they also make it unintelligible to their special client, the man in the street. Far from it. What they actually accomplish is the exact opposite. That is to say, it is precisely by this process of transmutation and emotionalization that they bring a given problem down to the level of that man's comprehension, and what is more important, within the range of his active sympathies. He is not interested in anything that does not stir him, and he is not stirred by anything that fails to impinge upon his small stock of customary appetites and attitudes. His daily acts are ordered, not by any complex process of reasoning, but by a continuous process of very elemental feeling. He is not at all responsive to purely intellectual argument, even when its theme is his own ultimate benefit, for such argument quickly gets beyond his immediate interest and experience. But he *is* very responsive to emotional suggestion, particularly when it is crudely and violently made, and it is to this weakness that the newspapers must ever address their endeavors. In brief, they must try to arouse his horror, or indignation, or pity, or simply his lust for slaughter. Once they have done that, they have him safely by the nose. He will follow blindly until his emotion wears out. He will be ready to believe anything, however absurd, so long as he is in his state of psychic tumescence.

In the reform campaigns which periodically rock our large cities,–and our small ones, too,–the newspapers habitually make use of this fact. Such campaigns are not intellectual wars upon erroneous principles, but emotional wars upon errant men: they always revolve around the pursuit of some definite, concrete, fugitive malefactor, or group of malefactors. That is to say, they belong to popular sport rather than to the science of government; the impulse behind them is always far more orgiastic than reflective. For good government in the abstract, the people of the United States seem to have no liking, or, at all events, no passion. It is impossible to get them stirred up over it, or even to make them give serious thought to it. They seem to assume that it is a mere phantasm of theorists, a political will-o'-the-wisp, a utopian dream–wholly uninteresting, and probably full of dangers and tricks. The very discussion of it bores them unspeakably, and those papers which habitually discuss it logically and unemotionally–for example, the New York *Evening Post*–are diligently avoided by the mob. What the mob thirsts for is not good government in itself, but the merry chase of a definite exponent of bad government. The newspaper that discovers such an exponent–or, more accurately, the newspaper that discovers dramatic and overwhelming evidence against him–has all the material necessary for a reform wave of the highest emotional intensity. All that it need do is to goad the victim into a fight. Once he has formally joined the issue, the people will do the rest. They are always ready for a man-hunt, and their favorite quarry is the man of politics. If no such prey is at hand, they will turn to wealthy debauchees, to fallen Sunday-school superintendents, to money barons, to white-slave traders, to unsedulous chiefs of police. But their first choice is the boss.

In assaulting bosses, however, a newspaper must look carefully to its ammunition, and to the order and interrelation of its salvos. There is such a thing, at the start, as overshooting the mark, and the danger thereof is very serious. The people must be aroused by degrees, gently at first, and then with more and more ferocity. They are not capable of reaching the maximum of indignation at one leap: even on the side of pure emotion they have their rigid limitations. And this, of course, is because even emotion must have a quasi-intellectual basis, because even indignation must arise out of facts. One fact at a time! If a newspaper printed the whole story of a political boss's misdeeds in a single article, that article would have scarcely any effect whatever, for it would be far too long for the average reader to read and absorb. He would never get to the end of it, and the part he actually traversed would remain muddled and distasteful in his memory. Far from arousing an emotion in him, it would arouse only *ennui,* which is the very antithesis of emotion. He cannot read more than three columns of any one subject without tiring: 6,000 words, I should say, is the extreme limit of his appetite. And the nearer he is pushed to that limit, the greater the strain upon his psychic digestion. He can absorb a single capital fact, leaping from a headline, at one colossal gulp; but he could not down a dissertation in twenty. And the first desideratum in a headline is that it deal with a single and capital fact. It must be "McGinnis Steals $1,257,867.25," not "McGinnis Lacks Ethical Sense."

Moreover, a newspaper article which presumed to tell the whole of a thrilling story in one gargantuan installment would lack the dynamic element, the quality of mystery and suspense. Even if it should achieve the miracle of arousing the reader to a high pitch of excitement, it would let him drop again next day. If he is to be kept in his frenzy long enough for it to be dangerous to the common foe, he must be led into it gradually. The newspaper in charge of the business must harrow him, tease him, promise him, hold him. It is thus that his indignation is transformed from a state of being into a state of gradual and cumulative becoming; it is thus that reform takes on the character of a hotly contested game, with the issue agreeably in doubt. And it is always as a game, of course, that the man in the street views moral endeavor. Whether its proposed victim be a political boss, a police captain, a gambler, a fugitive murderer, or a disgraced clergyman, his interest in it is almost purely a sporting interest. And the intensity of that interest, of course, depends upon the fierceness of the clash. The game is fascinating in proportion as the morally pursued puts up a stubborn defense, and in proportion as the newspaper directing the pursuit is resourceful and merciless, and in proportion as the eminence of the quarry is great and his resultant downfall spectacular. A war against a ward boss seldom attracts much attention, even in the smaller cities, for he is insignificant to begin with and an inept and cowardly fellow to end with; but the famous war upon William M. Tweed shook the whole nation, for he was a man of tremendous power, he was a brave and enterprising antagonist, and his fall carried a multitude of other men with him. Here, indeed, was sport royal, and the plain people took to it with avidity.

Mencken at the Baltimore Sun *in 1913 (courtesy of the Enoch Pratt Free Library)*

But once such a buccaneer is overhauled and manacled, the show is over, and the people take no further interest in reform. In place of the fallen boss, a so-called reformer has been set up. He goes into office with public opinion apparently solidly behind him: there is every promise that the improvement achieved will be lasting. But experience shows that it seldom is. Reform does not last. The reformer quickly loses his public. His usual fate, indeed, is to become the pet butt and aversion of his public. The very mob that put him into office chases him out of office. And after all, there is nothing very astonishing about this change of front, which is really far less a change of front than it seems. The mob has been fed, for weeks preceding the reformer's elevation, upon the blood of big and little bosses; it has acquired a taste for their chase, and for the chase in general. Now, of a sudden, it is deprived of that stimulating sport. The old bosses are in retreat; there are yet no new bosses to belabor and pursue; the newspapers which elected the reformer are busily apologizing for his amateurish errors,—a dull and dispiriting business. No wonder it now becomes possible for the old bosses, acting through their inevitable friends on the respectable side,—the "solid" business men, the takers of favors, the under-

writers of political enterprise, and the newspapers influenced by these pious fellows,—to start the rabble against the reformer. The trick is quite as easy as that but lately done. The rabble want a good show, a game, a victim: it does n't care who that victim may be. How easy to convince it that the reformer is a scoundrel himself, that he is as bad as any of the old bosses, that he ought to go to the block for high crimes and misdemeanors! It never had any actual love for him, or even any faith in him; his election was a mere incident of the chase of his predecessor. No wonder that it falls upon him eagerly, butchering him to make a new holiday!

This is what has happened over and over again in every large American city—Chicago, New York, St. Louis, Cincinnati, Pittsburg [*sic*], New Orleans, Baltimore, San Francisco, St. Paul, Kansas City. Every one of these places has had its melodramatic reform campaigns and its inevitable reactions. The people have leaped to the overthrow of bosses, and then wearied of the ensuing tedium. A perfectly typical slipping back, to be matched in a dozen other cities, is going on in Philadelphia to-day. Mayor Rudolph Blankenberg, a veteran warhorse of reform, came into office through the downfall of the old bosses, a catastrophe for which he had labored and agitated for more than thirty years. But now the old bosses are getting their revenge by telling the people that he is a violent and villainous boss himself. Certain newspapers are helping them; they have concealed but powerful support among financiers and business men; volunteers have even come forward from other cities—for example, the Mayor of Baltimore, himself a triumphant ringster. Slowly but surely this insidious campaign is making itself felt; the common people show signs of yearning for another *auto-da-fé*. Mayor Blankenberg, unless I am the worst prophet unhung, will meet with an overwhelming defeat in 1915. And it will be a very difficult thing to put even a half-decent man in his place: the victory of the bosses will be so nearly complete that they will be under no necessity of offering compromises. Employing a favorite device of political humor, they may select a harmless blank cartridge, a respectable numskull, what is commonly called a perfumer. But the chances are that they will select a frank ringster, and that the people will elect him with cheers.

Such is the ebb and flow of emotion in the popular heart—or perhaps, if we would be more accurate, the popular liver. It does not constitute an intelligible system of morality, for morality, at bottom, is not at all an instinctive matter, but a purely intellectual matter: its essence is the control of impulse by an ideational process, the subordination of the immediate desire to the distant aim. But such as it is, it is the only system of morality that the emotional majority is capable of comprehending and practicing; and so the newspapers, which deal with majorities quite as frankly as politicians deal with them, have to admit it into their own system. That is to say, they cannot accomplish anything by talking down to the public from a moral plane higher than its own: they must take careful account of its habitual ways of thinking, its moral thirsts and prejudices, its well-defined limitations. They must remember clearly, as judges and lawyers have to remember it, that the morality subscribed to by that public is far from the stern and arctic morality of professors of the science. On the contrary, it is a mellower and more human thing; it has room for the antithetical emotions of sympathy and scorn; it makes no effort to separate the criminal from his crime. The higher moralities, running up to that of Puritans and archbishops, allow no weight to custom, to general reputation, to temptation; they hold it to be no defense of a ballot-box stuffer, for example, that he had scores of accomplices and that he is kind to his little children. But the popular morality regards such a defense as sound and apposite; it is perfectly willing to convert a trial on a specific charge into a trial on a general charge. And in giving judgment it is always ready to let feeling triumph over every idea of abstract justice;

and very often that feeling has its origin and support, not in matters actually in evidence, but in impressions wholly extraneous and irrelevant.

Hence the need of a careful and wary approach in all newspaper crusades, particularly on the political side. On the one hand, as I have said, the astute journalist must remember the public's incapacity for taking in more than one thing at a time, and on the other hand, he must remember its disposition to be swayed by mere feeling, and its habit of founding that feeling upon general and indefinite impressions. Reduced to a rule of everyday practice, this means that the campaign against a given malefactor must begin a good while before the capital accusation—that is, the accusation upon which a verdict of guilty is sought—is formally brought forward. There must be a shelling of the fortress before the assault; suspicion must precede indignation. If this preliminary work is neglected or ineptly performed, the result is apt to be a collapse of the campaign. The public is not ready to switch from confidence to doubt on the instant; if its general attitude toward a man is sympathetic, that sympathy is likely to survive even a very vigorous attack. The accomplished mob-master lays his course accordingly. His first aim is to arouse suspicion, to break down the presumption of innocence—supposing, of course, that he finds it to exist. He knows that all storms of emotion, however suddenly they may seem to come up, have their origin over the rim of consciousness, and that their gathering is really a slow, slow business. I mix the figures shamelessly, as mob-masters mix their brews!

It is this persistence of an attitude which gives a certain degree of immunity to all newcomers in office, even in the face of sharp and resourceful assault. For example, a new president. The majority in favor of him on Inauguration Day is usually overwhelming, no matter how small his plurality in the November preceding, for common self-respect demands that the people magnify his virtues: to deny them would be a confession of national failure, a destructive criticism of the Republic. And that benignant disposition commonly survives until his first year in office is more than half gone. The public prejudice is wholly on his side: his critics find it difficult to arouse any indignation against him, even when the offenses they lay to him are in violation of the fundamental axioms of popular morality. This explains why it was that Mr. Wilson was so little damaged by the charge of federal interference in the Diggs-Caminetti case—a charge well supported by the evidence brought forward, and involving a serious violation of popular notions of virtue. And this explains, too, why he survived the oratorical pilgrimages of his Secretary of State at a time of serious international difficulty—pilgrimages apparently undertaken with his approval, and hence at his political risk and cost. The people were still in favor of him, and so he was not brought to irate and drum-head judgment. No roar of indignation arose to the heavens. The opposition newspapers, with sure instinct, felt the irresistible force of public opinion on his side, and so they ceased their clamor very quickly.

But it is just such a slow accumulation of pin-pricks, each apparently harmless in itself, that finally draws blood; it is by just such a leisurely and insidious process that the presumption of innocence is destroyed, and a hospitality to suspicion created. The campaign against Governor Sulzer in New York offers a classic example of this process in operation, with very skillful gentlemen, journalistic and political, in control of it. The charges on which Governor Sulzer was finally brought to impeachment were not launched at him out of a clear sky, nor while the primary presumption in his favor remained unshaken. Not at all. They were launched at a carefully selected and critical moment—at the end, to wit, of a long and well-managed series of minor attacks. The fortress of his popularity was bombarded a long while before it was assaulted. He was pursued with insinuations and innuendoes; various persons, more or less dubious, were led to make various charges, more or less vague, against him; the managers of the campaign sought to poison the plain people with doubts, misunderstandings, suspicions. This effort, so diligently made, was highly successful; and so the capital charges, when they were brought forward at last, had the effect of confirmations, of corroborations, of proofs. But, if Tammany had made them during the first few months of Governor Sulzer's term, while all doubts were yet in his favor, it would have got only scornful laughter for its pains. The ground had to be prepared; the public mind had to be put into training.

The end of my space is near, and I find that I have written of popular morality very copiously, and of newspaper morality very little. But, as I have said before, the one is the other. The newspaper must adapt its pleading to its clients' moral limitations, just as the trial lawyer must adapt *his* pleading to the jury's limitations. Neither may like the job, but both must face it to gain a larger end. And that end, I believe, is a worthy one in the newspaper's case quite as often as in the lawyer's, and perhaps far oftener. The art of leading the vulgar, in itself, does no discredit to its practitioner. Lincoln practiced it unashamed, and so did Webster, Clay, and Henry. What is more, these men practiced it with frank allowance for the naïveté of the people they presumed to lead. It was Lincoln's chief source of strength, indeed, that he had a homely way with him, that he could reduce complex problems to the simple terms of

Title page for a German book on anti-German propaganda in America during World War I, dedicated to Mencken

popular theory and emotion, that he did not ask little fishes to think and act like whales. This is the manner in which the newspapers do their work, and in the long run, I am convinced, they accomplish far more good than harm thereby. Dishonesty, of course, is not unknown among them: we have newspapers in this land which apply a truly devilish technical skill to the achievement of unsound and unworthy ends. But not as many of them as perfectionists usually allege. Taking one with another, they strive in the right direction. They realize the massive fact that the plain people, for all their poverty of wit, cannot be fooled forever. They have a healthy fear of that heathen rage which so often serves their uses.

Look back a generation or two. Consider the history of our democracy since the Civil War. Our most serious problems, it must be plain, have been solved orgiastically, and to the tune of deafening newspaper urging and clamor. Men have been washed into office on waves of emotion, and washed out again in the same manner. Measures and policies have been determined

Cartoons of Mencken as a war correspondent in World War I (courtesy of the Enoch Pratt Free Library)

by indignation far more often than by cold reason. But is the net result evil? Is there even any permanent damage from those debauches of sentiment in which the newspapers have acted insincerely, unintelligently, with no thought save for the show itself? I doubt it. The effect of their long and melodramatic chase of bosses is an undoubted improvement in our whole governmental method. The boss of to-day is not an envied first citizen, but a criminal constantly on trial. He is debarred himself from all public offices of honor, and his control over other public officers grows less and less. Elections are no longer boldly stolen; the humblest citizen may go to the polls in safety and cast his vote honestly; the machine grows less dangerous year by year; perhaps it is already less dangerous than a *camorra* of utopian and dehumanized reformers would be. We begin to develop an official morality which actually rises above our private morality. Bribe-takers are sent to jail by the votes of jurymen who give presents in their daily business, and are not above beating the street-car company.

And so, too, in narrower fields. The white-slave agitation of a year or so ago was ludicrously extravagant and emotional, but its net effect is a better conscience, a new alertness. The newspapers discharged broadsides of 12-inch guns to bring down a flock of buzzards–but they brought down the buzzards. They have libeled and lynched the police–but the police are the better for it. They have represented salicylic acid as an elder brother to bichloride of mercury–but we are poisoned less than we used to be. They have lifted the plain people to frenzies of senseless terror over drinking-cups and neighbors with coughs–but the death-rate from tuberculosis declines. They have railroaded men to prison, denying them all their common rights–but fewer malefactors escape to-day than yesterday.

The way of ethical progress is not straight. It describes, to risk a mathematical pun, a sort of drunken hyperbola. But if we thus move onward and upward by leaps and bounces, it is certainly better than not moving at all. Each time, perhaps, we slip back, but each time we stop at a higher level.

The final column in the series exemplifies the Germanophile/ Anglophobe stance that strained Mencken's connection to the Sunpapers *during World War I (excerpt from "The Free Lance,"* Baltimore Evening Sun, *23 October 1915, editorial page).*

Next to the merry effort of English blubberers and stay-at-homes to make capital of the Cavell incident, the most amusing affair of the moment is the gorgeous discrepancy between the Serbian war bulletins and the known facts. The glowing reports of victories that reached us, during August of last year, from Brussels via London, are now more than outdone by the optimistic fables sent from Nish via Athens. And why via Athens? Why not via Bucharest and Petrograd, or Cettinje and Rome? Obviously, because these bulletins are made especially for Greek consumption–because they are parts of a last desperate effort to convince the Greeks that the Central Powers cannot hack their way to Constantinople and the Suez Canal. But the scoundrelly bootblacks, alas, are too wise to be fooled. I quote here a high pro-Ally authority, Dr. E. J. Dillon, telegraphing to the London *Daily Telegraph* from Rome:

> The truth is that Greece and Roumania have been influenced by their rulers' dynastic predilections, by *general awe of Germany* and by a *certitude that the Allies would be worsted in the end.*

Gone the old general awe of England. Enter the general awe of Germany. . . . Incidentally, Dr. Dillon says that the Italian Black Handers are growing very restive. Their campaigns in the Trentino and before Görz have yielded them nothing, and they are beginning to feel that England has treated them very badly. Says Dr. Dillon:

> The general public here [in Italy] is dispirited at the generosity of the allied governments toward Greece [i. e., in the matter of Cyprus] compared with their business-like firmness when dealing with . . . Italy. . . .

But now that they are in the war, the poor Italians see no way of getting out. And as they observe the Central Powers making steady progress, they can look ahead and picture what is coming to them when Germany turns in their direction. "Atrocities" in Belgium? Pish! Wait for the big show! [. . .]

What could not be printed in a newspaper once America entered the war, owing to patriotic self-censorship as well as to government threats, appeared in Mencken's writings immediately afterward, when his cynicism was shared even by many veterans. A favorite target, as in this Smart Set *piece, was the propaganda swallowed by a gullible public ("Patriotic Propaganda,"* Smart Set *[April 1921]: 36).*

Various psychologists, dismayed by the harvest of blather that accompanied and followed the late war, yet profess to see some good in it, or at all events some necessity, in the paramount need of organizing the

Mencken (third from left) at Vilnius, Lithuania, on 30 January 1917 (courtesy of the Enoch Pratt Free Library)

courage of the plain people. Without a deliberate effort to arouse them, at whatever cost to sense and decency, it would have been impossible, so it is argued, to preserve their *morale*. This argument is only half-way sound. No sane rabble-rouser, in time of war, tries to pump up the *courage* of the plain people; what he actually tries to pump up is their *cowardice*. Thus in the late combat. The first selling point of all the boob-bumpers was the contention that the Germans (with gigantic wars on two fronts) were preparing to invade the United States, burn down all the towns, murder all the men, and carry off all the women. The second selling point was that the entrance of the United States would end the war almost instantly—that the Germans would be so colossally outnumbered, in men and guns, that it would be impossible for them to make any resistance. Neither argument showed the slightest belief in popular courage. Both were grounded upon the frank theory that the way to make the mob fight is to scare it half to death—and then show it a way to fight without any risk. Precisely the same thing happened in all the other warring countries. The boobs were unanimously scared into the war. It was only a small minority of men who went into the thing because they were courageous, or who sought and advocated such rules of combat as a truly courageous man demands.

What Mencken could write during the war proved his point. He amused himself by creating the notorious Bathtub Hoax. Despite his later attempts to undo it, the fictive history in this essay is still presented as fact in some reference works, and one of its details is the only thing that some people think they know about Millard Fillmore (excerpt from "A Neglected Anniversary," *New York Evening Mail, 28 December 1917, p. 9).*

On December 20 there flitted past us, absolutely without public notice, one of the most important profane anniversaries in American history, to wit, the seventy-fifth anniversary of the introduction of the bathtub into These States. Not a plumber fired a salute or hung out a flag. Not a governor proclaimed a day of prayer. Not a newspaper called attention to the day.

True enough, it was not entirely forgotten. Eight or nine months ago one of the younger surgeons connected with the Public Health Service in Washington happened upon the facts while looking into the early history of public hygiene, and at his suggestion a committee was formed to celebrate the anniversary with a banquet. But before the plan was perfected Washington went dry, and so the banquet had to be abandoned. As it was, the day passed wholly unmarked, even in the capital of the nation.

Bathtubs are so common today that it is almost impossible to imagine a world without them. They are familiar to nearly every one in all incorporated towns; in most of the large cities it is unlawful to build a dwelling house without putting them in; even on the farm they have begun to come into use. And yet the first American bathtub was installed and dedicated so recently as December 20, 1842, and, for all I know to the contrary, it may be still in existence and in use.

Curiously enough, the scene of its setting up was Cincinnati, then a squalid frontier town, and even today surely no leader in culture. But Cincinnati, in those days as in these, contained many enterprising merchants, and one of them was a man named Adam Thompson, a dealer in cotton and grain. Thompson shipped his merchandise by steamboat down the Ohio and Mississippi to New Orleans, and from there sent it to England in sailing vessels. This trade frequently took him to England, and in that country, during the 30s, he acquired the habit of bathing.

* * *

The bathtub was then still a novelty in England. It had been introduced in 1828 by Lord John Russell and its use was yet confined to a small class of enthusiasts. Moreover, the English bathtub, then as now, was a puny and inconvenient contrivance—little more, in fact, than a glorified dishpan—and filling and emptying it required the attendance of a servant. Taking a bath, indeed, was a rather heavy ceremony, and Lord John in 1835 was said to be the only man in England who had yet come to doing it every day. [. . .]

But it was the example of President Millard Fillmore that, even more than the grudging medical approval, gave the bathtub recognition and respectability in the United States. While he was still Vice-President, in March, 1850, he visited Cincinnati on a stumping tour, and inspected the original Thompson tub. Thompson himself was now dead, but the bathroom was preserved by the gentleman who had bought his house from his estate. Fillmore was entertained in this house and, according to Chamberlain, his biographer, took a bath in the tub. Experiencing no ill effects, he became an ardent advocate of the new invention, and on succeeding to the presidency at Taylor's death, July 9, 1850, he instructed his secretary of war, Gen. Charles M. Conrad, to invite tenders for the construction of a bathtub in the White House.

* * *

This action, for a moment, revived the old controversy, and its opponents made much of the fact that there was no bathtub at Mount Vernon or at Monticello, and that all the Presidents and other magnificoes of the past had got along without any such monarchical luxuries. The elder Bennett, in the New York "Herald," charged that Fillmore really aspired to buy and install in the White House a porphyry and alabaster bath that had been used by Louis Philippe at Versailles. But Conrad, disregarding all this clamor, duly called for bids, and the contract was presently awarded to Harper & Gillespie, a firm of Philadelphia engineers, who proposed to furnish a tub of thin cast iron, capable of floating the largest man.

This was installed early in 1851 and remained in service in the White House until the first Cleveland administration, when the present enameled tub was substituted. The example of the President soon broke down all that remained of the old opposition, and by 1860, according to the newspaper advertisements of the time, every hotel in New York had a bathtub, and some had two and even three. In 1862 bathing was introduced into the army by Gen. McClellan, and in 1870 the first prison bathtub was set up at Moyamensing Prison, in Philadelphia.

So much for the history of the bathtub in America. One is astonished, on looking into it, to find that so little of it has been recorded. The literature, in fact, is almost nil. But perhaps this brief sketch will encourage other inquirers and so lay the foundation for an adequate celebration of the centennial in 1942.

Mencken's "Monday Articles" for the Evening Sun *ran from 1920 to 1938, as the* Smart Set *editorship gave way to that of* The American Mercury *(1924–1933) and then, with the Great Depression, a partial eclipse. He was always at his best when the subject combined favorite topics on which he could work endless variations. Perennially these topics were religion, Prohibition, politics, and his own profession, as in this account of journalistic reactions to Al Smith, who was Catholic and "wet" ("Al and the Pastors,"* Baltimore Evening Sun, *6 August 1928, editorial page).*

I.

With the nomination of Al in the hot, hell-bent city of Houston, I resumed an old vice: the reading of denominational papers. Whether Catholic or Protestant, they are always full of amusing stuff, but especially when they are Protestant and evangelical. As of July 10 I subscribed to all the Baptist and Methodist organs south of the Potomac, and have been refreshing my soul with them ever since. They pour in at the rate of three or four a day, nearly every one with its furious, first-page blast against poor Al. From them I learn a great deal that is confidential and surprising about the

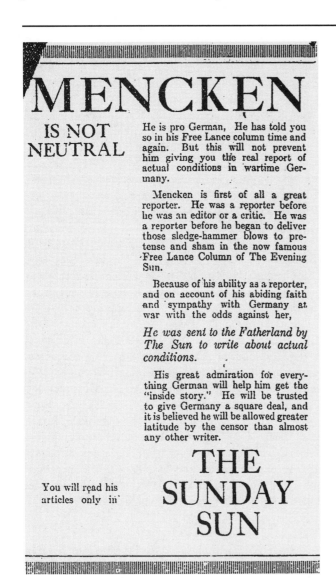

MENCKEN

IS NOT NEUTRAL

He is pro German, He has told you so in his Free Lance column time and again. But this will not prevent him giving you the real report of actual conditions in wartime Germany.

Mencken is first of all a great reporter. He was a reporter before he was an editor or a critic. He was a reporter before he began to deliver those sledge-hammer blows to pretense and sham in the now famous Free Lance Column of The Evening Sun.

Because of his ability as a reporter, and on account of his abiding faith and sympathy with Germany at war with the odds against her,

He was sent to the Fatherland by The Sun to write about actual conditions.

His great admiration for everything German will help him get the "inside story." He will be trusted to give Germany a square deal, and it is believed he will be allowed greater latitude by the censor than almost any other writer.

You will read his articles only in

THE SUNDAY SUN

Notice in the Sun *admitting its correspondent's partiality (courtesy of the Enoch Pratt Free Library)*

plot of the Pope to seize the United States, but even more about the troubles of his rivals of the Baptist and Methodist rites.

These brethren, I gather, are far from easy in mind. Convinced by their searchings of the Scriptures that the election of Al would cause the downfall of the Republic, they yet show a painful fear that the Solid South will nevertheless support him. What alarms them most is the attitude of the daily newspapers of the region, all of which have kissed the Tammany blarney stone. Thus they have to turn aside frequently from their slaughter of the Pope to rebuke these traitors, and the result is a division and dispersal of their fire.

Of all the sheets that come in for denunciation the most hotly denounced seem to be the Richmond *News-Leader,* the Jackson (Miss.) *News,* the Atlanta *Con-stitution* and the Raleigh *News and Observer.* All four are edited by consecrated, Christian men–the *News-Leader* by the gifted Dr. Douglas S. Freeman, the *News* by the Hon. Frederick Sullen, the *Constitution* by the Hon. Clark Howell, and the *News and Observer* by the eminent Josephus Daniels. Dr. Freeman is the leading Baptist layman of Richmond, Dr. Daniels is the leading Methodist of North Carolina, and the Hon. Mr. Sullen was converted by Dr. Billy Sunday and is to the front in all pious works. Nevertheless, all have dedicated their papers to Al, and so they are bitterly reviled by their colleagues of the evangelical press. The Richmond *Christian Advocate* even goes to the length of hinting darkly, though without saying it out loud, that Dr. Freeman is "now owned and controlled by Catholic and Jewish interests."

II.

Worse, there is a certain amount of treason within the fold of the pastors themselves. The case of Monsignor Warren A. Candler, the Methodist ordinary of Atlanta, has already got into the newspapers. He is a brother to Asa G. Candler, the coca-cola magnate, and hence has access to a great deal of money, and must be listened to when he speaks. Bishop Candler refuses to come out against Al; more, he warns the clergy of his diocese against taking the church into politics. Two of his colleagues on the bench of bishops join him. It is all very disturbing.

Nor is there any lack of dissent lower down the scale. I pick up the *Christian Index* of Atlanta, "the organ and property of the Baptists of Georgia," and find its whole first page given over to a solemn remonstrance by the Rev. John D. Mell. He addresses himself "to the Baptist preachers in Georgia," and says:

> The members of your churches are divided. Reason, judgment and prudence are going to be dethroned as the campaign progresses. If you take the high office to which you have been called down into the strife, and become a partisan in your community, you will lose the affection of nearly all of those you oppose, of many of those whose candidate you espouse, and you may, in some cases, even lose your pulpits. I have known, in my time, several strong preachers to lose their pulpits that way, and they were just as sincere as you are, and, perhaps, just as wise.

Editor Louie D. Newton, of the *Index,* gives his best space to this warning, but he makes no reference to it in his editorials. Instead, he gives over three pages to articles taking the opposite line–one a report of the dry conference at Asheville, N.C., on July 18 and 19, another a long treatise by the Rev. A. T. Robertson, professor of New Testament interpretation in the

Berlin, February 1, 1917.

Jetzt geht's los!   Across the front page of the
Tageblatt this morning runs the long-awaited, hat-in-the-ring-
throwing, much-pother-through-out-the-world-up-stirring headline:
Verkündung des uneingeschränkten U-Boot-Krieges! -- Proclamation
of the Unrestrained U-Boat War!   At last the big show!   The adjective used to be **rücksichtlos,** which is to say, reckless.   Late
it has been **verschärften:** sharpened.   Now it is **uneingeschränkten:**
unrestrained, unlimited, fast and loose, without benefit of clergy,
knock 'em down and drag 'em out.   But whatever the term used to
designate it, the thing itself remains, and out of that thing in
itself, unless I lose my guess, a lot of trouble is about to arise.
If the United States accepts this new slaughter of ships without
giving Graf von Bernstorff his walking papers, it will be a miracle.
And if it goes another month without horning into the war it will
be two miracles. . .

It got back to Berlin from Vilna and the Eastern front
late last night, tired, rheumatic and half-frozen, and rolled into
bed without stopping to hear the gossip in the Adlon bar.   This
morning I turned out just in time for the fireworks.   The first
American I encountered was Raymond Swing, of the Chicago **Daily News.**
I had borrowed a heavy overcoat and a pair of leather **Garmaschen**
from him to go into Lithuania, and I went to his office in Unter
den Linden to thank him for his amiability, and to offer him a
Leberwurst -- a sourvenir of the army slaughter-house at Novo

Page from the typescript for Mencken's unpublished journal written during his stint as a war correspondent (courtesy of the Enoch Pratt Free Library)

Alfred E. Smith, whose 1928 presidential campaign Mencken observed with great interest

Southern Baptist Theological Seminary, arguing that John the Baptist, if he were alive today, would be against Al, and a third by the Rev. T. F. Calloway, pastor of the First Baptist Church of Thomasville, Ga., full of hot stuff against the Pope. Dr. Robertson is one of the great whales of the Southern Baptist connection. He has many learned degrees, is the author of a textbook of New Testament Greek, and belongs to the American Philological Association. I offer the following specimen of his logic:

> It is better to have a head like that of John the Baptist and lose it for the sake of righteousness than not to have such a head and keep it.

III.

So far as I can make out, but one evangelical journal of the South has refused to join the hue-and-cry against Al. That is the *Southern Christian Advocate* of Columbia, S.C., the home of the celebrated Senator Cole L. Blease and (according to Dr. Blease himself) of some of the most accomplished booticians in the entire South. The editor of the *Southern Christian Advocate* went

to the Asheville conference and told the brethren there that "in South Carolina circumstances were such that all problems since 1876 had been worked out within the Democratic party, and that however many there might be who would never vote for Smith, few could be expected to vote for Hoover, and that the State would remain in the Democratic column."

The editor himself says that he will not vote for Al, and he gives plenty of space in his paper to those who advocate voting for Lord Hoover, but he refuses to go so far himself. Apparently, one of the considerations that keeps him in line is the fact that his Democratic State executive committee has decided that persons who confess that they will vote for Hoover cannot take any part in the Democratic primaries. He protests against this scheme to hog-tie dry Democrats, and says that it is "contrary to all fairness and the Constitution of a country of freemen." In other Southern States the same rule has been put into effect, and it has brought forth the same remonstrances. But the politicians stand pat, and so the pastors can only rage and roar.

Most of them do it with hearty goodwill. I can find but one, indeed, who pleads for Christian charity. He is the Rev. Livingston Johnson, editor of the *Biblical Record* of Raleigh, N.C., a Baptist organ. He says:

> Nothing can be gained, but much may be lost, by intemperate language or unkind conduct toward others. We should do our duty fearlessly, uninfluenced by what others may say or think, if our consciences are leading us to pursue courses different from theirs; but we should pray for grace to prevent us from saying anything that would alienate our friends, or create wounds that this life may be too short to heal.

Dr. Johnson adds to this plea the strange doctrine that "we preachers should remember that our chief work in the world is to offer the Bread of Life to hungry souls."

IV.

During the two weeks following Al's nomination there was but little mention of his religion. He was denounced simply as a wet, or as a member of Tammany. But now practically all of the denominational papers have at him as a Catholic, and devote a large part of their space to assaults upon the Pope. The principal charge leveled against His Holiness is that he is in politics, and eager to get political control of the United States. This ambition is opposed on the ground that church and state ought to be kept separate, but it is common for an embattled editor to argue in the very next column that it is not only permissible for the Bap-

"Only Four More Days, Boys–Do Your *Stuff!*"

November 2, 1928

Cartoon in the Sun *by Edmund Duffy, commenting on the alliance of the Ku Klux Klan and the Prohibitionists in opposition to the "wet" Catholic presidential candidate Smith (from S. L. Harrison,* The Editorial Art of Edmund Duffy *[Madison & Teaneck, N.J.: Fairleigh Dickinson University Press / London & Toronto: Associated University Presses, 1998]; reproduced by permission).*

tist and Methodist churches to go into politics, but even a moral duty.

Many of the reverend editors have been led by their researches to raise the old question, for long hotly debated by Southern theologians, whether a Catholic is a Christian at all. The Rev. A. M. Pierce, of the *Wesleyan Christian Advocate* of Atlanta, apparently thinks not: he is "strongly persuaded," he says, that Catholicism is only "a degenerate type of Christianity" and ought to be displaced by "a purer type." To that end, he says, "various Protestant churches are working on different mission fields." But other editors are not so sure. In the Richmond *Christian Advocate,* for example, space is given to a Norfolk contributor who appeals to Catholics as fellow-Christians, and says, "I have not yet, and I pray God I never will, knock any church that stands for Jesus Christ." Not many, however, go that far.

Meanwhile, it is curious to note that certain Romish practices have begun to get lodgment in the Bible Belt. For example, the *Biblical Record,* of Raleigh, gives over a column and a half on its first page to an account of a *retreat* at Ridgecrest, N. C., in June! More than sixty Baptists took part in it.

The term Bible Belt *was a Mencken creation. He enjoyed roiling the waters throughout the country, especially in the South, to provoke responses—the more violent the better. In this 1928 letter he encourages his editor, Hamilton Owens, to see that another Monday article concerning the Southern clergy during the Smith campaign gets wide circulation (typewritten letter with handwritten initial as signature at Enoch Pratt Free Library, Baltimore).*

H.L. MENCKEN
1524 HOLLINS ST.
BALTIMORE.

EVENING SUN *April 9, 1923.*

Saviors Of Civilization

By H. L. MENCKEN.

[*Copyright, 1923, The Evening Sun. Republication without credit not permitted.*]

I.

THE shattered Liberals, swinging endlessly between hope and indignation, now entertain the nobility and gentry of the Republic with heart-rending squawks against the French reign of assault and pillage along the Ruhr. The gallant Frogs, but lately battling heroically to save Christianity, democracy and all the rest of it from the hoof of the horrible Hun, have now, it appears, suddenly thrown off their gallantry, and devote themselves to enterprises that would almost cause a lifting of eyebrows in West Virginia, Arkansas or Northwestern Louisiana. Property is seized and carried off; peaceful citizens are flogged and murdered; women are outraged; children are brutally manhandled. The tale reads almost like a report on Ku Klux activities by the Knights of Columbus or B'nai B'rith. The English press agents imagined nothing worse during the German occupation of Belgium. Contemplating the appalling spectacle, the Liberals are so unpleasantly affected that they quite forget the regular weekly extermination of the whole Armenian nation by the Turks.

A depressing business, true enough, but nevertheless one that is not without its mirthless, sardonic humors. These are the same Frenchmen, remember, who but four short years ago were the deliverers of civilization, and these are the same Liberals who aided and abetted the delivery with exultant, falsetto applause. What has happened in the meanwhile? Are we to assume that the chivalrous and laborious Frogs, by some unprecedented act of God, have suddenly lost all their old high qualities and taken on the abhorrent sinfulness of their antagonists? Or are we to assume, alternatively, that what they are today is precisely what they have always been—in brief, that the whole dilemma reduces itself to the simple theory that the Liberals have been fooled again—as they were fooled by Woodrow, as they were fooled by the so-called Disarmament Conference, as they were fooled by the Irish settlement, and as they will be fooled according to their naïve and hopeful nature, over and over again, world without end?

II.

THE latter assumption, it seems to me, is by far the more plausible of the two: it is, indeed, so well supported by the evidence and by logic that, in the long run, even university professors of history will probably begin to flirt with it. There is, as a matter of fact, not the slightest reason for believing that the heroic French have changed in the slightest. They are today what they were before, during and immediately after the war—a race almost wholly devoid of the valiant and noble qualities so lately ascribed to them. There is no more actual altruism in a Frenchman than there is in a Greek. He is an extremely canny, realistic and avaricious fellow, eager for money and avid of power, and when he cannot get these things by honest industry, which is usually, he always tries to get them by force and fraud. The history of Europe for 500 years is simply a history of his successive efforts to swindle, pillage and dragoon his neighbors. The conduct of the French in the late war, far from being marked by a lofty courage and romantic idealism, as it was represented to be at the time by very much interested parties, was actually a grotesque compound of pathological furies and puerile despairs. There was never a moment from

French avarice, sordidness and uncleanliness. To say that these Americans came home with a high respect and admiration for the French would be a palpable exaggeration; they actually came home full of disgust and aversion. And so with the English. If the French are the most unpopular of peoples in England today, it is surely not due entirely to the political and economic conflict between the two countries; it is due just as much to millions of personal contacts during the war. The Belgians and Italians are not far behind. As for the Russians, they are well aware today how much French friendship was worth—how much genuine good will was in it and how much mere hope of gain.

Two salient facts, obscured by the violent propaganda of the war years, will emerge eventually and take their places in the history of the time. One is that the French habitually mistreated prisoners during the war, including the wounded—a circumstance which largely explains the special and extremely bitter character of the present German hatred of them. In almost every German community there is some soldier who spent a year or two in a French prison camp. He carries upon his body the marks of his experience, and his story is known to all of his neighbors and will be handed on to the generations of the future. The German prisoners in the hands of the English, Russians and Italians were nearly all decently treated; those in the hands of the French were treated to the humanity of savages. The remaining fact is this: that, alone among the nations engaged in the war, the French produced traitors who made deliberate efforts to deal with the enemy. A number of them, some in high places, were detected, but every well-informed German knows that there were plenty of others who were not detected.

IV.

IN view of all this, the discovery of the American Liberals that the French leopard has suddenly changed his spots, and become a sort of cross between a jackal and an hyena, is diverting, to say the least. But under its superficial humor there is a humor much more profound, and that lies in the fact that American Liberalism, at its best, is but little more than a feeble echo of English Liberalism—that the Liberals of the United States, even more than the general population of the United States, are delicately sensitive to English propaganda. Their present Francophobia, in brief, is significant chiefly because it is obviously the forerunner of something more general and powerful—something for which plans are already in the making.

The English fear that a France drunk with loot from the Ruhr, and made "gallant" beyond bounds by the facility with which an unarmed populace may be knocked about, will proceed to other and vaster enterprises of an heroic nature, and that they will presently offer a menace to British security. Worse, they fear that the French, with the largest standing army ever heard of on earth, an overwhelming superiority in the air, and the aid of such client states as Poland, Czecho-Slovakia, Belgium and Turkey, might prove an antagonist almost as formidable as Germany. I doubt that this is true; the English control of the seas would determine the issue of such a war, as it determined the issue of the last one. Nevertheless, the English believe it—and the situation at home, economically and politically, is plainly such

Mencken's Monday column for 9 April 1923, attacking both France and American liberals (courtesy of the Enoch Pratt Free Library)

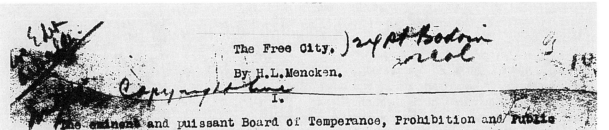

The Free City.

By H. L. Mencken.

I.

The eminent and puissant Board of Temperance, Prohibition and Public Morals of the Methodist Episcopal Church has at last discovered the obvious fact that the city of New York is not a Methodist village, and hence, by Methodist standards, not American. What is to be done about it? I gather that the remedy favored is force. The virtuous Wesleyans of the backwoods and mean streets are to march upon Babylon, with the usual rank of policemen in front of them, and reduce it to virtue with a big stick. The Jews and Catholics are to be chased out, all the public shows and stews are to be closed, and a new Zion is to be set up where the bootlegger now issues his low, lascivious cry, and the Middle Western butter-and-egg man pursues his gaudy mate.

Alas, for the good Methodist brethern, but these are evil days for all their lordlier hopes. Prohibition is dying on their hands, the wars upon the theatre, upon the cigarette, upon grand opera and upon loose literature are going badly, and it grows harder and harder, year by year, to shake down the suburban Sunday-schools. The American people, this year, will smoke 75,000,000,000 cigarettes ; fifteen years ago, before the Board of Temperance, Prohibition and Public Morals got under way, they smoked less than 8,000,000,000. There were two or three naughty magazines in the Republic then; now there are at least a hundred. The sight of a female ankle, in those days, drew bawling mobs; now the gals go stark naked upon the stage, and no one seems to care. Meanwhile, the chautauqua is in rapid decay, the hinds on the steppes are jazzing to the radio, and, as I have said, it is harder and harder to raise the moral wind. No wonder so many rural clergymen are forsaking the sacred desk for the safe salaries of the Y.M.C.A. and the good pickings of the Klan.

Typescript for Mencken's Monday column for 2 November 1925 (George H. Thompson Collection)

September 12th

Dear Hamilton:-

I suggest that it might be an idea to send my next Monday's article to various persons, clerical and otherwise, in the South. It may set some of them off. If you think well of the notion will you have your able staff send the clippings? Within are some names. I'll be in New York.

Today is my birthday. I have spent the whole day in prayer and soul-searching.

Yours,

M

In February 1999 a panel of experts assembled by the New York University School of Journalism listed Mencken's dispatches from the Scopes trial for the Evening Sun *as eighth among the top one hundred works of journalism of the twentieth century. They represent his most famous reporting, and he and his paper helped script the drama in 1925. John T. Scopes volunteered to test Tennessee's antievolution law; William Jennings Bryan volunteered to act as prosecuting attorney; and Dudley Field Malone, Arthur Garfield Hays, and (with Mencken's connivance) Clarence Darrow formed an impressive defense team. The* Sunpapers *sent a large contingent, posted Scopes's bond, and, after he was convicted, paid his fine. A letter to F. Scott Fitzgerald written shortly after the publication that year of the latter's* The Great Gatsby *mentions Mencken's eagerness to join the fray (typewritten letter with handwritten signature at Princeton University).*

Mencken, circa 1928, wearing a brown derby similar to Smith's trademark headgear after the Baltimore Post *arranged for its readers to vote for a boss of Baltimore, and Mencken was declared elected (courtesy of the Enoch Pratt Free Library)*

THE AMERICAN MERCURY
730 FIFTH AVENUE
NEW YORK

OFFICE OF THE EDITORS George Jean Nathan and H. L. Mencken

May 26th

Dear Fitz:-

When are you coming back to the Republic? You are missing a superb show. In a few weeks I am going down to Tennessee to see a school-teacher tried for teaching Evolution. Match that in your decayed principalities if you can! William Jennings Bryan is to prosecute, and Clarence Darrow and Dudley Field Malone are for the defense.

I am very eager to see the new novel. But two years is a hell of a long while. I hope you find time by the way to compose a piece for the above great family magazine. Why not a treatise on the very subject you discuss in your letter, i.e., novel-writing? It is much belabored, but seldom by anyone who has ever actually written a novel. La Wharton's fulminations in Scribner's scarcely constitute an exception. Her ideas are those of a high-school teacher.

As Law Enforcement grows rigider and rigider, New York grows wetter and wetter. Baltimore is now knee-deep in excellent beer. I begin to believe in prayer.

Sincerely yours,

H. L. Mencken

Mencken's reports from the Scopes trial supplied a series of classic caricatures that have largely replaced the real Bryan in the popular imagination. Beneath the humor is his familiar theme of the continual struggle between the "civilized minority" and the forces of ignorance ("Darrow's Eloquent Appeal Wasted on Ears That

Heed Only Bryan, Says Mencken," Baltimore Evening Sun, *14 July 1925, p. 1).*

Dayton, Tenn., July 14.–The net effect of Clarence Darrow's great speech yesterday seems to be precisely the same as if he had bawled it up a rainspout in the interior of Afghanistan. That is, locally, upon the process against the infidel Scopes, upon the so-called minds of these fundamentalists of upland Tennessee. You have but a dim notion of it who have only read it. It was not designed for reading, but for hearing. The clangtint of it was as important as the logic. It rose like a wind and ended like a flourish of bugles. The very judge on the bench, toward the end of it, began to look uneasy. But the morons in the audience, when it was over, simply hissed it.

During the whole time of its delivery the old mountebank, Bryan, sat tight-lipped and unmoved. There is, of course, no reason why it should have shaken him. He has those hill billies locked up in his pen and he knows it. His brand is on them. He is at home among them. Since his earliest days, indeed, his

Tennessee high-school teacher John T. Scopes at the time of his 1925 trial for teaching the theory of evolution

chief strength has been among the folk of remote hills and forlorn and lonely farms. Now with his political aspirations all gone to pot, he turns to them for religious consolations. They understand his peculiar imbecilities. His nonsense is their ideal of sense. When he deluges them with his theological bilge they rejoice like pilgrims disporting in the river Jordan.

Rumor Has Attorney-General Unsympathetic With Case.

The town whisper is that the local attorney-general, Stewart, is not a fundamentalist, and hence has no stomach for his job. It seems not improbable. He is a man of evident education, and his argument yesterday was confined very strictly to the constitutional points– the argument of a competent and conscientious lawyer, and to me, at least very persuasive.

But Stewart, after all, is a foreigner here, almost as much so as Darrow or Hays or Malone. He is doing his job and that is all. The real animus of the prosecution centers in Bryan. He is the plaintiff and the prosecutor. The local lawyers are simply bottle-holders for him. He will win the case, not by academic appeals to law and precedent, but by direct and powerful appeals to immemorial fears and superstitions of man. It is no wonder that he is hot against Scopes. Five years of Scopes and even these mountaineers would begin to

Cartoon in the Memphis Commercial Appeal *(6 April 1926), depicting Mencken as a monkey because of his support for the defense in the Scopes trial (© 1926 by the* Commercial Appeal, *Memphis, Tennessee; used with permission)*

laugh at Bryan. Ten years and they would ride him out of town on a rail, with one Baptist parson in front of him and another behind.

But there will be no ten years of Scopes, nor five years, nor even one year.

Trial Far From Farce.

Such brash young fellows, debauched by the enlightenment, must be disposed of before they become dangerous, and Bryan is here, with his tight lips and hard eyes, to see that this one is disposed of. The talk of the lawyers, even the magnificent talk of Darrow, is so much idle wind music. The case will not be decided by logic, nor even by eloquence. It will be decided by counting noses—and for every nose in these hills that has ever thrust itself into any book save the Bible there are a hundred adorned with the brass ring of Bryan. These are his people. They understand him when he speaks in tongues. The same dark face that is in his own eyes is in theirs, too. They feel with him, and they relish him.

I sincerely hope that the nobility and gentry of the lowlands will not make the colossal mistake of viewing this trial of Scopes as a trivial farce. Full of rustic japes and in bad taste, it is, to be sure, somewhat comic on the surface. One laughs to see lawyers sweat. The jury, marched down Broadway, would set New York by the ears. But all that is only skin deep.

Far Greater Struggle In Prospect.

Deeper down there are the beginnings of a struggle that may go on to melodrama of the first caliber, and when the curtain falls at least all the laughter may be coming from the yokels. You probably laughed at the prohibitionists, say, back in 1914. Well, don't make the same error twice.

As I have said, Bryan understands these peasants, and they understand him. He is a bit mangey and flea-bitten, but no means ready for his harp. He may last five years, ten years or even longer. What he may accomplish in that time, seen here at close range, looms up immensely larger than it appears to a city man five hundred miles away. The fellow is full of such bitter, implacable hatreds that they radiate from him like heat from a stove. He hates the learning that he cannot grasp. He hates those who sneer at him. He hates, in general, all who stand apart from his own pathetic commonness. And the yokels hate with him, some of them almost as bitterly as he does himself. They are willing and eager to follow him—and he has already given them a taste of blood.

Bryan Looks To Higher Fields.

Darrow's peroration yesterday was interrupted by Judge Raulston, but the force of it got into the air nevertheless. This year it is a misdemeanor for a country school teacher to flout the archaic nonsense of Genesis. Next year it will be a felony. The year after the net will be spread wider. Pedagogues, after all, are small game; there are larger birds to snare—larger and juicier. Bryan has his fishy eye on them. He will fetch them if his mind lasts, and the lamp holds out to burn. No man with a mouth like that ever lets go. Nor ever lacks followers.

Tennessee is bearing the brunt of the first attack simply because the civilized minority, down here, is extraordinarily pusillanimous.

I have met no educated man who is not ashamed of the ridicule that has fallen upon the State, and I have met none, save only Judge Neal, who had the courage to speak out while it was yet time. No Tennessee counsel of any importance came into the case until yesterday and then they came in stepping very softly as if taking a brief for sense were a dangerous matter. When Bryan did his first rampaging here all these men were silent.

State A Visible Antithesis.

They had known for years what was going on in the hills. They knew what the country preachers were preaching—what degraded nonsense was being rammed and hammered into yokel skulls. But they were afraid to go out against the imposture while it was in the making, and when any outsider denounced it they fell upon him violently as an enemy of Tennessee.

Now Tennessee is paying for that poltroonery. The State is smiling and beautiful, and of late it has begun to be rich. I know of no American city that is set in more lovely scenery than Chattanooga, or that has more charming homes. The civilized minority is as large here, I believe, as anywhere else.

It has made a city of splendid material comforts and kept it in order. But it has neglected in the past the unpleasant business of following what was going on in the cross roads Little Bethels.

The Baptist preachers ranted unchallenged.

Their buffooneries were mistaken for humor. Now the clowns turn out to be armed, and have begun to shoot.

The Rabble In Command.

In his argument yesterday Judge Neal had to admit pathetically that it was hopeless to fight for a

COMING! COMING!

To

DAYTON TENNESSEE

During the Trial of the Infidel Scopes

ELMER CHUBB, L.L.D., D.D.

FUNDAMENTALIST AND MIRACLE WORKER

MIRACLES PERFORMED ON THE PUBLIC SQUARE!

Dr. Chubb will allow himself to be bitten by any poisonous snake, scorpion, gila monster, or other reptile. He will also drink any poison brought to him.

In demonstration of the words of our Lord and Saviour Jesus Christ, as found in the 16th Chapter of the Gospel of St. Mark:

"And these signs shall follow them that believe: in my name shall they cast out devils, they shall speak with new tongues; they shall take up serpents, and if they drink any deadly thing it shall in no wise hurt them; they shall lay hands on the sick and they shall recover."

Public demonstration of healing, casting out devils, and prophesying. Dr. Chubb will also preach in Aramaic, Hebrew, Greek, Latin, Coptic, Egyptian, and in the lost tongues of the Etruscans and the Hittites.

TESTIMONIALS; All favorable but one:

With my own eyes I saw Dr. Chubb swallow cyanide of potassim.
—WILLIAM JENNINGS BRYAN,
Christian Statesman.

Dr. Chubb simply believes the word of God, and his power follows.
—REV. J. FRANK NORRIS.

I was possessed of devils, and Dr. Chubb cast them out of me. Glory to God.
—MAGDALENA RAYBACK,
R.F.D. 3, Duncan Grove, Mich.

When under the spell of divine inspiration Dr. Chubb speaks Coptic as fluently as if it were his mother tongue. As to Etruscan I cannot say.
—PROF. ADDISON BLAKESLEY,
Professor of ancient languages in Valparaiso University, Ind.

Chubb is a fake. I can mix a cyanide cocktail that will make him turn up his toes in thirty seconds.
—H. L. MENCKEN.

SPECIAL NOTICE: Dr. Chubb has never pretended that he had power to RAISE THE DEAD. The Bible shows that only the Saviour and the Twelve Apostles had that power.

Free will offering, dedicated to the enforcement of the anti-evolution law.

Satirical handbill by Edgar Lee Masters, who sent Mencken five hundred copies. Mencken hired some local boys to distribute them in Dayton. "They made absolutely no impression on the yokels gathered for the trial," he wrote, because "the miracles were old stuff in the Tennessee hills" (courtesy of the Enoch Pratt Free Library).

repeal of the anti-evolution law. The Legislature of Tennessee, like the Legislature of every other American State, is made up of cheap job-seekers and ignoramuses.

The Governor of the State is a politician ten times cheaper and trashier. It is vain to look for relief from such men. If the State is to be saved at all, it must be saved by the courts. For one, I have little hope of relief in that direction, despite Hays' logic and Darrow's eloquence. Constitutions, in America, no longer mean what they say. To mention the Bill of Rights is to be damned as a Red.

The rabble is in the saddle, and down here it makes its first campaign under a general beside whom Wat Tyler seems like a wart beside the Matterhorn.

***

(Excerpt from "Law and Freedom, Mencken Discovers, Yield Place to Holy Writ in Rhea County," Baltimore Evening Sun, 15 July 1925, p. 1.)

Dayton, Tenn., July 15.–[. . .]

Unitarians Regarded As Apollyons.

Two Unitarian clergymen are prowling around the town looking for a chance to discharge their "hellish heresies." One of them is Potter, of New York; the other is Birckhead, of Kansas City. So far they have not made any progress. Potter induced one of the local Methodist parsons to give him a hearing, but the congregation protested and the next day the parson had to resign his charge. The Methodists, as I have previously reported, are regarded almost as infidels in Rhea county. Their doctrines, which seem somewhat severe in Baltimore, especially to persons who love a merry life, are here viewed as loose to the point of indecency. The four Methodists on the jury are suspected of being against hanging Scopes, at least without a fair trial. The State tried to get rid of one of them, even after he had been passed; his neighbors had come in from his village with news that he had a banjo concealed in his house and was known to read the *Literary Digest*.

The other Unitarian clergyman, Dr. Birckhead, is not actually domiciled in the town, but is encamped, with his wife and child, on the road outside. He is on an automobile tour and stopped off here to see if a chance offered to spread his "poisons." So far he has found none.

Yesterday afternoon a Jewish rabbi from Nashville also showed up, Marks by name. He offered to read and expound Genesis in Hebrew, but found no takers. The Holy Rollers hereabout, when they are seized by the gift of tongues, avoid Hebrew, apparently as a result of Ku Klux influence. Their favorite among all the sacred dialects is Hittite. It sounds to the infidel like a series of college yells.

Reporters Laugh At Judge.

Judge Raulston's decision yesterday afternoon in the matter of Hays' motion was a masterpiece of unconscious humor. The press stand, in fact, thought he was trying to be jocose deliberately and let off a guffaw that might have gone far if the roar of applause had not choked it off. Hays presented a petition in the name of the two Unitarians, the rabbi and several other theological "reds," praying that in selecting clergymen to open the court with prayer hereafter he choose fundamentalists and anti-fundamentalists alter-

nately. The petition was couched in terms that greatly shocked and enraged the prosecution. When the judge announced that he would leave the nomination of chaplains to the Pastors' Association of the town there was the gust of mirth aforesaid, followed by howls of approval. The Pastors' Association of Dayton is composed of fundamentalists so powerfully orthodox that beside them such a fellow as Dr. John Roach Straton would seem an Ingersoll.

The witnesses of the defense, all of them heretics, began to reach town yesterday and are all quartered at what is called the Mansion, an ancient and empty house outside the town limits, now crudely furnished with iron cots, spittoons, playing cards and the other camp equipment of scientists. Few, if any, of these witnesses will ever get a chance to outrage the jury with their blasphemies, but they are of much interest to the townspeople. The common belief is that they will be blown up with one mighty blast when the verdict of the twelve men, tried and true, is brought in, and Darrow, Malone, Hays and Neal with them. The country people avoid the Mansion. It is foolish to take unnecessary chances. Going into the courtroom, with Darrow standing there shamelessly and openly challenging the wrath of God, is risk enough.

Warmer Things To Come.

The case promises to drag into next week. The prosecution is fighting desperately and taking every advantage of its superior knowledge of the quirks of local procedure. The defense is heating up and there are few exchanges of courtroom amenities. There will be a lot of oratory before it is all over and some loud and raucous bawling otherwise, and maybe more than one challenge to step outside. The cards seem to be stacked against poor Scopes, but there may be a joker in the pack. Four of the jurymen, as everyone knows, are Methodists, and a Methodist down here belongs to the extreme wing of liberals. Beyond him lie only the justly and incurably damned.

What if one of those Methodists, sweating under the dreadful pressure of fundamentalist influence, jumps into the air, cracks his heels together and gives a defiant yell? What if the jury is hung? It will be a good joke on the fundamentalists if it happens, and an even better joke on the defense.

As a student of religion, Mencken seized the opportunity to study evangelical Christianity while also reporting on the trial. The original version of this article appeared in the 13 July 1925 Evening Sun *as "Yearning Mountaineers' Souls Need Reconversion Nightly, Mencken Finds." It was revised for pub-*

lication in 1926 in Prejudices: Fifth Series *(excerpt from "The Hills of Zion," pp. 75–86).*

It was hot weather when they tried the infidel Scopes at Dayton, but I went down there very willingly, for I had good reports of the sub-Potomac bootleggers, and moreover I was eager to see something of evangelical Christianity as a going concern. In the big cities of the Republic, despite the endless efforts of consecrated men, it is laid up with a wasting disease. The very Sunday-school superintendents, taking jazz from the stealthy radio, shake their fire-proof legs; their pupils, moving into adolescence, no longer respond to the proliferating hormones by enlisting for missionary service in Africa, but resort to necking and petting instead. I know of no evangelical church from Oregon to Maine that is not short of money: the graft begins to peter out, like wire-tapping and three-card monte before it. Even in Dayton, though the mob was up to do execution upon Scopes, there was a strong smell of antinomianism. The nine churches of the village were all half empty on Sunday, and weeds choked their yards. Only two or three of the resident pastors managed to sustain themselves by their ghostly science; the rest had to take orders for mail-order pantaloons or work in the adjacent strawberry fields; one, I heard, was a barber. On the courthouse green a score of sweating theologians debated the darker passages of Holy Writ day and night, but I soon found that they were all volunteers, and that the local faithful, while interested in their exegesis as an intellectual exercise, did not permit it to impede the indigenous debaucheries. Exactly twelve minutes after I reached the village I was taken in tow by a Christian man and introduced to the favorite tipple of the Cumberland Range: half corn liquor and half coco-cola. It seemed a dreadful dose to me, spoiled as I was by the bootleg light wines and beers of the Eastern seaboard, but I found the Dayton illuminati got it down with gusto, rubbing their tummies and rolling their eyes. I include among them the chief local proponents of the Mosaic cosmogony. They were all hot for Genesis, but their faces were far too florid to belong to teetotalers, and when a pretty girl came tripping down the Main street, which was very often, they reached for the places where their neckties should have been with all the amorous enterprise of movie actors. It seemed somehow strange.

An amiable newspaper woman of Chattanooga, familiar with those uplands, presently enlightened me. Dayton, she explained, was simply a great capital like any other great capital. That is to say, it was to Rhea county what Atlanta was to Georgia or Paris to France. That is to say, it was predominantly epicurean and sinful. [. . .]

This newspaper woman, whose kindness covered city infidels as well as Alpine Christians, offered to take me back in the hills to a place where the old-time religion was genuinely on tap. The Scopes jury, she explained was composed mainly of its customers, with a few Dayton sophisticates added to leaven the mass. It would thus be instructive to climb the heights and observe the former at their ceremonies. The trip, fortunately, might be made by automobile. There was a road running out of Dayton to Morgantown, in the mountains to the westward, and thence beyond. But foreigners, it appeared, would have to approach the sacred grove cautiously, for the upland worshipers were very shy, and at the first sight of a strange face they would adjourn their orgy and slink into the forest. They were not to be feared, for God had long since forbidden them to practice assassination, or even assault, but if they were alarmed a rough trip would go for naught. So, after dreadful bumpings up a long and narrow road, we parked our car in a little woodpath a mile or two beyond the tiny village of Morgantown, and made the rest of the approach on foot, deployed like skirmishers. Far off in a dark, romantic glade a flickering light was visible, and out of the silence came the rumble of exhortation. We could distinguish the figure of the preacher only as a moving mote in the light: it was like looking down the tube of a dark-field microscope. Slowly and cautiously we crossed what seemed to be a pasture, and then we crouched down along the edge of a cornfield, and stealthily edged further and further. The light now grew larger and we could begin to make out what was going on. We went ahead on all fours, like snakes in the grass.

From the great limb of a mighty oak hung a couple of crude torches of the sort that car inspectors thrust under Pullman cars when a train pulls in at night. In the guttering glare was the preacher, and for a while we could see no one else. He was an immensely tall and thin mountaineer in blue jeans, his collarless shirt open at the neck and his hair a tousled mop. As he preached he paced up and down under the smoking flambeaux, and at each turn he thrust his arms into the air and yelled "Glory to God!" We crept nearer in the shadow of the cornfield, and began to hear more of his discourse. He was preaching on the Day of Judgment. The high kings of the earth, he roared, would all fall down and die; only the sanctified would stand up to receive the Lord God of Hosts. One of these kings he mentioned by name, the king of what he called Greece-y. The king of Greece-y, he said, was doomed to hell. We crawled forward a few more yards and began to see the audience. It was seated on benches ranged round the preacher in a circle. Behind him sat a row of elders, men and women. In front were the younger folk. We crept on cautiously, and individuals rose out of the ghostly gloom. A young mother sat suckling her baby, rocking as the preacher paced up and down. Two scared little girls hugged each other, their pigtails down their backs. An immensely huge mountain woman, in a gingham dress, cut in one piece, rolled on her heels at every "Glory to God!" To one side, and but half visible, was what appeared to be a bed. We found afterward that half a dozen babies were asleep upon it. [. . .]

A comic scene? Somehow, no. The poor half-wits were too horribly in earnest. It was like peeping through a knothole at the writhings of people in pain. From the squirming and jabbering mass a young woman gradually detached herself–a woman not uncomely, with a pathetic homemade cap on her head. Her head jerked back, the veins of her neck swelled, and her fists went to her throat as if she were fighting for breath. She bent backward until she was like half a hoop. Then she suddenly snapped forward. We caught a flash of the whites of her eyes. Presently her whole body began to be convulsed–great throes that began at the shoulders and ended at the hips. She would leap to her feet, thrust her arms in air, and then hurl herself upon the heap. Her praying flattened out into a mere

delirious caterwauling, like that of a Tom cat on a petting party. I describe the thing discreetly, and as a strict behaviorist. The lady's subjective sensations I leave to infidel pathologists, privy to the works of Ellis, Freud and Moll. Whatever they were, they were obviously not painful, for they were accompanied by vast heavings and gurglings of a joyful and even ecstatic nature. And they seemed to be contagious, too, for soon a second penitent, also female, joined the first, and then came a third, and a fourth, and a fifth. The last one had an extraordinary violent attack. She began with mild enough jerks of the head, but in a moment she was bounding all over the place, like a chicken with its head cut off. Every time her head came up a stream of hosannas would issue out of it. Once she collided with a dark, undersized brother, hitherto silent and stolid. Contact with her set him off as if he had been kicked by a mule. He leaped into the air, threw back his head, and began to gargle as if with a mouthful of BB shot. Then he loosed one tremendous, stentorian sentence in the tongues, and collapsed. [. . .]

Finally, we got tired of the show and returned to Dayton. It was nearly eleven o'clock–an immensely

Gene Kelly as E. K. Hornbeck, Donna Anderson as Rachel Brown, Dick York as Bertram T. Cates, and Spencer Tracy as Henry Drummond in a still from the 1960 movie adaptation of Jerome Lawrence and Robert E. Lee's play Inherit the Wind, *based on the Scopes trial. Hornbeck is modeled on Mencken, Cates on Scopes, and Drummond on Scopes's attorney Clarence Darrow. Fredric March played Matthew Harrison Brady, based on William Jennings Bryan (M-G-M).*

Clarence Darrow arguing for the defense at the Scopes Trial. The arrow points to Mencken (photograph by the Baltimore Sun).

late hour for those latitudes—but the whole town was still gathered in the courthouse yard, listening to the disputes of theologians. The Scopes trial had brought them in from all directions. There was a friar wearing a sandwich sign announcing that he was the Bible champion of the world. There was a Seventh Day Adventist arguing that Clarence Darrow was the beast with seven heads and ten horns described in Revelation xiii, and that the end of the world was at hand. There was an evangelist made up like Andy Gump, with the news that atheists in Cincinnati were preparing to descend upon Dayton, hang the eminent Judge Raulston, and burn the town. There was an ancient who maintained that no Catholic could be a Christian. There was the eloquent Dr. T. T. Martin, of Blue Mountain, Miss., come to town with a truck-load of torches and hymn-books to put Darwin in his place. There was a singing brother bellowing apocalyptic hymns. There was William Jennings Bryan, followed everywhere by a gaping crowd. Dayton was having a roaring time. It was better than the circus. But the note of devotion was simply not there; the Daytonians, after listening a while, would slip away to Robinson's drug-store to regale themselves with coca-cola, or to the lobby of the Aqua Hotel, where the learned Raulston sat in state, judicially picking his teeth. The real religion was not present. It began at the bridge over the town creek, where the road makes off for the hills.

Bryan died in Dayton on 26 July. The Sun *ran a "straight" obituary in parallel columns with Mencken's acerbic notice. A more polished version appeared in the latest* Prejudices *the next year (excerpt from "In Memoriam: W. J. B.," in* Prejudices: Fifth Series, *pp. 64–66).*

Has it been duly marked by historians that the late William Jennings Bryan's last secular act on this globe of sin was to catch flies? A curious detail, and not without its sardonic overtones. He was the most sedulous fly-catcher in American history, and in many ways the most successful. His quarry, of course, was not *Musca domestica* but *Homo neandertalensis*. For forty years he tracked it with coo and bellow, up and down the rustic backways of the Republic. Wherever the flambeaux of Chautauqua smoked and guttered, and the bilge of Idealism ran in the veins, and Baptist pastors dammed the brooks with the sanctified, and men gathered who were weary and heavy laden, and their wives who were full of Peruna and as fecund as the shad (*Alosa sapidissima*)—there the indefatigable Jennings set up his traps and spread his bait. He knew every country town in the South and West, and he could crowd the most remote of them to suffocation by simply winding his horn. The city proletariat, transiently flustered by him in 1896, quickly penetrated his buncombe and would have no more of him; the cockney gallery jeered him at every Democratic national convention for twenty-five years. But out where the grass grows high, and the horned

Mencken and Darrow in the dining room of Mencken's home at 704 Cathedral Street, Baltimore, in 1930 (courtesy of the Enoch Pratt Free Library)

cattle dream away the lazy afternoons, and men still fear the powers and principalities of the air—out there between the corn-rows he held his old puissance to the end. There was no need of beaters to drive in his game. The news that he was coming was enough. For miles the flivver dust would choke the roads. And when he rose at the end of the day to discharge his Message there would be such breathless attention, such a rapt and enchanted ecstasy, such a sweet rustle of amens as the world had not known since Johann fell to Herod's ax.

There was something peculiarly fitting in the fact that his last days were spent in a one-horse Tennessee village, and that death found him there. The man felt at home in such simple and Christian scenes. He liked people who sweated freely, and were not debauched by the refinements of the toilet. Making his progress up and down the Main street of little Dayton, surrounded by gaping primates from the upland valleys of the Cumberland Range, his coat laid aside, his bare arms and hairy chest shining damply, his bald head sprinkled with dust—so accoutred and on display he was obviously happy. He liked getting up early in the morning, to the tune of cocks crowing on the dunghill. He liked the heavy, greasy victuals of the farmhouse kitchen. He liked country lawyers, country pastors, all country people. He liked the country sounds and country smells. I believe that this liking was sincere—perhaps the only sincere thing in the man. His nose showed no uneasiness when a hillman in faded overalls and hickory shirt accosted him on the street, and besought him for light upon some mystery of Holy Writ. The simian gabble of the cross-roads was not gabble to him, but wisdom of an occult and superior sort. In the presence of city folks he was palpably uneasy. Their clothes, I suspect, annoyed him, and he was suspicious of their too delicate manners. He knew all the while that they were laughing at him—if not at his baroque theology, then at least at his alpaca pantaloons. But the yokels never laughed at him. To them he was not the huntsman but the prophet, and toward the end, as he gradually forsook mundane politics for more ghostly concerns, they began to elevate him in their hierarchy. When he died he was the peer of Abraham. His old enemy, Wilson, aspiring to the same white and shining robe, came down with a thump. But Bryan made the grade. His place in Tennessee hagiography is secure. If the village barber saved any of his hair, then it is curing gall-stones down there to-day. [. . .]

Best Minds

"HISTORY IS BUNK" HENRY FORD

SO IS SCIENCE

U. J. BRYAN

July 21, 1925

Sun cartoon by Duffy, who accompanied Mencken to the Scopes trial (from S. L. Harrison, The Editorial Art of Edmund Duffy *[Madison & Teaneck, N.J.: Fairleigh Dickinson University Press / London & Toronto: Associated University Presses, 1998]; reproduced by permission)*

Forty-five years later Scopes recalled Mencken in an interview for Esquire *(excerpt from Bynum Shaw, "Scopes Reviews the Monkey Trial: He became the pigeon by natural selection,"* Esquire, *74 [November 1970]: 86, 88, 90, 94).*

[. . .] As the trial date approached, Dayton became a circus. Pullman cars were ordered for railroad sidings to accommodate guests. A barbecue pit was dug on the courthouse lawn, and bleachers were erected for the convenience of itinerant evangelists. Stores displayed monkey signs and waved huge banners; J. R. Darwin, a Dayton haberdasher, found a little gold mine in his name. The press arrived, more than a hundred reporters and photographers, thirty of them sleeping on cots in a store loft and sharing one tap and a single outdoor privy. Most famous of the writers was H. L.

Mencken, down from Baltimore to mingle with "the local primates." (Scopes was not much impressed with Mencken, feeling that he was largely "a sensationalist." Over the years, he has more fondly remembered Baltimore's Frank R. Kent and a Hearst International News Service reporter, William K. Hutchinson, who at one important point in the trial gulled Judge Raulston into leaking his own secrets.)

Also represented in the news contingent was Radio Station WGN, of Chicago, which did the first live national broadcast of a trial.

Nuts and fanatics of every religious stripe rolled into Dayton. Mencken and Edgar Lee Masters dreamed one up and announced his arrival by handbill: Elmer Chubb, who would drink any known poison, work miracles and preach in eight tongues–

RILED BY MENCKEN SLURS, DAYTON CITIZENS WANT TO PUT HIM OUT

[By Gazette Times Private Wire—New York Times Service.]

DAYTON, TENN., July 16.—Dayton doesn't like H. L. Mencken. In fact, a considerable portion of Dayton's citizens have been considering and proposing to ask the editor of the American Mercury to leave town. Some have even suggested that he be taken "into an alley," but less irritable counselors have advised against it and Mr. Mencken remains in town, attending the trial and writing pieces which Dayton dislikes.

The resentment of the townspeople against Mr. Mencken became acute this morning after one of his syndicated articles, published in the Chattanooga News, had been read by practically everyone in the town. In it Mr. Mencken spoke of "Babbits," "morons," "hill-billies," "yokels," "peasants," "degraded nonsense" which country preachers are ramming and hammering into yokel skulls" and of Methodists being "regarded as infidels."

There were indignation meetings on the street corners and in stores. The Rev. A. C. Stribling, pastor of the Cumberland Presbyterian Church of Dayton, wrote a reply to Mr. Mencken, also published in the Chattanooga News, in which Mr. Mencken was taken to task for writing that the town was ignorant and that Tennesseans who were educated showed lack of courage in failure to fight the anti-evolution law.

"What cheap blatherskite of a pen-pusher," wrote Mr. Stribling, "can refer to courage while he is the guest of a great volunteer state? None but a nut suffering from a malignant case of Menckenitis. Let your gourd seed rattle, Buddy; they don't sprout."

The indignation of the Methodists, however, seemed to be greatest. The declaration of Mr. Mencken that the Baptists considered them infidels stirred a red-haired member of one of the Methodist churches to hardly restrained anger. He wanted Mr. Mencken to leave town at once. His friends approved the idea and others suggested they "take him into an alley." But A. P. Haggard, chief commissioner of Dayton, who also is president of the American National Bank and the town's leading citizen, prevailed upon them to leave Mr. Mencken alone.

"We don't like the things Mr. Mencken is writing and we want him to know it," said Mr. Haggard. "I hope nobody lays hands on him. I stopped them once, but I may not be there to dissuade them if it occurs to them again."

Newspaper item saved by Mencken, who subscribed to a clipping service (courtesy of the Enoch Pratt Free Library)

including "the lost languages of the Etruscans and Hittites." But the apparition was no more fantastic than reality: John the Baptist the Third; and the Bible Champion of the World; and the Absolute Ruler of the Entire World, Without Military, Naval, or Other

Caricature of Bryan on the cover of a leading humor magazine that covered the Scopes trial

Physical Force—hordes more like them were there in the flesh.

The twelve jurymen, when seated, included six Baptists and three Methodists, and with the panel thus stacked ("unanimously hot for Genesis," Mencken said) it was obvious from the beginning that Scopes would not fare well. It was not the intention of the defense, of course, to win acquittal. The idea was to force the case to the United States Supreme Court, where a decision could be rendered on the constitutionality of the Butler Act. As expected, Scopes was convicted (Mencken spoke of it as "bumping off the defendant") and fined $100 (which Mencken supplied), but the ultimate test was aborted when the Supreme Court of Tennessee voided the decision on a technicality.

The technicality was the fault of Judge Raulston, who under the law should have allowed the jury to fix the amount of the fine; however, he did not.

After all these years have passed, Scopes remembers Judge Raulston compassionately. "He did the best he could," Scopes said. "This trial was a new experience to him, as it was for me; it was far over his head, and over my head, too. He did a good job of listening; unfortunately, that wasn't enough."

Scopes is also charitable in his judgment of Bryan, who he thinks in some respects resembles today's liberals: "They think they're doing a good job, and they're not." Before the trial ever began, Scopes had first-hand acquaintance with the Great Commoner. Six years earlier, in graduation exercises at the Salem, Illinois, high school, John Scopes and three other students had erupted in uncontrollable sniggers during a Bryan speech. At Dayton, Bryan professed to remember it, and he treated Scopes as an old friend. Thinking back now on 1925 and the

Cartoons in the 18 July 1925 issue of Judge

Treatise on

The GODS

H. L. Mencken

Second edition: corrected and rewritten

New York: 1946
ALFRED A. KNOPF

Title page for the second edition (the first edition was published in 1930) of the work that Mencken considered his best book

Monkey Trial, Scopes believes Bryan was absolutely sincere in his rabid fundamentalism—though misguided. Over the years he has been bothered a little by the blatant attempts to peddle Florida real estate in Dayton: Bryan had large holdings in Florida. But Scopes bridles at Mencken's assessment of Bryan as "buffoon," "mountebank" and "buzzard."

He also disagrees with Mencken's characterization of the Dayton townsfolk and other trial spectators as "morons," "hillbillies" and "yokels." Scopes remembers the people there fondly and throughout the trial was on the best of terms with everybody. In turn, he was well-liked then and is well-liked now. In 1960, when he returned to Dayton for the premiere of the film, *Inherit the Wind,* he was presented the key to the city. The old ones in Dayton who remember him like to recall that the young Scopes, generally in open-throated white shirt, acted as porter for evolutionist and anti-evolutionist alike. [. . .]

Throughout his career Mencken advised the Sunpapers *on routine policy far more often than he conducted events like the Scopes Trial coverage. His most significant statement about the direction of a newspaper was in a 1929 letter to Paul Patterson, president of the parent A. S. Abell Company (typewritten letter at Enoch Pratt Free Library, Baltimore).*

July 21st

Dear Paul:-

During the past eight days (July 14-21, inc.) I have read the editorial page of The Sun very carefully, and after due prayer the following observations suggest themselves:

1. All the changes are for the better. In particular, the extra lead improves the appearance of the page. I also like the scheme of indenting important editorials (Dangerous Lethargy, July 10), but I don't think it is as good as putting them on Page 1. The page is the better for the abandonment of the headless editorials, but that is only because they were usually platitudinous. Vigorously written, they might be a valuable feature. The disappearance of the Bentztown Bard's column is a great relief. I think the page now looks better than it has ever looked in the past, but there is still plenty of chance to improve it. The heading on the letters looks amateurish to me. The double rule under the accompanying box is unnecessary. The cartoons, when they are done in chalk, are always badly printed and look messy. It would probably be wise to use pen-and-ink cartoons as often as possible. Duffy can be trained to draw them. He is young and full of ambition.

2. My doubts about "Down the Spillway," previously expressed, continue. The idea behind the column is an excellent one, but it seems to me that it is badly executed, The point of view that the stuff mirrors is somewhat feeble and obvious: it suggests that of a rather self-conscious young college professor—the sort of fellow who admires Christopher Morley and dreams of getting a whimsical essay into The Atlantic Monthly. In brief, the flavor of Sam Chew still hangs about it. I think there ought to be more robustness, more gusto in it. It is supposed to set forth the casual meditations, not of pedagogues running a literary magazine, but of practical men engaged upon a vigorous and enterprising newspaper. I suggest some questions to test contributions. Would Edward Bok think this was charming? Would it fit into the Hound & Horn, published at Harvard? Would William Lyon Phelps regret that he had not written it? One yes should be sufficient to exclude. Here, of course, I speak generally. All of the stuff is not

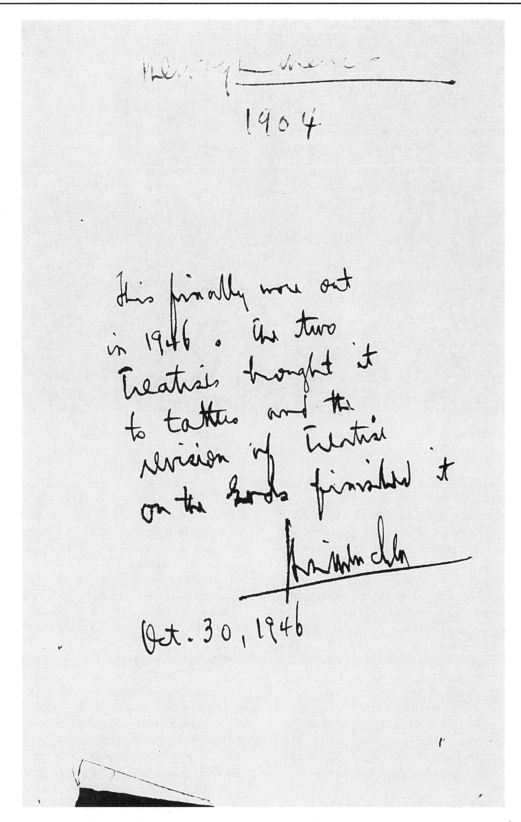

Inscription by Mencken in his copy of the Bible. His aim in Treatise on the Gods *and* Treatise on Right and Wrong *(1934)
was to undermine the authority of the Bible. The 1904 signature has faded (courtesy of the Enoch Pratt Free Library).*

Mencken with Paul Patterson, president of the Sunpapers *parent firm, A. S. Abell Company, in Atlanta, Georgia, in October 1926 (courtesy of the Enoch Pratt Free Library)*

alike. But enough of it recalls Agnes Repplier to make me uncomfortable.

3. The Letters to the Editor could stand a lot of improvement. Too many of them are quite pointless, too many are by numskulls, and too many are unsigned. Consider Long May He Play Politics and the Stock Market, July 14. The only reason for printing such a letter lies in the fact that it makes its author ridiculous. When his name is withheld the whole point is lost. Such letters as Dangerous Economy, July 18, either should be signed in full or submitted to the persons in interest before being printed. So with such palpable efforts at propaganda as Ritchie and Dennis, July 20. A letter column always tends to be monopolized by cranks and bores. Every effort should be made to exclude such puerilities as Peace Treaty Stamps, July 16, and Other Sides of Peale's Career, July 21. Matthew Page Andrews had better go on the black list. He is slipping into the shoes of the late Professor Henry E. Shepherd.

4. March of Events in Foreign Affairs seems to me to be very weak. In the main, it simply rehearses facts that have been printed, without adding anything to them. I can find no point of view in it. Whatever actual information it contains should be printed along with the news dispatches, in the Continental manner. The Associated Press has begun to send out explanations of foreign news, but there is room for more of them. I hate to see valuable space given over to the obvious. Encourage Parke to express opinions. His experience ought to make them worth hearing.

5. The editorial page miscellany is well selected, especially the longer pieces. Whoever gathers it should extend his reading as much as possible. Some of the best stuff is to be found in obscure publications. There is always a tendency in The Sun office to lean too heavily on one or two papers, notably the Manchester Guardian. The Guardian is by no means the masterpiece that it is sometimes represented to be. In many ways The Sun is already a far better paper, and there is no reason why it shouldn't be better in every way. Is anyone charged with going through the mass of propaganda papers and pamphlets that pass through the office? They are full of odd matter and useful suggestions. Stanley Reynolds, in his Evening Sun days, used to dredge superb stuff out of the Congressional Record. Some one should be told off to read it carefully. The same man should see that his name goes on the mailing-lists of all known propaganda organizations. They send out a great deal of amusing blather.

The Sun boardroom in 1929. Mencken is fifth from right (courtesy of the Enoch Pratt Free Library).

7. *[Note: There is no number 6.]* The editorials, it seems to me, are pretty well written, and the choice of subjects is good, but I believe that they are often a bit too cautious in tone. Dangerous Lethargy, before cited, offers a case in point. It is crippled by what seems to be an effort to be judicial. But why be judicial in such a situation? The Sun is not a court of justice; it is a newspaper of the Opposition. Its function is not to correct exercises in logic; it is to search out weaknesses in the Administration and expose them as dramatically as possible. When a Secretary of State is caught in an embarrassing predicament, made by an imbecile predecessor of his own party, it is not the business of an Opposition paper to make excuses for him. Let him do that for himself, with such aid as he can get from the organs of the Administration. It is not only the privilege of an Opposition paper to make him as uncomfortable as possible; it is its highest duty to do so, else free government becomes meaningless. For by making him uncomfortable it discourages the knaveries and idiocies that get public officers into such situations.

In many other editorials I sense the same excess of politeness, the same disinclination to come out with it. Apologies Were Made, July 20, and Unjust Proce-

dure, July 21, are typical. Here were two chances to do some vigorous and arresting writing; what got into the paper was simply mild remonstrance. I do not argue that invective is the only thing that ought to be printed in the editorial columns; all I argue is that when a scoundrel is on the block he ought to be denounced in plain terms, and without any judicial tenderness. So with fools. So with fool ideas. I believe that both Why Hide Facts?, July 20, and Needless and Dangerous, July 21, might have been far more effective than they are. In each case the method employed is relatively feeble; a forthright reductio ad absurdum would have been better. Moreover, The Sun should not wait for correspondents of The New Republic to bring it into action against such atrocities as the Capper-Johnson bill. One of its chief functions is to unearth such things and expose their viciousness. That exposure and the accompanying denunciation, it seems to me, should be free from unnecessary concessions. In order to carry conviction it is needful to have conviction. It is also needful to remember that most men are convinced, not by appeals to their reason, but by appeals to their emotions and prejudices. Such emotions and prejudices are not necessarily ignoble. It is just as creditable to hate injustice and dishonesty as it is to love the truth. One of the chief

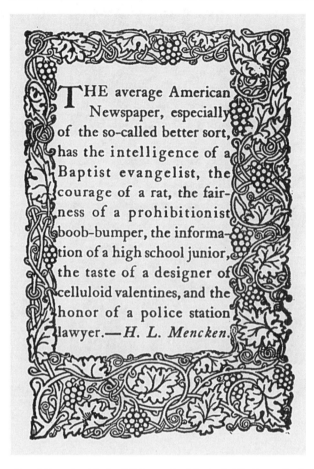

THE average American Newspaper, especially of the so-called better sort, has the intelligence of a Baptist evangelist, the courage of a rat, the fairness of a prohibitionist boob-bumper, the information of a high school junior, the taste of a designer of celluloid valentines, and the honor of a police station lawyer.—*H. L. Mencken.*

Broadside, printed in the 1930s, quoting Mencken's "On Journalism"
(Brown University Library)

should be denounced in plain terms and without reservations of any kind. In journalism, it seems to me, it is far better to be wrong than to be timorous. The papers that get attention are those that take a positive line, and stick to it with tenacity.

The opportunity lying before The Sun is almost unparalleled. Unlike most journals that play with ideas, it is rich, and can afford to do whatever it pleases. It has a competent editorial and news staff, and the salient men on that staff are in sympathy with its politics. Its good faith is generally admitted. It is not tied to any politician. Its only serious opposition is offered by the New York World, a paper in decay, and the St. Louis Post-Dispatch, which is far away. It has no local rivals of any dignity. I believe that it ought to assert itself, and that it will. I recommend that a steady increase in editorial vigor be made a matter of fixed policy, and that editorials be printed on Page 1 whenever it is possible. There is no need to be ashamed, certainly, of what it is doing now. But it can do more.

8. I believe that the editorial page could be made more attractive physically. Elmer Adler told me in New York a few weeks ago that he'd be glad to tackle it—and indeed the whole paper. Three columns of editorials are probably too much. It would be better to put some of the editorial writers to writing signed articles for the page. That has been tried in The Evening Sun, and with considerable success. I think The Sun could do it better.

9. Attached are the eight pages I have discussed, for reference.

purposes of The Sun, as I understand it, is to stir up such useful hatreds. I think it could go much further in that direction than it has gone.

Here, to be sure, I generalize rather gaily on somewhat meagre evidence. The week I have reviewed was a week of dulness. But I think it is still fair to say that The Sun has by no means made effective use of the opportunities standing before it to lead the Opposition. It has seldom assaulted the Administration with any vigor. The Kent articles have defended Hoover with great ingenuity, even when he was plainly caught with the goods; the paper itself has let him off with a few mild remonstrances. Thus the average reader, and especially the average intelligent reader, has probably got the notion that it is disposed to be friendly to him. The only way to dispose of that error is to tackle him head-on. Good chances offer themselves every day. An Opposition paper should seek them out and make the most of them. The acts of the Administration should be reviewed constantly, and with the deliberate purpose of finding weaknesses in them, and those weaknesses

Mencken reiterates some of these themes in a January 1937 memorandum to Patterson, but here he puts them in the context of the New Deal and the crisis in Europe. He was going against the local and national tide in his opposition to the policies coming out of Washington and to President Franklin D. Roosevelt's skillful use of the media (typewritten memo with handwritten emendations in the Enoch Pratt Free Library).

The primary aim of the <u>Sunpapers,</u> both in their news columns and on their editorial pages, must be simply and solely to tell the truth.

That aim is not to be attained by printing what every other paper prints. The ordinary flow of news is partial in two senses. It covers the field inadequately, and a large part of it is launched by persons with private interests to further. Not infrequently those private interests are adroitly disguised as public interests, but their real character remains. We must try to penetrate them and to counteract them. We must detect the falsities, whether of fact or of inference, in the news they launch, and set beside that news a kind that is more realistic and reliable.

At the present time that effort is especially necessary, for we confront a high development of government propaganda in both domestic and foreign affairs. Very little news emanating from Washington, even when it comes through our own bureau, is without bias, and very little news coming from Europe. It should be our fixed policy to be very suspicious of what is generally said and generally believed, and to set forth, whenever possible, the other side. We should bear in mind such facts as these: that H. M. Brailsford, considering his private politics, would be in favor of the Spanish government even if it were clearly wrong, and that all the congressional committees now functioning are looking for ammunition against capitalism, not for the truth about both capital and labor.

A lot may be accomplished by simply presenting the facts, but not everything. Some effort must be made to show their significance, and to expose the motives and methods of those who seek to sophisticate them. In other words, we must make some appeal to the sense of fair play, and even to the self-interest of readers. We'll get nowhere so long as we try to counteract a wholesale and highly skillful playing on the emotions with nothing more formidable than a resort to reasoning.

As for our general policy, I think it should be anti-Administration at all times. It has been so generally since the White Paper *[1919],* and it brings the power of sound information and impartial honesty against the immense effects of government propaganda, with its constant appeals to the lowest credulities of the people, and its playing on their tendency to believe in and even to worship conspicuous public officials. I do not propose that we denounce the Administration incessantly and unreasonably; I only propose that we view it skeptically, and refuse to assent to its devices and pretensions until we are sure that they are intelligent and sincere. Every public official with large powers in his hands should be held in suspicion until he proves his case, and we should keep him at all times in a glare of light. The fact, say, that Henry Wallace failed miserably and ignominiously at his own private business is a fact of capital importance, and it should be recalled often enough to keep it in the public mind.

At the time the <u>Sunpapers</u> were rehabilitated many of the persons chosen to man them, especially on the side of the foreign service, were of Liberal politics. Some of these persons have since become radicals. I believe that the safe and rational course for the papers themselves is still that of Liberalism, and that we should be watchful of radical propaganda by our own men. We should fight resolutely at all times for the chief Liberal goods, all of them well tested and of the highest

President Franklin D. Roosevelt, whose New Deal policies earned Mencken's scorn

value, <u>e.g.</u>, the limitation of governmental powers, economy in all the public services, complete publicity, the greatest tolerable degree of free speech, and a press secure against official pressure. There is nothing for a decent newspaper in radicalism. If it ever succeeds in this country our function will be gone, and with it our liberties. They will be gone equally whether the radicalism that comes in is of the Right or of the Left.

Having dispatched "the Archangel Woodrow" (Wilson), "Gamaliel" (Warren G. Harding), "Cal" (Calvin Coolidge), and "Lord Hoover" (Herbert Hoover), Mencken found his match in "Roosevelt Minor." On a famous occasion the biter was bit. At the Gridiron Club "roast" of Roosevelt on 8 December 1934 Mencken delivered a short speech with relatively mild jibes. FDR responded by reading a series of denunciations of American journalism that—as Mencken was the first to realize—were extracts from an essay of Mencken's that appeared in Prejudices: Sixth Series *(1927); the president revealed his source at the end. An embarrassed Mencken brushed the matter off at the time but never forgave Roosevelt for the joke. Nonetheless, he stood by his assessment of the profession (excerpt from "Journalism in America," in* Prejudices: Sixth Series, *pp. 9–16).*

Historical Notes
by our Cruise Member
Mr. Henry L. Mencken

The founder of the North German Lloyd, Captain Johann Gustav August Lloyd, launched his first *Schnellpostdampfer*, the *Columbus I*, in 1832. A year later it made the westward voyage from Bremen to New York in three months, two weeks, five days, 18 hours and 12 minutes. On this voyage the custom of making hat pools on the day's run was established. The first winner was a Mr. John R. Smith of Boston, Mass, who guessed that the run would be 35 sea-miles. On the 48th day out the pool was declared no bet, for the ship was blown backward 7 miles.

The *Columbus II*, launched in 1851, was the first Lloyd liner to have Pilsner on draught. It became so popular that passengers were bunked 15 in a room. Five slept from midnight to 8 a. m., five from 8 a. m. to 4 p. m., and the rest from 4 p.m. to midnight. The smokeroom was open continuously. This ship saw the first non sleeping smokeroom steward, Otto Kühne. On one voyage he remained on duty for eight days and sixteen hours.

The *Columbus III*, launched in 1874, was the first Lloyder worthy of the name of *Doppelschraubenschnellpostexpreßluxus- dampfer*. It made the run from the Scilly Islands to Sandy Hook in 16 days flat. This speed was considered dangerous, and was presently reduced to 18 days. The ship was very luxuriously outfitted. Every

male passenger had his own shaving mug and gold toothpick. The cabins were paved with Brussels carpets showing red roses 36 inches in diameter. There was a bathroom beside the boilerroom, and passengers could use it by applying to the head steward 48 hours in advance.

The *Columbus IV.*, which came in the 80's, was the first to have a library. This consisted of the Bible, "Die Familie Buchholz" and the bound reports of the N. G. L. back to 1832. In 1889 the works of Bulwer-Lytton were added. In 1890 followed those of Mrs. E. D. E. N. Southword. The Columbus IV. also had the first ship's band ever heard of on the high seas. It included many performers who afterward became famous, notably Richard Strauss, Gustav Mahler, and Igor Stravinsky. Strauss played the *Waldhorn* and Mahler the ophecleide. During the heavy storm off Nantucket, in 1893, the whole band was washed overboard, but the bass drum made a good lifeboat, and no one was lost.

The *Columbuses V, VI and VII* will be recalled by old travelers. On the first named four meals a day were served. This was increased to six on the *Columbus VI* and to nine on the *Columbus VII*. On the latter ship eightdoctors were carried. In 1903 the meals were reduced to five a day and a gymnasium was put in. Since then the great majority of passengers have been landed alive and under their own steam.

The *Columbus VIII* is our own ship. Its history is too complicated and romantic to be told here. More anon.

Lottery Results

The raffle which took place in the Main Lounge on Saturday afternoon was such a success that numbers were bought up to the very last minute, and we regret to say even later. The result was that $ 324 were collected, and prizes were bought for $ 296.25. This leaves $ 27.75 over, and the Cruise Staff sincerely hopes that it will meet with everyone's approval that this money has been given to the Widows' and Orphans' Fund of the North German Lloyd.

PERSONAL COLUMN
Review Of The "Scandals"

Mr. James F. McGrath — who sponsored and produced the "Scandals" has received a radiogram from Flo Ziegfeld offering him a job. Mc's selection of the ladies in the "Scandals Chorus" showed hidden talents.

* *

Senator Michael J. Ward was very happy in his position of toastmaster until someone suggested — he sings.

* *

Mr. Thompson Martin, or Martin Thompson, is an accomplished musician — if you are in doubt speak to the accordion.

* *

The two Pals, Locke & Martin outdid themselves; the impromptu way they sang pleased all of us.

* *

Mencken spoofing his profession in a contribution to a ship's newspaper (Jack R. Sanders Collection)

One of the agreeable spiritual phenomena of the great age in which we live is the soul-searching now going on among American journalists. Fifteen years ago, or even ten years ago, there was scarcely a sign of it. The working newspaper men of the Republic, of whom I have had the honor to be one since the last century, were then almost as complacent as so many Federal judges, movie magnates, or major-generals in the army. When they discussed their puissant craft at all, it was only to smack their chests proudly, boasting of their vast power in public matters, of their adamantine resistance to all the less tempting varieties of bribes, and of the fact that a politician of enlightened self-interest, giving them important but inaccurate news confidently, could rely upon them to mangle it beyond recognition before publishing it. I describe a sort of Golden Age, and confess frankly that I can't do so without a certain yielding to emotion. Salaries had been going up since the dawn of the new century, and the journalist, how-

ever humble, was beginning to feel his oats. For the first time in history he was paid as well as the human cranes and steam-shovels slinging rolls of paper in the cellar. He began to own two hats, two suits of clothes, two pairs of shoes, two walking-sticks, even two belts. He ceased to feed horribly in one-arm lunch-rooms and began to dine in places with fumigated waitresses, some of a considerable pulchritude and amiability, and red-shaded table lamps. He was, as much as such things are reckoned, happy. But at the heart of his happiness, alas, there yet gnawed a canker-worm. One enemy remained in his world, unscotched and apparently unscotchable, to wit, the business manager. The business manager, at will, could send up a blue slip and order him fired. In the face of that menace from below-stairs his literary superiors were helpless, up to and including the editor-in-chief. All of them were under the hoof of the business manager, and all the business manager ever thought of was advertising. Let an advertiser complain that his honor had been impugned or his *clavi* abraded, and off went a head.

It was the great war for human freedom, I suspect and allege, that brought the journalist deliverance from that last and most abominable hazard: he was, perhaps, one of the few real beneficiaries of all the carnage. As the struggle grew more savage on Flanders fields and business grew better and better at home, reporters of any capacity whatever got to be far too scarce to fire loosely. Moreover, the business manager, with copy pouring over his desk almost unsolicited, began to lose his old dread of advertisers, and then even some of his natural respect for them. It was a sellers' market, in journalism as in the pants business. Customers were no longer kissed; the lesser among them actually began to stand in line. The new spirit, so strange and so exhilarating, spread like a benign pestilence, and presently it began to invade even the editorial rooms. In almost every American city, large or small, some flabbergasted advertiser, his money in his hand, sweat pouring from him as if he had seen a ghost, was kicked out with spectacular ceremonies. All the principal papers, suddenly grown rich, began also to grow independent, virtuous, touchy, sniffish. No – – – – could dictate to them, God damn! So the old free reading notices of the Bon Marché and the Palais Royal disappeared, salaries continued to climb, and the liberated journalist, taking huge breaths of thrilling air, began to think of himself as a professional man.

Upon that cogitation he is still engaged, and all the weeklies that print the news of the craft are full of its fruits. He elects representatives and they meet in lugubrious conclave to draw up codes of ethics. He begins to read books dealing with professional questions of other sorts—even books not dealing with professional questions. He changes his old cynical view of schools of journalism, and is lured, now and then, into lecturing in them himself. He no longer thinks of his calling as a business, like the haberdasher's or tallow chandler's, or as a game, like the stockbroker's or faro-dealer's, but as a profession, like the jurisconsult's or gynecologist's. His purpose is to set it on its legs as such—to inject plausible theories into its practise, and rid it of its old casualness and opportunism. He no longer sees it as a craft to be mastered in four days, and abandoned at the first sign of a better job. He begins to talk darkly of the long apprenticeship necessary to master its technic, of the wide information and sagacity needed to adorn it, of the high rewards that it offers—or may offer later on—to the man of true talent and devotion. Once he thought of himself, whenever he thought at all, as what Beethoven called a free artist—a gay adventurer careening down the charming highways of the world, the gut-

ter ahead of him but ecstasy in his heart. Now he thinks of himself as a fellow of weight and responsibility, a beginning publicist and public man, sworn to the service of the born and unborn, heavy with duties to the Republic and to his profession.

In all this, I fear, there is some illusion, as there always is in human thinking. The journalist can no more see himself realistically than a bishop can see himself realistically. He gilds and engauds the picture, unconsciously and irresistibly. For one thing, and a most important one, he is probably somewhat in error about his professional status. He remains, for all his dreams, a hired man—the owner downstairs, or even the business manager, though he doesn't do it very often now, is still free to demand his head—, and a hired man is not a professional man. The essence of a professional man is that he is answerable for his professional conduct only to his professional peers. A physician cannot be fired by any one, save when he has voluntarily converted himself into a job-holder; he is secure in his livelihood so long as he keeps his health, and can render service, or what they regard as service, to his patients. A lawyer is in the same boat. So is a dentist. So, even, is a horse-doctor. But a journalist still lingers in the twilight zone, along with the trained nurse, the embalmer, the rev. clergy and the great majority of engineers. He cannot sell his services directly to the consumer, but only to entrepreneurs, and so those entrepreneurs have the power of veto over all his soaring fancies. His codes of ethics are all right so long as they do not menace newspaper profits; the moment they do so the business manager, now quiescent, will begin to growl again. Nor has he the same freedom that the lawyers and the physicians have when it comes to fixing his own compensation; what he faces is not a client but a boss. Above all, he is unable, as yet, to control admission to his craft. It is constantly recruited, on its lowest levels, from men who have little professional training or none at all, and some of these men master its chief mysteries very quickly. Thus even the most competent journalist faces at all times a severe competition, easily expanded at need, and cannot afford to be too saucy. When a managing editor is fired there is always another one waiting to take his place, but there is seldom another place waiting for the managing editor.

All these things plainly diminish the autonomy of the journalist, and hamper his effort to lift his trade to professional rank and dignity. When he talks of codes of ethics, indeed, he only too often falls into mere tall talk, for he cannot enforce the rules he so solemnly draws up—that is, in the face of dissent from above. Nevertheless, his discussion of the subject is still not wholly absurd, for there remain plenty of rules that he *can* enforce, and I incline to think that there are more of

enters into the common knowledge of educated men. There are managing editors in the United States, and scores of them, who have never heard of Kant or Johannes Müller and never read the Constitution of the United States; there are city editors who do not know what a symphony is, or a streptococcus, or the Statute of Frauds; there are reporters by the thousand who could not pass the entrance examination for Harvard or Tuskegee, or even Yale. It is this vast and militant ignorance, this wide-spread and fathomless prejudice against intelligence, that makes American journalism so pathetically feeble and vulgar, and so generally disreputable. A man with so little intellectual enterprise that, dealing with news daily, he can go through life without taking in any news that is worth knowing–such a man, you may be sure, is lacking in professional dignity quite as much as he is lacking in curiosity. The delicate thing called honor can never be a function of stupidity. If it belongs to those men who are genuinely professional men, it belongs to them because they have lifted themselves to the plane of a true aristocracy, in learning as well as in liberty–because they have deliberately and successfully separated themselves from the great masses of men, to whom learning is an insult and liberty an agony. The journalists, in seeking to acquire that status, put the cart before the horse. [. . .]

Hebrew title page that appeared in three of the twenty-five copies of Erez Israel *printed by B. P. Safran on the handpress of the New School for Social Research in New York in 1935. The book comprises revisions by Mencken of two of his* Sun *articles on the Jewish settlements in Palestine.*

One of Mencken's many attacks on FDR took the form of advocating the immigration of German Jews to America. This advocacy came in the wake of the president's restrictive policies and put Mencken well ahead of public and journalistic opinion. It was done out of genuine concern for a beleaguered minority and is an example of that professional duty to stand in opposition, resist propaganda, and tell the truth that he expounds in the Patterson memos. In light of the (mainly posthumous) charges of anti-Semitism brought against Mencken, this article–not to mention his earlier support for the Jewish settlement of Palestine–throws important light on a significant aspect of his character and career. His defense of the Jews is also an attack on another favorite target: the British imperium, whose influence on America's literature and foreign policy Mencken found malign. It is, perhaps, necessary to explain that Mencken is being ironic at the end of the article: there is "no prejudice" toward Eastern Jews in Russia only because of their putative socialism ("Help For The Jews," Baltimore Sun, *27 November 1938, editorial page).*

them than of the other kind. Most of the evils that continue to beset American journalism to-day, in truth, are not due to the rascality of owners nor even to the Kiwanian bombast of business managers, but simply and solely to the stupidity, cowardice and Philistinism of working newspaper men. The majority of them, in almost every American city, are still ignoramuses, and proud of it. All the knowledge that they pack into their brains is, in every reasonable cultural sense, useless; it is the sort of knowledge that belongs, not to a professional man, but to a police captain, a railway mail-clerk, or a board-boy in a brokerage house. It is a mass of trivialities and puerilities; to recite it would be to make even a barber beg for mercy. What is missing from it, in brief, is everything worth knowing–everything that

It is to be hoped that the poor Jews now being robbed and mauled in Germany will not take too seriously the plans of various foreign politicos to rescue them. Those plans, in all cases, smell pungently of national politics, and in not a few cases they are obviously fraudulent. The last is especially true of the English scheme to plant the victims in such forlorn and uninhabitable places as British Guiana, and of the American scheme to help them by goading and inflaming the Nazi Ku Kluxers, while at the same time refusing to take any substantial number into the United States, or to relax the drastic immigration laws which now bar out virtually all the really helpless.

It may be that some of the so-called *Ostjuden,* or Eastern Jews, could survive in British Guiana, for they are a tough people and used to hard scrabbling, but certainly it would be next door to murder to send any German Jews there, for most of them are more or less educated folk, and long accustomed to the ways and comforts of civilization. Try to imagine condemning a German-Jewish lawyer, or insurance man, or merchant, or schoolmaster to a place where the climate is that of a Turkish bath, and there are no roads, no towns, no food supply, and hardly any inhabitants save snakes and mosquitoes!

Tanganyika is almost as bad. As readers of Marius Fortie's recent and excellent book, "Black and Beautiful," must know, it has gone downhill ever since the English philanthropists took over the mandate. The unfortunate natives are so cruelly taxed that many of them are now quite destitute, and every effort to plant English settlers on the land has failed, The best that may be said of Tanganyika is that it is as good as the worst parts of Mexico. If a Jewish colony is planted there it will take at least a generation to make it self-sustaining, and the cost of supporting it meanwhile will make the millions poured out in Palestine seem puny.

—o—

THERE IS PLENTY of room for refugees in other and better British possessions. Canada could absorb 100,000, or even 200,000 with ease, and they would be useful acquisitions, especially in the western prairie provinces, which are dominated today by a low grade of farmers, without any adequate counter-balance of a competent middle class. Australia, now almost as exclusive as Sing Sing, which it somewhat resembles in population, could use quite as many, for more than a third of its population is crowded into two cities, and immense areas of good country behind the seacoast are undeveloped. As for New Zealand, it has less than the population of Maryland in an area ten times as large.

In all three of these Dominions the climate is at least as bearable as that of Northern Germany, and the beginnings of civilization are already visible. But in Tanganyika there is nothing but such bare land as the American pioneers saw when they crossed the Mississippi. An investment of billions would be needed to develop it even up to the point reached by, say, Venezuela or Haiti. Moreover, it would still remain a poor country, for its arable areas are remote from the world markets, and it lacks coal, oil and other essential minerals.

British Guiana is yet worse; indeed, it is so bad that nothing comparable to it can be found short of the Congo. The towns along its coast are malarious and miserable villages, the plowed area is less than 1/320 of the total territory, and all save a small strip fronting the sea is such a howling wilderness that even prisoners escaping from Devil's Island keep out of it. To transport the German Jews to such a hell hole would be even worse than condemning them to Devil's Island itself.

—o—

THE AMERICAN PLAN for helping the refugees is less openly brutal than the English plan, but almost as insulting to them, and even more futile. It confines itself, so far, to making bellicose speeches, passing inflammatory resolutions, collecting money to defend and glorify the assassin of the German attaché, and otherwise provoking Hitler to reprisals. In the same breath in which the Hon. Mr. Roosevelt declared that he "could scarcely believe that such things could occur in a Twentieth Century civilization," he assured the newspaper correspondents that he had no intention of proposing a relaxation of the immigration laws. In other words, he is sorry for the Jews, but unwilling to do anything about it that might cause him political inconvenience at home.

Such gross and disgusting pecksniffery is precisely what one might expect from the right hon. gentleman, and I only hope the American Jews who have swallowed so much of his other buncombe will not be fetched by it. The American newspapers, with their usual credulity, applauded it gravely—but not so the Negro papers. The dark comrades point out that Roosevelt has never been as solicitous about outrages on Negroes in this country. Says George S. Schuyler, perhaps the best of all the Aframerican journalists, in the Pittsburgh *Courier:*

> Imagine Roosevelt saying he "could scarcely believe" such atrocities could take place in this day and time when white people had just got through burning a schoolhouse and running Negroes out of Smyrna, Ga., and had just finished jabbing red-hot pokers into a Negro youth in Ruston, La.!

—o—

THERE IS only one way to help the fugitives, and that is to find places for them in a country in which they can really live. Why shouldn't the United States take in a couple of hundred thousand of them, or even all of them? I have heard, so far, but two objections to inviting them. The first is to the effect that there is far too much unemployment here now, and that a fresh immigration, even of so small a number, would only accentuate it. The second is that bringing them in would arouse the native Ku Kluxers, and perhaps launch a formidable anti-Semitic movement.

Both objections seem to me to be very feeble. The first is based on the theory that all the refugees would either join the unemployed themselves, or increase the roll to their own number by displacing Americans now at work. Neither effect is even remotely probable. The Jews will find work very quickly, and whatever they produce will be more than balanced by what they consume. They will not compete on the low level of the present dole-birds: they will compete on higher levels, and the chances are at least even that they will soon be adding more to the national income than they take away.

The Ku Klux fear is equally without ground. If they were planted in Mississippi, Arkansas or some other such jumping-off place, the local Ku Kluxers would undoubtedly protest, but not many Jews are likely to go to Mississippi or Arkansas. Instead they will stay in the larger cities—and there the number of their people is already so large that a few more will hardly be noticed. The present Jewish population of New York city is 1,765,000—more than four times the Jewish population of Palestine. It is absurd to argue that an increase of five or six per cent would set the patriotic Aryans to burning and slaying.

−o−

I AM HERE SPEAKING, of course, of German Jews, and of German Jews only. They constitute an undoubtedly superior group. Even their occasional rascals, so I was once told by a German police official, are far above the felonious common run. The question of the Eastern Jews remains, and it should be faced candidly. Many German Jews dislike them, and were trying to get them out of Germany before the present universal disasters came down. There is a faction of them that tends to be troublesome wherever they settle, and there is apparently ground for the general belief that in this country they incline toward the more infantile kinds of radicalism.

Fortunately, they are not numerous in German Jewry. The really large accumulations of them are in Poland and Rumania. It would be obviously impossible, even if it were prudent, for the United States to take them all in. But there is still plenty of room for them, and in a land where there is no prejudice against them, and their opportunities are immensely better than in Tanganyika or Guiana, or even Palestine. That land is Russia.

Roosevelt was on Mencken's mind when he gave a talk on editorial writing at a convention of the American Society of Newspaper Editors in Washington, D.C., on 16 April 1937 (from Proceedings: Fifteenth Annual Convention, American Society of Newspaper Editors, April 15–16–17, 1937 *[Washington, D.C.: National Press Club, 1937], pp. 45–49).*

Ladies and gentlemen, I will have to read. After all, we are writers and not speakers. Furthermore, my voice is bad, so maybe you will have to give me a little indulgence.

Any discussion of the situation of the American editorial page had better start with a fundamental question, to wit: Why should anyone read it at all? I must confess that, in looking over some of the pages now current, I find it impossible to imagine any sound reason.

The pull of the other pages is plain enough. The news pages, in the midst of a great deal of bosh and tosh, usually give the reader the essentials of the day's news, and news is something that all human beings crave, at all times and everywhere. Moreover, virtually all human beings crave the same kind. You will hear prigs protesting against the printing, say, of crime news, but it always turns out on cross-examination that they never miss reading it. A hanging is a good story to an archbishop, just as it is to a street-railway curve-greaser, and so is all the melodrama that precedes it.

The feature pages are almost as popular; indeed, in some papers they are more popular. The reason is not far to seek. They are aimed frankly at the actual tastes of the normal reader. They feed his (and especially her) vanity. They provide plenty of gossip and scandal, sometimes malicious. They are full of the puerile and inaccurate information that one picks up in barbershops. They offer a discussion of public questions by persons especially chosen for their fluent imbecility, which is to say, by columnists, of whom I have long had the honor to be one. Thus they meet a genuine need of readers who have gone through the intellectual shambles of the public schools, and it is no wonder that they are so popular.

The editorial page—by which I mean the section of actual editorials—meets no such need. It is, basically, an attempt to subject public questions to logical analysis—and logical analysis is something that nine human beings out of ten are incapable of and hence uninterested in. Their thinking is not done by that process. They have ideas, to be sure, and some of those ideas are furiously maintained, but they are not reached by syllogism; they are reached by desire and appetite, by yen and libido. At the time President Roosevelt launched his proposal for pulling the fangs of the Supreme Court certain newspapers sent reporters on the streets to find out what the plain people thought of it. The answers, in the main, were divided into two classes, neither of which showed anything more than simple feeling. The majority answered: "I am in favor of anything that Roosevelt wants." The rest answered, "I am against anything that Roosevelt is in favor of."

But while this was going on the editorial writers were filling their space with long and learned discussions of the matter, going back to history and heavy with subtle argumentation. The theory, I take it, was (and is) that there is a public eager for genuine light and leading. In all probability, such a public actually exists. It may be very small, but no doubt a thorough search of any American community would reveal it. But why, if it is real, should it give any serious consideration to anonymous editorials? Why should it follow wizards it doesn't know, whose qualifications it has no means of testing, and whose very convictions are often open to reasonable question?

I hope no one will think that I am here attempting to run down editorial writers. My belief is that there are many smart fellows among them, and the somewhat alarmed respect for them that I picked up in my early reportorial days still survives, though I have since been one myself, and have even hired and fired them. When I was a magazine editor I got a great deal of excellent stuff out of them, often to their own surprise. It amazed them to discover how well they could write, and what good ideas they had, once they had thrown off their false faces and begun to function as their own men. Some of them liked it so well that they quit their jobs and set up as independent publicists, and some of the some are making fairish livings at that trade to this day.

But how can any man be expected to do really effective writing under the conditions they commonly face? Only too often they must write at high speed, and with insufficient preparation, and at all times they must give primary consideration, not to what they may happen to think or feel themselves, but to what some higher functionary thinks or feels. And when that higher functionary himself does the actual writing, he is not uncommonly incommoded by trying to figure out, not what is the truth, but what is consistent with the paper's character, or past performances, or future plans, or what will please some still higher functionary.

All these allegations have been made against newspaper editorial writing by lay critics, and sometimes they have been resented hotly, as if they impugned the honor of newspapers. But all of us know

that they are generally true—if not on all newspapers, then at least on a great many. The job of the editorial writer is actually almost hopeless. He is expected to achieve effects under such cruel handicaps that they would cripple a writer of the first class, working with both arms free. Deprived of the chief strength of any writer—the force and color, such as they are, of his own personality—he carries on his art like a surgeon wearing boxing-gloves or an actor with a wooden leg.

Is there any remedy for this disease—any way to liberate him? Maybe not, but we can at least speculate. If I were the sole editor and proprietor of a newspaper, which God forbid, I think I'd start off by abolishing the editorial page as it now stands. It fails to interest the majority of readers and it fails to persuade the minority. It is a vestigial organ, and most of its old functions have now passed to the columnists and headline writers. It wastes a lot of excellent brain-power, and costs a lot more than it is worth, either to the paper or to the common good.

The first thing to do, it seems to me, is to let the editorial writers appear in their own persons, and the second thing is to take them off dealing with all things briefly and superficially, and to put them to dealing with a few things thoroughly and at length. The notion that people won't read long articles is nonsense. Those who can really read at all will read an acre—if it is well done. Many editorial writers, in my experience, know a great deal about this or that. If they had more elbow room they could set it forth much more persuasively than they do now, and if they did it over their own names they would take much more pains to set it forth charmingly.

Would the great masses of the plain people read them and heed them? Probably not. But that is only saying what I have said already—that the great masses are shy of logic, and can be reached only by appeals to their feelings. That appeal can never be made by intellectual devices. It must be made by the arts of the showman. I see no reason why a newspaper, in seeking to put over an idea, should not make use of the expedients already in use by its advertisers, and even by its feature writers. That is, I see no reason why it should not employ illustrations for the purpose, and vociferous typography, and the style of the radio fireside chat, the auction sale and the college yell. The primary object of public argumentation is not to show off the argufier's elegance; it is to set the customer to panting, sweating and beating his breast. That can never be done by putting the thing into small type, and under one-line heads.

The objection that any such hullabaloo would destroy the impartiality of the news columns is of very little force. The news columns are not actually impartial now, and they probably never can be. Those of you who argued against the New Deal in the last campaign—and so vainly—should know what I mean. While you were setting off your squibs on your editorial pages, your front pages roared with New Deal propaganda, most of it supplied at the cost of the taxpayer you were professedly trying to succor, but not a little of it concocted by your own men.

The tremendous development of this propaganda in late years has seriously corrupted the news. A great deal of it has become, in its raw state, only a kind of ballyhoo. I'll give you two examples, and then shut down. The first is provided by the proceedings of the LaFollette investigating committee. For weeks on end it filled the first pages with evidence that some of the larger employers of the country were setting spies upon their working people, fomenting disorders, and otherwise carrying on in an anti-social manner. This was important news, and it deserved to be printed. But not once during the whole uproar was there any hint that there had been any provocation from the other side. The employers were represented as mere criminals, and not a word was said about the forays and extortions that had scared them in the first place, and set them to doing the silly and brutal things that scared men always do.

The second example is less glaring but almost as significant. Last February the Department of Superintendence of the National Education Association was meeting at New Orleans. There were thousands of gogues in attendance, and they devoted a week to discussing the problems of their trade. What they said and did got very little space in the newspapers, and perhaps deserved even less. But on February 21, 30 of them put their heads together and sent a telegram to the White House, whooping up the raid on the Supreme Court. In one great paper that I could mention—but will not on advice of counsel—that telegram got a swell spot on Page 1, and then jumped to nearly a column on Page 2, with a full list of signers at the end. No one in the office seemed to notice that only 30 had signed out of more than 3,000 in attendance, that the telegram had been prepared by two professional radicals, and that it no more represented the general opinion of the assembled gogues than it did that of the Supreme Court itself.

I am not arguing that this telegram should have been ignored. It was actually, in its way, news, though certainly not important news. All I am arguing is that printing it without a gloss, like printing the LaFollette testimony without a gloss, was plainly misleading. In controversial matters the news can never be one side only; it must be both sides. It seems to me that the American newspapers, in the face of the immense propaganda now flooding them, have forgotten or neglected that capital fact. In an effort to let everyone be heard they have given all the advantage to the most vocal and enterprising side. They will never be doing their duty until they invent some way to strike a better balance. They will not be printing the true news until they show what is behind every effort to corrupt it.

But here I wander off into the news-room, which is not my present theme. The editorial-room, to return to it, is a much sadder sight. Its brave lads are trying to sweep back an ocean with brooms. Worse, they diligently avoid big brooms, and use only tiny little ones. Yet worse, every sweeper is blindfolded and knee-haltered before he begins, and confined to a few square feet of the shore. No wonder the waves roll in. (Applause)

Mencken was interviewed the following year for Editor & Publisher *magazine (Stephen J. Monchak, "H. L. Mencken Rides Again, Rowelling U. S. Newspapers,"* Editor & Publisher, *71 [10 September 1938]: 9, 14).*

BALTIMORE, Md., Sept. 5. The years have not mellowed Henry L. Mencken.

Outspoken, at times bitter, critic of things conservative, "the Baltimore Battler," as he often has been termed, still is the enfant terrible of conservative America. His winged shafts of criticism and caustic comment still fly as often as in the past.

One of the pet peeves of this brilliant, fretful, at times abusive, fault-finder, for years has been the American newspaper. In 1924, in an interview with EDITOR & PUBLISHER, he "shot the wad," as it were, stating, in essence, that American newspapers were getting rich and for that reason were getting respectable. He qualified his statement, then, however, pointing out that for the most part they were quacks and charlatans.

Has Never Changed His Mind

Today, more than a decade after, EDITOR & PUBLISHER again sought him out, this time in this traditional city of oysters and beer where he makes his home, to learn what, if any, change had entered into the picture, and invited him to comment freely on divers other related and unrelated subjects.

There has not been any change; Henry Louis Mencken of 1924 and Henry Louis Mencken of 1938 are the same man. His opening remarks for the record testify to that.

"I never changed my mind in my life," he snorted. "My view of the American press is unchanged. I believe that only a small minority of daily newspapers are intellectually respectable. Some of them are owned by racketeers, and even more by jackasses."

However, "the Scoffing Sage of Baltimore," a title to which he doesn't object, again was inclined to be optimistic and thought he perceived progress in improving this state of affairs. He attributed this advancement "mainly, if not solely, to the elimination of bankrupt and often venal papers."

After a few moments of contemplation there followed a flow of typical Menckenesque comment at times witty, but always critical. Warming to his subject and with tongue in cheek, it appeared, he placed a garland on the brow of the press, stating:

"I think the American newspapers cover news better than they did in my early days—much better," and then deftly removed it in the same breath with: "but the editorial pages have not improved. The editorial page is the weakest page on most American newspapers. On many it is filled with canned stuff. Very few editorial writers know their business. They tend to be literary essayists. A real editorial is not an essay; it is a stump speech."

Syndicated columns were next. Mr. Mencken believes their rise has damaged papers by making them too much alike. "Moreover, most of the columnists now in practice are fifth raters, with little information and less sense," he added.

However, all is not lost, for Mr. Mencken sees a great improvement in newspaper personnel in the past decade. "The oldtime boozing, grafting reporter has been pretty well eliminated," he observed. "I had the pleasure, back in 1905, of firing one of the last bunches of them in practice in Baltimore. The average reporter of today is a well educated, decent and a self-respecting man."

The curse of the newspaper trade, Mr. Mencken believes, "is the lure of press agent jobs, offering relatively high salaries. Whether newspapers can advance salaries sufficiently to put down this nuisance remains to be seen. I incline to think they can."

To Mr. Mencken's mind the entrance of labor leaders into newspaper editorial offices "will, at the start, cause confusion, and probably damage the better sort of men." This difficulty, however, will work out in time, he said. At present he believes the editorial unions are suffering from poor leadership, though he holds out hope that "sooner or later they will be run by superior men."

In Favor of Organization

Mr. Mencken said he was in favor of organization of working men, and that if he would have been eligible he would have joined the American Newspaper Guild. However, he thinks the guild's "present libido for pass-

Mencken, who later became "an honorary member of the International Association of Fire Chiefs," with the New Orleans chief in 1926 (courtesy of the Enoch Pratt Free Library)

ing resolutions is silly. It should stick to its proper business."

Mr. Mencken's admirable and lucid English is a pleasure to hear. He talks, if anything, better than he writes. Certainly, he can give a brilliant causerie on his proper subject. His talk is unforced and expresses him completely. He has no pretense in him and appears to like criticism and argument against his contentions. He is emphatic, and yet, appealing to his listener, he aims to be persuasive. In short, he doesn't pontificate.

At 58, he looks rosy and healthy, like some of the Rotarians he is wont to deplore. His face has rugged strength and shows much spirit. In an Oxford grey suit of summer cut, with shirt and tie to match, he looked prosperous and assured sitting across from the interviewer. Mr. Mencken doesn't look his age.

In recent years Mr. Mencken has stopped poking fun at "joiners," once his favorite target, in fact, ever since he became an honorary member of the International Association of Fire Chiefs. But he insists on the point that he is the only man in America, who is a celebrity in a manner, who is not weighted down with degrees. He is much opposed to academic distinctions.

Mr. Mencken's achievements are too well known to need recounting and most people know him for the truculent and dogmatic tone of his writings. Few will dispute that he is the greatest reviewer of his time. He has been called the dean of American critics but he is not pleased with the title, he indicates. In spite of his dragooning style and rough manners he is esteemed highly by the Fourth Estate.

Mr. Mencken threw a few rays of light into the dark corners of the literary cupboard even though he said: "I hate to discuss books in prospect." He said he was working on a book, which "in all probability, will be a volume of Solomonic advice to the young, cautioning them against politicians, reformers and other kinds of harlots.

"But it may be a volume of reminiscences of my first 12 years," he chuckled. "I don't know."

He was deeply earnest as he spoke again of newspapers.

"The American press is the only effective Opposition left in the U. S." he said. "Its main duty, it seems to me, is to keep a wary eye on the demagogues who operate on morons. Once a free press ceases to exist, the whole American system will collapse. It is the only remaining impediment to totalitarianism.

"That it will survive is not at all certain. Very few Americans actually believe in free speech. My guess is that by 1975 and may be by 1950 the press will be heavily policed."

He said the only way newspapers can serve the people is to tell the truth. "If the people refuse to heed it, that is not the outlook of newspaper men," he said. He quoted from an article which appeared under his signature in the *Baltimore Sunday Sun* Sept. 4, in which he discussed the present state of the nation.

In it he said "the New Deal is wrecking Democracy by reducing it to an absurdity—worse, to a patently dishonest absurdity." The real promoters of Fascism, against which he inveighed in his article, "are the New Deal's tinpot Hitlers and jitney Mussolinis," he said.

No Objection to Roosevelt Attacks

Discussing the recent attacks of President Roosevelt against the "Tory press," Mr. Mencken said he saw no objections to the President's action. "I see no objection to Roosevelt's attacks on the press," he stated. "Some of them are justified by the facts. But whether they are or they are not, he has a clear right to make them. I believe in free speech, and detest people who complain under attack. Roosevelt, of course, does it.

"Anything that concerns the welfare of the U.S. is within the province of the President. He should do a lot of talking. I regard Roosevelt as an unmitigated quack, but I greatly prefer him to such clams as Coolidge.

Quack or not, he is smart, and is thus worth a thousand Hoovers or Hardings.

"On the whole, it seems to me the American newspapers have done a good job under Roosevelt. The best of them have described him accurately. If the people like him as he stands, that is their business, not the newspapers'. A newspaper's function is to tell the truth, not to run things."

Mr. Mencken thinks a great many American newspapers have lost all definite character, "chiefly because they are filled with syndicated stuff." In the face of bitter controversy, they try to avoid offending any considerable faction, he said. "This may be prudent, but it is bad journalism," he observed. "I prefer outspoken people."

Newspaper chains, Mr. Mencken said, are sick and are falling to pieces by their own weight. He said there was no chain in America that could be called influential. "It is a sheer impossibility for one man to manage a dozen or more papers in different states," he growled. "He couldn't even read them in one day—in the way a newspaper man must read his own papers. I am glad to see the principal chains closing their ranks."

Mr. Mencken said he had no title with the Baltimore Sunpapers and has never had one since 1910, when he quit the Sunday desk of the *Sun* to help launch the Evening Sun. He added, however, that last spring he acted as editor of the Evening Sun for three months. Genial iconoclast, he retired as editor of *The American Mercury* in 1933.

Has No Official Title

"I have no office save the meager one of director in the Sun corporation," he said. "As such, I have no say in editorial matters." His editorship last spring, he said, was without significance. "It simply happened that the Sunpapers were an editor short, and I was doing nothing." Mr. Mencken said he made up the first editorial page of the Evening Sun in 1910, and has always written for it. Of late, his weekly article has been transferred to the Sunday Sun. "Again no significance," he said, "simply convenience."

Mr. Mencken's sage advice to aspiring journalists is to "work hard and try to learn. Write simply and try to improve your English. If you don't believe in your paper move to one you do believe in. Never take a copy reading job if you can help it."

On this theme Mr. Mencken found that the chances for advancement for good newspaper men are both better and worse than they were 30 years ago, when he first hung his hat on a Sun office hatrack. "They are better because more good men are needed than in those days," he said, "and worse because the

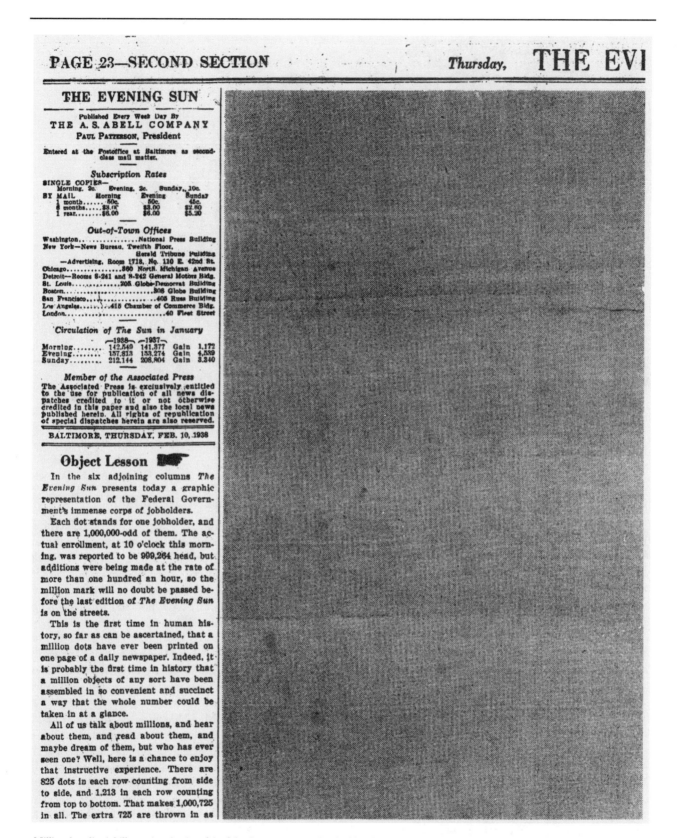

THE EVENING SUN

Published Every Week Day By

THE A. S. ABELL COMPANY

PAUL PATTERSON, President

Entered at the Postoffice at Baltimore as second-class mail matter.

Subscription Rates

SINGLE COPIES—
Morning, 3c.   Evening, 2c.   Sunday, 10c.

BY MAIL	Morning	Evening	Sunday
1 month......	50c.	50c.	45c.
6 months.....	$3.00	$3.00	$2.60
1 year........	$6.00	$6.00	$5.20

Out-of-Town Offices

Washington.................National Press Building
New York—News Bureau, Twelfth Floor.
    Herald Tribune Building
  —Advertising, Room 1718, No. 110 E. 42nd St.
Chicago.................360 North Michigan Avenue
Detroit—Rooms 8-241 and 8-242 General Motors Bldg.
St. Louis.............205 Globe-Democrat Building
Boston...........................308 Globe Building
San Francisco..................405 Russ Building
Los Angeles........415 Chamber of Commerce Bldg.
London........................40 Fleet Street

Circulation of The Sun in January

	1938	1937		
Morning........	142,549	141,377	Gain	1,172
Evening........	157,813	153,274	Gain	4,539
Sunday.........	212,144	208,804	Gain	3,340

Member of the Associated Press

The Associated Press is exclusively entitled to the use for publication of all news dispatches credited to it or not otherwise credited in this paper and also the local news published herein. All rights of republication of special dispatches herein are also reserved.

BALTIMORE, THURSDAY, FEB. 10, 1938

Object Lesson

In the six adjoining columns *The Evening Sun* presents today a graphic representation of the Federal Government's immense corps of jobholders.

Each dot stands for one jobholder, and there are 1,000,000-odd of them. The actual enrollment, at 10 o'clock this morning, was reported to be 999,264 head, but additions were being made at the rate of more than one hundred an hour, so the million mark will no doubt be passed before the last edition of *The Evening Sun* is on the streets.

This is the first time in human history, so far as can be ascertained, that a million dots have ever been printed on one page of a daily newspaper. Indeed, it is probably the first time in history that a million objects of any sort have been assembled in so convenient and succinct a way that the whole number could be taken in at a glance.

All of us talk about millions, and hear about them, and read about them, and maybe dream of them, but who has ever seen one? Well, here is a chance to enjoy that instructive experience. There are 825 dots in each row counting from side to side, and 1,213 in each row counting from top to bottom. That makes 1,000,725 in all. The extra 725 are thrown in as

Million-dot editorial illustrating the size of the federal government under the New Deal, published by Mencken during his three months as acting editor

The arch individualist and anticommunist Mencken reading the Communist Party paper, Daily Worker *(courtesy of the Enoch Pratt Free Library)*

improvement in newspaper personnel has sharpened competition."

"Men become impatient waiting for promotion. They forget that all the existing office dignitaries will be in hell in 15 years, and that their jobs will go to men now taking their orders. The choice will fall upon those who have ability, who work hard and do not complain too much about the slowness of time."

Leaning back in his swivel-chair, Mr. Mencken stuck his thumbs under his suspenders, drew them out and snapped them with conviction as he digressed a bit to observe that Labor Day in most American communities has become simply one more holiday. "It's idiotic imbecility," he sniffed. "Might as well have doctors' day or lawyers' day, or any other day. Its significance is lost. Few people connect it with labor. It has degenerated into the day when vacations are over. I detest mummeries."

Probably the greatest American exponent of argument in criticism, this man who has chosen to be chief jester for his own court—American journalism—thought it would be interesting to know his political philosophy. It came clearly, without hesitation and with sincere conviction.

A Libertarian in Politics

"I am a Libertarian," he asserted. "A Libertarian is simply one who believes in the utmost endurable measure of private freedom. I am against all laws which limit a man's right to say what he believes, however idiotic. I am for free speech even for Communists, who deny it to others, and I have hollered for them whenever they were attacked.

"I question both their intelligence and their bonafides, but nevertheless I think they have a clear right to be heard. The constitutional guarantees do not apply only to sensible and honest men; they extend just as well to rogues and damned fools."

In the past, Mr. Mencken has alienated certain people of perhaps too literal and serious a character by his tendency toward exaggeration and unqualified pronouncement. At times, too, he is accused of not infrequently pushing his well-known penchant for wit a little too ruthlessly. But it cannot be said he is ever other than honest, both with himself and with his target. Seeker after Nietzsche's "perfect man," nothing can stave his hand when he perceives a weak spot in the armor. The string is tautened, the barbed shaft is loosed and the ferreter of eccentricities again is on the warpath.

Straying from the sober realm of scholarship, Mr. Mencken passed lightly on "the Revolution." For it, this stanch free-thinker has nothing but contempt.

Dislikes Anonymous Editorials

Mr. Mencken said he was "a bad editorial writer," saying he can't operate comfortably save with his name plainly printed under the heading of the piece. "I think a writer signing his stuff should be given the utmost endurable freedom," he said. "I can't imagine asking a man to sign anything he doesn't believe. But I believe such freedom should be confined to men who actually have something to say, and can say it competently. Dull asses deserve no space, save maybe on Communist papers."

Discussing employer-employe relation, Mr. Mencken said he was keenly interested in the present American Civil Liberties Union controversy with the National Labor Relations Board in which the former is trying to have the NLRB differentiate between expressing opinion and intimidation. He said he believed that an employer should be free to discuss labor unions with his men.

"But it seems to me that it will be difficult to draw a safe line in the present controversy," he said. "To many workmen any utterance by the boss will seem to be a kind of intimidation. The prohibition in the Wagner Act is obviously inconvenient, and more than a little absurd, but modifying it will not be easy."

His concluding jibe, before he terminated the interview, was that schools of journalism are "staffed by broken-down editorial writers, than which there is nothing worse."

We walked out of the office together.

No, I thought, the years have not mellowed Henry L. Mencken.

Still attentive to the practical necessities of his craft, Mencken wrote most of the Stylebook *for the* Sunpapers. *It was the model for similar guides produced by other American newspapers ("Preface," in* Stylebook: The Sunpapers of Baltimore *[1944]), p. 3).*

This is only a preliminary print. After it has been subjected to thorough scrutiny it will be revised and reissued in more permanent form. It is hoped that all persons to whom it is handed will give it a very careful reading, *and suggest corrections and additions.* There is no objection to increasing its size, so long as its arrangement remains workable.

A stylebook does not pretend to lay down the rules of correct English. In America those rules are in

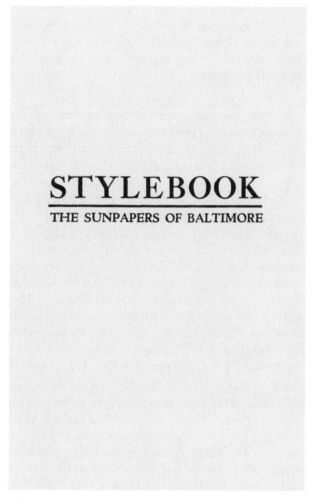

Title page for the Sunpapers *style manual (1944). Mencken wrote the preface and revised most of the work.*

a state of flux. They are determined, such as they are, not by the fiats of grammarians and schoolma'ms, but by the practice of good writers. The best a newspaper can do is to try to maintain a reasonable uniformity. Often it must choose arbitrarily between two forms, both of which have support in logic and good usage.

The use of banal counterwords, such as *angle, consistent, to contact* and *outstanding* is to be avoided. Also, there should be an avoidance of such affectations as the omission of the article at the beginning of a sentence, and the concoction of such clumsy forms as *Oil Tycoon Rockefeller* and *Columbia's President Butler.* A good newspaper man does not ape bad models.

On 30 June 1948, five months before the stroke that ended his career, Mencken was interviewed at the Library of Congress by the Sun *television editor. This interview is the only extant record-*

ing of Mencken speaking. From his replies may be extracted his views on fifty years in the profession of journalism (transcribed excerpts from Henry L. Mencken Interviewed by Donald H. Kirkley, Sr., *Library of Congress Recording Laboratory, PL18–PL19 [1948]).*

Most men that escaped college have a regret that pursues them, but I must confess I am much too vain to have any such regrets. I think that what I was doing when the boys in my generation were in college listening to idiot lectures and cheering football games and doing all the foolish and silly and useless things college boys do, I was a young reporter on the street. [. . .] I believe that a young newspaper reporter in a big city at that time led a life that has never been matched on earth, for romance and interest. [. . .] I never was a good reporter. [. . .] I never got a scoop in my life. They were the things that were esteemed in those days. They never seemed to me to have any sense. Most scoops were bad stories. And they were always exaggerated and played up in an idiot manner. No, I wasn't a good reporter except in one sense, that I worked. I was willing to work. I never shirked a job. [. . .]

One of the things that puzzles me about the modern young newspaper man is what does he do in his leisure. He has much more leisure than they did in my time. [. . .] I worked all the time. He works five days a week. What does he do? [. . .] Well, all those things [*golf, minding the children*] would have been considered not only degrading but impossible, psychologically, in my time. [. . .] The idea of a newspaper reporter with any self-respect playing golf is to me almost inconceivable. I hear that even printers now play golf. God almighty, that's dreadful to think of. I remember printers in my time–I knew a great many intimately–I always had to do with makeup on the papers and hence I knew the printers. And I was very fond of them, and they were fine fellows–but golf playing! It would just seem as incredible to hear of a printer going to a dance. Printers spent their leisure mainly in saloons and in summer on the shores down the rivers below Baltimore. They were intelligent men, the good ones. I learned a great deal more about the newspaper business from printers than I ever learned from editors. A great deal more. But now when you hear of a printer going out and dressing himself up and playing golf, the thing is really obscene. [. . .]

You could no more have a forty-hour week for a good newspaper reporter than you could have a forty-hour week for an archbishop. It's just not possible.

A good reporter, he simply refuses to let a story go when he's got his teeth into it. And he wants assignments. I remember, when I went down to the office in the morning, certainly the thing that interested me wasn't whether I'd get a lot of time off and go home early but whether I'd get some good assignments. If I got the good assignments, I didn't care how long I worked. I worked many a time all night. When the Baltimore Fire happened in February 1904, I was a young city editor. They dug me out of bed about eleven o'clock in the morning and said a big fire had started downtown. I went downtown. I never got my clothes off or slept until Wednesday morning at four o'clock. That's from Sunday to Wednesday. I suppose that's almost a record for continuous work. I grant you that there were moments when I drowsed at my desk, but I never stretched out to sleep until Wednesday morning. And far from looking on that as oppressive or keeping an account of overtime, I was delighted with the opportunity. I was young, I was ambitious, and I liked the job. I get the impression from the modern reporter that he doesn't really like his work. He wishes he were a druggist. Or he wishes he had a good job. [. . .] Well, no [*not a dramatist*], I wouldn't say that. The reporter with literary ambitions is one that I always respected. But most of the reporters that I encounter these days haven't even got literary ambitions. They never write anything outside the office. [. . .]

I think it [*newspaper ownership of television stations*] is a curse to newspapers, and I wish it could be separated from them. I am sorry that the Federal Communications Commission did not prohibit ownership of radio stations by a newspaper. I don't think it's a good thing in the public sense for any one agency to control rival news sources. They ought to be kept separate and in active rivalry. That's one objection to it. Secondly, human nature being what it is, as soon as a television or any kind of radio enterprise gets into a newspaper, an enormous number of men, including some of the best men, become radio crooners, not newspaper men. [. . .] Actors. Yeah, they get stagestruck, in brief, that's true. And it shows in the newspaper instantly. The way for newspapers to meet the competition of radio and television is simply to get out better newspapers. They can always keep miles ahead of these other agencies which haven't the machinery for doing what newspapers can do. Newspapers ought to print better papers. They are going downhill and any time you find a newspaper that's got a radio department you'll find a newspaper deteriorating.

Historian of Language: A National Endeavor

The American Language is generally considered Mencken's greatest work: in April 1999 the Modern Library ranked it ninth in a list of the twentieth century's one hundred best nonfiction books in English. It evolved from a series of articles, and because Mencken's pro-German views limited his journalism during World War I, he had time for longer projects. The book went through four editions between 1919 and 1936; each involved extensive rewriting on the basis of new information sent to him by scholars and by hundreds of ordinary people inspired to take an interest in their native tongue. Two large supplements appeared in 1945 and 1948, completing a life's work. The beginning was this article ("The Two Englishes," Baltimore Evening Sun, 10 October 1910, editorial page).

The English of England

Prof. Brander Matthews, that learned man, has been writing of late upon his favorite topic, the mutability of language. Words change and their meanings change. Idioms decay, dry up and blow away. Grammatical forms give birth to new grammatical forms. The same verb is conjugated differently in different ages, in different countries, on different sides of the street. The English people speak an English which differs enormously, in vocabulary and idiom, from the English spoken by Americans.

In proof of this last fact Professor Matthews cites the word university, which means one thing in England and quite a different thing in the United States—and yet other things in Germany and France. An English university would be called a group of colleges in the United States and a lunatic asylum in Germany. A German university, if set up among us, would be nominated a school of vice, a Chautauqua or an anti-Young Men's Christian Association. But enough of such subtleties. There are plenty of other words, more familiar to all of us, which show the great gaps which separate languages, and particularly the English and American languages.

Consider the common word shoe. In the United States it means—a shoe. In England it means a slipper.

The thing we call a shoe is known in England as a boot, and the thing we call a boot is known there as a Blucher. Their shoe is our slipper. "Ladies' boots" is a familiar sign in London. They call shoe polish boot blacking.

Treacle Vs. Molasses

To an Englishman all forms of grain are corn. The Corn laws were laws which placed a prohibitive duty upon foreign wheat. The thing we call corn is maize in England. In the English vocabulary a trolley car is a tram-car, a parlor is a drawing room (parlor, among the Britons, means the back room of a saloon), a saloon is a public house or "pub," a saloonkeeper is a licensed victualer, molasses is treacle, a locomotive engineer is an engine driver, a railway brakeman is a guard, a Methodist church is a chapel, the tin roof of a house is the leads, a trained nurse is a nursing sister, a newspaper reporter is a journalist, a chief of police is a chief constable and railway switches are points.

Even when the same word appears in both the English and American languages it is often spelled differently. The English word for jail, for example, is gaol. It is pronounced exactly like jail. So with the English word for tire, which is pronounced tire and spelled tyre. So with check, which is spelled cheque. They put an extra and useless "u" into labor, honor, harbor, color and ardor. They spell wagon with two "g's." They use an "x" instead of "ct" in such words as connection. They hang on, like grim death, to all superfluous "e's."

Their forms of address vary greatly from ours. They call a judge, not your Honor, but Your Worship or Your Lordship. A mayor is also Your Worship. A physician is always Doctor, as with us, but he is often without an M.D. degree. A surgeon, unless he has notoriously received an M.D., is always plain Mister—and it is seldom that he has an M.D. A nurse is addressed, not as Miss McGinnis, but as Nurse. A cook is called, not Maggie, but Cook. A ladies' maid is called, not Myrtle, but Brown or Simpson or Sweeny or whatever her surname happens to be. In England no preacher is called

-12-

to get ahead of.   These are so commonplace that we use them and hear them

without thought ; they seem as authentically parts of the English idiom as

to be left at the post or to curse God and die.   And yet, as the labors

of Thornton have demonstrated, all of them are of American ~~origin~~

(circumstances surrounding the)
nativity, and the origin of some of them has been accurately determined.

Many others are palpably the products of the great movement toward the West,
                      to strike it rich,   to rake in,
for example, to jump a claim, to pull up stakes, to die with one's boots on,
                      ^   (or bite)
to get the deadwood on, to get the drop, to back and fill (a steamboat

phrase used figuratively) and to get the bulge on.   And in many others
      authentic
the ^ American touch is no less plain, for example, in to kick the bucket, to

put a bug in his ear, to see the elephant, to crack up, to do up brown,

to bark up the wrong tree, to jump on with both feet, to go the whole hog,

to make a kick, to buck the tiger, to let it slide and to come out at the

little end of the horn.   To play possum obviously belongs to this list.

To it Thornton adds to knock him into a cocked-hat, despite its English

sound, and to have an ax to grind.   To go for, both in the sense of

belligerency and in that of partisanship, is also American, and so is

to go through (i.e., to plunder)   the coinage of the first half of the nineteenth century
                                                            that has,

      Of adjectives the list is no less long.   Among ~~those~~ in perfectly
                                                                  well-footed
good use today are ~~blooded (e.g. cattle)~~ non-commital, ~~and~~ highfalutin, ^
      played-out,   whole-souled   of first
down-town, flat-footed and true-blue.   The ~~former~~ appears in a

Senate debate of 1841; highfalutin in a political speech of the same
                     ^
decade,.   Both are useful words ; it is impossible ~~to~~ , not employing them,

to convey the ideas behind them without circumlocution.   The use of slim

in the sense of meagre, as in slim chance, slim ~~audiences~~ attendance and

slim support goes back still further.   The English always use small in

place of it.   Other, and less respectable ~~and~~ , contributions of the time

are brash, brainy, peart, locoed, no-account, pesky, picayune, scary,

well-heeled, hardshell (e.g., Baptist), low-flung, codfish (to indicate

opprobrium) and go-to-meeting.   The use of plumb as an adjective, as in

Page from the typescript for the first edition of Mencken's The American Language *(courtesy of the Enoch Pratt Free Library)*

MR. ALFRED A. KNOPF
announces the publication of
THE AMERICAN LANGUAGE

A Preliminary Inquiry Into the Development of English in the United States

By H. L. MENCKEN

This is the first comprehensive study of the subject since Schele de Vere's "Americanisms: the English of the New World" (1872). It is not a dictionary of Americanisms, but an attempt to investigate the lines of growth of the language in America, with particular attention to its spoken form. It embraces, among other things, the first serious inquiry into the grammar of colloquial American ever made, and presents discussions of a number of problems hitherto much neglected, for example, American spelling, the influence of immigrant languages upon English in America, and the mutations of American surnames and other proper names.

The book represents long and patient investigation, and its materials are admirably organized and clearly presented. The Bibliography alone is of great value to the student and teacher. Exhaustive indices facilitate reference, and offer a useful reinforcement to the existing dictionaries of Americanisms. No other work has ever pretended to cover the field so thoroughly.

Following is a brief digest of the contents:

Chapter I.
By Way of Introduction.—Varying definitions of *Americanism*. The national dialect as viewed by English and Continental writers and philologists. Its principal characteristics.

Chapter II.
The Beginnings of American.—Its differentiation from standard English in colonial days. Sources of word material. Colonial neologisms. Changed meanings. Early foreign influences. Pronunciation before 1812.

Chapter III.
The Period of Growth.—The rapid development of American after the War of 1812. The expanding vocabulary. The influence of the great immigrations. Western neologisms and the decay of New England dominance. The new American pronunciation.

Chapter IV.
American and English Today.—A detailed study of the differences between the two everyday vocabularies. American idioms and counter-words. Honorifics. Euphemisms and forbidden words.

Chapter V.
Tendencies in American.—The fundamental characters of the dialect. Foreign influences since the Civil War. Processes of word formation. Current pronunciation.

Chapter VI.
The Common Speech.—The vocabulary and grammar of vulgar spoken American. Studies of the verb, the pronoun, the adverb and the adjective. Pronunciation of the common speech.

Chapter VII.
Differences in Spelling.—Typical American spellings. Their influence upon English usage. Simplified spelling. General tendencies.

Chapter VIII.
Proper Names in America.—The Americanization of foreign surnames. Given names. Geographical names. Street names.

Chapter IX.
Miscellanea.—American proverbs. American slang. The future of the language.

The edition, consisting of only 1500 numbered copies, has been printed from type. IX + 394 pages; bound in blue buckram with gilt lettering; $4.00 net.

For sale at all bookshops or postpaid from the publisher on receipt of published price plus 5% additional for postage.

ALFRED A. KNOPF, *Publisher*, 220 West Forty-Second Street, New York

1919 announcement for Mencken's major scholarly work (courtesy of the Enoch Pratt Free Library)

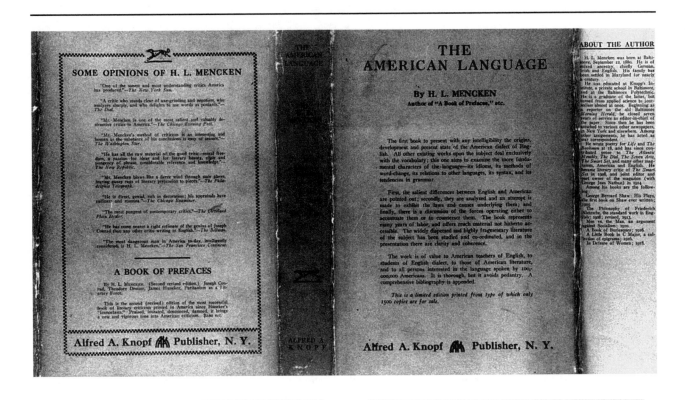

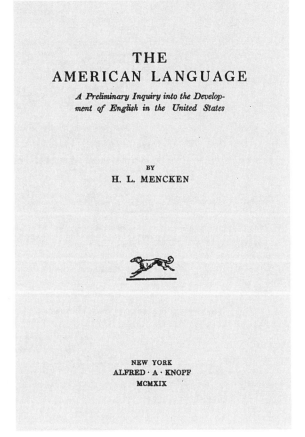

Dust jacket, certificate of limitation, and title page of the first edition of Mencken's magnum opus

Doctor unless he is an actual doctor of divinity. The American custom of addressing dancing masters, magicians, oyster shuckers, school teachers and acrobats as professor is unknown.

———

Other Strange English Words

Among the simple-minded barbarians over there a typewriter of either sex is known as a typist, a pass to the theatre is an order, the city editor of a newspaper is the chief reporter, the financial editor is the city editor, with a capital "C," a hardware dealer is an ironmonger, a delicatessen dealer is an Italian warehouseman, a dry goods merchant is a draper, a shoemaker is a bootmaker, a saleswoman is a lady clerk or a shop assistant, the president of a corporation is its chairman, the corporation itself is a public company, a party platform is a constitution, a candidate stands instead of running for office, the orchestra seats in a theatre are stalls, the orchestra circle is the pit, a letter carrier is a postman, a letter box is a pillar box, keeping company is walking out, a poorhouse is a workhouse, instead of studying medicine a medical student walks the hospitals, a fish dealer is a fishmonger, a locomotive fireman is a stoker, a dishwasher is a slavey, coal is coals, the room clerk of a hotel is the secretary, a round-trip ticket is a return ticket, a policeman is a constable and an apple pie is an apple tart.

———

There are many English words in common use across the ocean which have never become naturalized in America. The word chambers is an example. It means a bachelor's lodgings. The word don is another. It means a college dignitary. A host of ecclesiastical terms familiar to all Englishmen are seldom heard in this country. Of such sort are vicar, curate, canon, verger and prebendary. An usher over there means an assistant teacher. The principal of a school is called the head master or head mistress. Such English terms as subaltern, civil servant and moor are practically unknown in the United States. But we have adopted weekend, jam, tub and music hall.

———

Barrister; Solicitor

The Englishman is very careful to restrict the application of the word gentleman to men of some consideration, but he uses lady indiscriminately. Advertisements for lady typists, lady clerks and lady teachers fill the English papers. Barristers and solicitors differ vastly in

Professor Brander Matthews of Columbia University, who reviewed the first edition of The American Language

England, both in function and in public estimation, but among us there is no difference. An American lawyer may call himself advocate, barrister, solicitor, attorney or counselor, as he pleases. Candy, to the Britisher, is sweets, the fire department is the fire brigade, a floorwalker is a shopwalker, a store is a shop (we have begun to borrow the English term) and a warehouse is a store; oatmeal is porridge, boards are deals, a railway car is a carriage, freight is goods, a sidewalk is a footway, a subway is a tube, vegetables are greens, a street cleaner is a crossing sweeper, a job holder is a public servant, a railroader is a railway servant, store fixtures are shop fittings, lumber is timber, flathouses are mansions, window panes are lights, a drummer is a bagman or traveler, baggage is luggage, a trunk is a box, a satchel is a bag, a druggist is a chemist or apothecary and a doctor's office is his consulting room. The English have no bartenders or mixologists. Barmaids do the work.

H.L.M.

The wartime context of the first appearance of the book is seen in Mencken's 1918 letter to his friend, the Irish critic Ernest Boyd, written as he awaited a call that never came. The "George" mentioned is George Jean Nathan (typewritten letter with handwritten signature at Princeton University).

1524 Hollins Street
Baltimore, Md.

August 9th

Dear Boyd:-

We beat you to it! I expect to be called up for military service on September 5th. George is also eligible. This plays hell with the office. I wish to God you were in our midst. As a married man you would be exempt under the American law, and so you could take charge of the magazine. As it is, we have absolutely no one in sight. Could you get a permit to come out? I suppose not. The property is shaky enough now. If we have to pick up some flathead it will go to pot in four months. Incidently, my American Language book also seems to be finished.

Meanwhile, the Michelob flows freely, and I get down my share. Tell Mrs. Boyd that Baltimore has lately broken all weather records. On Monday of this week the official temperature was 105.4 degrees Fahrenheit -- almost unbearable. I couldn't do a stroke of work for two days -- and I am almost a salamander. My whole hide is burned and smarting.

What job I'll be assigned to I don't know. My experience fits me for the medical department, but that is already overcrowded, so, as a bachelor, I'll probably draw the infantry. Picture me, with my weight, digging ditches and learning the goose-step! After all, there are some humors in war.

Yours in Xt., H.L. Mencken

In 1963 Raven I. McDavid Jr. of the University of Chicago edited a one-volume abridgment of the complete work. On 21 October 1965 he gave the second annual Mencken Day lecture at Baltimore's Enoch Pratt Free Library, which had nurtured Mencken's intellectual growth. The lecture, which was published in the journal Menckeniana *the following year, helps to explain why Mencken should have been the first to undertake such a work (excerpt from "The Impact of Mencken on American Linguistics,"* Menckeniana, *17 [Spring 1966]: 1–2).*

[. . .] In discussing *The American Language* in the less urbane precincts of this Great Republic, I have had to explain what it was in Mencken's background that quali-

fied him to write so effectively on American English–a subject that no academic linguist, no professional lexicographer, no sociologist or historian had dared tackle in extenso. In Baltimore, however, we can take this background information for granted. No one in this audience needs to be reminded of the rich complexity of surrounding cultures including the Susquehanna Valley, the Eastern Shore, the old tobacco plantations, and what HLM fondly called "that great protein factory, the Chesapeake Bay." No one needs to be reminded of the variegated economic and social history of a city that has evolved from an outpost of the Virginia aristocracy through the cradle of the clippers, to the industrial center symbolized by the works at Sparrows Point. No one, I hope (despite the xenophobic idiocies of 1917), needs to be especially reminded of the civilizing effect that the German emigrés of 1830 and 1848 had on all American cities, or of the fact that by helping prevent the secession of Kentucky and Maryland and Missouri, they may have tipped the balance toward preserving the Union in its days of peril. No one who knew Henry Mencken needs to be reminded of the fact that, however much he delighted in ridiculing *homo boobensis Americanus,* he took equal delight in recording the variegated and often fantastic behavior of the species, especially its use of language–the most intimate and habitual and characteristic of human activities. None of you who come together tonight under the auspices of this institution needs to be reminded how important it is to a boy of bookish inclinations and free-wheeling tastes that he have untrammeled access to a rich collection of reading materials. All this background information, however, fails to explain genius, though it may help us to understand it. [. . .]

Not expecting large sales, Alfred A. Knopf limited the 1919 edition to 1,500 copies, which sold out completely. That fact, and the enormous nationwide correspondence that ensued (and would continue until Mencken's stroke in 1948), encouraged Knopf to print three more editions and the supplements. The fourth edition has gone through more than thirty printings. The novelty of Mencken's taking seriously the American language, as distinct from the King's English, may be gathered from his preface to the first edition (pp. v–viii).

The aim of this book is best exhibited by describing its origin. I am, and have been since early manhood, an editor of newspapers, magazines and books, and a critic of the last named. These occupations have forced me into a pretty wide familiarity with current literature, both periodical and within covers, and in particular into a familiarity with the current literature of England and America. It was part of my daily work, for a good many years, to read the principal English newspapers and reviews; it has been part of my work, all the time, to read the more important English novels, essays, poetry and criticism. An American born and bred, I early noted, as everyone else in like case must note, certain salient differences between the English of England and the English of America as practically spoken and written—differences in vocabulary, in syntax, in the shades and habits of idiom, and even, coming to the common speech, in grammar. And I noted too, of course, partly during visits to England but more largely by a somewhat wide and intimate intercourse with English people in the United States, the obvious differences between English and American pronunciation and intonation.

Greatly interested in these differences—some of them so great that they led me to seek exchanges of light with Englishmen—I looked for some work that would describe and account for them with a show of completeness, and perhaps depict the process of their origin. I soon found that no such work existed, either in England or in America—that the whole literature of the subject was astonishingly meagre and unsatisfactory. There were several dictionaries of Americanisms, true enough, but only one of them made any pretension to scientific method, and even that one was woefully narrow and incomplete. The one more general treatise, the work of a man foreign to both England and America in race and education, was more than 40 years old, and full of palpable errors. For the rest, there was only a fugitive and inconsequential literature—an almost useless mass of notes and essays, chiefly by the minor sort of pedagogues, seldom illuminating, save in small details, and often incredibly ignorant and inaccurate. On the large and important subject of American pronunciation, for example, I could find nothing save a few casual essays. On American spelling, with its wide and constantly visible divergences from English usages, there was little more. On American grammar there was nothing whatever. Worse, an important part of the poor literature that I unearthed was devoted to absurd efforts to prove that no such thing as an American variety of English existed—that the differences I constantly encountered in English and that my English friends encountered in American were chiefly imaginary, and to be explained away by denying them.

Still intrigued by the subject, and in despair of getting any illumination from such theoretical masters of it, I began a collection of materials for my own information, and gradually it took on a rather formidable bulk. My interest in it being made known by various articles in the newspapers and magazines, I began also to receive contributions from other persons of the same fancy, both English and American, and gradually my collection fell into a certain order, and I saw the workings of general laws in what, at first, had appeared to be

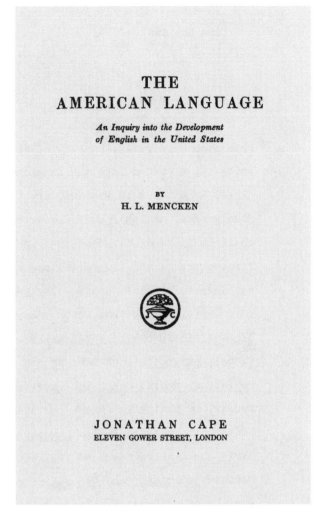

THE
AMERICAN LANGUAGE

*An Inquiry into the Development
of English in the United States*

BY
H. L. MENCKEN

JONATHAN CAPE
ELEVEN GOWER STREET, LONDON

*Title page for the first British edition (1922), based on the revised and
enlarged second American edition*

mere chaos. The present book then began to take form—its preparation a sort of recreation from other and far different labor. It is anything but an exhaustive treatise upon the subject; it is not even an exhaustive examination of the materials. All it pretends to do is to articulate some of those materials—to get some approach to order and coherence into them, and so pave the way for a better work by some more competent man. That work calls for the equipment of a first-rate philologist, which I am surely not. All I have done here is to stake out the field, sometimes borrowing suggestions from other inquirers and sometimes, as in the case of American grammar, attempting to run the lines myself.

That it should be regarded as an anti-social act to examine and exhibit the constantly growing differences between English and American, as certain American pedants argue sharply—this doctrine is quite beyond my understanding. All it indicates, stripped of sophistry, is a somewhat childish effort to gain the approval of English-

122 H.L.Mencken,
     1524 Hollins street,
     Baltimore, Md.

Jan 24 '26

Encyclopedia Britannica
14th Ed., 1929

Americanism, a term first used by John Witherspoon, president of
Princeton University, in 1781, designates (a) any word or combination of
words which, taken into the English language in the United States, has not
gained acceptance in England, or, if accepted, has retained its sense of
foreignness, and (b) any word or combination of words which, becoming archaic in England, has continued in good usage in the United States.   The
first class is the larger and has the longer history.   The earliest
settlers in Virginia and New England, confronted by plants and animals that
were unfamiliar to them, either borrowed the Indian names or invented
names of their own.   Examples are afforded by opossum(1610) , raccoon
(1608), chinkapin(1608) and squash (1642) among Indian words, and by
bull-frog, canvas-back, cat-bird and live-oak among inventions.   The
former, by the philological law of Hobson-Jobson, tended to take Anglicized
forms.   Thus the Indian isquontersquash (at least, that is how the
early chroniclers recorded it) became squantersquash and was then
reduced to squash, and otchock became wood-chuck. Many other words
came in as a pioneers gained familiarity with Indian life.   Such words
as hominy, moccasin, pone, tapioca and succotash remain everyday Americanisms to this day.

The archaisms, of course, showed themselves more slowly.   They had
to go out of use in England before their survival in America was noticeable.
But by the beginning of the Eighteenth Century there was already a considerable body of them, and all through that century they increased.   The
English language at home, chiefly under the influence of pedantry in the age
of Anne, was changing rapidly, but in America it was holding to its old forms.
There was very little fresh emigration to the colonies, and their own
people seldom visited England.   Thus by the end of the century " I guess"

First page from the typescript for Mencken's revision of the "Americanism" entry that had appeared in the previous edition of the Encyclopaedia
Britannica *(courtesy of the Enoch Pratt Free Library)*

men—a belated efflorescence of the colonial spirit, often commingled with fashionable aspiration. The plain fact is that the English themselves are not deceived, nor do they grant the approval so ardently sought for. On the contrary, they are keenly aware of the differences between the two dialects, and often discuss them, as the following pages show. Perhaps one dialect, in the long run, will defeat and absorb the other; if the two nations continue to be partners in great adventures it may very well happen. But even in that case, something may be accomplished by examining the differences which exist today. In some ways, as in intonation, English usage is plainly better than American. In others, as in spelling, American usage is as plainly better than English. But in order to develop usages that the people of both nations will accept it is obviously necessary to study the differences now visible. This study thus shows a certain utility. But its chief excuse is its human interest, for it prods deeply into national idiosyncrasies and ways of mind, and that sort of prodding is always entertaining.

I am thus neither teacher, nor prophet, nor reformer, but merely inquirer. The exigencies of my vocation make me almost completely bilingual; I can write English, as in this clause, quite as readily as American, as in this here one. Moreover, I have a hand for a compromise dialect which embodies the common materials of both, and is thus free from offense on both sides of the water—as befits the editor of a magazine published in both countries. But that compromise dialect is the living speech of neither. What I have tried to do here is to make a first sketch of the living speech of These States. The work is confessedly incomplete, and in places very painfully so, but in such enterprises a man must put an arbitrary term to his labors, lest some mischance, after years of diligence, take him from them too suddenly for them to be closed, and his laborious accumulations, as Ernest Walker says in his book on English surnames, be "doomed to the waste-basket by harassed executors."

If the opportunity offers in future I shall undoubtedly return to the subject. For one thing, I am eager to attempt a more scientific examination of the grammar of the American vulgar speech, here discussed briefly in Chapter VI. For another thing, I hope to make further inquiries into the subject of American surnames of non-English origin. Various other fields invite. No historical study of American pronunciation exists; the influence of German, Irish-English, Yiddish and other such immigrant dialects upon American has never been investigated; there is no adequate treatise on American geographical names. Contributions of materials and suggestions for a possible revised edition of the present book will reach me if addressed to me in care of the publisher at 220 West Forty-second Street, New York. I shall also be very grateful for the correction of errors,

some perhaps typographical but others due to faulty information or mistaken judgment.

In conclusion I borrow a plea in confession and avoidance from Ben Jonson's pioneer grammar of English, published in incomplete form after his death. "We have set down," he said, "that that in our judgment agreeth best with reason and good order. Which notwithstanding, if it seem to any to be too rough hewed, let him plane it out more smoothly, and I shall not only not envy it, but in the behalf of my country most heartily thank him for so great a benefit; hoping that I shall be thought sufficiently to have done my part if in tolling this bell I may draw others to a deeper consideration of the matter; for, touching myself, I must needs confess that after much painful churning this only would come which here we have devised."

MENCKEN.

Baltimore, January 1, 1919.

Having little that might be compared to it, reviewers of The American Language *sometimes had to grope for terms; but most, by far, were favorable. A notable theme—as in Francis Hackett's review in* The New Republic *and in an anonymous comment in the* Journal of the American Medical Association—*was Mencken's fearlessness in discussing both "raciness" and the absurd euphemisms that sometimes replaced it ("The Living Speech,"* New Republic, *19 [31 May 1919]: 155–156).*

Never has the flourishing personality of H. L. Mencken been so happily exercised as in this big book on the living speech of America. In Mr. Mencken there is something of the pedant and something of the anarchist. This book is compounded of both. It is the benign pedant, voracious and systematic and indefatigable, that has accumulated and organized the large mass of material that has gone into the volume; and it is the anarchist that has breathed fire into it. This anarchist, however, is not of the sallow kind. He is jocund and expansive, a Samson in girth and a Samson to send torches among the Philistines. He delights in raciness and has no fear of the grossest barbarism, yet he is cheerfully contemptuous of what he calls the "yokelry" and the "stupid populace" and the "gaping proletariat." He believes in a law at least to the extent of ascertaining it. He uses the tools of pedantry to give himself mastery. But he steers between the populace, on one hand, and "Prof. Balderdash," on the other. The result is a work which it is a platitude to call refreshing but which is actually refreshing in the deep sense as well as the obvious.

H. L. Mencken is a pioneer. He turns on the language we habitually use the mind and imagination of a fresh inquirer, an inquirer whose sophistication cannot

An entirely new version of a standard work

The AMERICAN LANGUAGE

By H. L. MENCKEN

Fourth Edition, Corrected, Enlarged and Rewritten. 800 pages, with a full word-list and an index. 325,000 words of text.

THIS famous book was first published in 1919. It was an immediate success, and has maintained steady sales ever since. It has been republished in England, and translated into German.

In 1921 the author brought out a second edition, considerably enlarged, and in 1923 a third, also enlarged. The present fourth edition is far more comprehensive than any of its predecessors. A few passages from the third edition are retained, but in the main it is a completely new work, offering an immense mass of novel, amusing and instructive material.

It lists more Americanisms than any existing dictionary of them. The growth of the American Language is dealt with historically, and everything that has been written about it in the past is noted. But the chief stress is laid on the language as it stands today. There is no other book on the subject which even remotely approaches the scope of this one.

$5.00 net

ALFRED·A·KNOPF · *Publisher* · 730 Fifth Avenue · New York

Advertisement for the 1936 edition of Mencken's work

be seriously questioned yet an inquirer who is not indentured to sophistication. And out of that fresh inquiry we are enabled to form a new view of our own spoken and written language. Mr. Mencken untiringly helps us to comprehend much that is obscure and irregular in the shifting courses of American expression. The living speech is a Mississippi which cannot easily be charted, but Mr. Mencken is a pilot who knows the new channels as well as the old, who steers us with the true current of the living stream. Many of us have no serene conviction in the matter of new idiom and new spelling and new locution. We grope rather blindly among the tendencies we are favoring and the tendencies we are resisting. We respond and we draw away, but we do not rationalize. Mr. Mencken comes titanically to our aid. Necessarily disregarding the prudes and the scholastic rhetoricians, he has opened his mind to receive every conceivable kind of data respecting the language now in use among the people of America, and with these usages to argue from he has created at least the beginning of an American rationale.

This does not mean that The American Language is sentimental radicalism. It is true that Mr. Mencken is hyperbolic at the beginning. He talks of the English dialect and the American dialect and he quotes someone who dwells on "the growing difficulties of intercommunication." Also he enjoys showing the enormous difference between unsophisticated American and sophisticated English, and he rather gleefully foreshadows the day when "me see she" will be common and therefore sound American usage. Without a parallel investigation of unsophisticated usages in English, I do not see how one can rest with such a conclusion. It is amusing to hurl the stink-pot of popular Americanisms among the grammarians, but Whitechapel and the Mile End Road and the Coombe and the rookeries of Glasgow could furnish similar weapons. The erosions of inflected speech are nominally more significant in America because language has a "general uniformity throughout the country," but it is one thing to produce the evidence of a common illiteracy, another thing to prove that the illiteracy is destined to supplant the corresponding literacy. "It is useless to dismiss the growing peculiarities of the American vocabulary and of grammar and syntax in the common speech as vulgarism beneath serious notice." Yes, if the "peculiarities" are definitely growing: but the actual repetition of a misuse from mouth to mouth is only one factor in deciding its eventual triumph. Does the misuse "work"? That is the qualitative test which must be met by such lazy and illogical locutions as "me see she."

But the great distinction of Mr. Mencken's book is his "the bee stang him" pragmatic method. "There are few forms in use," he quotes Lounsbury, "which, judged by a standard previously existing, would not be regarded as gross barbarisms." This extreme statement Mr. Mencken stupendously vindicates. In all the luxurious minutiae of his inquiry there is an impartial and scholarly use of evidence, yet his work cannot help serving as an antidote to snobs and snobbishness. "The attempt to make American uniform with English has failed ingloriously; the neglect of its investigation is an evidence of snobbishness that is folly of the same sort." These and simpler snobbishnesses are constantly corrected in his pages. Everyone knows the superior smile with which people who have the right shibboleth glance at one another when an outsider commits himself in their hearing—yet how often the right shibboleth is the index to the silliest kind of group complacency. Mr. Mencken exhibits many barbarisms such as "to ambition," "to compromit," "to happify." Right alongside them he prints words elevated to the peerage that were once similarly humble commoners. To advocate, to progress, to oppose, to derange, to appreciate (in value), lengthy, dutiable, reliable, bogus, influential, presidential—these were plebeians to start with, equally "bad form" and equally disdained. The same formalism is to be found in spelling, of course, and very often today an inherited American barbarism is cherished by the very person who shudders at a more recent one. In grammar, as Mr. Mencken says, there is also "a formalism that is artificial, illogical and almost unintelligible—a formalism borrowed from English grammarians, and by them brought into English, against all fact and reason, from the Latin." His list of popular conjugations, partly derived from Professor Ring Lardner, is a perfect

What Critics Say:

"A great book."
—Robert Bridges, late Poet Laureate of England.

"A learned and ingenious book."
—Dr. C. H. Grandgent, former head of the department of Romance Languages at Harvard University.

"A valuable book."
—Herbert Agar.

"A famous book."
—Dr. H. Lüdeke, in the "Deutsche Literaturzeitung."

"A brilliant argument and a luxuriant abundance of examples."
—Charles le Verrier, in "L'Europe Nouvelle."

"A well-known, extremely competent and exhaustive treatise."
—Wyndham Lewis.

"A splendid piece of scholarship."
—Providence Tribune.

"An independent and original treatment of the subject, the most comprehensive and arresting yet made."
—Dr. Louise Pound, former editor of "American Speech."

Blurbs for The American Language: *the critics raved*

museum of barbarism. It is also an extraordinary exhibition of professional zeal.

The great value of The American Language is, indeed, its sagacious thoroughness. It covers every sort of American idiosyncrasy in idiom, in spelling, in pronunciation, in grammar, in slang. To do so with piquancy was natural to Mr. Mencken, but the delight of the volume is its workmanship. And Mr. Mencken is not less marvelous in his ingenious generalizing than in his inexhaustible information.

He is not omniscient. He himself uses the archaic form 'round instead of round. He is surely not right in saying that the English vegetable marrow is the same thing as squash. He leaves out the American "ride" as an equivalent to the English "drive" (motor-ride). He says the English call a napkin a serviette and a coal-scuttle a coal-hod. Few English do. He says "diggings" is American for "habitation" whereas it is frequent English for "lodgings." Words like frisk and punk and sump and go-cart might be included to illustrate certain Americanizations. There are various Vanity Fair and Condé Nasty contributions to American—"undies" for underwear—that deserve to be noted.

But if a few unconsidered trifles have escaped Mr. Mencken, think of what he has captured and mounted. "'I like a belt more looser 'n what this one is.' 'Well, then, why don't you unloosen it more 'n you got it unloosened?'" To have an ear for this kind of speech, to preserve and diagnose it, is to do more than study the fauna and flora of language. It is to set the foundations for a more salient national literature. For what Mr. Mencken says at the end of his fascinating and inspiriting book is surely true; the American dialect is now apprehended "as something uncouth and comic. But that is the way that new dialects always come in—through a drumfire of cackles. Given the poet, there may suddenly come a day when our theirns and would'a hads will take on the barbaric stateliness of the peasant locutions of old Maurya in 'Riders to the Sea.' They seem grotesque and absurd today because the folks who use them seem grotesque and absurd. But that is too facile logic and under it is a false assumption. In all human beings, if only understanding be brought to the business, dignity will be found, and that dignity cannot fail to reveal itself, soon or late, in the words and phrases with which they make known their high hopes and aspirations and cry out against the intolerable meaninglessness of life." Beautifully said, and this is the flame which Mr. Mencken guards savagely from demons.

F. H.

* * *

(*"The Prudery of the Press,"* Journal of the American Medical Association, *72 [24 June 1919]: 1547*).

All efforts to diminish the spread of venereal diseases have encountered as a real obstruction a peculiar prudery in the American press. In his recent work on "The American Language" Mr. H. L. Mencken calls attention to the fact that the department of health in New York City in 1914 announced that its efforts to diminish venereal diseases were handicapped because "in most newspaper offices the words syphilis or gonorrhea are still taboo and without the use of these terms it is almost impossible to correctly state the problem." The Army Medical Corps in the early part of 1918 also encountered the same difficulty; most newspapers refused to print its bulletins regarding venereal disease in the Army. "One of the newspaper trade journals thereupon," Mencken says, "sought the opinions of editors upon the subject and all of them save one declared against the use of the two words." One editor placed the blame on the postoffice, and another reported that "at a recent conference of the Scripps Northwest League Editors" it was decided that "the use of such terms as gonorrhea, syphilis, and even venereal diseases would not add to the tone of the papers, and that the term vice diseases can be readily substituted." Mr. Mencken is of the opinion that the most Pecksniffian of American cities is Philadelphia, and he cites as a conspicuous example the change by the *Public Ledger* of the words "a virgin" to "a young girl." When the motion picture entitled "To Hell with the Kaiser" was advertised under government patronage, all of the Philadelphia billboards changed the announcement to read "To H— with the Kaiser." Most of our readers know the numerous synonyms used by the press for syphilis, among them "blood poisoning," "social evil" and "social disease." Apparently the press has been unable to coin a word for gonorrhea and the subject is merely tabooed. The campaign against venereal diseases depends largely on education of the public. Is the prudery of the press to continue to hinder such education?

Reviewers were fascinated with Mencken's thesis that the differences in English and American usage were so great as to warrant not only study but also celebration. This review by Lawrence Gilman conveys some of Mencken's own joy of discovery (excerpt from "The American Language," North American Review, *209 [May 1919]: 699–703).*

[. . .] What would an English school-teacher make of such an ordinary American sentence as this: "He had a skirt with him"? Is *skirt,* in this sense, "slang"? No doubt. But for concise and comprehensive and triumphant expressiveness, it is irreplaceable. Try to convey exactly the same sense, with the same economy, using any word that the *Spectator* would use. It can't be done. We have here an authentic addition to expressive speech, not merely a lazy substitute; and in five years you may find it in a New York *Times* editorial—without quotation-marks.

To anyone who has read Mr. H. L. Mencken's new book, the inspiration of the foregoing reflections will be obvious. Mr. Mencken in this book is more than engrossing. He is pestiferous. For is it not pestiferous to tie one to the tail of a 320-word [i.e., 320-page] book, in smallish print, from milking-time till sun-up? That is what will happen ("infall*y*ibly," as Mr. Barrie's Policeman says) to anyone whose trade is words, English or American; and it is probably what will happen to anyone else who is sufficiently interested to begin Mr. Mencken's book.

Every newspaper editor knows that an unfailing way to educe a torrent of correspondence from his readers is to start some verbal controversy. It is as certain to produce results as the throwing of a tomato omelette into an electric fan—an experiment which Mr. Oliver Herford (we believe) once declared to be the most urgent of his suppressed desires. We think Mr. Mencken has started something almost as exciting as the realization of Mr. Herford's secret ambition would be. His title alone is enough to rejoice the soul of any newspaper editor who might have thought to use it to initiate a discussion. "The American Language"! Does it exist? Is it different from standard English, "not merely in vocabulary, to be disposed of in an alphabetical list," but "in conjugation and declension, in metaphor and idiom, in the whole fashion of using words"? Mr. Mencken set out to prove that it is, and he has pulled off an achievement of extraordinary interest and importance.

This is no mere dictionary of Americanisms, as its publisher justly observes, but an attempt—an exceedingly able attempt—"to investigate the lines of growth of the language in America, with particular attention to its spoken form." Mr. Mencken examines the grammar of colloquial America, American spelling, the influence of immigrant languages upon English in America, the mutations of American surnames, American proverbs, American slang. It would be impossible to do justice to his book without carrying representation and discussion to an impracticable length. There is no help for it but to be unjust to his treatise, and unwillingly seem to contract its scope and comprehensiveness by dwelling upon one or two of its many significant aspects.

One's agreement with Mr. Mencken is so nearly one hundred per cent that one gets a certain low-lived satisfaction from disagreeing—when one can. Our chief difference with him is caused by what we feel to be a defect of emphasis. It seems to us that Mr. Mencken is too much dazzled by what he somewhere calls our "incomparable capacity for projecting hidden and often fantastic relationships into arresting parts of speech." Such a term as *rubberneck*, he thinks, is almost a complete treatise on national psychology. "It has in it precisely the boldness and disdain of ordered forms that are so characteristically American." The American "likes to make his language as he goes along." We

incline, he thinks, toward a directness of statement which, at its worst, lacks restraint and urbanity. So far, he thinks, we have escaped tall-talk, Johnsonese, machine-made jargon. We "rebel instinctively" against circumlocution. "There is more than mere humorous contrast between the famous placard in the wash-room of the British Museum: *These Basins Are For Casual Ablutions Only,* and the familiar sign at American railway crossings: *Stop! Look! Listen.*"

At our best, there is no denying the fact that we are wonders at inventing bold, vivid, concise, direct, and brilliantly expressive speech. *Joy-ride* is incomparable. So is *standpatter.* So are *lounge-lizard, high-brow, bone-head, tight-wad, road-louse; barrel* (for illicit affluence), *pork* (for public graft). There is no doubt that we have a creative way with language—let us admit it. But we think Mr. Mencken is a little too easy with us, a little under-critical. Along with this obvious tendency of the American language toward condensation, we must recognize—if we look steadily and honestly—another tendency, equally typical, in the opposite direction. We mean the patent American love for the verbally evasive, the verbally indirect, ambiguous, redundant.

We love the pretentious in speech, the absurdly ornate, the circumlocutory. It was our beloved America that invented *tonsorial parlor;* that adores the clumsily elaborate, the timidly genteel phrase; that prefers a shambling euphemism to a racy and swift directness. It was in America, in 1918, that the Army Medical Corps complained of the handicap imposed upon their work of essential public education because of the anserine squeamishness of the newspapers, which in most cases refused to print its bulletins regarding the prevalence of syphilis because as one blameless journalistic soul explained, "the use of such terms as 'gonorrhea,' 'syphilis,' and even 'venereal diseases' *would not add to the tone of the papers*" (the italics are ours). Such fatuous and panicky evasions as *statutory offense* for *adultery,* or *an interesting condition* for *pregnant,* are typically American. It is said that the New York *Evening Post* only recently permitted its reporters to use the bold term *street-walker.*

This trait, so far as it concerns language that touches upon the more urgent realities of the flesh, is due, of course merely to our irremediable Puritan hang-over. Mr. Mencken recognizes this truth, and has his fun with it. How can one thank him sufficiently for incidentally unearthing the fact that during the Victorean era in England the linguistic drapers, seeking a polite substitute for *bull,* which was banned as too gross for refined ears, hit upon and used the enchanting subterfuge, *gentleman-cow?* But while England has for the most part recovered from that ludicrous and horrible distemper, America has not. Mr. Mencken refers to a recent example of the use of *male-cow* for *bull* quoted in the *Journal* of the American Medical Association for November 17, 1917.

Mr. Mencken might point to the edifying fact that the American who now represents us abroad has not hesitated to use in public discourse such phrases as *going some,* and *hog* (as a verb). That is indeed all to the good. But Mr. Wilson is sufficiently expert in the use of language to know when to express himself like Walter Bagehot and when to express himself like the Man in the Street. Mr. Wilson's speech is, however, scarcely typical of the American language. Take a speech that is; not that of the motorman in New York, the ironworker in Pittsburgh, the corner grocer in St. Louis, the carpenter in Ohio: that, in the main, as Mr. Mencken says, is "a highly virile and defiant dialect," disdainful of precedent, without self-consciousness, "deriving its principles from the rough and ready logic of every day." Take the speech of the semi-educated American—the habitual speech of the American manufacturer, of the lower grade of Congressman, of the small-town matron, of the T. B. M., of the average newspaper-man—the American language that is used in a million prosperous provincial homes, a million business offices, a million newspaper "stories" and editorials. It is a speech that is flabby with timorous euphemism. It is shambling, mincing, cheaply "refined," indecently "respectable." It seems almost incapable of direct and honest speech. It not only says *limbs* when it means *legs* (which is merely the Puritan complex uttering a feebly shameful reminder of its dirty past), but it fails to say what it means even when it means something wholly unrelated to Sex and Sin. One would not expect a "nice" American woman to emulate the shameless English and call a female canine a *bitch.* She would be content with *dog;* or, if pressed, would take refuge in *lady-dog*—we have heard it. (Mr. Mencken admits this fact, but attempts to account for it by the delightfully naïve and excessively indulgent explanation that it is due "largely, perhaps," to the English people's "greater familiarity with country life.") But why does the average semi-educated, middle-class American (who, bless his amiable soul, rules our intellectual life) say *under the influence of liquor* when he means *drunk,* and *retire* when he means *go to bed?*

We think it is because the average American, despite his indisputable liking for the succinct and the vividly direct, has a concurrent, deep-seated, ineradicable inclination toward the euphemistic, the evasive, the stilted, the highfalutin'. This tendency permeates the speaking and writing of Americans, in regions of reflection and reaction where the Puritan complex does not enter at all. Is it because the American is really, for all his superficial raciness and vividness and impatience, at heart a quaking traditionalist, an incurable side-stepper? One sometimes suspects that this is so.

Mr. Mencken speaks of "the disdain of ordered forms" that is "so characteristically American." We think this "disdain" is largely superficial. In his heart of hearts, the American loves the old ways, the conventional ways. The art that he loves is saccharine, pretty, conventional—he infinitely prefers Howard Chandler Christy to Glackens; the Pretty-Girl, Little Tot, Lover-and-Sweetheart confections on the popular magazine covers to the drawings of Boardman Robinson or Art Young. He would willingly chuck Walt Whitman any day for Longfellow. He thrills at the *Méditation Religieuse* from "Thaïs" and goes to sleep over Moussorgsky.

But all this is hardly Mr. Mencken's fault. We have dwelt upon it merely because he did not, and we think his indulgence a defect in a book that is almost always sound, shrewd, discerning, just. This treatise is accomplished with humor, with brilliancy, with sympathetic imagination. And, as we began by saying, it is deplorably engrossing.

Professor Brander Matthews of Columbia University, "that learned man" whom Mencken mentioned in his initial essay on the American language, weighed in with a lengthy review. He brings Mark Twain into the discussion but was himself a man of letters in the mold of Twain's friend William Dean Howells and was one of the last of the type. Nonetheless, his strictures on Mencken's claim of a distinctly American language are fair-minded ("Developing the American from the English Language," New York Times Book Review, 30 March 1919, pp. 157, 164, 170).

Hidden in the second volume of Mark Twain's miscellaneous sketches and essays there is a paper entitled "Concerning the American Language." A footnote informs us that it was part of a chapter crowded out of "A Tramp Abroad." It purports to record a conversation supposed to have taken place between Mark and an Englishman in the same railway compartment. With captivating tactfulness the Englishman complimented Mark on his English, adding that Americans in general did not speak the English language as correctly as Mark did.

"I said I was obliged to him for his compliment—since I knew that he meant it for one—but that I was not fairly entitled to it, for I did not speak English at all—I only spoke American."

The Englishman laughed and said that this was a distinction without a difference; and Mark admitted that the difference was not prodigious, but still it was considerable. "The languages were identical several generations ago," Mark went on, "but our changed conditions and the spread of our people far to the south and far to the west have made many alterations in our

H. L. MENCKEN
1524 HOLLINS ST.
BALTIMORE.
March 16, 1944.

Dear Mr. Crockett:

I hear from C. J. Rosebault that you know something
about the history of the gin-rickey.   For the purpose of a
projected supplement to my old book, "The American Language,"
I am trying to find out precisely who Colonel Joe Rickey was.
Some accounts make him a bartender and say that he actually
invented the rickey.   Others are to the effect that he was
a Kentucky boozer whose name was borrowed for it by the actual
inventor.   Can you throw any light on this mystery?   If so,
it goes without saying that I'll be delighted to give you
credit in my forthcoming tome.

I seize the opportunity to hope that you are in good
health and spirits.

Sincerely yours,

Albert S. Crockett, Esq.,
320 east 42nd street,
New York City.

H. L. MENCKEN
1524 HOLLINS ST.   August 7, 1946.
BALTIMORE-23

Dear Mr. Kadison:

Those clippings are swell indeed, and I am delighted
to have them.   My very best thanks.

To waitress is surely a nifty verb, and almost the equal
of to architect.   Despite the hot weather, I am making fair
progress with my book, but I doubt that it will be finished until
next Spring.

My doctor has given me benadryl against my hay fever.
Whether or not it will work remains to be seen.   He warns me that
it may have unpleasant side effects, including headache, drowsiness
and nausea.   If any of them appear I'll throw the rest of the cap-
sules out of the window.

Sincerely yours,

Typical research letters, soliciting material and thanking contributors (Richard J. Schrader Collection)

pronunciation and have introduced new words among us and changed the meanings of many old ones."

Mark then proceeded to point out certain of the differences of pronunciation; but here I need not quote him, since this subdivision of the subject has recently been considered comprehensively and skillfully in Professor George Philip Krapp's illuminating little book on "The Pronunciation of Standard English in America," (Oxford University Press.) Nor need I copy here the ample collection of divergences of vocabulary and of usage with which Mark maintained his whimsical contention. I may note, however, that his ear was unusually acute, and that he was always keenly interested in linguistic peculiarities. I recall that once, when I asked him about his collaboration with Bret Harte in a play called "Ah Sin," Mark told me that the two partners had talked out the plot and that he had then played billiards, while Harte drafted the dialogue. "Of course, I had to go over his manuscript very carefully to get the dialect right. Bret never did know anything about dialect."

In his discussion with the Englishman in the railway compartment Mark adduced a serried catalogue of the differences he had noted between the English spoken by Americans and the English spoken by the British, and then he closed the debate by saying: "However, I won't tire you, but if I wanted to I could pile up differences here until I not only convinced you that English and American are separate languages, but that when I speak my native tongue in its utmost purity an Englishman can't understand me at all!"

To this the Englishman retorted: "I don't wish to flatter you, but it is about all I can do to understand you now."

The contention which Mark playfully put forward in this conversation has recently been seriously maintained by a leading American critic in an address before the American Academy of Arts and Letters. This scholar declared that he was shocked and grieved and saddened by the many evidences he had noticed that our speech in America was no longer conforming to the conventions of our kin across the sea in the little island where English had come to its maturity. He even went so far as to suggest that our English here in America was deteriorating and degenerating, as Greek had declined after it had entered on its decadence in the Hellenistic period when the centre of Greek civilization had migrated across the "tideless, dolorous, inland sea" from Athens to Alexandria.

And now comes H. L. Mencken, armed at all points, to maintain the same contention, not whimsically, like the American humorist, and not dolefully, like the American critic, but unhesitatingly and joyfully. He holds that the tongue which we speak on this side of the Western Ocean is no longer English, but is now American. He quotes George Ade in support of Mark Twain:

> The American must go to England in order to learn for a dead certainty that he does not speak the English language. * * * This pitiful fact comes home to every American when he arrives in London—that there are two languages, the English and the American.

Mr. Mencken does not consider the fact pitiful; he regards it as inevitable and satisfactory. He brings forward testimony to the same effect from the latest edition of the Encyclopaedia Britannica:

> It is not uncommon to meet with [American] newspaper articles of which an untraveled Englishman would hardly be able to understand a sentence.

Before considering the evidence that Mr. Mencken advances in support of his thesis it may be well to say that his book is interesting and useful; it is a book to be taken seriously; it is a book well planned, well proportioned, well documented, and well written. As I read its pages with both pleasure and profit I was reminded of an anecdote. Emerson once lent a translation of Plato to one of his rustic neighbors at Concord; and when the Yankee farmer returned it he did this with the characteristic remark: "I see Plato has a good many of my idees!" As I lingered over Mr. Mencken's successive and suggestive chapters I discovered that he had a good many of my ideas, and that I had a good many of his ideas. I supposed that the foundation of my assertion that Mr. Mencken's book is useful and interesting is to be found in the fact that I agree with many of his opinions. We are all of us the slaves of our personal equation, however much we may struggle to step off our own shadows.

Mr. Mencken would see nothing objectionable in the placard said to have been displayed in the window of a Swiss shop: "English Spoken and American Understood." He would accept this as a plain statement of an obvious fact. Everybody knows that there are a host of divergences between the English language as it is now spoken in the British Isles and as it is now spoken in the United States, differences of intonation, of pronunciation, of vocabulary, and even of grammar; but nobody has ever marshaled this host as amply, as logically, or as impressively as Mr. Mencken has done. There are half a dozen dictionaries of Americanism, all of them more or less heterogenous. Any helpful survey of the subject must begin by a classification of these so-called Americanisms to ascertain if they are rightly so called.

First of all there are the words which Americans gave to things unknown to the British—canoe, wig-

Advertisement for the first of the two supplementary volumes, published in 1945 and 1948, respectively

wam and moccasin, chowder and barbecue, caucus and gerrymander, telephone and phonograph. These are all American contributions to the English language; they are words in good standing because they are the only words to describe the things they designate. Then there are the good old words which have dropped out of use in Great Britain and which have survived in the United States: Fall, (Autumn;) wilt, (wither;) deck, (pack of cards.) These have never ceased to be good English, even if the British themselves do not know this. These survivals are so many that they supplied Senator Lodge with abundant material for an illuminating essay on "Shakespeare's Americanisms." Thirdly, there are the slang terms and phrases of indigenous origin and of ephemeral existence, springing up overnight, carried across the continent on the wings of the morning, and fading into contemptuous oblivion the day after tomorrow: Skiddoo, let her go, Gallagher; twenty-three for you. These inept expressions do not rise to the dignity of Americanisms. And finally there are the true Americanisms to be set over against the corresponding Briticisms: Elevator, (lift;) drugstore, (chemist's shop;) spool of thread, (reel of cotton.)

It is upon these that Mr. Mencken focuses our attention. He shows that American speech began to differentiate itself from British speech in the eighteenth century. He quotes from Thomas Jefferson (writing in 1813) an assertion that "'the new circumstances under which we are placed call for new words, new phrases, and for the transfer of old words to new objects: an American dialect will therefore be formed." And Mr. Mencken has found, in a dedicatory letter written to Benjamin Franklin, in 1789, a similar assertion by Noah Webster:

> Numerous local causes, such as a new country, new combinations of ideas in arts and sciences, and some intercourse with tribes wholly unknown in Europe, will introduce new words into the American tongue. These causes will produce, in a course of time, a language in North America as different from the future language of England as the modern Dutch,

Danish, and Swedish are from the German, or from one another.

This prediction of a hundred and thirty years ago has now been fulfilled, so Mr. Mencken maintains. Mark Twain and George Ade were justified in asserting that there are now two languages, English and American, the latter differentiated by "its impatient disdain of rule and precedent, and hence its large capacity (distinctly greater than that of the English of England) for taking in new words and phrases and for manufacturing new locutions out of its own materials," (Page 19.) The American is restless, impetuous, and swift to take short cuts. He is not, however,

> lacking in a capacity for discipline; he has it highly developed; he submits to leadership readily, and even to tyranny. But, by a curious twist, it is not the leadership that is old and decorous that fetches him, but the leadership that is new and extravagant. * * * A new fallacy in politics spreads faster in the United States than anywhere else on earth, and so does a new fashion in hats, or a new revelation of God, or a new means of killing time, or a new metaphor or piece of slang, (Page 22.)

As a result of the widening difference of our American speech from British speech is "not merely a difference in vocabulary," but "above all a difference in pronunciation, in intonation, in conjugation and declension, in metaphor and idiom, in the whole fashion of using words," (Page 34.)

These things may be admitted, all of them, and in fact they must be admitted, but this admission does not carry with it any acknowledgment that there are now two languages, or that there ever will be. Mr. Mencken is rejoiced by the vitality, the vigor, the freshness of the American language, and he looks forward to a time when the foremost American authors will cast off all allegiance to the traditions of the language as these came into being in England. Yet he has to regret that he can see no sign of any new departure in the writings of these foremost authors. Walt Whitman and Mark Twain and Mr. Howells are devoid of any colonial subservience to British standards, but what they wrote is still English and English of an indisputable purity. Even Mr. Mencken's own book is written in what he would call English and not in what he would call American.

The fact is that we Americans are all of us the children of Chaucer, the subjects of King Shakespeare, the coheirs of Milton and of Dryden; and we are proud of that ancient and honorable descent. There is really no probability that we shall ever renounce that inestimable heritage, however frankly we may free ourselves from outworn shackles and however bold and willful

we may be in verbal innovation. What is probable and increasingly probable, as Mr. Mencken himself is too shrewd not to see clearly, is that the British will prevent the gap between our speech and theirs from becoming wider than it is at present by accepting the best of our linguistic novelties. In a footnote [. . .] to the latest edition of the "Biglow Papers," Lowell declared that he could not take up a British journal without finding Americanisms. "The majority of Englishmen continue to make borrowings from the tempting and ever-widening American vocabulary," Mr. Mencken asserts; and "what is more, some of these loan-words take root, and are presently accepted as sound English, even by the most watchful," (Page 134.) And the exacerbated protests of a Frederic Harrison are significant admissions as to the ever-increasing penetration of American words and phrases into current British speech.

Mr. Mencken really gives up his case for the future development of a separate American Language when he tells us that "the American dialect of English * * * because it is already spoken by a far larger and more rapidly multiplying body of people" than the British dialect, will, very likely, "determine the final form of the language," (Page 317.) If the current speech of the United States is not to differ still more widely from that of the British Isles, it must be—and it will be—because the British will accept the best of the American contributions and modifications.

There is a significant remark, credited to Mark Twain and characteristic of his common sense, which I have never been able to find in his writings and which is to the effect that the King's English is the King's English no longer, "since it has gone into the hands of a stock company—and we Americans hold a majority of the stock." That is to say, the English of the future will be colored by the American of the present. In linguistic matters we shall pay little deference to contemporary British conventions, although we shall always be stanchly loyal to the traditions of our forefathers.

It has seemed best in this review to deal with Mr. Mencken's fundamental thesis and to resist the temptation to follow him into the alluring bypaths of linguistic inquiry. Yet there is one excursus I must permit myself. Mr. Mencken asks what effect upon the future of our speech is to be produced by the unassimilated folk of variegated ancestry who have been poured into the melting pot. I wish that he would give me an answer for one linguistic peculiarity which puzzles me. When a Scotsman says, "dinna ye fash yersel'," we see that this is the French "ne vous fachez pas"; and we may explain this as due to the intimate relations of France and Scotland in the days of Mary, Queen of Scots. But when an Irishman says of a portrait that it is "the very spit of him," we recognize the French "c'est son portrait tout

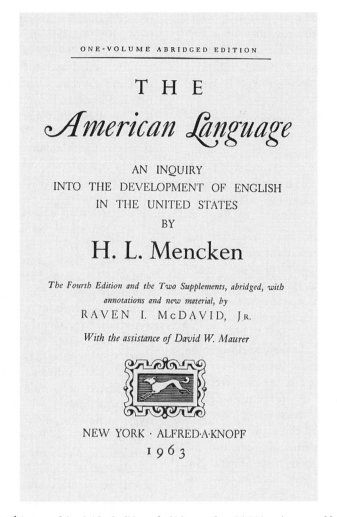

ONE-VOLUME ABRIDGED EDITION

THE

American Language

AN INQUIRY
INTO THE DEVELOPMENT OF ENGLISH
IN THE UNITED STATES
BY

H. L. Mencken

*The Fourth Edition and the Two Supplements, abridged, with
annotations and new material, by*
RAVEN I. McDAVID, Jr.

With the assistance of David W. Maurer

NEW YORK · ALFRED·A·KNOPF
1963

Title page of the abridged edition, of which more than 55,000 copies were sold

craché"; and we wonder how the men of Dublin and the men of Paris happened to hit on the same strange figure of speech. How is it that there are similar parallelisms between American colloquialisms and French? Our "that's the limit" is their "c'est un comble." Ludovic Halévy describes his heroine as "pas coquette pour un liard," and this runs in double harness with "she doesn't flirt for a cent." We call the ballyhoo man outside a show a "barker," and the same functionary in the Parisian fairs of the eighteenth century was known as the "aboyeur." And how is it that a common American affirmative is "sure!" and a corresponding Italian affirmative is "sicuro"?

I find I cannot quit Mr. Mencken without a little faultfinding. He avoids the violent vituperation which used to characterize linguistic debate; but he is not always so courteous as he might be toward the predecessors with whom he does not agree. He mentions the American Academy of Arts and Letters only to sneer at "the gifted philologs of that sanhedrim." He speaks slightingly of the late Thomas Raynesford Lounsbury, who deserved well of all linguistic inquirers; and he adds injury to insult by calling him Thomas S. Lounsbury. And he terms the writer of this review "a pundit." What have I ever done to deserve the stigma?

A British point of view is expressed by William McFee. He refers chiefly to the section "British Spelling in the United States" in the second edition ("Mencken and Menken or The Gift of Tongues," Bookman, 54 [December 1921]: 361–363).

There is something to be said for the Æsopian fox who lost his tail. He made the best of a bad job. By careless neglect he found himself bereft of a beautiful and useful part of his personality. Without loss of time he began a publicity campaign. He employed scientists who declared that tails were germ-carriers. He interested educators who discouraged tails in the schools. The vixen's clubs invited him to lecture, and passed a number of resolutions calling for legislation prohibiting tails everywhere. . . .

But what extenuation can one find for a fox, renowned for his courage and cunning, blessed with one of the finest, stiffest, and most bushy tails in the world, who preaches that not only are foxes better off without tails, but that the ideal fox has not sufficient sense to distinguish between the bark of a dog and the cluck of a hen?

To abandon the allegory, H. L. Mencken has demonstrated once more the eternal truth that very clever men must have their pet folly. It is most extraordinary how often a man of indubitable genius will founder in this most fatal quicksand of language-mongering. Many years ago, say in 1901, Bernard Shaw, then a newspaper man writing under a number of pen names, used phonetic spelling as an excuse to write immense letters to the press. The old "Morning Leader" would contain column after column of Shaw's amusing piffle about the mistakes we poor Englishmen made in pronouncing our own tongue. Spelling seems to have the same fascination for brilliant minds that perpetual motion and the punctureless tire have for young mechanics. But young mechanics have the great justification that they seek a stark utility beyond the realms of art. The spelling reformer has never betrayed the ultimate motives of his mania.

It is almost incredible that it should be necessary to call the attention of so shrewd a critic to the fact that a word may be logical and clear and correct, and ugly to look at. Yet Mr. Mencken seems never to have reflected that the beauty of a book may be enhanced not only by the arrangement of the words on the page but by the arrangement of the letters in the words. To take Mr. Mencken's own examples, *axe* and *centre* are prettier than *ax* and *center*. Which is possibly the reason why Mr. Mencken dislikes them. *Honour, harbour, tenour* are actual English words, not phonetic symbols like *mazda* and *veritite* and *oxide*. There is also another reason for that exasperating *u,* if I may whisper it. *Honour* is pronounced *honour,* not *honor,* whereas *ancestor* is pronounced that way, not *ancestour*. Of course, no one will ever believe an Englishman knows anything about pronouncing his own tongue. Scots, Celts, Welsh, Germans, and Americans unite in crushing him if he raise ever so mild a protest at their weird and wonderful emendations. Many English, out of

consideration for the foibles of others, change their own pronunciation to oblige, and for a quiet life.

In brief, words of the *honour* and *tenour* type are rightly spelled with the extra vowel not only because they are thereby identified with a particular meaning, but because the genius of the language demands it. One might almost say that we spell them that way for the same reason Mr. Mencken retains the double consonant in his name instead of dropping it as idiotic or nonsensical. Mr. Mencken demands further information about our peculiar fads, and it is singular that he never by any chance asks a question that an English man of letters cannot answer. Why add an *e* to *annex* and *form?* Because, your honour, *annex* is one thing and *annexe* another. Because *form* has a multitude of meanings active and substantive, whereas *forme* is a technical term. *Kerb* is a noun with a definite meaning, and *curb* is a noun and a verb of general application. When we come to *gaol* and *jail,* I am afraid Mr. Mencken will laugh if I contend that *gaol* is the better word. It has, to an Englishman, more significance than *jail*. Its appearance in a sentence has a sombre and foreboding effect upon that sentence. It is as much superior to *jail* as the German word *verloren* is to the French word *perdu*. Moreover, although I fear Mr. Mencken is by now so furious that he will not listen, we pronounce it *gaol,* not *jail*. . . . With regret one has to call attention to another point which Mr. Mencken has missed. Our word *superior* does not come direct from the French. It comes direct from the Latin. The French expression *Seine Supérieure* would be translated *Upper Thames* not *Superior Thames*. And it is the rule in English grammar when forming an adjective from a noun to modify the spelling. Mr. Mencken will find the same astounding idiosyncrasy in Italian. Mr. Mencken has not given this matter adequate attention. Twenty-five years ago English newspapers had *patent-insides*. I can remember them.

Mr. Mencken professes to ignore, in considering the new American Language, both "the jargon of the intellectual snobs and the gibberish of the vulgar." I think he is scarcely wise. To the stranger who comes to dwell in America both the jargon and the gibberish are revelations of the possibilities of the English tongue. What Mr. Mencken calls "the everyday discourse of ordinary educated folk" differs very little from the discourse of the same sort of folk in England. Nothing is more puzzling to an Englishman after reading American fiction and newspapers than to come here and find ordinary people speaking ordinary good English with practically no provincialisms or slang intermixed. The main difference is that the American attempts to explain to you how he *feels,* whereas an Englishman is reluctant to admit the existence of emotion at all.

But out in the open one can enjoy true sport. What joy to discover that when one needs a hair cut, one can enter a *tonsorial parlor!* And it almost robs the grave of victory and draws the sting of death to know that instead of an undertaker the family will call in a *mortuarian.* These, I take it, are what Mr. Mencken would call the jargon of the intellectual snobs. But "the gibberish of the vulgar" is equally alluring. It is the most vivid thing in the world. Mr. Mencken cannot persuade me he does not like it. I tell the world he does!

In all seriousness, however, the phrase "American Language" is scarcely needed yet except to indicate a certain peculiar offshoot of written English known as publicity writing. As far as I know there is nothing like it on earth. The Englishman tells you his pills are worth a guinea a box, or he begs you to "furnish with taste" at his store, or advises you to insist on a particular brand of mustard. The Frenchman or Spaniard hires a black-and-white artist who draws so extremely well that one simply has to pause and read the context. But the American publicity writer has lost touch with earth altogether. He has become so afflicted with the *cacoethes scribendi* that he will write whole pages of advertising about the cardinal virtues. I pick up a current periodical and I read:

> Towering above fear, buttressed with honor, meeting the assaults of circumstance with the strength of rightness, stands integrity.

Now to a European of average intelligence, this is a distinctly new departure—to write advertisements about an unmarketable abstraction. Of course the publicity man may argue that he is selling integrity. To that a European can offer no reply. It is something entirely beyond his experience.

To the man of letters, however, this particular adventure of the advertiser is serious. It implies that literature will have to abandon many forms and phrases and seek a means of expression not yet appropriated by the sales department. And the only means the present writer sees available at present is the continual use of good English. Mr. Mencken will never be able to use the American Language. It is already preempted. And in the future, when his own vigorous and sledgehammer style has been stolen by the publicity hounds, even Mr. Mencken may be forced to fall back on the despised English Language to distinguish his own essays from the advertisements.

After the first edition many contributions arrived unsolicited, but Mencken continued to canvass the country for word origins and linguistic novelties (transcriptions of letters [second letter is excerpted] at the New York Public Library).

February 26, 1935.

The Secretary,
National Selected Morticians,
520 N. Michigan Ave.,
Chicago, Ill.

Dear Sir:

May I introduce myself as the author of a book, The American Language, dealing at some length with the changes undergone by English in this country? It first appeared fifteen years ago and has since been republished in a number of editions. I am now engaged upon an extensive revision of it. In that revision I want to include some discussion of the word <u>mortician</u>. Can you tell me who invented it and when, precisely? When was the National Selected Morticians organized? Do you claim a monopoly on the use of the word, like that claimed by the National Real Estate Board on <u>realtor</u>?

If you can give me any help in this matter I'll be very grateful. I want to make my book as accurate as possible. The dictionaries are all very vague about the origin and history of <u>mortician</u>.

Sincerely yours,

(Signed) H.L. Mencken

* * *

November 11, 1943.

Dr. Logan Clendening,
Kansas City, Mo.
Dear Logan:

[. . .] I have been trying to find out the true meaning of the American verb <u>to goose</u> -- that is, I have been trying to find out what it is that makes a goosed man jump. Fishbein, of the Journal of the American Medical Association, has given me some help but he refuses to print an inquiry in his Notes and Queries column, apparently on the ground that it would be an indecorum. <u>To goose</u> doesn't appear in any American dictionary but the National Safety Council and other such agencies have issued many printed warnings against the practise. It is not an uncommon occurrence for a goosed man to fall off a high scaffold and hit a couple of other men on the

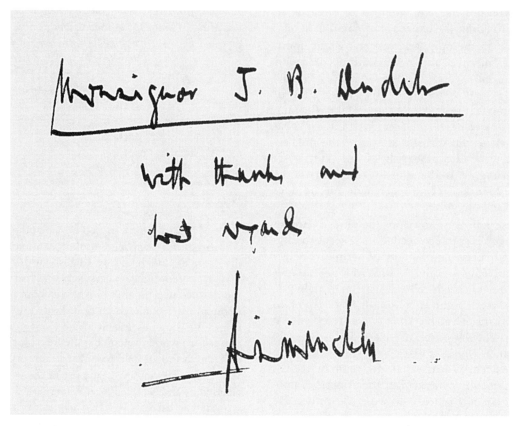

Inscription to Monsignor J. B. Dudek, an authority on the Czech language in America, in a copy of the second edition of The American Language, *published in 1921 (George H. Thompson Collection)*

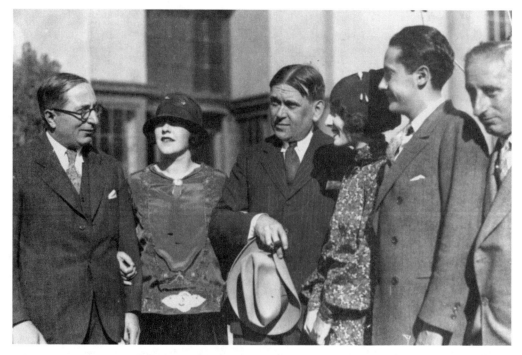

Mencken in Hollywood, 1926, with studio head Louis B. Mayer, actresses Aileen Pringle and Norma Shearer, and producers Irving Thalberg and Harry Rapf (courtesy of the Enoch Pratt Free Library)

way down. Fishbein suggests that the verb may come from an old custom of testing a goose by feeling of the fat in the anal region. Have you any ideas on the subject? I want to print something about the word in a supplement to The American Language, in progress.

Two other words that occupy me are <u>Charlie horse</u> and <u>glass arm</u>, formerly in wide use among baseball players. My impression is that <u>Charley horse</u> indicated a serious rupture or strain, whereas <u>glass arm</u> covered only a mild bursitis or synovitis. I can find nothing on the subject in the medical dictionaries, nor is there anything in the books at hand on traumatic surgery.

I surely hope that you and Mrs. Clendening are in the best of health and spirits. I am hard at work upon my book and have little time for anything else. Nevertheless, I manage now and then to get a really good dinner. I had one last night in the country not far from Baltimore. The excellent victuals were washed down with some prime Rhine wine.

Yours,

(Signed) H.L. Mencken

* * *

November 15, 1943.

Edgar Selwyn, Esq.,
MGM Studio,
Culver City, California.

Dear Edgar:

What precisely is an Oscar? I neglected to include it in my list of motion picture terms, but I think it ought to be there. My impression is there are a number of Oscars given -- one to the best actor, one to the best actress, another to the best photographer and so on. What precisely is the name of the body offering the prizes, and how many are given each year? I seem to have read somewhere that the actual prize is a statuette.

My apologies for bothering you again.

Yours,

(Signed) H.L. Mencken

One of the many professional and amateur authorities Mencken cites throughout the fourth edition of The American Language *is Monsignor J. B. Dudek, chancellor of the Roman Catholic diocese of Oklahoma City and Tulsa and an expert on the Czech language in America. Dudek's review, a carbon copy of which Mencken saw in advance, points to a* *feature of the book that is as responsible as the content for keeping it alive: its readability (excerpts from "A Philological Romance,"* Saturday Review of Literature, *14 [16 May 1936]: 10–11).*

This new edition of Mr. Mencken's magnum opus is a phenomenal achievement. To call it an "edition" is misleading. Not only has the book been thoroughly revised, rearranged, corrected, and brought up to date, but, saving a few passages, it has been so completely rewritten and so much new material has been added—the present volume is double the size of its immediate predecessor—that, excepting the title and the author's name, it is an entirely new work. Here we have a scholarly discussion, in 325,000 words, of the development of English in the United States, but so diverting a piece of writing withal that, from preface to index (of course there is an index!), one is scarcely aware that it is a scientific treatise of the first order. A bulky volume of 800 pages plus, which no one perhaps will set out to read seriatim, it nevertheless tempts the reader who opens it timorously to skip joyfully from one charming page to another. He encounters adventure, romance, mystery. Finally he is spellbound, and sitting up, away into the small hours of the night, reluctant to lay down this philological "Anthony Adverse" without seeing it through to the finish. The publisher's advance announcement recommended the book for the bedside. Prudently, nothing was said of it as a cure for insomnia, for in that capacity it would assuredly fail. Mr. Mencken is not a writer to be read half asleep. Lest any one be discouraged by a book obviously impossible to dispatch at one sitting, let it be observed here that each chapter is so complete in itself that it may be read independently. Thus, the book may be divided into convenient slices, which need not be taken in order.

The first edition of Mr. Mencken's "American Language" came out in March 1919. Limited to 1,500 copies, it was almost immediately exhausted. A second edition, revised and enlarged, appeared in December 1921, and a third, again revised and enlarged, in February 1923. This last has, heretofore, been the most familiar and popular. Although a relatively expensive book, sales were steady and comparatively large, five reprintings having been necessary. The work was published also in England, the first British edition being, with a few minor changes, the same as the American third; there is also a German translation, "Die Amerikanische Sprache," by Heinrich Spies (Berlin, 1927), much abbreviated, however, condensing in less than 200 pages (including index) the American third which contained over 400 pages of text, exclusive of a long bibliography and the index.

The formal bibliography is wisely omitted in the Fourth Edition, but bibliographical references are given in abundant footnotes, frequently as interesting and witty as the text. Those who enjoy a hearty guffaw should by no means miss the third footnote on page 498, or the one on page 501. The latter has a Rabelaisian piquancy, which though never obtrusive, is not absent elsewhere throughout the book. The List of Words and Phrases, expanded to seventy three-column pages, is a veritable dictionary of 12,000 Americanisms, including the earliest Colonial loan words as well as juicy examples of modern slang. Non-English words discussed in the text, especially in the Appendix, are not repeated in the word list, but the proper names occurring in Chapter X are.

To quote from the author's preface, the reader familiar with former editions will find that this one "not only presents a large amount of material that was not available when they were written, but also modifies the thesis that they set forth." [. . .] This argument, supported by conclusive evidence, is elaborated in Chapter I, "The Two Streams of English." Here is a delightful serio-comic essay on the discussions provoked by early Americanisms, the fury with which English reviewers and American pedagogues attacked them, the American writers' sympathetic attitude toward the "barbarisms," and their encounters with the English critics, in which the Americans patently scored. Not the least amusing is a discussion of sporadic efforts made in this country to impose the "United States" language by law.

The second, a very brief chapter, entitled "The Materials of Inquiry," setting forth the essential characteristics of the new language and enumerating the categories of Americanisms established by past observers, is partly reprinted from the previous edition but still considerably revamped. The third and fourth chapters are a history of the development of American-English from the arrival of the first settlers up to and including the Civil War, but words borrowed from Indian tongues, from the Dutch, French, and Spanish, are amply discussed, as also the fashioning of neologisms from English material. The period covered by Chapter IV was enormously fertile, and during it the language acquired most of its present distinguishing marks. The fifth chapter treats at length of word-formation processes now active. The sixth demonstrates the vast influence of American on parent English. It is here that Mr. Mencken most plausibly contends that the two languages remain definitely unlike, even in honorifics, euphemisms, *verboten* words, and expletives. Chapters VII and VIII deal admirably with American pronunciation and spelling, respectively, and in Chapter IX is the first formal grammar of the American vulgate ever essayed. Perhaps the finest chapter in the book is the tenth, "Proper Names in America." Surnames, given and place names receive hospitable attention, and there are startling revelations.

A book the size of Mr. Mencken's already formidable tome would not suffice for an adequate survey of American slang; but, within Chapter XI, he has compacted practically everything of permanent value to be extracted from the overwhelming, unstable mass of raw material that must be available. There is a section on the cant and argot of circus men, hoboes and other groups, including, *mirabile dictu*, pedagogues!

Chapter XII, "The Future of the Language," complements the opening chapter, and here Mr. Mencken becomes prophetic. The English language, he points out, is practically a world language; it still has sizeable competitors only in French and German. [. . .] He doubts that, as English spreads, it will be able to maintain its present (British) form: the foreigner must eventually make his choice between that and the American; but, despite differences, defects, and drawbacks, "English goes on conquering the world," and it is not difficult to predict which form is more apt to win.

The Appendix, on non-English dialects, is a book in itself. [. . .] Mr. Mencken has expanded to eighty-six pages a section which, in his third edition, filled but twenty-eight. Some knowledge of the various languages would be advantageous for an appreciation of this Appendix, but even the reader knowing only English (excuse me, American!) will chuckle over the disaster that has overtaken foreign tongues in the land of the free. Evidently, in linguistic matters there has been not only liberty but unbounded license. The setting up and proof-reading of this section must have driven more than one person insane, yet misprints are surprisingly few. Those discoverable will doubtless be corrected before the book is electrotyped. All in all, the volume is a magnificent piece of typography from the Plimpton Press.

It is hard to charge the learned author with mortal sins of commission, though Anglophiles, prudes, pedagogues, and purists will be prompt to tear him limb from limb. His main thesis will probably be denied *in toto*, but disproving it is quite another matter. As for sins of omission, every reader will think instantly of some pet word or phrase which Mr. Mencken should have included. This reviewer, for instance, searched vainly for the abomination "kiddie," which, for over fifteen years to his personal knowledge, has designated a child from the toddling age up to approaching puberty and has not yet died a richly deserved and horrible death. Even the noun "kid" is missing, though "kidding" is mentioned. "Kido," in the third edition, is omitted in this, probably as now obsolete. Among words overworked by the newspapers and at business men's luncheons, some of the "most outstanding," like "virtually," "group" (meaning anything from an insignificant sewing circle to the whole *corpus* of the R. C. Church), "visualize," and "alleged," are absent. After an "alleged" criminal has been sentenced to the electric chair, it seems the height of precaution and idiocy to keep on rehashing that he "allegedly" murdered the woman, an "alleged" underworld character, by strangulation after an "alleged" assault, etc., etc., when the possibility of legal action against the publisher by the *dramatis personæ* is exceedingly remote. Incidentally, there is no discussion of a hypothetical ukase compelling newspaper men to write, say, "Her head *virtually was* severed from her body," "U.S. *still is* neutral," "He *soon is* expected," or "*Almost it* is impossible," instead of constructions a normal person would use. There is the well known pedantry about the split infinitive, but what commandment forbids splitting a periphrastic tense?

But it is manifestly unfair to expect that Mr. Mencken should have included everything or that he should have made his book a mere lexicon. He sagely leaves that function to the compilers of "The Dictionary of American English on Historical Principles" now under way at the University of Chicago. Privately, I am informed that, for fear of scaring off readers, he rejected at least three times as much material, submitted to him by voluntary contributors, as he used. The job of judicious selection alone must have been a formidable one. Apparently, however, this penetrating observer, not only of the American but of the international scene, enjoyed his task hugely and his delight is infectious.

(Excerpt from a transcription of a letter at Princeton University.)

April 30, 1936.

Dear Monsignor:

Your review of "The American Language" really overwhelms me. I was frankly somewhat uneasy about it. The trouble with doing so large a book is that one almost inevitably gets lost in the midst of it. I was in fear that I had done that, and that the result was a vast accumulation of undigested materials. But your notice reassures me, and I needn't add that I offer my most profound thanks. It is not only very generous, it is also an excellent piece of writing, and if Canby is really a good editor he'll print it in full.

I was amazed the other day to receive a copy of America, a Jesuit weekly, containing a flaming advance notice of the book. Who wrote it I don't know. Hitherto America has treated me with great suspicion as an enemy of the True Faith and a corrupter of youth. I have always got along very amiably with the Commonweal, but not with America. Now, however, it gives me its imprimatur, and I begin to suspect that in the end I may really die in the odor of sanctity. [. . .]

Sincerely yours,

H. L. Mencken

Edmund Wilson, reviewing the fourth edition, noted that the first marked a stage in the nation's literary development and that the book had become a literary achievement in its own right (excerpt from "Talking United States," New Republic, *87 [15 July 1936]: 299–300).*

The articles razzing the New Deal which have been appearing in The American Mercury over the name of H. L. Mencken have sounded disconcertingly like the compositions supposed to be communicated from the other world by the spirits of Mark Twain, Oscar Wilde and William James. It is therefore reassuring to have authentically from Mencken's living hand this new edition of "The American Language."

This fourth edition of Mr. Mencken's "Inquiry into the Development of English in the United States" is more than twice as long as the "Preliminary Inquiry" of 1919; and it has been filled out, deepened and elaborated until the original tentative essay (of which little survives in this new version) has been brought to maturity as an authoritative work of the very first interest and importance. It is one of the few recent books of which it is really possible to say that it ought to be in every American library and that it ought to be read by every foreigner who wants to understand the United States. What is most remarkable about it is that a work which covers so much ground and which takes up so many philological matters in detail should remain for eight hundred pages so uniformly entertaining. It is rarely that a student of language is also a literary artist: Mr. Mencken has collected his Americanisms and exhibits them in the pages of this book with the loving appreciation of a naturalist mounting butterflies or labeling new fishes. Yet even this image conveys an impression too pedantic. One is made to feel throughout "The American Language" the movement and the pressure of the American people, vindicating their independence, filling out their enormous country, drawing and amalgamating with themselves the peoples of older nations, stamping that older world itself with their speech. We hear their voices, changing in intonation, creating a new vocabulary, breaking the language in to a new syntax–from the accents of Noah Webster acridly carrying though the Revolution against England in the realm of English spelling and pronunciation, to those of the latest arrivals in the back streets of the "foreign" sections of cities, where old tongues lose their primitive inflections under the attrition of the pebbles of the easy new speech, yet, in deliquescing (to change the figure), shoot their particles into the atmosphere around.

It is interesting to note certain important differences between this last edition of "The American Language" and the earlier ones. Seventeen years ago, Mr. Mencken was doubtful as to whether American usage would come eventually to dominate English or whether the two dialects would simply drift apart. But today he seems to have no doubt that English is destined "to become, on some not too remote tomorrow, a kind of dialect of American, just as the language spoken by the American was once a dialect of English." The first edition ended by venturing the following prophecy:

> Given the poet, there may suddenly come a day when our *theirns* and *would'a hads* will take on the barbaric stateliness of the peasant locutions of old Maurya in "Riders to the Sea." They seem grotesque and absurd today because the folks who use them seem grotesque and absurd. But that is too facile logic and under it is a false assumption. In all human beings, if only understanding be brought to the business, dignity will be found, and that dignity cannot fail to reveal itself, soon or late, in the words and phrases with which they make known their high hopes and aspirations and cry out against the intolerable meaninglessness of life.

That passage has now been omitted. The prophecy is already coming true. Since 1919 we have had Sinclair Lewis and O'Neill, Sherwood Anderson and Carl Sandburg, Hemingway and Dos Passos, Ring Lardner and Mencken himself.

And looking back today we can see that the first edition of "The American Language" marked a stage in the development of our literature. It marked the moment when the living tide of American had mounted so high along the sands of "correct English" that it became necessary to make some formal recognition of it—the moment when American writers were finally to take flight from the old tree and to trust for the first time to their own dialect. Six years later, in 1925, the review American Speech was started, and Sir William Craigie, one of the compilers of the big Oxford dictionary, sailed for the United States to begin work on a dictionary of American. To many readers of Mencken's first edition, the chapter on the syntax of "the common speech," in which he boldly seized the core of the subject, seemed either frivolous or shocking. Today it carries weight; we are not so sure of the grammar of the future. Looking back, we

must give Mencken credit for one of the really valuable services performed in our own day by American criticism for American writing. For the period of literary activity which reached its height just after the War, two critics of importance stand out: Mencken and Van Wyck Brooks. Brooks exposed the negative aspects of our literary tradition and urged us to get away from our governesses. Mencken showed the positive value of our vulgar heritage; and he did more than anyone else in his field to bring about that "coming of age" for which Brooks had sounded the hour. The publication of Mencken's "Book of Prefaces" in 1917, with its remarkable essay on Dreiser and its assault on "Puritanism as a Literary Force," was a cardinal event for the new American literature. Mencken did not precisely discover Dreiser, but he was able to focus him clearly for the first time as a figure of dignity and distinction, because he appreciated and made us taste the Americanism of Dreiser as Americanism, without attempting to write him down for not being something other than American. This *positive* treatment of Dreiser—so different from the negative attitude with which even sympathetic critics had in the past approached American writers like Mark Twain, was really a weight that tipped the scales. And the appearance of "The American Language" gave Mencken's position a scholarly base which it was not easy for the academically minded to dispose of. [. . .]

In an appendix to the second edition (1921) Mencken put theory into practice, inventing and also quoting "Specimens of the American Vulgate." They show what he meant by "American" at its most fundamental level and how he was both amused and appalled by it (excerpt from "The Declaration of Independence in American," pp. 388–389).

[The following is my own translation, but I have had the aid of suggestions from various other scholars. It must be obvious that more than one section of the original is now quite unintelligible to the average American of the sort using the Common Speech. What would he make, for example, of such a sentence as this one: "He has called together legislative bodies at places unusual, uncomfortable, and distant from the depository of their public records, for the sole purpose of fatiguing them into compliance with his measures"? Or of this: "He has refused for a long time, after such dissolutions, to cause others to be elected, whereby the legislative powers, incapable of annihilation, have returned to the people at large for their exercise." Such Johnsonian periods are quite beyond his comprehension, and no doubt the fact is at least partly to blame for the neglect upon which the Declaration has fallen in recent years. When, during the Wilson-Palmer saturnalia of oppressions, specialists in liberty began protesting that the

Declaration plainly gave the people the right to alter the government under which they lived and even to abolish it altogether, they encountered the utmost incredulity. On more than one occasion, in fact, such an exegete was tarred and feathered by the shocked members of the American Legion, even after the Declaration had been read to them. What ailed them was that they could not understand its eighteenth century English. I make the suggestion that its circulation among such patriotic men, translated into the language they use every day, would serve to prevent, or, at all events, to diminish that sort of terrorism.]

When things get so balled up that the people of a country have to cut loose from some other country, and go it on their own hook, without asking no permission from nobody, excepting maybe God Almighty, then they ought to let everybody know why they done it, so that everybody can see they are on the level, and not trying to put nothing over on nobody.

All we got to say on this proposition is this: first, you and me is as good as anybody else, and maybe a damn sight better; second, nobody ain't got no right to take away none of our rights; third, every man has got a right to live, to come and go as he pleases, and to have a good time however he likes, so long as he don't interfere with nobody else. That any government that don't give a man these rights ain't worth a damn; also, people ought to choose the kind of government they want themselves, and nobody else ought to have no say in the matter. That whenever any government don't do this, then the people have got a right to can it and put in one that will take care of their interests. Of course, that don't mean having a revolution every day like them South American coons and yellow-bellies and Bolsheviki, or every time some job-holder does something he ain't got no business to do. It is better to stand a little graft, etc., than to have revolutions all the time, like them coons and Bolsheviki, and any man that wasn't a anarchist or one of them I. W. W.'s would say the same. But when things get so bad that a man ain't hardly got no rights at all no more, but you might almost call him a slave, then everybody ought to get together and throw the grafters out, and put in new ones who won't carry on so high and steal so much, and then watch them. This is the proposition the people of the Colonies is up against, and they have got tired of it, and won't stand it no more. The administration of the present King, George III, has been rotten from the start, and when anybody kicked about it he always tried to get away with it by strong-arm work. Here is some of the rough stuff he has pulled: [. . .]

Ring Lardner, who contributed specimens of the argot of baseball players and actors for an appendix to the second edition of The American Language

Ring Lardner contributed to the appendix specimens of the argot of baseball players and actors. Mencken regarded Lardner as the author who was most successful in using common American speech. A footnote in the fourth edition includes a tribute (pp. 425–426).

Lardner died on Sept. 25, 1933, at the early age of 48. My own debt to him was very large. The first edition of the present work, published in 1919, brought me into contact with him, and for the second edition, published in 1921, he prepared two amusing specimens of the common speech in action. At that time, and almost until his death, he made penetrating and valuable suggestions. His ear for the minor peculiarities of vulgar American was extraordinarily keen. Once, sitting with him, I used the word *feller.* "Where and when," he demanded, "did you ever hear anyone say *feller?*" I had to admit, on reflection, that the true form was *fella,* though it is almost always written *feller* by authors. But never by Lardner. So far as I can make out, there is not

The writer Anita Loos, a contributor to Supplement II *of* The American Language. *Mencken wrote to her: "The Bavarian costume is superb. It makes me yodel."*

a single error in the whole canon of his writings. His first book of stories, You Know Me, Al, was published in 1915. He had many imitators, notably Edward Streeter, author of Dere Mable; New York, 1918; H. C. Witwer, who published more than a dozen books between 1918 and his death in 1929; and Will Rogers, who contributed a daily dispatch to a syndicate of newspapers, written partly in Standard English but partly in the vulgate, from 1930 to 1935. He also provided inspiration for the writers of popular songs and of captions for comic-strips. See Stabilizing the Language Through Popular Songs, by Sigmund Spaeth, *New Yorker,* July 7, 1934, and The English of the Comic Cartoons, by Helen Trace Tysell, *American Speech,* Feb., 1935. But these disciples never attained to Lardner's virtuosity.

Mencken's connection to Lardner is less surprising than that to Anita Loos, but his rejection of her advances was the inspiration for her Gentlemen Prefer Blondes *(1925). They remained friends for the rest of his life, and her long experience in Hollywood*

enabled her to make contributions such as this one in Supplement II *(1948). Elsewhere in the volume (p. 333, note 1) this student of flapperese was ranked just below Lardner: "He founded a school that has included such sharp observers as Anita Loos and Damon Runyon, but its members would all agree, I am sure, that he was facile princeps" (excerpt from "American Slang," pp. 697–698).*

[. . .] The argot of the movie-lots shows a good many loans from that of the theatre, but it has also produced some picturesque novelties of its own, chiefly having to do with the technical process of picture making. Most of the following specimens, assembled from various sources, were scrutinized and revised by Miss Anita Loos and the late Edgar Selwyn, to whose friendly aid I am much indebted:

Baby. A small spotlight.
Beard, muff, or feather-merchant. An extra with natural whiskers.
Beef. A laborer.
Best boy. The first assistant to a *gaffer,* which see.
Blupe. An unwanted sound on a sound track.

Dust jacket for Loos's novel, with a comment by Mencken

Boom-jockey. A sound man who follows the action with a microphone.

Bottle. A camera lens.

Breakaway. A chair or other object made of Balsa wood, which falls to pieces when one performer uses it to clout another; also, any simulated glass object made of clear sugar for the same purpose.

Bulber. A photographer.

Bungalow. The metal housing of a sound-proof camera.

Butterfly. A disk of gauze used to diffuse light, or a speck on the camera lens.

Canary. An unidentified noise.

Carbon-monkey. The man who renews the carbons in the lights used on a technicolor set. [. . .]

In a footnote in the fourth edition Mencken remarks on one of his own contributions to the American vulgate (p. 288, note 3).

I proposed the use of *bootician* to designate a high-toned big-city bootlegger in the *American Mercury,* April, 1925, p. 450. The term met a crying need, and had considerable success. In March, 1927, the San José *Mercury-Herald* said:

"Our bootleggers are now calling themselves *booticians.* It seems that *bootlegger* has some trace of odium about it, while *bootician* has none." (Reprinted in the Baltimore *Evening Sun,* April 4, 1927.) On July 23, 1931, according to the Associated Press, a man arrested in Chicago, on being asked his profession, answered proudly that he was a *bootician.*

In another footnote in the fourth edition Mencken modestly objects to his inclusion in a 1933 list compiled by W. J. Funk of Funk and Wagnalls. Along with such luminaries as Lardner, Damon Runyon, and Walter Winchell, he was one of "the ten most fecund makers of the American slang then current" (p. 560, note 1).

Mr. Funk added my own name to the list, but this, apparently, was only a fraternal courtesy, for I have never devised anything properly describable as slang, save maybe *booboisie.* This was a deliberate invention. One evening in February, 1922, Ernest Boyd and I were the guests of Harry C. Black at his home in Baltimore. We fell to talking of the paucity of words to describe the victims of the Depression then current, and decided to

Writer Damon Runyon, gossip columnist Walter Winchell, and Sherman Billingsley at Billingsley's Stork Club in New York. In a 1933 list compiled by W. J. Funk of the Funk and Wagnalls publishing firm, Mencken, Runyon, and Winchell were included among the "most fecund makers of the American slang."

remedy it. So we put together a list of about fifty terms, and on Feb. 15 I published it in the Baltimore *Evening Sun.* It included *boobariat, booberati, boobarian, boobomaniac, boobuli* and *booboisie.* Only *booboisie,* which happened to be one of my contributions, caught on. A bit later I added *Homo boobus,* and Boyd, who is learned in the tongues, corrected it to *Homo boobiens.* This also had its day, but its use was confined to the *intelligentsia,* and it was hardly slang. Even *booboisie* lies rather outside the bounds.

For all his affected disdain toward "chalky 'gogues," Mencken became a part of the linguistic establishment as many prominent scholars welcomed his work. Among his learned friends in the professoriat was Louise Pound of the University of Nebraska, who is known to literary historians as a mentor of Willa Cather and the first female president of the Modern Language Association. Mencken describes her contribution to the study of American near the beginning of the fourth edition (excerpt from "The Two Streams of English," in The American Language, *fourth edition, pp. 53–54).*

[. . .] The work of Dr. Pound has been especially productive, for whereas most of the other members of the Dialect Society have confined their investigations to the regional dialects of American, she and her pupils have studied the general speechways of the country.

She took her doctorate at Heidelberg under the distinguished Anglicist, Johannes Hoops, and soon afterward joined the English faculty of the University of Nebraska. Her first contribution to *Dialect Notes* was published in 1905; thereafter, for twenty years, she or her pupils were represented in almost every issue. In 1925, in association with Dr. Kemp Malone of the Johns Hopkins and Dr. Arthur G. Kennedy of Stanford, she founded *American Speech,* becoming its first editor. She continued in that capacity until 1933, when she was succeeded by Dr. William Cabell Greet of Barnard College, Columbia University. *American Speech,* even more than *Dialect Notes,* has encouraged the study of American: its files constitute a rich mine of instructive and often very amusing stuff. But it has got but little more support from American teachers of English than its predecessor. Though its first issues contained many articles addressed to them directly, they refused to be interested, and during its later years its pages have been supplied largely by lay students of the language. During its first five years its subscription list never reached 1500 names, and at the beginning of its sixth year it had but 329 subscribers. When Dr. Pound retired in 1933 it was taken over by the Columbia University Press. Today it continues to be published at a loss, though Dr. Greet and his associates make it a very useful journal. Beginning as a monthly, it is now a quarterly. [. . .]

Mencken with material for his A New Dictionary of Quotations on Historical Principles from Ancient and Modern Sources, *published in 1942 (courtesy of the Enoch Pratt Free Library)*

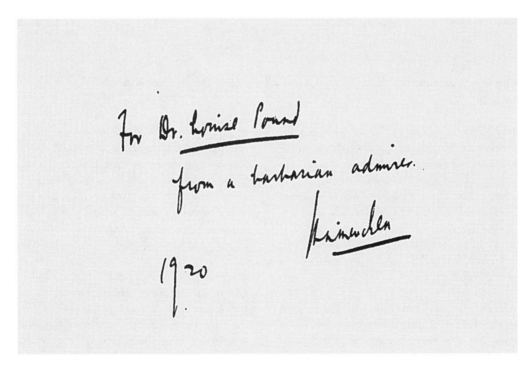

Inscription in the copy of Prejudices: Second Series *presented to Mencken's friend Louise Pound, a linguistics professor at the University of Nebraska (Richard J. Schrader Collection)*

Contents of the First Number of

AMERICAN SPEECH

(October, 1925)

The Americanization of Czech Given Names
By J. B. DUDEK
A painstaking and interesting study in the transmigration of words.

The Misuse of Medical Terms
By MORRIS FISHBEIN
How the layman slips up; slang in medical usage; the vagueness of many terms in common use. Dr. Fishbein is editor of the Journal of the American Medical Association.

A Linguistic Patriot
By KEMP MALONE
A study of Noah Webster and his first dictionary; Webster's trend toward distinctively American orthography.

A Ramble in the Garden of Words
By FRANK H. VIZETELLY
Some of the romance in the making of a great dictionary. Dr. Vizetelly is the editor-in-chief of the New Standard.

Trouper Talk
By GRETCHEN LEE
A delightful discussion of the patois behind the scenes in the vaudeville theater.

Irradiation of Certain Suffixes
By E. C. HILLS
A study of the sundry progeny of "cafeteria;" and of words formed from the suffixes "ery" and "orium."

Speech Tunes and the Alphabet
By ROBERT S. GILL
The inner nature of the famous (or infamous) goldfish cryptogram.

The Kraze for "K"
By LOUISE POUND
Activities of the petted favorite of the advertising man and propagandist; the kurious kraving for k in klever koinages.

Pudding-Time
By OLIVER F. EMERSON
A lexical note on an American use of the word.

Notes:
    Dr. Craigie and the dictionary of American English
    Spoken English in America
    Simplified Spelling in Russia
    Exclamations in American Speech

Book Reviews
Contributor's Column
    Curious and Humorous Notes from Everywhere

H. L. Mencken, critic and editor, in the September issue of THE AMERICAN MERCURY, says:

"Here, I believe, the American dialect shows far more bounce and vigor than the English of England. It rises to new situations with finer zest; it is immensely more resilient and picturesque. The news that Dr. Louise Pound, of the University of Nebraska, has set up a new journal, AMERICAN SPEECH, for its study is excellent indeed. Dr. Pound, trained at Heidelberg under Johannes Hoops, is one of the most competent philologians in America, but her learning is anything but stodgy. She and her pupils have carried on almost the only serious study of current American that has ever been attempted. Now she has the aid of Dr. Kemp Malone, of the Johns Hopkins, and of other scholars, ordained and lay. The material is endless and ever so tempting. AMERICAN SPEECH should quickly atone for the long neglect of the national vulgate by the great majority of American philologists."

Brochure, with encomium by Mencken, for a new journal edited by Louise Pound (courtesy of the Enoch Pratt Free Library)

In the last year of Mencken's working life fifty-five leading scholars collaborated on Literary History of the United States. *He was one of them, a natural choice for the chapter on the American language. In another chapter of this standard work, which went through three more editions, Robert E. Spiller offers an assessment of Mencken's great book that held up for the remainder of the century (excerpt from "The Battle of the Books," in volume 2 of* Literary History of the United States, *edited by Robert E. Spiller, Willard Thorp, Thomas H. Johnson, and Henry Seidel Canby [New York: Macmillan, 1948], p. 1145).*

[. . .] Mencken's essays may fade with time except for his occasional flashes of insight into the work of his contemporaries, but *The American Language* (1919), with its four revisions and its two supplements, will stand. Fortunately the partial suspension of free speech when the United States entered the First World War in 1917 turned his attention from his column on contemporary issues in the Baltimore *Evening Sun* and allowed him time to work on his long absorbing interest in American speech. For this work he combined the instinct of the scholar with the quick wit and shrewd insight of the journalist. The result was a book that, like the *Leaves of Grass,* grew by accretion and revision more in the manner of a living organism than of a card index. In itself a gigantic work of literature, it has given the American people their language as Emerson and Whitman gave them their literature by cutting the umbilical cord. Mencken does not deny the English, and behind that the Indo-Teutonic, origins of that language. He merely denies the authority of the historical scholar to legislate for the present as well as the past. By that simple device he has given new life to scholarship in one field of major importance. This is his final reconciliation with the "professors," some of whom like T. R. Lounsbury had been themselves working for the same ends by less sensational methods, but they came to him with the white flag. They found him at the old address on Hollins Street. [. . .]

Reprinted from
AMERICAN SPEECH
April, 1946

BULLETIN ON 'HON.'

H. L. MENCKEN
Baltimore, Maryland

WHEN, in 1937, the Hon. Jerry Voorhis, a new congressman from California, instructed the reporters for the *Congesssional Record* to cease and desist from describing him as *Hon.* in the Appendix thereof, they bucked with great stubbornness, and it was not until nearly three years later, on October 28, 1940, that he managed to exhort and threaten them into acquiescence. Why they bucked I do not know precisely, and the hon. gentleman tells me that he is somewhat uncertain himself, but I suspect that it was simply because Washington functionaries always fight to the death for any right or franchise, however irrational, that they have ever enjoyed. Once he had beaten them laboriously to their knees, Mr. Voorhis began hunting with fond hopes for recruits to his crusade, but during the years that have since rolled by he has roped only one, to wit, the Hon. Clare E. Hoffman of Michigan. It might be supposed that the lady members of the House—or, as its ground rules make them, the *gentlewomen*—would flock to Mr. Voorhis's flag, for *Hon.* in front of a female name still seems a bit incongruous to Americans, but not one of them has ever signed up. Indeed, all these stateswomen wallow and glory in the honorific, and sport it almost daily in the Appendix to the *Record,* notably the Hon. Clare Boothe Luce of Connecticut, the only congresswoman who may be described plausibly as both cerebral and beautiful, and the Hon. Mary T. Norton of New Jersey. La Norton, not contented with the frequent *Honing* she gets from the *Record's* reporters, once actually spoke of herself as 'I, *Hon.* Mary T. Norton' in a solemn House document.[1] The ex-*Hon.* Mr. Hoffman, it should be noted, is he, despite the fact that he and the Hon. Mrs. Luce bear the same given name.

It is hard to make out the rules whereby non-members quoted so

---

1. *Congressional Record,* May 6, 1938, p. 8467. All references hereafter, unless otherwise ascribed, will be to the *Record.* The presence of *A* before a page number indicates that the quotation is from the Appendix, a catchall in which members print extramural speeches by themselves and others, and a great assortment of other documents, including sentimental doggerel.

First page of an offprint of an article by Mencken from Pound's journal

The Sage of Baltimore: A Local, Ethnic,
and Individualist Voice

Mencken frequently celebrated the city of his birth, and he favored it over New York, where The Smart Set, The American Mercury, *and Alfred A. Knopf's books were edited and published. Though his work was nationally syndicated, his journalistic anchor was the* Baltimore Sun. *His audience always knew that the distinctive attitude that irritated or amused them was owed directly to Mencken's being a German-American libertarian from Baltimore—they always knew it because he kept such facts in the forefront, even when ethnic bias, shifts in the political winds, and geographical parochialism were marshaled against him. Van Wyck Brooks explains the importance of setting and heritage for Mencken's critical point of view, biases, limitations, and push for a culturally diverse American literature (excerpts from "Mencken in Baltimore," in Brooks,* The Confident Years: 1885–1915 *[New York: Dutton, 1952], pp. 455, 458–459, 471–472).*

In Gertrude Stein's Baltimore, where Henry L. Mencken was a newspaperman, few readers had ever heard of the story *Melanctha* or those other stories about Lena and Anna, the German servant-girls who had also lived in the city where Poe lay buried. In fact, few readers anywhere knew Gertrude Stein in 1910, or Veblen, or Ellen Glasgow, or Theodore Dreiser. The reigning American talents in fiction were Winston Churchill, Booth Tarkington, Richard Harding Davis and James Lane Allen, and most of the authors, already at work and emerging one by one, who interested readers later were still obscure. The playwrights of whom one heard were Augustus Thomas and Clyde Fitch, while the splenetic Paul Elmer More spoke in a measure for a circle of critics who were generally indifferent or hostile to the march of mind. On a lower level but still esteemed by a legion of popularizers, Hamilton Wright Mabie discussed "great books" and "culture,"–the last attenuation of the Anglo-American Goethean line by way of Emerson, Arnold and James Russell Lowell. This essayist perfectly fulfilled Leo Stein's characterization of the writing that is "like the running of water down hill," for, possessing no tension whatsoever, it followed the grooves of popular thought, purveying an easy sweetness and an easier light. [. . .]

The intersection of Charles and German Streets in Baltimore, circa 1890. German Street became Redwood during the anti-German hysteria of World War I (From Illustrated Baltimore: The Monumental City *[New York: American Publishing & Engraving Co., 1890]).*

Now Mencken had inherited, as he remarked, a "bias against the rabble" in his almost exclusively German Baltimore childhood, as the son of a German cigar-manufacturer who had married a German-American wife and who usually took him on Sundays to German beer-gardens. The family barber was a German too and so was the family farm-hand when the Menckens spent sufficient summers in the country to convince the boy that city life was "better," and Mencken had gone to a German school where they sang German *volkslieder* and the "pure American children" were regarded as "dunces." If Mencken was later inclined to regard most grown-up Americans as dunces too,–especially the "inferior" Anglo-Saxons *[(Footnote)* "Whenever the Anglo Saxon, whether of the English or of the American variety, comes into sharp conflict with men of other stocks, he tends to be worsted. . . . That this inferiority is real must be obvious to any impartial observer."– Mencken, *Prejudices: Fourth Series (The American Tradition)]*–it was partly because of these impressions that he gathered as a boy, impressions that could scarcely have been dispelled when he briefly attended a Sunday school kept by the author of *What a Young Man Ought to Know.* He acquired early the bourgeois traits that made him a good citizen, methodical, the most orderly of mortals, never late for trains, who never failed to appear in time for dinner, one who respected punctuality and solvency in others and who spent his life in one house in Baltimore. People lost in New York, he said, the sense of "abiding relationships" and the lares and penates that one found in this half-Southern city; and he liked what he described as the Baltimore "tradition of sound and comfortable living." Expressed in terms of a prosperous German cigar-manufacturer's house, this presupposed a contempt for the poor, for the shiftless and for workingmen who did not know their place, the peculiarly German contempt indeed that filled the mind of Nietzsche who regarded them as mere draught-animals to be used as tools. That Mencken should have been drawn to Nietzsche and his notion of the slave-proletariat,–a notion that was alien to Americans,–was preordained, as much as that he should have been drawn to Huneker if only as a lover of music who sketched for the piano ten or more sonatas. Mencken was a precocious composer of marches and waltzes. He was convinced, as a boy, for the rest, that life was essentially meaningless and that progress, democracy and religion were childish illusions, well summed up in the hullabaloo that amused him on street-corners when he stopped, looked and listened to the Salvation Army. Employed for a while in his father's factory, he went the rounds of cafés and saloons, taking orders for cigars and developing an epicure's palate; then, entering a newspaper-office, he became at eighteen a police reporter and was soon reviewing the theatre and music as well. He picked up the jargon and ways of thought of the city-room. When he came to compile his great work *The American Language,* Mencken was to know whereof he spoke. [. . .]

With all his reactionary cynicism, Mencken was a liberator who opened paths for writers and made straight their way by turning many of their obstacles into laughing-stocks, but his campaign against democracy lost any glamour it might have had when Hitler murdered seven million Poles and Jews. While much that Mencken said was true, the inevitable answer was that all other forms of government had proved to be

Mencken's house at 1524 Hollins Street

worse, that democracy, as Whitman put it, was the only safe system; and, when virtually every thinking German was only too happy to escape to America, Mencken's assaults on the country lost much of their force. Time broke the lance of the "literary uhlan," as the German-American societies had called him, and the critic who had said, "Most of the men I respect are foreigners," ceased to be a spokesman for the "mongrel and inferior" Yankees. It was almost forgotten that he had performed a major work of criticism in giving the *coup de grâce* to the colonial tradition, while, by fully recognizing the new interracial point of view, he contributed to the nationalizing of American letters. More than anyone else perhaps, Mencken broke the way for writers who were descended from "foreign" stocks and who were not yet assured of their place in the sun, and it was

Mencken in his office on the third floor of 1524 Hollins Street, circa 1928 (courtesy of the Enoch Pratt Free Library)

he who signalized Chicago as a literary centre and praised the new writers who used the "American language." Howells had long since welcomed George Ade and many another, but Mencken, who hailed Theodore Dreiser, was foremost in hailing Ring Lardner and praising with discrimination writers of his type. [*(Footnote)* "What amused Mark [Twain] most profoundly was precisely whatever was most worthy of sober admiration—sound art, good manners, the aristocratic ideal—and he was typical of his time. The satirists of the present age, although they may be less accomplished workmen, are at all events more civilized men. What they make fun of is not what is dignified, or noble, or beautiful, but what is shoddy, and ignoble, and ugly."–Mencken, *Prejudices: Fourth Series.*]

As for the question of colonialism,–still a live issue in 1920 [*(Footnote)* "The American social pusher keeps his eye on Mayfair; the American literatus dreams of recognition by the London weeklies; the American don is lifted to bliss by the imprimatur of Oxford or Cambridge; even the American statesman knows how to cringe to Downing Street."–Mencken, *Prejudices: Second Series* (1920).]–this was soon to be settled, thanks partly to him; and perhaps it could have been settled only by a critic of recent immigrant stock whose mind was entirely detached from the English tradition. Mencken's solution of the question was in certain ways

unfortunate precisely because of this and all it implied, but he performed an invaluable work in helping to establish the interracial American literature of the future. [. . .]

Brooks drew some of his phrases from an essay Mencken published in 1926, one of several such encomia (excerpts from "On Living in Baltimore," in Prejudices: Fifth Series, *pp. 237–238, 240–243).*

Some time ago, writing in an eminent Baltimore newspaper upon the Baltimore of my boyhood, I permitted myself an eloquent passage upon its charm, and let fall the doctrine that nearly all of that charm had vanished. Mere rhetoric, I greatly fear. The old charm, in truth, still survives in the town, despite the frantic efforts of the boosters and boomers who, in late years, have replaced all its ancient cobblestones with asphalt, and bedizened it with Great White Ways and suburban boulevards, and surrounded it with stinking steel plants and oil refineries, and increased its population from 400,000 to 800,000. I am never more conscious of the fact than when I return to it from New York. Behind me lies the greatest city of the modern world, with more money in it than all Europe and more clowns and harlots than all Asia, and yet it has no more charm than a

This text of my honorary address at the Polytechnic commencement, 1896, was founded out on the typewriter in my father's office

See p. 70

1

Ladies and Gentlemen:--

A ~~system~~ *course* of technical instruction now forms one of the most important departments of education in all civilized countries. The law, medicine and the clergy are no longer the only learned professions, for during the century which is about to close the natural sciences of steam-engineering and electricity have been born, and chemistry, phoenix-like, has risen from the ashes of its half-mythical, half-real progenitor--alchemy.

Each, in it's own field, is more useful to mankind than the other two; and each, although known to a greater or less extent to the ancients, has, in the last decade, grown from an experimental curiosity to such vast proportions that an estimate of it's value would, at best, be but approximate.

Electricity is undoubtedly the science of the future, which, in time, will revolutionize commerce and manufactures and effect an entire change in our social fabric. The noiseless motor car will soon supercede the puffing locomotive, just as the brilliant arc and incandescent lights have already replaced the flickering gas. Manual exertion, to all except the poorest, will become unnecessary and the race will physically degenerate. Distance has already been annihilated by the telegraph, and elecrical air-ships promise to become formidable rivals of the craft that plough the seas. Yet, although the locomotive will soon be a thing of the past, steam will always be as useful as it is today, because each advance in electrical science causes a corresponding necessity for more power, and the only practical method of producing this which is known at present is by employing the steam engine.

As the latter becomes more and more common in a nation that nation moves nearer and nearer toward perfect civilization. War and internal strife give way to the arts of peace and Prosperity and Affluence,

Page from the typescript for Mencken's high-school graduation address, delivered in 1896 (courtesy of the Enoch Pratt Free Library)

PREJUDICES
FIRST SERIES
BY H. L. MENCKEN

A COLLECTION of brief, but penetrating essays. While the subjects chosen deal mainly with books or authors, the general treatment is far from being either formal or stilted. The subjects range from "Arnold Bennett" to "The Genealogy of Etiquette," and from "The Late Mr. Wells" to "The Ulster Polonius."
(Mr. G. B. Shaw.)

Published by JONATHAN CAPE London

Dust jacket for the British edition (1921) of Mencken's essay collection, with a statement from George Bernard Shaw directed to an English audience

circus lot or a second-rate hotel. It can't show a single genuinely distinguished street. It hasn't a single park that is more lovely than a cemetery lot. It is without manner as it is without manners. Escaping from it to so ancient and solid a town as Baltimore is like coming out of a football crowd into quiet communion with a fair one who is also amiable, and has the gift of consolation for hard-beset and despairing men.

I have confessed to rhetoric, but I surely do not indulge in it here. For twenty-five years I have resisted a constant temptation to move to New York, and I resist it more easily to-day than I did when it began. I am, perhaps the most arduous commuter ever heard of, even in that Babylon of commuters. My office is on Manhattan Island and has been there since 1914; yet I live, vote and have my being in Baltimore, and go back there the instant my job allows. If my desk bangs at 3 P.M. I leap for the 3.25 train. Four long hours in the Pullman follow, but the first is the worst. My back, at all events, is toward New York! Behind lies a place fit only for the gross business of getting money; ahead is a place made for enjoying it. [. . .]

This concept of the home cannot survive the mode of life that prevails in New York. I have seen it go to pieces under my eyes in the houses of my own friends. The intense crowding in the town, and the restlessness and unhappiness that go with it, make it almost impossible for anyone to accumulate the materials of a home—the trivial, fortuitous and often grotesque things that gather around a family, as glories and debts gather around a state. The New Yorker lacks the room to house them; he thus learns to live without them. In the end he is a stranger in the house he lives in. More and more, it tends to be no more than Job No. 16432b from this or that decorator's studio. I know one New Yorker, a man of considerable means, who moves every three years. Every time he moves his wife sells the entire contents of the apartment she is leaving, and employs a decorator to outfit the new one. To me, at all events, such a mode of living would be unendurable. The charm of getting home, as I see it, is the charm of getting back to what is inextricably my own—to things familiar and long loved, to things that belong to me alone and none other. I have lived in one house in Baltimore for nearly forty-five years. It has changed in that time, as I have—but somehow it still remains the same. No conceivable decorator's masterpiece could give me the same ease. It is as much a part of me as my two hands. If I had to leave it I'd be as certainly crippled as if I lost a leg.

I believe that this feeling for the hearth, for the immemorial lares and penates, is infinitely stronger in Baltimore than in New York—that it has better survived there, indeed, than in any other large city of America—and that its persistence accounts for the superior charm of the town. There are, of course, thousands of Baltimoreans in flats—but I know of none to whom a flat seems more than a make-shift, a substitute, a necessary and temporary evil. They are all planning to get out, to find house-room in one of the new suburbs, to resume living in a home. What they see about them is too painfully not theirs. The New Yorker has simply lost that discontent. He is a vagabond. His notions of the agreeable become those of a vaudeville actor. He takes on the shallowness and unpleasantness of any other homeless man. He is highly sophisticated, and inordinately trashy. The fact no doubt explains the lack of charm that one finds in his town; the fact that the normal man of Baltimore is almost his exact antithesis explains the charm that is there. Human relations, in such a place, tend to assume a solid permanence. A man's circle of friends becomes a sort of extension of his family circle. His contacts are with men and women who are rooted as he is. They are not moving all the time, and so they are not changing their friends all the time. Thus abiding relationships tend to be built up, and when fortune brings unexpected changes, they survive those changes. The men I know and esteem in Baltimore are, on the whole, men I have known and esteemed a long while; even those who have come into my ken relatively lately seem likely to last. But of the men I knew best when I first began going to New York, twenty-five years ago, not one is a friend to-day. Of those I knew best ten years ago, not six are friends. The rest have got lost in the riot, and the friends of to-day, I sometimes fear, will get lost in the same way.

In human relationships that are so casual there is seldom any satisfaction. It is our fellows who make life endurable to us, and give it a purpose and a meaning; if our contacts with them are light and frivolous there is something lacking, and it is something of the very first importance. What I contend is that in Baltimore, under a slow-moving and cautious social organization, touched by the Southern sun, such contacts are more enduring than elsewhere, and that life in consequence is more agreeable. Of the external embellishments of life there is a plenty there—as great a supply, indeed, to any rational taste, as in New York itself. But there is also something much better: a tradition of sound and comfortable living. A Baltimorean is not merely John Doe, an isolated individual of *Homo sapiens,* exactly like every other John Doe. He is John Doe *of* a certain place—of Baltimore, of a definite *house* in Baltimore. It is not by accident that all the peoples of Europe, very early in their history, distinguished their best men by adding *of* this or that place to their names.

Mencken had only to be out of his natural habitat to be spotted for the arch-American that he was. Modern London comes off no better than New York in the encounter Beverley Nichols records (excerpt from "Two Plain and One Coloured," in Nichols, 25: Being a Young Man's Candid Recollections of His Elders and Betters *[New York: Doran, 1926], pp. 174–177).*

Quite the most amusing person I met at about this time was H. L. Mencken, whose books *Prejudices* so perfectly describe the particular standpoint in art which he has adopted. We met, as far as I remember, at some party or other at the Café Royal, but as it was impossible to talk in that establishment, under the distracting influence of Epsteins, Augustus Johns, Laverys and successive glasses of absinthe, we arranged to meet the next morning at his hotel. "And then I'll give you something that'll wake you up."

He did. And it did. When I called on him he was tramping backwards and forwards in his rooms, making a strange spluttering noise with his lips that suggested a large and angry bird stalking round its cage.

After refusing the inevitable double whisky which Americans apparently seem to consider an hourly necessity for Englishmen, I asked him what was the matter.

"Matter?" Again the spluttering noise, this time a little louder. "I've just been looking at London. What the devil are you doing to it? Do you want to make it another New York? A filthy sky-scraper in the Strand, half the most exquisite buildings being scrapped and thrown on the muck heap, and obscene advertising signs that are as bad as anything we've got on Broadway."

Splutter, splutter, splutter.

I thought it would be a good idea to ask him what he would do if he were suddenly given despotic powers over the reconstruction of London.

"The first thing I'd do," he said, lighting a cigar with a sort of aggressive courage that reminded one of firing a torpedo, "would be to hang every mother's son of an architect who was polluting one of the world's best cities. And when they were dangling high and dry, I'd go out with a packet of dynamite, blow up all the monstrosities in Regent Street, get hold of Nash's old plans, and slave-drive a few thousand British navvies until we'd got the thing back as it used to be—superb crescent, full of grace and beauty."

Splutter, splutter, splutter.

He resumed his perambulation round the room. "Then I'd invent a whole lot of brand-new tortures for any hulking Philistine of a manufacturer who started writing his blasted name on God's sky at night. Piccadilly Circus nowadays is an eyesore. It's bad enough in Broadway. But you can at least say there that the vast scale on which the signs are put up, the enormous size of the whole thing, does at least leave a certain feeling of awe on one's mind. Disgust too, but at least, *big.* Whereas in Piccadilly you've got a lot of footling little electric squares and circles, a yellow baby spitting fire, an undersized motor squiggling its wheels, a God-forsaken bottle pouring red liquid into a glass so damned small that it wouldn't make me tight if I drank out of it all night. Take 'em away!" (Splutter, splutter.) "Take 'em away! You're killing London!"

I think I have got in most of his adjectives. His conversation was also scattered with a good many examples of that word which Bernard Shaw employed with such effect in Pygmalion. These I have omitted.

He went on for some time in this strain, until I felt it time to point out to him that at least we were putting up a few new buildings that were quite worthy to stand by the old ones.

"Show 'em to me!" (Splutter, splutter.) "Take me along to see 'em. I'll stand you drinks for a month if what you say is true."

Display in the window of the Enoch Pratt Free Library, Baltimore, September 1940 (courtesy of the Enoch Pratt Free Library)

"Well, there's the new L.C.C. building on the other side of the Thames. Knott's the architect. One of the biggest buildings of its kind in the world, and one of the most beautiful."

He looked at me despairingly. "Oh, you ought to have been an American if you say a monstrosity like that's beautiful. I looked at it yesterday, and I spat in the Thames to show my contempt of it."

"But the line of it is perfect—the proportions are admirable . . ."

"Perfect rot. For one thing, what on earth induced the fool who built it to stick a hulking great red roof on top of it? All down that side of the Thames is grey. Grey old buildings, peering out of the mist, like veiled faces, tumble-down old ruins, wharfs, docks, bridges, grey, all grey. And then this fool comes along and sticks up a blasted Noah's Ark, covered with pillars and crowned with this futile roof. What's the good of that?"

I told him that if he were a real Londoner, he might not be so angry at the sight of an occasional touch of colour. He might not be so keen on his universal touch of grey if he had to live in it for ever. He might, if he had to cross the Thames day by day, year by year, come to welcome that red roof, sparkling across the grey water, and bringing even into the dullest days a flow of cheerfulness, as of reflected sunshine.

But he would have none of it. The roof should have been grey, and that was an end to the matter. I understood then why he had written three books called *Prejudices*.

None the less, a charming man, who is more American than he would care to think, for all his constant nagging at his own country. I said something vaguely derogatory of a certain section of American opinion, and he was down on me like a shot. I liked him best at that moment. [. . .]

An anonymous writer anticipated this visit and ignored Mencken's campaign to drive a wedge between the two great English-speaking peoples ("The Visit of Mr. Mencken," English Review, 35 [August 1922]: 142–143).

Whether or no the sea-serpent approaches these shores this season, we shall at least find consolation in the arrival of an indubitable portent, Mr. H. L. Mencken. The importance to literary and dramatic

England can hardly be over-estimated, for Mr. Mencken represents a phenomenon which is almost unknown in Europe, though conditions should, on the face of them, make its appearance much more likely:– The Man with the Hammer.

One of the absurd slogans that one sees hanging up in the offices of the less reputable firms in America is:–"Sell your hammer and buy a horn."

This cryptic injunction means that the whole duty of man is to "bring forth butter in a lordly dish" and see whether it will melt in the mouths of his compatriots.

Now Mr. Mencken has not discarded the horn; he has stood resolute and fought for people who had even a spark of genius. He, and he alone, has put America on the literary map. Without his intervention, we might still be standing by the conclusions of "Art in America" which appeared in THE ENGLISH REVIEW in 1912, instead of preparing a series of articles to tell Europe of how the Lord has made those dry bones live.

But Mr. Mencken has not sold his hammer. Practically single-handed, and mostly by means of an organ of a kind which, in Europe, could not possibly play a serious tune, he has made himself universally dreaded by the literary faker, who abounds in America to an extent which is quite unthinkable even in the shoddiest circles of Fleet Street to-day.

From Edgar Allen [sic] Poe, Brann of the Iconoclast, to William Marion Reedy, of The Mirror, America has been rather fortunate in possessing isolated Isaiahs. But of these Mr. Mencken is incomparably the most important. He has made his name dreadful to all literary and dramatic humbugs. His racy, cynical, exhilarating style compels the reader, and his contempt has been only the more deadly because of the good-humoured slang in which he couches it. The extent of his triumph may be gauged by the fact that he is writing in Harper's, the Century, and other former reactionary strongholds. Without declaring that his judgment is always impeccable, we can say that his critical acumen is at least equal to anything that we can show in Europe, and he has exercised his power with a decision and authority which is almost incomprehensible to people accustomed to the compromises of Fleet Street.

It is hardly too much to hope that his visit to Europe may be the beginning of the end of the flabbiness and half-heartedness of English criticism. He is a living witness to the fact that it is not necessary to acquiesce in the shoddy output of our literary linen-drapers any longer.

Mr. Mencken's motto has been: first right, then upright, and then downright.

Our national fear of saying something about an author whom we may possibly meet at dinner the following week has destroyed our national standards of literature, and, despite the Puritans and tradesmen of America, she is actually forging ahead of us because of our lack of independent criticism.

"Consider one fact: the civilisation that kissed Maeterlinck on both cheeks, and Tagore perhaps even more intimately . . . ."

That is typical of his smashing blow; may he lay about him heartily during his visit to Europe!

A later interview, recorded by H. Allen Smith, took place in Baltimore when Mencken was assembling his recollections for The New Yorker *and the* Days *books. His mellowness won him a new audience, but his fundamental outlook had not changed much over the years (excerpts from "Memoirs of an Ex-Columnist," in Smith,* Life in a Putty Knife Factory *[Garden City, N.Y.: Doubleday, Doran, 1943], pp. 171–177).*

[. . .] I found Mencken waiting for me at the offices of the Baltimore *Sun*. It was a steaming day–104 degrees in the shade. I had not seen Mencken in six years. I was startled when he walked into the room–shocked at the swiftness with which age had taken hold of him. He still seemed robust and alert, but age was showing in his face. He was well aware of it too. Several times during our long talk he spoke of the short time he had left.

I have at least one reason for hoping to outlive him. I have been written into his last will and testament. Readers of the Mencken memoirs will recall the story of the great Baltimore fire of 1904. At that time Mencken was city editor of the *Herald* and with the rest of the staff had to flee the newspaper's building when the flames took hold of it. Sometime later he returned to the gutted structure and managed to reach the floor where his desk had been. The desk was now no more than a layer of ashes on the floor but, prodding around in this mess, Mencken found his old copy hook–black and twisted but still intact. That copy hook has been one of his cherished mementos of the old days and, with all the audacity of an autograph nit, I once asked him if I might have it when he is finished with it. By letter he notified me:

> That copy hook will become yours the day I am translated to bliss eternal. I have left orders that my carcass is to be stuffed and deposited in the National Museum at Washington. I had planned to ask the taxidermist to put the copy hook in my hand, but that request is now canceled and you will get it in due course.

We had planned to go out to the Mencken house in Hollins Street, but it was altogether too hot to move around so we settled down in an office there at the *Sun*.

Mencken has written extensively about the three-story brick house, sandwiched in between buildings of the same approximate design, where he has lived almost all his life and where he has always done the major part of his work.

"The neighborhood has been going down steadily," he said. "In the last few years the Okies have been moving in. They are the mountain morons from Appalachia, and most of the old-timers of the neighborhood are moving out as these morons come in. Not me. I've lived in that house since 1883, save for the five years of my marriage. I intend to stay as long as I last. I may not last long, but that's where I intend to finish out my days."

He lives at the house with his bachelor brother, August, an engineer who is about ten years younger than Henry. August looks a good deal like "Harry" and is an author in his own right, having produced a recent book concerned with famous hangings. The brothers keep a couple of household servants and Henry has a secretary—a lady of middle years who comes in mornings, takes dictation, and goes home to write it. Mencken describes her as possessing asbesto [sic] ears.

He's a prodigious worker and his home is a veritable warehouse of raw materials for his labor. His mother never threw away any piece of paper with writing on it, and her literary son, engaged in recent years on autobiographical projects, has had a stupendous cargo of source material to aid him in setting down his reminiscences. It has not been necessary for him to visit the public library or the newspaper morgues to ascertain the price of hominy in 1883. He even dredged up the doctor's bill for his own birth. A certain Dr. Buddenbohn assessed the Menckens ten dollars for fetching Henry Louis on a September Sunday evening in 1880. I contend that was the biggest ten dollars' worth this country ever got.

During the last few years Mencken has been furrowing through these acres of material and writing his autobiography in sections. Thus far three volumes have been finished—*Happy Days, Newspaper Days,* and *Heathen Days,* and any person who can read those books and succeed in disliking their author—well, that person has a hive of maggots for a brain.

There in Baltimore I was interested, chiefly, in the kind of life Mencken is leading these days. He said he's still having fun.

"The chief pleasure I get out of life is my work," he said. "I get no pleasure in games. I hate sports. The one thing I love to do is travel, but a man can't travel any more. I don't want to see South America. I might get down there and get stuck in one of those rattraps. I've been everywhere and I think I know people in every town in America. It becomes a tough proposition for me to go to a town and try to see it and soak it up. People I know in each town want to entertain me and it's hard to get out of such things. What I really like to do is just wander around the streets and look at the morons."

Mencken is still the moving spirit of the Saturday Night Club—a small group of amateur musicians which has been holding weekly meetings since 1905. They gather in a room in a downtown office building and start playing their music at 8:15 P.M. Mencken plays second piano and they usually keep going until ten o'clock, at which time they adjourn to a beer resort for the remainder of the evening.

"I'm the only original member left," he said. "There are no written regulations and no officers. To become a member a man has to meet with unanimous approval. No guests are permitted to wander into our concerts. A member may bring a guest but he's got to be sure of his man and he's responsible for the guest's behavior. A guest is not permitted to criticize the music. He can sit and listen to it, but he can't say he likes it or dislikes it. If he says anything at all about it, we throw him the hell out."

Mencken no longer writes regularly for the *Sun,* though he is on the board of directors. He has no office at the newspaper and my meeting with him took place in the office of the publisher, Paul Patterson. Mencken generally rides a trolley car from his home to the *Sun* building. [. . .]

After a couple of hours the time came for me to leave. I had to catch an airline coach at the Lord Baltimore Hotel across the street from the *Sun.* Mencken went with me. In the elevator he spoke almost affectionately with the Negro operator, asked about his health and the health of his family, and said, "I missed you around here the other day. I thought maybe you were in Europe fighting the Huns."

We walked across the street and stood at the entrance to the hotel.

"I'd go in with you while you make the arrangements about the coach," he said, "but maybe you already noticed that the chiropractors of America are having their convention in this hotel. You know how I have handled the chiropractors down through the years. I wouldn't be safe in there. They'd ambush me in thirty seconds if I stepped into that lobby. They'd throw me to the floor and dismantle my spinal column and play marbles with my vertebrae."

So we stood there and talked for about ten more minutes and then he left, swinging briskly up the street, nobody paying him a bit of mind. I stood and watched him. To me he was the greatest man in Baltimore, in Maryland, perhaps even in the United States. Yet there in the heart of Baltimore scores of people passed him without giving him a second glance. He had on a flat straw hat and a dull business suit and there was a black cigar stuck in his face. He didn't look like a great man. He might have been a plumber, taking a day off and heading for a Rita Hayworth movie. He stopped at the corner where the traffic light was against him, and turned around and saw that I had been watching him. He raised his arm and waved good-by, and I tingled all over like a high-school girl being introduced to Victor Mature.

I went into the hotel and up to the transportation desk where I had to wait a few minutes. A Baltimore taxi driver was standing at my elbow. I asked him if he knew H. L. Mencken.

"Sure," he said. "Newspaper guy. His column ain't as popular as it used to be, though. He's again Roosevelt." [. . .]

A distant relative of Mencken's, Johann Burkhard Mencken, published De Charlataneria Eruditorum *in 1715. Based on lectures that Johann Mencken had given at the University of Leipzig, it attacked the frauds of that day. Mencken commissioned a translation of the book, and he wrote a preface for it. The book was both an act of piety to his relative and a last great assertion of his cultural affinity with the Germany he had defended for so long (excerpt from "Editor's Preface," in* Johann Burkhard Mencken, The Charlatanry of the Learned, *translated by Francis E. Litz [New York & London: Knopf, 1937], pp. 44–45).*

[. . .] The Napoleonic wars, which ended the line of Mencken scholars at Leipzig, Halle, Helmstedt and Wittenberg, also seem to have wiped out the book. It belonged, indeed, to an era that was then definitely closing; it looked back to the revolutionary Seventeenth Century, not forward to the revolutionary Nineteenth, and it was, in its small way, one of the monuments marking the last stage of the Renaissance. I was forty years old before I ever read it, or any other of Mencken's writings. I may be pardoned, I hope, for recording that it astonished me, and no little delighted me, to find that a man of my name, nearly two hundred years in his grave, had devoted himself so heartily to an enterprise that had engaged me day in and day out in a far country–the tracking down of quacks of all sorts, and the appreciative exhibition of their multifarious tricks to catch coneys. Nor was my delight lessened when I noted that the quacks he had thus belabored in Eighteenth Century Europe were still flourishing mightily in

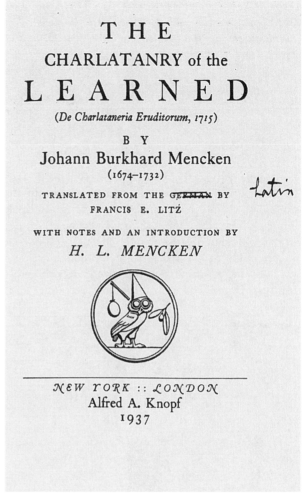

Title page, with correction by Mencken, of a book by his distant relative (courtesy of the Enoch Pratt Free Library)

Twentieth Century America, along with many reinforcements that he had never dreamed of. Old Johann was not my ancestor; I am descended from his father's cousin, Lüder (1658–1726), professor of law at Leipzig, and *Viva Lex* (The Living Law-Book). But if the two were alive today I suspect that I'd greatly prefer the company of Johann to that of Lüder, so my editing of Dr. Litz's translation of "De Charlataneria Eruditorum" takes on a sort of filial character, and will be granted the indulgence, perhaps, that goes therewith. [. . .]

Mencken's correspondence with his friend and early publisher Philip Goodman includes an extemporized comic history of a German-Jewish world that was largely imaginary. The collection was published in 1996 as Do You Remember? *In this letter Mencken refers to the manuscript for his* In Defense of Women, *published on 17 September 1918;*

many fictional persons; and a new play, The Tongue of the World, *by Goodman. Goodman's reply is missing from the correspondence (transcription of a letter at the Enoch Pratt Free Library, Baltimore).*

Baltimore, Md.
February 6th (1918)

Dear Goodman:

You will get the woman book, such as it is, by March 15. I am glad of the chance to rewrite and embellish Opus XV. I'll make it a really good book. Your selling plans inflame me. But a man trained under old man Bornschein in the carpet business surely ought to know how to make them buy.

A disgusting detail has been overlooked. I always put publishers in the press, and squeeze 25 free copies out of them, instead of the usual 10. This is my sole ganovry. As for royalties and so on, I trust to Kent J. Goldstein, my lawyer. He can always prove that something is due me. You will become well acquainted with his young process-server, I. Mortimer Hartogensis.

Yes, I have heard the story of the Buchsbaum-Gundelfinger combat, but always from prejudiced parties. Anton Roesser, the anti-Semite, was always talking about it at the Turnverein Vorwärts. Old Buchsbaum himself never mentioned it in my hearing. I have an open mind. Let me hear the kosher version.

My congratulations. I'll probably be in New York on March 3rd, and shall be present at the ringside. I hope the piece is as good as "Alone in London".

In Xt.

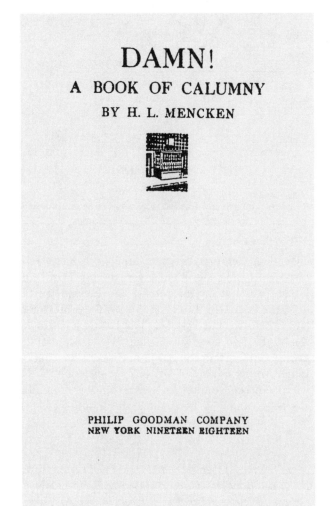

Title page for the first of Mencken's books to be published by Goodman

The basis of Mencken's sympathy for Germany may be seen in an essay on Nietzsche that he published in The Atlantic Monthly *in November 1914. He had earlier written* The Philosophy of Nietzsche *(1908)–the first book in English on the philosopher–and* The Gist of Nietzsche *(1910); later, he translated Nietzsche's* The Antichrist *(1920). This piece is a challenge to the Anglophile establishment in one of its own organs. He always argued that that establishment propagandized America into World War I, the horrors of which could not yet be fully imagined when this essay appeared (excerpt from "The Mailed Fist and Its Prophet,"* Atlantic Monthly, *114 [November 1914]: 606–607).*

[. . .] Go through *Thus Spake Zarathustra* from end to end, and you will find that nine tenths of its ideas are essentially German ideas, that they coincide almost exactly with what we have come to know of the new German spirit, just as the ideas of Aristotle were all essentially Greek, and those of Locke essentially English. Even its lingering sneers at the Germans strike at weaknesses which the more thoughtful Germans were themselves beginning to admit, combat, and remedy. It is a riotous affirmation of race-efficiency, a magnificent defiance of destiny, a sublime celebration of ambition.

Not even Wilhelm himself ever voiced a philosophy of vaster assurance. Not even the hot-heads of the mess-table, drinking uproariously to *der Tag*, ever flung a bolder challenge to the gods. "Thus," shouts Zarathustra, "would I have man and woman: the one fit for warfare, the other fit for giving birth; and both fit for dancing with head and legs"–that is, both lavish of energy, careless of waste, pagan, gargantuan, inordinate. And then, "War and courage have done more great things than charity. Not your pity, but your bravery lifts up those about you. Let the little girlies tell you that 'good' means 'sweet' and 'touching.' I tell you that 'good' means 'brave.' . . . The slave rebels against hardships and calls his rebellion superiority. Let *your* superiority be an *acceptance* of hardships. . . . *Let your commanding be an obeying.* . . . Propagate yourself *upward.* . . . I do not spare you. . . . Die at the right time. . . . *Be hard!*"

I come to the war: the supreme manifestation of the new Germany, at last the great test of the gospel of strength, of great daring, of efficiency. But here, alas, the business of the expositor must suddenly cease. The streams of parallel ideas coalesce. Germany becomes Nietzsche; Nietzsche becomes Germany. Turn away from all the fruitless debates

DIE AMERIKANISCHE SPRACHE
(DAS ENGLISCH DER VEREINIGTEN STAATEN)

VON

H. L. MENCKEN

DEUTSCHE BEARBEITUNG

VON

HEINRICH SPIES

1927

VERLAG UND DRUCK VON B. G. TEUBNER / LEIPZIG UND BERLIN

Title page for a German translation of The American Language, *one of several of Mencken's works to appear in German*

FRANZ BLEI

❋

DAS GROSSE BESTIARIUM DER MODERNEN LITERATUR

❋

1922

ERNST ROWOHLT VERLAG

BERLIN

Title page for the first book published on the European Continent to mention Mencken

over the responsibility of this man or that, the witless straw-splitting over non-essentials. Go back to Zarathustra: "I do not advise you to compromise and make peace, *but to conquer.* Let your labor be fighting and your peace victory. . . . What is good? All that increases the feeling of power, the will to power, power itself in man. What is bad? All that proceeds from weakness. What is happiness? The feeling that power increases, that resistance is being overcome. . . . Not contentment, but more power! Not peace at any price, but war! Not virtue, but efficiency! . . . The weak and the botched must perish: that is the first principle of our humanity. *And they should be helped to perish!* . . . I am writing for the lords of the earth. . . . You say that a good cause hallows even war? . . . *I tell you that a good war hallows every cause!*"

Barbarous? Ruthless? Unchristian? No doubt. But so is life itself. So is all progress worthy the name. Here at least is honesty to match the barbarity, and, what is more, courage, the willingness to face great hazards, the acceptance of defeat as well as victory. "Ye shall have foes to be hated, but *not* foes to be despised. Ye must be proud of your foes . . . The new Empire has more need of foes than of friends. . . . Nothing has grown more alien to us than that 'peace of the soul' which is the aim of Christianity. . . . And should a great injustice befall you, then do quickly five small ones. A small revenge is better than none at all."

Do we see again those grave, blond warriors of whom Tacitus tells us—who were good to their women, and would not lie, and were terrible in battle? Is the Teuton afoot for new conquests, a new tearing down, a new building up, a new transvaluation of values? And if he is, will he prevail? Or will he be squeezed to death between the two mill-stones of Christianity and Mongol savagery? Let us not assume his downfall too lightly: it will take staggering blows to break him. And let us not be alarmed by his possible triumph. What did Rome ever produce to match the Fifth Symphony?

The critic Stuart P. Sherman, who wrote a scathing review of Mencken's A Book of Prefaces (photograph by Doris Ulman)

America's entry into the war gave Mencken's enemies their chance for personal attacks on his ancestry and patriotism. Stuart P. Sherman's ostensible review of Mencken's recently published A Book of Prefaces *makes sarcastic use of the blurbs on its dust jacket while tarring many others of German (and Jewish) heritage with the same brush ("Beautifying American Literature,"* Nation, *105 [29 November 1917]: 593–594).*

Mr. Mencken is not at all satisfied with life or literature in America, for he is a lover of the beautiful. We have nowadays no beautiful literature in this country, with the possible exception of Mr. Dreiser's novels: nor do we seem in a fair way to produce anything aesthetically gratifying. Probably the root of our difficulty is that, with the exception of Mr. Huneker, Otto Heller, Ludwig Lewisohn, Mr. Untermeyer, G. S. Viereck, the author of "Der Kampf um deutsche Kultur in Amerika," and a few other choice souls, we have no critics who, understanding what beauty is, serenely and purely love it. Devoid of aesthetic sense, our native "Anglo-Saxon" historians cannot even guess what ails our native literature. For a competent historical account of our national anaesthesia one should turn, Mr. Mencken assures us, to a translation, from some foreign tongue—we cannot guess which—by Dr. Leon Kellner.

Thus one readily perceives that Mr. Mencken's introductions to Conrad, Dreiser, and Huneker and his discourse on "Puritanism as a Literary Force" are of the first importance to all listeners for the soft breath and finer spirit of letters.

Though a lover of the beautiful, Mr. Mencken is not a German. He was born in Baltimore, September 12, 1880. That fact should silence the silly people who have suggested that he and Dreiser are secret agents of the Wilhelmstrasse, "told off to inject subtle doses of *Kultur* into a naïf and pious people." Furthermore, Mr. Mencken is, with George Jean Nathan, editor of that staunchly American receptacle for *belles-lettres,* the *Smart Set.* He does indeed rather ostentatiously litter his pages with German words and phrases—*unglaublich, Stammvater, Sklavenmoral, Kultur, Biertische, Kaffeeklatsch, die ewige Wiederkunft, Wille zur Macht* . . . u. s. w. He is a member of the Germania Männerchor, and he manages to work the names of most of the German musicians into his first three discourses. His favorite philosopher happens to be Nietzsche, whose beauties he has expounded in two books—first the "philosophy," then the "gist" of it. He perhaps a little flauntingly dangles before us the seductive names of Wedekind, Schnitzler, Bierbaum,

Schoenberg, and Korngold. He exhibits a certain Teutonic gusto in tracing the "Pilsner motive" through the work of Mr. Huneker. His publisher is indeed Mr. Knopf. But Mr. Knopf disarms anti-German prejudice by informing us that Mr. Mencken is of "mixed blood—Saxon, Bavarian, Hessian, Irish, and English"; or, as Mr. Mencken himself puts it, with his unfailing good taste, he is a "mongrel." One cannot, therefore, understand exactly why Mr. Knopf thinks it valuable to announce that Mr. Mencken "was in Berlin when relations between Germany and the United States were broken off"; nor why he adds, "Since then he has done no newspaper work save a few occasional articles." Surely there can have been no external interference with Mr. Mencken's purely aesthetic ministry to the American people.

As Mr. Mencken conceives the æsthetic ministry, there is nothing in the world more dispassionate, disinterested, freer from moral, religious, or political significance. The "typical American critic," to be sure, is a pestilent and dangerous fellow; he is a Puritan; he is obsessed by non-æsthetic ideas; he is ever bent on giving instruction in the sphere of conduct; he is always talking about politics and morals. But Mr. Mencken assures us, "criticism, as the average American 'intellectual' understands it, is what a Frenchman, a German, or a Russian would call donkeyism." Now, though Mr. Mencken is not a German, he has an open mind. One may even say that he has a "roomy" mind. And by that token he is quite certainly not a typical American critic. We imagine that he may fairly be taken as a representative of the high European critical outlook over "beautiful letters"—as he loves to call such finely sensitive work as that of Mr. Dreiser. He does not wander over the wide field of conduct with a birch rod; he simply perceives and feels and interprets the soul of loveliness in art—to use his own expressive phrase, he beats a drum for beauty.

One who does not fix firmly in mind Mr. Mencken's theoretical *Standpunkt* is likely to be somewhat confused by his practice. The careless and cursory reader of these *belles pages* of his will probably not, it is true, be impressed with their æsthetic purity and serenity, not at first. One's first impression, indeed, is that Mr. Mencken has as many moral and political irons in the fire as the "typical American critic"—the poor native whose blood is not so richly tinctured with Saxon, Bavarian, and Hessian elements. He has a dozen non-æsthetic standards which he incessantly employs in the judgment of books and authors. He has a "philosophical theory," "politics," "social ideas," "ideas of education," and "moral convictions," with all which a piece of literature has to square, if it is to please him. These general ideas he treats by no means as trifles; he

thrusts them into one's face with peculiar emphasis and insistence. So that presently one begins to suspect that his quarrel with American criticism is not so much in behalf of beauty as in behalf of a *Kultur* which has been too inhospitably received by such of his fellow-citizens as look to another *Stammvater* than his. Of course, the true explanation is that Mr. Mencken's culture-propaganda is what a drummer (for *das Schöne*) would call his "side-line." Beauty is the main burden of his pack.

Though Mr. Mencken's *Kultur* is not German, it reminds one faintly of the German variety as described by Professor Eucken in October, 1914: "Our German Kultur has, in its unique depth, something shrinking and severe; it does not obtrude itself, or readily yield itself up; it must be earnestly sought after and lovingly assimilated from within. This love was lacking in our neighbors; wherefore they easily came to look upon us with the eyes of hatred." Mr. Mencken's culture is like this in that one must love it ere it will seem worthy of one's love. For example, his fundamental philosophical idea is, that "human life is a seeking without finding, that its purpose is impenetrable, that joy and sorrow are alike meaningless." Then there are his political notions. The good Mr. Knopf—the good and helpful Mr. Knopf—tells us that in politics our lover of beautiful letters is "an extreme Federalist." We had divined that. Mr. Mencken himself shrinkingly betrays the fact that he considers the hopes and professions of democracy as silly and idle sentimentality. Then there are his social ideas: he is for a somewhat severe male aristocracy; he firmly points out "how vastly the rôle of women has been exaggerated, how little they amount to in the authentic struggle of man." Then there are his educational ideas. The useful Mr. Knopf informs us that Mr. Mencken "attended no university." We had divined that also. Does he not explicitly declare that "college professors, alas, never learn anything"? Does he not steadily harp on "the bombastic half-knowledge of a school teacher"? Does he not note as a sign of Mr. Huneker's critical decadence the fact that he has spoken civilly of a Princeton professor? Does he not scornfully remark, "*I* could be a professor if I would"? Then there are his moral convictions. He is anti-Christian. He is for the *Herrenmoral* and against the "Sklavmoral that besets all of us of English speech." He holds with Blake that "the lust of the goat is also to the glory of God." Finally there are his national and racial feelings and convictions. He holds that the Anglo-Saxon civilization excels all others as a prolific mother of quacks and mountebanks. Mr. Mencken's continuous tirade against everything respectable in American morals, against everything characteristic of American soci-

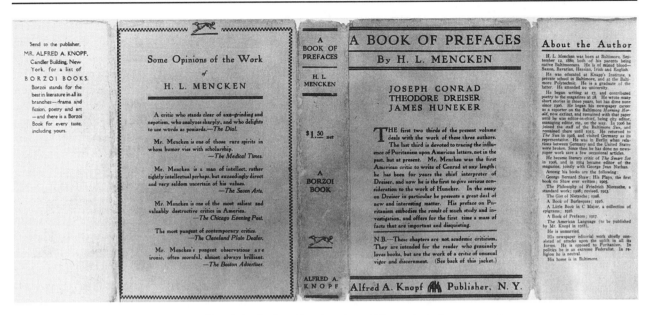

Dust jacket for the volume that triggered Sherman's wrath

ety, and against everything and everybody distinguished in American scholarship and letters, is not precisely and strictly *æsthetic* criticism; indeed, an unsympathetic person might say that it is not criticism at all, but mere scurrility and black-guardism. His continuous laudation of a Teutonic-Oriental pessimism and nihilism in philosophy, of anti-democratic politics, of the subjection and contempt of women, of the *Herrenmoral,* and of anything but Anglo-Saxon civilization, is not precisely and strictly *æsthetic* criticism; an unsympathetic person might call it infatuated propagandism. But, of course, all these things are properly to be regarded as but the *obiter dicta* of a quiet drummer for beauty.

Still, for the æsthetic critic, it is a pleasure to turn from Mr. Mencken's somewhat polemical general ideas to the man himself as revealed by the subtle and finely woven garment of his style. Though not a German, Mr. Mencken has a beautiful style; and though he could be a professor if he would, he has a learned style. To his erudition let stand as witnesses the numberless choice words calculated to send the vulgar reader to a dictionary: "multipara," "chandala," "lamaseries," "coryza," "lagniappe," "umbilicarii," "Treuga Dei," "swamis," "gemaras," "munyonic," "glycosuria." This is clearly the vocabulary of an artist and a scholar. As an additional sign of his erudition, consider his discovery that Mr. Dreiser "stems" from the Greeks; also his three-line quotation from a Greek dramatist—in the original Greek. To prove the beauty of his phrasing and his general literary feeling, one has but to open

the book and dip in anywhere. Here, in Dryden's words, is "God's plenty." How gently he touches the decline of religious faith in New England: "the old God of Plymouth Rock, as practically conceived, is now scarcely worse than the average jail warden or Italian padrone." How nobly he lays to rest the moral faith of our fathers: "the huggermugger morality of timorous, whining unintelligent and unimaginative men—envy turned into law, cowardice sanctified, stupidity made noble, Puritanism." How adequately he interprets the spirit of our emancipators: "The thing that worried the more ecstatic Abolitionists was their sneaking sense of responsibility, the fear that they themselves were flouting the fire by letting slavery go." What a felicitous image of Emerson!—"a diligent drinker from German spigots"; alas, poor Emerson, he left the German taproom too soon, and so remained a "dilettante" all his life. And here are jewels three words long that on the forefinger of Belles Lettres will sparkle forever: "professional sinhound," "blackmailing Puritan," "campaigns of snouting and suppression," "the pall of Harvard quasi-culture," "college pedagogues," "the gifted pedagogue," "Philadelphia, that depressing intellectual slum," "pedants lecturing to the pure in heart," "a leap to the Victorians, the crêpe-clad pundits, the bombastic word-mongers of the *Nation* school," "the kept idealists of the *New Republic,"* "the pious gurglings of Longfellow," the "giggle" and "kittenishness" of Mr. Howells, "Rufus Wilmot Griswold, that almost fabulous ass," "the era of cuspidors," the "sonorous platitudes" [of Mr. Brownell], the "calm superior numskullery that was Victorian," "eminent excoriators of the Rum Demon," "the intolerable prudishness and dirtymindedness of Puritanism"–"one ingests a horse-doctor's dose of words, but fails to acquire any illumination."

The sheer verbal loveliness of writing like this can never pass away. It is the writing of a sensitive intellectual aristocrat. It has the quality and tone of high breeding. It is the flower and fragrance of a noble and elevated mind that dwells habitually with beauty. Does not one breathe a sigh of relief as one escapes from the ruck and muck of American "culture" into the clear and spacious atmosphere of genuine æsthetic criticism? If, by exchanging our American set of standards for his "European" set, we could learn to write as Mr. Mencken does, why do we hesitate? Well, as a matter of fact, there is already a brave little band of sophomores in criticism who do not hesitate. These humming Ephemera are mostly preserved in the pure amber of Mr. Mencken's prose. At everything accepted as finely and soundly American, swift fly the pebbles, out gushes the corrosive vapor of a *discriminating* abuse. The prospect for beautiful letters in America is visibly brightening.

Mencken's civic contributions as a German American of international reputation were recognized as late as 1965, when Baltimore mayor Theodore R. McKeldin delivered a speech honoring Mencken to the Independent Citizens Committee German Day Celebration on September 19. The speech was reported in the Sun *and, in German, in the* Baltimore Correspondent *("Baltimore, My Baltimore,"* Menckeniana, *16 [Winter 1965]: 1–2).*

Of all the distinguished contributions that citizens of German extraction have made to Baltimore, the most famous was the late H. L. Mencken. Because he was an extremely bold and forthright critic, he made enemies; and some were so infuriated by his manner that they were never able to consider calmly the matter presented in his writing. Thus, to this day, one finds honest and otherwise intelligent people who are unable to understand why so much of Baltimore delighted in Mencken while he lived and still cherishes his memory.

Yet it is quite simple. Mencken embodied four of the characteristics that have won for German-Americans the affection and respect of their neighbors, not only in Baltimore, but everywhere. He loved music and laughter, and he revered learning and freedom. In that he was typically German. Grant that this was not the whole man. Grant that if

he exalted Beethoven, he also exalted Nietzsche. Yet the fact remains that he strove mightily to teach us to hate tyranny and injustice, and to despise fraud and pretense. In view of that service, we can afford to ignore the fact that he was a somewhat stern schoolmaster who did not spare the rod.

I invite your attention, also, to the fact that there are some people who contend that Mencken's greatest contribution to Baltimore is yet to be realized. This is the amazingly vivid picture he painted of the nineteenth-century city in the series of *Days* books–*Happy Days, Newspaper Days,* and *Heathen Days.* Technically, they constitute an autobiography, but actually they tell us much less about the man, Mencken, than about the city, Baltimore, in those last decades before it was hurled into the perplexities and confusion of the twentieth century.

It is not for us to judge exactly how important this is, because we are still in the midst of the perplexities and confusions. But it may be plausibly argued that a future generation, in more tranquil times, will find in these books the record of a civilization filled with gusty humors, but also filled with abounding vitality, with self-confidence, and with energy that will make it highly attractive to men of the closing decades of this century.

If that should prove to be the case, then all that Mencken did for Baltimore during his lifetime will be outweighed by the returns from his labor that will be received long after his death. For he has given a kind of legend–far, indeed, from the Arthurian cycle, or the Song of Roland, or the Homeric epics, but still a legend that men of future generations will read with pleasure.

A great legend is immortal, and even a small one lasts far longer than the Psalmist's "threescore years and ten." I do not pretend to think that Baltimore-before-1914 will last like the Camelot of King Arthur, or the Aachen of Charles the Great, or "the topless towers of Ilion." But I do suspect that Mencken has given it a lease on life that will continue when most of us here today are forgotten; and that is no small gift.

Be that as it may, we know that if he excited the emotions of the town, he also excited its intelligence; which means that a great gulf separates him from the demagogues who foment hysteria without even a tinge of thought. We know, too, that in praising music and puncturing fraud he added enormously to the gaiety of the city. Perhaps the best one-sentence description of Mencken ever written is Walter Lippmann's remark: "he denounces life and makes you want to live."

It seems to me, therefore, that the Germanic element in the city of Baltimore may take just pride in the fact that it was one of theirs who most vociferously urged upon this town love of the arts, specifically the art of music, love of the laughter that wrecks pompous falsehood, and love of liberty for all men, regardless of race or creed or national origin. To have produced such a force is a badge of honor, and you Baltimore Germans should wear it proudly.

Music was an integral part of Mencken's life and work. His stereotypical fondness for German music, alluded to by the mayor, led him to promote forthcoming concerts by the Baltimore Symphony Orchestra, the first publicly supported symphony orchestra in America. He was knowledgeable on the subject and a competent pianist. Especially when they involve programmatic description, his many writings on music are better than his criticism of poetry, which he thought inferior to prose because it (like music) appealed primarily to the emotions. Here Mencken describes for Baltimoreans Robert Schumann's Symphony No. 1, which the orchestra was to play the following Friday (excerpts from "O Fruehling, Wie Bist Du So Schoen!" Baltimore Evening Sun, 12 April 1916, editorial page).

[. . .] The Spring Symphony, as I have twice remarked, opens with a rousing theme for trumpet and French horns, the which is at once repeated by the full orchestra *fortissimo.* It is, as Schumann himself said, the call of Spring, the summons to be up and cavorting. A fiery passage follows, with the fiddles squeaking high up the E string, and the cellos and bull-fiddles haw-hawing far below. Pan is loose; the woods are awakening. Then comes, very softly, a fragmentary restatement of the trumpet theme, this time for wood-wind, and then a cadenza-line solo passage for the first flute, and a sudden hurrying of the tempo. A few measures further on the introduction glides beautifully into the first movement proper. It opens with a gay theme made of the trumpet call, and to the tail of it is hooked a rustling passage for the strings, delightfully suggestive of the breeze blowing through greening trees. The second subject, first given out by the clarinets and bassoons and kept in the wood-wind throughout the movement, is a simple and plaintive song, but the development is almost exclusively concerned with the first subject, which is worked out with the utmost ingenuity and effectiveness. Early in the development section Schumann introduces the triangle, and in one place actually gives it the theme. This use of it caused a musical scandal in 1842, for the triangle, up to that time, had not appeared in serious orchestral writing. (Today, with tom-toms and wind-machines grown commonplace, it seems old-fashioned.) Toward the end of the movement, a third theme is heard, chiefly sung, like the second, by clarinets and bassoons. But it is, as it were, an afterthought, and soon after it appears the movement comes to a brilliant close.

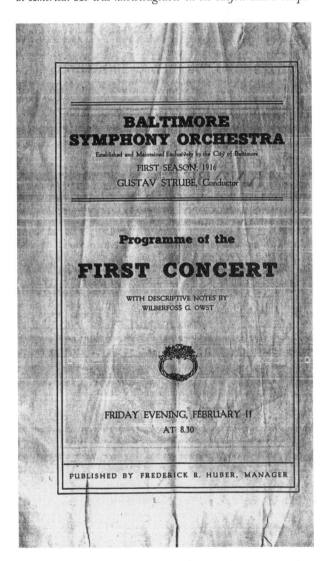

Cover of the program for the first performance of the orchestra whose concerts Mencken promoted in his newspaper pieces (Arthur J. Gutman Collection)

§4.

The slow movement is a lovely song, at first for the violins, and then, after a moment in the wood-wind, for the cellos. Toward the end it goes back to the wood-wind. One theme suffices for the whole; the second is no more than an echo of the first. Fragments from the two are woven into an exquisite fabric in the middle, but there is no real development, and the whole thing, first and last, is no more than a song with orchestral accompaniment. In this respect it suggests

Page from the sheet music for a waltz written by Mencken in his teens (courtesy of the Enoch Pratt Free Library)

Mencken playing the piano on 12 July 1932; photograph by Carl Van Vechten (courtesy of the Enoch Pratt Free Library and the Van Vechten Estate)

The Saturday Night Club in its quarters at 619 St. Paul Street, Baltimore, 24 April 1937. Mencken (far right) played second piano (courtesy of the Enoch Pratt Free Library).

the last movement of Schubert's Unfinished Symphony, another example of unsurpassable beauty wedded to the starkest simplicity of design. As Philip H. Goepp says, "the *larghetto* is one simple, sincere song, a stay of merriment; but there is no sadness, rather a settled, deep content." One lies under the trees and listens to the birds. In the *Gasthaus* down under the hill there is a pretty *Biermad'l*. It is May Day. [. . .]

The prime example of the "abiding relationships" of which Mencken wrote in "On Living in Baltimore" was the famous Saturday Night Club, founded in 1904 and not formally disbanded until 1950. Its members met primarily for the purposes of playing music and drinking. It varied in size over the years and consisted of amateur and professional musicians, as well as nonplaying friends who enjoyed the gemütlichkeit. A notable member was the composer Louis Cheslock, who compiled an anthology of Mencken's writings on music in which he described his first encounter with Mencken's piano playing at the home of the conductor of the Baltimore Symphony Orchestra (excerpt from "Postlude," in H. L. Mencken on Music, *edited by Cheslock [New York: Knopf, 1961], pp. 212–213).*

[. . .] I first heard Henry Mencken play the piano more than thirty years ago at the home of Gustav Strube.

The program opened with the Cesar Franck symphony. From the first notes it was obvious that Mencken knew his music. With each new shift in tempo and tonality he was the soul of the ensemble. Sudden *pianissimo*–and he hushed the bass and horn. He signaled each entry. And so it went through exposition, development, recapitulation and into the coda. And at the end he let out an enormous whoop. [. . .]

In his obituary for his longtime friend Albert Hildebrandt, Mencken mentions the long-remembered attempt of the club to perform a heroic feat (excerpt from "The End of a Happy Life," Baltimore Evening Sun, *21 November 1932, editorial page).*

[. . .] On the secular side he got through almost everything written for the cello. For twenty-five years he went to the late Frederick H. Gottlieb's house every Sunday night to engage in chamber music, and for even longer he played every Saturday night with another club. Nor was that all, for he put in many evenings playing with his wife, his daughter and his sister-in-law, and in the earlier days there were weeks when he made music every night. He was always ready to drop everything for a session with his cello. Once, years ago, I

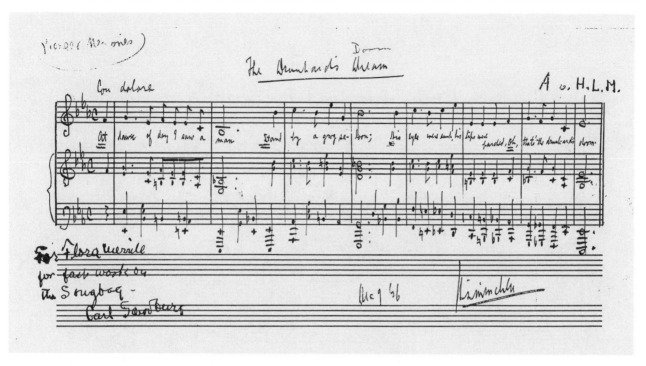

Manuscript for Mencken's contribution to Carl Sandburg's American Songbag *(1927) (Richard J. Schrader Collection)*

Shield of the Saturday Night Club, which now hangs in the Mencken Room of the Enoch Pratt Free Library

happened into his place one afternoon when a German exchange student was calling on him. The German allowed that he was a fiddler, and Al suggested a couple of trios. We played from 4 to 6.30, went out to dinner, returned at 7.30, and kept on until 11. Another time he was a party to a desperate scheme to play the first eight Beethoven symphonies *seriatim*. We began late one afternoon, and figured that, allowing for three suppers, one breakfast, one lunch, and five pauses for wind and beer, the job would take 24 hours. But we blew up before we got to the end of the Eroica. [. . .]

Mencken maintained close friendships all his life and was person-
ally liked even by many of his opponents once they got to know
him. Nonetheless, he earned a reputation as a misanthrope
because of the "bias against the rabble" that, as Brooks
remarked, he inherited from his German Baltimore childhood.
That bias turned him against democracy, which, he thought, frus-
trated creativity and individuality by giving power to third-raters
who ruled out of envy and stifled their superiors. As long as he
was attacking such world-savers as the prohibitionists, the Com-
stocks, and the opponents of evolution, and as long as the economy
was good, he was widely admired as the chief libertarian gadfly
and even as a political theorist. As his friend and editor Hamilton
Owens said in a reminiscence (included below), Mencken's prime
interest as a literary critic "was not literary expression for its own
sake but rather the use of that expression for social criticism. In

Page from the sheet music for a song that was a favorite part of the Saturday Night Club's repertoire. The work was first transcribed and published by Mencken (Yale Collection of American Literature, Beinecke Rare Book and Manuscript Library).

Europe, where his writings were almost always available in translation, his role was accepted as that of social philosopher, which was precisely what Baltimoreans had known him to be all the time." Though he mocked the doctrinaire creeds of others, Mencken was induced by Forum *magazine to create one of his own for a series it was running in 1930; the series was published in book form the following year. The essay is a clear statement of what underlies his libertarianism and agnosticism (excerpts from* Living Philosophies, *by Mencken, Albert Einstein, and others [New York: Simon & Schuster, 1931], pp. 179–183, 187–193).*

"Faith," said the unknown author of the Epistle to the Hebrews, "is the substance of things hoped for, the evidence of things not seen."

The definition, in these later days, seems to be pretty well forgotten, especially by those master forgetters, the Christian theologians, for it is common to hear them discussing (and denouncing) the beliefs of men of science as if they were mere articles of faith. The two things, of course, are quite distinct. Belief is faith in something that is known; faith is belief in something that is not known. In my own credo there are few articles of faith; in fact, I have been quite unable, in ten days and nights of prayer and self-examination, to discover a single one.

What I believe is mainly what has been established by plausible and impartial evidence, *e.g.,* that the square on the hypotenuse of a right triangle is equal to the squares on the other two sides, that water is composed of oxygen and hydrogen, and that man is a close cousin to the ape. Further than that I do not care to go. Is there a life after death, as so many allege, wherein the corruptible puts on incorruption and the mortal immortality? I can only answer that I do not know. My private inclination is to hope that it is not so, but that hope is only a hope, and hopes and beliefs, it seems to me, can have nothing in common. If, while the taxidermists are stuffing my integument for some fortunate museum of anatomy, a celestial catchpole summons my psyche to Heaven, I shall be very gravely disappointed, but (unless my habits of mind change radically at death) I shall accept the command as calmly as possible, and face eternity without repining.

Most of the sorrows of man, I incline to think, are caused by just such repining. Alone among the animals, he is dowered with the capacity to invent imaginary worlds, and he is always making himself unhappy by trying to move into them. Thus he underrates the world in which he actually lives, and so misses most of the fun that is in it. That world, I am convinced, could be materially improved, but even as it stands it is good enough to keep any reasonable man entertained for a lifetime.

As for me, I roll out of my couch every morning with the most agreeable expectations. In the morning paper there is always massive and exhilarating evidence that the human race, despite its ages-long effort to imitate the seraphim, is still doomed to be irrevocably human, and in my morning mail I always get soothing

FORM OF BEQUEST

I give and bequeath unto Henry Louis Mencken, alias H. L. Mencken, a citizen of Baltimore, in the Maryland Free State, the sum of ....

....dollars, of the present standard of weight and fineness, and free of all inheritance taxes and other imposts, whether inflicted by the United States or by any State or Territory thereof, in testimony of my appreciation of his altruistic and unrelenting services to his country as patriot and Christian, in consideration of his probable bodily and spiritual needs in his declining years, and for value received.

Passed as to legality by Messrs. Goldfarb, Feinberg, Spritzwasser and O'Shaunnessy.

The Bureau of Prohibition holds that wines and liquors may be devised by will only to "the widow, children or other relations residing in the dwelling of the deceased owner at the time of his death." But this inhuman restriction, of course, will be null and void when the Volstead Act is repealed.

Example of the kind of joke that Mencken often included in letters to his friends

proof that there are men left who are even worse asses than I am.

It may be urged that such satisfactions are lowly; nevertheless, the fact remains that they are satisfactions. Would the tinsel world that idealists pant for be better? Would it be really habitable at all? I am ready to doubt it formally. It would be swept, at best, by chill winds; there would be no warming glow of human folly. There would be no Lindberghs in it, to risk their necks preposterously and charmingly; there would be no Comstocks and Wayne B. Wheelers, no Hoovers and Coolidges; there would be no poets with their pretty bellyaches; above all, there would be no theologians. And maybe no Americans.

One hears complaint that the existing world is being Americanized, and hence ruined. It may be that my steadfast refusal to join in that complaint is patriotism; if so, make the most of it. Here in these States, if we have accomplished nothing else, we have at least brought down all the more impossible varieties of human aspiration to absurdity, and so made life the more endurable. Alone among the great nations of history we have got rid of religion as a serious scourge—and by the simple process of reducing it to a petty nuisance. Alone again, we have rid ourselves of the worst curses that lie in politics—and by the easy and obvious device of making politics comic.

The Fathers of the Republic, I believe, were far cleverer fellows than they are commonly represented to be, even in the schoolbooks. If it was not divine inspiration that moved them, then they must have drunk better liquor than is now obtainable on earth. For when they made religion a free-for-all, they prepared the way for making it ridiculous; and when they opened the doors of office to the mob, they disposed forever of the delusion that government is a solemn and noble thing, by wisdom out of altruism. The bald facts stand before every eye to-day; it is a joyous and instructive business to contemplate them. And it is even more joyous and instructive to contemplate the sad heavings of those who still refuse to face them, but try to get rid of them by the arts of the prestidigitator and the rhetorician.

When I travel abroad, which is no oftener than I can help it, I am always depressed by the gloom of the so-called intellectuals. My acquaintance among them, in most of the countries of Europe, is somewhat large, and so I can't escape their agonies. Everywhere they fret themselves to death over the problem of government. Everywhere they plan to bring in Utopia by turning this gang out and putting that gang in. Everywhere they believe in wizards and messiahs. It seems to me that we in America—that is, those of us who have become immune to rhetoric—have got beyond that naïveté, and that we are the sounder and happier for it. Reconciling

ourselves to the incurable swinishness of government, and to the inevitable stupidity and roguery of its agents, we discover that both stupidity and roguery are bearable—nay, that there is in them a certain assurance against something worse.

The principle is surely not new in the world: everyone ought to know by this time that a mountebank, thinking only of to-morrow's cakes, is far safer with power in his hands than a prophet and martyr, his eyes fixed frantically upon the rewards beyond the grave. So a prudent man prefers Hoover to Stalin or Mussolini, or even to Ramsay MacDonald, a Scotsman and hence a fanatic. No doubt Al Smith would have been better, if only on Burke's theory that politics is at its best when it is most closely adjusted, not to reason, but to human nature. But Hoover is natural enough for all every-day purposes; and where his timidity makes him fall short, his failure is concealed by the glorious labors of such corn-doctors as Borah, Jim Watson, Charlie Curtis, Andy Mellon, and Old Joe Grundy.

Here I do not argue that mountebanks are more admirable than honest men; I merely argue that, in such fields as those of politics and religion—to which, of course, the master-quackery of pedagogy ought to be added—they are socially safer and more useful. The question before us is a practical one: how are we to get through life with a maximum of entertainment and a minimum of pain? I believe that the answer lies, at least in part, in ridding solemn ponderosities of their solemn ponderosity, in putting red noses on all the traditional fee-faw-fo-fums.

That enterprise, by the cunning of the Fathers, we have been able to carry further in the United States than it is carried anywhere else. Do strong men blubber against the outrage of prohibition? Then smell their breaths to see how real their grievance is. Are there protests against the clubs of the police? Then compare a few amiable bumps on the head to a quart of Mussolini's castor oil? Do jobholders consume the substance of the people? Then ask the next Englishman you meet to show you his income tax bill. And are the high places of the land held by trashy and ignoble fellows, bent only upon their own benefit? Then take a look at the scoundrels who constitute the state in France. [. . .]

The common view of science is that it is a sort of machine for increasing the race's store of dependable facts. It is that only in part; in even larger part it is a machine for upsetting *un*dependable facts. When Copernicus proved that the earth revolved around the sun, he did not simply prove that the earth revolved around the sun; he also proved that the so-called revelation of God, as contained in the Old Testament, was rubbish. The first fact was relatively trivial: it made no difference to the average man then, as it makes no dif-

And [Elisha] went up from thence
into Beth-el: and as he was going up
by the way, there came forth little
children out of the city, and mocked
him, and said unto him, Go up,
thou bald head; go up, thou bald
head.

And he turned back and looked on
them, and cursed them in the name of
the Lord. And there came forth
two she bears out of the wood, and
tare forty and two children of them.

Handwriting sample submitted by Mencken for graphological analysis. It is one of his favorite biblical passages, 4 Kings 2:23–24 (from Jerome S. Meyer, Mind Your P's and Q's *[New York: Simon & Schuster, 1927].*

ference to him to-day. But the second fact was of stupendous importance, for it disposed at one stroke of a mass of bogus facts that had been choking the intelligence and retarding the progress of humanity for a millennium and a half.

So with every other great discovery in the physical world: it had immediate repercussions in the world of ideas, and often they were far more important than its immediate effect. The long line of glorious workers in medicine are not to be regarded merely as cheaters of the grave, for the grave, in the long run, has cheated every one of them in turn; their service to man was that they dissuaded him from laying vain blames for his ills and making vain and ignominious appeals for aid against them, and set him to examining them, and himself with them, in a rational and self-respecting manner. That medicine saves to-day thousands who must have died yesterday is a fact of small significance, for most of them will leave no more marks upon the history of the race than so many June bugs; but that all of us have been persuaded thereby to turn from priests and magicians when we are ill to doctors and nurses—that is a fact of massive and permanent importance. It benefits everybody worthy of being called human at all. It rids the thinking of mankind of immense accumulations of intellectual garbage. It increases the dignity of every honest man and it diminishes the puissance of every fraud. [. . .]

The supply, unluckily, still remains very large. Its reservoir is the mob, uneducable and irrational, and along the banks of that reservoir many enterprising frauds—theological, political, and philosophical—find profitable fishing. There are impatient men who long to heave the whole company overboard at one swoop: they are the fashioners of Utopias. But human progress, of course, can never be so facile. It must be carried on, not with the cosmic engines of gods, but with the puny machinery at hand; and that machinery, as everyone knows, is always breaking down.

The Fathers of the Republic, despite the sagacity that I have been praising, were a bit too confident and impatient. I suppose they believed that by setting religion adrift they had got rid of it, but all they had really done was to make it ready for self-wrecking years after their day was done. Again and even worse, they bent their hardest endeavors to setting up a government of the most sagacious, the most honorable, the most fit—but all they actually achieved was to let in the least fit, and a century and a half afterward we are still struggling to get rid of the Hardings, Coolidges, and Hoovers.

Things would move faster if there were a general agreement as to the goal, but that is too much to hope for. There are men in the world, and some of them not unintelligent men, who have a natural appetite for the untrue, just as there are others who have a natural appetite for the ugly. A bald fact somehow affrights them: they long to swathe it in comforting illusions. Thus one hears from them that it is somehow immoral for an artist to depict human life as it actually is: the spectacle of the real must be ameliorated by an evocation of the ideal, which is to say, of the *un*real. So Thomas Hardy becomes a bad artist, and the author of *Pollyanna* a good one.

One hears again, and from the same men, that religious faith is a valuable thing *per se,* even if it be faith in propositions revolting to the most elementary intelligence. And one hears that it is an evil business to dwell upon the gross and intolerable failures of democracy, lest the general belief in democracy itself be converted into doubt. The facts, it appears, are nothing; the important thing is to retain a hopeful and pleasant frame of mind. The most valuable philosopher is that one who conjures up glittering universes in which two and two make five, six, or even ten; the most despicable is the fellow who keeps on insisting that they make only four.

Of such sort are the reconcilers of science and religion, the more naïve variety of Liberals in politics, and the various disciples of Hamilton Wright Mabie and Edward W. Bok in the arts. I daresay the first-named were an active and expectant party in the day of Copernicus; if so, they must have given a great deal less comfort to Copernicus than to Pope Paul III. They continue energetically to-day, proving that Genesis and the Darwinian hypothesis are not in conflict, that curved space is still reconcilable with the Book of Revelation, and that, in any case, it is better to go to church on Sunday than to stay away.

The tragedy of such men is that, in the long run, they are bound to find that they are holding empty bags. The Popes, soon or late, always go over to Copernicus, as Dr. Andrew D. White once proved in two noble tomes. The truth, battered and torn, yet survives all the pretty nothings that beset it. Out of the welter of hopes and fears, of cautions and evasions, there always arises in the end the gaunt, immovable figure of a solid fact.

Certainly the Liberals in our midst should have learned long ago how dangerous it is to tackle such facts with no better weapons than hosannas. Is it so soon forgotten that they once believed in Roosevelt? And then in Wilson? And then in the War to End War? And then in a long series of other impostures, ranging from the initiative and referendum to the direct primary, and from woman suffrage to prohibition? There is more here than mere innocence; there is also, it seems to me, a downright libido for the improbable, a thirst to believe what can scarcely be imagined as true. [. . .]

Such is the will to believe. Holding it to be a great nuisance in the world, and worse even than the will to power, I try to keep myself as free of it as I can. On gloomy days I speculate as to the probable state of modern man if it had ever been universal. We'd still be following Pope Paul; nay, not the Pope of that name but the Saint, with his cocksure ignorance and his Little Bethel moral scheme. Perhaps we'd be even further back than that—among the sheiks of the Palestine plateau and the primitive shamans of the Central Asian wilderness. It seems to me that such prophets as Dr. Robert A. Millikan, when they flirt gravely with the rev. clergy, ask us to go back almost that far.

Are the clergy true teachers or false? Is the body of ideas that they merchant true or not true? If it is not true, then I can imagine no prudent and profitable traffic with them. They have a right, of course, to be heard, but they have no more right to be attended to than the astrologers and necromancers who were once their colleagues and rivals.

There is only one man who has a right to be attended to, and that is the man who is trying, patiently, fairly, earnestly, diligently, to find out the truth. I am willing to give him my ear at any time of the day or night, year in and year out. But I am not willing to listen to the man who argues that what might be or ought to be true is somehow superior to what *is* true. One Copernicus, it seems to me, is worth all the Popes who ever lived, and all the bishops and archbishops, and all save a baker's dozen of the holy saints.

The title of this article is far too wide. No man, within the space allotted me, could make anything approaching a complete or even a fair statement of his credo. I must content myself, after the foregoing prolegomenon, with a few random notes.

I believe that religion, generally speaking, has been a curse to mankind—that its modest and greatly overestimated services on the ethical side have been more than overborne by the damage it has done to clear and honest thinking.

I believe that no discovery of fact, however trivial, can be wholly useless to the race, and that no trumpeting of falsehood, however virtuous in intent, can be anything but vicious.

I believe that all government is evil, in that all government must necessarily make war upon liberty; and that the democratic form is at least as bad as any of the other forms.

I believe that an artist, fashioning his imaginary worlds out of his own agony and ecstasy, is a benefactor to all of us, but that the worst error we can commit is to mistake his imaginary worlds for the real one.

I believe that the evidence for immortality is no better than the evidence for witches, and deserves no more respect.

I believe in complete freedom of thought and speech, alike for the humblest man and the mightiest, and in the utmost freedom of conduct that is consistent with living in organized society.

I believe in the capacity of man to conquer his world, and to find out what it is made of, and how it is run.

I believe in the reality of progress.

I—

But the whole thing, after all, may be put very simply. I believe that it is better to tell the truth than to lie. I believe that it is better to be free than to be a slave. And I believe that it is better to know than to be ignorant.

One of Mencken's earliest books was Men versus the Man: A Correspondence between Robert Rives La Monte, Socialist, and H. L. Mencken, Individualist *(1910). La Monte was one of those "fashioners of Utopias" decried by Mencken in* Living Philosophies. *A 1924 note by Burton Rascoe provides a good introduction to the work ("Mencken: Shirtsleeve Autocrat," in Rascoe,* A Bookman's Daybook, *edited by C. Hartley Grattan [New York: Liveright, 1929], pp. 195–196).*

Friday, January 25.

Mencken once engaged in a book-length debate, in the form of letters, with Robert Rives La Monte on the subject of "Men vs. the Man." Mencken argued fiercely for individualism, *les droits de seigneur,* aristocracy, and the right of the few to exploit the weak. La Monte argued with equal heat for the rights of the proletariat, the need for Socialism, and the blessings of altruism and the equal chance. The joke of it is that Mencken at the time was sweating away in his shirt sleeves at a newspaper job, while La Monte was taking his ease on a beautiful country estate in Connecticut.

The flavor of the dialogue with La Monte may be gathered from the last word, which is given to Mencken (excerpt from "Mencken's Reply to La Monte's Sixth Letter," in Men versus the Man: A Correspondence between Robert Rives La Monte, Socialist, and H. L. Mencken, Individualist, *pp. 245–247).*

[. . .] But even admitting the idle and rich son of a millionaire to be entirely and perniciously useless, I fail to see what can be fairly done about it. His father received from the public certain enormous sums for certain services, which, by the law of supply and demand, bore a high market value, and, as I have shown before, they went to him upon the distinct understanding that he was to have the free use of them. If he had chosen to devote them to useful public purposes, no one would have objected; and if he had chosen to pay them, on his deathbed, into the public treasury, even you Socialists would have hailed him as moral. Why should he be denounced, then, because he chose to hand them over to his dissolute and half-imbecile son? Would it be fair or honest, after making a definite treaty with him, to abrogate it without his consent? And would it be even expedient? Isn't it plain enough that his idle son is the worst of all possible foes to impregnable wealth?

And now for the other objections. Do the greatest rewards really go to the most efficient and worthy? Doesn't the struggle for existence, by warring upon weak bodies, sometimes rob the world of incomparable minds? And doesn't luck play the principal part in the struggle? I answered most of these questions, I believe, in a former letter, but it may be well to repeat my general answer here. It is this: that I am concerned in this discussion with the world as it is, and not with the world as it might or should be. If it were possible, by a human act, to nullify the law that the fittest shall survive, Socialism and all other schemes of that sort would become reasonable—I grant only their reasonableness, mind you, and not their truth—but as things stand it seems to me that they are almost beyond the pale of debatable ideas. Whether for woe or weal, nature provides that the strong shall have an advantage over the weak, and that the fortunate shall outrun the luckless in the race. It is scarcely worth while for us to attempt to judge nature here. All we may safely do is to make a note of the fact that this scheme of things, whatever its horrors, at least makes for progress; and to thank whatever gods there be that we, personally, are measurably removed from the bottom of the scale.

I am not a religious man, but I cannot think upon my own good fortune in life without a feeling that my thanks should go forth, somewhere and to someone. Wealth and eminence and power are beyond my poor strength and skill, but on the side of sheer chance I am favored beyond all computation. My day's work is not an affliction, but a pleasure; my labor, selling in the open market, brings me the comforts that I desire; I am assured against all but a remote danger of starvation in my old age. Outside my window, in the street, a man labors in the rain with pick and shovel, and his reward is merely a roof for to-night and tomorrow's three meals. Contemplating the difference between his luck and mine, I cannot

fail to wonder at the eternal meaninglessness of life. I wonder thus and pity his lot, and then, after awhile, perhaps, I begin to reflect that in many ways he is probably luckier than I.

But I wouldn't change places with him.

Sincerely,

MENCKEN.

The book brought forth a response from Marcus Hitch (excerpt from "Marxian vs. Nietzschean," International Socialist Review, *10 [May 1910]: 1024–1025).*

[. . .] When disputants cannot agree on the facts, the debate as to the cause of these facts, who suffers or profits by them, and what results any proposed changes would have, is a waste of breath. Mencken claims that the exploitation of the workers is small; that there is no forced unemployment; that capitalists do useful work;—in fact, that there is no criterion by which we can tell what work is useful and what not useful; that everyone gets the actual value of his work in the open market; that there is no waste in competition; that human labor power is only muscle power, ox power; that the necessity of getting a livelihood and supporting one's offspring, which is effective in the case of wild beasts, is powerless to overcome the congenital laziness of the ordinary human being; that nothing but the magic touch of exploitation for private profit will work this miracle; that the difference between the high-caste man and the low-caste is congenital, not economic; but apparently he fears that the removal of the economic difference would destroy the congenital difference.

Well, if these things are true, then Mencken's philosophy appears reasonable and debate is useless. Mencken is unwilling to pay men anything merely for the labor of being alive; we too. We are also unwilling to pay men anything merely for the labor of being property-owners.

Mencken is grieved because low-caste men cannot understand the binomial theorem. That is nothing. We have tried a hundred times and have never yet found a high-caste man (outside the socialists) who could grasp the axiomatic proposition that the abolition of exploitation in industry would necessarily cut away the foundation of graft in politics and make an honest government possible; or the equally evident proposition that although you cannot change men's actions directly by legislation, nevertheless you can change industrial and property conditions by legislation, and that these changed conditions would in turn affect men's actions. That is an "epigram in Persian" to the high-caste man; on economic subjects he cannot

on AUG

For WHO'S WHO IN AMERICA (Vol. 16, 1930-1931)

NOTE The following personal sketch appears in the last edition of WHO'S WHO IN AMERICA issued about two years ago. It is sent to you for revision, with a view to inclusion in the forthcoming new edition, *subject to editorial approval.* Please read the sketch with care, making necessary alterations, using typewriter if possible.

The leading essentials of every sketch are: *Full name, place and date of birth, full names of parents, education, college degrees (including dates), marriage (including full name and date).*

THE A. N. MARQUIS COMPANY, Chicago, Ill., U. S. A.

Please do not rewrite this sketch, which is now in type. Make your corrections on this sheet.

PAID ORDER   23634

MENCKEN, Henry Louis, author, editor; b. Baltimore, Md., Sept. 12, 1880; s. August and Anna (Abhau) M²; ed. pvt. sch. and Baltimore Polytechnic; unmarried. Reporter, 1899, city editor, 1903-05, Baltimore Morning Herald; editor Evening Herald, 1905-06; on staff Baltimore Sun, 1906-10; Evening Sun, 1910-16, 1918—; corr. German army, 1916-17; lit. critic Smart Set, 1908-23; co-editor same, 1914-23; editor The American Mercury 1924—; contbg. editor The Nation, 1921—; contbr. to Atlantic Monthly, Century, Yale Review, New Republic, London Nation, Neue Rundschau, etc.; corr. at Scopes trial, nat. conventions, etc. *Author:* Ventures Into Verse, 1903; George Bernard Shaw—His Plays, 1905; The Philosophy of Friedrich Nietzsche, 1908; The Artist (play), 1912; A Book of Burlesques, 1916; A Little Book in C Major, 1916; A Book of Prefaces, 1917; In Defense of Women, 1917; Damn—a Book of Calumny, 1917; The American Language, 1918; Prejudices—First Series, 1919, Second Series, 1920; Third Series, 1922, Fourth Series, 1924, Fifth Series, 1926, Sixth Series, 1927; Notes on Democracy, 1926. Part author: Men vs. the Man, 1910; Europe After 8:15, 1914; The American Credo, 1920; Heliogabalus (play), 1920. Editor: The Players' Ibsen, 1909; The Free Lance Books, 1919. *Home:* 1524 Hollins St., Baltimore, Md. *Office:* 730 Fifth Av., New York, N.Y.

; The Bode, 1930.

(also 37 Bedford Square, London WC 1, England.)

To obviate the necessity of sending out another proof, please return this sketch even if no change be made. Every sketch must be accounted for before the book can go to press.

Please furnish here both home and business address, if not already correctly given above.

Home Address...

Business Address...

672-10   Printed in U. S. A.

Proof, corrected by Mencken, for his biographical entry (Arthur J. Gutman Collection)

truly think, as Mencken would say. He has a contempt for the "master equation" of economic determinism which reveals sociological truths; but master equations in any other department of human knowledge are acceptable and indicate a high-caste mind.

As the oyster cannot free himself from his shell, so the typical individualist cannot free himself from the idea that the "natural" function of public government is to enforce private contracts by the artificial means of courts. This whole philosophy is based on the delusion that under bourgeois freedom the contracts and business customs of men, which grow into laws, arise out of industrial relations which are the result of the deliberate choice of the parties; in other words, that men choose their methods of social industry according to their varying tastes or whims. [. . .]

Mencken stated his Darwinian-Nietzschean opinion concisely for Edward Silvin (from Why I Am Opposed to Socialism: Original Papers by Leading Men and Women, *edited by Silvin [Sacramento, Cal., 1913], pp. 6–7).*

I am opposed to Socialism because, in general, it means a vain and costly attack upon the immutable natural law that the strong shall have advantage over the weak. I do not defend that law as perfect, nor do I even maintain that it is just. If I had the world to make over I should probably try to find something to take its place, something measurably less wasteful and cruel. But the world is as it is and the law is as it is. Say what you will against it, you must at least admit that it works, that it tends to destroy the botched and useless, that it places a premium upon enterprise and courage, that it makes for health and strength, that it is the most powerful of all agents of human progress. Would brotherhood, supposing it to be achieved, do as well? I doubt it. Brotherhood would help the soft man, the clinging man, the stupid man. But would it help the alert and resourceful man? Answer for yourself. Isn't it a fact that difficulties make daring, that effort makes efficiency? Do not functions develop by use? Does the cell act or react?

Meanwhile, I grant all schemes of brotherhood one indubitable merit. Socialism shares it with Christianity. It is this: that they are eternally impossible of carrying out, that men cannot actually live them. The Beatitudes, after 2,000 years, are still mere poetry. No human fiat will ever repeal the law of natural selection. No rebellion of slaves will ever break down that great barrier which separates slaves from masters.

Religion is the response of the weak, Mencken observes in a section of his 1926 work Notes on Democracy *(excerpt from "The Democrat as Moralist," pp. 152–154).*

Liberty gone, there remains the majestic phenomenon of democratic law. A glance at it is sufficient to show the identity of democracy and Puritanism. The two, indeed, are but different facets of the same gem. In the psyche they are one. For both get their primal essence out of the inferior man's fear and hatred of his betters, born of his observation that, for all his fine theories, they are stronger and of more courage than he is, and that as they go through this dreadful world they have a far better time. Thus envy comes in; if you overlook it you will never understand democracy, and you will never understand Puritanism. It is not, of course, a specialty of democratic man. It is the common possession of all men of the ignoble and incompetent sort, at all times and everywhere. But it is only under democracy that it is liberated; it is only under democracy that it becomes the philosophy of the state. What the human race owes to the old autocracies, and how little, in these democratic days, it is disposed to remember the debt! Their service, perhaps, was a by-product of a purpose far afield, but it was a service none the less: they held the green fury of the mob in check, and so set free the spirit of superior man. Their collapse under Flavius Honorius left Europe in chaos for four hundred years. Their revival under Charlemagne made the Renaissance possible, and the modern age. What the thing was that they kept from the throat of civilization has been shown more than once in these later days, by the failure of their enfeebled successors. I point to the only too obvious examples of the French and Russian Revolutions. The instant such a catastrophe liberates the mob, it begins a war to the death upon superiority of every kind—not only upon the kind that naturally attaches to autocracy, but even upon the kind that stands in opposition to it. The day after a successful revolution is a blue day for the late autocrat, but it is also a blue day for every other superior man. The murder of Lavoisier was a phenomenon quite as significant as the murder of Louis XVI. We need no scientists in France, shouted MM. of the Revolutionary Tribunal. Wat Tyler, four centuries before, reduced it to an even greater frankness and simplicity: he hanged every man who confessed to being able to read and write. [. . .]

By 1926 Mencken's "mob" was visible to him at every election and whenever a literary experiment was censored. By then they had outlawed alcohol and evolution and tried to ban an issue of

The American Mercury. *And in a form that would grow less novel as the century wore on, they exploited and vulgarized "personalities" who could become nationally famous overnight because of the new media of radio and the cinema. Now and then a "superior man" was trapped by his fame, as Mencken relates about one of the most remarkable encounters of the 1920s. It was arranged by a Hollywood connection, the actress Aileen Pringle (who, like Anita Loos, felt that she had been jilted by Mencken). Mencken describes the event in a 1926 letter to Ernest Boyd and in an essay in* Prejudices: Sixth Series, *published in 1927 (typewritten letter with handwritten initial as signature at Princeton University).*

H. L. MENCKEN
1524 HOLLINS ST.
BALTIMORE

July 26th

Dear Boyd:-

It was an excellent evening. The weather had dam nigh finished me that day, but I was full of life in the morning. Let us have more of them. I suggest going to Meyer's Hotel in Hoboken for dinner the next time. The victuals are very fair, and the beer is superb--the best in the East.

I am sending a copy of the suppressed May Mercury by this mail. Don't let it be seen. Its circulation might complicate our legal difficulties. Both injunctions have been appealed, and we will have to begin a long and expensive struggle in the Fall. The Postoffice, in particular, will be hard to knock out. It will probably drag us to the Supreme Court of the United States.

I am innocent, mon colonel. I made no attempt upon that beautiful artiste. She invited me to meet Rudolph Valentino next day, and I had a very instructive session with him. We sat in our shirt sleeves and discussed Art. He is, it appears, an Intellectual. But surely not a bad fellow.

I am in my usual low state, and full of gloomy forebodings about the future of Christianity.

In Xt. M

* * *

(*"Valentino," in* Prejudices: Sixth Series, *pp. 305–311*).

By one of the chances that relieve the dullness of life and make it instructive, I had the honor of dining with this celebrated gentleman in New York, a week or so before his fatal illness. I had never met him before, nor seen him on the screen; the meeting was at his instance, and when it was proposed, vaguely puzzled

FREE VISTAS · VOL. II

A LIBERTARIAN OUTLOOK ON LIFE & LETTERS · EDITED BY JOSEPH ISHILL

PUBLISHED BY THE ORIOLE PRESS AT BERKELEY HEIGHTS, N. J.

· MCMXXXVII ·

Cover for an issue of a magazine that included two congratulatory letters from Mencken

me. But soon its purpose became clear enough. Valentino was in trouble, and wanted advice. More, he wanted advice from an elder and disinterested man, wholly removed from the movies and all their works. Something that I had written, falling under his eye, had given him the notion that I was a judicious fellow. So he requested one of his colleagues, a lady of the films, to ask me to dinner at her hotel.

The night being infernally warm, we stripped off our coats, and came to terms at once. I recall that he wore suspenders of extraordinary width and thickness—suspenders almost strong enough to hold up the pantaloons of Chief Justice Taft. On so slim a young man they seemed somehow absurd, especially on a hot Summer night. We perspired horribly for an hour, mopping our faces with our handkerchiefs, the table napkins, the corners of the table-cloth, and a couple of towels brought in by the humane waiter. Then there came a thunder-storm, and we began to breathe. The hostess, a

The movie star and romantic idol Rudolph Valentino, with whom Mencken had dinner shortly before the actor's death

woman as tactful as she is charming, disappeared mysteriously and left us to commune.

The trouble that was agitating Valentino turned out to be very simple. The ribald New York papers were full of it, and that was what was agitating him. Some time before, out in Chicago, a wandering reporter had discovered, in the men's wash-room of a gaudy hotel, a slot-machine selling talcum-powder. That, of course, was not unusual, but the color of the talcum-powder was. It was pink. The news made the town giggle for a day, and inspired an editorial writer on the eminent Chicago *Tribune* to compose a hot weather editorial. In it he protested humorously against the effeminization of the American man, and laid it light-heartedly to the influence of Valentino and his sheik movies. Well, it so happened that Valentino, passing through Chicago that day on his way east from the Coast, ran full tilt into the editorial, and into a gang of reporters who wanted to know what he had to say about it. What he had to say was full of fire. Throwing off his 100% Americanism and reverting to the *mores* of his fatherland, he challenged the editorial writer to a duel, and, when no answer came, to a fist fight. His masculine honor, it appeared, had been outraged. To

the hint that he was less than he, even to the extent of one half of one per cent., there could be no answer save a bath of blood.

Unluckily, all this took place in the United States, where the word honor, save when it is applied to the structural integrity of women, has only a comic significance. One hears of the honor of politicians, of bankers, of lawyers, even of the honor of the United States itself. Everyone naturally laughs. So New York laughed at Valentino. More, it ascribed his high dudgeon to mere publicity-seeking: he seemed a vulgar movie ham seeking space. The poor fellow, thus doubly beset, rose to dudgeons higher still. His Italian mind was simply unequal to the situation. So he sought counsel from the neutral, aloof and aged. Unluckily, I could only name the disease, and confess frankly that there was no remedy—none, that is, known to any therapeutics within my ken. He should have passed over the gibe of the Chicago journalist, I suggested, with a lofty snort—perhaps, better still, with a counter gibe. He should have kept away from the reporters in New York. But now, alas, the mischief was done. He was both insulted and ridiculous, but there was nothing to do about it. I advised him to let the dreadful farce roll along to exhaustion. He protested that it was infamous. Infamous? Nothing, I argued, is infamous that is not true. A man still has his inner integrity. Can he still look into the shaving-glass of a morning? Then he is still on his two legs in this world, and ready even for the Devil. We sweated a great deal, discussing these lofty matters. We seemed to get nowhere.

Suddenly it dawned upon me—I was too dull or it was too hot for me to see it sooner—that what we were talking about was really not what we were talking about at all. I began to observe Valentino more closely. A curiously naïve and boyish young fellow, certainly not much beyond thirty, and with a disarming air of inexperience. To my eye, at least, not handsome, but nevertheless rather attractive. There was an obvious fineness in him; even his clothes were not precisely those of his horrible trade. He began talking of his home, his people, his early youth. His words were simple and yet somehow very eloquent. I could still see the mime before me, but now and then, briefly and darkly, there was a flash of something else. That something else, I concluded, was what is commonly called, for want of a better name, a gentleman. In brief, Valentino's agony was the agony of a man of relatively civilized feelings thrown into a situation of intolerable vulgarity, destructive alike to his peace and to his dignity—nay, into a whole series of such situations. It was not that trifling Chicago episode that was riding him; it was the whole grotesque futility of his life. Had he achieved, out of nothing, a vast and dizzy success? Then that success was hollow as well as vast—a colossal and preposterous nothing. Was he acclaimed by yelling multitudes? Then every time the multitudes yelled he felt himself blushing inside. The old story of Diego Valdez once more, but with a new poignancy in it. Valdez, at all events, was High Admiral of Spain. But Valentino, with his touch of fineness in him—he had his commonness, too, but there was that touch of fineness—Valentino was only the hero of the rabble. Imbeciles surrounded him in a dense herd. He was pursued by women—but what women! (Consider the sordid comedy of his two marriages—the brummagem, star-spangled passion that invaded his very death-bed!) The thing, at the start, must have only bewildered him. But in those last days, unless I am a worse psychologist than even the professors of psychology, it was revolting to him. Worse, it was making him afraid.

I incline to think that the inscrutable gods, in taking him off so soon and at a moment of fiery revolt, were very kind to him. Living, he would have tried inevitably to change his fame—if such it is to be called—into something closer to his heart's desire. That is to say, he would have gone the way of many another actor—the way of increasing pretension, of solemn artiness, of hollow hocus-pocus, deceptive only to himself. I believe he would have failed, for there was little sign of the genuine artist in him. He was essentially a highly respectable young man, which is the sort that never metamorphoses into an artist. But suppose he had succeeded? Then his tragedy, I believe, would have only become the more acrid and intolerable. For he would have discovered, after vast heavings and yearnings, that what he had come to was indistinguishable from what he had left. Was the fame of Beethoven any more caressing and splendid than the fame of Valentino? To you and me, of course, the question seems to answer itself. But what of Beethoven? He was heard upon the subject, *viva voce,* while he lived, and his answer survives, in all the freshness of its profane eloquence, in his music. Beethoven, too, knew what it meant to be applauded. Walking with Goethe, he heard something that was not unlike the murmur that reached Valentino through his hospital window. Beethoven walked away briskly. Valentino turned his face to the wall.

Here, after all, is the chiefest joke of the gods: that man must remain alone and lonely in this world, even with crowds surging about him. Does he crave approbation, with a sort of furious, instinctive lust? Then it is only to discover, when it comes, that it is somehow disconcerting—that its springs and motives offer an affront to his dignity. But do I sentimentalize the perhaps transparent story of a simple mummer? Then substitute Coolidge, or Mussolini, or any other poor devil that you can think of. Substitute Shakespeare, or Lincoln, or Goethe, or Beethoven, as I have. Sentimental or not, I confess that the predicament of poor Valentino touched me. It provided grist for my mill, but I couldn't quite enjoy it. Here was a young man who was living daily the dream of millions of other young men. Here was one who was catnip to women. Here was one who had wealth and fame. And here was one who was very unhappy.

Ten years later Mencken found that the "mob" was being directed by a master demagogue over the radio (excerpt from "The More Abundant Dialectic," Baltimore Evening Sun, *20 April 1936, editorial page).*

I

[. . .] I often wonder that no one has undertaken a formal history of demagogy. If I had the time I think I'd take on the job myself, but too many other jobs stand in the way, some spiritual and some secular. The notion that the thing is a modern imposture seems to be widely held, but it is in error. It actually arose in the dark backward and abysm of history, and it has been throwing off renowned and even immortal practitioners for many, many centuries. Indeed, the thing we call history is to a large extent only a serial biography of such charlatans. But it would be a mistake to dismiss them as mere swindlers. Like the inventors of bogus religion, they have often convinced themselves of their own inspiration, and not a few of them have suffered martyrdom. The last to go to the stake, as connoisseurs will recall, was William Jennings Bryan, LL. D. He needed no executioner to set him afire. He was consumed by the natural heat of his own dreadful fury against his betters.

II

Aside from that fury, there is precious little to be discovered in the New Deal metaphysic. It is a puerile amalgam of exploded imbecilities, many of them in flat contradiction of the rest. It proposes to give people more to eat by destroying food, to lift the burden of debt by encouraging fools to incur more debt, and to husband the depleted capital of the nation by outlawing what is left of it. It heads in all directions at once, and gets precisely nowhere. No two of the Brain Trust wizards appear to agree, save of course upon the constant need for more money. They give at least as much time to brawling among themselves as they give

The socialist Emma Goldman, whose deportation in 1925 was criticized by Mencken (National Archives)

to the actual promotion of their discordant and preposterous Utopias.

With a change of a few words, a large part of Dr. Roosevelt's harangue to the local come-ons might have been converted into the spiel of a quack doctor addressing yokels at a county fair. Its obvious purpose was to scare them into believing that something awful ailed them, and then to offer them an infinite series of sure cures. "If the first bottle doesn't relieve you, come back and we'll try another"—of course, for another 25 cents. Show me anything else in the speech, and I'll eat a copy of it soaked in one-hundred-proof strychnine. It was not only silly; it was shameless. There was no pretense of rational discussion. It was pure and unadulterated demogogy. [. . .]

Mencken's support of individual liberty took forms other than potshots in reaction to New Deal attempts at fixing the Depression. He actively defended—in writing and in person—the right to expound utopian visions, even those far more repulsive to him than Roosevelt's. Left-wing radicals could count on this antisocialist's voice during the Red Scare; to Mencken, the superior person does not fear the contending of ideas but uses whatever power he or she has to protect free speech—it is the mob that flails at whatever seems threatening. One celebrated case involved the deportation of a pair of anarchists (excerpts from "As H. L. M. Sees It: The United States Sustains A Loss In Berkman And Emma

Goldman," Baltimore Evening Sun, *25 April 1925, editorial page; originally written for the* Chicago Tribune, *where it appeared on 26 April as "Two Wasted Lives").*

One commonly hears of such persons as Emma Goldman and Alexander Berkman only as remote and horrendous malefactors, half human and half reptilian. Editorial writers, on dull days, exhume ancient bills of complaint against them and give thanks to God that they are safely beyond these Christian shores, and for good. They are denounced by orators before the American Legion, by suburban pastors and by brave Congressmen. While they were still in our midst one heard only that *Polizei* were hot on their trail, that the gallant catchpolls of the so-called Department of Justice were about to trap them, that the hoosegow at Atlanta was being warmed for them. Since the Buford sailed the science of jurisprudence has made immense progress among us. Had it leaped a step Berkman would have had a padlock through his snout, and La Goldman, I suspect, would have been outfitted with *ceinture de patriotisme.*

All this indignation, unfortunately, conceals something, and that is the somewhat disconcerting fact that both are extremely intelligent—that once their aberrant political ideals are set aside they are seen to have very sharp wits. They think clearly, unsentimentally and even a bit brilliantly. They write simple, glowing and excellent English. Their feelings, far from being those of yeggmen, cannibals and prohibition enforcement officers, are those of highly civilized persons. How, then, is their political nonsense to be explained–their childish belief in the proletariat, their life-long faith in Utopia? Go ask me something easier! I am no professor of morbid psychology. But I know a very intelligent man, a scientist of national fame, who believes that drinking a glass of beer is a mortal sin. I know another man, eminent in public life, who patronizes chiropractors. I know a third, worth at least $10,000,000, who believes in thought transference. I know a fourth–[. . . .]

Now to my point: It was a great mistake, I am convinced, to let so shrewd, forthright and frank a fellow go, and La Goldman with him. The defect in our system is that it utilizes men badly–that it throttles more talent than it makes any use of. The Bolsheviki seem to be surviving Berkman's devastating onslaught; it may even strengthen them at home, if only by making them more careful. But in the United States, where such criticism is needed quite as sorely as in Russia and where it could be turned to use ten times as well–here the only thing we can think of doing to such a man as Berkman is to lock him up in jail. Because his fulminations alarm a few profiteers, we hunt him as if he were a mad dog–and finally kick him out of the country. And with him goes a shrewder head and a braver spirit than has been seen in public life among us since the Civil War.

Mencken writes about another famous exile in his long review of Leon Trotsky's My Life. *He is fair in judging the book on its own terms, while noting the author's ideological limitations (a man of prejudices like himself) and, as was his custom, not sparing America when the opportunity arises. Not only is there no triumphalism, but a qualified admiration emerges in the essay (*"The Russian Phantasmagoria,"* American Mercury, 20 [July 1930]: 381–383).*

"An nescis, mi filli," wrote Axel Oxenstjerna to his son, "quantilla prudentia mundus regatur?"–Don't you know, my son, with what little sense the world is governed? Oxenstjerna died in 1654, but there has been no improvement since. On the contrary there has been a further decline, for democracy selects out the least competent by a sort of natural instinct, and nowhere in the world today is a genuinely first-rate man at the head of a civilized state. Thus the business of governing becomes a somewhat shabby and dubious avocation, comparable to fortune-telling, running a street carnival or biting off puppies' tails. That this is true in the United States must be manifest to anyone who puts in a month reading the *Congressional Record,* or gives an eye to the statistics of criminality among recent Governors of the States. That it is true also at the other end of the scale, in Soviet Russia, is made abundantly plain by Trotsky's book. The whole General Staff of the Bolsheviki marches across his pages, and he pronounces judgment upon each hero as he passes. Half of them, it appears, are idiots, and the other half are scoundrels. One exception should be noted: the late Lenin. But the chief merit of Lenin, it appears quickly, was that he usually agreed with Trotsky, and always praised him. Otherwise, he too would have probably dropped to the level of Zinoviev, Pyatakov, Voroshilov, Kuybyshev, Dzerzhinsky, Menzhinsky, Kamenev, Stalin and the rest.

Trotsky plainly fancies himself as a writer, and makes frequent reference to his literary services to the holy cause, and to the fact that his first dream in life was to be a great author. It must be said for him that he tells his story well, but it cannot be added that his personality, as he depicts it himself, shows any charm. The man is obviously hard, brittle, pedantic, self-righteous, more than a little pharisaical. He is forever parading his learning and deriding that of other men. Now and then a sort of Rooseveltian bombast gets into him, and even more often he falls into the evangelical sing-song of Woodrow Wilson. That he has a certain ability, both for intrigue and for command, is probable, but that it is of anything properly describable as high quality is far from apparent. The fact that he managed, as chief of the Red army, to throw off the White invasions which began in 1918 seems to have been due a great deal less to his own military capacity than to the stupidity of his opponents. When, in 1920, he faced the Poles he got a dreadful beating. True enough, he says that he opposed this ill-favored venture, and tries to put all the blame for it on Stalin, but the fact remains that it is the business of a military leader to win, whether he is in favor of the current war or not. Certainly one who has been beaten by Poles cannot claim to be a Napoleon.

All these campaigns seem to have been carried on from the Bolshevik side much as our own Civil War, at least in its first stages, was carried on from the side of the North. That is to say, the majority of generals in the field were political appointees, and there was constant interference from the politicians at home. Trotsky opposed this interference, but could not resist the temptation to play politics himself. The result was a vast pestilence of wire-pulling, tale-bearing and well-poisoning. Factions split off from the main party of world-savers, and individual prophets jumped from one to another. The whole story, read as it is here set down, takes on a comic opera aspect. The Bolsheviki were not only amateurs

Mencken with Senator Joseph F. Guffey of Pennsylvania at the hearing on antilynching legislation before a subcommittee of the Senate Judiciary Committee, 14 February 1934 (courtesy of the Enoch Pratt Free Library)

at military strategy; they were also amateurs at government, and many of them seem to have been amateurs, too, at common decency. Meanwhile, the country starved and groaned. Thousands were dying while the corps of doctrinaires debated this or that fine point of Marxian theory, or scrambled for one another's jobs. Over all reigned Lenin, leaning first this way and then that way.

Trotsky's account of his own downfall is far less clear than it might be. He lays it simply to a secret conspiracy of all the members of the Politbureau save himself, led by Stalin. They agreed, he says, to talk him down and themselves up. They organized branches of their cabal in the local Bolshevik organizations, and systematically promoted subordinates who were known to be against him. But why against him? This is never stated plainly. All this went on while Lenin was lying ill. When he died the conspirators came out into the open. In January, 1925, Trotsky was relieved of his duties as Commissary for War, and soon afterward he was interned in three small offices, none of them of the slightest impor-

tance. In January, 1927, he was exiled to Central Asia, and a year later he was put out of Soviet territory altogether. He is now living in Turkey, trying in vain to get permission to visit either England or Germany. He says he needs medical attention.

The first part of his book is the more interesting, for it describes what must have been a very pleasant childhood in Little Russia. Papa Bronstein (the family name) was a rich farmer and also carried on various other enterprises, including a machine-shop and a flour mill. Young Lev Davydovich, in those days, was innocent of political ideas; it was not until he got to the high-school at Odessa that he began to listen to spellbinders. They made short work of him, and before he was twenty he belonged to a subversive organization and was being watched by the police. He had a talent for mathematics and his father wanted him to become an engineer, but his first arrest broke that up, and presently he was bound for Siberia. He escaped and made his way across Russia and the rest of Europe to London, where he met Lenin. In a few years he was back in Russia and condemned to Siberia again, only to escape again, and thereafter, until the collapse of the Russian monarchy in 1917 he was a wanderer, living successively in all countries from Spain to Norway and from Austria to the United States.

Trotsky disposes in his narrative of all the gaudy legends that have grown up about his stay in New York. He was in the city, he says, but two months, and he met none of the persons who now claim intimate acquaintance with him. "If all the adventures ascribed to me," he says, "were banded together in a book they would make a far more entertaining biography than the one I am writing here. But I must disappoint my American readers. My only profession in New York was that of a revolutionary Socialist. . . . I wrote articles, edited a newspaper, and addressed labor meetings." All of his speeches, he says, were made either in Russian or in German. "My English was even worse then than it is today, so that I never thought of making public addresses in it." Nevertheless, it seems to have been good enough for reading purposes, for he says he "studied the economic history of the United States assiduously" in one of the New York libraries. But maybe he studied it in Russian or German, or in Yiddish. He has little to say about those days, and that little is not very complimentary. Obviously, Manhattan made a somewhat dubious impression upon him.

One thing he constantly overlooks in his book, and that is the matter of his sustenance. How did he live during all those years in exile? How did he pay for his costly and extensive journeys? Certainly it is hard to believe that he got a living by his writing, for he contributed only to hole-in-the-wall papers of small circulation. Nor is it easy to think of him keeping himself and his wife and family on the fees of a labor orator. He says that a purse was made up for him when he started home to Russia, but the amount was small and could not have paid for his passage. How, indeed, is he maintaining himself today? If his enemies in Moscow are supporting him, how much are they giving him? Here are details that are sadly missing in his story. It would be interesting to know what the average income of a revolutionist is, and what his pension amounts to when his day is done. But on these points good Lev Davydovich is magnificently silent.

Mencken was opposed to the death penalty and frequently denounced the ultimate denial of civil rights: lynching. Such barbarity was common not only in the South but also on Maryland's Eastern Shore, and Mencken's denunciations were often met with physical threats. Here he describes some responses to

his latest attack (excerpt from "Sound and Fury," Baltimore Evening Sun, 14 December 1931, editorial page).

I

What with their grandiose effort to stampede and paralyze Baltimore with threats of boycott, ruin and desolation, their even more grandiose effort to terrify the sinful *Sunpapers* into leaping to the mourners' bench and accepting lynching as a Christian sacrament, and their announced determination, come what may, to save the Republic and the True Faith from the hellish conspiracies of the Russian Bolsheviki, the Salisbury fee-faw-fums are giving a very gaudy show—so gaudy, indeed, that I marvel to see Baltimoreans so indifferent to it. It is quite as good as any of the similar shows that are set up from time to time in the deeper reaches of the Bible Belt, and it has the prime virtue of being all our own. But very few Baltimoreans seem to be aware that it is going on, and those few take no apparent interest in it.

The local papers of the lower Shore, for a week past, have been bursting with incandescent and highly instructive stuff. They have not only mirrored faithfully the emotions of a pious and patriotic people at an heroic moment; they have also printed a number of new facts about the sublime event of December 4. One item, which I take from the Berlin-Ocean City *News,* is that the ceremony was not performed in churchly silence, as the *Sunpaper's* correspondents reported, but to the tune of "kicking and screaming." Nor was this kicking and screaming, it appears, done by the lynchee, for he was in a strait-jacket and had his head tightly bound, but by the six Salisbury boosters who led the lynchers.

Another interesting item is that the rope was not flung over the fatal tree by "several men," as the lying *Sunpaper* reported, but by a gallant Salisbury "schoolboy"—no doubt a graduate of some seminary in ropecraft, chosen for his talent. A third item I lift from the celebrated *Marylander and Herald* of Princess Anne, a leader in the current movement to bust Baltimore by boycott:

One member of the mob took his knife and cut off several toes from the Negro's feet and carried them away with him for souvenirs.

What has become of these souvenirs the *Maryland and Herald* does not say. No doubt they now adorn the parlor mantelpiece of some humble but public-spirited Salisbury home, between the engrossed seashell from Ocean City and the family Peruna bottle. I can only hope that they are not deposited eventually with the Maryland Historical Society, or sent to Archbishop James Cannon, Jr., the most eminent of all the living natives of Salisbury.

Do not look at the Negro.

His earthly problems are ended.

Instead, look at the seven WHITE children who gaze at this gruesome spectacle.

Is it horror or gloating on the face of the neatly dressed seven-year-old girl on the right?

Is the tiny four-year-old on the left old enough, one wonders, to comprehend the barbarism her elders have perpetrated?

Rubin Stacy, the Negro, who was lynched at Fort Lauderdale, Florida, on July 19, 1935, for "threatening and frightening a white woman," suffered PHYSICAL torture for a few short hours. But what psychological havoc is being wrought in the minds of the white children?

National Association for the Advancement of Colored People notice with comment by Mencken ("Souvenir of the Confederacy") at the top. Mencken enclosed it in a 2 January 1936 letter to Theodore Dreiser (Theodore Dreiser Papers, Rare Book and Manuscript Library, University of Pennsylvania).

II

My remarks in this place on December 7, under the heading of "The Eastern Shore *Kultur*," seem to have upset the *Marylander and Herald,* for it devotes the better part of two columns of black type on its first page to a calm and well-reasoned refutation of them. The essence of this refutation is that, along with the Hon. Bernard Ades, LL. B., I am affiliated with "anarchist and Communist groups, composed for the most part of men and women from the lowest strata of the mongrel breeds of European gutters." To this the Cambridge *Daily Banner* adds the charge that I am a lyncher myself, for didn't I once propose to take William Jennings Bryan "to the top of the Washington Monument in Washington, disembowel him, and hurl his remains into the Potomac"?

This proposal, unfortunately, I can't recall, but no doubt the editor of the *Daily Banner* has a better memory than I have. In any case, I am constrained to acknowledge it on the general ground that a theologian is capable of anything. The *Worcester Democrat,* of Pocomoke City, though it does not mention my ghastly designs on Dr. Bryan, joins the *Daily Banner* in denouncing me as a lyncher, and offers to bet that both Dr. Edmund Duffy, the *Sunpaper*'s wicked cartoonist, and I "are cussing the luck which prevented [us] from getting [our] hands on the rope that swung 'Mister' Williams to a tree." Going further, it ventures the view that both of us

> could have danced with glee around the bonfire of human flesh; and could easily have imagined a barbecue was on hand; could have eaten the flesh of the carcass, and smacked [our] lips over the fine flavor of the gasoline.

This fancy, which I leave to the Freudians, warms up the Pocomoke brother, and he proceeds as follows:

> Mencken's soul, if he has one, must have come from a hyena, a rattlesnake, or a skunk. There must have been present at his birth a flock of leathern-winged bats, a nest of rattlesnakes, a swarm of hornets, and a colony of toad frogs—all contributing to his special form of life. There must have been some such scene attending his later existence as portrayed by the immortal

William where the witches concoct a charm made up of poisoned entrails, fillet of a fenny snake, eye of newt, toe of frog, wool of bat, tongue of dog, adder's fork, blind worm's sting, lizard's leg, scale of dragon. . . . and all cooled with baboon's blood. With all this, his body was smeared good and plenty, and behold! the creature in its present form! [. . .]

The articles on lynching and Mencken's appearance on 14 February 1934 before the Senate Judiciary Committee were decisive in the passage of the Costigan-Wagner Anti-Lynching Bill. He was the only journalist to testify in person (excerpt from a press release by the Press Service of the National Association for the Advancement of Colored People, p. 1).

[. . .] Another star witness was H. L. Mencken, the celebrated critic, who said "No government pretending to be civilized can go on condoning such atrocities. Either it must make every possible effort to put them down, or it must suffer the scorn and contempt of Christendom." He suggested that "the best plan will be to make a beginning by passing that bill,

Cartoon by Edmund Duffy (from S. L. Harrison, The Editorial Art of Edmund Duffy *[Madison & Teaneck, N.J.: Fairleigh Dickinson University Press / London & Toronto: Associated University Presses, 1998]; reproduced by permission)*

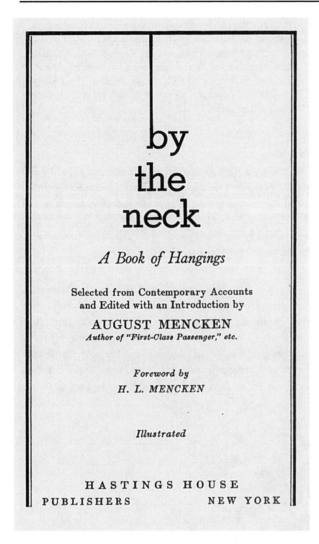

by
the
neck

A Book of Hangings

Selected from Contemporary Accounts
and Edited with an Introduction by
AUGUST MENCKEN
Author of "First-Class Passenger," etc.

Foreword by
H. L. MENCKEN

Illustrated

HASTINGS HOUSE
PUBLISHERS   NEW YORK

Title page for a 1942 book edited by Mencken's younger brother

and then waiting for the proper courts to pass upon it. . . . Nothing can be accomplished until an actual experiment is undertaken." [. . .]

Mencken's last article before the stroke that incapacitated him was an attack on the segregation laws of the very city that had nurtured his tolerant, if outspoken, spirit ("Mencken Calls Tennis Order Silly, Nefarious," Baltimore Evening Sun, 9 November 1948, editorial page).

When, on July 11 last, a gang of so-called progressives, white and black, went to Druid Hill Park to stage an inter-racial tennis combat, and were collared and jugged by the cops, it became instantly impossible for anyone to discuss the matter in a newspaper, save, of course, to report impartially the proceedings in court.

The impediment lay in the rules of the Supreme Bench, and the aim of the rules is to prevent the trial of criminal cases by public outcry and fulmination. I am, and have always been, in favor of the aim. I was in favor of it, in fact, long before any of the judges now extant arose to the bench from the underworld of the bar, and I argued for it at great length in the columns of the *Sunpapers*.

But four months is a long while for journalists to keep silent on an important public matter, and if I bust out now it is simply and solely because I believe that the purpose of the rule has been sufficiently achieved. The accused have had their day in court, and no public clamor, whether pro or con, has corrupted the judicial process. Seven, it appears, have been adjudged guilty of conspiring to assemble unlawfully and fifteen others have been turned loose.

–o–

To be sure, the condemned have petitioned the Supreme Bench, sitting *en banc,* for new trials, but it is not my understanding that the rule was designed to protect the reviewing lucubrations of the Supreme Bench. I simply can't imagine its members being swayed by newspaper chit-chat; as well think of them being swayed by the whispers of politicians. Moreover, I have no desire to sway them, but am prepared to accept their decision, whatever it is, with loud hosannahs, convinced in conscience that it is sound in both law and logic. As for the verdict of Judge Moser below, I accept it on the same terms precisely.

But there remains an underlying question, and it deserves to be considered seriously and without any reference whatever to the cases lately at bar. It is this: Has the Park Board any right in law to forbid white and black citizens, if they are so inclined, to join in harmless games together on public playgrounds? Again: Is such a prohibition, even supposing that it is lawful, supported by anything to be found in common sense and common decency?

I do not undertake to answer the first question, for I am too ignorant of law, but my answer to the second is a loud and unequivocal No. A free citizen in a free state, it seems to me, has an inalienable right to play with whomsoever he will, so long as he does not disturb the general peace. If any other citizen, offended by the spectacle, makes a pother, then that other citizen, and not the man exercising his inalienable right, should be put down by the police.

–o–

Certainly it is astounding to find so much of the spirit of the Georgia Cracker surviving in the Maryland Free State, and under official auspices. The public parks are supported by the taxpayer, including the colored taxpayer, for the health and pleasure of the whole people. Why should cops be sent into them to separate those people against their will into separate herds? Why should the law set up distinctions and discriminations which the persons directly affected themselves reject?

If the park tennis courts were free to all comers no white person would be compelled to take on a colored opponent if he didn't care to. There would be no such vexations and disingenuous pressure as is embodied, for example, in the Hon. Mr. Truman's Fair Employment Practices Act. No one would be invaded in his privacy. Any white player could say yes or no to a colored challenger, and any colored player could say yes or no to a white. But when both say yes, why on earth should anyone else object?

It is high time that all such relics of Ku Kluxery be wiped out in Maryland. The position of the colored people, since the political revolution of 1895, has been gradually improving in the State, and it has already reached a point surpassed by few other states. But there is still plenty of room for further advances, and it is irritating indeed to see one of them blocked by silly Dogberrys. The Park Board rule is irrational and nefarious. It should be got rid of forthwith.

–o–

Of equal, and maybe even worse, irrationality is the rule regarding golf-playing on the public links, whereby colored players can play on certain links only on certain days, and white players only on certain other days. It would be hard to imagine anything more ridiculous. Why should a man of one race, playing *in forma pauperis* at the taxpayers' expense, be permitted to exclude men of another race? Why should beggars be turned into such peculiarly obnoxious choosers?

I speak of playing *in forma pauperis* and that is precisely what I mean. Golf is an expensive game, and should be played only by persons who can afford it. It is as absurd for a poor man to deck himself in its togs and engage in its witless gyrations as it would be for him to array himself as a general in the army. If he can't afford it he should avoid it, as self-respecting people always avoid what they can't afford. The doctrine that the taxpayer should foot the bills which make a bogus prince of pelf of him is New Dealism at its worst.

–o–

I am really astonished that the public golf links attract any appreciable colored patronage. The colored people, despite the continued efforts of white frauds to make fools of them, generally keep their heads and retain their sense of humor. If there are any appreciable number of them who can actually afford golf, then they should buy some convenient cow-pasture and set up grounds of their own. And the whites who posture at the taxpayers' expense should do the same.

In answer to all the foregoing I expect confidently to hear the argument that the late mixed tennis matches were not on the level, but were arranged by Communists to make trouble. So far as I am aware this may be true but it seems to me to be irrelevant. What gave the Communists their chance was the existence of the Park Board's rule. If it had carried on its business with more sense they would have been baffled. The way to dispose of their chicaneries is not to fight them when they are right.

Magazine Editor

Mencken's most important early collaborator was George Jean Nathan, his co-editor at both The Smart Set *and, for a time,* The American Mercury. *During their reign at the former (1914–1923)—and for several years earlier, when they achieved national fame as reviewers for it—their mission was to clear away sentimental and puritanical literature and encourage the realism and naturalism that had blossomed in the last decades of the nineteenth century. The magazine was important not only for their continued commentary but because of the authors they promoted. For instance, they were the first in the United States to publish work by James Joyce. Mencken saw fiction as the best medium for exposing his ideas on life and art, and Theodore Dreiser was his battletank. Nathan was far less interested in politics than was Mencken; his chief concern was the theater, and for forty years he was the dean of American drama critics. In* Pistols for Two *(New York: Knopf, 1917), co-authored by Mencken and Nathan under the pseudonym Owen Hatteras, they provide verbal portraits of each other that, while not always literally true, generally hit the mark and convey the spirit that enlivens the pages of* The Smart Set *(excerpt from "George Jean Nathan," pp. 5–7).*

He was born in Fort Wayne, Indiana, February 14 and 15 (the stunning event occurred precisely at 12 midnight) 1882.

His boyhood ambition was to be an African explorer in a pith helmet, with plenty of room on the chest ribbon for medals that would be bestowed upon him by the beauteous Crown Princess of Luxembourg.

He was educated at Cornell University and the University of Bologna, in Italy.

He is a man of middle height, straight, slim, dark, with eyes like the middle of August, black hair which he brushes back *à la française,* and a rather sullen mouth.

He smokes from the moment his man turns off the matutinal showerbath until his man turns it on again at bedtime.

He rarely eats meat.

He lives in a bachelor apartment, nearly one-third of which is occupied by an ice-box containing refreshing beverages. On the walls of his apartment are the pictures of numerous toothsome creatures. He is at the present time occupied in writing a book describing his sentimental adventures among them.

He has published the following books: "Europe After 8:15," in collaboration with Mencken and Mr. Willard Huntington Wright; "Another Book on the Theater," "Bottoms Up," and "Mr. George Jean Nathan Presents."

He has written for almost every magazine in America, except *Good Housekeeping* and *The Nation.*

He dresses like the late Ward McAllister and wears daily a boutonnière of blue corn flowers.

He dislikes women over twenty-one, actors, cold weather, mayonnaise dressing, people who are always happy, hard chairs, invitations to dinner, invitations to serve on committees in however worthy a cause, railroad trips, public restaurants, rye whisky, chicken, daylight, men who do not wear waistcoats, the sight of a woman eating, the sound of a woman singing, small napkins, Maeterlinck, Verhaeren, Tagore, Dickens, Bataille, fried oysters, German soubrettes, French John Masons, American John Masons, tradesmen, poets, married women who think of leaving their husbands, professional anarchists of all kinds, ventilation, professional music lovers, men who tell how much money they have made, men who affect sudden friendships and call him Georgie, women who affect sudden friendships and then call him Mr. Nathan, writing letters, receiving letters, talking over the telephone, and wearing a hat.

In religion he is a complete agnostic, and views all clergymen with a sardonic eye. He does not believe that the soul is immortal. What will happen after death he doesn't know and has never inquired.

He is subject to neuralgia. He is a hypochondriac and likes to rehearse his symptoms. Nevertheless, a thorough physical examination has shown that he is quite sound. His Wassermann reaction is, and always has been, negative. He is eugenically fit.

He never reads the political news in the papers. He belongs to a college fraternity and several university societies.

The room in which he works is outfitted with shaded lamps and heavy hangings, and somewhat sug-

George Jean Nathan and Mencken. The photograph was taken by Alfred A. Knopf at his summer home in Purchase, New York, in 1923, shortly before the three launched The American Mercury *(courtesy of the Enoch Pratt Free Library).*

gests a first-class bordello. He works with his coat on and shuts the windows and pulls down all the curtains. He writes with a pencil on sheets of yellow paper. He cannot use a typewriter.

He detests meeting people, even on business, and swears every time a caller is announced at *The Smart Set* office. He never receives a woman caller save with his secretary in the room.

He wears an amethyst ring. In his waistcoat pocket he carries an elegant golden device for snapping off the heads of cigars. He has his shoes shined daily, even when it rains.

Like the late McKinley, he smokes but half of a cigar, depositing the rest in the nearest spitbox. Like Mark Twain, he enjoys the more indelicate varieties of humor. Like Beethoven, he uses neither morphine nor cocaine. Like Sitting Bull and General Joffre, he has never read the Constitution of the United States. [. . .]

In a pamphlet from around 1915, signed by both men but written by Mencken, Mencken and Nathan spelled out what they

did and did not want in contributions to The Smart Set *(excerpts from* A Note to Authors *[New York: Smart Set, n.d.], pp. 1–3, 5–6).*

The aim of The Smart Set, in general, is to interest and amuse the more civilized and sophisticated sort of reader—the man or woman who has lived in large cities, and read good books, and seen good plays, and heard good music, and is tired of politicians, reformers, and the newspapers. It is not what is known as a popular magazine; it hasn't a circulation of 1,000,000 a month, and it never will have. This fact frees it from any necessity to take a hand in the uplift, or to pretend that it is made sad by the sorrows of the world. It assumes that its typical reader, having a quarter in his pocket to spend for a magazine without either gaudy pictures in it or "inspirational" rubbish, is quite satisfied with both the world and himself, and that even if he isn't, there are times when he doesn't want to worry over schemes of improvement. It is at such times that The Smart Set tries to reach him. It offers him, on a small scale, the kind of intelligent

Nathan and Mencken at the Stork Club in New York City, 24 March 1948 (courtesy of the Enoch Pratt Free Library)

entertainment that such a play as Shaw's "Caesar and Cleopatra" offers him on a large scale, or Strauss' "Der Rosenkavalier" on a still larger scale.

That is, as we have said, it *tries* to do so. The fact that it often falls a good deal short is one to which we are already painfully privy. We do the best we can with the means at hand. If Joseph Conrad's "Youth" were yet unpublished, and if Conrad offered it to us tomorrow, we'd mortgage our salaries to buy it, and stop the presses to get it into the next number. For Anatole France's "The Revolt of the Angels" we'd do the same. Or for anything by Arthur Schnitzler as good as "Anatol." Or for a play by Lord Dunsany comparable to "The Green Gods from the Mountains." Or (supposing it new) for John Millington Synge's "Riders from the Sea." Or for one of John Masefield's sea songs. Or for a ballad by Otto Julius Bierbaum. Or for an essay by Walter Pater. Or for a single epigram by Oscar Wilde. . . Failing such masterpieces, we take the next best that offers, and whether that next best be by so well-known a man as Dunsany or Dreiser, or by some clever youth just out

of college, it is all one to us. We read personally every piece of printable manuscript that comes into this office, and we are unfeignedly delighted every time a newcomer sends in something that is good.

With this programme, it must be plain that we do *not* want the conventional sentimentality of the cheap magazines, the rubber-stamp stuff that presents old ideas, old situations, old points of view. For example, we don't want war stories; they were all written when Zola wrote "The Attack on the Mill," and the best of them that are now getting into type are feeble and empty. Again, we don't want newspaper stories, or stories of the Canadian Northwest, or stories about prostitutes, or political stories, or stories of the occult, or stories of A.D. 2,000, or stories of the cow country, or stories about artists or authors: we believe that all of these have been overdone, and that civilized readers are tired of them. Yet again, we don't want plays in which, as the curtain rises, the heroine is explaining the plot into a telephone, or in which either burglars or married women come to the apartments of rich New York bach-

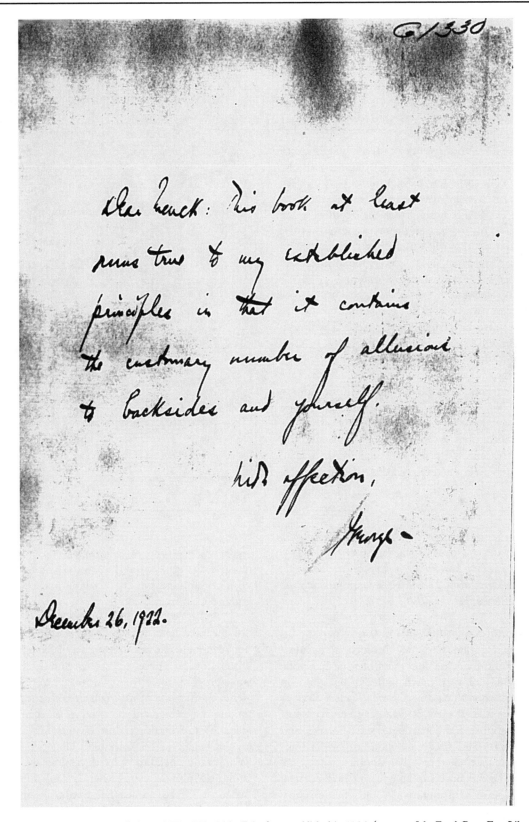

Inscription in Mencken's copy of Nathan's The World in Falseface, *published in 1923 (courtesy of the Enoch Pratt Free Library)*

elors, or in which husbands come home unexpectedly to find their wives kissing their best friends: we believe that these, too, have been done to death. Yet again, we don't want anything "delightfully optimistic," whether in play form, in story form, or in any other form: we believe that the persons who enjoy such mush know where to get it, and that they do not look for it in The Smart Set. [. . .]

Poetry? We print twenty or thirty poems every month, and a good many of them get into the anthologies. But don't send us sentimental things of the Poet's Corner variety; we are tired of odes to the meadow thrush, and war-songs arguing that the death of a soldier is a grief to his mother, and clumsy attempts at *vers libre,* and lyrics of amour in which "heart" rhymes with "part." . . . Our short prose pieces, no doubt, you know; a dozen other magazines are imitating them. We want novelty, cleverness, good writing: a little prose poem, a piece of wit, a felicitous turn of phrase–above all, what we have never had before. And so with epigrams. Please don't send us puns, or platitudes, or cribs from Oscar Wilde. We have never had half enough good epigrams. . . .

In conclusion, there are two things for authors to remember. First, we employ no readers, and all manuscripts not downright impossible are read by one of the two of us. Secondly, we try to make every decision within a week, and every accepted manuscript is paid for immediately, without any regard to the date of publication.

Cover for the first issue of the magazine edited by Mencken and Nathan

Mencken revealed the formula for a successful magazine in a 1919 essay discussing The Magazine in America, *by "Prof. Dr. Algernon Tassin, a learned birchman of the great university of Columbia" (excerpt from "The American Magazine," in* Prejudices: First Series, *pp. 176–180).*

[. . .] Dr. Tassin, apparently in fear of making his book too nearly good, halts his chronicle at its most interesting point, for he says nothing of what has gone on since 1900–and very much, indeed, has gone on since 1900. For one thing, the *Saturday Evening Post* has made its unparalleled success, created its new type of American literature for department store buyers and shoe drummers, and bred its school of brisk, business-like, high-speed authors. For another thing, the *Ladies' Home Journal,* once supreme in its field, has seen the rise of a swarm of imitators, some of them very prosperous. For a third thing, the all-fiction magazine of Munsey, Robert Bonner and Street & Smith has degenerated into so dubious a hussy that Munsey, a very moral man, must blush every time he thinks of it. For a fourth thing, the moving-picture craze has created an entirely new type of magazine, and it has elbowed many other types from the stands. And for a fifth thing, to make an end, the muck-raking magazine has blown up and is no more.

Why this last? Have all the possible candidates for the rake been raked? Is there no longer any taste for scandal in the popular breast? I have heard endless discussion of these questions and many ingenious answers, but all of them fail to answer. In this emergency I offer one of my own. It is this: that the muck-raking magazine came to grief, not because the public tired of muck-raking, but because the muck-raking that it began with succeeded. That is to say, the villains so long belabored by the Steffenses, the Tarbells and the Phillipses were either driven from the national scene or forced (at least temporarily) into rectitude. Worse, their places in public life were largely taken by nominees whose chemical purity was guaranteed by these same magazines, and so the latter found their occupation gone and their following with it. The great masses of the plain people, eager to swallow denuncia-

Cover for one of the issues that included work by Fitzgerald

tion in horse-doctor doses, gagged at the first spoonful of praise. They chortled and read on when Aldrich, Boss Cox, Gas Addicks, John D. Rockefeller and the other bugaboos of the time were belabored every month, but they promptly sickened and went elsewhere when Judge Ben B. Lindsey, Francis J. Heney, Governor Folk and the rest of the bogus saints began to be hymned.

The same phenomenon is constantly witnessed upon the lower level of daily journalism. Let a vociferous "reform" newspaper overthrow the old gang and elect its own candidates, and at once it is in a perilous condition. Its stock in trade is gone. It can no longer give a good show—within the popular meaning of a good show. For what the public wants eternally—at least the American public—is rough work. It delights in vituperation. It revels in scandal. It is always on the side of the man or journal making the charges, no matter how slight the probability that the accused is guilty. The late Roosevelt, perhaps one of the greatest rabble-rousers the world has ever seen, was privy to this fact, and made it the corner-stone of his singularly cynical and effective politics. He was forever calling names, making

accusations, unearthing and denouncing demons. Dr. Wilson, a performer of scarcely less talent, has sought to pursue the same plan, with varying fidelity and success. He was a popular hero so long as he confined himself to reviling men and things—the Hell Hounds of Plutocracy, the Socialists, the Kaiser, the Irish, the Senate minority. But the moment he found himself on the side of the defense, he began to wobble, just as Roosevelt before him had begun to wobble when he found himself burdened with the intricate constructive program of the Progressives. Roosevelt shook himself free by deserting the Progressives, but Wilson found it impossible to get rid of his League of Nations, and so, for awhile at least, he presented a quite typical picture of a muck-raker ham-strung by blows from the wrong end of the rake.

That the old appetite for bloody shows is not dead but only sleepeth is well exhibited by the recent revival of the weekly of opinion. Ten years ago the weekly seemed to be absolutely extinct; even the *Nation* survived only as a half-forgotten appendage of the *Evening Post*. Then, of a sudden, the alliance was broken, the *Evening Post* succumbed to Wall Street, the *Nation* started on an independent course—and straightway made a great success. And why? Simply because it began breaking heads—not the old heads of the *McClure's* era, of course, but nevertheless heads salient enough to make excellent targets. For years it had been moribund; no one read it save a dwindling company of old men; its influence gradually approached *nil.* But by the elementary device of switching from mild expostulation to violent and effective denunciation it made a new public almost over-night, and is now very widely read, extensively quoted and increasingly heeded. . . . I often wonder that so few publishers of periodicals seem aware of the psychological principle here exposed. It is known to every newspaper publisher of the slightest professional intelligence; all successful newspapers are ceaselessly querulous and bellicose. They never defend any one or anything if they can help it; if the job is forced upon them, they tackle it by denouncing some one or something else. The plan never fails. Turn to the moving-picture trade magazines: the most prosperous of them is given over, in the main, to bitter attacks upon new films. Come back to daily journalism. The New York *Tribune,* a decaying paper, well nigh rehabilitated itself by attacking Hearst, the cleverest muck-raker of them all. For a moment, apparently dismayed, he attempted a defense of himself—and came near falling into actual disaster. Then, recovering his old form, he began a whole series of counter attacks and cover attacks, and in six months he was safe and sound again. . . .

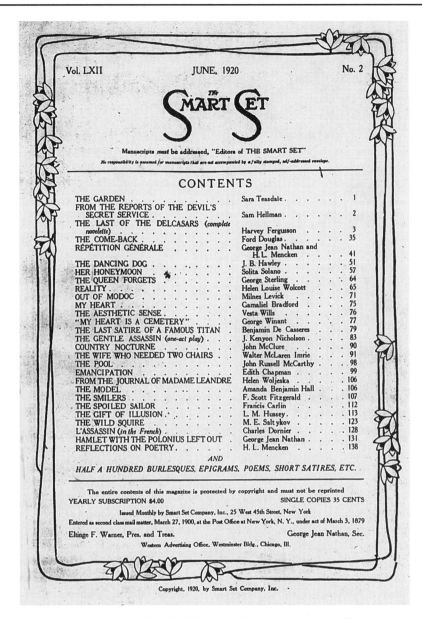

Contents page for an issue that includes work by several frequent contributors

In My Life as Author and Editor, *published posthumously in 1993, Mencken left a description of the office of* The Smart Set *circa 1916 that contrasts sharply with what may be found in a pamphlet,* Suggestions to Our Visitors, *nearly all of which was written by Mencken. Eltinge F. Warner was the publisher, and Stella Golde was the office assistant (excerpt from the typescript at the Enoch Pratt Free Library, Baltimore, for* My Life as Author and Editor).

[. . .] When Warner decided that we ought to have a rug in our office we sent Golde [*(Footnote)* Pronounced Goldie. We always thought of Goldie as her given-name. In fact, I had known her for four or five years before I learned that it was her surname.] to a Brooklyn department-store that she recommended as elegant, with instructions to buy the best rug she could find for $12.50. She returned with a Turkey-red one so dreadful that we could not help howling with delight when we saw it. Once it was on the floor we decided that the office deserved decorations to fit it, and thereafter gave over our leisure to amassing them. One of the principal items of the wall <u>decor</u> was a series of posters issued by the French Association Against Alcohol, showing the effect of alcohol upon various organs of the body—full size and in full color. To them we added photographs of a dozen or more of the most abhorred characters of the time—for example, Lieut. Charles Becker and the German Crown Prince—each purportedly inscribed by the subject to either Nathan or me. On our desks stood plaster statues, hideously colored, of the sort that Italian vendors used to sell on the street, and above Nathan's desk hung the pennants of various colleges, beginning with his own Cornell and Warner's Princeton, and running down to the Ohio Wesleyan, the Texas Christian and Tuskegee. Warner's office was decorated with originals of the covers of Field and Stream and the stuffed carcasses of fish that he had caught, so we hung the covers of the Parisienne in ours and added a couple of stuffed fish that Nathan bought at a junkshop in Third avenue. In the course of a few months the walls were covered up to the ceiling. [. . .]

(Suggestions to Our Visitors [New York: Smart Set, n.d.].)

1. The editorial chambers are open daily, except Saturdays, Sundays and Bank Holidays, from 10.30 A. M. to 11.15 A. M.

2. Carriage calls at 11.15 A. M. precisely.

3. The Editors sincerely trust that guests will abstain from offering fees or gratuities to their servants.

4. Visitors expecting telephone calls while in audience will kindly notify the Portier before passing into the consulting rooms.

5. Dogs accompanying visitors must be left at the garde-robe in charge of the Portier.

6. Visitors are kindly requested to refrain from expectorating out of the windows.

7. The Editors regret that it will be impossible for them, under any circumstances, to engage in conversations by telephone.

8. The Editors assume no responsibility for hats, overcoats, walking sticks or hand luggage not checked with the Portier.

9. Solicitors for illicit wine merchants are received only on Thursdays, from 12 o'clock noon until 4.30 P. M.

10. Interpreters speaking all modern European languages are in daily attendance, and at the disposal of visitors, without fee.

11. Officers of the military and naval forces of the United States, in full uniform, will be received without presenting the usual letters of introduction.

12. The House Surgeon is forbidden to accept fees for the treatment of injuries received on the premises.

13. Smoking is permitted.

14. Visitors whose boots are not equipped with rubber heels are requested to avoid stepping from the rugs to the parquetry.

15. A woman Secretary is in attendance at all interviews between the Editors, or either of them, and lady authors. Hence it will be unnecessary for such visitors to provide themselves with either duennas or police whistles.

16. Choose your emergency exit when you come in; don't wait until the firemen arrive.

17. Visiting English authors are always welcome, but in view of the severe demands upon the time of the Editors, they are compelled to limit the number received to 50 head a week.

18. The objects of art on display in the editorial galleries are not for sale.

19. The Editors regret that they will be unable to receive visitors who present themselves in a visibly inebriated condition.

20. Cuspidors are provided for the convenience of our Southern and Western friends.

21. The Editors beg to make it known that they find it impossible to accept invitations to public dinners, memorial services or other functions at which speeches are made, or at which persons are present who ever make speeches elsewhere.

22. The Editors assume that visitors who have had the honor of interviews with them in the editorial chambers will not subsequently embarrass them in public places by pointing them out with walking sticks.

23. Photographs of the Editors are on sale at the Portier's desk.

24. Members of the hierarchy and other rev. clergy are received only on Thursdays from 12 o'clock noon to 4.30 P. M.

25. The Editors cannot undertake to acknowledge the receipt of flowers, cigars, autographed books, picture postcards, signed photographs, loving cups or other gratuities. All such objects are sent at once to the free wards of the public hospitals.

26. Positively no cheques cashed.

*In another pamphlet Mencken assesses the achievement of the magazine up to 1921, when the price rose from twenty-five to thirty-five cents. He mentions obliquely three "money-makers": these were what he elsewhere called his "louse magazines"—*Parisienne, Saucy Stories, *and* Black Mask—*which he and Nathan founded and then sold as a way of supporting their more serious endeavors. The piece is a clear statement, free of Nietzschean thunder, of the relationship of their editorial policy to Mencken's views on the superior person versus the "booboisie" that is the product of democracy and the target audience of more conventional magazines. Echoes of his classic "The National Letters," which had recently appeared in* Prejudices: Second Series *(1920), can be heard (excerpt from* A Personal Word *[New York: Smart Set, n.d.], pp. 1–8).*

George Jean Nathan and I took over the editorial direction of THE SMART SET in the Summer of 1914, just after the outbreak of the late war. I had been doing my monthly book article since November, 1908, and

Nathan had been doing his article about the theatres since a month or two later. It never occurred to me, in those years, that I should ever assume a large share of editorial responsibility for the magazine. John Adams Thayer, then the publisher and majority stockholder, had offered me the editorship several times, but I had always refused it for a single and simple reason: I didn't want to live in New York, which seemed to me then and seems to me now a most uncomfortable city. My home was and is in Baltimore, which I like much better.

But in the summer of 1914 that impediment was suddenly removed. Thayer disposed of the magazine to Eltinge F. Warner, publisher of The Warner Publications, and his associates. Some time before this, by one of the trivial accidents of life, Warner had met Nathan on a ship bound home from England; the two happened to be wearing overcoats of the same kind, and stopped to gabble idly, as fellow passengers will, on deck one morning. They had a few drinks together, parted at the dock, and never thought to meet again. But when Warner looked into the magazine that he was to manage, he found the name of Nathan on the list of regular contributors, and, recalling their brief meeting, sought him out and asked him to take the editorship. Nathan said that he would do it if I agreed to help him. There ensued negotiations, and the upshot was an arrangement that is still in force.

Our authority as editors is exactly equal; nevertheless, we are never in conflict. I read all the manuscripts that are sent to us, and send Nathan those that I think are fit to print. If he agrees, they go into type at once; if he dissents, they are rejected forthwith. This veto is absolute, and works both ways. It saves us a great many useless and possibly acrimonious discussions. It takes two yeses to get a poem or essay or story into the magazine, but one no is sufficient to keep it out. In practice, we do not disagree sharply more than once in a hundred times, and even then, as I say, the debate is over as soon as it begins. I doubt that this scheme has ever lost us a manuscript genuinely worth printing. It admits prejudices into the matter, but they are at least the prejudices of the responsible editors, and not those of subordinate manuscript readers. We employ no readers, and take no advice. Every piece of manuscript that comes into the office passes through my hands, or those of Nathan, and usually through the hands of both of us. I live in Baltimore, but come to New York every other week.

So much for editorial management. Our financial organization is equally simple. Warner made over some of the capital stock of the magazine to Nathan and me, and we three continue in joint control today. Warner's problem, when we took charge, was to pay off the somewhat heavy floating debt of the property, and put

Mencken in the Smart Set *office, 1921 (courtesy of the Enoch Pratt Free Library)*

it on a sound basis. This he accomplished before the end of 1915. From the moment he came into the office THE SMART SET has paid all authors immediately on the acceptance of their manuscripts, paid all printers' and paper bills promptly—and absorbed not a cent of new capital. Warner operates all of his enterprises in that manner. We trust his judgment in all business matters, as he trusts ours in editorial matters. The usual conflict between the editorial room and the business office is never heard of here.

II.

An impression seems to be abroad that THE SMART SET, selling at 35 cents, makes an enormous profit, and that Warner, Nathan and I have got rich running it. This is not true. Warner is a man of many enterprises and has made a great deal of money, and Nathan and I are both able to exist comfortably without looking to the magazine. Had we been inclined, we might have turned it into a very productive money-maker. This is not merely tall-talk; we actually did the thing with three other magazines. But from the start we viewed THE SMART SET as, in some sense, a luxury rather than a means of profit, and this view of it has always conditioned our management of it. We have

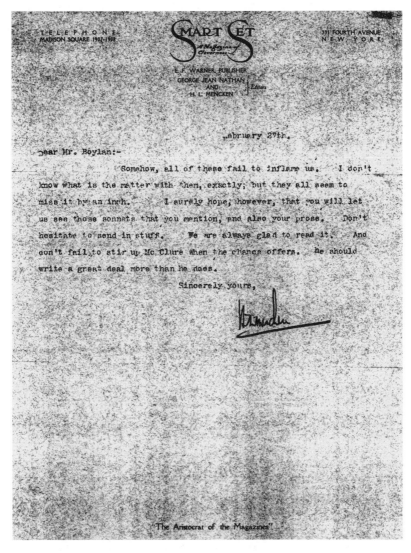

SMART SET

TELEPHONE
MADISON SQUARE 1902-1903

371 FOURTH AVENUE
NEW YORK

E. F. WARNER, PUBLISHER
GEORGE JEAN NATHAN
AND   } Editors
H. L. MENCKEN

February 27th.

Dear Mr. Boylan:-

Somehow, all of these fail to inflame us. I don't
know what is the matter with them, exactly; but they all seem to
miss it by an inch. I surely hope, however, that you will let
us see those sonnets that you mention, and also your prose. Don't
hesitate to send in stuff. We are always glad to read it. And
don't fail to stir up McClure when the chance offers. He should
write a great deal more than he does.

Sincerely yours,

"The Aristocrat of the Magazines".

Typically gentle rejection letter (Richard J. Schrader Collection)

never made any effort to attract readers in large numbers; we have always sought to print, not the most popular stuff we could find, but the best stuff. And we have never made any effort to load the magazine with advertising: it prints less than any other magazine of its class. This desire to be free—to run the thing to suit ourselves without regard to either popular taste or the prejudices of advertisers—has cost us much revenue, and the fact has not only deprived us of good profits, but also made it impossible for us to compete with the more popular magazines in bidding for manuscripts. But we have never regretted our policy. The authors who expect and demand enormous prices for their wares—the Carusos and Babe Ruths of letters—are but seldom the sort of authors we are interested in. It has been our endeavor, not to startle the booboisie with such gaudy stars, but to maintain a hospitable welcome for the talented newcomer—to give him his first chance in good company, and to pay him, if not the wages of a moving picture actor, then at least enough to reward him decently for his labor. We believe that this scheme has cost us very few manuscripts worth printing. We have not only brought out by it more novices of first-rate ability than any other American magazine; we have also had the pleasure of printing some of the best work of contemporary American authors of assured position, including Dreiser, Cabell, Sherwood Anderson and Miss Cather. Such authors, we believe, regard the atmosphere of THE SMART SET as different from that of the commercial magazines.

But our purpose, of course, has not been altruistic. We are surely not uplifters, either as critics or as editors. We have run our magazine as we have written our books—primarily to please ourselves, and secondarily to entertain those Americans who happen, in general, to be of our minds. We differ radically in many ways. For example, Nathan is greatly amused by the theatre, even when it is bad, whereas I regard it as a bore, even when it is good. Contrariwise, I am much interested in politics, whereas Nathan scarcely knows who is Vice-President of the United States. But on certain fundamentals we are thoroughly agreed, and it is on the plane of these fundamentals that we conduct THE SMART SET, and try to interest a small minority of Americans. Both of us are against the sentimental, the obvious, the trite, the maudlin. Both of us are opposed to all such ideas as come from the mob, and are polluted by its stupidity: Puritanism, Prohibition, Comstockery, evangelical Christianity, tin-pot patriotism, the whole sham of democracy. Both of us, though against socialism and in favor of capitalism, believe that capitalism in the United States is ignorant, disreputable and degraded, and that its heroes are bounders. Both of us believe in the dignity of the fine arts, and regard Beethoven and Brahms as far greater men than Wilson and Harding. Both of us stand aloof from the childish nationalism that now afflicts the world, and regard all of its chief spokesmen, in all countries, as scoundrels.

We believe that there are enough other Americans of our general trend of mind to give a reasonable support to a magazine voicing such notions. We believe that such men and women have the tolerance that is never encountered in the nether majority—that they like a certain amount of free experimentation in the arts. We thus try to assemble for them the novelties that seem to us to be genuinely worth while—not the tawdry monkey-shines of Greenwich Village, but the new work of the writers who actually know how to write. Thus we printed the plays of Eugene O'Neill when he was still an unknown newcomer, and the strange, sardonic short stories of Ben Hecht before ever he started to write "Erik Dorn," and the sketches of Lord Dunsany before his vogue began. As I say, we do not pursue neologism for its own sake: THE SMART SET avoided all the extravagances of the free verse movement, as it is now avoiding the extravagances of such foreign crazes as Expressionismus and Dadaism. We try to entertain the reader who can distinguish between genuine ideas and mere blather. It is for this reason, perhaps, that our poetry, to some readers—and especially to many of the new poets—seems excessively conservative. But here conserva-

tism, we believe, has served a good purpose, for we have certainly printed as much sound poetry, during the past seven or eight years, as any of the magazines devoted to *vers libre,* and a great deal more than most. Practically all the genuine poets of the country have been in the magazine during that time, and most of them have been in it very often. [. . .]

The editors used form rejections slips, but now and then Mencken wrote personally. His letters were usually comical and upbeat, briefly pointing out the reasons for rejection and inviting further submissions, as in this note, probably written in 1915, to his friend Louis Untermeyer (typewritten letter, with handwritten initial as signature, at the University of Virginia).

SMART SET
A Magazine of Cleverness

E. F. WARNER, PUBLISHER
GEORGE JEAN NATHAN
AND
H. L. MENCKEN *Editors*
456 FOURTH AVENUE, NEW YORK

May 25th.

Dear Bierbaum:-

The more I read these, the less I like them. What is the answer? Does my mind decay, or are you trying to work off some stickers on me? Detailed remarks:

"Here Lies --". I have bought 3 or 4 when-I-am-gones lately, f.o.b. New York and Chicago, and Nathan is already wearing crape on his arm. This one, I grant you, is ingenious; the technique tickles; but we must stop plucking the low, sad C string.

"Resurrection". Imprimis, you have used the ideer before. Zum zweiten, the Christians will think we are trying to kid the Rev. Dr. J. C. Josephson, deceased.

"Nocturne. . .B Minor". Not poetry, but a conservatory exercise.

"A Winter Lyric". Immoral, decadent, lewd.

"An Old Song": A sound lyric ideer, albeit shop-worn, but corrupted by lines tortured to make rhymes. How in hell can a redstart scatter the heat? Do you mean a snow-bird? Also elsewhere. The thing seems artificial. Am I right?

Send me, in Goddes name, a simple love song. I offer 2 to 1 that you have a barrel of them in your cellar. If not, what is easier than writing a couple?

Meanwhile, how are you, anyhow?

Yours, <u>M</u>

"The Aristocrat of the Magazines"

1524 HOLLINS STREET
BALTIMORE, MD., U. S. A.

February 14th

Dear Johns:-

I am voting for the poem, but with " in Winter"
expunged from the title. Why not simply "Nocturne"? All our
winter numbers are printed, and a winter piece during the summer would
probably arouse the suspicions of the Secret Service. I trust
that your unfailing sagacity will approve this change.
What else have you? I constantly suspect that you have a
bale of good stuff, all unprinted. Why not send it to me some day,
prose and verse, and let me go through it?

Yours,

The Second Coming of Christ is announced at Sandy Spring,
a small town in Maryland.

Letter of acceptance to Orrick Johns. "Nocturne" appeared in the January 1919 issue of The Smart Set *(Richard J. Schrader Collection).*

The joy of the editorial collaboration, even toward the end, is communicated by Burton Rascoe in a 1923 note. Nathan and "Heine" Mencken compiled The American Credo *in 1920. Contrary to what Rascoe says, Mencken was about a year and a half older than Nathan (excerpts from "How Mencken and Nathan Play," in Rascoe's* A Bookman's Daybook, *edited by C. Hartley Grattan [New York: Liveright, 1929], pp. 81–84).*

Thursday, January 16.

To lunch to-day with H. L. Mencken and George Jean Nathan, and Mencken told me that Nathan was about to retire from active life because he had been done for good and proper in a review by Johnny Weaver last week; "and Alec Woollcott has been getting after me," said Mencken; "I'll have to tell his brother to give him a spanking." "Heine has been expounding a theory," said Nathan, "that the demoralization brought on by the war has been responsible for the decline of the one great social virtue of the Germans—that of keeping appointments on time. It's all nonsense. The Germans never did keep appointments. I am going to send Heine a book called 'The American Credo,' item 979 of which is that Germans appear promptly for appointments.

Heinie is the victim of most of the superstitions set forth in that valuable little book." [. . .]

Amid the banter and the disparagement of some of our contemporaries we got in many good words of agreement on the question of the genius of Don Marquis, the high qualities in Dreiser and the work of Sherwood Anderson. Mencken told me that it was Dreiser who first discovered Anderson, that Jefferson Jones asked Dreiser to read "Windy McPherson's Son" and that Dreiser was very enthusiastic about it and wrote so to Mencken at the time. "Dreiser was always discovering great geniuses," said Mencken, "and they all turned out to be flivvers, except Sherwood Anderson. Dreiser thought Harris Merton Lyon, who was the nearest he came to discovering another genius, was as great as De Maupassant; and he was always getting all het up about some new man. There was the Fort fellow who wrote 'The Book of the Damned.' Dreiser thought Fort was greater than Zola and Maupassant put together. That's a side of Dreiser that has always been overlooked; he was always going out of his way to boost other novelists. He had a genuine altruistic interest in the development of American literature. He was never afraid or too selfish to take up a new novelist and work hard to win recognition for him. His trou-

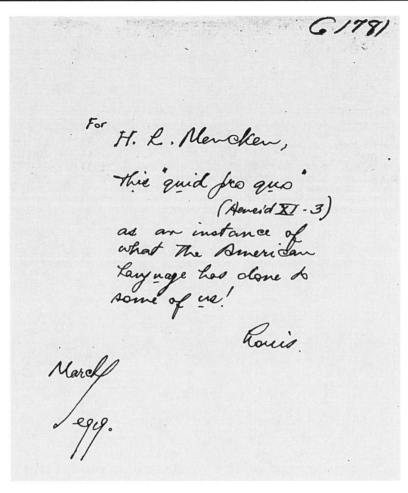

Inscription by Louis Untermeyer in his New Era in American Poetry *(1919), published the same year as Mencken's* The American Language
(courtesy of the Enoch Pratt Free Library)

ble was that his judgment was faulty. He uncovered too many flivs."

In the current issue of *Vanity Fair* Aldous Huxley has an article, not a good one, in which he has a good line about the young critics who are trying desperately to write like old men, and in reading it I thought at once of the contrast to that of the spectacle of Mencken and Nathan. They are both in their forties; they are men of wit, erudition, information, taste and intelligence, and yet neither of them has as yet drawn a long face and put on a judicial or professorial air. They are much younger in spirit, in outlook, in verve, in manner, than most of the younger critics not long out of college, two of whom Ben Ray Redman once characterized viciously by saying: "They have achieved senility before reaching maturity."

Mencken and Nathan are such inveterate playboys that they are always consuming a great deal of time and energy playing practical jokes. On St. Valentine's Day I always get from Mencken one of those comic valentines I have not seen on sale since I was a child, with a grotesque picture and some verses calling me a red-nosed sot who ought to straighten up and be a man, and not long ago I got an invitation to join an anti-Semitic organization, of which J. Montmorency Lubowitz, Sir Hamar Cohen and Anatole Knopf were members, all worked up at some expense of time and money on authentic-looking stationery. Louis Untermeyer gets Yom Kippur greetings from Mencken every year, with scrolls and doves and embossed designs; and I get from Mencken about once a month some sect's printed pamphlets announcing the second coming of the Messiah, with some such penned inscription from Mencken as "Pass the word on to Percy Hammond. This is authentic. Get ready." Nathan sends me advertisements of medical devices and notices telling where I can get a hand-tailored suit for $14.98; and Mencken sends me marked copies of *The Congressional Record* and bulletins of the Michigan Authors' Soci-

Form rejection slip

appalling dose, certainly! How many books have I reviewed, noticed, praised, mocked, dismissed with lofty sneers? I don't know precisely, but probably fully two thousand. But how many have I *read*? Again, I must guess, but I should say at least twice as many. What? Even so. The notion that book reviewers often review books without having read them is chiefly a delusion; it may happen on newspapers, but certainly not on magazines of any pretensions. I remember printing notices of a number of books that were so dull, at least to me, that I couldn't get through them, but in every such case I printed the fact frankly, and so offered no complete judgment. Once, indeed, I read part of a book, wrote and printed a notice denouncing it as drivel, and then, moved by some obscure, inner necessity, returned to it and read it to the end. This experience gave me pause and taught me something. One cylinder of my vanity—the foul passion that is responsible for all book reviewers above the rank of slaves, as it is for all actor-managers, Presidents and archbishops—urged me to stick to my unfavorable notice, but the other cylinder urged me to make handsome amends. I did the latter, and trust that God will not forget it. I trust, too, that He will not overlook my present voluntary withdrawal from this pulpit. The insurance actuaries say that my expectation of life is exactly twenty-five years; in twenty-five years I might write and print three hundred more articles—another million and a half words. If I now resign the chance and retire to other scenes, then perhaps it may help me a few inches along the Eight-Fold Path. Men have been made saints for less. [. . .]

III

Glancing back over the decade and a half, what strikes me most forcibly is the great change and improvement in the situation of the American imaginative author—the novelist, poet, dramatist, and writer of short stories. In 1908, strange as it may seem to the literary radicals who roar so safely in Greenwich Village today, the old tradition was still powerful, and the young man or woman who came to New York with a manuscript which violated in any way the pruderies and prejudices of the professors had a very hard time getting it printed. It was a day of complacency and conformity. Hamilton Wright Mabie was still alive and still taken seriously, and all the young pedagogues who aspired to the critical gown imitated him in his watchful stupidity. This camorra had delivered a violent wallop to Theodore Dreiser eight years before, and he was yet suffering from his bruises; it was not until 1911 that he printed "Jennie Gerhardt." Miss Harriet Monroe and her gang of new poets were still dispersed and inarticulate; Miss Amy Lowell, as yet unaware of Imagism, was

ety. Where they find time for all this fooling I don't know; but Nathan looks about eighteen, and Mencken, who is actually younger than Nathan, about twenty-eight.

Mencken and Nathan resigned their editorship of The Smart Set *with the December 1923 issue. Mencken wrote a valedictory in which he compares the state of American letters then with what it had been when his work first appeared in the magazine (excerpts from "Fifteen Years,"* Smart Set *[December 1923]: 138, 139–401).*

I

I began to write these book articles for THE SMART SET in November, 1908–that is, the first of them appeared in the magazine for that month. Since then, counting this one, I have composed and printed no less than one hundred and eighty-two—in all, more than nine hundred thousand words of criticism. An

writing polite doggerel in the manner of a New England schoolmarm; the reigning dramatists of the nation were Augustus Thomas, David Belasco and Clyde Fitch; Miss Cather was imitating Mrs. Wharton; Hergesheimer had six years to go before he'd come to "The Lay Anthony"; Cabell was known only as one who provided the text for illustrated gift-books; the American novelists most admired by most publishers, by most readers and by all practising critics were Richard Harding Davis, Robert W. Chambers and James Lane Allen. It is hard, indeed, in retrospect, to picture those remote days just as they were. They seem almost fabulous. The chief critical organ of the Republic was actually the Literary Supplement of the New York *Times*. The *Dial* was down with diabetes in Chicago; the *Nation* was made dreadful by the gloomy humors of Paul Elmer More; the *Bookman* was even more saccharine and sophomoric than it is today; the *Freeman,* the *New Republic* and the *Literary Review* were yet unheard of. When the mild and *pianissimo* revolt of the middle 90's—a feeble echo of the English revolt—had spent itself, the Presbyterians marched in and took possession of the works. Most of the erstwhile *revoltés* boldly took the veil—notably Hamlin Garland. The American Idealism now preached so pathetically by Prof. Dr. Sherman and his fellow fugitives from the Christian Endeavor belt was actually on tap. No novel that told the truth about life as Americans were living it, no poem that departed from the old patterns, no play that had the merest ghost of an idea in it had a chance. When, in 1908, Mrs. Mary Roberts Rinehart printed a conventional mystery story which yet managed to have a trace of sense in it, it caused a sensation. (I reviewed it, by the way, in my first article.) And when, two years later, Dr. William Lyon Phelps printed a book of criticism in which he actually ranked Mark Twain alongside Emerson and Hawthorne, there was as great a stirring beneath the college elms as if a naked fancy woman had run across the campus. If Hergesheimer had come into New York in 1908 with "Cytherea" under his arm, he would have worn out his pantaloons on publisher's benches without getting so much as a polite kick. If Eugene O'Neill had come to Broadway with "The Emperor Jones" or "The Hairy Ape," he would have been sent to Edward E. Rose to learn the elements of his trade. The devilish and advanced thing, in those days, was for a fat lady star to give a couple of matinées of Ibsen's "A Doll's House." [. . .]

At the apex of Mencken's career the writer and editor Carl Van Doren offered an assessment of his historic importance. He evaluated not only Mencken the editor but Mencken the reviewer, literary critic, and social satirist, his other aspects at The

Smart Set. While admiring Mencken's growing stature as a man of letters, Van Doren also pointed out the limits of smartness ("Smartness and Light," in Van Doren's Many Minds: Critical Essays on American Writers *[New York: Knopf, 1924], pp. 120–135).*

The democratic dogma has had its critics in America ever since the priests and magistrates of the first colonies began to note the restive currents which stirred among their people. Critics of the same temper roared at the Revolution, and lost. During the probationary years of the republic there were Federalists, and then Whigs, and eventually Republicans, to say nothing of Bourbons of different varieties from time to time. Most of these skeptic voices have been merely political, but not all. Poe, for instance, was a poet, concerned with art and beauty, and a critic who spread death among the idols of popular taste. H. L. Mencken is a wit, concerned less with art or beauty than with the manners of his nation, who aims his wrath at the very heart of democracy, announces that the system is no less a nuisance than a failure, and proclaims the empire of excellence. Like Poe, he uses every critical method except that of mercy, and, like Poe, he wins applause at every death he deals. He could not win this if there were not an alert minority which delights in the victories of criticism over commonplace.

2

Mr. Mencken, at whom academic circles still cock a frigid or a timid eye, grows steadily more significant. Before the war, of which he says that he neither advised nor approved it, he was a useful conduit leading to the republic from Shaw and Nietzsche and Ibsen. The war played into his hands, it begins to look, as into those of hardly any other literary American. Heretofore, to change the figure, he had been but an intern in the hospital of his American kind, satisfied with an occasional run in the ambulance, an occasional appendix to cut out, an occasional skull to help trepan. Now he was suddenly invited to apply diagnosis, surgery, or the lethal chamber in such a range of cases as no native satirist had ever been allowed to practise on. He found hundreds of politicians palsied with incompetence, thousands of journalists and educators and preachers flatulent with prophecy, millions of patriots dropsical with sentimentalism. He found idealists who had delusions of grandeur, scholars who suffered from obsessions of hatred, business men who had been shell-shocked out of all self-control, women whose long-repressed instincts burst into frenzies of cruelty. He found, what seemed to him the source and cause of all these maladies, the plain people turned into a vast standard mass, now dumb and snuffling like a flock of

-114-

made an immense success, and was soon earning $4,000 a month. The total capital put into it was $500, and we got this back in four months. Once the Comstocks tackled it, but it was really quite harmless, and the case was thrown out on a demurrer. I tired of this nonsense very soon, despite its profitableness, and in 1916 Nathan and I sold our interest to Warner and Crowe. We got a very good price: it put both of us, in fact, into easy waters.

There existed, meanwhile, a 15-cent thriller called Snappy Stories, beloved of shop girls. Col. Mann had started it shortly after he had sold the Smart Set, and had appropriated for it the two long S's of the latter's cover. The fact irked us. We found that we could do nothing about it legally. So we decided to start a long S imitation of our own. The result was Saucy Stories, which still exists. (The Parisienne suspended two or three years ago. When the American troops got home, all things French began to lose popularity). Saucy Stories made a great success, but Nathan and I tired of it, and sold it to Warner and Crowe. A year or two later we started the Black Mask, devoted to stories of mystery. It, also, was a success. Its readers included many judges, statesmen, and other such Eminentisimos. Nathan and I sold our interest in it to Warner and Crowe after running it for six months. Such enterprises begin as good sport, but soon become bores. Crowe was then near death. He was a very rich man, and liked us. He therefore gave us an excellent price. This price, with what we had already got out of the organization, sufficed to relieve Nathan and me from want permanently. Since then we have done nothing primiarily for money -- that is, in the magazine field. The Black Mask still

Page from the typescript for "Autobiographical Notes 1925," prepared by Mencken for Isaac Goldberg, his first biographer (courtesy of the Enoch Pratt Free Library)

sheep, now loud and savage like a pack of wolves. All the folly which overwhelmed him had, to his eyes, the symptoms of having risen from the body of democracy. No wonder, given his conception of life, that he should have laid aside his scalpel and have taken to the jolly bludgeon as the only tool he needed. No wonder, given the consequences of the madness he observed, that he should finally have declared the worst result of the war to be the fact that so many Americans survived it.

The wonder is, rather, that Mr. Mencken should have waked so many echoes among his countrymen. No other contemporary critic is so well known in the colleges. No other is so influential among the latest generation of boys and girls of letters. Substantial citizens and sound students who cannot agree with a half or a quarter of what he says, nevertheless delight in the burly way in which he says it and find themselves agreeing with more than they thought they could. He has endowed the decade with a whole glossary of words which breathe contempt for its imbecilities. It is in part because his voice is the least uncertain of all the critic voices that he is so clearly heard; but it is also in part because there was among Americans already a strong vein of discontent with democracy which needed only to be tapped to send forth gushers of criticism and ridicule. Idealism and optimism had been orthodox too long for their own health; suspicion had been gathering under the surface of the national temper. The war, by straining idealism to the point of reaction and optimism to the point of collapse, had considerably discredited both of them. The young and the irresponsible, looking at the mess the mature and the responsible had made of human life on the planet, lost what respect they had and broke out of bounds. Irreverence for institutions and ribald laughter for respectability and a hard directness of speech succeeded the older modes. And when the dispersed thousands who felt this new spirit cast about for a spokesman, they rapidly realized that in Mr. Mencken the hour had found its man.

3

What first attracted them was pretty certainly his impudence, as it attracts most readers to him at first. He is as brash as a sophomore is supposed to be. He has never heard of a head too sacred to be smitten. That something is taboo merely makes him want to try it once. He walks briskly into shrines and takes a cheerful turn through cemeteries. Here is what Mr. Mencken says of Lincoln's Gettysburg address, before which hardly an American has ever ventured to lift his voice unless he lifted it to hymn: "It is eloquence brought to a pellucid and almost child-like perfection—the highest emotion reduced to one graceful and irresistible gesture. . . . But let us not forget that it is oratory, not logic;

beauty, not sense. . . . The doctrine is simply this: that the Union soldiers who died at Gettysburg sacrificed their lives to the cause of self-determination—'that government of the people, by the people, for the people,' should not perish from the earth. It is difficult to imagine anything more untrue. The Union soldiers in that battle actually fought against self-determination; it was the Confederates who fought for the right of their people to govern themselves. . . . The Confederates went into the battle an absolutely free people; they came out with their freedom subject to the supervision and vote of the rest of the country—and for nearly twenty years that vote was so effective that they enjoyed scarcely any freedom at all. Am I the first American to note the fundamental nonsensicality of the Gettysburg address? If so, I plead my aesthetic joy in it in amelioration of the sacrilege."

His final sentence is, it may be said, much the kind of impudence which led this critic in an earlier book to call an archbishop "a Christian ecclesiastic of a rank superior to that attained by Christ." Both comments at least reveal a keen pleasure in the saying of sharp things. But in the whole comment upon Lincoln there is a larger sagacity which grows upon Mr. Mencken as he widens his inquiries and leaves mere witticism behind him. Those whom he first attracts by his impudence he holds by his sagacity. He may play upon the saxophone with the gesticulations of jazz, but he knows many important harmonies and he constantly brings them into his performance. Regarding theology, politics, philosophy, law, medicine, art, business, morals, character, language, he has said some of the shrewdest things in his American generation. Not all are new, not all are true, but they proceed from a singularly powerful intelligence expressing itself in a singularly untrammeled speech. It happens to be a tory intelligence, impatient of whatever is untried, unimpressed by the bombastic, the heroic, the altruistic, scornful of the unsophisticated; an intelligence which holds that the vast majority of men are supine; that those who are not supine are foolish; that those who are not foolish are knavish; and that the few who have brains or virtues must stand together or they will be smothered in the mass. It happens also to be radical intelligence, cutting away excrescences of verbiage, challenging sluggish habits of thought, daring to drive through morasses of emotion to the solid ground of sense beyond, carrying the guidon of reason into desperate breaches. Tory or radical, this intelligence has a reach and thrust which make it noticeable, no matter of what persuasion its observers may at any moment be.

Such an intelligence, however, unaided by other qualities, could never have got Mr. Mencken his audience. Instead of being astringent, as his doctrine might

Répétition Générale

By H. L. Mencken and George Jean Nathan

§1

*P*ATRIOTISM.—Of all men, the Englishman is the only one whose patriotism has about it an air of dignity. The Englishman loves his country in the way that a man loves a patient, faithful and sympathetic woman to whom he has been married for years on end and whose life with her has been replete with comfort and peace. The Frenchman, on the other hand, loves his country as he would a gaudy chorus nymph whose anatomy had fascinated him; the German, his, as a sophomore loves his college football team; and the American, his, as Jumbo loved Barnum.

§2

Hedonism.—Every man is a hedonist. The only difference between the two varieties of the sons of Aristippus is that one hedonist seeks his goal of pleasure on earth and that the other seeks his in heaven. The latter, posturing his anti-Cyrenaic doctrine, is actually the more selfish and more positively hedonistic of the two, since where the former seeks only the transitory and impermanent pleasures that the earth and his days upon it can vouchsafe to him the other seeks instead, under the gaudy labels of altruism, idealism, etc., with which he self-deceptively plasters himself, the everlasting and immutable pleasures of the world hereafter.

§3

The Denaturized Gob.—Few phenomena offer more refined and instructive entertainment to the public psychologist than the American navy's decline in popularity during the past twenty-five years. At the time of the Spanish-American War, as everyone sentient in those days will recall, it was easily the premier service in the popular regard, and in even the least of its exploits the great masses of the plain people took a violent and vociferous pride. They were proud, too, of the army, and its heroic feats against the Hunnish hordes of Spain, and one of the great captains of that army was made President for his stupendous feats of blood and blather in the field; but it was the navy that they cherished most, and the popular heroes that it produced were more numerous than those of the army, and in the main they were far more fondly cherished. Even the immortal Roosevelt, it will be remembered, was half a navy man, and what got him into the White House, I believe, was less his colossal butcheries in the land battles of the war, important though they were to the cause of human liberty, than his long antecedent struggles to free the navy from the politicians, and make it fit to fight. The navy, indeed, was popular before the war began, or even threatened. The army could tackle and massacre a whole tribe of Indians without causing half the public thrill that followed the bombardment of a Venezuelan coast village by the White Squadron, with a total loss of but one blind cripple crippled in the other leg. This White Squadron, I more than suspect, was the actual cause of the war itself. From the day it first put to sea the booboisie watched it with glowing pride, and longed for a

First page of the June 1920 installment of a regular feature in The Smart Set

have made him, he is amazingly full of the sap of life and comedy. Not since Poe has an American critic taken such a fling or enjoyed it more. The motive of criticism, he maintains, "is not the motive of the pedagogue, but the motive of the artist. It is no more and no less than the simple desire to function freely and beautifully, to give outward and objective form to ideas that bubble inwardly and have a fascinating lure in them, to get rid of them dramatically and make an articulate noise in the world. . . . It is the pressing yearning of every man who has ideas in him to empty them upon the world, to hammer them into plausible and ingratiating shapes, to compel the attention and respect of his equals, to lord it over his inferiors." Yet even this exciting conception of the art of criticism had to be joined with a particular endowment if Mr. Mencken was to be the personage he is. That endowment is gusto, and gusto he possesses in a degree which no one of his contemporaries can rival. In a decade of which too many of the critics have dyspepsia, Mr. Mencken, as he might say, "goes the whole hog."

There comes to mind a curious parallel with Whitman, drunk with joy in the huge spectacle of his continent filled with his countrymen. Sitting in New York or Camden, he sent his imagination out over the land, across all its mountains and prairies, along all its rivers, into all its cities, among all its citizens at their occupations. He accepted all, he rejected nothing, because his affection was great enough to embrace the entire republic. His long panoramas, his crowded categories, are evidence that he gloated over the details of American life as a lover gloats over the charms of his mistress or a mother over the merits of her baby. So, in his different fashion, Mr. Mencken gloats over the follies of the republic. But is his fashion so different from Whitman's as it appears at first glance? His intellectual position compels him to see a side which Whitman overlooked. What to Whitman seemed a splendid turbulence, to Mr. Mencken seems a headless swirl. What to Whitman seemed a noble cohesiveness, seems to Mr. Mencken a herd-like conventionality. What to Whitman seemed a hopeful newness, seems to Mr. Mencken a hopeless rawness. Yet the satirist no less than the poet revels in the gaudy spectacle. "The United States, to my eye," Mr. Mencken explicitly says, "is incomparably the greatest show on earth. It is a show which avoids diligently all the kinds of clowning which tire me most quickly—for example, royal ceremonials, the tedious hocus-pocus of *haut politique,* the taking of politics seriously—and lays chief stress upon the kinds which delight me unceasingly—for example, the ribald combats of demagogues, the exquisitely

ingenious operations of master rogues, the pursuit of witches and heretics, the desperate struggles of inferior men to claw their way into Heaven. We have clowns in constant practice among us who are as far above the clowns of any other great state as a Jack Dempsey is above a paralytic—and not a few dozens or score of them, but whole droves and herds. Human enterprises which, in all other Christian countries, are resigned despairingly to an incurable dullness—things that seem devoid of exhilarating amusement by their very nature—are here lifted to such vast heights of buffoonery that contemplating them strains the midriff almost to breaking."

4

Is Mr. Mencken, then, an enemy of his people? "Here I stand," he contends, "unshaken and undespairing, a loyal and devoted Americano, even a chauvinist, paying taxes without complaint, obeying all laws that are physiologically obeyable, accepting all the searching duties and responsibilities of citizenship unprotestingly, investing the sparse usufructs of my miserable toil in the obligations of the nation, avoiding all commerce with men sworn to overthrow the government, contributing my mite toward the glory of the national arts and science, spurning all lures (and even all invitations) to go out and stay out . . . here am I, contentedly and even smugly basking beneath the Stars and Stripes, a better citizen, I daresay, and certainly a less murmurous and exigent one, than thousands who put the Hon. Warren Gamaliel Harding beside Friedrich Barbarossa and Charlemagne, and hold the Supreme Court to be directly inspired by the Holy Spirit, and belong ardently to every Rotary Club, Ku Klux Klan, and Anti-Saloon League, and choke with emotion when the band plays the 'Star-Spangled Banner,' and believe with the faith of little children that one of Our Boys, taken at random, could dispose in a fair fight of ten Englishmen, twenty Germans, thirty Frogs, forty Wops, fifty Japs, or a hundred Bolsheviki." Whitman, with whatever other tones or arguments, never exhibited his essential Americanism more convincingly. Have Americans no speech but praise? Have they no song but rhapsody?

The truth of the matter is, Mr. Mencken is one of the most American things we have. Both his art and his success spring from the gusto which draws him to the comic aspects of the life around him—draws him with as great an eagerness as if he accepted all he saw and acclaimed it. To read him, even while dissenting from his doctrine on every page, is to gasp and whoop with recognition. Thus, for instance, he illustrates "Eminence," without a

NEW YORK, October 10, 1923.

The undersigned announce that they are relinquishing the editorship of THE SMART SET with the issue for December, 1923, and that they have disposed of all their holdings in The Smart Set Company, Inc.

They have had this step in mind for several years; lately, on their completion of nine years' service as editors of the magazine, they decided upon it definitely. For six years before they assumed the editorship they were regular members of the staff. Thy have thus put in fifteen years of continuous service.

They are withdrawing from the work so long carried on together because they believe that, in so far as it is accomplishable at all, the purpose with which they began in 1908 has been accomplished. That purpose was to break down some of the difficulties which beset the American imaginative author, and particularly the beginning author, of that time—to provide an arena and drum up an audience for him, and to set him free from the pull of the cheap, popular magazine on the one side and of the conventional "quality" magazine, with its distressing dread of ideas, on the other—above all, to do battle for him critically, attacking vigorously all the influences which sought to intimidate and regiment him. This work is obviously no longer necessary. The young American novelist, dramatist or poet is quite free today, and the extent of his freedom is shown by the alarm and dudgeon of the pedants who still protest so vainly against it. That protest, in 1908, was yet potent and damaging; today it is only ridiculous.

The undersigned have enjoyed the combat and do not tire of it. They are not eager for a rest; they are eager for another round. But their desires and interests now lead them beyond belles lettres and so outside the proper field of THE SMART SET. They could not carry the magazine with them without changing its name, completely revolutionizing its contents, and otherwise breaking with its traditions—a business plainly full of practical difficulties. They have thought it wiser and more comfortable to withdraw from the editorship, dispose of their stock in the publishing company, and devote themselves to setting up an entirely new magazine. This they are now engaged upon in association with Mr. Alfred A. Knopf, the publisher. The new magazine will be THE AMERICAN MERCURY; its purpose will be to discuss realistically, not only American letters, but the whole field of American life. The first issue will be as of January, 1924.

Letter from Mencken and Nathan announcing the end of their editorship of The Smart Set *and the founding of their new magazine,* The American Mercury *(courtesy of the Enoch Pratt Free Library)*

word of commentary: "The leading Methodist layman of Pottawattamie county, Iowa. . . . The man who won the limerick contest conducted by the Toomsboro, Ga., *Banner*. . . . The President of the Johann Sebastian Bach *Bauverein* of Highlandtown, Md. . . . The girl who sold the most Liberty Bonds in Duquesne, Pa. . . . The man who owns the best bull in Coosa County, Ala. . . . The oldest subscriber to the Raleigh, N. C., *News and Observer*. . . . The author of the ode read at the unveiling of the monument to General Robert E. Lee at Valdosta, Ga. . . . The old lady in Wahoo, Neb., who has read the Bible 38 times. . . . The professor of chemistry, Greek, rhetoric, and piano at the Texas Christian University, Fort Worth, Tex. . . . The leading dramatic critic of Pittsburgh. . . . The night watchman in Penn Yan, N. Y., who once shook hands with Chester A. Arthur"—and on and on with Rabelaisian fecundity. Nothing petty, nothing absurd, nothing grotesque, nothing racy of the soil, seems to have escaped Mr. Mencken's terrible eye. Though he has not traveled very widely in the United States, he knows the map as well as any continental drummer. Though he has taken only a journalist's hand in actual politics, he is virtually the first to hoot at any new political asininity. As if with a hundred newspapers and a hundred clubs for his whispering gallery, he appears to have heard every secret and every scandal. Nor does he content himself with random citation of what he hits upon. He hoards them and makes treatises. With George Jean Nathan, his dapper David, this rugged Jonathan has collected nearly a thousand vulgar beliefs in *An American Credo;* by himself he has composed a large first and a huge second edition of *The American Language.* He has, in short, the range of a journalist, the verve of a comic poet, the patience of a savant. Among American humorists no one but Mark Twain has had more "body" to his art than Mr. Mencken.

5

Poe, Whitman, Mark Twain—are they unexpected companions for a former editor of the *Smart Set?* Perhaps; and yet Mr. Mencken, laying aside to some extent the waggish elements in his constitution, begins to have the stature of an important man of letters. Unlike Poe, he has in him nothing of the poet and he has written nonsense about poetry. Unlike Whitman, he has not deeply studied the common man at first hand and he dismisses such persons with the insolence of a city wit. Unlike Mark Twain, he despises the miserable race of man without, like Mark Twain, also pitying it. What Mr. Mencken most conspicuously lacks, indeed, is the mood of pity, an emotion which the greatest satirists have all exhibited now or then. Even Swift, as indisposed to forgive a fool as Mr. Mencken is, occasionally let fall a glance of compassion upon folly. This is the particular penalty of smartness: though it may have plenty of light, it fears, even for a moment, to be sweet. Embarrassed in the presence of nothing else, it is embarrassed in the presence of ungirt emotions. Far from suffering fools gladly, it finds it difficult to overlook the dash of folly which appears in enthusiasm and heroism. Any habitual addiction to smartness makes almost impossible that highest quality of the mind, magnanimity. Mr. Mencken is but rarely magnanimous. It seems significant that he, passionately devoted as he is to music, so often misses the finer tones of eloquence when, as in poetry or prophecy, they are attended by expressed ideas which his reason challenges. Unless he can take his music "straight," he suspects it. The virtue of his quality of suspicion is that it helps him to see through things; its vice is that it frequently keeps him from seeing round them.

The writer and editor Carl Van Doren, who assessed Mencken's importance in his Many Minds *(1924)*

At the same time, however, Mr. Mencken is an utter stranger to parsimonious or ungenerous impulses. No one takes a trouncing more cheerfully than he; no one holds out a quicker hand of encouragement to any promising beginner in literature or scholarship. The stupidity against which he wages his hilarious war is the stupidity which, unaware of its defects, has first sought to shackle the children of light. It is chiefly at sight of such attempts that his indignation rises and that he rushes forth armed with a bagpipe, a slapstick, a shillalah, a pitchfork, a butcher's cleaver, a Browning rifle, a lusty arm, and an undaunted heart. What fun, then! Seeing that the feast of fools has still its uses, he elects himself boy-bishop, gathers a horde of revelers about him, and burlesques the universe. Of course he profanes the mysteries, but the laughter with which he does it and the laughter which he arouses among the by-standers have the effect of clearing the packed atmosphere. When the saturnalia ends, sense settles down again with renewed authority. If it is a service to Mr. Mencken's country for him to be so often right in his quarrels and to bring down with his merry bullets so many giant imbecilities, even though with his barrage he not seldom slays some honest and charming idealism; so also it is a service to his country for him, even while he is vexing a few of the judicious with his excess of smartness, to enrich the nation with such a powerful stream of humor as no other American is now playing upon the times.

In the Alfred A. Knopf firm's self-congratulatory The Borzoi 1925 *Mencken recalls how he became acquainted with the man who printed most of his great books—and printed them beautifully—as well as* The American Mercury. *His relationship with Knopf was the second great collaboration of his life ("Memorandum," in* The Borzoi 1925: Being a Sort of Record of Ten Years of Publishing *[New York: Knopf, 1925], pp. 138–141).*

It must have been in 1913 or thereabout that I first met him—a very tall, very slim young fellow, but lately out of college, with a faint and somewhat puzzling air of the exotic about him. I recall especially his mustache: so immensely black that it seemed beyond the poor talents of nature, and yet so slender, so struggling that it was palpably real. How he got into my office in Baltimore I don't remember: I was fat in those days, and lazy and very busy, and I did not see any visitors that I could avoid. No doubt he fetched me by raising the name of Joseph Conrad. He was, it appeared, in communication with Conrad; he had a Conrad letter in his pocket. Astounding and interesting! He unfolded a scheme to gather all the Conrad books together—they were printed, as I recall it, by eleven different publishers—and reissue them decently in one series. We were, of course, on good terms at once. It is a curious fact that we are on good terms still, despite innumerable transactions between us, steadily increasing in complexity and many of them involving money. I can recall no other New Yorker with whom I have communed peacefully so long.

That was before he set up shop on his own account. He worked for Doubleday, Page & Company, his backers in the Conrad enterprise, and a bit later for Mitchell Kennerley. I saw him two or three times a year, as he reached Baltimore on his rounds. A highly serious young man. He had a great many ideas, and was surely not backward about exposing them. One and all, they related to the single subject: the making of books. He believed that taste was improving in America: that good books would find a larger public year after year. He believed that Americans were beginning to notice books as works of art:

the way they were printed, the paper in them, the binding, even the dust covers. He carried around specimens of somewhat startling novelties in that line, chiefly out of Leipzig and Munich. He outlined projects for duplicating them, improving on them, going far ahead of them. It appeared quickly that a young man with so many notions would not long survive as a hireling. One day he told me that he planned to set up shop for himself. I daresay my eyebrows lifted: it was surely not a propitious time for ventures involving the intellect. The World War was less than a year old; doubts and fears consumed the Republic; people were reading newspapers, not books. He cheerfully threw in additional difficulties. He had, it appeared, no money, or very little. He hadn't even an office: a small space in his father's quarters would be enough. Worst of all, he had a girl, and would have a wife come Whitsun.

So the ship put out in October, 1915, with a jury mast, sails out of the rag-bag, and a crew of one boy and one girl. The girl, in fact, was not yet aboard; she shipped early the following Spring. For a number of months I heard nothing from the skipper. He was hard at work, vastly at work, almost desperately at work. Then I caught a glimpse of the ship. It had two masts now, and new sails, and a new and challenging ensign under the main-truck: on a field of white a spectral dog, leaping into space. This dog, I learned, was a borzoi; I know no more about it to this day. The ship now began to appear off my coast more frequently. It sprouted a third mast, and then a fourth. Sailors began to show on the deck, apparently well filled with proteins and carbohydrates. A smoke-stack arose, and belched smoke. Deck grew upon deck. I began to hear a band, and the shuffle of dancing in the evening. There were stewards, officers in blue and brass, a purser, a boots. A bar opened. In an imperial suite lolled the sybarite, Joe Hergesheimer. In 1917 I engaged passage myself, taking a modest room on D deck. It seemed only polite to pay my respects to the skipper. I found him immersed in books up to his neck—big books and little books, books sober and staid and books of an almost voluptuous gaudiness, books of all ages and in all languages, books in the full flush of beauty, ready for the customer and books stripped down to their very anatomical elements. And all the talk I heard, to the end of that first voyage, was of books, books, books.

It was five or six years, perhaps, before I ever heard him mention any other subject. No, that is too sweeping. Once—it must have been toward the end of 1915—he told me about the bride-elect: her willingness to make the voyage in that first crazy barque, her interest in books—nay, in type, paper, ink. Pres-

Alfred A. Knopf, who published The American Mercury *and Mencken's books beginning with* A Book of Prefaces *(1922)*

ently, I had a view of her: she seemed too young and too charming for it to be true. But I believed it later when I found her on deck, magnificently navigating the craft while the skipper took to the land, and visited the trade in Buffalo, Detroit and St. Paul. He went off talking books, and he came back talking books. Always books. One day, quite by accident, I discovered that he was also interested in music. We launched into Brahms instantly–but in ten minutes were back to the books. I tried Beethoven: he lasted longer. Bach: longer still. But even old Johann Sebastian, in the end, yielded to books.

That was in the days of hard struggle. Of late, with the waters calm, the decks crowded with passengers, and the holds full of–books!–I have noticed a growing expansiveness. There is more time to listen to the band, even to grab a clarinet and essay a few toots. One night, lately, we put in a solid hour belaboring Richard Strauss; not a type clicked, not a rose fluttered upon William Heinemann's grave. There have been conferences, too, on the subject of Moselle, its snares and mysteries, and on the hotels of London, Paris and Berlin, and on dogs, and even on the Coolidge statecraft. If I were younger and less bilious in my prejudices, there would be discourse, I suspect, on golf: I have seen the grotesque clubs of the game in a corner. There is a son to think of. There is a large and complicated organization, ever growing, ever presenting problems. There is the *American Mercury*. It has changed both of us, if only by

enormously multiplying our contacts, East, West, North, South. But to Alfred, I believe, it is still visible primarily as a book. Into it have gone all the ideas that buzzed in his head back in 1915. It is a sort of service stripe for him, marking off his first ten years as a publisher.

A piece in an anonymously published book gives the official view of the early days of The American Mercury *("Embryo," in* Three Years, 1924–1927: The Story of a New Idea and Its Successful Adaptation, *with a Postscript by H. L. Mencken [New York: American Mercury, 1927], pp. 3–6).*

All the ideas buzzing, as H. L. Mencken recently wrote, in Alfred Knopf's head as far back as 1915 have gone into *The American Mercury*. "It is," he continued, "a sort of service stripe for him, marking off his first ten years as a publisher." And Mr. Knopf himself has written that the desire for a magazine to fit in with his publishing programme had for a long time beset him. "But it takes," said Mr. Knopf, "an editor even more than a publisher, who will pay the printer's bills, to publish a first class review. The jobs are and must be kept separate and distinct. I had, therefore, first to find my editor." Co-incidentally, Mr. Mencken, dissatisfied with the old *Smart Set* and determined to change its policy or desert it altogether, was thinking of a review more to his liking.

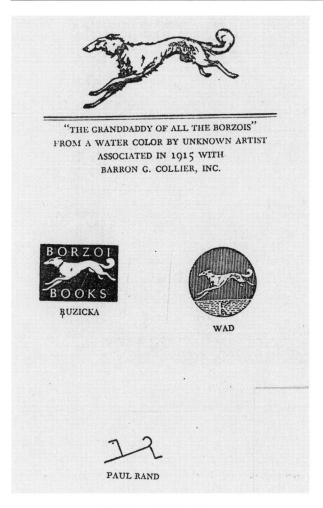

"THE GRANDDADDY OF ALL THE BORZOIS"
FROM A WATER COLOR BY UNKNOWN ARTIST
ASSOCIATED IN 1915 WITH
BARRON G. COLLIER, INC.

BORZOI BOOKS
RUZICKA

WAD

PAUL RAND

Variations of the Knopf logo

In 1913, Alfred Knopf and H. L. Mencken met. "We were, of course, on good terms at once," wrote Mr. Mencken. And in 1917, two years after Mr. Knopf had begun his career as an independent publisher, H. L. Mencken found under the sign of the Borzoi a congenial home for his writings. The commercial and cultural success of the venture may be read of in Isaac Goldberg's successful biography, "The Man Mencken" (Simon and Schuster). "Mencken brought," wrote Mr. Goldberg, "new prestige to the house of Knopf; to the books of Mencken, Knopf brought a business acumen that was heightened by a flair for experiment, commercial adventure, novelty, individualism."

The association, so agreeable to both men, naturally developed into even closer contact when Mr. Knopf chose Mr. Mencken to edit his new review. Since the forthcoming *American Mercury* was to concern itself wholly with American life, the editor could be no other than H. L. Mencken, who had for years given his most amused atten-

tion to the goings on in America. His mighty labor "The American Language" was itself sufficient reason for the selection. To have named another person would have been as absurd as hiring Queen Marie of Roumania.

In the Summer and Autumn of 1923 Mr. Knopf discussed plans for the review with Mr. Mencken and Mr. George Jean Nathan. Mr. Nathan was to act as co-editor at Mr. Mencken's request, and he remained so until July 1925 (withdrawing then because of his desire to be freed from the technological details of editing, but continuing as a contributing editor.) Mr. Samuel Knopf, father of Alfred Knopf, assumed the part of business manager, bringing to the venture the wisdom and experience of a long and interesting business career.

Announcements were made in the newspapers and a considerable amount of interest and suspense created. Mr. Mencken scouted for material for the initial number with all the delectation of Kit Carson hunting Indians. Extra office space was made and several fair young ladies engaged to care for the Founder Subscribers. Elmer Adler designed the handsome format of the magazine, and The Haddon Craftsmen were entrusted with the printing. The date of the first issue was set for December 25th.

Meanwhile there was a time of prayer. Friends were, naturally enough, encouraging and enthusiastic. The book trade was interested, and the press unfailingly cordial. Certainly there was reason to be sanguine. A few skeptical persons, it is true, insisted that the new undertaking could never be so good as the editor and publisher promised to make it. Such variety of material and general excellence, they said, could not be maintained. Others, doubtless mistaking Mr. Mencken's famous philippics against sham for radicalism, were openly hostile. They would be divinely condemned, they told the world, if they would pay fifty cents for a poisonous and expensive periodical. How curiosity overcame their prejudice will be revealed in the comments quoted farther on.

That *The American Mercury* was to be concerned only with American life and letters was disappointing to certain Tories. And the editor's denial of any evangelizing motive was ill received by the reformers. There was, however, a middle group, seemingly unknown to most editors, to whom the new magazine was dedicated. These were readers, intelligent, civilized and fair. On such an audience the editor and publisher of *The American Mercury* believed they could depend. It was, they thought, necessarily a limited group. And how, in ordering a first printing of only ten thousand copies for the first number, they greatly underestimated its size will be told.

At the press in Camden the new magazine was being put together. Its paper, the finest Scotch featherweight, sewn to a rich green cover so that the book could be opened flat on a table, and the beauty and dignity of its format gave a new note of elegance to the

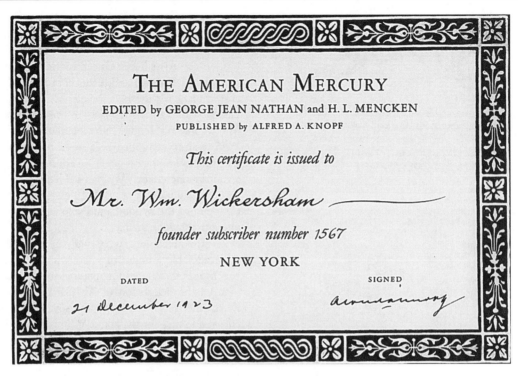

THE AMERICAN MERCURY

EDITED by GEORGE JEAN NATHAN and H. L. MENCKEN

PUBLISHED by ALFRED A. KNOPF

This certificate is issued to

Mr. Wm. Wickersham

founder subscriber number 1567

NEW YORK

DATED

SIGNED

21 December 1923

Certificate for charter subscriber (Richard J. Schrader Collection)

making of magazines. Elmer Adler, in *The New York Evening Post Literary Review,* wrote, "The editors, publisher and printers met to discuss the typography of the new magazine, how best to express its ideas in type form. The problem was definite. There were to be no illustrations. The type must first be legible, then only sufficiently decorative to relieve the otherwise plain pages. It must not be obtrusive nor interfere with free expression. It must be set both close enough to permit an easily read line and to present a not-too-difficult production problem. These were some of the main considerations. The decision was Garamond type." The result was a strikingly handsome yet dignified appearance which sets *The American Mercury* apart from its tasteless and gaudy newsstand neighbors.

The first issue of The American Mercury *was dated January 1924, the month following the departure of the co-editors from* The Smart Set. *It had an even wider audience and broader concerns than the earlier magazine.* The American Mercury *was the most respected journal of literature and politics of the 1920s, and its famous green covers marked the reader as a member of the "civilized minority." Those broad concerns, as stated in Mencken's contribution to* The Writer's Market, *explain why Nathan took less interest than before and resigned as co-editor in 1925 (from* The Writer's Market, *edited by Aron M. Mathieu [Cincinnati: Writer's Digest, 1930], p. 13).*

Its theory is that quacks give good shows and offer salubrious instruction, if only in the immemorial childishness of mankind. Nor are all of them clad in obvious motley. They exist within the circle of the American Medical Association as well as under rustic flambeaux, and in the great universities as well as beneath the banners of Communism, Kiwanis and the New Thought. To these austerely respectable quacks, in particular, loving attention has been given.

The American Mercury does not neglect *belles lettres,* but it makes no apology for devoting relatively little space to mere writing. Its fundamental purpose is to depict and to interpret the America that is in being; not the America that might be or ought to be. It would print more short stories if more good ones could be found. But not many are being written in the United States today. There are, or would seem to be, two reasons for this. One is that the form is probably in decay—that all of its potentialities have been worked out and nothing remains save to chase tails. Various ardent experimentalists try to overcome or evade its natural limitations but none of them, so far, has solved the problem. The other reason is that the market for bad short stories is so wide and lucrative at the moment that only romantic idealists try to write good ones. On the one hand there is the demand of the magazines of huge circulation for standardized stuff that will interest their vast hordes of morons and offend no one—in other words, for trash that will be turned into movie scenarios. And on the other

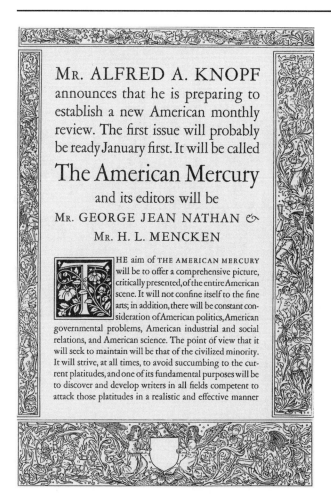

MR. ALFRED A. KNOPF announces that he is preparing to establish a new American monthly review. The first issue will probably be ready January first. It will be called

The American Mercury

and its editors will be

MR. GEORGE JEAN NATHAN &
MR. H. L. MENCKEN

THE aim of THE AMERICAN MERCURY will be to offer a comprehensive picture, critically presented, of the entire American scene. It will not confine itself to the fine arts; in addition, there will be constant consideration of American politics, American governmental problems, American industrial and social relations, and American science. The point of view that it will seek to maintain will be that of the civilized minority. It will strive, at all times, to avoid succumbing to the current platitudes, and one of its fundamental purposes will be to discover and develop writers in all fields competent to attack those platitudes in a realistic and effective manner

First page of the publisher's announcement of the new venture (Yale Collection of American Literature, Beinecke Rare Book and Manuscript Library)

hand there is the demand of the innumerable all-fiction magazines for trade goods on an even lower level–stories, indeed, for readers who are just able to read at all.

The magazine's aims and early progress are detailed in a 1924 letter soliciting a contribution from Untermeyer (typewritten letter with handwritten signature at The Lilly Library, Indiana University).

THE AMERICAN MERCURY
Published monthly by ALFRED A. KNOPF
Edited by GEORGE JEAN NATHAN & H. L. MENCKEN
220 WEST FORTY-SECOND STREET
NEW YORK

February 1st

Dear Louis:-

Unluckily, it is just too late, alas, alas! We have decided to cut out contributed reviews, and to revert to the Fundamentalism of my old book articles in The Smart Set -- in brief, an obscene show once a month. But what of an article? What ideas have you? What of your next book? Is there anything in it we could use?

Our scheme, in brief, is to stick to the Republic as closely as possible, at least for the first year. No treatises on Czecho-Slovakian politics or Bulgarian ideals. No translations from the Norse, Basque and Modern Greek. In general, no Dial complex.

The baby seems to be doing very well. We had to reprint the first number twice and the second number once, and our print order for No. 3 will be beyond 25,000. But Knopf is still losing his shirt. The grass paper and the fine printing are very expensive, and so far, of course, advertising lags. But it is growing, and when it reaches 32 pages a month Alfred will be able to buy two gross of new yellow neckties. Let us pray.

How long are you staying in Vienna? You are missing a superb show at home, what with Teapot Dome, the Anderson trial and half a dozen other such gaudy spectacles. Poor Cal is sweating blood. But I believe that he will be renominated and re-elected. He is a fine Christian man. Yours,

<u>Mencken</u>

Another piece in Three Years *crows about the quality of work in the magazine from 1924 to 1927 ("Conspicuous Articles and Authors," in* Three Years, 1924 to 1927: The Story of a New Idea and Its Successful Adaptation, *pp. 23–28).*

That an unusual and varied group of writers contribute to *The American Mercury* is the direct result of Mr. Mencken's extraordinary editorial policy. Famous and familiar figures of reputations long established are of course represented. And so are others, little known or unknown, who have something to say and can say it interestingly and clearly. Mr. Mencken in his weekly column in the Chicago *Tribune* has described the pleasure of discovering these new Dreisers, Cathers, and Hergesheimers. "A publisher (or editor) when he finds anything good in the garbage that gurgles over his desk all day is so happy that he sends for his bootlegger and kisses his wife." Seven hundred manuscripts come to the editorial room of *The American Mercury* every month. Of this deluge enough first rate work is selected to fill the magazine. Only contributions of the highest quality are accepted. Even distinguished writers, who are occasionally tempted to water milk for other magazines, are required to deliver cream to *The American Mercury.*

It will hardly be denied that H. L. Mencken has encouraged and published more young writers than any other American editor or critic. Word from Ruth Suckow, F. Scott Fitzgerald, Thyra Samter Winslow, and Countee Cullen, to cite only a few, would convince the skeptical. In *The American Mercury* new names have been developed and will continue to be as long as young Americans have the talent and the urge to write beautifully and well.

The distinguished amateur is encouraged to express himself, as he does authoritatively, on subjects on which he is better informed than the professional writer. Physicians, business men, lawyers, and even clergymen and hoboes have been heard. The hack writer never receives attention, his shoddy work being particularly anathema to the editor of *The American Mercury*.

The great names in American life and letters, with the new men and amateurs, form an exceptional company. There are mingling in the pages of *The American Mercury* aristocrats of literature and heroes and writers of picaresque adventure: Joseph Hergesheimer and Carl Van Vechten with Jim Tully and Frank Harris; Bishop Fiske of the Episcopal Church with Clarence Darrow; George Jean Nathan with Countee Cullen, the negro poet, to name only a few.

From the United States Senate in May 1925 a thousand barbed arrows were shot forth by the Honorable James Reed of Missouri in his article "The Pestilence of Fanaticism." And Arthur Krock's amazingly sympathetic piece "Jefferson's Stepchildren," appearing in February 1926, broke a seismograph in Washington. Amused and appreciative letters on this article were received by the magazine from three governors of states, and not all three of them Republicans. Famous figures of the past have been appropriately canonized, in particular Grover Cleveland, John Peter Altgeld, and William Jennings Bryan, in three separate studies from the diamond-pointed pen of Edgar Lee Masters. And Mr. Coolidge was examined by Frank Kent, the distinguished Washington correspondent, in an article in the August 1924 issue which was according to the New York *Evening World,* "the subject of conversation throughout the country." "The Shroud of Color" was published in November 1924, and Countee Cullen, the fine young poet, became famous, like Byron, overnight. Another poet, Edwin Markham, old and now but rarely heard, offered in August 1926 his "Ballad of the Gallows-Bird," acclaimed as equal in merit to "The Man With a Hoe," his most famous poem. Very little poetry has been published in *The American Mercury* but that little memorable and good.

Clarence Darrow is a frequent contributor, his article "The Ordeal of Prohibition" in August 1924 drawing this comment from the New York *World:* "Clarence Darrow, at present in the limelight as counsel for the defense in the Franks case, has more enduring

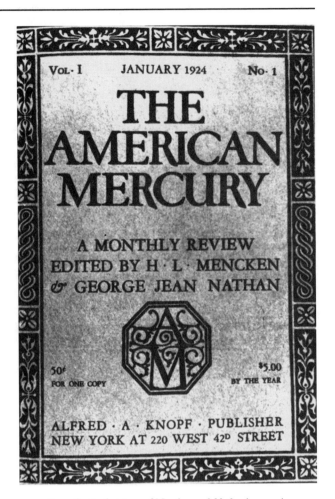

Cover for the first issue of Mencken and Nathan's magazine

claims to fame, among them an article in *The American Mercury* on 'The Ordeal of Prohibition'!"

Among many prominent men of science whose advanced ideas are welcomed by *The American Mercury* are Paul de Kruif, Raymond Pearl of the Johns Hopkins Institute, Emmet Raid Dunn of Smith College and Morris Fishbein editor of the *Journal of the American Medical Association.* Harry Elmer Barnes, professor of historical sociology at Smith College wrote "The Drool Method in History" for the January 1924 number and musty historical societies are still discussing it indignantly. A year later, in the January 1925 number Oswald Garrison Villard's brilliant satire, "Creating Reputations Ltd." brought forth much comment in the New York newspapers, Herman Hagedorn of the Roosevelt Memorial Society desiring to have a reprint of the article.

Sinclair Lewis in "Self-Conscious America" so enraged Harold Stearns, an American writer in Paris, that he threatened to return to America and administer violent injury to our contributor's body. This was in October 1925 and Mr. Lewis is as yet unharmed.

When "Aesthete: 1924 Model" by Ernest Boyd appeared in the January 1924 number, Burton Rascoe, devoting several columns in the New York *Tribune* to the reaction to the article, wrote: "Two hours after the magazine appeared upon the stands Greenwich Village was in an uproar." The satire aroused, as the New York *Times* put it, "an amusing and tasteless outburst on the part of certain young men who saw themselves spoofed in it."

Carl Dreher wrote "The Psychopathology of Business" in April 1925 and Orrick Johns "The Advertising Agent" in August 1924. Both articles were commented on and reprinted in advertising trade journals. "Shrines of Opportunity" by George A. Scott in August 1925 amused certain sophisticated business men and occasioned much comment.

In the realm of American Literature the nobility is well represented. Joseph Hergesheimer's latest contribution is "Art" in the November 1926 issue, an amusing philippic against current æsthetic cant. His beautiful portrait of Lillian Gish in April 1924 was enthusiastically commented on by a well-known motion-picture critic, "Such calm, carefully considered analyses coming in the midst of all the rabid and unrestrained gush that daily fills the movie journals are like a snatch of fresh air after an enervating trip in the subway."

Carl Van Vechten has written charming essays on tights, breakfasts, and one, "Mutations Among Americans," received especial praise both at home and abroad. Theodore Dreiser's story "Convention" is memorable. "All God's Chillun Got Wings" by Eugene O'Neill, appeared in *The American Mercury* for February 1924 before it was acted and was much commented on in the New York newspapers. That number, the second issue of the magazine, is now sold at some bookstores for ten dollars.

The various phases of religion have received a good deal of attention. In 1926 articles have appeared on the Methodists, Baptists, Lutherans, and Episcopalians. An article "The Catholic Press," one of the latest of the series is in the December 1926 number. These critiques are for the most part secular in tone, but occasionally a divine is persuaded to explain his particular brand of mysticism. These studies of contemporary religion go beyond this. They discuss religion in all its phases, especially in its overlapping the profane life of politics and the arts. Bishop Fiske's article "Bringing in the Millennium" in which he expresses his determination to continue resisting the commercialized welfare movements of today was agreeably received by the New York *Evening World* which announced "If this be heresy, let propagandists and paid servants of the 'uplift' make the most of it."

Lewis Mumford has written on architecture, Ernest Newman on music, Louis Untermeyer (a poet as well as a jeweler) on jewelry. Mr. Mencken's monthly journal and his book review department known as The Library are featured. Of one of these reviews Heywood Broun wrote in the New York *World:* "In the current (September 1924) number of *The American Mercury,* Henry Mencken has an essay on a medical theme which contains more wisdom than almost any doctor is capable of dispensing." George Jean Nathan regularly writes dramatic criticism and clinical notes. And there always is "Americana," that very comic, frequently tragic department, of which an editorial in the New York *World* writes that it is "made up of the most imbecile clippings from the American press; the material is furnished by thousands of contributors; it is without doubt the most fearful and wonderful digest of American thought now appearing in any American periodical."

Mencken enjoyed "stirring up the animals," and the magazine was attacked from all sides. His clipping service kept him informed of national rumblings, enabling him and his future wife, Sara Haardt, to collect and arrange the barbs in a dictionary of abuse (Schimpflexikon). *In the chapter on his editorial work the two connoisseurs listed almost exclusively the contributions from the right-wing and the ridiculous (excerpts from "As an Editor," in* Menckeniana: A Schimpflexikon *[New York: Knopf, 1928], pp. 65–66, 67, 68, 70–71).*

If anyone will send me the *Mercury,* I will inspect Mr. Mencken's pus collections, but I refuse to be salivated at my own expense.
JOHN HIGGINBOTHAM, *in the Springfield* (Mass.) Union. [. . .]

THIS PUTRID public pest, H. L. Mencken, is a significantly named public nuisance. His initials are H. L., meaning the first and last of the word Hell. He publishes a magazine called the *American Mercury,* and any doctor will tell you that nobody takes mercury but degenerates who have acquired the most loathsome social sexual disease known after an illicit honeymoon with some unwashed Lazar or Lazarette of the highways.

The Yellow Jacket. [. . .]

READ MENCKEN *passim,* especially his "Americana" department of monthly rakings by means of clipping bureaus from the entire press of America, with everything winnowed out save those scraps that tend to belittle our civilization. One Mencken in a generation is positively all that we can endure.
PROFESSOR FRED LEWIS PATTEE, *in the Christian Advocate.* [. . .]

Mencken in 1923

MERCURIANITY is the name of a new religion, the Bible of which is a green-covered monthly magazine. Its followers include blasé disciples of Bohemianism; young people in college who believe that anything which tears down is good; seekers after literary and æsthetic thrills, and a host of men and women who are discontented with contemporary American culture.

THE REV. LOUIS I. NEWMAN, *of San Francisco.* [. . .]

A TEACHER at one of the great Chicago universities said: "The one thing that makes me fear for the future is the number of our students who read the *American Mercury.* On the campus, you can see copies of it under every arm. Not only do they read it, but they absorb everything it says–they live with it. It is the greatest single danger that exists in American life today."

FLORA WARREN SEYMOUR, *in the Step-Ladder.*

H. L. MENCKEN, editor of the *American Mercury,* is known in New York as one of its brightest men. He is also openly, notoriously and positively its meanest. He makes meanness pay. Nothing is sacred to Mencken, from the character of George Washington to the divine form of beautiful woman.

The Idaho Statesman (Boise). [. . .]

Late in 1930 Mencken assessed for his readers the magazine's achievement even as its influence had begun to wane ("The Editor Reviews His Magazine," American Mercury, *21 [September 1930]: xxxiv–xxxv).*

Despite the effort of those who dislike it to credit it with this or that sinister programme, THE AMERICAN MERCURY is, in reality, quite devoid of propagandist aim. It belongs to no school, and proposes no new and thrilling remedy for all the sorrows of the world. Its pages are open to writers of all shades of belief, provided only they believe in something not revolting to an enlightened man and are able to argue for it in a good-humored and amusing manner. It naturally gives

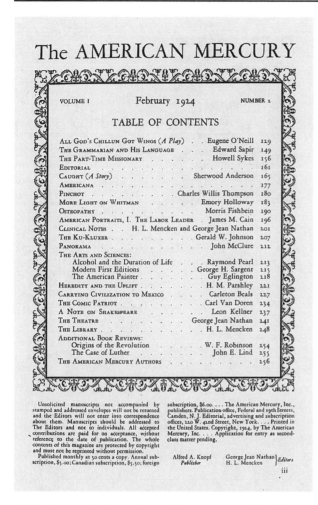

The AMERICAN MERCURY

Unsolicited manuscripts not accompanied by stamped and addressed envelopes will not be returned and the Editors will not enter into correspondence about them. Manuscripts should be addressed to The Editors and not to individuals. All accepted contributions are paid for on acceptance, without reference to the date of publication. The whole contents of this magazine are protected by copyright and must not be reprinted without permission. Published monthly at 50 cents a copy. Annual subscription, $5.00; Canadian subscription, $5.50; foreign subscription, $6.00. . . . The American Mercury, Inc., publishers. Publication office, Federal and 19th Streets, Camden, N. J. Editorial, advertising and subscription offices, 220 W. 42nd Street, New York. . . . Printed in the United States. Copyright, 1924, by The American Mercury, Inc. . . . Application for entry as second-class matter pending.

Alfred A. Knopf   George Jean Nathan | Editors
Publisher   H. L. Mencken

iii

Table of contents for the second issue of the magazine, considered the best in its history

no space to such imbecilities as astrology, Christian Science, communism, spiritualism, and the New Humanism, but otherwise it is very tolerant, and has been hospitable, *inter alia,* to both the most implacable defenders of capitalism and its most enterprising and pertinacious critics. In the field of beautiful letters it is likewise very catholic. It has made room for both decorous sonneteers and the contrivers of the most advanced varieties of free verse, and for writers of fiction of all schools, from the Victorian to the post-Joycean. The one thing it insists upon is decent writing. However its contributors may differ otherwise, they are all indubitably literate.

The magazine makes its appeal to the more skeptical and unimpassioned class of Americans; naturally enough, they tend to be somewhat well-to-do. It does not try to convert them to anything; it simply tries to give them civilized entertainment. Those persons who

chance to have been born with a firm faith in the incredible do not often read it, for they find it disturbing and uncomfortable. Thus it cannot hope to interest Methodists, or the ladies of the D. A. R., or the professional heroes of the American Legion, or Ku Kluxers, or believers in the Noble Experiment, or anyone else of that general sort. But it offers a steady supply of pleasant (and sometimes instructive) reading to those who view the world more blandly and more accurately, and there are enough of them in the United States, by God's inscrutable will, to keep up its circulation and warm its advertisers.

All the principal American authors, at one time or another, have contributed to its contents, but it is written mainly by writers who are not professionals. Among them have been men ranging from a United States Senator to a cotton-mill worker, from a college president to a trained nurse, and from a judge on the bench to a learned hobo. One of its most memorable articles, a truly magnificent piece of writing, was done by a man who, before it got into type, went to the electric chair for murder. Another came from a laborer in a lumber-mill, since turned author. It has always been very hospitable to such novelties, and it has printed far more of them than any other American magazine. They are presented because they help Americans to understand one another, and because they tend to be extraordinarily interesting. Many more of the same sort are in prospect.

THE AMERICAN MERCURY, with its first appearance, set a new standard in printing. It has been widely imitated ever since, but no other magazine has been able to keep up with its constant improvements. It is addressed to readers who want the best, both in contents and in investiture. It has been a substantial success, and is in a sound and secure position today.

In the last issue that he edited Mencken reviewed a translated abridgment of Adolf Hitler's Mein Kampf *and four other books on the nascent Third Reich. This document is an example of his turning to social and political criticism with greater frequency toward the end of his editorship. More important, it is typical of the writings that gave ammunition to friend and foe alike regarding Mencken's attitudes toward Hitler and the Jews. It should be noted that because of his temperament, upbringing, and journalistic training he had the habit of classifying and stereotyping people, largely within an American perspective. Thus, it should not be surprising that he classifies Hitler with William Jennings Bryan as an archdemagogue when one remembers that he hated Bryan. But he could not hate the German people, and his faith in their essential decency was tragically misplaced ("Hitlerismus,"* American Mercury, 30 [December 1933]: 506–510).

MY BATTLE, by Adolf Hitler; abridged and translated by E. T. S. Dugdale. $3. 5¼ x 8; 297 pp. Boston: *The Houghton Mifflin Company.*

THE EXPERIMENT WITH DEMOCRACY IN CENTRAL EUROPE, by Arnold J. Zurcher. $2.50. 5¼ x 8; 328 pp. New York: *The Oxford University Press.*

HITLER'S REICH: THE FIRST PHASE, by Hamilton Fish Aarmstron. $1. 5^1/$_8$ x 7^3/$_8$; 73 pp. New York: *The Macmillan Company.*

GERMANY ENTERS THE THIRD REICH, by Calvin B. Hoover. $2.50. 5^5/$_8$ x 8^5/$_8$; 243 pp. New York: *The Macmillan Company.*

THE BROWN BOOK OF THE HITLER TERROR AND THE BURNING OF THE REICHSTAG, prepared by the World Committee for the Victims of German Fascism. $2.50 5 x 7^5/$_8$; 348 pp. New York: *Alfred A. Knopf.*

I list a few of the first-comers among what promises to be a long procession of Hitler books. We are in for a great flood of them, like the flood of Russian books two or three years ago. At the time these lines are written Hitler has just flung his defiance to the world, and no man can say what his position may be by the time they come into print. On the one hand, he may have forced France and England into something resembling acquiescence in his demands, though they will never, of course, admit categorically that they have yielded; and on the other hand, they may be preparing to dislodge him by force, and have even proceeded to do so. But whatever the issue, it must be manifest that he has given Europe its greatest scare since the Bolsheviki reached the gates of Warsaw in 1920, and that the newspapers will print many a black headline before the debate over him is ended, and he sinks at last into the gray gloom of exploded and forgotten politicians.

The most surprising thing about him, it seems to me, is that his emergence should have been surprising. He was, in fact, implicit in the Treaty of Versailles, and, indeed, in what passed, toward the end of the war, as the Allies' statement of war aims. The underlying purpose of the whole uproar, we were told, was to heave out the Hohenzollerns, and give the German people the great boon of democratic government. There was no sign that any considerable portion of them longed for it, but nevertheless it was to be given to them. Ostensibly, the aim here was purely philanthropic: the Germans were to be lifted up in spite of themselves. But under that lofty purpose there lurked a scarcely concealed desire to make and keep them weak, and it was generally believed that both birds might be brought down with the same stone. The old imperial army, though it had been beaten at last, had held out against all the rest of Europe for four long years, and the evidences of its

A STATEMENT BY THE EDITOR

THE AMERICAN MERCURY

is quite devoid of propagandist purpose. It labors under no yearning to "educate" its public, or to put down Babbittry or Bolshevism, or to spread a new gospel of Beauty, or to save the World. Its one aim is to offer civilized entertainment to civilized readers. It is not alarmed and enraged by Babbittry and Bolshevism—two almost identical symptoms of the common rage of inferior men to instruct and run their betters —but amused by them. ∿ ∿ Its function is to depict America for the enlightened sort of Americans— realistically, with good humor, and wholly without cant. It is read wherever a civilized minority survives the assaults of the general herd of yawpers and come-ons. Its aim is to entertain that minority— and give it some consolation.

Flier, drawn from Mencken's contributions to Knopf's Three Years, 1924–1927: The Story of a New Idea and Its Successful Adaptation *(1927), that was inserted into books published by the firm*

appalling prowess were on every side. No one wanted another dose out of the same bottle, and it was felt that a good way to avoid it would be to turn out the undivided and highly military Hohenzollerns and set up a gang of democratic politicians, who could be trusted to spend most of their time and energy fighting one another, and so have little left for the external foes of their country.

This was wise reasoning so far as it went, but unfortunately it overlooked some unpleasant corollaries. The politicians who began practise in Berlin actually behaved, at least for eight or ten years, precisely as the Allied metaphysicians had expected. That is, they devoted themselves wholeheartedly to getting and keeping jobs for themselves and their friends, and were willing to make almost any imaginable sacrifice of their country's interest to that end. They agreed to the Dawes Plan, the Young Plan and a dozen other such fine schemes, all of them designed to keep Germany bankrupt and impotent. They were quite willing, on the one hand, to ruin German capital, and on the other hand, to enslave German labor, if only they and their gangs could continue in office thereby. When, as and if any German protested he was proceeded against with great vigor by the *Polizei,* and if he proceeded from talk to acts he was denounced to the common enemy, and in not a few cases actually put in the way of losing his life. Meanwhile, these stupid and often knavish politicos were depicted in the Allied and American press as great statesmen, and the fact was conveniently overlooked that a huge gulf was beginning to yawn between the German government and the German people.

The situation became so unendurable a year or two ago that even the Allied diplomats, an extraordinarily stupid class of men, began to realize that if it were not relieved there would be an explosion. Accordingly, certain concessions to the realities began to be made. Unfortunately, they were made grudgingly and did not go far enough; worse, they were arrived at after open and often raucous debate, so that everyone, including the more intelligent Germans, could see plainly that there was little honest good-will in them, but mainly only the yearning of England to get ahead of France, or *vice versa,* or the desire of Mussolini to shine as a world statesman. As for the common people in Germany, they began to despair. The prevailing politicians, at best, were only too plainly duffers, and it began to be obvious that the country would go to pot if they continued in power.

The German masses were thus ripe for demagogues, and the preaching of new and revolutionary arcana. Both appeared promptly, for both had been in waiting since the first dreadful years after the war. There were two gangs of these demagogues. The one preached Communism and the other a kind of Fascism. Each promised, if put into power, to proceed at once to the elimination of the other. The Communists, with the horrible writhings of Russia so close and so full of warning, found it impossible to convince any considerable number of sensible men, but they made good progress among university innocents of the type of our own Brain Trust, and they found it easy to round up millions of recruits among the proletariat, which had nothing to lose but its chains. The Fascists appealed rather to the middle class, which had been ruined once by the Berlin politicians and was in fear of being ruined again. They made but little more impression on the enlightened minority than the Communists, but what they proposed was at least less cannibalistic than Communism, and most of them, at the worst, were at any rate Germans, so they began to gather support in the upper income brackets, and to enjoy the advantages

that go with having money to pay for newspapers, parades and brass bands.

The ensuing combat was depicted by most of the American correspondents resident in Berlin as a low comedy comparable to one of our own presidential campaigns, and few of them believed that either the Communists or the Fascists would fetch the great body of non-political and naturally conservative Germans, most of whom, and especially the farmers, had a certain nostalgia for the Hohenzollerns, and were eager only to be let alone, that they might work hard and reaccumulate the capital wasted by the war, the subsequent inflation, and the pestilence of politicians. Many of these correspondents apparently believed that the Communists had the better of it; I can recall only one who predicted formally that the Fascists would really attain to power. The rest overlooked two things. The first was that the Fascists had much more money than the Communists, and could thus give a better show. The second was that they had developed in one Adolf Hitler, an obscure Austrian, a demagogic rhetorician of the first calibre—indeed, a fit match for either William Jennings Bryan or David Lloyd George, or for the two taken together.

This Hitler began modestly, and for a long while was a very minor figure in German politics. Down to 1923, when he got involved in some riots instigated by General Ludendorff and was jailed for a few months, he was scarcely heard of outside Bavaria. His political ideas, at that time, were somewhat vague. He had started out in Vienna as a Socialist enemy of the Hapsburgs, but had afterward shopped around among the small and often preposterous minor parties that arose in Germany after the war. Put up to speak, from time to time, for these discordant causes, he discovered an extraordinary talent as a mob orator, and was soon, as he himself says in "My Battle," "a master of this craft." It was a common feat for him to face a hostile audience of three or four thousand, and bring it galloping to the mourner's bench in an hour. German politics, in those days as in these, ran to rough-house, and Hitler did not disdain the protection of strong-arm men, but three times out of four he really didn't need it. He achieved on one occasion the impressive feat of talking down a hall full of Communists: many of them, in fact, rushed up to join him at the end, though neither he nor they knew where he was headed.

It is easy to see from Hitler's book that he is anything but a political philosopher. What he says in it is often sensible enough—for example, when he argues that Germany's first big task is to collar Austria and so consolidate the German people, and again when he argues that its natural route of expansion is along the Baltic, and yet again when he argues that it can never

Page from the March 1928 issue of The American Mercury. *The monthly column, prepared by Mencken, inspired national outrage.*

hope to make an honest friend of France—but always it has an air of second hand. In this it greatly resembles Bryan's "The First Battle," another effort by a mob orator to make effective rhetoric of the ideas of other men. Hitler was tutored as he went along by various theorists, but he quickly translated their theories into catch-words of his own, and he is quite as far from some of them today as Stalin is from Trotzky or Roosevelt from Moley. As an orator he is incomparable, at least in Germany. England may have his match in Lloyd George, as we had his match in Bryan, but the Germans have not seen his like in modern times. It is thus no wonder that they wallow

in his terrific eloquence, and forget to notice that what he says is often absurd.

His anti-Semitism, which has shocked so many Americans, is certainly nothing to marvel over. Anti-Semitism is latent all over Western Europe, as it is in the United States, and whenever there are public turmoils and threats of public perils it tends to flare up, as it did in France in 1894, when the French feared a new Franco-German war, and in Austria during the lunatic days following the war. The disadvantage of the Jew is that, to simple men, he always seems a kind of foreigner. He practises a religion that is not common, he has customs that seem strange to the general, and only

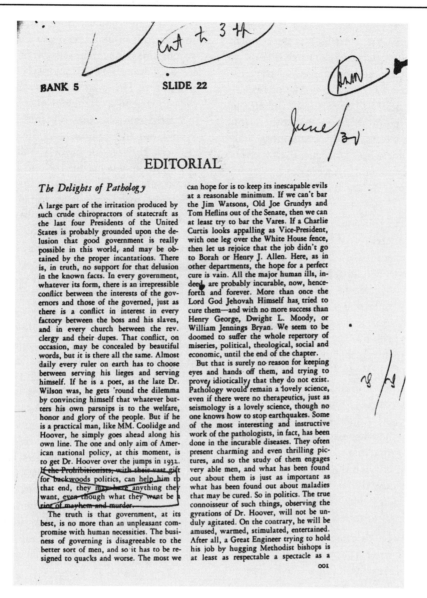

Proof sheet, corrected by Mencken, for the June 1930 issue of The American Mercury *(courtesy of the Enoch Pratt Free Library)*

too often he indulges imprudently in talk about going back to his own country some day, and reviving the power and glory of his forefathers. He is commonly a fierce patriot in whatever land he lives in, and he certainly was, at least in most cases, in Germany during the war, but his patriotism is always ameliorated, despite its excess, by a touch of international-mindedness born of his history, and in consequence he is commonly held suspect by patriots who can't see beyond their own frontiers. Thus he is an easy mark for demagogues when the common people are uneasy, and it is useful to find a goat. He has served as such a goat a hundred times in the past, and he will probably continue in the rôle, off and on, until his racial differentiation disappears or he actually goes back to his

fatherland. In Germany, as in Poland, Austria and France, he has been made use of by demagogues for many years, precisely as the colored brother has been made use of in our own South.

But at the time Hitler began to prowl the land the Jew was suspect in Germany for another reason, to wit, his entanglement with Bolshevism. This entanglement, in large part, was imaginary, and at best it was much exaggerated, but nevertheless it had some reality, at least in the plain man's eye. There were plenty of Jews among the Moscow master-minds, and they had proved their puissance by putting down Jew-baiting in Russia, for long the chief field sport of the Christian masses there. Moreover, the bloody *Räterepublik* at Munich—long forgotten elsewhere, but only too well remembered in Germany—had been set up and bossed by a Jew, and there were other Jews high in the councils of the Communist party, which proposed openly to repeat the Munich pillages and butcheries all over the country. It was thus easy for Hitler to convince his customers that there was peril in Israel, and in the end he managed to convince the more credulous of them that even the Jewish bankers, judges, doctors and store-keepers of Berlin were suspicious characters, though actually nine-tenths of them were quite as orthodox, politically speaking, as the men of their several classes in New York.

What followed was certainly not creditable to the German people, nor indeed to the human race in general. Once the paranoiacs on the lower levels were turned loose they proceeded instantly to extravagant barbarities, and the most innocent man, when he came under their fire, was no safer than the actually guilty. If Hitler had been able to confine the hunting to Communists there would have been no complaint in the United States and very little in England, for the Communists openly condone the even worse brutalities that have gone on in Russia, and would repeat them all over the world if they had the means. But when the Brown Shirts began to harass and intimidate, flay and murder perfectly innocent and helpless people, some of them Jews but probably more of them Christians, and very few of them Communists, then the world was shocked indeed, and Hitler has now discovered that shocking it is a very serious and dangerous business, with results not to be disposed of by oratory.

In such matters what is done cannot be undone; the main question, as I write, is how long the orgy will last, and whether it will wear itself out or have to be put down by external force. If the latter is resorted to, and it takes the form of military pressure, we are probably in for another World War, though it may not follow immediately. The Germans, of course, without adequate arms, could not resist the French, but once the French got across the Rhine it would be difficult if not impossible for them to come back, and their presence there would inevitably set off a general conflagration. A general boycott would not be as dangerous, but its effect, I think, would be to strengthen rather than weaken Hitler at home, where his theory of a huge conspiracy against Germany would begin to be believed in by millions who now doubt it. Moreover, such a boycott would be resisted elsewhere in the world, and here in the United States it might easily launch a formidable anti-Semitic movement, especially in view of the fact that many of the current Jewish leaders in this country are very loud and brassy fellows, with an unhappy talent for making the *Goyim* Jew-conscious.

There remains the remedy of sober second thought. It can be relied on to cure even the wildest and wooliest of public manias soon or late, but unfortunately it takes time. That a majority of Germans will go on yielding to Hitler *ad infinitum* is hard to believe, and in fact downright incredible. Either he will have to change his programme so that it comes into reasonable accord with German tradition and the hard-won principia of modern civilization, or they will rise against him and turn him out. He has the bayonets today and so he seems irresistible, but it is not to be forgotten that those same bayonets, on some near tomorrow, may be turned against him, and that he has only one throat to cut. Mussolini, to be sure, has lasted since 1922 and the Bolsheviks of Moscow since 1917. But I incline to think that the Germans are much less likely to follow Slav and Latin example in this matter than to stick to the ways of their own blood.

Bryan, in all probability, was actually elected President of the United States in 1896, and yet by 1904 he was already a comic character, and before he died his old huge following had shrunk to a feeble rabble of half-wits. Lloyd George was the sole and absolute proprietor of Great Britain in 1919, but today he bosses only himself.

The Ku Klux Klan in 1920 had millions of members, could count upon close to a majority in Congress, and controlled at least twenty States, but by 1925 it was dispersed and impotent, and its Hitler was in jail. The American Legion ran amuck at about the same time, and somewhere in my files are at least twenty pounds of newspaper clippings describing the heroic mauling of unarmed and helpless persons, including many Jews, by its brave lads. Yet the legion, today, is simply a gang of professional pension-grabbers, and even politicians kick it about.

Mencken's partial eclipse on the national stage began with the Great Depression and lasted until he regained an audience with the fourth edition of The American Language *(1936) and retained it with his mellow reminiscences in the* Days *books of the 1940s. The last issue of* The American Mercury *edited by Mencken was published in December 1933; Henry Hazlitt replaced him. Theodore Maynard, a poet at Mt. St. Mary's College in Emmitsburg, Md., summarized Mencken's achievement as editor and critic. The prediction that Mencken had no more to say was not fulfilled (excerpts from "Mencken Leaves 'The American Mercury,'"* Catholic World, *139 [April 1934]: 10–20).*

Let me make two preliminary remarks. The first is that I know Henry Mencken and have a great respect and liking for him. Therefore perhaps I write with a bias in his favor, though it should be said that I respected him long before I knew him. The second remark is that I do not propose offering here a general

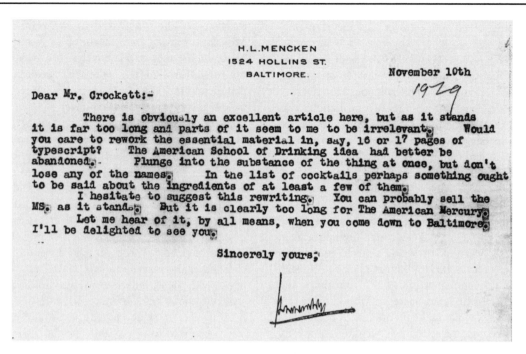

H.L.MENCKEN
1524 HOLLINS ST.
BALTIMORE.

November 10th
1929

Dear Mr. Crockett:-

There is obviously an excellent article here, but as it stands it is far too long and parts of it seem to me to be irrelevant. Would you care to rework the essential material in, say, 16 or 17 pages of typescript? The American School of Drinking idea had better be abandoned. Plunge into the substance of the thing at once, but don't lose any of the names. In the list of cocktails perhaps something ought to be said about the ingredients of at least a few of them.

I hesitate to suggest this rewriting. You can probably sell the MS. as it stands. But it is clearly too long for The American Mercury.

Let me hear of it, by all means, when you come down to Baltimore. I'll be delighted to see you.

Sincerely yours,

Rejection letter from The American Mercury *(Richard J. Schrader Collection)*

discussion of the life and miracles of the Sage of Baltimore, or even of his literary work as a whole. My concern is primarily with his editorship of *The American Mercury*.

Of his early work on Baltimore newspapers, or on *The Smart Set* from 1908–23, I do not know enough to speak with any competence, though I am aware that this should be considered in any final estimate of Mencken. But as nothing so ambitious as such an estimate is to be attempted, there is hardly any need for an apology. And, after all, *The Smart Set* was conducted in a mood of sardonic cynicism, the trashy stories being offered to what Mencken loves to call the "booboisie," and the mordant criticism (which was the real purpose of the magazine) to what some people, but never Mencken himself, love to call the "intelligentsia." It was in *The American Mercury* that Mencken really set up a pulpit from which he could address the country. So distinctive a thing did he make of it that it is difficult to conceive of it without him. We may get a very good magazine from Mr. Hazlitt, but it is bound to be a different magazine under the old name. I wish it all success, but the terms "Mencken" and "Mercury" will remain always inseparable in my mind. I shed a few tears of regret before continuing.

In January, 1924, the first number of *The American Mercury* appeared under the editorship of H. L. Mencken and George Jean Nathan. All the characteristic features of the magazine had been carefully thought

out, so that during ten years it has received practically no modification. From the beginning it was a smashing success, the first issue having to be printed twice. In fact, its success was greater at the start than later on. The depression caused sales to drop off; but even had the Coolidge boom kept up, *The Mercury* would probably have declined somewhat. Mencken had done his work so thoroughly that everybody who had read the early issues had a pretty good inkling as to what would be in the later ones. He had thumped his point home so well that there was no longer much need of doing any thumping at all. Yet I am reliably informed that *The Mercury* was almost alone among magazines of its class in the fact that it ended 1933 with a profit.

From the start it was Mencken's magazine. He had, indeed, stipulated that Nathan should be associated with him; but it was plain that the association was merely nominal. There were for some time joint "Clinical Notes" (mainly written by Nathan), and some pages of dramatic criticism, wholly written by him. But it is clear that his function was that of an advisory contributor. After the first year it was announced as such, and eventually he retired altogether. It is no reflection upon him to say that he never really fitted into *The Mercury*. His keen intelligence takes little interest in the turbulent life of the world, though nobody could make more bitingly satirical comments upon some of its more superficial aspects. In politics he has no interest whatsoever. As Mencken once said of him, he probably could not name the Vice-President of the United States. Without precisely living in an ivory tower, his life is mainly spent in the theater.

But Mencken's preoccupation was with the whole of American life, though his riotous taste in humor led him to prefer its gaudier manifestations. His gusto at first sight leaves one with the impression that he was willing to gobble everything down without discrimination. But with that gusto goes a delicate epicureanism: none of his cannibal banquets is quite complete without a Methodist bishop or a dry senator to grace the board. These were his larks' wings and nightingales' tongues. On the other hand, those Anti-Saloon League ecclesiastics and politicians who thought of Mencken as a dreadful ogre who could be satisfied with nothing except their raw flesh, were in error. He enjoyed morticians and beauticians and horticians almost as much. On lean days he would even tear a Lion limb from limb, and track a Shriner to the inmost recesses of his shrine. He has even been known to make do upon such coarse fare as insurance company executives, realtors, publicity experts, shoe-salesmen, radio-announcers, chiropractors and taxi-drivers, with a little juice squeezed out of the bones of bootleggers and baseball-players as a sauce. Not always could he roll upon his voluptuous tongue the blood of Y. M. C. A. secretaries or prohibition enforcement officers. No doubt Mencken is a monster, but only on holydays of obligation did he fasten his vampire teeth on a justice of the Supreme Court or a founder of a new religion.

Yet in spite of somewhat rowdy fun at times, *The Mercury's* articles were almost always well-informed. Mencken saw to that. If he had a way of jazzing up the contributions to his magazine, he was also careful to check statements of fact. One may think his point of view warped, or dislike his style, but I cannot recall where any of his critics convicted him of serious error. Never once has he been sued for libel, despite his years of outspoken controversy. *The Mercury* told us many things which we could not easily learn about elsewhere; and it was generally safe to rely upon what we were told. Despite his fondness for wild humor, Mencken has an extremely orderly mind, chock-full of practicality and common sense, and detests inaccuracy as much as any other form of slovenly inefficiency.

The Mercury was above all else *The American Mercury,* and confined itself to life in this country. It never contained articles about happenings in Europe, unless they were concerned with the way Americans disported themselves in, say, Paris or Majorca. Even European books received scant attention, when they were noticed at all.

Many Americans were very naturally indignant at some of the aspects of the American scene that were exposed, and at the irreverence with which many of their most cherished traditions were handled. As Mencken himself put it, he for years spilled ink "denouncing that hypocrisy that runs, like a hair in a hot dog, through the otherwise beautiful fabric of American life." With loud scoffs he derided all the politicians and wowsers and members of Rotary who unctuously proclaimed that their lives were dedicated to the social uplift. [. . .]

No doubt Mencken would be the first to admit that Rotarians are a very harmless bunch of fellows. If he derided them, it was because they laid themselves wide open to the shafts of satire. He understood very well that by making them look absurd he would help to discredit all those other well-meaning but fatuous groups of people whose complacent good-nature tends to smother the spread of ideas. It was no good trying to argue with them; indeed there was nothing very much that one could argue about. The only thing that could be done was to try and laugh them out of existence.

As these were the very people that the mass of Americans had been taught to admire and imitate, there was a good deal of bewilderment and indignation when they were attacked. Mencken was therefore denounced by them as being un-American, a dangerous radical, a Jew, the Teuton Blond Beast, an Anglophile, and what not. He laughed at the anger he aroused, kept (and later published) a scrapbook of the terms of abuse used against himself, and let fly another quiver of arrows—with devastating effect. There was no need for him even to take the trouble to defend himself against the charge of being un-American. Though a German in blood he has none of the marks of a German about him, unless it be a liking for beer and music and methodical industry. But so far from being ponderous or stodgy, his mind clicks to a hair-trigger, and his flow of ideas is fantastic and prolific rather than deep. It would be hard to find a more representative American. However much he might make fun of American life and American institutions, one could not imagine him living anywhere except in America, or having been produced by any country but America. He had nothing in common with those æsthetic fellow-countrymen of his who, after a brief acquaintance with England or France, are never able to be happy again anywhere except abroad. When Mencken is asked why he does not clear out of the United States, since he holds the opinions he does, he answers very simply that it is because he would not for worlds miss the spectacle of rich absurdity provided for his entertainment here. That is his way of saying that he likes America too much to leave. He might add (but as he never will, I must do it for him) that he loves America too much to leave. He would warmly repudiate any suggestion that he stays for his country's good. He loathes all reformers and

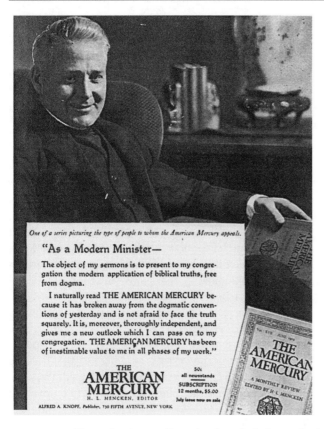

House advertisements illustrating the magazine's appeal to independent thinkers (courtesy of the Enoch Pratt Free Library)

up-lifters. But he is doing what he can to increase the dignity and honesty and charm of American life. No doubt he does relish to the full the antics of the people he derides; but were he merely the detached spectator he would at most sneer at them. His furious and boisterous propaganda at their expense would have no meaning, did he not hope to do his part in exterminating them as pests. It would be a sad day for him when the last of them perished; but upon his conscience there rests the inexorable duty of working towards that day.

If Mencken has, as his chief assets, humor and honesty and good sense, his chief deficiency would seem to be philosophical. Not that he is without a philosophy, but it does not strike one as being very important. Thousands will laugh and cheer when he goes on the warpath against the Babbitts, where hardly one will listen when he begins to expound his system. He may be said to have a huge following, but no disciples. As Ernest Boyd says in his book on Mencken, he has had "a Nietzschean education, and he is loyal to his old teacher, but his philosophy of life and art has little of Nietzsche in it, and their points of contact are probably fewer than their points of divergence. Their one fundamental point of agreement is their rejection of Christianity and democracy." Even if we are to take the

somewhat sportive *In Defense of Women* (thoroughly repudiated by Mencken in practice since his marriage) as owing something to Nietzsche, it would still be true that Mencken is a Nietzschean in a Pickwickian sense. Even where the views of the two philosophers coincide—that is, concerning Christianity and democracy— the coincidence is far from perfect. With little of Nietzsche's bitter rancor, Mencken attacks a corrupt congressman rather than the philosophical idea of democracy; Elmer Gantry rather than Christianity. A believer in Christianity and democracy must not only approve of all this, but the more sincere his conviction, the stronger must be his approval. In the specific case Mencken is nearly always right; his general principle may be unsound, but is of little consequence one way or the other.

I must confess having always been mildly amused at Mencken's announcing himself as an aristocrat. For he is the most sociable and accessible of mortals, without a particle of "side," a good mixer, positively exuding bonhomie. Now I am aware that a real aristocrat has no need to cultivate an icy aloofness. In fact that is generally the mark of the parvenu. But the easy and affable manners of the aristocrat will have also at all times a touch of distinction. Mencken, on the other hand, is thoroughly *bourgeois,* though in the best sense: cheerful, sturdy, independent, comfortable. I do not question the sincerity of his aristocratic principle. But I recall another, and a far more fierce, upholder of that principle: Coventry Patmore. He was all that Mencken is not: arrogant, intolerant, but quite content to let the world go to the devil in its own way. If I am obliged to applaud his greater consistency, I confess that I much prefer Mencken's "aristocracy" on all other grounds.

Mencken's political theory boils down to this: that there should be honesty and competence in politics, and that under the parliamentary system we rarely get either. Both points may be admitted by the firmest believer in democracy. But it must be immediately added that the aristocratic system offers no better guarantee of our obtaining them, if as good a one. All that a man of intelligence and public spirit can be expected to do is to expose chicanery and stupidity wherever they appear. This Mencken always does. His practice being what it is, his political theory may be whatever he chooses to call it.

Moreover, Mencken, being the man he is, does not stop to argue with anyone of whom he disapproves. He takes a battle-ax, and tries to split his enemy's skull—which, after all, is the most effective method of controversy. He is deterred by no feelings for exalted personages, or by any concessions to respectability. Presidents Harding, Coolidge and Hoover were each in turn served in much the same way; and, though at the time many people thought Mencken was using almost blasphemous language, it would seem that the country has come very generally to share his opinions of its former heroes. [. . .]

What it all comes to is this: Mencken makes no pretense to being a "constructive critic." He is purely destructive, but is, as such, decidedly beneficial to society. Contrary to what is generally held concerning a destructive critic, I cannot see that he is obliged to have something better to put in the place of the evil thing he would destroy. By sitting down to write a perfect constitution for future generations, he would give the scoundrels he was out to attack every chance to escape, or, perhaps, even to go, still secure in place and profit, to their graves. [. . .]

To what extent Mencken's criticism of certain Protestant sects has been fair, and to what extent unfair, I must leave those sects themselves to determine. But there can be no doubt whatever that, however noble the motive may have been, this country has lain under the harrow of the Anti-Saloon League, and that this was a machine of outrageous religious tyranny. There can be no doubt that American Catholics have suffered from intolerance and bigotry, deliberately directed against them by the same ecclesiastical groups who ran the Anti-Saloon League. On this score Catholics are deeply indebted to Mencken. He has done valiantly in helping to discredit our bitterest enemies.

But it is not merely because Mencken has been the enemy of those groups from which we have suffered most, that Catholics owe him a debt of gratitude. His friendly feelings towards us are shown in more positive ways. His references to the Church are kindly and respectful, because, as he says, "It is manifestly more honest, intelligent and urbane than any of the dominant Protestant sects." Now and then, it is true, he has pilloried Catholics in "Americana"; but only rarely has this happened. I recall one such case. A Catholic family in New Jersey while eating a dessert of Jello, found that the fragments left upon one of the plates resembled a statue of the Little Flower. The miraculously formed statue was exhibited to their pious (and moronic) neighbors. Well, I believe such assininity ought to be ridiculed. There are fools among Catholics, as among other people. Whether it is because Catholics more rarely make fools of themselves than, say, Baptists, which I hope is the reason, or whether it is because Mencken has a more friendly feeling for Catholics, it is certainly true that they have no reason to complain of their treatment at his hands. There is no human likelihood of his ever becoming a Catholic. Nevertheless Catholics have received a good deal of aid and comfort from him.

But if Mencken had never said a word in our favor, his strenuous fight against cant and sentimentality and humbug, by clearing the air, tends to our advantage. With the battle over literary censorship the Church officially has no concern. We have our own *Index,* which is designed primarily as a barrier against the dissemination of heresy. The individual conscience has to be the guide with regard to works stained with pornography.

When the law steps in at this point the question becomes hopelessly confused. All Catholics of course hold that works likely to have an immoral effect should be neither written nor read; and some Catholics have supported their suppression by the State. The result is merely that works which may not be sent through the mails, may be sent by express. Furthermore it would seem to be impossible for the law to decide intelligently as to what works are immoral. I take a case in point. James Joyce's *Ulysses* has until recently been banned. Now that enormous work has sections in which the limit of obscenity is reached, in the sense of Joyce's using all the nine unprintable Anglo-Saxon monosyllables. Nevertheless *Ulysses* is about as far as anything could be from an incitement to sin. On the other hand books of all kinds which assume the right to adultery and the rectitude of abortion are freely circulated.

*Mencken and Sarah Haardt Mencken on their wedding day,
27 August 1930*

I am aware that I am not making an adequate discussion of the censorship. All I am trying to maintain is that there are practical as well as theoretical difficulties in its way, so that a protest against Comstockery is both valid and valuable. While Mencken has fought against the censorship, he is not obsessed on the subject, and *The Mercury* has been very harmless in the nature of its contributions. Even the attempt, some years ago, to suppress an issue of *The Mercury* in Boston because of a story it contained, resulted, after Mencken went there to force his arrest, in his acquittal, and in the death of the local Comstock shortly after from chagrin. The story was a mild affair.

Mencken's literary criticism has really been directed against exploding every form of hokum. The man, being perfectly honest and forthright, has a keen sense of the possession or lack of these qualities in other people. He has been all in favor of vigorous writing by people who have something to say, and against, as he says in *The American Language,* "the typical literary product of the country . . . a refined essay in *The Atlantic Monthly* manner, perhaps gently jocose but never rough."

Against the whole tribe of professors he has waged unceasing war. Of one of these gentlemen he says that he "devotes a chapter to proving that 'of the 10,565 lines of *Paradise Lost* 670, or 6.3 per cent, contain each two or more accentuated alliterating vowels,' another to proving that in such word-groups as rough and ready, 68 per cent put the monosyllable first and the dissyllable second, and 42 per cent put the dissyllable first and the monosyllable second." [. . .]

A great day for him was when, in 1925, Boni and Liveright published a novel by a Baptist minister. Mencken's long review of it was screamingly funny, but it is too long to quote. Here, however, is the knock-out blow:

"Dr. Dixon is a Baptist clergyman. The Baptists are not commonly regarded as artists. One hears of them chiefly as engaged in non-æsthetic or anti-æsthetic enterprises—ducking one another in horse-ponds, scaring the darkeys at revivals, acting as stool-pigeons for Prohibition agents, denouncing the theater and the dance, marching with the Klan. But here is one who has felt the sweet kiss of beauty; here is a Baptist who can dream."

Since Dr. Dixon's preposterous novel was rather easy game, it should be said that Mencken does not hesitate to take the button off the foils with writers like H. G. Wells, Arnold Bennett, Stuart Sherman and Paul Elmer More. Nor do his friends escape when they write nonsense, as may be seen by his reviews of Edgar Lee Masters' *Mirage* and Sinclair Lewis's *Ann Vickers*. Here is criticism that is always astringent and bracing. The only serious defects I can find in it are a comparative failure to appreciate delicate shades of meaning in prose, and a suspicion of poetry. Yet he reads verse, though he regards it as nothing but charming lying; and his first book was in verse. Much of it is not at all bad (though Mencken has since completely repudiated it) being ingenious and well-constructed. One might describe it (by slightly altering a line of Belloc's) as

Much in the style of Kipling, only worse.

This attempt, never since then renewed, at the writing of verse proves that Mencken, whatever else he is, is not a poet.

But we cannot expect everything. If Mencken's mind lacks sensitiveness, he makes up for it by his grip upon actuality, his coarse refreshing common sense. And he writes in a style which, if heavily loaded with slang, is for that reason all the more pungent. There is never any doubt about what it is that he is trying to say, or his complete ability to say it. Masculine, sinewy and lucid—we must put him, despite important differences, with Swift and Cobbett. All three are earth-bound, but all three make a virtue of their limitations.

It is a question whether any of Mencken's work is likely to survive. So essentially journalistic is it, that I must confess that (despite the pleasure I always take in his writing when I first read it) I find it hard to go back to it. The effect is immediate, not lasting. Probably of all men who have ever written, Mencken is least concerned with the judgment of posterity. It is sufficient for his purpose that he can arrest the attention of his contemporaries, if only for a fleeting instant. This is writing thrown out because of the urgent spur of the occasion, and may be considered as merely printed conversation. His talk is in exactly the same vein, rapid-fire, explosive, humorous. We should take what he writes in the same way, as the expression of what he means at the moment, but about which he may change his mind, and which in any case is not to be taken too literally. He should be allowed a little leeway for the play of fancy. At the same time his sincerity should be acknowledged: we must not confound seriousness and solemnity.

The man, upon a first personal acquaintance, may surprise, and yet he and his work constitute a single entity. However cruel some of his criticism seems, it springs from his honesty. Here is a man kindly and courteous, who, though he talks exuberantly, is quite willing to listen to what other people may have to say, however dull it may be. This pitiless foe of Babbittry is unmasked as a man full of all the common and commonplace virtues. There is about him nothing of the æsthete. Literary men do not often look the part, yet few of them look less like it than Mencken. A man of his somewhat squat stocky figure, and large round face suggests the proprietor of a thriving delicatessen store. His ties look as though they had been picked in a hurry from the fifty cent bargain counter. He is the very embodiment of normality.

His cordiality puts one instantly at ease. Nobody can meet him and not like him, and his amiability is so great that when, after having fought a man upon paper for years, Mencken encounters him in the flesh, his sociability has a way of overcoming his aversion.

The first time I met him was shortly after his marriage. It was entertaining to see how tremendously he was enjoying being married, and to notice the attitude of his young wife towards her celebrated husband. She looked at him with the eye a mother would cast upon a precociously clever urchin, admiration and indulgence mingled together.

At lunch he ate voraciously of a Southern dish, the recipe for which he had got, so he told me, from

Carl Van Vechten. And it pleased him that I enjoyed my food, and took a second and third helping. He apologized that he was at the moment out of beer—for he is vain of his prowess as a brewer—but, as a bottle of wine was produced, I was content to forego even the best Volstead-era home-brew. Then he said, "Maynard, look behind you! That was a wedding-present from my brother." It was a picture six feet by four that must once have hung in a saloon, and it showed a brewery going full blast.

Some time afterwards, G. K. Chesterton told me how his host in New York had written to Mencken in the hope of bringing the two men together. Mencken had replied, "I am very sorry I cannot go to meet Chesterton. For I have long cherished an ambition to take him out and make him drunk, and then hand him over to the police while he was in that condition, to the shame of Holy Mother Church."

I told Mencken afterwards of Chesterton's comment, "Why, I could put Mencken under the table any day!" "Yes," said Mencken, "I suppose he could."

What he will do now that he has left *The Mercury,* I do not know. A treatise on morals is in preparation, and this, I think, is likely to be better than his excursion into theology. But it is not likely to contain anything new. His work is completed. His plea that no magazine should keep an editor for more than ten years, can be only a way of his admitting that he has said what he had to say, that there is no more to say. *The American Mercury* has fulfilled its destiny.

For several years past it had grown steadily less interesting. Not that the actual value of its contents declined; but the subjects suitable for treatment in its pages were growing fewer. Even "Americana" was less funny than in the days of yore. Was it that Revivalists and Rotarians had, because of the *Mercury* lash, become more circumspect in their behavior? Whatever the reason, the crop of absurdity was thinning. And as Burton Rascoe has said of Mencken, he is now in the unhappy position of a born disputant who finds no one to disagree with him.

But if he has been a little too successful, the country should still be grateful to him. It is a better place to live in now (despite the depression) than it was in the old boom days. And while it would be fantastic to suggest that the higher level of intelligence is due to Mencken, it is no more than plain justice to acknowledge his efforts in behalf of decency and honesty. There is much that escaped his ken. His range is limited. There is no prophetic fire in the man. He has never itched to steer humanity in any particular course. He set himself one task—exposing fools and hypocrites. And that task has been accomplished.

Cover for an issue of the journal of opinion for which Mencken became a contributing editor in 1921

Mencken's impending resignation was noted in an anonymously published article that reflects a changing nation's exhaustion ("Mr. Mencken Leaves the Mercury," Christian Century, *50 [18 October 1933]: 1292).*

The retirement of Mr. Mencken from the editorship of the American Mercury may not mark an epoch in American literature but it has significance as one of the signs of the passing of a type of criticism which during the past decade has had a vogue disproportionate to its value. Mr. Mencken's scorn of the "booboisie" and his Rabelaisian laughter at the queer antics of the "Bible belt" have been his conspicuous contributions to the interpretation of American culture. His monthly exhibits of "Americana," for the most part culled from the provincial press, have constituted a continuing satire on the manners and customs of what he considered the benighted elements of the country—a satire unique in that it made the unlucky dogs tie cans to their own tails. It was clever stuff, without a doubt. No one can do the sort of thing that Mr. Mencken does any better than he. But it is not the thing that most needs to be done at present. One had already begun to sense a disquieting

untimeliness in these keen cynicisms which professed to be so absolutely timely. Their subject-matter was of today, but their spirit was of yesterday. We are fed up with cynicism. "Oh yeah" has lost its charm. Criticism must pass into a somewhat more sober and disciplined mood to get a favorable hearing. We no longer relish being told that we are fools. We have heard it often enough, and have admitted it. To continue rubbing it in seems scarcely good sportsmanship; in any case it is not good journalism. Perhaps the American Mercury will lead in a new direction, as it has so competently though often exasperatingly led in the old, or perhaps it will just cease to lead. Whichever happens, Mencken's abandonment of his post as the mentor of American mores is symptomatic of a change in the American mood.

Though he disagreed with its politics, Mencken became a contributing editor of The Nation *in 1921; his articles appeared in it as late as 1934. In 1926 he explained the significance of the magazine, finding it a rare exception to the rule that American magazines ignore the civilized minority ("The Nation," in* Prejudices: Fifth Series, *pp. 255–262).*

One often hears lamentation that the American weeklies of opinion are not as good as their English prototypes—that we have never produced anything in that line to equal, say, the *Athenæum* or the *Saturday Review*. In the notion, it seems to me, there is nothing save that melancholy colonialism which is one of the curses of America. The plain fact is that our weeklies, taking one with another, are quite as well turned out as anything that England has ever seen, and that at least two of them, the *Nation* and the *New Republic,* are a great deal better. They are better because they are more hospitable to ideas, because they are served by a wider and more various range of writers, and because they show an occasional sense of humor. Even the *New Republic* knows how to be waggish, though it also knows, especially when it is discussing religion, how to be cruelly dull. Its Washington correspondence is better than any Parliamentary stuff in any English weekly ever heard of, if only because it is completely devoid of amateur statesmanship, the traditional defect of political correspondence at all times and everywhere. The editors of the English weeklies all ride political hobbies, and many of them are actively engaged in politics. Their American colleagues, I suspect, have been tempted in that direction more than once, but happily they have resisted, or maybe fate has resisted for them.

Of all the weeklies—and I go through at least twenty each week, American and English, including the Catholic *Commonweal* and a Negro journal—I like the

Nation best. There is something charming about its format, and it never fails to print an interesting piece of news, missed by the daily newspapers. Moreover, there is always a burst of fury in it, and somewhere or other, often hidden in a letter from a subscriber, a flash of wit—two things that make for amusing reading. The *New Republic,* I suspect, is more authoritative in certain fields,—for example, the economic—but it is also more pontifical. The *Nation* gets the air of a lark into many of its most violent crusades against fraud and folly; one somehow gathers the notion that its editors really do not expect the millennium to come in to-morrow. Of late they have shown many signs of forsaking Liberalism for Libertarianism—a far sounder and more satisfying politics. A Liberal is committed to sure cures that always turn out to be swindles; a Libertarian throws the bottles out the window, and asks only that the patient be let alone.

What the circulation of the *Nation* may be I don't know. In its sixtieth anniversary number, published in 1925, there was a hint that the number then sold each week ran far ahead of the 11,000 with which E. L. Godkin began in 1865. I have heard gabble in the saloons frequented by New York publishers that the present circulation is above 30,000. But no one, so far as I know, has ever suggested that it equals the circulation of even a third-rate daily paper. Such dull, preposterous sheets as the New York *Telegram,* the Washington *Star,* the Philadelphia *Public Ledger* and the Atlanta *Constitution* sell two or three times as many copies. Such magazines for the herd as *True Stories* and *Hot Dog* sell fifty times as many. Nevertheless, if I were a fellow of public spirit and eager to poison the Republic with my sagacity, I'd rather be editor of the *Nation* than editor of any of the other journals that I have mentioned—nay, I'd rather be editor of the *Nation* than editor of all of them together, with every other newspaper and magazine in America, save perhaps four or five, thrown in. For the *Nation* is unique in American journalism for one thing: it is read by its enemies. They may damn it, they may have it barred from libraries, they may even—as they did during the war—try to have it put down by the Postoffice, but all the while they read it. That is, the more intelligent of them—the least hopeless minority of them. It is to such minorities that the *Nation* addresses itself, on both sides of the fence. It has penetrated to the capital fact that they alone count—that the ideas sneaked into them to-day will begin to sweat out of the herd day after to-morrow.

Is the Creel Press Bureau theory of the late war abandoned? Is it impossible to find an educated man who is not ashamed that he succumbed to the Wilson buncombe? Then thank the *Nation* for that deliverance, for when it tackled Wilson it tackled him alone. Is the Coolidge Golden Age beginning to be sicklied o'er with a pale cast of green? Then prepare to thank the *Nation* again, for it began to tell the harsh, cold truth about good Cal at a time when all the daily journals of America, with not ten exceptions, were competing for the honor of shining his shoes. I often wonder, indeed, that the great success of the *Nation* under Villard has made such little impression upon American journalists—that they are so dead to the lessons that it roars into their ears. They all read it—that is, all who read anything at all. It prints news every week that they can't find in their own papers—sometimes news of the very first importance. It comments upon that news in a tart and well-informed fashion. It presents all the new ideas that rage in the world, always promptly and often pungently. To an editorial writer the *Nation* is indispensable. Either he reads it, or he is an idiot. Yet its example is very seldom followed—that is, forthrightly and heartily. Editorial writers all over the land steal ideas from it daily; it supplies, indeed, all the ideas that most of them ever have. It lifts them an inch, two inches, three inches, above the sedimentary stratum of Rotarians, bankers and ice-wagon drivers; they are conscious of its pull even when they resist. Yet very few of them seem to make the inevitable deduction that the kind of journalism it practices is better and more effective than the common kind—that they, too, might amount to something in this world if they would imitate it.

In such matters, alas, change is very slow. The whole press of the United States, I believe, is moving in the direction of the *Nation*—that is, in the direction of independence and honesty. Even such papers as the New York *Herald-Tribune* are measurably less stupid and intransigeant than they used to be, in their news if not in their opinions. But the majority of active journalists in the higher ranks were bred on the old-time party organs, and it is very difficult for them to reform their ways. They still think, not as free men, but as party hacks. On the one side they put the truth; on the other side they put what they call policy. Thus there are thousands of them who still sit down nightly to praise Coolidge—though to the best of my knowledge and belief there is not a single journalist in the whole United States who ever speaks of Coolidge in private without sneering at him. This resistance to change grows all the more curious when one observes what happens to the occasional paper which abandons it. I offer the Baltimore *Sunpaper* as an example—an especially apposite one, for the influence of the *Nation* upon it must be apparent to everyone familiar with its recent history. It was, a dozen years ago, a respectable but immensely dull journal. It presented the day's news in a formal, unintelligent fashion. It was accurate in small things, and free from sensationalism, but it seldom if ever went beyond the overt event to the causes and motives behind it. Its editorial opinions were flabby, and without influence. To-day it is certainly something far different. It must still go a long, long way, I suspect, before it escapes its old self altogether, but that must be a dull reader, indeed, who cannot see how vastly it has improved. It no longer prints the news formally; it devotes immense energy to discovering and revealing what is behind the news. In opinion it has thrown off all chains of faction and party, and is sharply and often intelligently independent. Its reaction to a new public problem is not that of a party hack, but that of a free man. It is, perhaps, sometimes grossly wrong, but no sane person believes that it is ever deliberately disingenuous.

Well, the point is that this new scheme has been tremendously successful—that it has paid in hard cash as well as in the usufructs of the spirit. There is no sign that the readers of the *Sunpaper*—barring a few quacks with something to sell—dislike its new vigor, enterprise and independence. On the contrary, there is every evidence that they like it. They have increased greatly in numbers. The paper itself rises in dignity and influence. And every other newspaper in America that ventures upon the same innovations, from the *World* in New York to the *Enquirer-Sun* down in Columbus, Ga., rises in the same way. It is my contention that the *Nation* has led the way in this reform of American journalism—that it will be followed by many papers to-morrow, as it is followed by a few to-day. Its politics are sometimes outrageous. It frequently gets into lamentable snarls, bat-tling for liberty with one hand and more laws with the other. It is doctrinaire, inconsistent, bellicose. It whoops for men one day, and damns them as frauds the next. It has no sense of decorum. It is sometimes a bit rowdy. But who will deny that it is honest? And who will deny that, taking one day with another, it is generally right—that its enthusiasms, if they occasionally send it mooning after dreamers, at least never send it cheering for rogues—that its wrongness, when it is wrong, is at all events not the dull, simian wrongness of mere stupidity? It is disliked inordinately, but not, I believe, by honest men, even among its enemies. It is disliked by demagogues and exploiters, by frauds great and small. They have all tasted its snickersnee, and they have all good reason to dislike it.

Personally, I do not subscribe to its politics, save when it advocates liberty openly and unashamed. I have no belief in politicians: the good ones and the bad ones seem to me to be unanimously thieves. Thus I hope I may whoop for it with some grace, despite the fact that my name appears on its flagstaff. How my name got there I don't know; I receive no emolument from its coffers, and write for it very seldom, and then only in contravention of its ideas. I even have to pay cash for my annual subscription—a strange and painful burden for a journalist to bear. But I know of no other expenditure (that is, of a secular character) that I make with more satisfaction, or that brings me a better return. Most of the papers that I am doomed to read are idiotic even when they are right. The *Nation* is intelligent and instructive even when it is wrong.

The Antipuritan Critic: Champion of a New Literature

Mencken's early journalistic career included drama criticism, and, starting in 1908, this work overlapped his book reviewing for The Smart Set. *He had further prepared himself to be an arbiter of "beautiful letters" by publishing fiction and poetry since his teens. Harrison Hale Schaff contributed to the first full-length biography of Mencken a letter that documents crucial moments in the establishment of Mencken's national reputation as a literary critic. The book on George Bernard Shaw was the first ever published on the Irish playwright. The book on Friedrich Nietzsche was the first in English on the German philosopher. Schaff, who also helped Mencken put together a brief anthology titled* The Gist of Nietzsche *(1910), provides a good overview of Mencken's intellectual development through the early days of* The American Mercury. *Mencken had by then completed four of the six volumes in the* Prejudices *series for Knopf. Schaff's gentle advice at the end might have resulted in Mencken's influence carrying through the Depression years if it had been heeded, but he would not have been the same Mencken that Schaff describes so well (letter from Schaff, in Isaac Goldberg,* The Man Mencken: A Biographical and Critical Survey *[New York: Simon & Schuster, 1925], pp. 371–377).*

Broadlands, Southborough, Mass.

My dear Dr. Goldberg:–

In the spring of 1905 the firm of John W. Luce and Company, with which I was then and am still associated, received a letter calling their attention to the possibility of an increased interest in the plays of George Bernard Shaw. Our correspondent pointed out that *Candida* had been produced the previous season with some success and that in the fall Arnold Daly would inaugurate another season of Shaw plays. Up to that time Shaw's representation in American publication lists was limited to 'Plays Pleasant and Unpleasant,' brought out by Herbert Stone of Chicago, without attracting special attention, and a slender little volume on our list, Shaw's brilliant essay, "On Going to Church." Probably, as our firm was one of the few which at that time thought Shaw good enough to print, the writer, who signed himself Henry L. Mencken, ventured to approach us with a proposal to write a volume of

The Irish playwright George Bernard Shaw, of whose work Mencken was an early champion

202

twenty to thirty thousand words of descriptive and critical comment on the then published plays of Mr. Shaw and offered to prepare and submit a portion of the manuscript if we approved the plan and would entrust the work to him.

Mencken at that time had some newspaper experience and had contributed to several magazines. He assured us that we had never heard of him, which was the fact, and gave us as a reference Ellery Sedgwick, at present editor of the *Atlantic Monthly,* who was known to us. We did not, however, trouble Mr. Sedgwick for his opinions. I mention the reference in justice to both gentlemen as significant that at the outset of their careers, both of which became distinguished, each recognized in the other capacities of accomplishment and judgment now fully realized.

We wrote Mencken at once that his proposal interested us and if his manuscript came up to his expectations and our hopes we would undertake the publication.

Then followed the exchange of a number of long letters in which Mencken outlined more fully the plan of his book which was in the main to follow Shaw's own essay on the *Quintessence of Ibsenism,* and we, our suggestions on various points. In due course a portion of the manuscript was submitted and returned for revision. The introduction was entirely re-written. Both Mencken and ourselves were anxious that the book should be creditable and he spared no pains nor labor in his work. If a criticism, or a suggestion of omission or addition was made and met his approval, he at once went to work and incorporated it in his manuscript. On the other hand, if he questioned the advisability of doing so he stated his reasons fully, interestingly and with the warmth characteristic of his personality. Along in the fall of that year the book was published and at once attracted favorable and extended criticism from the literary editors and enjoyed a very fair and steady sale.

Mencken was gratified by the reception accorded his book and was anxious to follow it up with another volume. His suggestion was a book for playgoers in which he proposed to embody a digest and criticism of the current drama. In his capacity as dramatic critic he had accumulated a large amount of material for such a book and had to a certain extent tabulated it. We, however, were not very enthusiastic over the proposal and suggested that he now undertake the work of presenting to the English reading public the philosophy of Frederich [*sic*] Nietzsche. It happened that, in replying to Mencken's first letter proposing the Shaw book, I mentioned our plan to have such a volume prepared as it was apparent that the Nietzschean philosophy had exerted a strong influence on the English and Continen-

George Bernard Shaw His Plays

BY

HENRY L. MENCKEN

BOSTON AND LONDON
JOHN W. LUCE & CO.
1905

Title page for the first book published on Shaw

tal dramatists including Mr. Shaw on which he was proposing to write. In replying at that time he said: 'Truly there must be something in mental telepathy for just as your note of the 14th reached me I was thinking of an article showing how Nietzsche has influenced, not only Sudermann, Hauptmann and Company, but also Kipling and Roosevelt, and how Nietzsche himself was merely the successor of Spencer.–But though I am tolerably familiar with Nietzsche and know Maeterlinck, Sudermann and Hauptmann pretty well and Ibsen and Pinero better, I scarcely feel that I could undertake the book you suggest. That is because I think the writing of it would involve a close study of a good many lesser men–philosophers and playwrights–of Germany and Scandinavia. Of these I know little and my German is so bad that I would encounter enormous difficulties in

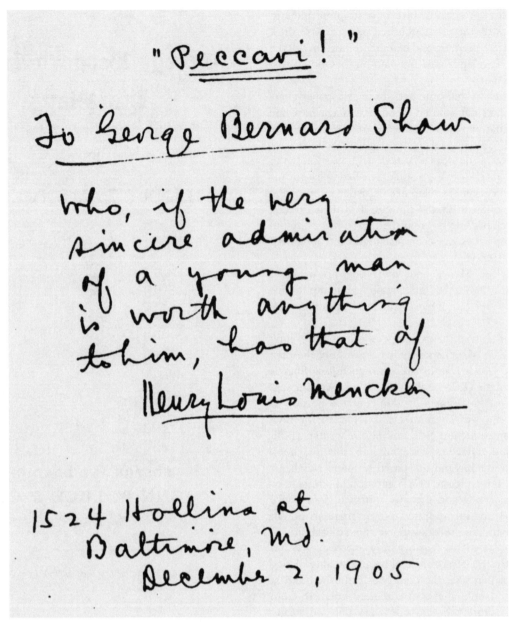

Inscription by Mencken in the copy of George Bernard Shaw: His Plays *that he presented to Shaw (Harry Ransom Humanities Research Center,*
The University of Texas at Austin)

trying to learn more. Besides, the task is one for a man of ample leisure and thorough scholarship. I have little of the former and make no pretense to the latter. Nevertheless, it was on my purpose to work in part along those lines in the proposed book on Shaw.'

With increased confidence in himself as the result of the success of his Shaw book Mencken re-considered his qualifications as a German scholar and proceeded to read the endless volumes of Nietzsche's æsthetic and philosophic works in the original and as in the case of the Shaw book outlined very fully his plan of the work. Taking this with me I went to Baltimore and discussed the matter with him at some length. As in the case of the Shaw book the various instalments of manuscript gave rise to no little criticism, suggestion and changes to which Mencken responded as before with arguments, acquiescence, rejection, infinite good temper and a willingness to contribute unending industry.

To those familiar with his style it will be no surprise when I say that among the bones of contention were some of the bizarre and extravagant expressions with which the manuscript was garnished. Stoutly he contended for the retention of many of them,—and some survived. Others in the spirit of compromise were modified or eliminated.

The German philosopher Friedrich Nietzsche, another figure of whom Mencken was an early supporter

Following the work on Nietzsche we undertook with Mencken a new translation of the Ibsen plays under his editorship, but only two volumes were issued, "The Doll's House" and "Little Eyolf." A variety of reasons contributed to the dropping of the undertaking, not the least of which was the increased demand on Mencken's time incident to his growing responsibilities on the *Smart Set.*

Following the Ibsen adventure, a preface or two, and that amazing little play, "The Artist," which stands out as one of the very finest of modern satires in any language, complete the list of Mencken's work published through our firm.

While it is true that the years in which he was in close touch with John W. Luce and Company were at the outset of his career and on the whole a formative period for him, it should not be forgotten that Mencken came to us with a by no means indifferent equipment. He had to his credit several years of active and varied newspaper work under editors who

Clarity, force in expression and something of the element of surprise were what Mencken wanted, and very rightly. He was one of the early ones to discover that words are not invariably to be used as the exact dimensional factors in a problem of ideas but at times as symbols by which the creative literary artist suggests the vibrant, colorful, tonic panorama of his thoughts.

On publication, *The Philosophy of Friedrich Nietzsche* was an immediate success and gave the author a firm position in the field of letters and seriously threatened to establish him as a philosopher of truly academic pretensions. This latter prospect frightened him nearly to death. On the other hand our firm would have been glad to have had him plant himself on that firm ground and devote his efforts to the serious and somewhat formal exposition of the varying currents of modern philosophy and social psychology. But to be branded as academic was the last thing in the world that Mencken desired and with a naturally philosophic and scholarly turn of mind he went to every length to record an antagonism to all the formalities that make up the traditions of that cult.

THE PHILOSOPHY OF FRIEDRICH NIETZSCHE

BY HENRY L. MENCKEN

I shall be told, I suppose, that my philosophy is comfortless — because I speak the truth; and people prefer to believe that everything the Lord made is good. If you are one such, go to the priests, and leave philosophers in peace!

Arthur Schopenhauer.

LUCE ET LABORE

BOSTON
LUCE AND COMPANY
MCMVIII

Title page for the first book in English on Nietzsche

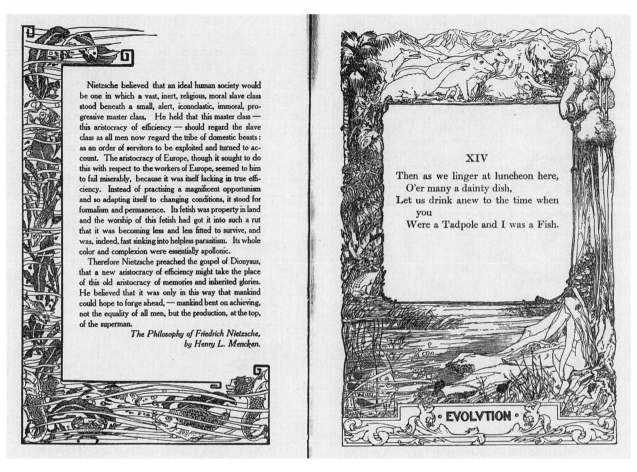

Nietzsche believed that an ideal human society would be one in which a vast, inert, religious, moral slave class stood beneath a small, alert, iconoclastic, immoral, progressive master class. He held that this master class — this aristocracy of efficiency — should regard the slave class as all men now regard the tribe of domestic beasts : as an order of servitors to be exploited and turned to account. The aristocracy of Europe, though it sought to do this with respect to the workers of Europe, seemed to him to fail miserably, because it was itself lacking in true efficiency. Instead of practising a magnificent opportunism and so adapting itself to changing conditions, it stood for formalism and permanence. Its fetish was property in land and the worship of this fetish had got it into such a rut that it was becoming less and less fitted to survive, and was, indeed, fast sinking into helpless parasitism. Its whole color and complexion were essentially apollonic.

Therefore Nietzsche preached the gospel of Dionysus, that a new aristocracy of efficiency might take the place of this old aristocracy of memories and inherited glories. He believed that it was only in this way that mankind could hope to forge ahead, — mankind bent on achieving, not the equality of all men, but the production, at the top, of the superman.

The Philosophy of Friedrich Nietzsche,
by Henry L. Mencken.

XIV

Then as we linger at luncheon here,
O'er many a dainty dish,
Let us drink anew to the time when
you
Were a Tadpole and I was a Fish.

· EVOLVTION ·

Excerpt from Mencken's book on Nietzsche reprinted as part of the commentary on Langdon Smith's poem Evolution: A Fantasy *(1909)*

took pains to train their young men in the best traditions of journalism. He had published privately a book of poems and contributed a number of stories and articles to different magazines. To this must be added a wide reading in the fields of literature which reflected the highest type of intellectual development of that day, philosophy and drama. The novel then, as now, with rare exception, had nothing to offer; intellectual literary progress was and had been for some time in the hands of the European dramatists who translated into a popular form of presentation the work of the philosophers.

Mencken's judgment in general and particularly of what he read was surprisingly mature. He had acquired the foundation of a style and had definite ideas as to how he hoped to develop it. Already he was orienting himself to the viewpoint he has maintained in recent years and if his philosophic foundations were somewhat nebulous, gathered as they had been largely through the presentation of the dramatists, he was thoroughly impregnated with them. His work on the Shaw volume and the Nietzsche clarified and crystallized these ideas. The influ-

ence of those two books has been wide but to none so intense as to the author himself; the Shaw, in matters of personality and temperament, the Nietzsche, as to fundamental ideas. To them I wish we might have added a volume of æsthetics, but then of course was not the time for Mencken to even consider such a work. And to all this should be joined the dynamic energy of ambition and industry coupled with good temper and a boundless reserve of pure fun.

Philosophically Mencken is an aristocrat, jealously guarding personal dignity by the suppression of any vulgar display of his emotional reactions, which are many, highly sensitive and inclined to be sentimental. Temperamentally, he is the mediæval Latin student of John Addington Symonds' "Wine, Women and Song"—a counter balance in nice adjustment, which limits the complete realization of either his philosophic or temperamental tendencies.

If the creative artist is interesting in retrospect he is doubly so in the potentialities of the future and though speculation as to the trend of future events and accomplishment is always hazardous, there is a

The music, art, and literary critic James Gibbons Huneker, a major influence on Mencken's attitudes and style

major social and political problems. His mind, if anything, is more alert, his reactions quicker, his powers of penetration greater. There is even a suggestion of a slowly dawning moderation, not by any means a re-valuation of values, but a more constructive taste in the selection of material for valuation, and with it will come, I suspect, a realization that tolerance rather than prejudice is the aristocratic gesture of disdain; then we shall see a period of brilliant creative accomplishment that Mencken's fine capacity for sound scholarship so well qualifies him to achieve.

HARRISON HALE SCHAFF

Boston,
August, 1925

Mencken's intellectual development was most influenced by Nietzsche and nineteenth-century science (the Darwinian branch, especially), his literary taste by realists and naturalists. His attitude and the famous style that went with it had many fathers, but none was more important than the critic James Gibbons Huneker (1857–1921). Through his writings on literature and the other arts, and, just as importantly, through his gifts as a raconteur, Huneker gave Mencken access to the larger aesthetic world. Mencken describes their first encounter (excerpt from "Huneker: A Memory" in Prejudices: Third Series, *pp. 66–68).*

[. . .] In his early days, when he performed the tonal and carnal prodigies that he liked to talk of afterward, I was at nurse, and too young to have any traffic with him. When I encountered him at last he was in the high flush of the middle years, and had already become a tradition in the little world that critics inhabit. We sat down to luncheon at one o'clock; I think it must have been at Lüchow's, his favorite refuge and rostrum to the end. At six, when I had to go, the waiter was hauling in his tenth (or was it twentieth?) *Seidel* of Pilsner, and he was bringing to a close *prestissimo* the most amazing monologue that these ears (up to that time) had ever funnelled into this consciousness. What a stew, indeed! Berlioz and the question of the clang-tint of the viola, the psychopathological causes of the suicide of Tschaikowsky, why Nietzsche had to leave Sils Maria between days in 1887, the echoes of Flaubert in Joseph Conrad (then but newly dawned), the precise topography of the warts of Liszt, George Bernard Shaw's heroic but vain struggles to throw off Presbyterianism, how Frau Cosima saved Wagner from the libidinous Swedish baroness, what to drink when playing Chopin, what Cézanne thought of his disciples, the defects in the structure of "Sister Car-

world-old urge to venture into that doubtful field. In the last twenty years Mencken has not changed fundamentally. A wider experience and increased activities have simply given to him a greater facility and smoothness in operation. It still amuses him that a president of the United States should have been vapid enough to qualify as a good Elk and his successor so crude as to make a doubtful addition to the Rotarians. Methodists still serve him as a symbol of social and cultural development, while the inherent ignorance and vulgarity of the masses (which is an obvious and accepted fact that long since ceased to occasion the slightest wonder or resentment on the part of those capable of sensing conditions), still serve him as a phenomenon on which to expatiate with a vocabulary of ascending invective that becomes more and more difficult to make effective as its intensity increases, and which if persisted in must become as toneless as a tuning fork vibrating in those high ranges that the ear fails to record. On the other hand Mencken's field of vision has broadened notably and with it has come an interest in

The writer Joseph Conrad, whose work Mencken admired and praised

rie," Anton Seidl and the musical union, the complex love affairs of Gounod, the early days of David Belasco, the varying talents and idiosyncrasies of Lillian Russell's earlier husbands, whether a girl educated at Vassar could ever really learn to love, the exact composition of chicken paprika, the correct tempo of the Vienna waltz, the style of William Dean Howells, what George Moore said about German bathrooms, the true inwardness of the affair between D'Annunzio and Duse, the origin of the theory that all oboe players are crazy, why Löwenbräu survived exportation better than Hofbräu, Ibsen's loathing of Norwegians, the best remedy for Rhine wine *Katzenjammer,* how to play Brahms, the degeneration of the Bal Bullier, the sheer physical impossibility of getting Dvořák drunk, the genuine last words of Walt Whitman. . . .

I left in a sort of fever, and it was a couple of days later before I began to sort out my impressions, and formulate a coherent image. Was the man allusive in his books—so allusive that popular

report credited him with the actual manufacture of authorities? Then he was ten times as allusive in his discourse—a veritable geyser of unfamiliar names, shocking epigrams in strange tongues, unearthly philosophies out of the backwaters of Scandinavia, Transylvania, Bulgaria, the Basque country, the Ukraine. And did he, in his criticism, pass facilely from the author to the man, and from the man to his wife, and to the wives of his friends? Then at the *Biertisch* he began long beyond the point where the last honest wife gives up the ghost, and so, full tilt, ran into such complexities of adultery that a plain sinner could scarcely follow him. I try to give you, ineptly and grotesquely, some notion of the talk of the man, but I must fail inevitably. It was, in brief, chaos, and chaos cannot be described. But it was chaos made to gleam and corruscate with every device of the seven arts—chaos drenched in all the colors imaginable, chaos scored for an orchestra which made the great band of Berlioz seem like a fife and drum corps. [. . .]

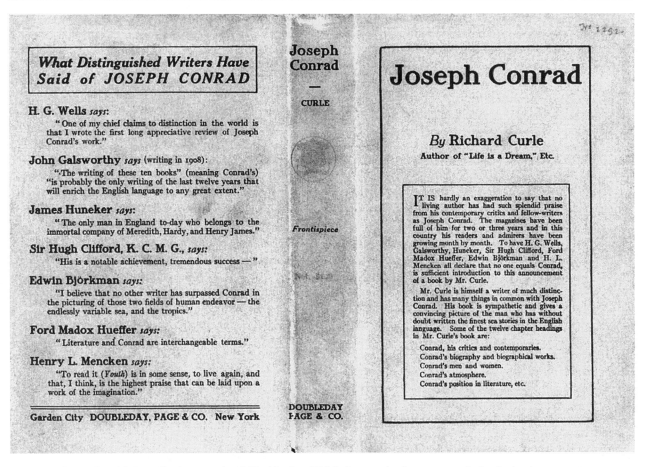

Dust jacket with the earliest-known testimonial by Mencken (1914), for an author he was among the first in America to promote

Mencken was among the earliest critics to recognize the greatness of Joseph Conrad, whose first novel appeared in 1899. He always promoted Conrad's work and used it as a standard. What he found in it may be seen in his reaction on first reading A Traveller at Forty, *by Theodore Dreiser, who was, for Mencken, Conrad's American equivalent (excerpt from a typewritten 16 November 1913 letter, with handwritten initials as signature, at the University of Pennsylvania).*

THE SUN
BALTIMORE, MD.

Sunday.

Dear Dreiser:-

[. . .] But don't assume from the foregoing that the book has disappointed me. Far from it. You have got into it, not only a definite revelation of your personality, but also a clear statement of your philosophy. Do you know that this last is substantially identical with Joseph Conrad's? You will find his confession of faith in "A Personal Record". He stands in wonder before the meaninglessness of life. He is an agnostic in exactly the same sense that you are -- that is to say, he gives it up. [. . .]

Yours,
HLM

Mencken's A Book of Prefaces *was published by Knopf in October 1917. It includes the essay "Joseph Conrad," and Conrad did not take long to respond to it (handwritten letter at the Enoch Pratt Free Library, Baltimore).*

Capel House,
Orlestone,
NR Ashford
11 Nov 17.

Dear Mr Mencken

Thanks for your friendly note. The book too has arrived—and I need not tell you that the appreciation of a mind so alert, so penetrating and so unprejudiced is a matter of the greatest possible gratification and interest to me. I can't help feeling that you make perhaps too much of what there is in me. But as on one hand I have the greatest respect for your critical faculty (respect as apart from admiration which is there too) and on the other I am conscious of absolute sincerity (as I look back on my work) well then, I suppose, it must be so. It remains for me to thank you warmly for the generous terms in which you express your judgment, for the tone of friendliness toward the man–and his effort.

There are a few little matters of fact: as for instance the impression (spread by dear Clifford) that I ever hesitated between French and English. I could not have done so. If I hadn't had the English to write I would never have written at all. You may take my word for it. I certainly was not writing or even working at Alm: Folly for five years. I carted it about with me for that length of time, simply because I have the habit of sticking to things but I had even no opportunities to think about it (still less to toil over it). The MS (which J. Q. has got right enough) is the freest from erasures of all my MSS. What did I care–what did I know then? To address my fellow-men at large on any subject or even with a yarn, did not seem to me a serious occupation. I have learned since, by arduous experience that it is–or that it can be. But the experience (very bitter at times) was purely personal, belonging to "ma vie intérieure" as the French say. No MS of mine–not a single one–was hawked about. Unwin accepted A's Folly and asked for the next. Henley accepted the Nigger on the strength of 3 chapters for the "New Review," and Heinemann did the same for book form of that work. The contract for Typhoon stories was signed 3 years before the book appeared. I sent Karain to Mr. Blackwood (and marked my own price on it) who accepted it. Everything else that appeared in Maga was asked for and Heart of Darkness was written by special request for the M number of that venerable periodical. My contracts here with Methuen and now with Dent were business transactions for works unseen–unwritten.

The difficulty was the writing: ill health, blank weeks, nay months, that won't (in the words of Winnie Verlac) bear thinking about. And for the rest I can only say: Nous avons vécu. One boy of 19 at the front since 1915–another of 11 at school, and the solitude and silence (conditions of life) so loyally shared without a shadow of repining by my wife go on–as before. Two, three more books may yet come out of it. Quien sabe?

I was specially pleased by your references to Nostromo. A new ed^{on} is coming out with a short preface. I shall send you a copy. I enclose here a photograph taken in Poland in 1914. Something that hasn't been knocking about in ill^d papers.

                                        Yours cordially
                                        Joseph Conrad.

The "Shaw book" discussed by Schaff broke the ground for all future books on the subject, but Mencken's stated aims were modest (excerpt from the preface to George Bernard Shaw: His Plays, *p. vii).*

This is a little handbook for the reading tables of Americans interested enough in the drama of the day to have some curiosity regarding the plays of George Bernard Shaw, but too busy to give them careful personal study or to read the vast mass of reviews, magazine articles, letters to the editor, newspaper paragraphs and reports of debates that deal with them. Every habitual writer now before the public, from William Archer and James Huneker to "Vox Populi" and "An Old Subscriber" has had his say about Shaw. In the pages following there is no attempt to formulate a new theory of his purposes or a novel interpretation of his philosophies. Instead, the object of this modest book is to bring all of the Shaw commentators together upon the common ground of admitted fact, to exhibit the Shaw plays as dramas rather than as transcendental treatises, and to describe their plots, characters, and general plans simply and calmly, and without reading into them anything invisible to the naked eye. [. . .]

The anonymous reviewer for the Chicago Tribune *spotted the Menckenian elements in the book, though he had never heard of the author–and failed to mention the title ("An Interpretation of Shaw," 2 January 1906, p. 8).*

Mr. Henry L. Mencken, an author of whom the reviewer is lamentably ignorant, is under the impression that some persons may be too much occupied with other matters to read in full the plays of George Bernard Shaw, and he has obligingly, if not altogether fairly, offered them the scenario of each play filled out with his own interpretation. The first sentences of his outline of "Candida" is submitted that the true Shawite may judge of the reliability of the author's interpretation:

"'Candida,'" says Mr. Mencken, "is a latter day essay in feminine psychology after the fashion of 'A Doll's House,' 'Monna Vanna,' and 'Hedda Gabler.' Candida Morell, the heroine, is a clergyman's wife, who, lacking an acquaintance with the philosophies and face to face with the problem of earning her daily bread, might have gone the muddy way of Mrs. Warren. As it is, she exercises her fascinations upon a moony poet, arouses him to the mad dog stage of passion, drives her husband to the verge of suicide–and then, with bland complacency and unanswerable logic, reads both an excellent lecture, turns the poet out of doors, and falls into her husband's arms, still chemically pure. It is an edifying example of the influence of mind over matter."

Mr. Mencken has read Huneker, William Archer, Cunningham Graham, and the other epigrammatic critics, and having something of a turn for epigram himself he has made a readable book and one likely to further the stirring habit of disputation. He regards Mr. Shaw as an indubitable searcher for truth. The drama, he points out, is the record of conflict. Shaw's conflicts are between the orthodox and the heterodox. "Darwin," says Mr. Mencken, "made this war between the faithful and the scoffers the chief concern of the time, and the sham-smashing that is now going on in all the fields of human inquiry might be compared to the crusades that engrossed the world in the middle ages. Every one, consciously or unconsciously, is more or less directly engaged in it, and so, when Shaw chooses conspicuous fighters in the war as the chief characters of his plays, he is but demonstrating his comprehension of human nature as it is manifested today."

This is quite self-evidently true. Mr. Shaw has been trying to help men and women to understand themselves. He has invited them to come out from behind their own hypocrisy and stand in the open and fight for what they are secretly and actually thinking. The only difficulty is that in presenting a type a dramatist labors under the disadvantage that each man, conscious of the variant instincts, impulses, dreams, and principles of his own personality, finds the coincidence between himself and the depicted character too slight to admit of genuine sympathy of a subjective sort. While, on the other hand, Mr. Shaw's manifest coldness toward the creations of his extraordinary fancy causes the public, also, to regard with alien eyes these odd specimens of humanity whom he has caught and speared to his paper for the scientific scrutiny of the pessimistic.

The real trouble with Shaw is, cognizant of almost everything though he is, he has failed at the last to be cognizant of what is best in men and women. He has counted in almost everything except such little matters as simplicity, ideality, direct, instinctive sacrifice, and genuine natural affection. It is by these things that the greater part of humanity moves, and for them the complex play of ulterior motives and unconfessed temptations is no more than the dancing of phosphorus over the water. It is there for an hour, giving to the familiar scene a curious unreality and lending an evil enchantment of its own, but presently it is gone and the wholesome sea lies under the morning sun taking and giving of the fair elements of life. The deeps are not disturbed. When Mr. Shaw becomes aware of these deeps in the human soul and pays to humanity the tribute which it really deserves he will be better understood.

Mr. Mencken has, however, shown more of a sense of fitness than to make such trite remarks as those above. He has brought a satirist's comprehension to a greater satirist's work. The book is worth adding to the shelf of Shawana—if one has such a thing. (John W. Luce & Co., Boston and London, publishers.)

Mencken also, in effect, introduced Nietzsche to America by means of the other major book discussed in the Schaff letter, The Philosophy of Friedrich Nietzsche. *His aims this time were not modest. That philosophy informed his thinking on both politics and literature; and even more than in his writings on exemplary literary figures he was here the critic as advocate, however objective the book might appear (excerpt from the introduction to* The Philosophy of Friedrich Nietzsche, *p. vii).*

The philosophy of Friedrich Nietzsche and the music (and quasi-music) of Richard Strauss: herein we have our modern substitutes for Shakespeare and the musical glasses. There is no escaping Nietzsche. You may hold him a hissing and a mocking and lift your virtuous skirts as you pass him by, but his roar is in your ears and his blasphemies sink into your mind. He has colored the thought and literature, the speculation and theorizing, the politics and superstition of the time. He reigns as king in the German universities—where, since Luther's day, all the world's most painful thinking has been done—and his echoes tinkle, harshly or faintly, from Chicago to Mesopotamia. His ideas appear in the writings of men as unlike as Roosevelt and Bernard Shaw; even the newspapers are aware of him. He is praised and berated, accepted and denounced, canonized and damned. Pythagorus had no more devout disciples and Spinoza had no more murderous and violent foes. Wherefore it may be a toil of some profit to examine his ideas a bit closely; to differentiate between what he said in his books and what his apostles and interpreters and enemies say or think he said; and in the end, perhaps, to find out what he meant. [. . .]

The anonymous New York Times *reviewer was not intimidated ("An Account of Nietzsche,"* New York Times Book Review, *15 February 1908, p. 90).*

In this volume, "Friedrich Nietzsche," by Henry L. Mencken, (Luce & Co.,) we are given in the introduction a clear notion of the writer's own attitude toward the great German, as well as some conception of his fitness to write upon and to translate him. It is evident that Mr. Mencken possesses the requisite sympathy, and withal a certain clear, forceful, even ardent style, a keen and thoroughgoing intellect, knowledge of

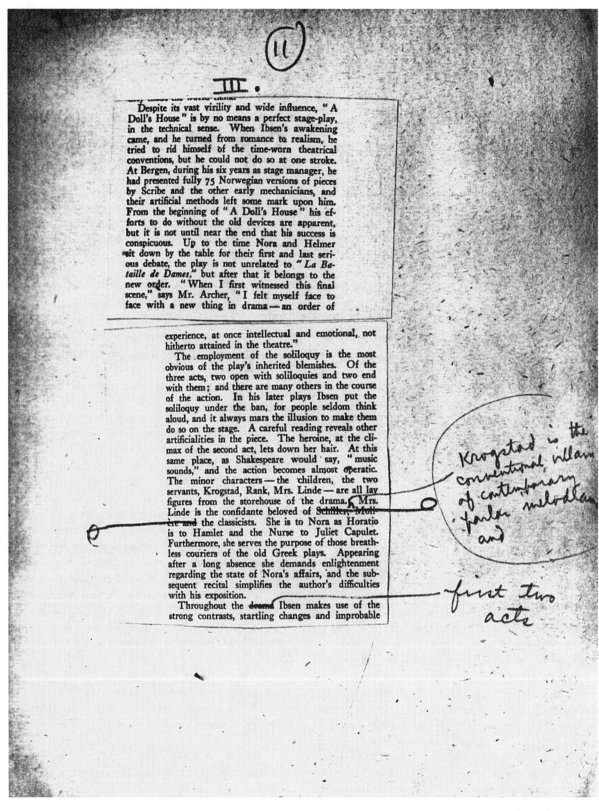

Page with pasted-on clippings from Mencken and Holger A. Koppel's translation of Henrik Ibsen's A Doll's House *(1909), showing Mencken's revisions for a planned second edition. This work and their translation of Ibsen's* Little Eyolf *(1909) did not sell well, however, and the proposed revised edition was abandoned (courtesy of the Enoch Pratt Free Library).*

men, and a sense of humor. He is not hampered by prejudice nor dismayed by traditions, and he is able to leave out inessentials without destroying the harmony of what remains. He has made a good book and gives us a pretty fair conception of just what Nietzsche was and what he stood for.

In the sketch given of the philosopher's life we get an impression as of a sick and fretful eagle confined to a barnyard, maddened by its senseless chatter, with a far eye on rocky, desolate heights, tearing with fierce beak and claws at the prized and awe-inspiring erections with which the sleek fowls have been fenced in and guarded from the real world without. "Is it true?" was Nietzsche's one question to everything life or man opposed to him. A terrible sincerity held him in its grasp, an intolerance of the least sham, the slightest cowardice. He would not be happy at the price of truth, or what he conceived to be truth. He died at the age of 56, after several years of insanity, nursed and coddled like a little child—gentle, docile, saying to the sister who devoted herself to him: "You and I, my sister—we are happy!"

The succeeding chapters, under such heads as "The Superman," "Truth," "Christianity," "Women and Marriage," &c., give us the structure made by Nietzsche to express his conceptions of the universe, and his idea as to how this universe should be and could be improved.

Whether one agrees with any or all of his conclusions is not here to the point. The important thing is that Mr. Mencken has given us in this book, easily held in the hand and written for the layman without mysteries and involutions, the opportunity of seeing just what Nietzsche thought and wrote, and the privilege of making up our individual minds as to the truth and value of this thought. He also quotes from many of the German's critics, and seeks to define his value as a teacher.

Holger A. Koppel assisted Mencken in the translation of Henrik Ibsen's A Doll's House *(1909). Mencken prized the author for the reasons stated by Schaff: he was one of "the European dramatists who translated into a popular form of presentation the work of the [contemporary] philosophers." Mencken's theory is grounded on his predecessor Howells's call for the commonplace in literature, but, like the Young Turks of the 1890s, such as Stephen Crane and Frank Norris, he wanted it to go beyond Howells's "reticent realism" (excerpt from the introduction to* A Doll's House, *pp. x–xii).*

[. . .] Into this peaceful scene "A Doll's House" came like a bomb. Turning his back upon poetry and romance, and upon the great reputation which his past achievements had won for him, Ibsen stood forth as a realist of the realists. To the astonished public of the time, his play seemed something incredible and outrageous. It had no hero; it had scarcely a hint of love-making; it provoked neither the ready laugh nor the willing tear. Instead of presenting anew the conventionalized figures play-goers were habituated to seeing on the stage, it presented a small group of personages who resembled, in a startling manner, the people they saw about them in the world every day. The dramatist removed one wall from an ordinary sitting-room, and showed a husband and wife at their fireside. And as the action proceeded it became evident that the drama was planned, not only to depict a veritable man and woman, but also to analyze and test the relation which bound them together. In a word, it put a question mark after the word marriage.

Thus the play was remarkable for two reasons: first, because it conveyed a sense of photographic reality; and secondly, because it presumed to criticize an institution which the vast majority of human beings held to be impeccable. The particular question asked by "A Doll's House" would not greatly excite the world to-day, for familiarity has robbed it of its old indecorum. But in 1879, with anthropomorphism still triumphant and the literal accuracy of the Pentateuch still a matter of debate, it was daring to the verge of blasphemy. To achieve an equal sensation to-day a play would have to question something which the world yet accepts as undoubted and indubitable—the value of family loyalty, for example, or the utility of political liberty. [. . .]

Theodore Dreiser gives an account of his first meeting with his greatest champion, which occurred while Dreiser was editing The Delineator *magazine. Later in the year of this writing (1925), real and imagined slights led to a break in their friendship. Some of the articles Mencken ghosted for Leonard K. Hirshberg appeared in* What You Ought to Know about Your Baby *(1910), nearly all of which was written by Mencken without credit ("Henry L. Mencken and Myself," in Isaac Goldberg,* The Man Mencken: A Biographical and Critical Survey, *pp. 378–381).*

It was sometime during the Spring or Summer of 1908, and my second year of editorial control of the Butterick Publications, that there came to me a doctor by the name of Leonard K. Hirshberg who explained that besides being a physician of some practice in Baltimore he was a graduate of Johns Hopkins and interested in interpreting to the lay public if possible the more recent advances in medical knowledge. There had been various recent developments, as there always are. Some phases of these he proposed to describe in articles of various lengths. And then it was that he announced that, being a medical man and better equipped technically in that line than as a writer, he had joined with a newspaper-man or editorial writer then connected with the Baltimore *Sun,* Henry L. Mencken. The name being entirely unfamiliar to me at the time, he proceeded to describe him as a young, refreshing and delightful fellow of a very vigorous and untechnical literary skill, who, in combination with himself, would most certainly be able to furnish me with articles of exceptional luminosity and vigor. Liking two or three of the subjects discussed, I suggested that between them they prepare one and submit it. In case it proved satisfactory, I would buy it and possibly some of the others.

In less than three weeks thereafter I received a discussion of some current medical development which seemed to me as refreshing and colorful a bit of semi-scientific exposition as I had read in years. While setting forth all the developments which had been indicated to me, it bristled with gay phraseology and a largely suppressed though still peeping mirth. I was so pleased that I immediately wrote Hirshberg that the material was satisfactory and that I would be willing to contract with him and his friend for one of the other subjects he had mentioned.

And then some weeks later in connection with that or some other matter, whether to discuss it more fully or merely to deliver it or to make the acquaintance of the man who was interested in this new literary combination, there appeared in my office a taut, ruddy, blue-eyed, snub-nosed youth of twenty eight or nine whose brisk gait and ingratiating smile proved to me at once enormously intriguing and amusing. I had, for some reason not connected with the basic mentality you may be sure, the sense of a small town roisterer or a college sophomore of the crudest and yet most disturbing charm and impishness, who, for some reason, had strayed into a field of letters. More than anything else he reminded me of a spoiled and petted and possibly over-financed brewer's or wholesale grocer's son who was out for a lark. With the sang-froid of a Cæsar or a Napoleon he made himself comfortable in a large and impressive chair which was designed primarily to reduce the over-confidence of the average beginner. And from that particular and unintended vantage point he beamed on me with the confidence of a smirking fox about to devour a chicken. So I was the editor of the Butterick Publications. He had been told about me. However, in spite of *Sister Carrie,* I doubt if he had ever heard of me before this. After studying him in that almost arch-episcopal setting which the chair provided, I began to laugh. "Well, well," I said, "if it isn't Anheuser's own brightest boy out to see the town." And with that unfailing readiness for any nonsensical flight that has always characterized him, he proceeded

The author Theodore Dreiser, whose work was defended by Mencken

to insist that this was true. "Certainly he *was* Baltimore's richest brewer's son and the yellow shoes and bright tie he was wearing were characteristic of the jack-dandies and rowdy-dows of his native town. Why not. What else did I expect? His father brewed the best beer in the world." All thought of the original purpose of the conference was at once dismissed and instead we proceeded to palaver and you-hoo anent the more general phases and ridiculosities of life, with the result that an understanding based on a mutual liking was established, and from then on I counted him among those whom I most prized—temperamentally as well as intellectually. And to this day, despite various disagreements, that mood has never varied.

Subsequent to this there were additional contacts based on this instantaneous friendship. He visited me at my apartment in New York and I in turn repaired to Baltimore. We multiplied noisy and roistering parties. Sometime during 1908 or 9—or whenever it was that the old Col. Mann's *Smart Set,* owing to various scandals in connection with its management, was reorganized and a new editor sought, a managing editor of mine came to me with the news of this thing. He was a capable fellow but not as I saw it suited to the particular work he was doing for me—nor to the editorship of the *Smart Set* for that matter. Yet, because I had been pon-

WHAT YOU OUGHT TO KNOW ABOUT YOUR BABY

By LEONARD KEENE HIRSHBERG, B.A., M.D.

⊞

A Text Book for Mothers
on the Care and Feeding
of Babies, with Questions
and Answers Especially
Prepared by the Editor

⊞

PUBLISHED BY
THE BUTTERICK PUBLISHING COMPANY
BUTTERICK BUILDING   1910   NEW YORK

*Title page for a volume largely ghostwritten by Mencken and published
by the firm for which Dreiser served as managing editor. The questions
and answers were the only parts not written by Mencken.*

dering how to replace him without injury to himself, I now encouraged him in the thought with which he had come to me–i.e.–that with my approbation and aid he would apply for the editorship of the same. And why not he as well as another? If they did not like him, they could soon get rid of him, could they not–said I. So I stirred him with the plausibility of the idea and he immediately proceeded to apply for the place, and, to my satisfaction, as well as astonishment, secured it.

But as was the custom of some others whom I had advised in this fashion in times past, he soon returned to me with the request that I aid him in outlining a policy and suitable staff or list of contributors for his magazine. And, in discussing what regular and permanent features might be introduced and who would be most likely to lend lustre to the magazine by their

work, I suggested that as intriguing as anything would be a Book Department with a really brilliant and illuminating reviewer. Instantly the one name that appealed to me as ideal for this work was that of Mencken. I insisted that he could not do better than get this man and that he should engage him at once. This he did. And this was the beginning of Mencken's connection with the *Smart Set,* which subsequently led to its control by himself and George Jean Nathan who was already doing dramatics for the magazine, if I am not mistaken, when my youthful aspirant and assistant moved in.

THEODORE DREISER

New York,
    August 24, 1925

Mencken's first review of a Dreiser work appeared in The Smart Set. *It was an uncharacteristic rave about the novel that is perhaps Dreiser's finest aesthetic achievement, and Mencken saw in it the influence of the new literature of Europe (excerpt from "A Novel of the First Rank,"* Smart Set *[November 1911]: 153).*

If you miss reading "JENNIE GERHARDT," by Theodore Dreiser (*Harpers*), you will miss the best American novel, all things considered, that has reached the book counters in a dozen years. On second thought, change "a dozen" into "twenty-five." On third thought, strike out everything after "counters." On fourth thought, strike out everything after "novel." Why back and fill? Why evade and qualify? Hot from it, I am firmly convinced that "JENNIE GERHARDT" is the best American novel I have ever read, with the lonesome but Himalayan exception of "Huckleberry Finn," and so I may as well say it aloud and at once and have done with it. Am I forgetting "The Scarlet Letter," "The Rise of Silas Lapham" and (to drag an exile unwillingly home) "What Maisie Knew"? I am not. Am I forgetting "McTeague" and "The Pit"? I am not. Am I forgetting the stupendous masterpieces of James Fenimore Cooper, beloved of the pedagogues, or those of James Lane Allen, Mrs. Wharton and Dr. S. Weir Mitchell, beloved of the women's clubs and literary monthlies? No. Or "Uncle Tom's Cabin" or "Rob o' the Bowl" or "Gates Ajar" or "Ben Hur" or "David Harum" or "Lewis Rand" or "Richard Carvel"? No. Or "The Hungry Heart" or Mr. Dreiser's own "Sister Carrie"? No. I have all these good and bad books in mind. I have read them and survived them and in many cases enjoyed them.

And yet in the face of them, and in the face of all the high authority, constituted and self-constituted, behind them, it seems to me at this moment that "JENNIE GERHARDT" stands apart from all of them, and a bit above them. It lacks the grace of this one, the humor of that one, the perfect form of some other one; but taking it as it stands, grim, gaunt, mirthless, shapeless, it remains, and by long odds, the most impressive work of art that we have yet to show in prose fiction–a tale not unrelated, in its stark simplicity, its profound sincerity, to "Germinal" and "Anna Karenina" and "Lord Jim"–a tale assertively American in its scene and its human material, and yet so European in its method, its point of view, its almost reverential seriousness, that one can scarcely imagine an American writing it. [. . .]

Mencken's funniest review of Dreiser also appeared in The Smart Set. *It was more characteristic than the previous in that, as was usually the case, he conceded at length the manifest weaknesses in his subject's writing, thereby disconcerting the relatively humorless Dreiser (excerpt from "A Literary Behemoth,"* Smart Set *[December 1915]: 150–151).*

On page 703 of Theodore Dreiser's new novel, "THE 'GENIUS'" (*Lane*), the gentleman described by the title, Eugene Tennyson Witla by name, is on his way to a Christian Scientist to apply for treatment for "his evil tendencies in regard to women." Remember the place: page 703. The reader, by this time, has hacked and gummed his way through 702 large pages of fine print: 97 long chapters: more than 300,000 words. The stage-hands stand ready to yank down the curtain; messieurs of the orchestra, their minds fixed eagerly upon malt liquor, are up to their hips in the finale; the weary nurses are swabbing up the operating room; the learned chirurgeons are wiping their knives upon their pantaloons; the rev. clergy are swinging into the benediction; the inexorable embalmer waits in the antechamber with his unescapable syringe, his Mona Lisa smile. . . . And then, at this painfully hurried and impatient point, with the *coda* already under weigh and even the most somnolent reaching nervously for his galoshes, Dreiser halts the whole show to explain the origin, nature and inner meaning of Christian Science, and to make us privy to a lot of chatty stuff about Mrs. Althea Johns, the lady-like healer, and to supply us with detailed plans and specifications of the joint, lair or apartment-house in which this fair sorceress lives, works her miracles, trims her boobs, and has her being!

Believe me, I do not spoof. Turn to page 703 and see for yourself. There, while the fate of Witla waits and the bowels of patience are turned to water, we are instructed and tortured with the following particulars about the house: [. . .]

Such is novel-writing as Dreiser understands it–a laborious and relentless meticulousness, an endless piling up of small details, an almost furious tracking down of

Publisher's promotional brochure quoting a Mencken review

ions, electrons and molecules. One is amazed and flabbergasted by the mole-like industry of the man, and no less by his lavish disregard for the ease and convenience of his reader. A Dreiser novel, at least of the later canon, cannot be read as other novels are read, *e.g.,* on a winter evening or a summer afternoon, between meal and meal, travelling from New York to Boston. It demands the attention for at least a week, and uses up the strength for at least a month. If, tackling "The 'Genius,'" one were to become engrossed in the fabulous manner described by the newspaper reviewers and so find oneself unable to put it down and go to bed before the end, one would get no sleep for three days and three nights. A man who can prove that he has

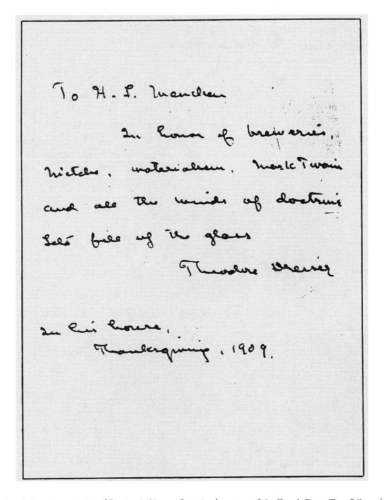

Inscription in a reprint of Dreiser's Sister Carrie *(courtesy of the Enoch Pratt Free Library)*

read such a novel without medical assistance should be admitted to the *Landwehr* at once, without thesis or examination, and perhaps even given the order *pour la mérite*. A woman of equal attainments is tough enough to take in washing or to sing Brünnhilde. . . .

And yet, and yet—well, here comes the inevitable "and yet." For all his long-windedness, for all his persistent refusal to get about his business, for all his mouthings of things so small that they seem to be nothings, this Dreiser is undoubtedly a literary artist of very respectable rank, and nothing proves it more certainly than this, the last, the longest and one is tempted to add the damnedest of his novels. [. . .]

For his support over the years, notably in the battle against censorship—Mencken organized the international protest when The "Genius" *was banned, and the two were jointly attacked as German Americans in the war years by superpatriotic critics—Dreiser presented Mencken with the manuscript for* Sister Carrie. *This exchange occurred after they had repaired their friendship. The movie*

of Sister Carrie *was not made until 1951, with Jennifer Jones and Laurence Olivier in the lead roles (handwritten [Dreiser] and typewritten [Mencken] letters at the New York Public Library and the University of Pennsylvania, respectively).*

THEODORE DREISER

June 16, '39

Dear Mencken:

I am truly glad to hear that the original ms of Sister Carrie will not be dust for a while, anyhow. It was courteous of you to look after it. Sometime I may want to look over the script and now it is possible. What does a photo-stat copy cost?

Barring the indescribably mental and financial fluctuations of this area Sister Carrie is sold—as a movie The price is between $40,000 and $50,000, but commissions, income tax etc come out of that, so it isn't so much. Pending the amicable adjudication of certain

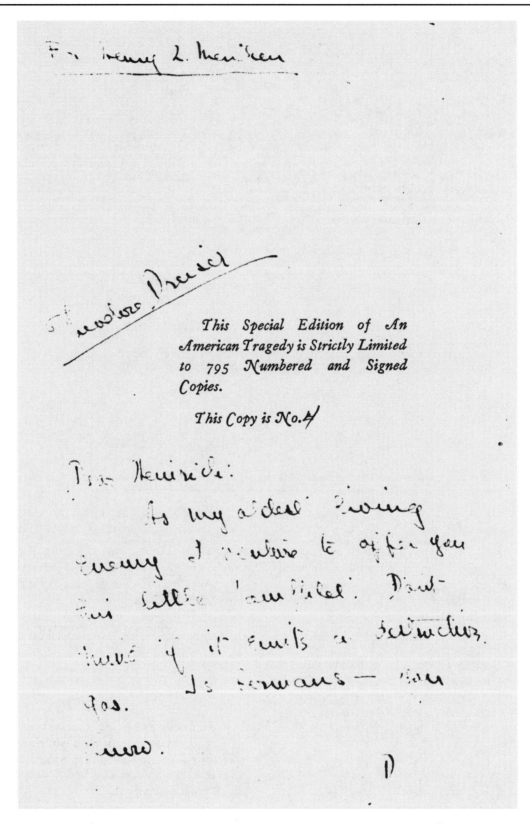

Inscription in Mencken's copy of Dreiser's novel. It reads, "Dear Heinrich: As my oldest living enemy I venture to offer you this little pamphlet. Don't mind if it emits a destructive gas. Us Germans–you know" (courtesy of the Enoch Pratt Free Library and The Dreiser Trust).

Caricature of Dreiser that he inscribed to Mencken in 1916 (Astor, Lenox and Tilden Foundations, New York Public Library)

Look who's here. Theodore Dreiser, whose power and force have placed him in the forefront of American novelists, and who has demonstrated that he can write a realistic novel with something real in it.

H. L. MENCKEN
1524 HOLLINS ST.
BALTIMORE.

June 27, 1939.

Dear Dreiser:

It is excellent news that you have placed "Sister Carrie" with the movies. However much the money may be diminished by fees and taxes, it still remains money found. As you know, I have always believed that "Sister Carrie" would make a really first-rate movie. In the days when it was first discussed the movies were in a crude state; today they are at least better than they were then. My guess is that the Hays office will not make any real difficulties.

The manuscript was mounted by hand at the expense of the New York Public Library. I placed it in the Library's custody simply because I thought it

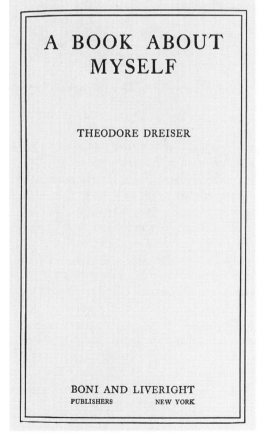

A BOOK ABOUT MYSELF

THEODORE DREISER

BONI AND LIVERIGHT
PUBLISHERS   NEW YORK

Title page for a 1922 book that Mencken edited for Dreiser without acknowledgment. "It was a dreadful specimen of Dreiser's writing at its worst, and I put in long hours trying to claw it into plausible English," Mencken wrote (My Life as Author and Editor, 1993).

moral points with the Hays office—(believe it or not the book is still immoral because—harken—Carrie isn't punished for her crime)—a fairly solid binder has been handed over free and clear. And they'll work to get that back if they have to turn it into comedy. It's total history certainly constitutes one.

I work very hard. Every day. This region is stuffed with hard boiled savage climbers, stuffed and mounted shirts, the lowest grade of political grafter, quacks not calculable as to number or variety, all grades of God-shouters—(now welcoming Heywood Broun) and loafers, prostitutes, murderers and perverts. In the bland sunshine here they multiply like germs in the Canal Zone. What saves it is the wisdom, taste, honor and virtue of the moving picture industry.

I am—barring possible incarceration—As ever

Dreiser

* * *

Sinclair Lewis, in whose novels Mencken saw fictionalized versions of his own social criticism

should be taken care of better than I could do it. The understanding is that nobody is ever to have access to it in your lifetime without your written permission. If, by any extraordinary and incredible manifestation of God's grace, I survive you, then they will have to come to me. After we are both in Paradise it will be in the custody of the Library.

My guess is that making a photostat would be rather expensive. The thing, as it stands, is accessible to you, of course, at all times.

I have just returned from Indianapolis, where I spent five days attending the convention of the Townsendites. It was a dreadful show, but somehow amusing.

Yours,
M

The other author of the era with whom Mencken is particularly associated is Sinclair Lewis, the first American to win the Nobel Prize in literature (1930). Mencken promoted Lewis because he saw, in novels such as Main Street *(1920) and* Babbitt *(1922), fictionalized versions of his own social criticism, as he*

gleefully states in his review of the latter (excerpt from "Portrait of an American Citizen," Smart Set *[October 1922]: 139).*

[. . .] Let me confess at once that this story has given me vast delight. I know the Babbitt type, I believe, as well as most; for twenty years I have devoted myself to the exploration of its peculiarities. Lewis depicts it with complete and absolute fidelity. There is irony in the picture; irony that is unflagging and unfailing, but nowhere is there any important departure from the essential truth. Babbitt has a great clownishness in him, but he never becomes a mere clown. In the midst of his most extravagant imbecilities he keeps both feet upon the ground. One not only sees him brilliantly; one also understands him; he is made plausible and natural. As an old professor of Babbittry I welcome him as an almost perfect specimen—a genuine museum piece. Every American city swarms with his brothers. They run things in the Republic, East, West, North, South. They are the

MAIN STREET   263

on what a fool Dr. McGanum was to try to use that cheap X-ray outfit of his on an epithelioma, repaired a frock, drowsily heard Kennicott stoke the furnace, tried to read a page of Thorstein Veblen—and the day was gone.

Except when Hugh was vigorously naughty, or whiney, or laughing, or saying "I like my chair" with thrilling maturity, she was always enfeebled by loneliness. She no longer felt superior about that misfortune. She would gladly have been converted to Vida's satisfaction in Gopher Prairie and mopping the floor.

II

Carol drove through an astonishing number of books from the public library and from city shops. Kennicott was at first uncomfortable over her disconcerting habit of buying them. A book was a book, and if you had several thousand of them right here in the library, free, why the dickens should you spend your good money? After worrying about it for two or three years, he decided that this was one of the Funny Ideas which she had caught as a librarian and from which she would never entirely recover.

The authors whom she read were most of them frightfully annoyed by the Vida Sherwins. They were young American sociologists, young English realists, Russian horrorists; Anatole France, Rolland, Nexo, Wells, Shaw, Key, Edgar Lee Masters, Theodore Dreiser, Sherwood Anderson, Henry Mencken, and all the other subversive philosophers and artists whom women were consulting everywhere, in batik-curtained studios in New York, in Kansas farmhouses, San Francisco drawing-rooms, Alabama schools for negroes. From them she got the same confused desire which the million other women felt; the same determination to be class-conscious without discovering the class of which she was to be conscious.

Certainly her reading precipitated her observations of Main Street, of Gopher Prairie and of the several adjacent Gopher Prairies which she had seen on drives with Kennicott. In her fluid thought certain convictions appeared, jaggedly, a fragment of an impression at a time, while she was going to sleep, or manicuring her nails, or waiting for Kennicott.

These convictions she presented to Vida Sherwin—Vida Wutherspoon—beside a radiator, over a bowl of not very good

Page from Lewis's 1920 work. Mencken was named in many novels of the 1920s.

originators and propagators of the national delusions—all, that is, save those which spring from the farms. They are the palladiums of 100% Americanism; the apostles of the Harding politics; the guardians of the Only True Christianity. They constitute the Chambers of Commerce, the Rotary Clubs, the Kiwanis Clubs, the Watch and Ward Societies, the Men and Religion Forward Movements, the Y.M.C.A. directorates, the Good Citizen Leagues. They are the advertisers who determine what is to go into the American newspapers and what is to stay out. They are the Leading Citizens, the speakers at banquets, the profiteers, the corruptors of politics, the supporters of evangelical Christianity, the peers of the realm. Babbitt is their archetype. He is no worse than most, and no better; he is the average American of the ruling minority in this hundred and forty-sixth year of the Republic. He is America incarnate, exuberant and exquisite. Study him well and you will know better what is the matter with the land we live in than you would know after plowing through a thousand such volumes as Walter Lippmann's "Public Opinion." What Lippmann tried to do as a professor, laboriously and without imagination, Lewis has here done as an artist with a few vivid strokes. It is a very fine piece of work indeed. [. . .]

Mencken also promoted what are now fashionably called "the marginalized." He tried to open the canon to their writing as he had opened The American Language *to their voices. He did not patronize or condescend to minorities; he held their work to the same standards as he held those of white authors, calling for the same realism, the same avoidance of sentimentalism and idealism that he found in Dreiser. In a review of* The Shadow, *by Mary White Ovington, he states what he thinks should be the agenda of the Negro writer—although he is mistaken about Ovington's race and marital status (excerpt from "Gropings in Literary Darkness,"* Smart Set *[October 1920]: 140–141).*

[. . .] Nevertheless, the author shows skill, observation, a civilized point of view. Let her forget her race prejudices and her infantile fables long enough to get a true, an unemotional and a typical picture of her people on paper, and she will not only achieve a respectable work of art, but also serve the cause that seems to have her devotion. As she herself points out, half of the difficulties between race and race are due to sheer ignorance. The black man, I suppose, has a fairly good working understanding of the white man; he has many opportunities to observe and note down, and my experience of him convinces me that he is a shrewd observer—that few white men ever fool him. But the white man, even in the South, knows next to nothing of

the inner life of the negro. The more magnificently he generalizes, the more his ignorance is displayed. What the average Southerner believes about the negroes who surround him is chiefly nonsense. His view of them is moral and indignant, or, worse still, sentimental and idiotic. The great movements and aspirations that stir them are quite beyond his comprehension; in many cases he does not even hear of them. The thing we need is a realistic picture of this inner life of the negro by one who sees the race from within—a self-portrait as vivid and accurate as Dostoyevsky's portrait of the Russian or Thackeray's of the Englishman. The action should be kept within the normal range of negro experience. It should extend over a long enough range of years to show some development in character and circumstance. It should be presented against a background made vivid by innumerable small details. The negro author who makes such a book will dignify American literature and accomplish more for his race than a thousand propagandists and theorists. He will force the understanding that now seems so hopeless. He will blow up nine-tenths of the current poppycock. But let him avoid the snares that fetched Mrs. Ovington. She went to Kathleen Norris and Gertrude Atherton for her model. The place to learn how to write novels is in the harsh but distinguished seminary kept by Prof. Dr. Dreiser. [. . .]

Mencken's contribution to the Harlem Renaissance was fully acknowledged in Charles Scruggs's The Sage in Harlem: H. L. Mencken and the Black Writers of the 1920s *(Baltimore & London: Johns Hopkins University Press, 1984). "He seemed to know what they knew," Scruggs writes, "that beneath the smug surface of American life was a core of rottenness" (p. 25). Richard Wright recorded the moment of his discovery of this fact in his* Black Boy: A Record of Childhood and Youth *(New York: Harper, 1945). It is the most famous account of what was a frequent occurrence: a young writer taking courage and direction from Mencken (excerpt from chapter 13, pp. 214–219).*

One morning I arrived early at work and went into the bank lobby where the Negro porter was mopping. I stood at a counter and picked up the Memphis *Commercial Appeal* and began my free reading of the press. I came finally to the editorial page and saw an article dealing with one H. L. Mencken. I knew by hearsay that he was the editor of the *American Mercury,* but aside from that I knew nothing about him. The article was a furious denunciation of Mencken, concluding with one, hot, short sentence: Mencken is a fool.

I wondered what on earth this Mencken had done to call down upon him the scorn of the South. The only people I had ever heard denounced in the

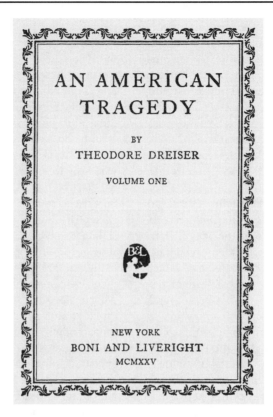

Title page for the first edition of the novel that, the critic Irving Babbitt noted, had been "hailed in certain quarters as the 'Mt. Everest' of recent fiction"

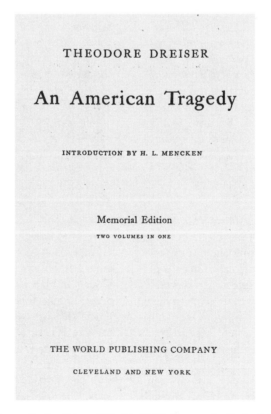

Title page for the edition published in 1946, the year after Dreiser's death

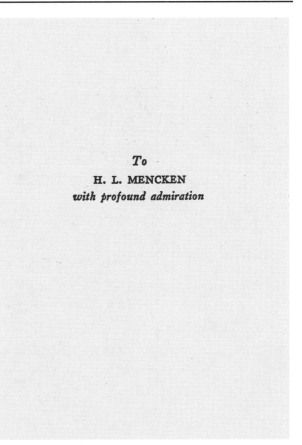

To
H. L. MENCKEN
with profound admiration

Dust jacket and dedication page for Lewis's 1927 novel

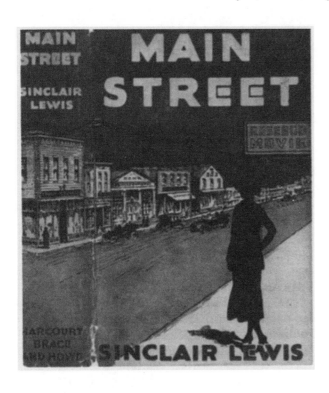

Dust jackets for two of Lewis's novels, published in 1920 and 1922, respectively, that reflect Mencken's attitudes towards the "Booboisie."

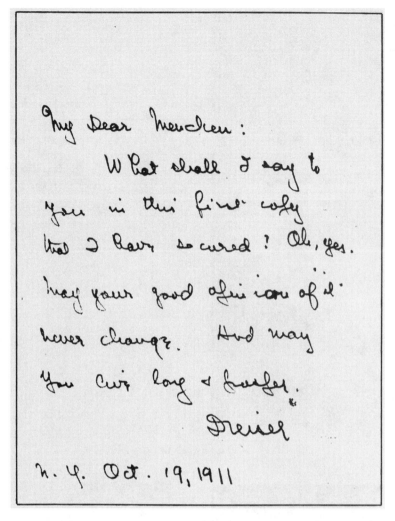

Inscription in Dreiser's Jennie Gerhardt *(courtesy of the Enoch Pratt Free Library)*

South were Negroes, and this man was not a Negro. Then what ideas did Mencken hold that made a newspaper like the *Commercial Appeal* castigate him publicly? Undoubtedly he must be advocating ideas that the South did not like. Were there, then, people other than Negroes who criticized the South? I knew that during the Civil War the South had hated northern whites, but I had not encountered such hate during my life. Knowing no more of Mencken than I did at that moment, I felt a vague sympathy for him. Had not the South, which had assigned me the role of a non-man, cast at him its hardest words?

Now, how could I find out about this Mencken? There was a huge library near the riverfront, but I knew that Negroes were not allowed to patronize its shelves any more than they were the parks and playgrounds of the city. I had gone into the library several times to get books for the white men on the job. Which of them would now help me to get books? And how could I read them without causing concern to the white men with whom I worked? I had so far been successful in hiding my thoughts and feelings from them, but I knew that I would create hostility if I went about this business of reading in a clumsy way. [. . .]

There remained only one man whose attitude did not fit into an anti-Negro category, for I had heard the white men refer to him as a "Pope lover." He was an Irish Catholic and was hated by the white Southerners. I knew that he read books, because I had got him volumes from the library several times. Since he, too, was an object of hatred, I felt that he might refuse me but would hardly betray me. I hesitated, weighing and balancing the imponderable realities.

Richard Wright, a writer who, as a young man, took courage from Mencken

Dust jacket for Wright's 1945 autobiography

One morning I paused before the Catholic fellow's desk.

"I want to ask you a favor," I whispered to him.

"What is it?"

"I want to read. I can't get books from the library. I wonder if you'd let me use your card?"

He looked at me suspiciously.

"My card is full most of the time," he said.

"I see," I said and waited, posing my question silently.

"You're not trying to get me into trouble, are you, boy?" he asked, staring at me.

"Oh, no, sir."

"What book do you want?"

"A book by H. L. Mencken."

"Which one?"

"I don't know. Has he written more than one?"

"He has written several."

"I didn't know that."

"What makes you want to read Mencken?"

"Oh, I just saw his name in the newspaper," I said.

"It's good of you to want to read," he said. "But you ought to read the right things."

I said nothing. Would he want to supervise my reading?

"Let me think," he said. "I'll figure out something."

I turned from him and he called me back. He stared at me quizzically.

"Richard, don't mention this to the other white men," he said.

"I understand," I said. "I won't say a word."

A few days later he called me to him.

"I've got a card in my wife's name," he said. "Here's mine."

"Thank you, sir."

"Do you think you can manage it?"

"I'll manage fine," I said.

"If they suspect you, you'll get in trouble," he said.

"I'll write the same kind of notes to the library that you wrote when you sent me for books," I told him. "I'll sign your name."

He laughed.

"Go ahead. Let me see what you get," he said.

That afternoon I addressed myself to forging a note. Now, what were the names of books written by H. L. Mencken? I did not know any of them. I finally wrote what I thought would be a fool-proof note: *Dear Madam: Will you please let this nigger boy*—I used the word "nigger" to make the librarian feel that I could not possibly be the author of the note—*have some books by H. L. Mencken?* I forged the white man's name.

I entered the library as I had always done when on errands for the whites, but I felt that I would somehow slip up and betray myself. I doffed my hat, stood a respectful distance from the desk, looked as unbookish as possible, and waited for the white patrons to be taken care of. When the desk was clear of people, I still waited. The white librarian looked at me.

"What do you want, boy?"

As though I did not possess the power of speech, I stepped forward and simply handed her the forged note, not parting my lips.

"What books by Mencken does he want?" she asked.

"I don't know, ma'am," I said, avoiding her eyes.

"Who gave you this card?"

"Mr. Falk," I said,

"Where is he?"

"He's at work, at the M-- Optical Company," I said. "I've been in here for him before."

"I remember," the woman said. "But he never wrote notes like this."

Oh, God, she's suspicious. Perhaps she would not let me have the books? If she had turned her back at that moment, I would have ducked out the door and never gone back. Then I thought of a bold idea.

"You can call him up, ma'am," I said, my heart pounding.

"You're not using these books, are you?" she asked pointedly.

"Oh, no, ma'am. I can't read."

"I don't know what he wants by Mencken," she said under her breath.

I knew now that I had won; she was thinking of other things and the race question had gone out of her mind. She went to the shelves. Once or twice she looked over her shoulder at me, as though she was still doubtful. Finally she came forward with two books in her hand.

"I'm sending him two books," she said. "But tell Mr. Falk to come in next time, or send me the names of the books he wants. I don't know what he wants to read."

I said nothing. She stamped the card and handed me the books. Not daring to glance at them, I went out of the library, fearing that the woman would call me back for further questioning. A block away from the library I opened one of the books and read a title: *A Book of Prefaces*. I was nearing my nineteenth birthday and I did not know how to pronounce the word "preface." I thumbed the pages and saw strange words and strange names. I shook my head, disappointed. I looked at the other book; it was called *Prejudices*. I knew what that word meant; I had heard it all my life. And right off I was on guard against Mencken's books. Why would a man want to call a book *Prejudices*? The word was so stained with all my memories of racial hate that I could not conceive of anybody using it for a title. Perhaps I had made a mistake about Mencken? A man who had prejudices must be wrong.

When I showed the books to Mr. Falk, he looked at me and frowned.

"That librarian might telephone you," I warned him.

"That's all right," he said. "But when you're through reading those books, I want you to tell me what you get out of them."

That night in my rented room, while letting the hot water run over my can of pork and beans in the sink, I opened *A Book of Prefaces* and began to read. I was jarred and shocked by the style, the clear, clean, sweeping sentences. Why did he write like that? And how did one write like that? I pictured the man as a raging demon, slashing with his pen, consumed with hate, denouncing everything American, extolling everything European or German, laughing at the weaknesses of people, mocking God, authority. What was this? I stood up, trying to realize what reality lay behind the meaning of the words . . . Yes, this man was fighting, fighting with words. He was using words as a weapon, using them as one would use a club. Could words be weapons? Well, yes, for here they were. Then, maybe, perhaps, I could use them as a weapon? No. It frightened me. I read on and what amazed me was not what he said, but how on earth anybody had the courage to say it.

Occasionally I glanced up to reassure myself that I was alone in the room. Who were these men about whom Mencken was talking so passionately? Who was Anatole France? Joseph Conrad? Sinclair Lewis, Sherwood Anderson, Dostoevski, George Moore, Gustave Flaubert, Maupassant, Tolstoy, Frank Harris, Mark Twain, Thomas Hardy, Arnold Bennett, Stephen Crane, Zola, Norris, Gorky, Bergson, Ibsen, Balzac, Bernard Shaw, Dumas, Poe, Thomas Mann, O. Henry, Dreiser, H. G. Wells, Gogol, T. S. Eliot, Gide, Baudelaire, Edgar Lee Masters, Stendhal, Turgenev, Huneker, Nietzsche, and scores of others? Were these men real? Did they exist or had they existed? And how did one pronounce their names?

I ran across many words whose meaning I did not know, and I either looked them up in a dictionary or, before I had a chance to do that, encountered the word in a context that made its meaning clear. But what strange world is this? I concluded the book with the conviction that I had somehow overlooked something terribly important in life. I had once tried to write, had once reveled in feeling, had let my crude imagination roam, but the impulse to dream had been slowly beaten out of me by experience. Now it surged up again and I hungered for books, new ways of looking and seeing. It was not a matter of believing or disbelieving what I read, but of feeling something new, of being affected by something that made the look of the world different.

As dawn broke I ate my pork and beans, feeling dopey, sleepy. I went to work, but the mood of the book would not die; it lingered, coloring everything I saw, heard, did. I now felt that I knew what the white men were feeling. Merely because I had read a book that had spoken of how they lived and thought, I identified myself with that book. I felt vaguely guilty. Would I, filled with bookish notions, act in a manner that would make the whites dislike me?

I forged more notes and my trips to the library became frequent. Reading grew into a passion. My first serious novel was Sinclair Lewis's *Main Street*. It made me see my boss, Mr. Gerald, and identify him as an American type. I would smile when I saw him lugging his golf bags into the office. I had always felt a vast distance separating me from the boss, and now I felt closer to him, though still distant. I felt now that I knew him, that I could feel the very limits of his narrow life. And this had happened because I had read a novel about a mythical man called George F. Babbitt.

The plots and stories in the novels did not interest me so much as the point of view revealed. I gave myself over to each novel without reserve, without trying to criticize it; it was enough for me to see and feel something different. And for me, everything was something different. Reading was like a drug, a dope. The novels created moods in which I lived for days. But I could not conquer my sense of guilt, my feeling that the white men around me knew that I was changing, that I had begun to regard them differently.

Whenever I brought a book to the job, I wrapped it in newspaper—a habit that was to persist for years in other cities and under other circumstances. But some of the white men pried into my packages when I was absent and they questioned me.

"Boy, what are you reading those books for?"

"Oh, I don't know, sir."

"That's deep stuff you're reading, boy."

"I'm just killing time, sir."

"You'll addle your brains if you don't watch out."

The poet, novelist, diplomat, lawyer, and civil rights leader James Weldon Johnson, whose writing Mencken promoted

I read Dreiser's *Jennie Gerhardt* and *Sister Carrie* and they revived in me a vivid sense of my mother's suffering; I was overwhelmed. I grew silent, wondering about the life around me. It would have been impossible for me to have told anyone what I derived from these novels, for it was nothing less than a sense of life itself. All my life had shaped me for the realism, the naturalism of the modern novel, and I could not read enough of them. [. . .]

The extraordinary James Weldon Johnson—poet, novelist, diplomat, lawyer, and civil rights leader—was one of Mencken's informants on black life in the United States. Mencken published his work and so did Knopf, at Mencken's urging. Here Johnson recalls his first meeting with Mencken, which occurred around 1915 (excerpt from Johnson, Along This Way *[New York: Viking, 1933], pp. 305–306).*

The first new contact I made was with H. L. Mencken, then one of the editors of *Smart Set*. Mr.

GOD'S TROMBONES

SEVEN NEGRO SERMONS IN VERSE

By JAMES WELDON JOHNSON

The inspirational sermons of the old-time Negro preachers are here set down as poetry. Mr. Johnson tells in his preface of hearing these same themes treated by famous preachers in his youth; some of the sermons are still current, and like the Spirituals they have a significant place in Negro folk-material. The poet has not only given them a form in which they will survive; he has transmuted their essence into original and moving poetry. The Negro artist, Aaron Douglas, has made eight arresting interpretations.

James Weldon Johnson has published one other volume of poems, and has edited *The Book of American Negro Poetry* and the two *Books of American Negro Spirituals*. In 1925 he received the Spingarn Medal, and in 1926 one of the Harmon awards, for distinguished contributions to Negro culture. He is Secretary of the National Association for the Advancement of Colored People.

H. L. MENCKEN calls *Go Down Death* (page 27) "one of the most remarkable and moving poems of its type ever written in America."

30 IRVING PLACE *The Viking Press* NEW YORK CITY

Back of the dust jacket for Johnson's book of verse. Mencken had published "Go Down Death" in The American Mercury.

Mencken had made a sharper impression on my mind than any other American then writing, and I wanted to know him. As a reason for going to see him, I took along a one-act play, *Mañana de Sol,* which I had translated from the Spanish of Serafín and Joaquín Álvarez Quintero. I sent my name in, feeling not entirely confident that I should see Mr. Mencken, but he came out almost promptly. We sat and talked for thirty, forty, perhaps forty-five minutes; and I kept wondering how a man as busy as he could give so much time to a mere stranger. I had never been so fascinated at hearing anyone talk. He talked about literature, about Negro literature, the Negro problem, and Negro music. He declared that Negro writers in writing about their own race made a mistake when they indulged in pleas for justice and mercy, when they prayed indulgence for shortcomings, when they based their protests against unjust treatment on the Christian or moral or ethical code, when they argued to prove that they were as good as anybody else. "What they should do," he said, "is to single out the strong points of the race and emphasize them over and over and over; asserting, at least on these points, that they are *better* than anybody else." I called to his attention that I had attempted something of that sort in *The Autobiography of an Ex-Colored Man.* He was particularly interested in Negro music, and I afterwards sent him copies of songs by Burleigh and Cook and Johnson. Through some correspondence which we had about the songs, I discerned that his chief interest in them was not that of an editor but of a musician. Mr. Mencken did not accept the play, but my visit was the beginning of a very pleasant relation. His parting advice was that I center my efforts on prose rather than poetry; I gathered that his opinion of poetry and poets was not exceedingly high. When I left him I felt buoyed up, exhilarated. It was as though I had taken a mental cocktail. [. . .]

Johnson had used the last phrase in an earlier piece. Referring to Mencken's "Mr. Cabell of Virginia," he takes issue with the racial reasons for the cultural inferiority of Southern white trash to blacks, preferring the political. The article is but one example of how Mencken for years stimulated discussion on the nation's primary social problem ("American Genius and Its Local[e]," New York Age, 20 July 1918, editorial page).

We have often referred to the writings of H. L. Mencken. His English is a mental cocktail, an intellectual electric shock. Anybody who habitually dozes over conventional English ought to take Mencken at least once or twice a week in order to keep the moss and cobwebs out of their brains. Mr. Mencken writes excellently on a wider range of subjects than any other one writer in the United States, and whatever his topic may be, he is always interesting. But he is at his best when he is talking about the theatre or literature or music or philosophy or feminism or criticism. On these subjects he is an authority.

The chief charm of Mencken is that he always has a fresh point of view on even the oldest subject. If the subject is one that does not admit of a fresh point of view, Mencken does not touch it, he considers it as already finished, exhausted; as a subject to be left in an embalmed state in the tomb of literature. It is into this very pit that Mencken always avoids that so many writers fall; they do not even know when a subject is exhausted. For that reason so many fledgling poets attempt to write odes to birds and flowers (skylarks, nightingales, daisies and roses), not realizing that Keats and Shelley and Burns and a host of others have done the job to a finish.

Mencken's style is all his own; nobody in the country writes like him. Sometimes we know that he is laughing at his readers, and sometimes we suspect that he is laughing at himself. We might call him a humorous cynic; and when he is most cynical, he is most enjoyable. He is the cleverest writer in America to-day.

But those who look merely for cleverness in Mencken are missing the best part of him; the best part of Mencken is truth. He gets at truth because he is devoid of the sentimental and mawkish morality which seems to be the curse of nearly everybody who writes in the English language. In other words, he is free and is therefore not

afraid to write the truth. Many a writer is sincere enough, but bound by so many traditions and conventions that he cannot write the truth. Mencken pays no regard to traditions and conventions as such; he has absolutely no respect for them merely on account of their age.

———

The other day we picked up an article headed, "Mr. Cabell of Virginia." The article was by H. L. Mencken. Of course we were at once interested in Mr. Cabell because Mr. Mencken was talking about him. The article was a critical estimate of Mr. Cabell's work as a novelist. We know very little about that work, never having read any of Mr. Cabell's books; but Mr. Mencken puts high value on him, and we have made up our mind to read at least one of those books at the first opportunity. The critic gives as one of the reasons why Cabell should be read the following: "he is the only indubitably literate man left in the late Confederate States of America." Then he goes on to say:

> Let the last consideration engage us first. What I mean to say is that Cabell is the only first-rate craftsman that the whole South can show. In all that vast region, with its 30,000,000 or 40,000,000 people and its territory as large as half a dozen Frances or Germanys, he is the only author worth a damn—almost the only one who can write at all. The spectacle is so strange that I can't keep my eyes from it. Imagine an empire as huge as the Holy Roman, and with no more literature than Pottstown, Pa., or Summit, N. J.—not a poet, not a serious historian, not a critic good or bad, not a dramatist dead or alive, and but one novelist!

Then Mr. Mencken takes up the question of the lack or rather the absence of literary men and women in the South, and says:

> The causes of this paucity I have hitherto discussed and guessed at. Perhaps the soundest theory is that which holds that the civil war destroyed the whole civilization of the region and well-nigh exterminated the civilized Southerner. The few who survived came North, leaving the soil to the Ethiop and the poor white trash. The latter now struggle for possession in the manner of dogs and cats, with the odds increasingly in favor of the black. Of the two, he alone shows any cultural advance; he begins to produce artists, and even sages. But the poor white trash, now politically dominant in all the southern states, produce only traders, schemers, politicians and reformers—in brief, bounders.

There is an interesting question raised here. Why is it that the South produces no first-rate literature? As Mr. Mencken says, this whole wide region with "not a poet, not a serious historian, not a critic good or bad, not a dramatist dead or alive." We think we can shed a little light on this question. Mr. Mencken thinks the condition may be due to the fact that "the civil war destroyed the whole civilization of the region and well nigh exterminated the civilized Southerner." But why should not the poor white trash produce something? Is it possible that they can be so innately inferior to the Southern aristocracy? Were they any more handicapped than the "Ethiop," who, Mr. Mencken says, "alone shows any cultural advance"?

We do not think that the destruction of the old Southern civilization or any innate inferiority of the poor white trash is the reason; the real reason is that the white South of to-day is using up every bit of its mental energy in this terrible race struggle. All of the mental efforts of the white South run through one narrow channel; the life of every Southern white man as a man and a citizen, most of his financial activities and all his political activities, are impassably limited by the ever present "Negro problem." All of the mental power of the whole South is being used up in holding the Negro back, and that is the reason why it does not produce either great literature or great statesmen or great wealth. That is, the white South is less intensely interested in forging ahead than it is in keeping the Negro from forging ahead. Witness: in Alabama there is opposition to a compulsory education law because under it Negro children would be compelled to go to school.

On the other hand, the Negro is not using up any of his strength in trying to hold anybody back, he is using every ounce of it to move forward himself. His face is front and toward the light; when the white man tries to force him back he, the white man, turns from the light and faces backward. Unless the white people of the South right-about on this question, the Negro will in the long run distance them in the higher and finer achievements.

Mencken had favorably reviewed The Autobiography of an Ex-Colored Man, *which first appeared anonymously in 1912. Because of him, the second edition was published by Knopf in 1927 (typewritten 1924 letter with handwritten initial as signature at the Enoch Pratt Free Library, Baltimore).*

H. L. MENCKEN
1524 HOLLINS ST.
BALTIMORE.

November 27th

Dear Alfred:–

1. I forgot to tell you that James Weldon Johnson, the chief man in the Association for the Advancement of Colored People, is preparing to write his reminiscences. He has had a very remarkable career and writes very well. You will get the book automatically. I may be able to use parts of it in The American Mercury.

M

Pittsburgh Courier *columnist George S. Schuyler, whose work Mencken published frequently in his magazine* The American Mercury

One of the leading black newspapers was the Pittsburgh Courier, *which featured distinguished columnists of various political stripes. On the right was George S. Schuyler, whose work Mencken published in the last six years of* The American Mercury *more frequently than that of any other author. Mencken wrote to the* Courier *in 1947 that Schuyler was the best columnist in the United States. In 1927 he wrote to Schuyler, soliciting contributions for* The American Mercury *(typewritten letter with handwritten signature at New York Public Library).*

THE AMERICAN MERCURY
730 FIFTH AVENUE
NEW YORK

August 25th

Dear Mr. Schuyler:–

Have you anything in hand or in mind that would fit into The American Mercury? If so, I'll be delighted to hear of it. I mean something done realistically and fearlessly, like your excellent stuff in the Pittsburgh Courier.

THE REVIEWER
A Monthly Magazine
Richmond, Va.

EDITORS

EMILY CLARK   HUNTER STAGG
MARY STREET   MARGARET FREEMAN

The Editors of The Reviewer announce the continuation of the magazine in enlarged form as a monthly, beginning October 1, 1921. Subscriptions for six months, ending with the issue of March 1, 1922, will be taken for $1.50.

What Various Critics Say:

The New York Times Book Review says:

> The Reviewer is valiantly attempting to concentrate the literary fluctuations of the South, and is carrying well-written reviews—The Reviewer continues to blaze its way through the literary sand flats of the South.

Atlanta Journal:

> Of the greatest interest to all lovers of the best in literature, and those patriotic Southerners who love southern traditions, but who enjoy these traditions with a modern note, is the new southern magazine, The Reviewer.

Douglas Freeman, in the News Leader, Richmond, Va., says:

> Richmond's youngest periodical, The Reviewer, has completed a half year of semi-monthly publication. During that time it has received more encouragement from the foremost writers of the country than any Southern magazine ever has received. Some of the most distinguished of American authors have given to The Reviewer articles that would have commanded the best prices of the greatest American periodicals. The result is that The Reviewer could print a "contributors column" for its first volume that would rival if not excel in the names it included any that the most famous American monthly·could boast.

H. L. Mencken, in The Smart Set, says:

> As I write, The Reviewer—which comes out twice a month—has reached its ninth number. It has no endowment, but is wholly sustained by the energies of the four enthusiasts—Emily Clark, Hunter Stagg, Mary Street, and Margaret Freeman—who edit it. Its contents throw an illuminating light, not only upon the causes of the intellectual stagnation of the South, but also upon the way out. The editors apparently know what sort of stuff they need to break down the old Southern tradition and prepare the path for better things. Here is the opportunity of The Reviewer, if the Richmond fog proves breathable long enough for it to get under way. It is young, it is unhampered by ties, and it shows, beneath all its superficial yieldings, a very palpable discontent with the Southern scene of to-day. Its peril is that it may sink into the puerile literary formalism that already curses the South, and so disappear beneath a sea of sweetened bilge.

Pages 1 and 3 of a four-page brochure, published during the literary magazine's first year, noting Mencken's approval
of the periodical (Jack R. Sanders Collection)

A while back I made some effort to get an article showing how the whites look to an intelligent Negro. Various dark literati of my acquaintance tried their hands at it, but all of them, it seemed to me, missed it. They couldn't get rid of politeness. Does the idea interest you? If so, I'll be glad to discuss it further.

> Sincerely yours,
> H. L. Mencken

Mencken's most notorious challenge to white supremacy in the arts, particularly in the South, was "The Sahara of the Bozart." The original 1917 article did not cause much of a stir, but the expanded version in Prejudices: Second Series *(1920) provoked an uproar. Black authors generally welcomed it; some of its theses are addressed above, having appeared elsewhere in Mencken's writings. When the desert threatened to bloom, Mencken was there to encourage the process, as in his support for the fledgling magazine* The Reviewer. *Emily Clark, an editor, recorded his assistance (excerpt from "H. L. Mencken," in Clark,* Innocence Abroad *[New York & London: Knopf, 1931], pp. 111–113).*

[. . .] This editor had been in correspondence with him since the spring before, when the magazine was started *[1921]*. He had written a half-serious but wholly cordial welcome to the magazine in the Baltimore *Evening Sun,* quickly followed by a sharp slap from him, in the same paper, on the appearance of its second issue. Part of the contents of this issue represented that Southern period when the phrase "postwar" meant a heightening of illusion rather than a complete loss of it. I wrote him in defence of the magazine, explaining that we had no money, only the goodwill of subscribers and contributors, and that the South, especially, must be encouraged as well as aroused. Since, at that time, I was unbelievably naïve, holding firmly to the faith that *The Reviewer* was as vitally absorbing to all intelligent persons as it was to me, I sent this letter by special delivery late at night, as soon as I had read his article. And the day that he received it, in May 1921, he replied, at amazing length, and in paragraphs of advice neatly and Teutonically numbered 1, 2, 3, 4, and 5: "I think that your plan, fundamentally, is quite sound. You are starting from the sea-level, so to speak. That is, you are giving a fair hearing to every Virginian, and keeping your magazine in the charac-

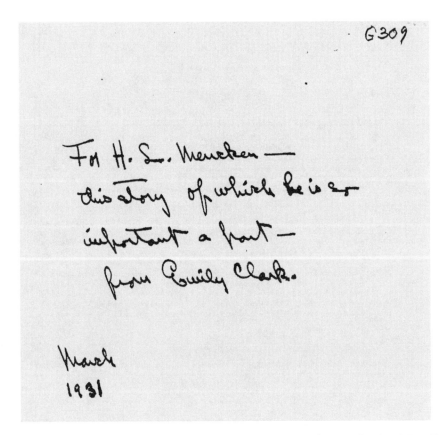

Inscription in Mencken's copy of Clark's Innocence Abroad, *published in 1931 (courtesy of the Enoch Pratt Free Library)*

The journalist Gerald W. Johnson, who reviewed Mencken's "The Sahara of the Bozart" in 1923

ter of the country. It seems to me to be far better to move away from the unconventional criticism of the South gradually than to run amok like the New Orleans group. The *Double-Dealer* is wholly un-Southern; *The Reviewer* is thoroughly of the South. . . . Some time ago someone sent me a bulletin issued by the Atlanta Public Library containing an excellent article on Cabell. The author of it, whoever he or she is, should be able to do good stuff for you." This was Frances Newman. I had not heard of her before. "There is a woman, Mrs. Peterkin, at Lang Syne Plantation, S. C., who is doing very interesting stuff. . . . In general, your chief aim should be to develop new Southern authors. The South is beginning to emerge from its old slumber. You have a capital chance to lead the way. Cabell's aid and interest, of course, are invaluable, but you can't help Cabell." This letter, also, brought me my first news of Julia Peterkin. A week later he wrote: "Criticism and progress, to be effective, must be iconoclastic and pugnacious. Before a sound literature can arise in the South, the old nonsense must be knocked down, and

from within. It will be useless to attempt a compromise. You must arm yourself and take to the highroad, ready to cut throats whenever it is necessary. The thing must be done boldly, and, in order to get a crowd, a bit cruelly." He had not, at that time, it is scarcely necessary to say, beheld any editor of *The Reviewer*. Later still: "On the whole, I think that you had better avoid all Northerners. What the South needs, beyond everything, is new growth from within. If you let in a Northerner, try to make him discuss some Southern topic." [. . .] In August, in regard to his first *Reviewer* contribution, for October 1921, he wrote: "I am firmly convinced that the preliminary work must be rough, but I'll be very polite and pianissimo. I hear from Arkansas that the Ku Klux Klan down there is after me. I shall introduce a few references to these heroes, and also to such cads as Candler, the Coca-Cola man." [. . .]

One of the more temperate white responses to "The Sahara of the Bozart" was by Gerald W. Johnson. In it one can see a prophecy of William Faulkner. Though a liberal, Johnson was later recruited by Mencken for the Sunpapers *(excerpts from "The Congo, Mr. Mencken,"* Reviewer, *3 [July 1923]: 889–893).*

[. . .] "The Sahara of the Bozart" he called the South. I think, as I shall explain later, that his figure was ill chosen; but it must be admitted that he supported his assertion with an impressive wealth of detail. Any doubts that survived his whirlwind attack must be resolved by this indisputable fact: such Southerners as have achieved national reputation in letters have, with rare exceptions, done the bulk of their good work elsewhere than in the South. The New England school flourished and perished in New England. The Far Westerners thrive on the Pacific coast. The Indianans find Indianapolis quite habitable. William Allen White and Ed Howe manage to survive even in Kansas. But the South seems to be afflicted with some tremendous centrifugal force that hurls artists across her borders like stones from a sling. The heavier the man the farther he flies. Lafcadio Hearn landed in Japan.

There have been exceptions, of course, but the rule holds good; and where such a rule holds good there is obviously something highly peculiar in the artistic and intellectual life of the region.

It is not to be explained by poverty and ignorance, for Elizabethan England was far poorer and more ignorant than the South ever was. It is not by our illiterates that we are differentiated sharply from the rest of the country. Cole L. Blease is no illiterate, nor Vardaman of Mississippi, nor William Joseph Simmons, founder of the Ku Klux Klan. Benton, the eulogist of

Senator Linn, was no illiterate, and John Temple Graves is educated, not to say learned. These men have gained more than local notoriety by widely varying means; but they have in common a certain wild fantasticality, whether it be expressed merely by the employment of rolling, sonorous periods, or swashbuckling defiance of the civilized world, or meeting by the light of the moon in weird garb to mutter spells and incantations in unknown tongues. They are Southerners, and their mad success in the South is certainly indicative of the fact that they embody Southern ideals much more successfully than such comparatively matter-of-fact persons as—to choose three ejected North Carolinians—Joseph G. Cannon, Walter Hines Page and Benjamin N. Duke. [. . .]

Mr. Mencken spoke of the South as "The Sahara of the Bozart." I submit that he could hardly have chosen a worse figure. The Sahara, as I am informed and believe, is for the most part a treeless waste, denuded alike of animal and of vegetable life. The South resembles more Sierra Leone, where, according to Sir Harry Johnston, "the mammalian fauna of chimpanzis, monkeys, bats, cats, lions, leopards, hyenas, civets, scaly manises, and large-eared earth-pigs, little-known duiker bush-buck, hartebeeste, and elephant, is rich and curious." So is the literary flora; and if Mr. Mencken presumes to doubt it, I invite him to plunge into the trackless waste of the Library of Southern Literature, where a man might wander for years, encountering daily such a profusion of strange and incredible growths as could proceed from none but an enormously rich soil.

The South is not sterile. On the contrary, it is altogether too luxuriant. It is not the Sahara, but the Congo of the Bozart. Its pulses beat to the rhythm of the tom-tom, and it likes any color if it's red. [. . .]

Can anything rare and exquisite survive under such conditions? Certainly. Orchids. Edgar Allan Poe grew them long ago, and Sidney Lanier, and James Branch Cabell grows them today. But in the tropics one soon wearies of orchids. There the exotic would be a trim, English garden * * * or, if we must have luxuriance, the stately, ordered luxuriance that Sir Thomas Browne could create.

Before there can be fair gardens in the South, though, there must be Herculean labor performed in clearing away the jungle growths—labor involving the use of sharp steel, swung vigorously. It is within the bounds of probability that some laborers will perish miserably, stung to death by noxious insects, or rent limb from limb by the mammalian fauna. But such things must be at every famous victory.

Furthermore, this very negroid streak that gives to the bulk of Southern writing at present the startling appearance of an African chief parading through the town arrayed in a stove-pipe hat, monocle, frock coat and no trousers, may prove in the future an asset of first-rate value. The chances are that it will at least prevent us from falling into drab monotony. [. . .]

He who has the vision to see Southern literature coming at all—and I profess to have it—needs must see it stepping high, for that is of its walk the way. It could not be otherwise. It has the pulse of the tom-toms in its veins, the scents of the jungle are in its nostrils and the flaming colors of the jungle in its eyes. It will be colorful beyond belief, instead of a discreet maquillage it will come wearing smears of paint like a witch-doctor. It may be outlandish, but it will not be monotonous. It may be gorgeously barbaric, but it will not be monotonous. For all I know, it may be in some manifestations tremendously evil—it may wallow in filth, but it will not dabble in dirt. I think we may even have a hint of it now in Clement Wood's ghastly, soul-sickening and damnable true "Nigger." That, at least, is a possible line along which it may come.

In the meantime, though, we have with us today a public fascinated by the flashy, even though it may be false. Instead of poets and authors we have poetesses and authoresses, poetets and authorets. At Richmond, Cabell plucks abstractedly the strings of his medieval lyre; at Charleston, away off to one side, DuBose Heyward and Hervey Allen are tentatively trying out their harp and 'cello combination; at the University of North Carolina the Playmakers are trying to play a fantasia on toy trumpets. Others are scattered here and there with rare and beautiful instruments. But the centre of the stage and the attention of the audience are engaged by a literary equivalent of Isham Jones's jazz band engaged in a spirited rendition of "Bang Away at Lulu." [. . .]

Women writers were as welcome as African Americans in the pages of Mencken's magazines. Indeed, one of the few exceptions to his strictures on the South was "the violet in the Sahara," Frances Newman. Mencken offered corrections of her first novel, The Hard-Boiled Virgin *(1926), in proof. Here he reviews her posthumous letters, edited by Hansell Baugh ("The Lady From Georgia,"* American Mercury, *19 [March 1930]: 382–383).*

In this collection Mr. Baugh has done an excellent job of editing. It was not easy in dealing with the letters of a writer as pawkily malicious as Frances Newman, to avoid outraging tender susceptibilities, but he has managed to do it admirably, and without leaving out anything of any importance. His selections are judicious, and his comments and explanations all show good sense. Not many authors are so fortunate in their *post-*

Mencken with the writer Frances Newman in Atlanta, October 1926 (courtesy of the Enoch Pratt Free Library)

mortem editors, as the sad case of Stuart P. Sherman was but lately recalling. The dull pedagogues who stuffed his remains would have made a sorry spectacle, I daresay, of so vivid and unconventional a person as Miss Newman. But Baugh preserves her essence, and so he does a valuable service to her memory.

She was a woman of diverse and unusual talents. Her first novel, "The Hard-Boiled Virgin," though it broke most of the ancient rules of its genus—there was, for example, not a line of dialogue in it—was so penetrating in its psychology and so charming in its style that it overcame even the handicap of its own instant *succès de scandale.* Her first and only short story, "Rachel and Her Children" (published in THE AMERICAN MERCURY for May, 1924), made a success almost as great; it got into all the anthologies at once, and brought her so many orders for more like it that she might have settled down to steady and profitable work in that field. As for her criticism, it was extraordinarily pungent, unhackneyed and stimulating. No one else could have written "The Short Story's Mutations." The soul that there adventured among masterpieces was quite unlike any other soul. For to the end of her days, though she

became increasingly literary, Miss Newman retained the freshness and piquancy of the strange girl who astonished Atlanta, back in 1915 or thereabouts, by printing immensely learned and brilliant reviews in the local *Journal.*

This prentice work was plainly the product of an extraordinary personality, but it took Frances six or eight years to really learn her trade. Her first reviews, for all their brilliancy, were more or less gushing and chaotic. She had so much to say, so vast a stream of mere information to pour out of the vast reservoir of her reading, that she slapped down sentences without giving much care to their sequence. The result was an uneven and difficult style—highly artificial one minute, and artless and naïve the next. It is to her credit as a practical critic that she became keenly conscious of its defects, and set about resolutely to remedy them. The result was a complete change in her manner of writing, first visible in "Rachel and Her Children." Abandoning her dark allusiveness and her heavy snarls of phrase, she began to write simply and clearly. Sentence began to follow sentence in a limpid and charming procession. This transformation, despite its difficulties in psychology, was very happily achieved, and toward the end of her life Miss Newman wrote with almost crystalline clarity. There is, indeed, many a lesson in writing in "The Hard-Boiled Virgin," and there would have been more in the works that were to have followed it.

Another transformation, I believe, was under way at the time of her premature and ever to be lamented death. She was getting over her somewhat too keen delight in shocking the stupid, born of her early life in the South. There would have been no more such atrocities as the title of "The Hard-Boiled Virgin." That title was put on the book against the unanimous advice of the author's elders, and it served only to stick a label on her that she certainly did not deserve. The enterprises she had in mind in her last days were quite free from any such factitious naughtiness. She had begun to take her business very seriously, and there is not the slightest doubt that she would have made her mark in it. She showed a curious combination of qualities, most of them good. There was in her a feline cleverness that was completely feminine, but beside it ran a shrewd and tolerant humor that was almost masculine. She was very intelligent and immensely industrious. She realized her own deficiencies, and was determined to put them down. The combination would have taken her, given ten more years, much further than she ever actually went.

As a person she was singularly attractive, mainly because of her uncommon courage. It took a lot of it, I suspect, to break through her Southern inhibitions; it took even more to face the resulting uproars in the capital of Ku Kluxia. In the end, facing what seemed to be incurable illness and the collapse of her work, she chose to slip from life quietly, serene to the last. She will be remembered beyond her generation. And Mr. Baugh has given her a dignified memorial, full of understanding.

Dust jacket for Newman's first novel, which the author had asked Mencken to read in proof during his Atlanta visit

Mencken's favorite female poet was his fellow Baltimorean Lizette Woodworth Reese. Her work, and one sonnet in particular, served as the standard in his criticism, as in this review of a Sara Teasdale collection (review of Rivers to the Sea, Smart Set *[May 1916]: 310).*

Saving only Lizette Woodworth Reese, Miss Teasdale (by book and bell, Mrs. Filsinger) is easily the first of living American lyric poets. Between the two, indeed, there are many resemblances. Each works in fragile and delicate forms; each returns always, after whatever excursion, to the *chant triste;* each shows a curious liking for the bald monosyllable, and particularly for the Anglo-Saxon monosylla-

ble. Here, for example, is a little song that either might have written:

> The roofs are shining from the rain,
> The sparrows twitter as they fly,
> And with a windy April grace
> The little clouds go by.
>
> Yet the back-yards are bare and brown
> With only one unchanging tree—
> I could not be so sure of Spring
> Save that it sings in me.

The author here, it so happens, is Miss Teasdale, but if it had come to me unsigned I should have guessed Miss Reese. I do not hint, I need not add, at imitation. Miss Teasdale is too genuine a poet to need to borrow from anyone. But the concept of beauty cherished by the one woman is obviously nearly identical with the concept cherished by the other, and both give voice to it with the same apparent artlessness that conceals profound and dignified art. Miss Reese, it seems to me, is the better poet; at all events, Miss Teasdale has yet to

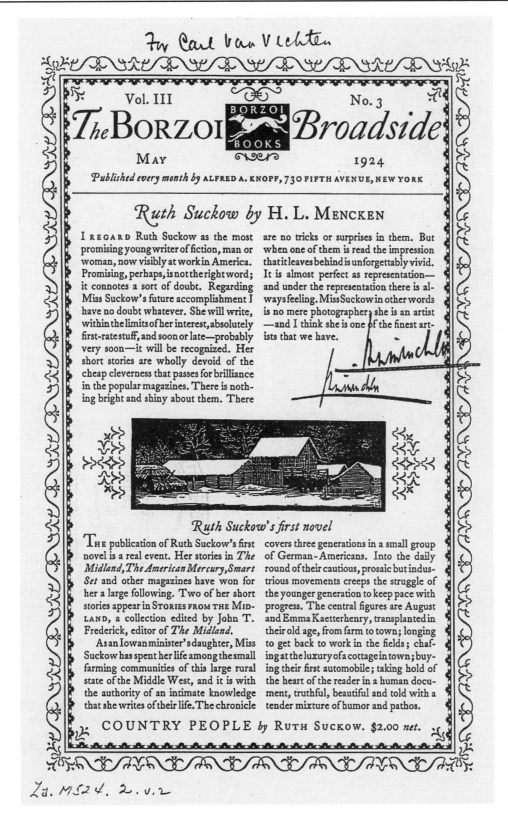

For Carl Van Vechten

Vol. III   The BORZOI Broadside   No. 3

BORZOI BOOKS

MAY   1924

Published every month by ALFRED A. KNOPF, 730 FIFTH AVENUE, NEW YORK

Ruth Suckow *by* H. L. MENCKEN

I REGARD Ruth Suckow as the most promising young writer of fiction, man or woman, now visibly at work in America. Promising, perhaps, is not the right word; it connotes a sort of doubt. Regarding Miss Suckow's future accomplishment I have no doubt whatever. She will write, within the limits of her interest, absolutely first-rate stuff, and soon or late—probably very soon—it will be recognized. Her short stories are wholly devoid of the cheap cleverness that passes for brilliance in the popular magazines. There is nothing bright and shiny about them. There are no tricks or surprises in them. But when one of them is read the impression that it leaves behind is unforgettably vivid. It is almost perfect as representation—and under the representation there is always feeling. Miss Suckow in other words is no mere photographer; she is an artist —and I think she is one of the finest artists that we have.

Ruth Suckow's first novel

THE publication of Ruth Suckow's first novel is a real event. Her stories in *The Midland, The American Mercury, Smart Set* and other magazines have won for her a large following. Two of her short stories appear in STORIES FROM THE MIDLAND, a collection edited by John T. Frederick, editor of *The Midland*.

As an Iowan minister's daughter, Miss Suckow has spent her life among the small farming communities of this large rural state of the Middle West, and it is with the authority of an intimate knowledge that she writes of their life. The chronicle covers three generations in a small group of German-Americans. Into the daily round of their cautious, prosaic but industrious movements creeps the struggle of the younger generation to keep pace with progress. The central figures are August and Emma Kaetterhenry, transplanted in their old age, from farm to town; longing to get back to work in the fields; chafing at the luxury of a cottage in town; buying their first automobile; taking hold of the heart of the reader in a human document, truthful, beautiful and told with a tender mixture of humor and pathos.

COUNTRY PEOPLE *by* RUTH SUCKOW. $2.00 *net.*

Za. M524. 2. v. 2

Alfred A. Knopf brochure, inscribed to Carl Van Vechten, with a notice by Mencken of Ruth Suckow, one of the women writers Mencken published in his magazines. Parts of this notice appeared on the dust jacket of the novel (Yale Collection of American Literature, Beinecke Rare Book and Manuscript Library).

The poet Sara Teasdale, whose collection River to the Sea *Mencken reviewed in 1916 (photograph by Williamina Parrish)*

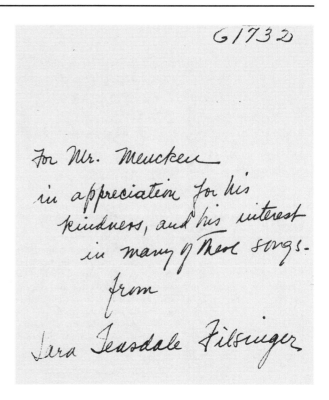

Inscription in Teasdale's Love Songs, *published in 1917 (courtesy of the Enoch Pratt Free Library and Special Collections, Margaret Clapp Library, Wellesley College)*

write anything of the noble rank of the sonnet, "Tears." But with the simple lyric, often of but eight lines, the latter has achieved effects that no poet writing in English to-day has surpassed. In these songs one finds the very acme of simple melodiousness; they sing exquisitely, and they fix a mood with sure enchantment. Nothing, indeed, could excel the beauty of such things as "Morning," "The Sea-Wind," "Gifts" and "The Kiss," in the present volume. In more ambitious forms Miss Teasdale is less successful. But what of it? She has written at least twenty perfect songs, and that is more than most poets do in all their lives. [. . .]

Mencken's great manifesto, "The National Letters," appeared in 1920. Here his criticism of a society fearful of those new voices he promoted merges with his assault on the lack of audacity in American literature. It is the fanfare for a decade (excerpt from Prejudices: Second Series, *pp. 69–70, 98–101).*

[. . .] Obviously, that order cannot constitute a genuine aristocracy, in any rational sense. A genuine aristocracy is grounded upon very much different principles. Its first and most salient character is its interior security, and the chief visible evidence of that security is the freedom that goes with it—not only freedom in act, the divine right of the aristocrat to do what he jolly well pleases, so long as he does not violate the primary guarantees and obligations of his class, but also and more importantly freedom in thought, the liberty to try and err, the right to be his own man. It is the instinct of a true aristocracy, not to punish eccentricity by expulsion, but to throw a mantle of protection about it—to safeguard it from the suspicions and resentments of the lower orders. Those lower orders are inert, timid, inhospitable to ideas, hostile to changes, faithful to a few maudlin superstitions. All progress goes on on the higher levels. It is there that salient personalities, made secure by artificial immunities, may oscillate most widely from the normal track. It is within that entrenched fold, out of reach of the immemorial certainties of the mob, that extraordinary men of the lower orders may find their city of refuge, and breathe a clear air. This, indeed, is at once the hall-mark and the justification of an aristocracy—that it is beyond responsibility to the general masses of men, and hence superior to both their degraded longings and their no less degraded aversions. It is nothing if it is not autonomous, curious, venturesome, courageous, and everything if it is. It is the custodian of the qualities that make for change and experiment; it is the class that organizes danger to the service of the race; it pays for its high prerogatives by standing in the forefront of the fray. [. . .]

I have described the disease. Let me say at once that I have no remedy to offer. I simply set down a few ideas, throw out a few hints, attempt a few modest inquiries into causes. Perhaps my argument often turns upon itself: the field is weed-grown and paths are hard to follow. It may be that insurmountable natural obstacles stand in the way of the development of a distinctively American culture, grounded upon a truly egoistic nationalism and supported by a native aristocracy. After all, there is no categorical imperative that ordains it. In such matters, when the conditions are right, nature often arranges a division of labor. A nation shut in by racial and linguistic isolation—a Sweden, a Holland or a France—is forced into autonomy by sheer necessity; if it is to have any intellectual life at all it must develop its own. But that is not our case. There is England to hold up the torch for us, as France holds it up for Belgium, and Spain for Latin America, and Germany for Switzerland. It is our function, as the younger and less confident partner, to do the simpler, rougher parts of the joint labor—to develop the virtues of the more elemental orders of men: industry, piety, docility, endurance, assiduity and ingenuity in practical affairs—the wood-hewing and water-drawing of the race. It seems to me that we do all this very well; in these things we are better than the English. But when it comes to those larger and more difficult activities which concern only the superior minority, and are, in essence, no more than products of its efforts to *demonstrate* its superiority—when it comes to the higher varieties of speculation and self-expression, to the fine arts and the game of ideas—then we fall into a bad second place. Where we stand, intellectually, is where the English non-conformists stand; like them, we are marked by a fear of ideas as disturbing and corrupting. Our art is imitative and timorous. Our political theory is hopelessly sophomoric and superficial; even English Toryism and Russian Bolshevism are infinitely more profound and penetrating. And of the two philosophical systems that we have produced, one is so banal that it is now imbedded in the New Thought, and the other is so shallow that there is nothing in it either to puzzle or to outrage a school-marm.

Nevertheless, hope will not down, and now and then it is supported by something rather more real than mere desire. One observes an under-current of revolt, small but vigorous, and sometimes it exerts its force, not only against the superficial banality but also against

the fundamental flabbishness, the intrinsic childishness of the Puritan *Anschauung*. The remedy for that childishness is skepticism, and already skepticism shows itself: in the iconoclastic political realism of Harold Stearns, Waldo Frank and company, in the grouping questions of Dreiser, Cabell and Anderson, in the operatic rebellions of the Village. True imagination, I often think, is no more than a function of this skepticism. It is the dull man who is always sure, and the sure man who is always dull. The more a man dreams, the less he believes. A great literature is thus chiefly the product of doubting and inquiring minds in revolt against the immovable certainties of the nation. Shakespeare, at a time of rising democratic feeling in England, flung the whole force of his genius against democracy. Cervantes, at a time when all Spain was romantic, made a headlong attack upon romance. Goethe, with Germany groping toward nationalism, threw his influences on the side of internationalism. The central trouble with America is conformity, timorousness, lack of enterprise and audacity. A nation of third-rate men, a land offering hospitality only to fourth-rate artists. In Elizabethan England they would have bawled for democracy, in the Spain of Cervantes they would have yelled for chivalry, and in the Germany of Goethe they would have wept and beat their breasts for the Fatherland. To-day, as in the day of Emerson, they set the tune. . . . But into the singing there occasionally enters a discordant note. On some dim to-morrow, perhaps, perchance, peradventure, they may be challenged.

Mencken's rhetorical ploy is to draw one to his side by implying that to agree with him is to join the civilized minority, an aristocracy of the mind. H. T. Stagg is representative of those who were charmed by the style of the essay and not offended by those undemocratic implications (excerpt from review of Prejudices: Second Series, Reviewer, *1 [15 February 1921]: 26).*

[. . .] The rest of it is well worth reading, as Mencken is always well worth reading, whether for laughter, anger, both or neither, but it is there that the unwelcome suggestion of the possible fate of our best literary critic rises. In "The National Letters," however, he is on his own ground, where sincere feeling, deep concern and wide knowledge cannot be obscured by glittering perversity, capriciousness and pugnacity of manner. As the title of this essay indicates it is a survey of the condition in which American literature finds itself to-day and the causes which have produced that condition. It is the survey of a telescopic eye and an uncompromising judgment, written in a style that is a joy to read for its own sake in this day of shoddy, inflexible prose. It is severe—cruelly so—but none too severe to meet the occasion as most readers will admit. True, not being omnipotent, Mencken may now and then be guilty of slight injustice, but all the same on the subject of the national letters he offers his best and we have no one at present who can surpass it. [. . .]

The usually sympathetic Walter Lippmann, on the other hand, represents those who did take offense ("The Near Machiavelli," New Republic, 31 [31 May 1922]: 12–14).

Mr. H. L. Mencken has given public notice that he is engaged in writing a treatise which will teach the enlightened minority how to govern the unenlightened majority. The usual thing to do, I realize, is to wait for the treatise before discussing it. But in Mr. Mencken's case such academic prudence is quite unnecessary. Mr. Mencken has already published the blurb for the jacket and an outline of his principles. And as he has taught us how unnecessary it is to read a book before reviewing it, I see no reason why I should not review his book before he writes it.

There are a number of Menckens of varying excellence. There is Mencken the philologist for whom I have the greatest admiration. There is Mencken the literary critic whom I respect as I would a somewhat discriminating one-eyed bull in a china shop. But there is another and more pretentious Mencken,–the author of an American Dunciad and the prophet of a new aristocracy. It is a book by this third Mencken which I am venturing to review.

"The problem of democratic government," he tells us, "narrows down to this: how is the relatively enlightened and reputable minority to break the hold of such mountebanks (the present office-holding class) upon the votes of the anthropoid majority? . . . The man of education and self respect may not run with the mob and he may not yield to it supinely, but what is to prevent him deliberately pulling its nose? What is to prevent him playing upon its fears and credulities to good ends as a physician plays upon them by giving its members bread pills, or as a holy clerk seeking to bring it up to relative decency, scares it with tales of a mythical hell? In brief, what is to prevent him from swallowing his political prejudices . . . in order to channel and guide the prejudices of his inferiors? It may be, at first blush, an unsavory job–but so is delivering a fat woman of twins an unsavory job. Yet obstetricians of first skill and repute do it–if the fee be large enough."

Thus spoke Henry Louis Zarathustra. "Some of the principles of the new science already begin to clarify in my mind." Let us see how far they have clarified.

The human race, according to Mr. Mencken, consists of the mob and the enlightened minority. The mob is "congenitally uneducable" and has an "incurable distrust" of the truth. The "intelligent minority," on the other hand, is characterized by an "incurable thirst for knowledge." It is this congenitally and incurably thirsty minority which is going to be taught by Mencken's "new science" how to pull the nose of the incurably and congenitally uneducable mob. The minority is to do it, however, and of course, for "good ends."

At once you look around for the intelligent minority which is to turn the trick. You do not ever learn from Mr. Mencken who compose it. But he leaves you in no doubt as to who are not members in good standing of the educable and thirsty minority. "The lower orders of men" you can dismiss at once. With equal certainty you can eliminate the whole church-going population of the United States, since Mr. Bryan goes to church. Business men, of course, are excluded ipso facto because there are Rotary Clubs, Boards of Trade and other boob-thumping organizations among them. Lawyers likewise. The whole "body of teachers in Christendom" is eliminated at one stroke. As for the professors, if they escape with their lives they may well rejoice. Newspaper men as a whole are quite ineligible, and so, if I am not mistaken, are women of all classes and professions. The politicians, high and low, have the "honesty of a press agent and the dignity of a bawdy house keeper." The eligible list grows smaller. Republicans, Democrats, Socialists, Anarchists all take the count. And as for the liberals, men like Bryce, Wells, and those who take more or less the same line, they are as poor frauds as Senator Lusk and the Ku Klux Klan.

There are left Mr. Mencken, Mr. Nathan, their publisher Mr. Knopf, and the enlightened minority who read the Smart Set. I don't know them all by name, but for the purpose of the argument I am willing to grant Mr. Mencken a few thousand bona fide members of his intelligent minority.

Now his theory is that they ought to take charge of human affairs. He knows they cannot do it by force, but he does think they can do it by acting "boldly and vigorously" on the principles of the "new science" which he is about to expound to them as Machiavelli expounded politics to the Medici. The basic principle of that new science is simplicity itself. Mr. Mencken will teach his new aristocrat how to make all the rest of us "exult" and "tremble." Then "knowing that much he will be master of the whole art of practical politics under democracy."

This is the most touching exhibition of human credulity that I have encountered in many a day. You have here a faith in the power of words that is complete. For Mr. Mencken thinks that if a small minority could only utter the right words they would take possession of human society. Mr. Mencken will therefore create a science which will teach the intelligent minority how to use phrases that will make the rest of us exult or tremble and they will be masters of the world. Somebody has been pulling Mr. Mencken's leg.

For he has taken in as if it were the gospel the whole current buncombe that you can do anything by publicity and advertising. Mr. Mencken has contracted the disease he set out to cure. What else is at the bottom of those features of American life to which Mr. Mencken so violently and so rightly objects, except this same childlike faith in the omnipotence of words? What is at the bottom of our prohibiting and censoring except a belief that by incantation you can make people righteous? What is at the bottom of the business hokum, which Christopher Morley recently immortalized in his Ginger Cubes, except the belief that you can do immense things by working up the proper verbal excitement? On what are the Pollyanna inspirations and the quack religions founded but this same superstition that the Word is the Thing? And then along comes Mr. Mencken and proposes to regenerate human society by adopting the same superstitions, but for "good ends." The bold and fearless critic, the Holy Terror among the Academics, steps forward with the proposal that a little group of serious thinkers can make themselves masters of civilization by uttering a few scarifying phrases.

How did the mountain manage to bring forth such a mouse?

Mr. Mencken likes words. They are concrete and important objects in his life, and collecting them has been his most serious intellectual interest. Words are, moreover, his only means of action and his sole occupation. By words he has achieved a considerable reputation. His victories have been won in battles of words, and in human fashion, he likes to believe that the universe is ruled by words. Lacking any first hand knowledge or enough realistic sense of social organization to ask himself, for example, why parties endure though the slogans change, he concludes that the slogans of politics are the essence of politics, and that if you could discover the superslogan you would be the superman.

This belief in the magic of words is intellectually not one bit more respectable than the wearing of a rheumatism string, or any of the other follies which Mr. Mencken loves to cite as evidence of the folly of politicians. Mr. Mencken, to be sure, thinks he is superior to superstition because he proposes to use words cynically, whereas the victims of his criticism believe

them more or less naively. But the superstition does not disappear because Mr. Mencken despises it. If he thinks, as he does, that slogans are the ultimate force in society, his belief is a superstition, and it makes no difference whether he is awestruck by the fact or cynical about it. His science is of the same stuff at bottom as Mr. Bryan's or Billy Sunday's.

And like them he is so determined to have the universe what he would like it to be that he will not stop to find out what it is. For Mr. Mencken has a dream. He would like as an expert in words to recreate the world by words in the image of that dream. What does he see in that dream? He sees himself as the companion of a small masterful minority who rule the world and who, because it is so simple to rule the world, have ample leisure for talk. In that circle Mencken is the gayest spirit of the lot, the literary pope, of course, but with a strong flavor of Rabelais and Voltaire about him. The hard work of the world is left to the subject masses, who are uneducable, and are therefore destined to feed him, clothe him, keep him warm, and print books for him.

I think this is a sincere dream. I think Mencken really cares for fine things of a sort, though simple things untranslated into art are not significant to him. But what I wonder is whether he ever realizes how little he exemplifies the aristocratic type which he would so much like to be. I am not speaking merely of the fact that he is so often vulgar about vulgarity, and that he frequently makes you think he feels he must make a show because you may not have heard that he recently acquired a reputation. I am speaking rather of the inner commotion which directs his troubled vitality.

For the quality that marks him off from the genuine intellectual aristocrat is the absence of settled assurance within. There is no point in Mencken where you ever reach serenity, no point at which anything justifies itself. Everything has to be fortified by bounce and brag if he is to hold fast to it. The good things have to be kept vital by feverishly thumping the bad ones. Mr. Mencken would not dare to stop contemplating his dislikes for fear of being left contemplating a vacuum.

But there is a rudimentary honesty about him, not a complete honesty because his critical faculties are not searching enough for many of the things of which he speaks ex cathedra, but an honesty of feeling. And so I wonder whether in his most honest moments he realizes how much he is the victim of the vices he hates, whether he knows how deeply the modern city's fever has gotten into his blood, and how much like Cinderella with flat feet he seems when he cries for an aristocracy in the pages of the Smart Set.

F. Scott Fitzgerald's review of Prejudices: Second Series *is favorable but not deferential. His familiarity with the Mencken canon enables him to point out what is new and what is perennial ("The Baltimore Anti-Christ,"* Bookman, *53 [March 1921]: 79–81).*

The incomparable Mencken will, I fear, meet the fate of Aristides. He will be exiled because one is tired of hearing his praises sung. In at least three contemporary novels he is mentioned as though he were dead as Voltaire and as secure as Shaw with what he would term "a polite bow." His style is imitated by four-fifths of the younger critics—moreover he has demolished his enemies and set up his own gods in the literary supplements.

Of the essays in the new book the best is the autopsy on the still damp bones of Roosevelt. In the hands of Mencken Roosevelt becomes almost a figure of Greek tragedy; more, he becomes alive and loses some of that stuffiness that of late has become attached to all 100% Americans. Not only is the essay most illuminating but its style is a return to Mencken's best manner, the style of "Prefaces," with the soft pedal on his amazing chord of adjectives and a tendency to invent new similes instead of refurbishing his amusing but somewhat overworked old ones.

Except for the section on American aristocracy there is little new in the first essay "The National Letters": an abundance of wit and a dozen ideas that within the past year and under his own deft hand have become bromides. The Knights of Pythias, Right Thinkers, On Building Universities, Methodists, as well as the corps of journeyman critics and popular novelists come in for their usual bumping, this varied with unexpected tolerance toward "The Saturday Evening Post" and even a half grudging mention of Booth Tarkington. Better than any of this comment, valid and vastly entertaining as it is, would be a second Book of Prefaces say on Edith Wharton, Cabell, Woodrow Wilson—and Mencken himself. But the section of the essay devoted to the Cultural Background rises to brilliant analysis. Here again he is thinking slowly, he is on comparatively fresh ground, he brings the force of his clarity and invention to bear on the subject—passes beyond his function as a critic of the arts and becomes a reversed Cato of a civilization.

In "The Sahara of the Bozart" the dam breaks, devastating Georgia, Carolina, Mississippi, and Company. The first trickle of this overflow appeared in the preface to "The American Credo"; here it reaches such a state of invective that one pictures all the region south of Mason-Dixon to be peopled by moron Catilines. The ending is gentle—too gentle, the gentleness of ennui.

To continue in the grand manner of a catalogue: "The Divine Afflatus" deals with the question of inspiration and the lack of it, an old and sad problem to the man who has done creative work. "Examination of a Popular Virtue" runs to eight pages of whimsical excellence—a consideration of ingratitude decided at length with absurd but mellow justice. "Exeunt Omnes," which concerns the menace of death, I choose to compare with a previous "Discussion" of the same subject in "A Book of Burlesques." The comparison is only in that the former piece, which I am told Mencken fatuously considers one of his best, is a hacked out, glued together bit of foolery, as good, say, as an early essay of Mark Twain's, while this "Exeunt Omnes," which follows it by several years, is smooth, brilliant, apparently jointless. To my best recollection it is the most microscopical examination of this particular mote on the sun that I have ever come across.

Follows a four paragraph exposition of the platitude that much music loving is an affectation and further paragraphs depreciating opera as a form. As to the "Music of Tomorrow" the present reviewer's ignorance must keep him silent, but in "Tempo di Valse" Mencken, the modern, becomes Victorian by insisting that what people are tired of is more exciting than what they have just learned to do. If his idea of modern dancing is derived from watching men who learned it circa thirty-five, toiling interminably around the jostled four square feet of a cabaret, he is justified; but I see no reason why the "Bouncing Shimmee" efficiently performed is not as amusing and as graceful and certainly as difficult as any waltz ever attempted. The section continues with the condemnation of a musician named Hadley, an ingenious attempt to preserve a portrait of Dreiser, and a satisfactory devastation of the acting profession.

In "The Cult of Hope" he defends his and "Dr. Nathan's" attitude toward constructive criticism—most entertainingly—but the next section "The Dry Millennium," patchworked from the Ripetizione Generale, consists of general repetitions of theses in his previous books. "An Appendix on a Tender Theme" contains his more recent speculations on women, eked out with passages from "The Smart Set."

An excellent book! Like Max Beerbohm, Mencken's work is inevitably distinguished. But now and then one wonders—granted that, solidly, book by book, he has built up a literary reputation most to be envied of any American, granted also that he has done more for the national letters than any man alive, one is yet inclined to regret a success so complete. What will he do now? The very writers to the press about the blue Sabbath hurl the bricks of the buildings he has demolished into the still smoking ruins. He is, say, forty; how of the next twenty years? Will he find new gods to dethrone, some eternal "yokelry" still callous enough to pose as intelligenzia before the Menckenian pen fingers? Or will he strut among the ruins, a man beaten by his own success, as futile, in the end, as one of those Conrad characters that so tremendously enthrall him?

Mencken's nonfiction prose remains unsurpassed in the twentieth century. New fashions in critical theory have in no way marred his readability nor lessened the insight he provides into the works on which he comments. Such is the case even when he is writing informally, as in this bringing together of a couple of his predecessors in a letter written in 1919 or 1920 to his lover, Marion Bloom. For all his advocacy of the modern, he was highly conscious of the larger tradition (typewritten letter with handwritten initial as signature at the Enoch Pratt Free Library, Baltimore).

H. L. MENCKEN
1524 HOLLINS ST.
BALTIMORE.

December 11th

Dear Marion:–

You get the books whenever you get the house. I'll give you your free choice of any of my own books. I have almost too many, and a good number of them I never look at.

It doesn't surprise me that you dislike old Mark. He was the eternal skeptic and you are the eternal believer. You are in error, however, when you assume that he was an utter materialist. He was a mechanist, but that is something different. He, too, had his dreams, as you will see plainly in Joan of Arc, and you must also see in the lyrical passages of Life on the Mississippi and Huckleberry Finn. Don't assume that the only idealism is that of one who believes in Jesus. Christians, in the main, are scarcely idealists at all. They love God on a salary–that is, all their devotion is selfish: they expect to be rewarded for it. Also, don't assume that Greek idealism found its expression in the Rome of the Empire. Rome was always a third-rate country–a sort of England, even a sort of United States. It was run by commercial cads. But the Greece of Pericles' day was something far different. The Greeks were not immoral. That is, they did not reject duty. On the contrary, they had a very lofty conception of duty. But it differed vastly from the conception of the modern Christian. They were not snufflers and they were not time-servers.

What is Man, of course, is not profound. But it shows the rare quality of honesty–it tries to examine

the truth. The fact is, of course, that there is no truth. You always assume that, because Christianity seems to me to be piffle, I believe in some contrary theory–that, because I laugh at Christian Science, I therefore swallow all the childish hocus-pocus of incompetent family doctors practising up side streets. This is absurd. My skepticism is more thorough-going than you imagine. I doubt everything, including even my own doubts.

Don't take my books too seriously. My motto is that of Swift: "the chief end I propose to myself in all my labors is to vex the world rather than divert it". It thus tickles me (probably much to your bepuzzlement) to find my stuff violently attacked, particularly on such grounds as those stated by the Boston Transcript, Sherman, etc. If I can make such persons unhappy–and I can–it gives me pleasure. I seldom attack them personally; they seem to me to be too small. But I enjoy attacking their idols and filling them with fears and doubts. [. . .]

Yours,
H

To help sell the Knopf edition of Gulliver's Travels "the American Swift" wrote an introduction that throws light on his points of departure from the Victorian era, to which he was otherwise beholden (excerpt from the introduction to Jonathan Swift, Gulliver's Travels [New York: Knopf, 1925], pp. v–vi).

The name of Swift, I daresay, will always lie under the cloud of Thackeray's dreadful invective. Every schoolboy is familiar with the picture of the poor Dean lying in wait for his enemies "in a sewer" and disposing of them with "a coward's blow and a dirty bludgeon." How much truth is in it? Probably very little. Thackeray was led into libel and nonsense by his own colossal sentimentality. He was a true son of the Victorian age, as Swift was a true son of the age of Anne, and between the two there could be no sympathy and little understanding. Swift's crime quickly becomes apparent. He was wholly devoid of the fundamental Victorian virtues: uxoriousness, philoprogenitiveness, love of the hearth. His view of marriage was so harsh that it ranged him among "madmen"; when he spoke of children he became a downright "ogre." What other Englishman, ancient or modern, would have dared to propose handing the little dears over to the cook, and so getting something out of them beyond mere spiritual delights and usufructs? The jocosity wounded Thackeray where he was tenderest. It was, to one who took a fierce, Christian pride in both his stomach and his loins, a veritable blow below the belt. Hence his celebrated philippic, and hence the lingering notion that Swift was a low and knavish fellow, armed with his grand-mother's shinbone, and ready to crack a friend's head for the price of a pair of silver buckles.

He was, of course, nothing of the sort. He was simply a premature and lonely forerunner of the modern age–a Voltaire born in the wrong country and a couple of generations too soon. He was the first great enemy of the immemorial anthropocentric delusion. Long before him, stretching back into the remotest shadows, there had been critics of man, and some of them had laid on with vast ferocity, but he was the first to go the whole hog–he was the first to deny the very premises with which all the rest began. When he regarded *Homo sapiens* he did not see a god with a few lamentable defects; he saw a poor worm with no virtues at all, but only a crushing burden of follies, weaknesses and imbecilities. He saw a coward and an idiot, a fraud and a scoundrel. Was this preposterous quadruped made in the image of God? Then God Himself was not fit to be lord of the noble horse, the august lion, the brave and honest rat. Was it any wonder that the "Thoughts on Religion" had "scarce a Christian character" and that they were, at bottom, "merely a set of excuses for not professing disbelief"? The fact outraged another of Thackeray's sentimentalities, and so added to his indignation. But he was wrong again, as he had been wrong before. A Christian character, forsooth! It was precisely Swift's merit that he was superior to all such sweet bilge–that he somehow managed to rid himself of the romantic baggage of his race, and to stand upon a hilltop regarding it, with sharp and horrible eyes. [. . .]

Mencken introduced dozens of other works. His forewords, along with the texts he chose and sometimes edited, were another means of communicating his critical agenda and philosophical outlook, as is pointed out in Joseph Wood Krutch's review of the first five Free Lance Books. The works, by Pío Baroja, E. W. Howe, Edwin Muir, James N. Wood, and Nietzsche (The Antichrist, *translated by Mencken), were published by Knopf. The sixth and last, a new edition of Mencken's* In Defense of Women, *appeared in 1922 ("Antichrist and the Five Apostles,"* Nation, *113 [21 December 1921]: 733–734.)*

H. L. Mencken once called himself a liaison officer between the American intelligentsia and European ideas, but he is something much more impassioned than that. He is a sort of heathen missionary zealously endeavoring to convert the barbarian Christians away from the false gods of Humility and Restraint, and his method is the method of the popular evangelist who expounds the Sermon on the Mount in the vocabulary of slang. Like Billy Sunday he preaches in his shirtsleeves and any furniture about the platform is in danger of a smashing. The only essential difference is that Mr. Mencken knows what he is talking about. When he is finished, Nietzsche is still recognizably Nietzsche, while as much cannot be said for Mr. Sunday's Christ.

This also Mr. Mencken has in common with the popular preacher; his real genius is for denunciation. Words and phrases of gorgeous contempt like "boob-bumper," "spy-hunter," "emotion-pumper," and "propaganda-monger" flow readily from his pen, and a sort of immoral indignation is his specialty. Above all else, he is generally surer of what he doesn't want than of what he does. Let any man attack "the boobery" with sufficient violence, be it in the cause of naturalism, of aestheticism, of the aristocracy, or, as in the case of E. W. Howe, of mere common sense, and that man is Mr. Mencken's friend, for he is far too much interested in the slaying of Philistines to care whose jaw-bone it is done with. Thus he can welcome the naturalism of Theodore Dreiser because it outrages the populace, and he can welcome Edwin Muir's denunciation of naturalism because that denunciation does not proceed upon an ethical basis.

Whatever in Mr. Mencken's creed is not negative comes from Nietzsche, and consciously or unconsciously he has pretty well confined himself to the Nietzschean in selecting the volumes for his Free Lance series. All are full of protest, but they have more in common than this, and the promise that "no point of view which is sincere and intelligible will be excluded" has not so far been kept, though there is no reason, of course, why it should be. Each of the books is a gospel, and they might all be bound together in one book without offering more difficulty to the synthesizer than is offered, let us say, by the books of the two Testaments. To be a Free Lance is not only to be egotistical and intransigent; it is to raise egotism and intransigency to the position of a creed. All, with the exception of E. W. Howe, have confessedly fallen under the spell of Nietzsche, and the Naumburg Antichrist has taught them that anti-respectability need not be mere defiance. Your Baudelaires and your Swinburnes traded upon the thrill of wickedness and paid their respects to conventional virtues by worshiping sin, but the post-Nietzscheans disdain self-conscious naughtiness. By the familiar process heresy has become orthodoxy, and pride, self-assertion, and egotism, ceasing to be gorgeous sins, have become the true virtues.

Even E. W. Howe, that astounding provincial philosopher who is furthest from the norm of the series, is a Nietzsche *manqué*. Of sentiment and of outward deference to morality and tradition merely because they are morality and tradition he has as little as Mr.

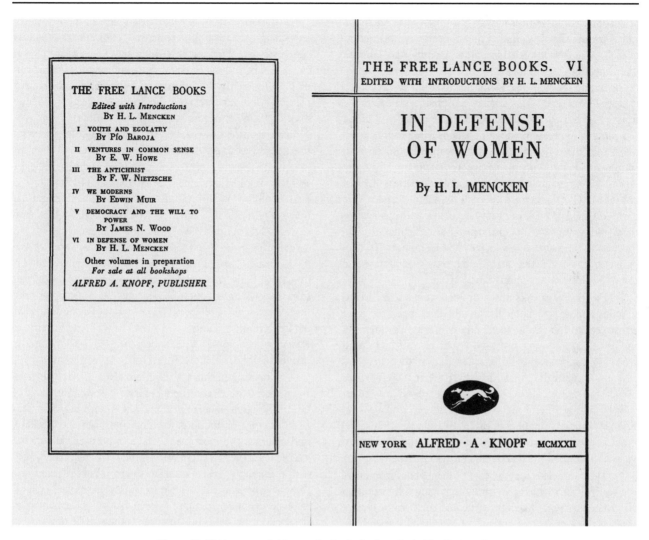

THE FREE LANCE BOOKS

Edited with Introductions
By H. L. MENCKEN

I YOUTH AND EGOLATRY
By Pío Baroja

II VENTURES IN COMMON SENSE
By E. W. Howe

III THE ANTICHRIST
By F. W. Nietzsche

IV WE MODERNS
By Edwin Muir

V DEMOCRACY AND THE WILL TO
POWER
By James N. Wood

VI IN DEFENSE OF WOMEN
By H. L. Mencken

Other volumes in preparation
For sale at all bookshops

ALFRED A. KNOPF, PUBLISHER

THE FREE LANCE BOOKS. VI
EDITED WITH INTRODUCTIONS BY H. L. MENCKEN

IN DEFENSE
OF WOMEN

By H. L. MENCKEN

NEW YORK   ALFRED · A · KNOPF   MCMXXII

Verso of half-title page and title page for the final volume in the Free Lance series

Mencken himself, and he is as impatient as Nietzsche at sentimental deference to weakness and incompetence. He has little fault to find with any part of the world except those who would make it better, and though he is not ferocious his general assumption is that the under dog is just where he belongs. If you haven't what you want, he suggests that you try to get it and that if you cannot you had best not look for sympathy, because it is probably your own fault anyway. He rails constantly at the assumption that there is anything necessarily or inherently good in humility or poverty, and his constant insistence upon the superiority of the man who does something over the dreamer or philosopher may be seen, upon translation into the Nietzschean lingo, to be nothing more than a shrewd rustic preference for the Dionysian over the Apollonian. It happens that his ideal of the man who does something is the man who runs a business or improves a plow rather than the Nietzschean ideal of a man reaching up to a plane of activity removed from the ordinary business of feeding

and propagating, but the difference is largely the result of environment. Nourish an intransigent individualism and a hatred of sentimental incompetence upon German metaphysics and you get Nietzsche; nourish it upon American materialistic common sense and you get Howe.

In the reading of "Ventures in Common Sense" there are more of those internal chuckles which come with the appreciation of a clean thrust well delivered than in the reading of any of the other books of the Free Lance series, and the series cannot perform a better service to American literature than to gain a wider audience for Mr. Howe's intellectual honesty. That this Kansas philosopher can flout certain traditional American assumptions and still remain so completely American is explained partly by certain limitations of his own and partly by a traditional American inconsistency. Things which are fundamentally American as distinguished from those which are only sentimentally such are bred in his bone. Honesty, industry, hustle are as dear to him as they were to Franklin, and by no possible philosophy could he be led away from his instinctive admiration for the simple virtues. There is nothing in his preference for result over intentions, for a comfortable house over fine ideas, and for a substantial success over a romantic or intangible one that is not and has not always been typically American. His originality consists solely in the frankness with which he admits his materialism and in the clearness of expression which he attains by refusing to veil or to mix his practical philosophy with religion, or with sentiment. Paying no lip-service to vague idealism, he writes: "Women are more chaste than men because lack of chastity is less dangerous for men than for women. The strongest motive back of every safe, sane, and respectable man and woman is not principle, but selfishness." And there is nothing in this to shock except its honesty. In general, it may be said that Howe preaches what ninety-nine out of a hundred Americans practice.

Pio Baroja speaks much of Nietzsche, and he toyed with his philosophy, but in the end the doctrine of the Antichrist proved too strenuous for the artistic temperament of the Spaniard and after using Nietzscheism to free himself from current restraints he relapsed into aestheticism and cast his lot with the Apollonians. Of the remaining three books, one is by Nietzsche himself and the other two are merely highly interesting corollaries to his philosophy—Edwin Muir meditating upon its literary and spiritual implications and James Wood using it as the basis for a vicious critique of the democratic form of government.

Whatever else may be said of their philosophy or of the source from which they draw it, it cannot be said that Nietzsche was without a very strenuous idealism or that he evolved his destructive critique of Christianity merely to make the world safe for either aesthetes like Baroja or for common-sense materialists like Mr. Howe. It is no paradox to say that whatever his vagaries he has reaffirmed what humanitarianism as well as many other modern philosophies were in danger of forgetting, and that is that man does not live by bread alone. In the introduction to "We Moderns" [by Muir] Mr. Mencken writes: "One cannot read some of the modern medical literature, particularly on the side of public hygiene, without giving one's sympathy to the tubercle bacilli and the spirochaetae. Science of that sort ceases to be a fit concern for superior men, gentlemen; it becomes a concern for evangelists, uplifters, bounders. Its aim is no longer to penetrate the impenetrable, to push forward the bounds of human knowledge, to overreach the sinister trickeries of God; its aim is simply to lengthen the lives of human ciphers and to reinforce their delusions that they confer a favor upon the universe by living at all. Worse, it converts the salvation of such vacuums into a moral obligation, and sets up the absurd doctrine that human progress is furthered by diminishing the death-rate in the Balkans, by rescuing Georgia crackers from the hookworm, and by reducing the whole American people, the civ-

ilized minority with the barbarian mass, to a race of teetotaling ascetics, full of pious indignation and Freudian suppressions." The essential thing behind this exercise in exaggeration and the essential thing behind the Nietzschean philosophy of Mr. Muir and Mr. Wood is not the callous contempt for humanity but the appreciation of something essentially noble—of knowledge, of power, and of fortitude cultivated for their own sakes—and a contempt for an exclusive concern with the material comforts of man.

To the truly aspiring spirit mere mortality has always seemed vile. The medieval Christian looked to the glory of heaven, and only with the decay of Christianity came the religion of humanity—the idea, that is, that though to care exclusively for one's own food and raiment was vile, to care for everybody's food and raiment was somehow, through mere magnitude, noble. Nietzscheism is a reaffirmation of faith in excellence itself, in greatness as distinct from a mere aggregation of littlenesses. Its contempt for the mob was born not of wanton cruelty but of a spiritual craving for genuine greatness and a disgust with scientific materialism which found the highest human activity in the provision of health and comfort for the greatest number.

Christian humility was originally a species of hero-worship; it was an abasement before the power and glory of God. Humanitarianism, gradually relinquishing God, has fixed its worship not upon the glory but upon the humility, and invented the most meaningless of phrases, "the divine average," as though there were something essentially excellent in the mere lack of excellence. From Nietzscheism one may at least learn that while to abase oneself before God may be tolerable, to abase oneself before abasement is to deny excellence and thus to commit the suicide of the soul. If the God of humanity is to be man, then humanity must worship not the average but the godlike man.

Humanitarianism, the most characteristic product of the materialistic age, may not only be accused of applying the merely quantitative standard in the measurement of human values, but may be seen also as a hatred of life itself because it seeks by alleviation and equalization to diminish life's intensity. It would, if possible, abolish tragedy and hence belittle life, because suffering is an essential part of man's grandeur. When Mr. Santayana recently attempted to solve the problem of evil by saying that contemplation was the greatest good and that since evil was, equally with good, material for contemplation, he was expounding the Nietzschean view on the passive side. To the Nietzschean life is the only good, and since suffering and happiness are equally intense forms of life, suffering is good. Thomas Hardy, says Mr. Muir, "sets out in his books to prove that life is a mean blunder; and, in spite of himself, the tragedy of this blunder becomes in his hands splendid and impressive, so that life is enriched even while it is defamed. Art . . . refutes his pessimism and turns his curses into involuntary blessings." The modern, robbed of God and of heaven, can prevent the world from shrinking into intolerable pettiness only by worshiping the noble in man and the sublime in life.

That new world beside whose birth-bed Matthew Arnold sat agonizing has been an unconscionable time in getting itself born. Certainly no "new world" in the sense which he meant has come into being, for the year 1921 is still a part of that period of questioning of which he spoke and has as few certitudes as the year 1855. Three points of view are current: there is aestheticism, there is the scientific optimism of the socialist-ameliorist group, and there is the excellence-worship of the Nietzschean aristocracy. The first is obviously sterile and parasitic. The second offers little beyond a general leveling, and promises no way in which anybody can be better than many now are. It invites us simply, if we cannot be satisfied with mere food and raiment, to do as the two castaways did in W. H. Mallock's "The New Paul and Virginia" when they found drinking an insufficiently noble pleasure. They, it may be remembered, decided to call it altruism—each being happy over the champagne which the other drank. Nietzscheism offers at least an ideal of the glorified man which is more attractive than the humanitarian ideal of well-fed mediocrity. It reestablishes the idea of excellence as a goal, and if it is cruel, cruelty is no more than a scientific age has been led to expect.

The direction for the modern writer that Richard Wright discovered in A Book of Prefaces *could be found monthly in Mencken's magazine reviews, sometimes even more frequently in his newspaper notices. They provide a running commentary on the development—or backsliding—of contemporary literature. Some of the authors he held up for praise have vanished from the canon, despite his best efforts. Perhaps the most notable such figures in his stable were Joseph Hergesheimer and James Branch Cabell. The latter he regarded as an exception to the cultural deadness of the South. Cabell's* Jurgen (1919), *the subject of this review, had later to be defended from the charge of obscenity (excerpt from "The Flood of Fiction,"* Smart Set *[January 1920]: 139–140).*

[. . .] In brief, a very simple tale, and as old in its fundamental dolorousness as arterio sclerosis. What gives it its high quality is the richness of its detail—the prodigious gorgeousness of its imagery, the dramatic effectiveness of its shifting scenes, the whole glow and gusto of it. Here, at all events, it is medieval. Here Cabell evokes an atmosphere that is the very essence of charm. Nothing could be more delightfully done than some of the episodes—that of Jurgen's meeting with Guenevere in the Hall of Judgment, that of his dialogue with old King Gogyrvan Gawr, that of his adventure with the Hamadryad, that of the ceremony of the Breaking of the Veil, that of his invasion of the bed-chamber of Helen of Troy. The man who could imagine such scenes is a first-rate artist, and in the matter of their execution he proves the fact again. Time and again they seem to

be dissolving, shaking a bit, going to pieces—but always he carries them off. And always neatly, delicately, with an air. The humor of them has its perils; to Puritans it must often seem shocking; it might easily become gross. But here it is no more gross than a rose-window. . . . Toward the end, alack, the thing falls down. The transition from heathen Olympuses and Arcadies to the Christian Heaven and Hell works an inevitable debasement of the comedy. The satire here ceases to be light-fingered and becomes heavy-handed: "the religion of Hell is patriotism, and the government is an enlightened democracy." It is almost like making fun of a man with inflammatory rheumatism. Perhaps the essential thing is that the book is a trifle too long. By the time one comes to Calvinism, democracy and the moral order of the world one has begun to feel surfeited. But where is there a work of art without a blemish? Even Beethoven occasionally misses fire. This "Jurgen," for all such ifs and buts, is a very fine thing. It is a great pity that it was not written in French. Done in English, and printed in These States, it somehow suggests Brahms scoring his Fourth Symphony for a jazz band and giving it at an annual convention of the Knights of Pythias.

Mencken had his blind spots. He overlooked other talented Southerners, never reviewing Thomas Wolfe or William Faulkner. He also did not think highly of Ernest Hemingway, but he did recognize from the beginning the talent of their mutual

Dust jacket for Fitzgerald's first novel, published in 1920. Mencken joined the critical chorus that welcomed the work.

friend F. Scott Fitzgerald. In The Smart Set *Mencken joined the chorus that welcomed* This Side of Paradise. *He wrote two reviews of* The Great Gatsby, *including a guarded one for* The American Mercury, *in which it is grouped with three other novels now forgotten (excerpt from "Books More or Less Amusing–II,"* Smart Set *[August 1920]: 140).*

[. . .] The best American novel that I have seen of late is also the product of a neophyte, to wit, F. Scott Fitzgerald. This Fitzgerald has taken part in THE SMART SET's display of literary fireworks more than once, and so you are probably familiar with his method. In "This Side of Paradise" he offers a truly amazing first novel–original in structure, extremely sophisticated in manner, and adorned with a brilliancy that is as rare in American writing as honesty is in American statecraft. The young American novelist usually reveals himself as a naïve, sentimental and somewhat disgusting ignoramus–a believer in

Photograph of Mencken taken by Fitzgerald at Fitzgerald's home near Baltimore, 1932 (courtesy of the Enoch Pratt Free Library)

F. Scott Fitzgerald

Great Causes, a snuffler and eye-roller, a spouter of stale philosophies out of Kensington drawing-rooms, the doggeries of French hack-drivers, and the lower floor of the Munich Hofbräuhaus. Nine times out of ten one finds him shocked by the discovery that women are not the complete angels that they pretend to be, and full of the theory that all of the miners in West Virginia would become instantly non-luetic, intelligent and happy if Congress would only pass half a dozen simple laws. In brief, a fellow viewing human existence through a knot-hole in the floor of a Socialist local. Fitzgerald is nothing of the sort. On the contrary, he is a highly civilized and rather waggish fellow–a youngster not without sentiment, and one even cursed with a touch or two of pretty sentimentality, but still one who is many cuts above the general of the land. More, an artist–an apt and delicate weaver of words, a clever hand, a sound workman. The first half of the story is far better than the second half. It is not that Fitzgerald's manner runs thin, but that his hero begins to elude him. What, after such a youth, is to be done with the fellow? The author's solution is anything but felicitous. He simply drops his Amory Blaine as Mark Twain dropped

As a matter of fact, Mr Mencken, I stuck your
name in on page 224 in the last proof—
partly, I suppose, as a vague bootlick
and partly because I have since adopted
a great many of your views. But the
other literary opinions, especially the
disparagement of Cobb, were written
when you were little more than a
name to me—

This is a bad book full of good
things, a novel about flappers written
for philosophers, an exquisite burlesque
of Compton McKenzie with a pastiche
of Wells at the end—

F. Scott Fitzgerald
March 20th, 1920

Inscription in Mencken's copy of This Side of Paradise *(courtesy of the Enoch Pratt Free Library and by permission of Harold Ober Associates Inc. ©
1980 by Frances Scott Fitzgerald Smith)*

Dust jacket for Fitzgerald's best-known novel, published in 1925. Mencken reviewed the book in The American Mercury.

imer, Miss Cather. Fitzgerald, though he had no such struggle, now tries to make it for himself. "The Great Gatsby" is full of evidences of hard, sober toil. All the author's old slipshod facility is gone; he has set himself rigorously to the job of learning how to write. And he shows quick and excellent progress. "The Great Gatsby" is not merely better written than "This Side of Paradise"; it is written in a new way. Fitzgerald has learned economy of words and devices; he has begun to give thought to structure; his whole attitude has changed from that of a brilliant improvisateur to that of a painstaking and conscientious artist. I certainly don't think much of "The Great Gatsby" as a story. It is in part too well-made and in part incredible. But as a piece of writing it is sound and laudable work.

At Fitzgerald's urging, Mencken took notice of Hemingway's Men without Women; *but he did so in an omnibus review that also dealt with five other works, including Thornton Wilder's* The Bridge of San Luis Rey *(excerpt from "Fiction,"* American Mercury, *14 [May 1928]: 127).*

Huckleberry Finn, but for less cogent reason. But down to and including the episode of the love affair with Rosalind the thing is capital, especially the first chapters. Not since Frank Norris's day has there been a more adept slapping in of preliminaries.

* * *

("New Fiction," American Mercury, *5 [July 1925]: 382.)*

Of these novels, the one that has given me most pleasure is Fitzgerald's, if only because it shows the author to be capable of professional advancement. He is still young and he has had a great success: it is a combination that is fatal to nine beginning novelists out of ten. They conclude at once that the trick is easy—that it is not worth while to sweat and suffer. The result is a steady and melancholy decline; presently the best-selling *eminentissimo* of yesterday vanishes and is heard of no more. I could adorn this page with a list of names, but refrain out of respect for the dead. Most of the novelists who are obviously on solid ground today had heavy struggles at the start: Dreiser, Cabell, Hergeshe-

Ernest Hemingway, whose novel Men Without Women *(1927) Mencken reviewed at Fitzgerald's urging*

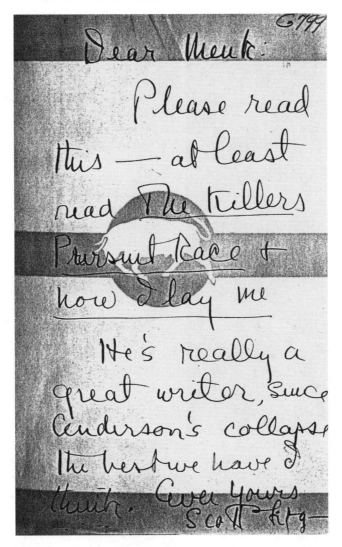

Fitzgerald's message in Hemingway's Men without Women, *which prompted Mencken to review the book (courtesy of the Enoch Pratt Free Library and by permission of Harold Ober Associates Inc. © 1980 by Frances Scott Fitzgerald Smith)*

[. . .] Mr. Hemingway and Mr. Wilder have made huge successes of late and received a great deal of uncritical homage. I believe that both are too sagacious to let it fool them. It is technical virtuosity that has won them attention; it is hard and fundamental thinking that must get them on, if they are to make good their high promise. I gather from both of them the feeling that they are yet somewhat uncertain about their characters—that after their most surprising bravura passages they remain in some doubt as to what it is all about. As a result, their work often seems fragmentary: it charms without leaving any very deep impression. But that is a defect that the years ought to cure. Meanwhile, Mr. Hemingway's "Fifty Grand," first printed in the *Atlantic*, and "The Killers," first printed in *Scribner's* and Mr. Wilder's "The Marquesa de Montemayor" and "Uncle

Pio" are things to be sincerely thankful for. They may not be masterpieces, but masterpieces might surely be written in their manner. [. . .]

Mencken had many blind spots when it came to poetry. While finding much to admire in imagism, he was not happy with the directions in which modernism was taking verse. In another omnibus review, he seized the occasion to make a sweeping theoretical statement and to criticize both poets and critics, with his friend Louis Untermeyer's The New Era in American Poetry *as the central text (excerpt from "The Coroner's Inquest," Smart Set [July 1919]: 138–140).*

In all the days of my pastorate in this place, now running, boy and man, to eleven year, I have faced no

ing begins. Even the elaborate expositions of Amy Lowell and Ezra Pound have left a lot to be said, for Miss Lowell always demolishes her theories by printing dithyrambs embodying them, and Pound is so steadily and heroically indignant that he usually leaves one with the notion that all poetry is evil, including even the kind he advocates. Here Untermeyer stands shoulders above the rest. He is clear, he is positive, he is full of a fine gusto, and yet he keeps his head from first to last, and avoids getting into a sweat over ideas that, after all, may still need a certain amount of revision before they take rank with the binomial theorem. Not that he is timorous, vacillating, temporizing. Far from it, indeed. He thinks he knows what he thinks he knows, and he states it with bounce. But the messianic note that gets into the bulls and ukases of Pound and Miss Lowell is happily absent from his treatise, and so it is possible to follow him amiably even when he is wrong.

And that is not seldom. At the very start, for example, he permits himself a lot of highly dubious rumble-bumble about the "inherent Americanism" and soaring democracy of the new poetry movement. "Once," he says, "the most exclusive and aristocratic of the arts, appreciated and fostered only by little *salons* and erudite groups, poetry has suddenly swung away

Mencken's friend, the poet Louis Untermeyer (photograph by
Lotte Jacobi)

such stately pile of critical works as that which now rears itself before me. Enumerated, they come to fourteen volumes, and in size they range from Vincent Starrett's thin monograph on Arthur Machen (*Hill*), with its thirty-five duodecimo pages, to the lordly bulk of the second book of "The Cambridge History of American Literature" (*Putnam*), tilting the hay-scales at two pounds eight ounces. [. . .]

The most stimulating of all these volumes, despite many curious aberrations of the judgment and the fancy, is undoubtedly Untermeyer's, if only because it is the first cogent and exhaustive statement of the case for the new poetry by one who has helped to give it form and direction. The critical literature of the movement, hitherto, has been very unsatisfactory. I need only point to the windy, chautauqua-like pronunciamentos of Vachel Lindsey, the vague and often contradictory announcements of the Imagists, and the hollow guff of Dr. Kreymborg and the other third-raters of Greenwich Village. Mountebankery has too often corrupted the thing; in Lindsey himself, perhaps the most original of the whole boiling, it is often impossible to say where serious purpose ends and mere boob-bump-

The poet Ezra Pound, whom Mencken compared unfavorably
to Untermeyer

H. L. Mencken
replies to a letter which asks his opinions
On Book Reviews

Dear Sir:

I have your note of April 6th, addressed to Mr. S. Mencken. The only S. Mencken I know of is my uncle Sigmund. He is in the lime and cement business, and knows nothing of book reviewing.

My own view is that a book review, first and foremost, must be entertaining. By this I mean that it must be dexterously written, and show an interesting personality. The justice of the criticism embodied in it is a secondary matter. It is often, and perhaps usually, quite impossible to determine definitely whether a given book is 'good' or 'bad'. The notion to the contrary is a delusion of the defectively intelligent. It is almost always accompanied by moral passion. But a critic may at least justify himself by giving his readers civilized entertainment. If he is genuinely competent he very frequently gives them much better entertainment than they could find in the book reviewed.

There are, of course, certain standards and criteria. A book may be full of errors in fact. It may be dishonest. It may be illiterate. But beyond that it is difficult to determine values exactly. What remains is simply the critic's personal reaction. If he is a well-informed man and able to write decently, anything he writes about anything will divert his readers. If he is an ass, he will only bore them.

Sincerely yours,

H. L. Mencken

Broadside publication of Mencken's letter to a reader that includes Mencken's philosophy of book reviewing (Harry Ransom Humanities Research Center, The University of Texas at Austin)

from its self-imposed strictures and is expressing itself once more in terms of democracy." Pondering excessively, I can think of nothing that would be more untrue than this. The fact is that the new poetry is neither American nor democratic. It started, not in the United States at all, but in France, and its exotic color is still its most salient characteristic. Practically every one of its practitioners is palpably under some strong foreign influence, and most of them are no more Anglo-Saxon than a samovar or a toccata. The extravagant strangeness of Pound, his almost bellicose anti-Americanism, is a mere accentuation of what is in every other member of the fraternity. Many of them, like Frost, Fletcher, H.D. and Pound, have deliberately exiled themselves from the republic. Others, such as Oppenheim, Sandburg, Giovannitti, Benét and Untermeyer himself, are palpably Continental Europeans, often with Levantine traces. Yet others, such as Miss Lowell and Masters, are little more than translators and adapters—from the French, from the Japanese, from the Greek. Even Lindsey, the most thoroughly national of them all, has also his alien smear, for whatever is most novel and significant in his verse is based plainly upon the rude folk-song of the negroes of the South. Let Miss Lowell herself be a witness. "We shall see them," she says at the opening of her essay on E. A. Robinson,

the subject matter of their verse with its position in the national consciousness. Oppenheim, Sandburg and Lindsey are democrats, just as Whitman was a democrat, but their poetry is no more a democratic phenomenon than his was, or than, to go to music, Beethoven's Eroica Symphony was. Many of the new poets, in truth, are ardent enemies of democracy, for example, Pound. Only one of them has ever actually sought to take his strophes to the vulgar. That one is Lindsey—and there is not the slightest doubt that the yokels welcomed him, not because they were interested in his poetry, but because it struck them as an amazing and perhaps even a fascinatingly obscene thing, for a sane man to go about the country on any such bizarre and undemocratic business.

Thus burdened at the start, Untermeyer quickly throws off his theories and gives us some extraordinarily sound and penetrating criticism of his contemporaries. Now and then, as in the case of

---

Books by

JIM TULLY

—

BEGGARS OF LIFE
JARNEGAN
CIRCUS PARADE
SHANTY IRISH

"*I*F Tully were a Russian, read in translation, all the Professors would be hymning him. He has all of Gorky's capacity for making vivid the miseries of poor and helpless men, and in addition he has a humor that no Russian could conceivably have. In 'Shanty Irish,' it seems to me, he has gone far beyond any of his work of the past. The book is not only brilliantly realistic; it also has fine poetic quality."

—H. L. MENCKEN

Mencken blurb on a preliminary page of his friend Tully's Shanty Irish *(1928)*

"ceding more and more to the influence of other, alien, peoples. . . ." A glance is sufficient to show the correctness of this observation. There is no more "inherent Americanism" in the new poetry than there is in the new American painting and music. It lies, in fact, quite outside the main stream of American culture.

Nor is it democratic, in any intelligible sense. The poetry of Whittier and Longfellow was democratic. It voiced the elemental emotions of the masses of the people; it was full of their simple, rubber-stamp ideas; they comprehended it and cherished it. And so with the poetry of James Whitcomb Riley, and with that of Walt Mason and Ella Wheeler Wilcox. But the new poetry, grounded firmly upon novelty of form and boldness of idea, is quite beyond their understanding. It seems to them to be idiotic, just as the poetry of Whitman seemed to them to be idiotic, and if they could summon up enough interest in it to examine it at length, they would undoubtedly clamor for laws making the confection of it a felony. The mistake of Untermeyer, and of others who talk to the same effect, lies in confusing the beliefs of poets and

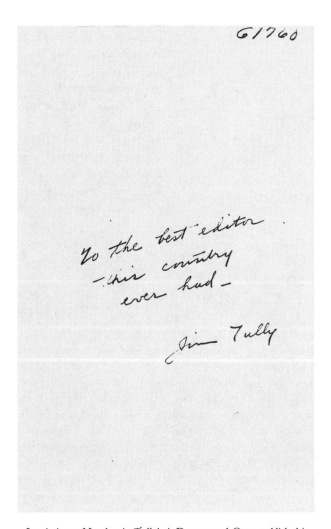

Inscription to Mencken in Tully's A Dozen and One, *published in 1943 (courtesy of the Enoch Pratt Free Library)*

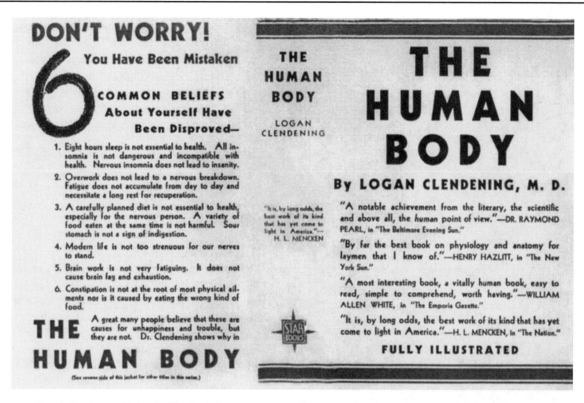

Dust jacket for a medical book. Mencken's far-ranging interests (and hypochondria) made his opinion noteworthy in this field.

Giovannitti, he allows himself too much praise, and now and then, as in the case of Pound, he halts his analysis before he has done full justice, but in the main he is accurate, thorough and fair. His essay on Robert Frost is far better than Miss Lowell's, and I think he also does better with E. A. Robinson than she does. Furthermore, his book is much wider in scope than hers; covers a great many more poets, and so gives a more comprehensive view of the general movement. Finally, he finds space for a brief consideration of various poets who stand quite outside it, among them, Sara Teasdale and Lizette Woodworth Reese, who are much greater artists than any of the bards within the fold. In this outer Alsatia he is less sure-handed than inside. His astounding under-estimate of John McClure in the *New Republic,* happily not included in the present book, will, I trust, become historical and cause him to blush on the gallows. But, taking his bitter with his sweet, he has achieved a book of criticism that is readable, sagacious and good-tempered—in short, quite the best critical work that the new fermentation of minnesingers has yet thrown up.

As for the relative and absolute worth of these rebels against Stedman's Anthology and McGuffey's Sixth Reader, I shall probably discourse upon it pro-foundly in the future. At the moment, my impression is that Sandburg and Oppenheim are the best of them—the one an incisive and shocking realist and the other a sonorous rhapsodist, almost biblical in his stately eloquence. Miss Lowell is the schoolmarm of the movement—a pedagogue with brief moments of illumination. She has done half a dozen excellent poems in the Imagist manner, and a great many dull doggerels. There is a good deal that is extra-poetical in her celebrity; if she were Miss Tillie Jones, of Allentown, Pa., we'd hear a great deal less about her. Masters, I believe, is already extinct. What made the great fame of "The Spoon River Anthology" was not so much its grim truthfulness as the public notion that it was improper. It fell upon the country at the height of the sex wave. All of Masters' later poetry is pishposh. Lindsey? Alas, he has done his own burlesque. Frost? A standard New England poet, with a few changes in phraseology, and the substitution of sour resignationism for sweet resignationism. Whittier without the whiskers. Pound? The American in headlong flight from America—to England, to Italy, to the Middle Ages, to ancient Greece, to Cathay and points East. The most picturesque and pugnacious man and withal the sharpest, most resilient mind in the movement. The Others group, the

tiful. There was something milky about his complexion and cerulean in his blue eyes, and he looked much more the boy than the man. He was, in fact, less than twenty-three years old. [. . .]

Pound wrote to me about Joyce from England on February 2, 1915, and gave me his address in Trieste, where he was making a miserable living as a teacher of languages. Pound hailed from Idaho and was the son of a minor functionary in the Philadelphia Mint, but he had been living in England for some years before this, and was a leading figure in a New Poetry Movement then under way there. I had reviewed his "Provenca" at some length in the <u>Smart Set</u> for April, 1911, and his translations of Guido Cavalcanti in the issue for April, 1913, and had suggested to Boyer and then to Wright that he be invited to contribute to the magazine. He was a diligent propagandist for other authors of his general way of thinking, and the first letter from him that I can recover is one to Boyer dated February 26, 1914, recommending Richard Aldington. I got into direct communication with him during 1914, and when Nathan and I took over the <u>Smart Set</u> his suggestions became frequent. When he wrote to me about Joyce I asked him to send me some of Joyce's short stories, and this he did at once. They were "The Boarding-House" and "A Little Cloud." Nathan and I liked them so much that we decided to print both of them in the next number to be made up, which was that for May, 1915. They were the first things by Joyce ever to appear in an American magazine.[. . .]

With the passing of 1917 there came a bucking-up, and by March, 1918, we were printing a novelette by Thyra Samter Winslow, followed the next month by one by Hugh Kahler. [. . .] An even greater improvement was shown in our one-act plays. This last, indeed, began before the end of 1917, for in the October issue of that year we published Eugene O'Neill's "The Long Voyage Home," a really distinguished piece of work. In May, 1918, we followed with his "Ile" and in August with "The Moon of the Caribbees." It was ordinarily Nathan's job to rustle for one-act plays, but O'Neill fell to me, and it is my recollection that it was Louis Untermeyer who suggested trying to recruit him. He had published a volume of one-acters, by title "Thirst and Other One-Act Plays," in 1915, but it had made no impression, and he was virtually unknown save in Greenwich Village, where he had recently lived in drunken squalor with Louise Bryant, afterward the wife, in succession, of John Reed and of William C. Bullitt, ambassador to France. He had been married himself, in 1909, to a Greenwich Village belle named Kathleen Jenkins, but they separated soon afterward, and in 1918 he married Agnes Boulton, an occasional contributor to the <u>Smart Set</u>. Two of his plays, "Bound

The playwright Eugene O'Neill, several of whose works Mencken published in The Smart Set

Greenwich vers librists, the Socialist trombonists? They are the street-boys following the calliope. [. . .]

Mencken left behind a reminiscence of his first meeting with Fitzgerald—and vignettes of many other bright lights—in his posthumously published My Life as Author and Editor *(1993). His stature made it inevitable that he would encounter nearly every major and minor author of the period (excerpts from the typescript for* My Life as Author and Editor *at Enoch Pratt Free Library, Baltimore, pp. 678, 215–216, 534–536, 671–673).*

I met Francis Scott Key Fitzgerald in June or thereabout, 1919, and his first contribution to the <u>Smart Set</u>, a short story called "Babes in the Wood," was printed in the issue for September of that year, to be followed in November with a one-act play, "The Debutante." It is my recollection that I first saw him in George Nathan's apartment in the Royalton, and that George had picked him up somewhere or other a little while before. He was then a slim, blonde young fellow, tall and straight in build and so handsome that he might even have been called beau-

Inscription in O'Neill's Moon of the Caribbees, *published in 1919 (courtesy of the Enoch Pratt Free Library and Yale University)*

East for Cardiff" and "Thirst," were produced by the Provincetown Players at their wharf theatre in Provincetown in 1916, and later the company brought the former to New York, but, though it showed signs of growing skill it was lost in the welter of one-acters then being put on in Little Theatres centered in and radiating from the Village, and I believe that Nathan had not seen it. At all events, it fell to me to deal with O'Neill and I must have begun negotiations with him soon after my return from the war. [. . .]

Beside La Speyer the Smart Set's recruits in 1919 included Willa Sibert Cather and F. Scott Fitzgerald. I had been reviewing Cather's books favorably since the appearance of "Alexander's Bridge" in 1912. It was a palpable imitation of Edith Wharton, but it was a very good imitation; indeed, it seemed to me to be better than anything La Wharton herself had done save "Ethan Frome."[. . .] I gave a brief but equally friendly notice to "O Pioneers!" in October, 1913, and said of "The Song of the Lark," in January, 1916: "I have read no late novel with a greater sense of intellectual stimulation." In 1918 came "My Ántonia," which I reviewed at length in the issue for March, 1919, saying of the author: "There is no other American author of her sex, now on view, whose future promises so much." I must have had some communication with her after my

review of "The Song of the Lark," for I find a letter from her, dated May 12, 1916, in which she discusses the suggestion (apparently made by me, though not in my review) that the heroine of the story was Lillian Nordica (1859–1914). I gather from this letter that she actually had Nordica in mind, but had been careful to conceal the fact as much as possible, for the singer's last husband, George Washington Young, was still alive, and he was known to be a bellicose and litigious fellow. Cather's associations, in those days as in her later years, were largely with musicians and music-lovers. She was one of the most assiduous concert-goers New York ever saw, and apparently had no social life save that connected with music. Her publisher, in the 1912–1919 period, was the Houghton Mifflin Company of Boston, but she had been greatly taken by the sightly format of the books brought out by Knopf, and one day she walked into his office and proposed that he take over. This must have been in 1918. Unfortunately, it was difficult to get rid of her contract with Houghton, and the first of her books to appear with the Knopf imprint was "Youth and the Bright Medusa," which came out in 1920 and was reviewed by me in the Smart Set for December of that year. I must have written to her in 1918, proposing that she do something for the magazine, for I find a letter from her,

The writer Willa Cather, whom Mencken recruited for The Smart Set *in 1919*

Early in June, 1919, I proposed that he turn over "In Defense of Women" to Knopf, who had already taken over "Damn," and they entered into negotiations at once. These negotiations were carried on in the best Jewish manner, and on June 20 I was writing to Goodman:

(small type)

Knopf's bookkeeper, Miss Rabinowitz, who listened in on your palaver, tells me that there were many dramatic episodes. She says that when Knopf bared his breast and invited you, with his voice full of sobs, to cut out his heart and have done, she was deceived by the realism of it and came dam nigh fainting. [. . .] Miss Rabinowitz inclines to think that you might have got 1 1/8 cents more a copy if you had not drunk that doped raisin wine. She carried off a high appreciation of your forensic talents, and has mentioned you to her sister, Miss Birdie, who is stenographer to Morty Schiff. [. . .]

(end small type)

dated December 6, 1918, saying that she was projecting "several shorter things" and would let me see them when they were finished. On May 2, 1919, she sent in "Her Boss" and we printed it in the October issue. Dreiser and Lord Dunsany were also represented in that issue, but otherwise it was undistinguished. Some time a bit later she sent me another story, saying frankly that it had been declined by T. R. Smith, then managing editor of the *Century,* and offering it "at a bargain price—a hundred dollars."

Other contractual matters appear in My Life as Author and Editor, *including the dickering between Mencken's two best friends over transfer of what would become one of his most popular books,* In Defense of Women, *which was published by Philip Goodman (excerpt from the typescript for* My Life as Author and Editor *at the Enoch Pratt Free Library, Baltimore, pp. 612–614).*

[. . .] By this time it was obvious that he could not sell the book -- indeed, it was obvious that his publishing venture was a complete failure -- and he was already preparing to try theatrical management.

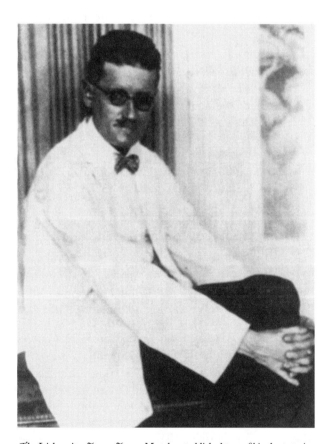

The Irish writer James Joyce. Mencken published two of his short stories in The Smart Set *in May 1915—the first of Joyce's works to appear in an American magazine.*

Philip Goodman, who published some of Mencken's early books (Jack R. Sanders Collection)

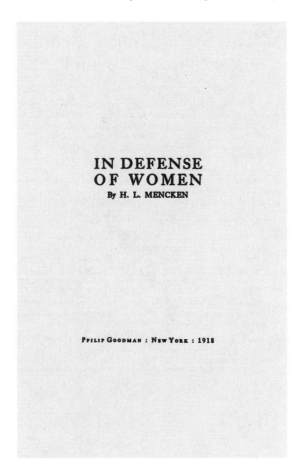

*Title page for the first edition of Mencken's book, with the
publisher's first name misspelled*

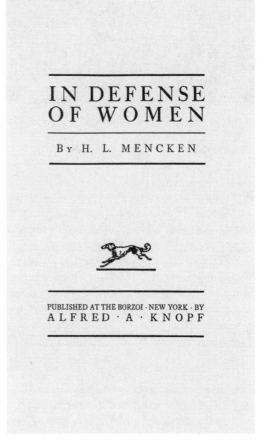

*Title page for the Knopf issue, made up from Goodman's
remainder sheets (1919)*

friend's future (excerpts from the typescript at Enoch Pratt Free Library, Baltimore, entry for 11 October 1945, pp. 1–3).

[. . .] In theory, he has been at work on his autobiography, but in fact he has done nothing. He showed me a single page of much interlined and wholly unintelligible manuscript, and told me that it represented seven hard days of effort. This sounded incredible, but it is plain that he can't write. He is full of complaints against Knopf for letting most of his books go out of print and melting the plates, but they went out of print simply because they had ceased to sell, and the plates were melted under a government order that those of all books that had sold less than so many copies for a year past must be turned in for the metal in them. Knopf is preparing to bring out a new edition of "The Three Black Pennies," but it is delayed by the paper shortage, greatly to Joe's discontent. He blames Knopf, but is quite irrational. He thinks that Knopf should keep all of his books in print, despite the fact that some of them had no sales for years. I proposed that he pick out four or five that

Inscribed photograph of the novelist Joseph Hergesheimer, whose work Mencken continued to champion even as Hergesheimer's reputation went into eclipse (courtesy of the Enoch Pratt Free Library)

When they came to terms -- just what those terms were I do not recall -- Knopf bound Goodman's remaining sheets in the neat blue binding, with gilt stamping, that he had adopted for my books, and by the end of 1919 he had worked off the whole stock in hand and In Defense of Women went out of print. It needed, as it stood, a considerable revision, for a large and important part of it dealt with the extension of the suffrage to women, and that extension, since the date of its first publication, had been converted from a mere threat or prospect into a reality.

Joseph Hergesheimer has been mentioned several times in contexts that indicate his status as a major novelist whose reputation, it appeared, would long outlive him. Now he seldom merits more than a line in literary histories. Mencken stood by Hergesheimer, whom he had promoted since the Smart Set *days; but by the time of this entry in his posthumously published diary he had few illusions about his*

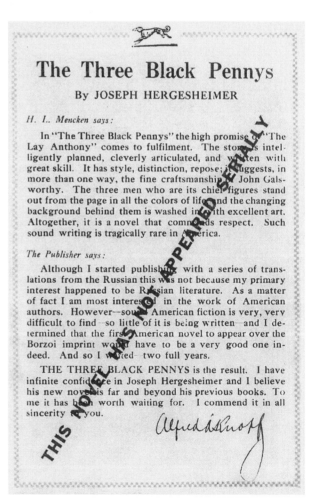

Back of dust jacket for the first novel published by Knopf (1917)

he really cherishes, and prepare them for reprinting. Then, if Knopf refuses to reset them, he can turn to some other publisher. I suggested Scribner. [. . .]

I always enjoy palavering with Joe, even when, as now, he is uncomfortable and intermittently peppery. He and I have been close friends since 1914, and have never had a serious difference. Despite his inability to write, he still talks amusingly, and shows no other sign of mental decay. His case is most distressing, and more than a little mysterious. I am his age precisely, and I am full of ills, but I have written and published five books since I was sixty, and all of them have been well enough done to sell well and get preponderantly favorable notices. I am in hopes that when Dr. Benjamin M. Baker gets home from the war, about Christmas, I'll be able to induce Joe to see him. The quacks he has consulted have done him no good. Though his blood count is about 200, they tell him that he needs no treatment save a mild diet – and then let him drink beer. Certainly it would be easy to imagine a more salubrious drink for a diabetic. But Joe insists that he is <u>not</u> a diabetic. [. . .]

Passport photo of Mencken and his wife, Sara Haardt Mencken, taken on 29 December 1933 (courtesy of the Enoch Pratt Free Library)

A writer who never had more than a modest reputation was Mencken's wife, Sara Haardt. She published a novel, The Making of a Lady *(1931), and after her death Mencken collected her stories as* Southern Album *(1936). The nation was amused when the author of the sardonic* In Defense of Women *found a bride in 1930 at the age of fifty. He had enjoyed her company and her collaboration for some years before that, and he knew when he married her that she did not have long to live. In his diary he reflected on her passing. The quotation from Goethe means "Deny yourself; you must deny yourself" (excerpts from the typescript at Enoch Pratt Free Library, Baltimore, entry for 31 May 1940, pp. 1, 5).*

Sara is dead five years today -- a longer time than the time of our marriage, which lasted but four years and nine months. It is amazing what a deep mark she left upon my life -- and yet, after all, it is not amazing at all, for a happy marriage throws out numerous and powerful tentacles. They may loosen with years and habit, but when a marriage ends at the height of its success they endure. It is a literal fact that I still think of Sara every day of my life, and almost every hour of the day. Whenever I see anything that she would have liked I find myself saying that I'll buy it and take it to her, and I am always thinking of things to tell her. There was a tremendous variety in her, and yet she was always steadfast. I can recall no single moment during our years together when I ever had the slightest doubt of our marriage, or wished that it had never been. I believe that she was equally content. We had our troubles, especially her illnesses, but they never set up any difference between us: they always drew us closer and closer together. Indeed, it was only the last year or so that

was darkened by them, for before that she always recovered quickly, and seemed to be making a steady gain in health. I knew all the while that her chances of life were not too good, but nevertheless the overt situation was usually reassuring, and so I put fears out of my mind. What I wrote of her courage in the preface to "Southern Album" was all true. It was seldom that she ever showed any sign of discouragement. I remember once --when she developed an eye infection, and Alan C. Woods, always forthright, told her that it was probably tuberculous. She came home from his office in a state close to collapse, and I had a hard time quieting her. But in a couple of days she had recovered her fortitude, and soon afterward the infection cleared up. She had a dreadful vulnerability to tuberculosis, and yet a compensatory capacity for throwing it off. Her two spells of pleurisy were both severe, and yet she recovered quickly. [. . .]

We had often talked of death, for she was well aware that her own chances of life were less than the average. She insisted that she would die first, but it always seemed to me to be improbable, for I was her senior by 18 years, and had been badgered by all sorts of illnesses for years. A complete skeptic, she made me promise, in case she died first, to have her body cre-

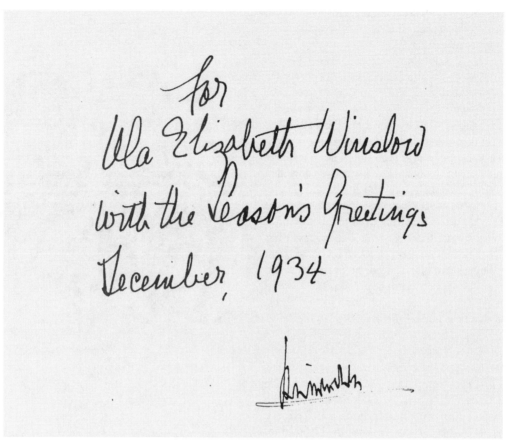

Inscription by Sara Mencken to a former teacher, subscribed by Mencken (Richard J. Schrader Collection)

mated. When she died on that lovely May day I was uneasy about this, for I feared that her sisters might object. But when they got to Baltimore it turned out that she had told them her wish, and that they approved. I did not go to the crematory. What was left of her was taken there by my two brothers and her brother John. Her ashes are buried at the foot of the grave of my mother, and beside her there is room for mine. Thinking of her, I can well understand the great human yearning that makes for a belief in immortality, but I do not believe in it, and neither did she. We have parted forever, though my ashes will soon be mingling with hers. I'll have her in mind until thought and memory adjourn, but that is all. Whether or not it is better so I do not know, but there is the fact as I see it. We were happy together, but all beautiful things must end. Entbehren sollst; du sollst entbehren.

In the same year, Robert van Gelder interviewed Mencken for The New York Times Book Review *of 11 February, giving him a chance to survey the literary scene from his heyday to the present. The piece was reprinted in a collection of van Gelder's*

interviews *("Mencken on Literature and Politics," in van Gelder,* Writers and Writing *[New York: Scribners, 1946], pp. 20–22).*

Russia and Roosevelt are responsible for a ten-year decline in the quality of American writing, said H. L. Mencken.

"The writers fell for the current blah, and no good art can come from men who believe in the blah of their times. The writers of the Thirties have been enslaved by the bushwah of the Pinks."

It was a typical Mencken interview. "Print it!" Mr. Mencken would say after delivering himself of what appeared on the surface to be the grossest libel. "I've known so-and-so for years and in my considered opinion he is a jackass and a simple-minded stooge."

The setting was the comfortably furnished board room and library of the Knopf offices on Madison Avenue, where Mr. Mencken had spent a part of the morning writing autograph cards for insertion into copies of his new book, "Happy Days: 1880–1892."

"Imbecile, boob, idiot," said Mr. Mencken, talking of politics and Pinks. He has a way of pressing his cigar against an ashtray and pushing it around when he is emphasizing his opinion of the editors of *The New Republic* or *The Nation,* or when he is talking of members of President Roosevelt's Cabinet. Naturally, the cigar frequently goes out. The wonder is that it remains lighted as well as it does.

He credits the World War and the peace that followed it with the rise of literature during the second and third decades of this century. Artists could stand aside and see through the abject falsehoods, the rosy glow of optimism, that warmed the common man in the years immediately after the war, and as a result they performed their true functions as artists.

"Red Lewis. His 'Babbitt' was incomparable, wonderful, great. As George Nathan said of 'The Merry Widow': 'Nobody wrote it—God wrote it.' You can say that same thing, truthfully, about 'Babbitt.' Babbitt at that time was the greatest man in the country, he was America. And Lewis saw him truly and fully, had a little fun with him, too.

"Then he wrote 'Elmer Gantry.' We had prohibition and Elmer was the great man behind prohibition. Some people said he exaggerated Elmer. Nonsense, I know those fellows. Elmer was one of the best of them; he was a scholar and a gentleman compared to some I've known, a prince among his kind. Lewis had a little fun with him, too, but basically it was a true portrait.

"But Red is a humble fellow. What other good novelist do you know who speaks well of other novelists? None of 'em do—none of 'em. That's proof of Red's humility. He always speaks well of other novelists. And probably because of that basic humility of his he was caught up in politics. He lambasted the Fascists and then turned around and tried to lambast the Communists in the worst novel ever written in America. That was—let's see, yes, 'The Prodigal Parents.' Frightful stuff. Imbecilic."

The main trouble with American literature, says Mr. Mencken, is that other writers also went into politics, and lost their gift of disbelief.

"The kids came out of college with degrees that weren't worth anything. They couldn't cash in, they couldn't get jobs, they hadn't anything to sell. So they turned to Messiahs—to Russia and to Roosevelt.

"They believed that Roosevelt was going to make America more wonderful than it ever had been before. They believed that the Russians had found a system of government that would permit every one to be comfortable and happy.

"Believing and trusting, they were out of the hurricane, free of the loneliness—but they weren't artists. They couldn't perform the artist's function. They were enslaved by the Pinks."

Best of the up-from-slavery writers, Mr. Mencken believes, is James T. Farrell. "Wonderful stuff in those Chicago tales. Whoever doesn't like Farrell is an idiot or a liar." Farrell had considerable critical backing three or four years ago, has been less prominently mentioned since. Mr. Mencken puts that down to politics. "Farrell refused to go along with Stalin's boys, and as a critic he took a fall out of new authors they were bringing up. So they ganged him." Farrell's latest effort, a tale of the Christian Front, does not appeal to Mr. Mencken, who found it "idiotic, imbecilic, rot." "But, after all, every writer may crack up occasionally."

He also likes William Saroyan: "the only one of the 'advanced' writers with pungency, with something fresh to say and a new way of saying it."

John Steinbeck "has a great talent, but he must have been flattered by the pigs. The political essays in 'Grapes of Wrath' are terrible. They might have been written by one of the kept idealists of the liberal magazines that run on a deficit. But the story is wonderful. I assume that he'll outgrow the stupid politics."

Beyond promoting artists who "could stand aside and see through the abject falsehoods, the rosy glow of optimism, that warmed the common man in the years immediately after the war," Mencken endured trial by combat. He laid out his antipuritanism early on, and it is the thread connecting nearly all of his advocacy. The great early statement is in A Book of Prefaces *(1917), where he discusses fear of sex (excerpt from "Puritanism as a Literary Force," pp. 274–276).*

[. . .] So beset, it is no wonder that the typical American maker of books becomes a timorous and ineffective fellow, whose work tends inevitably toward a feeble superficiality. Sucking in the Puritan spirit with the very air he breathes, and perhaps burdened inwardly with an inheritance of the actual Puritan stupidity, he is further kept upon the straight path of chemical purity by the very real perils that I have just rehearsed. The result is a literature full of the mawkishness that the late Henry James so often roared against— a literature almost wholly detached from life as men are living it in the world—in George Moore's phrase, a literature still at nurse. It is on the side of sex that the appointed virtuosi of virtue exercise their chief repressions, for it is sex that especially fascinates the lubricious Puritan mind; but the conventual reticence that thus becomes the enforced fashion in one field extends itself to all others. Our fiction, in general, is marked by an artificiality as marked as that of Eighteenth Century poetry or the later Georgian drama. The romance in it runs to set forms and stale situations; the revelation, by such a book as "The Titan," that there may be a glamour as entrancing in the way of a conqueror of men as in the way of a youth with a maid, remains isolated and exotic. We have no first-rate political or religious novel; we have no first-rate war story; despite all our national engrossment in commercial enterprise, we have few second-rate tales of business. Romance, in American fiction, still means only a somewhat childish amorousness and sentimentality—the love affairs of Paul and Virginia, or the pale adulteries of their elders. And on the side of realism there is an almost equal vacuity and lack of veracity. The action of all the novels of the Howells school goes on within four walls of painted canvas; they begin to shock once they describe an attack of asthma or a steak burning below stairs; they never penetrate beneath the flow of social concealments and urbanities to the passions that actually move men and women to their acts, and the great forces that circumscribe and condition personality. So obvious a piece of reporting as Upton Sinclair's "The Jungle" or Robert Herrick's "Together" makes a sensation; the appearance of a "Jennie Gerhardt" or a "Hagar Revelly" brings forth a growl of astonishment and rage. [. . .]

Burton Rascoe reviewed A Book of Prefaces *for the* Chicago Tribune; *he later expanded the review for a Knopf brochure on Mencken. He would not be the last to find a kind of puritanism in Mencken's own intolerance (excerpt from "Fanfare," in* H. L. Mencken *[New York: Knopf, 1920], pp. 3–7).*

Pour être un bon critique il faut avoir une forte personalité—REMY DE GOURMONT.

I

When H. L. Mencken unpacks his idiomatic brasses, tunes up his verbal strings, and gets in readiness his phrasal woodwinds to orchestrate a fugue in damnation or in praise of man, god or book, his all too meagre audience cancels all other engagements to be on hand at the initial presentation. The result, that audience knows, will be an experience of pure enjoyment. His musicianship is unfailing. His program is unsatisfactory only in its impermanence. Though the theme he proposes is invariably Mencken—Mencken apropos of this or that—he gives it infinite and intricate variations.

It is, then, as an artist in words that Mr. Mencken is first to be considered. He has the true marks of a stylist: a rich and varied vocabulary and an aptitude for connotation. The baldly obvious, the commonplace in expression, are to him impossible. If he possesses an illusion, it is that word arrangements matter. In the employment of hackneyed, lifeless similes, down-at-the-heel metaphors, and shopworn nouns and adjectives, he sees a dull intellect plodding pathetically along,

redeemed only if it express with dubious clarity a new or vital idea. Knowing that the style is the man and that any one who has something definite to express gives to it naturally a form that commands attention in itself, he respects the manner as much as the content, cultivates the gipsy phrase in his own compositions, and values it in the work of others.

He is distinctly aware. He dwells in no ivory tower, aloof and austere. The whole process of daily life in this republic, its utterly serious concern with fallacies and foibles, its flatulent popular idols, its puerile preferences in literature, art, politics, amusements and moral schemes, its lusty and pretentious *vulgus,* its self-styled *intelligenzia,* all furnish him with ammunition for his critical *mitrailleuse.* He reads everything that has a bearing upon the life about him, from the latest bad novel to the latest papal bull, and from handbills to decisions of the Supreme Court. His vivid combinations, his apt coinages of words are traceable to a close observation and appraisal of daily affairs. Add a nimble and often grotesque imagination and you have the formula of his style—the most vigorous, the most individual, and the most frequently imitated in this country. He owes much of it to his early studies of Nietzsche. It has the slash, the incisiveness, and the gusto of the apothegmatic "Will to Power." It is the style of a satirist and humourist of a high order, one equal to compact and devastating epithets. It moves with an irregular tempo, replete with dissonances. It is imagistic, colourful, dynamic.

II

American literature has been, and is, singularly deficient in established critics who have anything like a rational conception of their jobs. The majority, initiate in a few of the patent rituals of Aristotle and Quintilian, don the forbidding robes of high priests to Sweetness and Light, and go about their business much as if the idea were to keep all they know to themselves.

The æsthetic criteria of these Neo-Boussets are the pulpit criteria of the early nineteenth century. They are unaware that psychologists long ago made a division between ethical values and reactions to æsthetic stimuli. One of the chief among them is aghast at Sainte-Beuve's catholicity of taste and sheds a righteous tear of regret that the great Frenchman was not a family man and a Scotch Presbyterian. Another—whose flare for discovering a new Balzac in every third potboiler who sends him a novel and whose genius for being quoted on the ash cans of the publishing alleys make him probably the most sinister drawback to the advancement of American letters—this professor, in a work on the English novel, hangs an unbecoming and unnecessary halo above the head of Mark Twain, finds moral tracts in every fiction, and leaves out entirely two or three of the really important novelists of the present day. Criticism, so practised, becomes an exercise in hieroglyphics, a requiem high mass at 4 o'clock in the afternoon–anything save a sane, intelligent effort to get at a writer's intention and to judge him as to whether he has achieved it, well or ill.

This effort Mencken makes in "A Book of Prefaces," dealing with Conrad, Dreiser, and Huneker, with an added chapter on "Puritanism as a Literary Force." It is a book of creative criticism in a sense unusual in American letters. It is an assault upon the cultural pharisaism which leads us to ballyhoo third-rate Russian, French, Italian, Japanese, and Hindu poets and novelists, issuing them in translations with roycroftie bindings to lie unopened on library tables, while men nearer home, eminently more deserving of artistic consideration, are neglected or, what is worse, pilloried by smug reviewers. It is a work of appraisement and appreciation by a man who can write coherently and with effect, who knows several literatures and yet is not a don, who has taste and discrimination and yet is not a prig, who can pass judgment on a writer and yet not assume that the destiny of the race is thus determined by his words, and who can be a critic and yet be human.

To get the full force of his writings, of course, one must at least know the A B C's of literary history, but one must also know that this is the twentieth century. A pedant will miss as many of his allusions as will a parlour maid or a chauffeur. He has, to be sure, his share of intellectual fourflush; he, too, is an American. He shows, at times, an offensive intellectual arrogance and a vainglorious trick of parading names of unfamiliar writers through the pages of his discourse. He has an intolerance as definite in its way as the intolerance of the Methodism and Puritanism he fights. He has a sentimental bias for the melancholy as against the joyous temperament. At heart he is a Puritan, as was Nietzsche and is Shaw. And he has his regular fling at *bourgeoisie* baiting, a pastime he pleasingly alternates with badgering the "intellectuals." It is great fun for him and for his readers. With an adjective and a noun he can strip a Chautauqua pundit of every stitch of his pretentious accoutrements and leave him shivering in the altogether, a pathetic and ridiculous spectacle.

He is at best as a critic in dealing with prose. He has little patience with or appreciation for poetry and with characteristic impromptu he is likely to consign to the limbo of his estimates, along with a hack versifier, a poet of high calibre, whose methods and aims he does not immediately apperceive. It is this intolerance, these snap and final judgments, this delight in an occasional display of cultural *bijouterie*, that lessen his stature as a critic. Some of us hope that in the long run he will shed that fault and gain a trifle more of poise and balance, without losing thereby his gem-like quality of phrase.

This consummation, in fact, he has in large measure achieved in "A Book of Prefaces." His occasional sacrifice of clear perspective to the pungent line is here absent. He has approached Conrad, Dreiser, and Huneker with an unwonted chastity of critical materials and given an equitable estimate and a keen analysis of the artistic aims of these men. He inspires one with a desire to find pleasure in their writings, or, if one is already familiar with them, to cherish a more intimate acquaintance with them. This is, of course, the mission–if he have a mission–of the critic. He perhaps reads in Dreiser and Conrad that which is not, a habit he abominates in others. But that is only one more evidence that there is no such thing as a purely objective criticism. A critic invariably treats of himself in considering the work of others, and he is worth while only in so far as he is of intellectual interest and consequence as a man.

Mencken has rooted lustily for Dreiser ever since the latter first appeared upon the literary scene. He early discerned in the Indianan a new and vital force in American letters, a sincere and unflinching artist, pledged to present faithfully life as he had seen it. And when Dreiser was down and gasping under the onslaught of public and professional critics, Mencken stepped in, wielding his mighty cutlass, decapitated some half dozen of the more weighty anthropophagites, and drove the rest to cover. The fight is not over, but Mencken is holding them at bay and others have enlisted in his aid. He knows Dreiser's faults, of which there are many, and he points them out in his book, but he also knows Dreiser's merits. [. . .]

Randolph Bourne developed similar ideas in his review and pointed to Mencken's own brand of moralism. The word comstockery *is derived from Anthony Comstock (1844–1915), a crusader against obscene literature, special agent for the Post Office Department, and a leader of Boston's Watch and Ward Society who caused the destruction of fifty tons of books and gave his name to the so-called Comstock Law (1873), which barred sexually oriented matter from the mails ("H. L. Mencken,"* New Republic, *13 [24 November 1917]: 102–103).*

Mr. Mencken gives the impression of an able mind so harried and irritated by the philistinism of American life that it has not been able to attain its full power. These more carefully worked-over critical essays are, on the whole, less interesting and provocative than the irresponsible comment he gives us in his magazine. How is it that so robust a hater of uplift and puritanism becomes so fanatical a crusader himself? One is forced to call Mr. Mencken a moralist, for with him appraisement has constantly to stop while he tilts against philistine critics and outrageous puritans. In order to show how good a writer is, he must first show how deplorably fatuous, malicious or ignorant are all those who dislike him. Such a proof is undoubtedly the first impulse of any mind that cares deeply about artistic values. But Mr. Mencken too often permits it to be his last, and wastes away into a desert of invective. Yet he has all the raw material of the good critic—moral freedom, a passion for ideas and for literary beauty, vigor and pungency of phrase, considerable reference and knowledge. Why have these intellectual qualities and possessions been worked up only so partially into the finished attitude of criticism? Has he not let himself be the victim of that paralyzing Demos against which he so justly rages? As you follow his strident paragraphs, you become a little sorry that there is not more of a contrast in tone between his illumination of the brave, the free and the beautiful, and the peevish complaints of the superannuated critics of the old school. When are we going to get anything critically curative done for our generation if our critical rebels are to spend their lives cutting off hydra-heads of American stodginess?

Mr. Mencken's moralism infects the essay on Conrad perhaps the least. With considerable effort the critic shakes himself loose from the clutches of his puritan enemies and sets Conrad very justly in relation to his time. "What he sees and describes in his books," Mr. Mencken says, "is not merely this man's aspiration or that woman's destiny, but the overwhelming sweep and devastation of universal forces, the great central drama that is at the heart of all other dramas, the tragic struggles of the soul of man under the gross stupidity and obscene joking of the gods." He likes Dreiser for the same reason, because "he puts into his novels a touch of the eternal Weltschmerz. They get below the drama that is of the moment and reveal the greater drama that is without end." Mr. Mencken discusses Dreiser with admirable balance, and his essay is important because it criticizes him more harshly and more searchingly than many of us dare to do when we are defending him against the outrageous puritan. The essay on Huneker is perhaps the most entertaining. If "to be a civilized man in America is measurably less difficult, despite the war, than it used to be, say, in 1890" (when Mr. Mencken, by the way, was ten years old), it is to Mr. Huneker's gallant excitement that part of the credit is due.

Dreiser and Huneker Mr. Mencken uses with the utmost lustiness, as Samson used the jaw-bone, to slay a thousand Philistines, and his zeal mounts to a closing essay on Puritanism as a Literary Force, which employs all the Menckenian artillery. Here Mr. Mencken, as the moralist contra moralism, runs amuck. It is an exposure that should stir our blood, but it is so heavily documented and so stern in its conviction of the brooding curtain of bigotry that hangs over our land, that its effect must be to throw paralyzing terror into every American mind that henceforth dares to think of not being a prude. Mr. Mencken wants to liberate, but any one who took his huge concern seriously would never dare challenge in any form that

engine of puritanism which derives its energy from the history and soul of the American people. Mr. Mencken is much in earnest. His invective rises above the tone of scornful exaggeration. But his despair seems a little forced. I cannot see that the younger writers—particularly the verse-writers—are conscious of living under any such cultural terrorism as he describes. Mr. Mencken admits that the puritan proscription is irrational and incalculable in its operation. Surely as long as there are magazines and publishers—as there are in increasing numbers—who will issue vigorous and candid work, comstockery in art must be seen as an annoying but not dominating force. Mr. Mencken queerly shows himself as editor, bowing meekly under the puritan proscription, acting as censor of "a long list of such things by American authors, well-devised, well-imagined, well-executed respectable as human documents and as works of art—but never to be printed in mine or any other American magazine." But what is this but to act as busy ally to that very comstockery he denounces? If the Menckens are not going to run the risk in the name of freedom, they are scarcely justified in trying to infect us with their own caution.

The perspective is false that sees this persecution as peculiar to America. Was not Lemonnier prosecuted in Paris? Did not Baudelaire, Flaubert, Zola suffer? Did not Zola's publisher in England die in prison? Has not D. H. Lawrence's latest novel been suppressed in England before it had even a chance to be prosecuted here? It is England not America that has an official censorship of plays. Comstockery is not so much a function of American culture as it is of the current moralism of our general middle-class civilization. The attack must be, as Nietzsche made it, on that moralism rather than on its symptoms. But Mr. Mencken is not particularly happy in his understanding of Nietzsche. He wrote the book from which a majority of the Americans who know about Nietzsche seem to have gotten their ideas. How crude a summary it is may be seen by comparing it with the recent study of Nietzsche by another American, W. M. Salter. One wishes Mr. Mencken had spent more time in understanding the depth and subtleties of Nietzsche, and less on shuddering at puritanism as a literary force, and on discovering how the public libraries and newspapers reviewers are treating Theodore Dreiser.

Mr. Mencken's mode of critical attack thus plays into the hands of the philistines, demoralizes the artist, and demoralizes his own critical power. Why cannot Demos be left alone for a while to its commercial magazines and its mawkish novels? All good writing is produced in serene unconsciousness of what Demos desires or demands. It cannot be created at all if the artist worries about what Demos will think of him or do to him. The artist writes for that imagined audience of perfect comprehenders. The critic must judge for that audience too.

Nonetheless, Comstockery persisted. Because of its frankness, Henry Miller's Tropic of Cancer *could not be published in the United States until 1961. Mencken read the edition published in France in 1934 (transcription of a letter at the New York Public Library).*

January 25, 1936.

Henry Miller, Esq.
Barbizon Plaza,
New York City.

Dear Mr. Miller:

Your letter from Paris has just reached me, and I assume that you have already arrived at the Barbizon Plaza. If so, will you please let me hear of it. I may be in New York in a week or two and I'd like to see you.

I read Tropic of Cancer a month ago. It seems to me to be a really excellent piece of work, and I so reported to the person who sent it to me. Of this, more when we meet.

Yours,
(Signed) H.L. Mencken

Wrapper for the 1934 French edition of Miller's novel, the one Mencken read

Henry Miller, whose novel Tropic of Cancer *(1934) was banned in the United States until 1961*

OF - BY - AND ABOUT HENRY MILLER a collection of pieces by Miller – Herbert Read – Nicola Chiaromonte – Wallace Fowlie – Paul Rosenfeld – H. L. Mencken – Pierre Fauchery – William Carlos Williams – Cyril Connolly – Aldous Huxley – Blaise Cendrars – Edmond Wilson – Ralph Thompson – Wladimir Weidle – Dorothy Dudley – Conrad Moricand.

Printed by
Leo Porgie for the Alicat Bookshop Press
At 287 South Broadway, Yonkers, N. Y.
In June, 1947
Of this edition of 1000 copies,
only 750 copies are for sale.
Copyright 1947 by Oscar Baradinsky,
Alicat Bookshop.

Title page for a book by Mencken and other antipuritans

~ H. L. MENCKEN ~
Super-Puritan
Lend him your prayers

Frontispiece caricature from Harvey Wickham's The Impuritans
(New York: Dial, 1929)

As both friends and enemies pointed out, Mencken was a bourgeois Baltimorean who did have his limits. Harvey Wickham, writing when Mencken's influence as a critic was beginning to wane, finds irony in the fact (excerpt from "The Meaning of Mencken," in Wickham, The Impuritans *[New York: Dial, 1929], pp. 232–233).*

[. . .] Mencken is really a Superpuritan rather than an Impuritan. That is, instead of carrying Puritan faults to excess and so arriving at licence through the bursting of strait-lacing, in the way which is now so common, he seeks a golden and older mean—to be himself mediæval, in short, without knowing it. He has listened agape to too many Puritan old wives' tales to be able to give his tendencies the right name. Nevertheless he would like to undo some of the harm which a too hasty evacuation of Rome brought upon us, would be very

pleased indeed to find at least some substitutes for various useful things which we inadvertently left behind us in our flight. He struggles valiantly to educate the "moron"; to teach him some history, even if it be only his own; to get him to recognize some authority, if it be only the new authority of science not too narrowly understood. Mencken simply cannot live without common sense. Even his pro-sex campaign, undertaken in the days when that dog had a bad name, stopped short of trying to make a god out of glands. [. . .]

Some years earlier Winthrop Parkhurst had found in the vigor of Mencken's demolition a kind of reverse puritanism, while also exposing the vast wasteland he confronted (review of Prejudices: First Series, Dial, *68 [February 1920]: 267–272).*

A certain king once gave to three of his courtiers, in order to determine their wisdom, three hollow crystal globes which were filled with a golden wine and sealed so that none of the fluid might escape therefrom.

Said the first courtier to himself:

"Wine is to be drunk. I will break the glass and taste this stuff, for I am sure it will prove very excellent on the tongue."

So he broke his crystal globe, and before he could catch any of the wine it was spilled upon the ground.

Said the second courtier to himself:

"This crystal of mine is beautiful to the eye, but it is stained inside with a yellow liquid. If I remove the liquid my crystal globe will then be transparent and exquisite."

And, boring a small hole in the side of it, he broke his globe into a thousand fragments.

Said the third courtier to himself:

"This crystal which the king has given me is round like the dome of the sky. Moreover, it is filled with a golden wine which, if drunk, would doubtless make me happy for an hour but which may not be removed, I fear, without breaking the glass and spilling the wine upon the ground. Therefore I will only hang my globe in my window that, seeing it each morning, I may contemplate infinity and be drunk in my imagination on the wine which is within."

And he hung the king's gift in his window.

And when the king saw what the courtier had done he was pleased. And he said to the courtier:

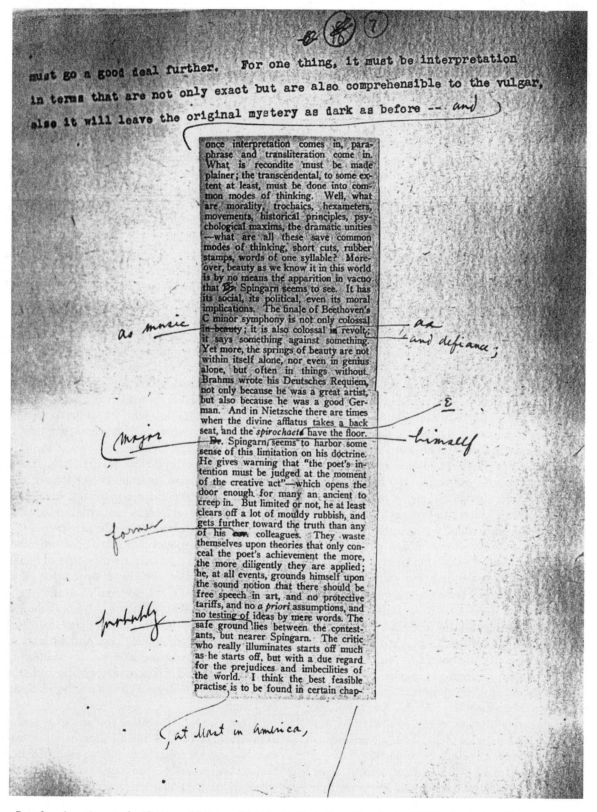

must go a good deal further. For one thing, it must be interpretation in terms that are not only exact but are also comprehensible to the vulgar, else it will leave the original mystery as dark as before -- *and*

once interpretation comes in, paraphrase and transliteration come in. What is recondite must be made plainer; the transcendental, to some extent at least, must be done into common modes of thinking. Well, what are morality, trochaics, hexameters, movements, historical principles, psychological maxims, the dramatic unities —what are all these save common modes of thinking, short cuts, rubber stamps, words of one syllable? Moreover, beauty as we know it in this world is by no means the apparition in vacuo that Spingarn seems to see. It has its social, its political, even its moral implications. The finale of Beethoven's C minor symphony is not only colossal in beauty; it is also colossal in revolt; it says something against something. Yet more, the springs of beauty are not within itself alone, nor even in genius alone, but often in things without. Brahms wrote his Deutsches Requiem, not only because he was a great artist, but also because he was a good German. And in Nietzsche there are times when the divine afflatus takes a back seat, and the *spirochaetœ* have the floor. Dr. Spingarn seems to harbor some sense of this limitation on his doctrine. He gives warning that "the poet's intention must be judged at the moment of the creative act"—which opens the door enough for many an ancient to creep in. But limited or not, he at least clears off a lot of mouldy rubbish, and gets further toward the truth than any of his colleagues. They waste themselves upon theories that only conceal the poet's achievement the more, the more diligently they are applied; he, at all events, grounds himself upon the sound notion that there should be free speech in art, and no protective tariffs, and no *a priori* assumptions, and no testing of ideas by mere words. The safe ground lies between the contestants, but nearer Spingarn. The critic who really illuminates starts off much as he starts off, but with a due regard for the prejudices and imbecilities of the world. I think the best feasible practise is to be found in certain chap-

as music *as* *and defiance;*

ε

major *himself*

former

probably

, at least in America,

Page from the setting copy for "Criticism of Criticism of Criticism" in Prejudices: First Series *(1919), showing how Mencken produced the* Prejudices *volumes by cutting and pasting clippings from his newspaper and magazine articles (courtesy of the Enoch Pratt Free Library)*

"For your wisdom and understanding you shall be rewarded. I hereby make you the First Critic of the Land."

"Criticism is the last of all literary forms; it will perhaps end by absorbing them all. It is admirably adapted to a very civilized society whose memories are rich and whose traditions are already age-old. It is peculiarly suited to a curious, learned, and polished race of men. In order that it may prosper it demands more cultivation than all other literary forms."

So, once upon a time, spake Anatole France; and if that curious, learned, and polished Frenchman spake accurately it is scarcely surprising that literary criticism in the United States, if not a lost art, is one which only tentatively has been found. For American traditions are young, American society is but superficially civilized, and American memories are rich principally in terms of Wall Street and the Stock Exchange. It is true that we have produced such men as Whitman, Poe, and Emerson. It is true, also, that we have bred Abraham Lincoln and Samuel Clemens—one the author of an immortal prose-poem, the other the author of Huckleberry Finn. It is likewise true that we are far from hostile to the published dreams of an ancient world: we glibly read Plato and Nietzsche and Shakespeare and Shaw and Shelley; and, at least when our bugles are mute and our flags are furled in peace, we listen as hungrily to Beethoven and Wagner as we do to Bizet and Sir Edward Elgar. We are, in fact, taken by and large, most generous patrons of the arts; for we build museums, erect libraries, construct theatres, endow orchestras, and generally support the aesthetic edifices with a hand seldom closed in avarice and often opened wide in opulence. We let few chances slip of dropping several million dollars in the hat of a passing band of *skomorokhi,* and we count that day lost whose low-descending sun views from our pocket-books no aesthetic benefaction done.

But one fact remains: our art is almost entirely imported. Our dreams are not dreamed, but bought. Our museums, libraries, theatres, orchestras, and aesthetic edifices generally, are erected by our own hands— and then filled with the treasures of other men. As yet the United States Senate has produced for us neither a Burke nor a Macaulay; St. Patrick's Cathedral has given us neither a Rubens nor a Michelangelo; our slums breed no Balzacs or Zolas; and our aristocracy has failed to furnish us with a single Chopin, Liszt, or Tchaikowsky. At times, we may have seemed to be, artistically, a precociously fecund race. But if we have given this impression we have done so, with very few exceptions, by merely playing foster-mother to the arts. We have seldom conceived beauty or borne it in travail and patient sorrow: for the most part we have bought beauty outright and dandled it proudly on our knee.

In the face, then, of this painful shortage of native material on which a critic may judiciously engage his teeth, it is not astonishing that most of our current criticism should be chiefly a garrulous expression of starvation. Without national maturity you cannot have art, and without art you cannot have an adequate appreciation or criticism of art. That we possess any critics at all is, indeed, more a matter for amazement than that the majority of our critics are cadaverous in phrase and lean in understanding. For, on the one hand, they are confronted by the bleak and rocky Charybdis of creative aridity; and, on the other, they are buffeted and tossed about, as in a storm, by the Scylla of popular puritanical opinion.

This whirlpool of popular opinion is, in truth, a more vicious and dangerous phenomenon than even those barren cliffs beyond which the American critic must swim before reaching the shores of his Sicily; for it is formed of a watery emotionalism whipped high and furious by the winds of puritanical doctrine. And though a critic may, with no very serious difficulty, steer clear of such barren promontories as, say, the novels of Robert Chambers or Elinor Glyn, he will find himself being sucked down, if he is not a careful navigator, in the maelstrom made for his destruction by the preachers of art-for-morality's-sake, of art-for-Anthony-Comstock's-sake, of art-for-everyone's-and-everything's-sake except the artist and his art.

Now, the belief that art should teach a fine moral lesson has, of course, a certain excuse for existence. As long as men believe that it is preferable to tell the truth rather than to lie, as long as men visit condemnation on thieves and encomiums on public benefactors—as long, in brief, as some modes of conduct are considered right and others wrong, so long are the pages of literature a fit and proper place for the dramatization of ethical ideas. The error of the doctrine of art-for-morality's-sake lies not in asking literature to bespeak the cause of righteousness; it lies in demanding that literature bespeak the cause of nothing else. And the error of contemporary criticism lies, likewise, in stimulating this one-sided demand for soothing syrups and teething-rings and failing to cry out always for the whole apothecary shop.

Let us take an example. You are, let us say, a high-minded citizen of the Untied States, intent on national security and the sanctity of the Seventh Mosaic Law. Full of democratic idealism and a respect for American womanhood, you observe, in a book you are reading, that a German spy, by name Schmidt, has plotted for the overthrow of the American Government and has succeeded, incidentally, in effecting the ruin of a beautiful American girl. You are disgusted. You are repelled. You are horrified. And as a loyal citizen of the United

States you are patriotically thrilled to learn that this same German spy is captured on page 256, sentenced on page 258, shot on page 281, and buried without honours on page 285. Your patriotic soul, forsooth, probably soars into the very empyrean on discovering that so dastardly a criminal has come to so judicious and timely an end. But as an artist, as a critic, even as an intelligent reader, do you care a whit whether Schmidt is dead or alive? You do not. For as an artist, as a critic, or as an intelligent reader your politics are neither German nor American, and your morals are as international as the sun. You may be incidentally pleased over the vindication of some of your personal beliefs. But this pleasure is merely the pleasure of the patriot and the moralizer. In so far as you are an artist your delight is solely in the clash of idea with idea, the impact of personality on personality, and the battle of creed against creed. And you realize that to demand the downfall of iniquity and the triumph of good, as most of our critics are fond of doing, is equivalent to saying that minor keys in music are very sad, that sadness often leads to suicide, and that Beethoven's Fifth Symphony, being in the minor mode, should therefore be suppressed at once because it tends to depopulate the world.

Such juvenile standards of art criticism are not merely prevalent in this country: they are well-nigh universal. Fortunately, for every war there is a hero, for every Hellespont there is a Leander, and at every critical feast there is at least one guest who knows how to handle a fork. Mr. Mencken's table manners are frequently astonishing to the *epigoni* of letters, but his skill in disposing of current literature by the mouthful is so obviously neat and effective as to disarm reproach with admiration. Finding the fare good, he has bluntly shaken his head in approval; finding the fare tolerable, he has eaten it with a growl; finding the fare atrocious, he has overturned the table entirely and brought all the china crashing to the floor. His critical vehemence is sometimes alarming. But it always is healthy, for it bespeaks an insatiable appetite for nourishment, as well as an open demand for the best in the larder, that seldom has been exhibited either this side of the Atlantic or of the Nineteenth Century. The author of Prejudices realizes that to err is human. He knows, also, that critically to forgive is asinine. Therefore he never forgives, never cleans his plate for the sake of good form, never makes pretty farewell speeches about having had a good time. If the food pleases him—as it does occasionally—he eats it at once and holds out his plate for more. If it displeases him, on the contrary—and this happens less occasionally—he rejects it straightway and stormily goes home to bed. And if the world hears promptly of his pleasure, the very stars are made privy to his pain.

There is, as I have said, refreshing honesty in this thunderous approval and denunciation of current American literature. It is honesty, moreover, that has seldom been matched either here or abroad. Poe, grinding his heel in the dust to hollow out a grave for Longfellow, was not more courageous than Mr. Mencken, who has struck down by name any of his contemporaries whom he considers silly, weak, or ephemeral. Nor is his onslaught merely brutal. His bludgeon is fitted with a keen blade. If he lived in the Eighteenth Century and wrote with a quill, he would, one feels, be sharpening it constantly. His opinions are edged with a remarkably penetrating style; and there is weight behind his blow no less certainly than there is a knife in front of his axe-head.

With such critical equipment a man is certain to travel far. That Mr. Mencken has travelled farther in his examination of present-day literatures than any other American, excepting perhaps Mr. Huneker, is a statement which only the timid would end with an interrogation mark and only the blind would not begin at all. That he suffers from a defect, however, which cripples many of his judgements and warps no inconsiderable part of his views is a statement which equally demands the light. And the humour and tragedy of this particular shortcoming are born of the fact that the very evil of Puritanism which Mr. Mencken continually embattles has infected him locally with a disease which, if less dangerous, is no less virulent than the one he is seeking to destroy. It is almost as though, going forth to kill the typhus germ, he had inadvertently contracted malaria of the soul. His actual theories of criticism are sound; and his elucidation of the holy business of critics, at the beginning of the volume, is as compact and forceful an example of zetetical writing as his later review of Elsie Clews Parsons' Fear and Conventionality, and his mordant exposure of Clayton Hamilton. It is when he sets out to apply these theories that all his pent-up hatred of Presbyterianism, Puritanism, and the seven deadly virtues comes gushing out in a stream of blinding indignation. There is not room here, unfortunately, to notice the men he douses under it or the paradoxical manner in which the hose sometimes gets partially turned on himself. I can only advise you to read the book through for yourself, turning to page 16, where he observes, outraged, that "'This girl is pretty,' says the artist. 'But she has left off her undershirt,' protests the head-master," and do your own wondering as to whether or not, if Mr. Mencken took a part in the conversation, it would not run: "'This girl is pretty,' says the artist. 'But she has put her undershirt on!'"

Or, turning to page 26, conclude for yourself if a critic, reviewing the later novels of H. G. Wells, and announcing that "once a critic begins to suffer from a messianic delusion his days as a serious artist are ended," might not with equal propriety develop that aesthetic formula and state frankly that "once a critic begins to suffer from a diabolic delusion his days as a bigoted critic are begun."

But these exterior flaws, after all, are more the flaws of critical vehemence than of actual critical vice. They mar the surface of Mr. Mencken's prejudices, but they are cracks which give outer indications of an internal, high-pressure revolt against the stupidities of the day. They show that his prejudices, inside, are really opinions.

Those opinions are not always tempered with tolerance, and his defence of the Goethe-Arnold-Spingarn-Croce theory of aesthetics sometimes talks so loud, as Emerson would have put it, that you cannot quite hear what it says. But again this is probably less Mr. Mencken's fault than the fault of the land and age in which he lives. In a country which has produced little art you cannot expect much criticism of art that is sober, mature, or restrained. In such a land you should be grateful if occasionally you discover one more man who, if only at times, is content to hang the crystal globes of literature in his window and say, looking at them without rancour and with very little impatience, "Je n'impose rien; Je ne purpose rien; J'expose."

Stuart P. Sherman's review of Prejudices: First Series *appeared in* The New York Times Book Review *and was reprinted in a collection of his essays. Unapologetic for his ad hominem attack on* A Book of Prefaces, *the jingoistic "Beautifying American Literature" (1917; see pp. 130–133, above), Sherman manages to document, in his hatred, much of what Mencken stood for: realism, antipuritanism, Anglophobia, Germanophilia, and destructive criticism. Moreover, the review is a sweeping denunciation and bitter caricature of the youths who sought intellectual leadership from Mencken ("Mr. Mencken, the Jeune Fille, and the New Spirit in Letters," in Sherman,* Americans *[New York: Scribners, 1922], pp. 1–12).*

A woman whose husband has made money in the war likes to have her portrait painted and her friends coming in to admire it. So a new public, grown conscious of itself, demands a new literature and a new literature demands a new criticism. Fine gentlemen with a touch of frost above the temples, sitting at ease in quiet old clubs under golden-brown portraits of their ancestors, and turning the pages of the *Athenæum* or Mr. More's *Nation,* have seen with disdainful yet apprehensive glance through plate-glass windows the arrival of all three: the formation of a reading public of which they are not a part, the appearance of a literature which they do not care to read, the development of a criticism in which their views are not represented. Since a critic is of no importance except with reference to what he criticizes, you will please bear with me while I bring in the new literature and the new readers. When the stage is properly set, Mr. Mencken will appear.

How shall one indicate the color and spirit of it?– this new public now swarming up the avenues of democratic opportunity; becoming prosperous, self-conscious, voluble; sunning itself in the great cities; reaching out greedily to realize its "legitimate aspirations." This latest generation of Americans, so vulgar and selfish and good-humored and sensual and impudent, shows little trace of the once dominant Puritan stock and nothing of the Puritan temper. It is curiously and richly composed of the children of parents who dedicated themselves to accumulation, and toiling inarticulately in shop and field, in forest and mine, never fully mastered the English definite article or the personal pronoun. It is composed of children whose parents or grandparents brought their copper kettles from Russia, tilled the soil of Hungary, taught the Mosaic law in Poland, cut Irish turf, ground optical glass in Germany, dispensed Bavarian beer, or fished for mackerel around the Skagerrack. The young people laugh at the oddities of their forbears, discard the old kettles, the Mosaic Law, the provincial dialect, the Lutheran pastor. Into the new society breaking without cultural inheritance, they derive all their interests and standards from their immediate environment, and gravitate towards refinement through more and more expensive gratifications of the senses.

The prettiest type of this swift civilization–and I must have something pretty to enliven a discourse on current criticism–the prettiest type is the *jeune fille,* who, to modernize the phrase of an old poet, aspires to a soul in silken hosiery and doeskin boots. She springs, this young creature with ankles sheathed and shod like a Virginia deer–ankles whose trimness is, aesthetically speaking, quite the finest thing her family has produced in America–she springs from a grandmother who clumped out in wooden shoes to milk a solitary cow in Sweden. She has no soul, the young thing, but she trusts that the tailor, the milliner, the bootmaker, the manicurist, the hairdresser, and the masseuse can give her an equivalent. Wherever art can work on her surfaces, she is finished. When the car is at the door in the morning–"a distinctive body on a distinguished *chassis*"–and she runs down the steps with somewhat more than a flash of her silken perfections, she is exquisite, what though the voice is a bit hard and shrill with which she calls out, "H'lo, kiddo! Le's go't Brentano's."

She is indeed coming–the new reader! She will bring home an armful of magazines, smelling deliciously of the press, books with exciting yellow jackets, plays newly translated and imported, the latest stories, the most recent ideas, all set forth in the current fashion, and all, as it will seem to her, about herself, her sort of people, her sort of world, and about the effort which her fair young ego is making to emerge from the indiscriminated mass and to acquire physical form and line congruous with that "distinctive body mounted on a distinguished chassis," which bears her with such smooth speed up Riverside Drive. She will have no American literature of the "classical period" in her library; for the New England worthies who produced it wrote before the public of which she is a part began to read or to be noticed in books. The *jeune fille,* though a votary of physical form, feels within herself an exhilarating chaos, a fluent welter, which Lowell and Longfellow and James and Howells do not, but which her writers must, express.

Therefore, she revels in the English paradoxers and mountebanks, the Scandinavian misanthropes, the German egomaniacs, and, above all, in the later Russian novelists, crazy with war, taxes, hunger, anarchy, vodka, and German philosophy. She does enjoy, however, the posthumous pessimism of Mark Twain—it is "so strong and virile"; and she relishes his pilot oaths—they are "so sincere and unconventional." She savors Mr. Masters' hard little naturalistic sketches of "passion" on Michigan Boulevard; they remind her of her brother. Sherwood Anderson has a place on her shelves; for by the note of revolt in *Winesburg, Ohio* she recognizes one of her own spirit's deserted villages. Lured by a primitive instinct to the sound of animals roving, she ventures a curious foot into the fringes of the Dreiserian wilderness vast and drear; and barbaric impulses in her blood "answer the wail of the forest." She is not much "intrigued" by the frosty fragilities of imagist verse; but at Sandburg's viking salute to the Hog-Butcher of the World she claps her hands and cries: "Oh, boy, isn't it gorgeous!" This welter of her "culture" she plays, now and then, at organizing on some strictly modern principle, such as her father applies to his business, such as her brother applies to his pleasures—a principle of egotistical combat, a principle of self-indulgence, cynical and luxurious. She is not quite happy with the result. Sometimes, I imagine, she wishes that her personal attendants, those handmen and maidens who have wrought so wonderfully with her surfaces, could be set at work upon her interior, so that her internal furnishing and decoration could be brought into measurable concord with the grace and truth of her contours, the rhythm of her hair.

Imagine a thousand *jeunes filles* thus wistful, and you have the conditions ready for the advent of a new critic. At this point enters at a hard gallop, spattered with mud, H. L. Mencken high in oath—thus justifying the Goethean maxim: *Aller Anfang ist schwer.* He leaps

from the saddle with sabre flashing, stables his horse in the church, shoots the priest, hangs the professors, exiles the Academy, burns the library and the university, and, amid the smoking ashes, erects a new school of criticism on modern German principles, which he traces through Spingarn to Goethe, but which I should be inclined to trace rather to Eckermann.

Of my own inability to interpret modern Germany, however, I have recently been painfully reminded by an 86-page pamphlet sent to me from Hamburg, with blue-pencil marks kindly inserted by the author, one Hansen—apparently a German-Schleswigian-American who has studied rhetoric in Mr. Mencken's school—inquiring what the masses can possibly know of the real Germany, "so long as the Shermans squat like toads in the portals of the schools and the Northcliffes send their Niagaras of slime through the souls of the English-speaking peoples." I was amused, of course, to find a great lord of the press so quaintly bracketed with an obscure teacher of literature in a Middle Western university as an effective obstacle between the sunlight and Germany. All the same, my conscience was touched; and I remembered with satisfaction that, on the appearance of Mr. Mencken's *Prefaces,* I made a conscientious effort to tell my countrymen where they should go, namely, to Mr. Mencken, if they desired a really sympathetic presentation of the modern Teutonic point of view with reference to politics, religion, morals, women, beer, and *belles-lettres.*

On the appearance of Mr. Mencken's new volume, *Prejudices*—continuing my humble service as guide to what I am not thoroughly qualified to appreciate—I can only say that here I find again the Nietzschean "aristocrat" of yesteryear, essentially unchanged. He is a little sadder, perhaps, since democracy has unhorsed the autocrats; but his skepticism of democracy is unshaken. He is a shade more cynical since the extension of women's suffrage; but he is as clear as ever that he knows what girls were made for. He is a little more sober since the passage of the national prohibition act, and a bit less lyrical about the Pilsener-motive in the writings of Mr. Huneker; but, come rain or shine, he still points with pride to a digestion ruined by alcohol. In other respects, former patrons of his school for beautifying American letters will find his familiar manners and customs essentially unaltered.

If we are to have a Menckenian academy, Mr. Mencken shows the way to set it up—with vigor and rigor, with fist and foot, with club and axe. The crash of smashed things, the knocking of heads together, the objurgations which accompany his entrance have a high advertising value, fascinating to all the gamins of the press and attractive to our *jeune fille,* who will pay for a copy of *Prejudices* and form her taste upon it. And far be it from me to deny that she may learn something from her heavy-handed disciplinarian. Mr. Mencken, like most men, has his merits, of which it is a pleasure to speak. He is alive; this is a merit in a good man and hardly a defect even in a bad critic. He has a rough, prodding wit, blunted by thrusting at objects which it cannot pierce, but yet a wit. He is passionately addicted to scoffing; and if by chance a sham that is obnoxious to him comes in his way, he will scoff at a sham. He has no inclination to the softer forms of "slush" or to the more diaphanous varieties of "pishposh." He has a style becoming a retired military man—hard, pointed, forcible, cocksure. He likes a sentence stripped of baggage, and groups of sentences that march briskly off at the word of command, wheel, continue to march, and, at word of command, with equal precision, halt. He has the merits of an efficient rhetorical drill-sergeant. By his services in pointing out to our fair barbarian that she need not, after all, read Mr. Veblen, she should acknowledge that he has earned the royalty on her copy of *Prejudices*. He has given her, in short, what she might expect to get from a stiff freshman course in rhetoric.

When he has told her who fits sentences together well and who ill, he has ended the instruction that was helpful to her. He can give her lessons in derision, lessons in cynicism, lessons in contempt; but she was mistress of all these when she entered his school. He can offer to free her from attachment to English and American literary traditions; but she was never attached to these traditions. He will undertake to make her believe that Baptists and Methodists, professors and academicians, prohibition societies and marriage covenants are ridiculous; but she always thought them ridiculous. He is ready to impregnate her mind with the wisdom of "old Friedrich," Stirner, Strindberg, and the rest of the crew; but her mind is already impregnated with that sort of wisdom. "When one has turned away from the false and the soft and the silly," this is the question she is asking, "where does one go to find true and beautiful things?" She has heard somewhere by chance, poor girl, that one who pursues truth and beauty is delivered from the grosser tyrannies of the senses, escapes a little out of the inner welter and discovers serenity widening like a fair dawn in the land, with a certain blitheness and amenity. This is æsthetic liberation.

For one seeking æsthetic liberation there is a canon of things to be thought on which the worldliest of sound critics, Sainte-Beuve, pronounced as clearly and insistently as Saint Paul. The Germans, as the great Goethe explained to the saucer-eyed Eckermann, are "weak on the æsthetic side." Aesthetic appreciation is superficially an affair of the palate, and at bottom an affair of the heart, embracing with elation whatsoever things are lovely. Mr.

Mencken has no heart; and if he ever had a palate he has lost it in protracted orgies of literary "strong drink." He turns with anguish from the pure and simple flavors that please children as the first gifts of nature, and that delight great critics as the last achievements of art. His appetite craves a fierce stimulation of sauces, a flamboyance and glitter of cheeses, the sophisticated and appalling ripeness of wild duck nine days old.

He devotes, for example, two pages to leading the *jeune fille* away from Emerson as a writer of no influence. He spends several more in showing her that Howells has nothing to say. He warns her that Mr. Garland's *Son of the Middle Border* is amateurish, flat, banal, and repellant. He gives a condescending *coup de pied* to the solider works of Arnold Bennett and singles out for intense admiration a scarlet-lattice scene or so in his pot-boilers. As the author of a work on the American language, over-ambitiously designed as a wedge to split asunder the two great English-speaking peoples, and as an advocate of an "intellectual aristocracy," it has suddenly occurred to him that we have been shamefully neglecting the works of George Ade; accordingly, he strongly commends to our younger generation the works of Mr. George Ade. But the high light and white flame of his appreciation falls upon three objects as follows: the squalid story of an atrocious German bar-maid by Sudermann; an anonymous autobiographical novel, discovered by Mr. Mencken himself, which exhibits "an eternal blue-nose with every wart and pimple glittering," and is "as devoid of literary sophistication as an operation for gallstones"; and, third and last, the works of Mr. Mencken's partner, Mr. George Jean Nathan, with his divine knack at making phrases "to flabbergast a dolt."

I imagine my bewildered seeker for æsthetic liberation asking her mentor if studying these things will help her to form "the diviner mind." "Don't bother me now," exclaims Mr. Mencken; "don't bother me now. I am just striking out a great phrase. Aesthetic effort tones up the mind with a kind of high excitement. I shall say in the next number of the *Smart Set* that James Harlan was the *damnedest ass* that America ever produced. If you don't know him, look him up. In the second edition of my book on the American language I shall add a new verb—to *Menckenize*—and perhaps a new noun, *Menckenism*. The definition of these words will clear up matters for you, and summarize my contribution to the national *belles-lettres*. It is beginning to take—the spirit is beginning to spread."

While Mr. Mencken and the *jeune fille* are engaged in this chat on the nature of beauty, I fancy the horn of a "high-powered" automobile is heard from the street before the Menckenian school. And in bursts Mr. Francis Hackett, looking like a man who has just performed a long and difficult operation under the body of his car, though, as a matter of fact, he has only just completed a splashing, shirt-sleeve review for *The New Republic.* "Let's wash up," cries Mr. Hackett, stripping off his blouse of blue jeans, "and go out to luncheon."

"Where shall we *fressen?*" says Mr. Mencken.

"At the Loyal Independent Order of United Hiberno-German-Anti-English-Americans," says Mr. Hackett. "All the New Critics will be there. Colum, Lewisohn, Wright, and the rest. I tried to get Philip Littell to come along. He's too gol darned refined. But I've got a chap in the car, from the West, that will please you. Used to run a column in the World's Greatest. Calls Thomas Arnold of Rugby 'that thrice-damned boor and noodle.'"

"Good!" Mr. Mencken exclaims. "A Menckenism! A Menckenism! A likely chap!" And out they both bolt.

The *jeune fille,* with a thoughtful backward glance at Mr. Hackett's blouse, goes slowly down into the street, and, strolling up the walk in the crisp early winter air, overtakes Mr. Littell, who is strolling even more slowly. He is reading a book, on which the first snowflake of the year has fallen, and, as it falls, he looks up with such fine delight in his eye that she asks him what has pleased him.

"A thought," he replies gently, "phrased by a subtle writer and set in a charming essay by a famous critic. Listen: "*Où il n'y a point de délicatesse, il n'y a point de littérature.*" *[(Footnote)* Translated: "When one begins to Menckenize, the spirit of good literature flees in consternation."*]*

"That's a new one on me," says the *jeune fille.*

The New Humanist critic Irving Babbitt, who attacked Mencken's antipuritan views in the journal The Forum *in 1928 (photograph by Notman Photo Co.)*

In Mencken's analysis, neopuritanism took hold especially among the lowly, but, as he wrote in 1934, it was finally about envy and power (excerpt from Treatise on Right and Wrong, *pp. 269–270).*

[. . .] The neo-Puritanism which prevails in rural America makes a powerful appeal to men at the bottom of the human ladder, for it makes virtues of the abstinences that fate forces upon them, and permits them to feel pleasantly superior to their betters. Thus a Baptist rustic in Mississippi is consoled when he compares his wife to the houris he sees in the movies, or the white mule he swigs behind the barndoor to the hellish wines consumed in New York. His guides spiritual and moral, in the main, are hinds like himself, and have little learning, even in theology. It does not daunt them when their theorizings bring them into plain conflict with the text of Holy Writ, as happened in the case of Prohibition. There are few of them who do not pretend, by inference if not explicitly, to be better than Jesus. What animates them is mainly an insatiable thirst for power: it explains their frequent excursions into politics, and their general lack of conscience. When Bishop James Cannon, Jr., taken in flagrant stock gambling, protested that he had no love for money *per se,* he was laughed at by many, yet he probably told the truth. He wanted money simply to increase and consolidate his already for-

midable power, both ecclesiastical and political—in his own jargon, to extend the Kingdom. Cadging money from the faithful, among his colleagues of the evangelical sects, is always spoken of as "Kingdom work." No wonder they are all fond (as the bishop himself is) of quoting John Wesley's sermon on money, beginning "Make all you can." For it not only justifies their own insatiable demands for more and more of it; it also gives a flavor of piety to the practices of their chief lay supporters, who are the bankers and industrialists of the Bible country. Whenever there has been a strike of millhands down there the local evangelical clergy have been almost unanimously in favor of the employers, and for a sound reason: the employers build their churches and pay their salaries. [. . .]

Firing the first shot in what is known as the Humanist counterattack, Irving Babbitt aimed at Mencken's subjectivity and at his conception of classical puritanism. In the process, Babbitt condemned the very outlook on life that made possible the kind of realism and naturalism that

Mencken promoted (excerpts from "The Critic and American Life," Forum, 79 *[February 1928]: 161–176).*

A frequent remark of the French about Americans is: "They're children"; which, interpreted, means that from the French point of view Americans are childishly uncritical. The remark is relevant only in so far as it refers to general critical intelligence. In dealing with the special problems of a commercial and industrial society Americans have shown that they can be abundantly critical. Certain Americans, for example, have developed a critical keenness in estimating the value of stocks and bonds that is nothing short of uncanny. The very persons, however, who are thus keen in some particular field are, when confronted with questions that call for general critical intelligence, often puerile. Yet in an age like the present, which is being subjected to a constant stream of propaganda in everything from the choice of its religion to its cigarettes, general critical intelligence would seem desirable.

As a matter of fact, most persons nowadays aspire to be not critical but creative. We have not merely creative poets and novelists, but creative readers and listeners and dancers. Lately a form of creativeness has appeared that may in time swallow up all the others—creative salesmanship. The critic himself has caught the contagion and also aspires to be creative. He is supposed to become so when he receives from the creation of another, conceived as pure temperamental overflow, so vivid an impression that, when passed through his temperament, it issues forth as a fresh creation. What is eliminated in both critic and creator is any standard that is set above temperament and that therefore might interfere with their eagerness to get themselves expressed.

This notion of criticism as self-expression is important for our present subject, for it has been adopted by the writer who is, according to the last edition of the *Encyclopædia Britannica,* "the greatest critical force in America"–Mr. H. L. Mencken. "The critic is first and last," says Mr. Mencken, "simply trying to express himself; he is trying to achieve thereby for his own inner ego the grateful feeling of a function performed, a tension relieved, a katharsis attained which Wagner achieved when he wrote *Die Walküre,* and a hen achieves every time she lays an egg." This creative self-expression, as practiced by himself and others, has, according to Mr. Mencken, led to a salutary stirring up of the stagnant pool of American letters: "To-day for the first time in years, there is strife in American criticism. . . . Heretics lay on boldly and the professors are forced to make some defence. Often going further they attempt counterattacks. Ears are bitten off, noses are bloodied. There are wallops both above and below the belt."

But it may be that criticism is something more than Mr. Mencken would have us believe, more in short than a squabble between Bohemians, each eager to capture the attention of the public for his brand of self-expression. To reduce criticism indeed to the satisfaction of a temperamental urge, to the uttering of one's gustos and disgustos (in Mr. Mencken's case chiefly the latter) is to run counter to the very etymology of the word which implies discrimination and judgment. The best one would anticipate from a writer like Mr. Mencken, possessing an unusual verbal virtuosity and at the same time temperamentally irresponsible, is superior intellectual vaudeville. One must grant him, however, certain genuine critical virtues–for example, a power of shrewd observation within rather narrow limits. Yet the total effect of his writing is nearer to intellectual vaudeville than to serious criticism.

The serious critic is more concerned with achieving a correct scale of values and so seeing things proportionately than with self-expression. His essential virtue is poise. The specific benefit he confers is to act as a moderating influence on the opposite insanities between which mankind in the lump is constantly tending to oscillate–oscillations that Luther compares to the reelings of a drunken peasant on horseback. The critic's survey of any particular situation may very well seem satirical. The complaint that Mr. Mencken is too uniformly disgruntled in his survey of the American situation rather misses the point. Behind the pleas for more constructiveness it is usually easy to detect the voice of the booster. A critic who did not get beyond a correct diagnosis of existing evils might be very helpful. If Mr. Mencken has fallen short of being such a diagnostician, the failure is due not to his excess of severity but to his lack of discrimination.

The standards with reference to which men have discriminated in the past have been largely traditional. The outstanding fact of the present period, on the other hand, has been the weakening of traditional standards. An emergency has arisen not unlike that with which Socrates sought to cope in ancient Athens. Anyone who is untraditional and seeks at the same time to be discriminating must almost necessarily own Socrates as his master. As is well known, Socrates sought above all to be discriminating in his use of general terms. The importance of the art of inductive defining that he devised may perhaps best be made clear by bringing together two sayings, one of Napoleon–"Imagination governs mankind"–and one of John Selden–"Syllables govern mankind." Before allowing one's imagination and finally one's conduct to be controlled by a general term, it would seem wise to submit it to a Socratic scrutiny.

It is, therefore, unfortunate that at a time like the present, which plainly calls for a Socrates, we should instead have got a Mencken. One may take as an example of Mr. Mencken's failure to discriminate adequately, his attitude toward the term that for several generations past has been governing the imagination of multitudes—democracy. His view of democracy is simply that of Rousseau turned upside down, and nothing, as has been remarked, resembles a hollow so much as a swelling. A distinction of which he has failed to recognize the importance is that between a direct or unlimited and a constitutional democracy. In the latter we probably have the best thing in the world. The former, on the other hand, as all thinkers of any penetration from Plato and Aristotle down have perceived, leads to the loss of liberty and finally to the rise of some form of despotism. The two conceptions of democracy involve not merely incompatible views of government but ultimately of human nature. The desire of the constitutional democrat for institutions that act as checks on the immediate will of the people implies a similar dualism in the individual—a higher self that acts restrictively on his ordinary and impulsive self. The partisan of unlimited democracy on the other hand is an idealist in the sense of that the term assumed in connection with the so-called romantic movement. His faith in the people is closely related to the doctrine of natural goodness proclaimed by the sentimentalists of the eighteenth century and itself marking an extreme recoil from the dogma of total depravity. The doctrine of natural goodness favors the free temperamental expansion that I have already noticed in speaking of the creative critic.

It is of the utmost importance, however, if one is to understand Mr. Mencken, to discriminate between two types of temperamentalist—the soft and sentimental type, who cherishes various "ideals," and the hard, or Nietzschean type, who piques himself on being realistic. As a matter of fact, if one sees in the escape from traditional controls merely an opportunity to live temperamentally, it would seem advantageous to pass promptly from the idealistic to the Nietzschean phase, sparing oneself as many as possible of the intermediary disillusions. It is at all events undeniable that the rise of Menckenism has been marked by a certain collapse of romantic idealism in the political field and elsewhere. The numerous disillusions that have supervened upon the War have provided a favoring atmosphere.

The symptoms of Menckenism are familiar: a certain hardness and smartness and disposition to rail at everything that, rightly or wrongly, is established and respected; a tendency to identify the real with what Mr. Mencken terms "the cold and clammy facts" and to assume that the only alternative to facing these facts is to fade away into sheer romantic unreality. These and similar traits are becoming so widely diffused that, whatever one's opinion of Mr. Mencken as a writer and thinker, one must grant him representativeness. He is a chief prophet at present of those who deem themselves emancipated but who are, according to Mr. Brownell, merely unbuttoned.

The crucial point in any case is one's attitude toward the principle of control. Those who stand for this principle in any form or degree are dismissed by the emancipated as reactionaries or, still graver reproach, as Puritans. Mr. Mencken would have us believe that the historical Puritan was not even sincere in his moral rigorism, but was given to "lamentable transactions with loose women and fiery jugs." This may serve as a sample of the assertions, picturesquely indiscriminate, by which a writer wins immediate notoriety at the expense of his permanent reputation. The facts about the Puritan happen to be complex and need to be dealt with very Socratically. It has been affirmed that the point of view of the Puritan was Stoical rather than truly Christian, and the affirmation is not wholly false. The present discussion of the relationship between Puritanism and the rise of capitalism with its glorification of the acquisitive life also has its justification. It is likewise a fact that the Puritan was from the outset unduly concerned with reforming others as well as himself, and this trait relates him to the humanitarian meddler or "wowser" of the present day, who is Mr. Mencken's pet aversion.

Yet it remains true that awe and reverence and humility are Christian virtues and that there was some survival of these virtues in the Puritan. For a representative Puritan like Jonathan Edwards they were inseparable from the illumination of grace from what he terms "a divine and supernatural light." In the passage from the love and fear of God of an Edwards to the love and service of man professed by the humanitarian, something has plainly dropped out, something that is very near the centre. What has tended to disappear is the inner life with the special type of control it imposes. With the decline of this inner control there has been an increasing resort to outer control. Instead of the genuine Puritan we then have the humanitarian legalist who passes innumerable laws for the control of people who refuse to control themselves. The activity of our uplifters is scarcely suggestive of any "divine and supernatural light." Here is a discrimination of the first importance that has been obscured by the muddy thinking of our half-baked intelligentsia. One is thus kept from perceiving the real problem, which is to retain the inner life, even though one refuse to accept the theological nightmare with which the Puritan associated it. More is involved in the failure to solve this problem than the Puritan tradition. It is the failure of our contemporary life in general. Yet, unless some solution is reached by a full and free exercise of the critical spirit, one remains a mere modernist and not a thoroughgoing and complete modern; for the modern spirit and the critical spirit are in their essence one.

What happens, when one sets out to deal with questions of this order without sufficient depth of reflection and critical maturity, may be seen in Mr. Sinclair Lewis's last novel. He has been lured from art into the writing of a wild diatribe which, considered even as such, is largely beside the mark. If the Protestant Church is at present threatened with bankruptcy, it is not because it has produced an occasional Elmer Gantry. The true reproach it has incurred is that, in its drift toward modernism, it has lost its grip not merely on certain dogmas but, simultaneously, on the facts of human nature. It has failed above all to carry over in some modern and critical form the truth of a dogma that unfortunately receives much support from these facts–the dogma of original sin. At first sight Mr. Mencken would appear to have a conviction of evil–when, for example, he reduces democracy in its essential aspect to a "combat between jackals and jackasses"–that establishes at least one bond between him and the austere Christian.

The appearance, however, is deceptive. The Christian is conscious above all of the "old Adam" in himself: hence his humility. The effect of Mr. Mencken's writing, on the other hand, is to produce pride rather than humility, a pride ultimately based on flattery. The reader, especially the young and callow reader, identifies himself imaginatively with Mr. Mencken and conceives of himself as a sort of morose and sardonic divinity surveying from some superior altitude an immeasurable expanse of "boobs." This attitude will not seem especially novel to anyone who has traced the modern movement. One is reminded in particular of Flaubert, who showed a diligence in collecting bourgeois imbecilities comparable to that displayed by Mr. Mencken in his *Americana*. Flaubert's discovery that one does not add to one's happiness in this way would no doubt be dismissed by Mr. Mencken as irrelevant, for he has told us that he does not believe in happiness. Another discovery of Flaubert's may seem to him more worthy of consideration. "By dint of railing at idiots," Flaubert reports, "one runs the risk of becoming idiotic oneself."

It may be that the only way to escape from the unduly complacent cynicism of Mr. Mencken and his school is to reaffirm once more the truths of the inner life. In that case it would seem desirable to disengage, so far as possible, the principle of control on which the inner life depends from mere creeds and traditions and assert it as a psychological fact; a fact, moreover,

that is neither "cold" nor "clammy." The coldness and clamminess of much so called realism arises from its failure to give this fact due recognition. A chief task, indeed, of the Socratic critic would be to rescue the noble term "realist" from its present degradation. A view of reality that overlooks the element in man that moves in an opposite direction from mere temperament, the specifically human factor in short, may prove to be singularly one-sided. Is the Puritan, John Milton, when he declares that "he who reigns within himself and rules passions, desires, and fears is more than a king," less real than Mr. Theodore Dreiser when he discourses in his peculiar dialect of "those rearranging chemisms upon which all the morality or immorality of the world is based"? [. . .]

One may illustrate from Mr. Dreiser's *American Tragedy,* hailed in certain quarters as the "Mt. Everest" of recent fiction. He has succeeded in producing in this work something genuinely harrowing; but one is harrowed to no purpose. One has in more than full measure the tragic qualm but without the final relief and enlargement of spirit that true tragedy succeeds somehow in giving, and that without resort to explicit moralizing. It is hardly worth while to struggle through eight hundred and more very pedestrian pages to be left at the end with a feeling of sheer oppression. The explanation of this oppression is that Mr. Dreiser does not rise sufficiently above the level of "rearranging chemisms," in other words, of animal behavior. Tragedy may admit fate–Greek tragedy admits it–but not of the naturalistic variety. Confusion on this point may compromise in the long run the reputation of writers more eminent than Mr. Dreiser–for example, of Thomas Hardy. Fatalism of the naturalistic type is responsible in large measure for the atmosphere of futility and frustration that hangs heavily over so much contemporary writing. One finally comes to feel with a recent poet that "dust" is the common source from which

stream

The cricket's cry and Dante's dream.

Anyone who admits reality only in what derives from the dust, whether in a cricket or a Dante, must, from the point of view of the religious or the humanistic realist, be prepared to make substantial sacrifices. In the first place, he must sacrifice the depth and subtlety that arise from the recognition in some form of the duality of man's nature. For the interest that may arise from the portrayal of the conflict between a law of the spirit and a law of the members, the inordinate interest in sex for its own sake promoted by most of the so-called realists is a rather shabby substitute. A merely naturalistic realism also involves the sacrifice of beauty in almost any sense of that elusive term. Closely related to this sacrifice is the sacrifice of delicacy, elevation, and distinction. The very word realism has come to connote the opposite of these qualities. When we learn, for example, that someone has written a realistic study of a great man, we are sure in advance that he has devoted his main effort to proving that "Plutarch lied." The more the great man is reduced to the level of commonplace or worse, the more we feel he has been "humanized."

Mr. Sherwood Anderson has argued ingeniously that, in as much as we ourselves are crude, our literature, if it is not to be unreal and factitious, should be crude likewise. But the writer who hopes to achieve work of importance cannot afford to be too deeply immersed in the atmosphere of the special place and passing moment. Still less can he afford to make us feel, as writers like Mr. Anderson and Mr. Dreiser and Mr. Sinclair Lewis do, that, if there were any lack of vulgarity in what they are depicting they would be capable of supplying the defect from their own abundance. More is involved here than mere loss of distinction. We have come, indeed, to the supreme sacrifice that every writer must make who does not transcend a naturalistic realism. He must forego the hope of the enduring appeal—the hope that every writer worthy of his salt cherishes in some degree. In the absence of humanistic or religious standards, he is prone to confound the real with the welter of the actual, and so to miss what Dr. Johnson terms the "grandeur of generality." [. . .]

A genuinely critical survey would make manifest that the unsatisfactoriness of our creative effort is due to a lack of the standards that culture alone can supply. Our cultural crudity and insignificance can be traced in turn to the inadequacy of our education, especially our higher education. Mr. Mencken's attack on the "professors" is therefore largely justified; for if the professors were performing their function properly Mr. Mencken himself would not be possible. [. . .]

As it is, our institutions of learning seem to be becoming more and more hotbeds of "idealism." Their failure, on the whole, to achieve standards as something quite distinct from ideals on the one hand, and standardization on the other, may prove a fact of sinister import for the future of American civilization. The warfare that is being waged at the present time by Mr. Sinclair Lewis and others against a standardized Philistinism continues in the main the protest that has been made for several generations past by the temperamentalists, hard or soft, against the mechanizing of life by the utilitarian. This protest has been, and is likely to continue to be, ineffectual. The fruitful opposite of the standardized Philistine is not the Bohemian, nor again the hard temperamentalist or superman, as Mr. Mencken conceives him, but the man of leisure. Leisure involves an inner effort with reference to standards that is opposed to the sheer

The conservative critic Paul Elmer More, mentioned in Mencken's review of T. S. Eliot's For Lancelot Andrewes

expansion of temperament, as it is to every other form of sheer expansion. [. . .]

[. . .] My end has been accomplished if I have justified in some measure the statement with which I started as to the importance of cultivating a general critical intelligence. James Russell Lowell's dictum that before having an American literature we must have an American criticism was never truer than it is to-day. The obvious reply to those who call for more creation and less criticism is that one needs to be critical above all in examining what now passes for creation. A scrutiny of this kind would, I have tried to show, extend beyond the bounds of literature to various aspects of our national life and would converge finally on our higher education.

We cannot afford to accept as a substitute for this true criticism the self-expression of Mr. Mencken and his school, unless indeed we are to merit the comment that is, I am told, made on us by South Americans: "They are not a very serious people!" To be sure, the reader may reflect that I am myself a critic, or would-be critic. I can only express the hope that, in my magnifying of the critical function, I do not offer too close a parallel to the dancing-master

DITHYRAMBS ON ALCOHOL

BY

H. L. MENCKEN

Envy of the other fellow lies at the root of all prohibition legislation, insists H. L. Mencken, chanting the praise of potable alcohol for its contentment-bringing qualities. Even excessive drinking has its high uses, the satirist argues, since a man who yields to it is a man the world is well rid of.

Title page for an unauthorized collection of four Mencken pieces opposing prohibition (1918)

in Molière who averred, it will be remembered, that "all the mistakes of men, the fatal reverses that fill the world's annals, the shortcomings of statesmen, and the blunders of great captains arise from not knowing how to dance."

Among Mencken's replies was this review of T. S. Eliot's For Lancelot Andrewes *("The New Humanism," American* Mercury, *18 [September 1929]: 123–124).*

In this little volume Mr. Eliot lets a pale and chromovitreous but none the less searching light into the pseudo-Humanism which now enchants so many young American college professors, with Professor Irving Babbitt serving as its Bishop Cannon, Dr. Paul Elmer More as its Mrs. Willebrandt, and the late Stuart P. Sherman as its martyred Wayne B. Wheeler. What is revealed, of course, is what everyone unaffected by the movement knew was there all the while, namely, a somewhat sickly and shame-faced Christian mysticism. The Humanist of the current model, at his best, is what Mr. Eliot seems to be himself: a natural

Catholic who finds it impossible to swallow a church ruled by an Italian paleographer and so compromises on one ruled (at least transiently) by a Scotch labor agitator. At his worst, he is what Dr. Sherman was: a rustic Methodist somewhat flustered by what passes for learning among us, but still unable to throw off the feeling that all city men are sinful and will go to Hell. At one place, with sly humor, Mr. Eliot compares Professor Babbitt to Socrates. "How far Socrates believed," he says, "and whether his legendary request of the sacrifice of a cock was merely gentlemanly behavior or even irony, we cannot tell; but the equivalent would be Professor Babbitt receiving extreme unction, and that I cannot at present conceive." This, plainly enough, is a figure of speech: its name, unless I forget my schoolbooks, is antiphrasis. I herewith predict formally that Dr. Babbitt, when his time comes, will heave his Phi Beta Kappa key out of the window and demand the holy oils—that is, if the clergy of the Presbyterian rite administer them. For he is not only a Christian, his protestations to the contrary notwithstanding; he is also a Calvinist, though he may not know it. So are all the other hortatory pedagogues, including Dr. Robert A. Millikan, the reconciler of Einstein and the International Sunday-school Lessons. To call such denizens of the catacombs Humanists is as absurd as it would be to call Mr. Chief Justice Taft a Liberal.

Mr. Eliot began life as one of Professor Babbitt's disciples, but hard study at the British Museum convinced him that the current Humanism was full of buncombe. His present point of view, he says, "may be described as classicist in literature, royalist in politics, and Anglo-Catholic in religion." Parts of this, as he himself confesses, are vague and savor of clap-trap; it is hard, for example, to think of the author of "The Waste Land" as a genuine classicist. But on the religious side there is no reason to doubt the author's seriousness. He proves it by exhuming various sacerdotal obscurities from oblivion, and arguing gravely that they were profound thinkers—nay, even gifted stylists. The enterprise is not new; I have heard Christian Scientists maintain that even Mrs. Eddy was a sound writer. But Mr. Eliot carries it off with more than the usual grace, for he writes very effectively himself, and is full of that odd and useless learning which gives an air of persuasiveness to otherwise bald and unconvincing disputation. For one, I remain unconvinced that either Bishop Andrewes or his brother Bramhall could write, but I confess that reading about them was pleasant, and did me no harm.

It is, however, when he discusses religion *per se* that Mr. Eliot is at his best. The failure of the so-called Humanists to get rid of it plainly delights him, as his exposure of that failure must delight the more malicious sort of reader. The moment they begin to lay down their cock-sure rules as to what is virtuous and what is not, they find themselves, willy nilly, toying with a concept of the will of God, and the moment they admit that concept to their exhortations and

Mencken at NBC in New York for his radio interview on beer, 1933 (courtesy of the Enoch Pratt Free Library)

objurgations "then some doctrine of Grace must be admitted too." The rest is a primrose path, and at the end lies a state church–maybe not the political Methodism which now afflicts the United States, but nevertheless a church. Some of the Humanists peer longingly through the area windows of Rome; others, like Mr. Eliot himself, succumb to the imperial pomps of the Anglican communion; yet others, such as Dr. Millikan, bring all their compromises to a head by embracing the arch-compromise of Unitarianism. As for Professor Babbitt, "his Humanism is, . . . to my mind, alarmingly like the very Liberal Protestant theology of the Nineteenth Century; it is, in fact, a product–a by-product–of Protestant theology in its last agonies." I can imagine no definition of the movement which would define it more precisely.

While it was necessary, the "ombibulous" Mencken laid in a huge supply of alcohol, had a network of "booticians" to accommodate him in his travels, and crusaded against the ultimate neopuritan attempt at control in this country: Prohibition. It drove him to the kind of satiric hyperbole that left him open to attacks like Babbitt's, as in this piece ("Real Issues at Last," Baltimore Evening Sun, *23 July 1928, editorial page).*

[. . .] Prohibition is essentially a yokel idea. It mirrors alike the farmer's fear of himself and his envy of city men. Unable to drink at all without making a hog of himself, he naturally hates those who can. When a city man goes on a grand drunk, the police take charge of him humanely and he is restrained from doing any great damage. The worst that happens to him is that his wife beats him and he loses his job. But when a farmer succumbs to the jug his unmilked cows burst, his hogs and chickens starve, his pastor denounces him as an atheist (or even an Episcopalian), and he is ruined. Thus he favors Prohibition, especially if he is given to heavy drinking–first because he hopes it will protect him against himself, and secondly because it harasses his superior and enemy, the city man. [. . .]

The personal effects of the drought were remembered long afterward (excerpt from "The Noble Experiment," in Heathen Days, 1890–1936, *pp. 200–202).*

Prohibition went into effect on January 16, 1920, and blew up at last on December 5, 1933–an elapsed time of twelve years, ten months and nineteen days. It seemed almost a geological epoch while it was going on,

first draft — stenographic notes 1933

The six months of beer has been a sort of vaccination. They have got immunized to the old gin, and we can go directly from theory to fact and show that is true. It is a notorious fact that women are drinking beer now who were drinking gin up to last April.

M. B. C. Oct 18, 1933

This is true of women?

Yes, thousands and millions of them.

Is this true also of the young?

Reports from colleges are universally in one direction. Boys have got back to beer, which is a harmless drink. And there is another form of vaccination. They have got used to a relatively mild beer, much milder than bootleg beer. It tastes better, and experience shows it is safer, more salubrious beer. Brewmasters tell me there is no reason why they should make beer substantially stronger than 3.2. If it can be raised to 3.6 or 3.8 it might be better, and that beer would not be substantially more intoxicating than 3.2. We are on a beer diet. What bootleggers are going to discover to their horror is that their market is shot to pieces. Beer is safer and better. Probably the ideal beer would be about 3.6 or 3.7. That would enable them to get enough material in the beer to make any conceivable flavor within the limits of their skill, and at the same time wouldn't put in enough alcohol to make the beer dangerous for any rational person.

Is there any *relation between the* alcohol content of beer *and its taste or flavor?*

Yes. To some extent. Alcohol is one of the flavors of beer without any question. In addition, it is obvious the very

Page from the transcript of Mencken's beer interview (courtesy of the Enoch Pratt Free Library)

Mencken drinking the first glass of beer drawn at the Rennert Hotel in Baltimore on the night of the repeal of Prohibition, 5 December 1933 (courtesy of the Enoch Pratt Free Library)

and the human suffering that it entailed must have been a fair match for that of the Black Death or the Thirty Years' War, but I should say at once that my own share of the blood, sweat and tears was extremely meagre. I was, so far as I have been able to discover, the first man south of the Mason and Dixon line to brew a drinkable home-brew, and as a result my native Baltimore smelled powerfully of malt and hops during the whole horror, for I did not keep my art to myself but imparted it to anyone who could be trusted—which meant anyone save a few abandoned Methodists, Baptists and Presbyterians, most of them already far gone in glycosuria, cholelithiasis or gastrohydrorrhea, and all of them soon so low in mind and body that they could be ignored.

My seminary was run on a sort of chain-letter plan. That is to say, I took ten pupils, and then each of the ten took ten, and so on *ad infinitum*. There were dull dogs in Baltimore who went through the course forty or fifty times, under as many different holders of my degrees, and even then never got beyond a nauseous *Malzsuppe,* fit only for policemen and Sunday-school superintendents. But there were others of a much more

shining talent, and I put in a great deal of my time in 1921 and 1922 visiting their laboratories, to pass judgment on their brews. They received me with all the deference due to a master, and I was greatly bucked up by their attentions. In fact, those attentions probably saved me from melancholia, for during the whole of the twelve years, ten months and nineteen days I was a magazine editor, and a magazine editor is a man who lives on a sort of spiritual Bataan, with bombs of odium taking him incessantly from the front and torpedoes of obloquy harrying him astern.

But I would not have you think that I was anything like dependent, in that abominable time, upon home-brew, or that I got down any really formidable amount of it. To be sure, I had to apply my critical powers to many thousands of specimens, but I always took them in small doses, and was careful to blow away a good deal of the substance with the foam. This home-brew, when drinkable at all, was a striking proof of the indomitable spirit of man, but in the average case it was not much more. Whenever the mood to drink purely voluptuously was on me I preferred, of course, the product of professional brewmasters, and, having been

Mencken at the door to his wine cellar, 1941 (courtesy of the Enoch Pratt Free Library)

born lucky, I usually found it. Its provenance, in those days, was kept a kind of military secret, but now that the nightmare is over and jails no longer yawn I do not hesitate to say that, in so far as my own supply went, most of it came from the two lowermost tiers of Pennsylvania counties. Dotted over that smiling pastoral landscape there were groups of small breweries that managed successfully, by means that we need not go into, to stall off the Prohibition agents, and I had the privilege and honor of getting down many a carboy of their excellent product both in Baltimore, where I lived, and in New York, where I had my office. [. . .]

Had Prohibition been the only assault on his liberties, these episodes of circumventing the law would be only a comic leitmotif. Far more serious—and, Mencken would argue, of a piece with it— were the many instances of censorship that he had to combat. The man most associated with this branch of puritanism was Anthony Comstock. Mencken described Comstock's effect on discussion about sex in Prejudices: Fifth Series *(1926), published in the same year in which Mencken fell afoul of the Watch and Ward Society himself (excerpt from "Comstockery," pp. 16–18).*

[. . .] I have been reviewing current American fiction pretty steadily since 1908. The change that I note

is immense. When I began, a new novel dealing frankly with the physiology and pathology of sex was still something of a novelty. It was, indeed, so rare that I always called attention to it. To-day it is a commonplace. The surprise now comes when a new novel turns out to be chemically pure. Try to imagine an American publisher, in these days, getting alarmed about Dreiser's "Sister Carrie" and suppressing it before publication! The oldest and most dignified houses would print it without question; they print far worse every day. Yet in 1900 it seemed so lewd and lascivious that the publisher who put it into type got into a panic of fright, and hid the whole edition in the cellar. To-day that same publisher is advertising a new edition of Walt Whitman's "Leaves of Grass," with "A Woman Waits for Me" printed in full!

What ruined the cause of the Comstocks, I believe, was the campaign of their brethren of sex hygiene. The whole Comstockian case, as good Anthony himself used to explain frankly, was grounded upon the doctrine that virtue and ignorance were identical—that the slightest knowledge of sin was fatal to virtue. Comstock believed and argued that the only way to keep girls pure was to forbid them to think about sex at all. He expounded that doctrine often and at great length. No woman, he was convinced, could be trusted. The instant she was allowed to peek over the fence she was off to the Bad Lands. This notion he supported with many texts from Holy Writ, chiefly from the Old Testament. He was a Puritan of the old school, and had no belief whatever in virtue *per se*. A good woman, to him, was simply one who was efficiently policed. Unfortunately for him, there rose up, within the bounds of his own sect, a school of uplifters who began to merchant quite contrary ideas. They believed that sin was often caused by ignorance—that many a virtuous girl was undone simply because she didn't know what she was doing. These uplifters held that unchastity was not the product of a congenital tendency to it in the female, but of the sinister enterprise of the male, flowing out of his superior knowledge and sophistication. So they set out to spread the enlightenment. If all girls of sixteen, they argued not unplausibly, knew as much about the dreadful consequences of sin as the average police lieutenant or midwife, there would be no more seductions, and in accordance with that theory, they began printing books describing the discomforts of parturition and the terminal symptoms of lues. These books they broadcasted in numerous and immense editions. Comstock, of course, was bitterly against the scheme. He had no faith in the solemn warnings; he saw only the new and startling frankness, and he believed firmly that its one effect would be to "arouse a libidinous passion . . . in the mind of a modest woman." But he was spiked and hamstrung by the impeccable respectability of the sex hygienists. Most of them were Puritans like himself; some were towering giants of Christian rectitude. One of the most active, the Rev. Dr. Sylvanus Stall, was a clergyman of the first chop—a sorcerer who had notoriously saved thousands of immortal souls. To raid such men, to cast them into jail and denounce them as scoundrels, was palpably impossible. Comstock fretted and fumed, but the thing got beyond him. [. . .]

Things had not changed so much that Dreiser completely escaped the Comstocks. They attempted to suppress The "Genius" *in the summer of 1916, holding against him his German heritage as well as a few objectionable passages in the book. Mencken fought for him by, among other things, collecting signatures for a petition. It was signed by more than 120 American writers and endorsed by seven from England ("A Protest Against the Suppression of Theodore Dreiser's* The 'Genius'").

We, the undersigned, American writers observe with deep regret the efforts now being made to destroy the work of Theodore Dreiser. Some of us may differ from Mr. Dreiser in our aims and methods, and some of us may be out of sympathy with his point of view, but we believe that an attack by irresponsible and arbitrary persons upon the writings of an author of such

Inscribed photograph of James Branch Cabell, whose novel Jurgen *(1919) Mencken defended against obscenity charges (courtesy of the Enoch Pratt Free Library)*

manifest sincerity and such high accomplishments must inevitably do great damage to the freedom of letters in the United States, and bring down upon the American people the ridicule and contempt of other nations. The method of the attack, with its attempt to ferret out blasphemy and indecency where they are not, and to condemn a serious artist under a law aimed at common rogues, is unjust and absurd. We join in this public protest against the proceeding in the belief that the art of letters, as carried on by men of serious purpose and with the co-operation of reputable publishers, should be free from interference by persons who, by their own statement, judge all books by narrow and impossible standards; and we advocate such amendments of the existing laws as will prevent such persecutions in future:—

Among the villains was the New York Society for the Suppression of Vice, which struck against another friend of Mencken's a few years later. Mencken joined the committee of protest and contributed to a report (letter in Jurgen and the Censor: Report of

HATRACK
483

heaven, but Hatrack remained a harlot in Farmington. Every Sunday night for years she went through the same procedure. She was hopeful always that someone would speak to her and make a place for her, that the brothers and sisters who talked so volubly about the grace and the mercy of God would offer her some of the religion that they dripped so freely over everyone else in town. But they did not, and so she went back down the street to the Post Office, swishing her skirts and offering herself to all who desired her. The men who had been waiting for her, and who had known that she would come, leered at her and hailed her with obscene speech and gesture. And she gave them back leer for leer, meeting their sallies with giggles, and motioning with her head toward the cemeteries.

And so she went up the hill. A little while later a man left the group, remarking that he must go home. He followed her. And a moment after that another left, and then another, until behind Hatrack was a line of men, about one to a block, who would not look at one another, and who looked sheepishly at the ground when they met anyone coming the other way. As each man accosted her in turn Hatrack inquired whether he was a Protestant or a Catholic. If he was a Protestant she took him into the Catholic cemetery; if he was a Catholic they went into the Masonic cemetery. They paid her what they liked, or nothing, and she was grateful for whatever she received. It was Hatrack who made the remark that was famous in our town for many years. To a stranger who offered her a dollar she said:

"You know damned well I haven't got any change."

Last page of the Herbert Asbury article that appeared in the April 1926 edition of The American Mercury *and led to Mencken's arrest in Boston on obscenity charges*

Mencken with his lawyer, Arthur Garfield Hays (left), and Detective Garrett at his arrest in Boston, April 1926
(courtesy of the Enoch Pratt Free Library)

Hays and Mencken holding copies of the banned issue of The American Mercury *(courtesy of the Enoch Pratt Free Library)*

the Emergency Committee Organized to Protest against the Suppression of James Branch Cabell's *Jurgen* [New York: Privately printed, 1920], pp. 53–54).

H. L. Mencken
1524 Hollins Street
Baltimore

The raid on *Jurgen* is the crowning absurdity. The book is not only a sound and honest piece of work; it is also an unquestionable work of art; and perhaps the finest thing of its sort ever done in America. In any civilized country such a book would be received with enthusiasm by every educated man; here it is exposed forthwith to the stupid attack of persons without either intelligence or taste.

The laws under which such outrageous assaults upon decent books and decent authors are made were drawn up by the late Comstock to suit his private convenience, and are so worded that it is practically impossible for an accused publisher to make an effective defense. They are unjust, oblique and dishonest. I believe that no movement against Comstockery can have any force until these laws are

materially amended. It will take a hard fight to amend them, but it can be done. Certainly no Legislature, once it is made aware of the disgusting facts, will ever ratify the proceedings that now go on under them.

If you undertake this agitation you must expect to be attacked viciously. Comstockery is a profitable business, and those who live by it are without decency. But you will be doing a valuable work for American letters. Call on me for any help that I can give.

Sincerely yours,
H. L. Mencken

Then it was Mencken's turn to face court proceedings, when the April 1926 issue of The American Mercury *was challenged because of an item it contained. Opposing him were the Reverend J. Franklin Chase and the New England Watch and Ward Society. Mencken completed an account of the case in 1937; it was published in 1988 as* The Editor, the Bluenose, and the Prostitute *(excerpts from the typescript for "The 'Hatrack' Case 1926–27 Fair Copy," in the Enoch Pratt Free Library, Baltimore, volume 1, pp. 1, 6–10).*

Brimstone Corner in Boston, during Mencken's arrest in the "Hatrack" case (photograph by the Baltimore Sun)

The assault upon the American Mercury for printing Herbert Asbury's "Hatrack" was certainly not unanticipated in the office of the magazine. Since its first issue, in January, 1924, it had been decidedly out of favor with the Puritans of the country, East, West, North and South, and had devoted a great deal of its space to exposing and ridiculing them. Among its contributors had been some of the most conspicuous foes of the blue-nose moral scheme, for example, Clarence Darrow, Senator James A. Reed of Missouri, James Branch Cabell, Albert Jay Nock, and Margaret Sanger, the prophetess of birth-control. There had been many demands in the religious press, and even in the newspapers, that it be suppressed, and at frequent intervals it had been barred from the news-stands of various communities, though there was never anything in it that could be described, with the remotest approach to accuracy, as subversive of civilized decency. In its department of "Americana," made up of printed imbecilities gathered from all parts of the country, there were many amusing examples of Puritan intolerance and hypocrisy.[. . .]

Chase's astonishing power in Boston seemed to me to be worth an article in the American Mercury, and early in 1925 I began to hunt for some one to write it. I approached several Boston newspaper men, but without success, for the newspapers there, with few exceptions, were almost as completely intimidated by

the Watch and Ward Society as the booksellers and newsdealers. Indeed, Chase boasted in his annual report for 1924-25 that "no book interdicted by the Boston Booksellers Committee [i.e., by Chase himself] has been circulated by the book firms of this State, or advertised, or reviewed by our newspapers." Moreover, he also boasted in private that he had forced the dismissal of John Macy, erstwhile literary editor of the Boston Herald, for denouncing his operations. I accordingly turned elsewhere, and finally unearthed one A. L. S. Wood, a book-reviewer for the Springfield Union, ambitious for larger deeds and a wider audience. Wood went to Boston, had an interview with Chase, gathered some material about him from others, and wrote a brief article describing his practises. That article was certainly not literature, and it was even no great shakes as reporting, but it was the best I could get, and I printed it, under the title of "Keeping the Puritans Pure," in the American Mercury for September, 1925.

The magazine had barely come out when news arrived from J. J. Crowley, a magazine promotion agent of Boston, that Chase was furious and full of threats of revenge. In fact, he told the local wholesalers in undisguised gloating that the American Mercury would soon be banned from his diocese, and even talked grandly of having it barred from the mails, though on what ground he did not say. He was certainly not mollified when I printed a second article, under the title of "Bos-

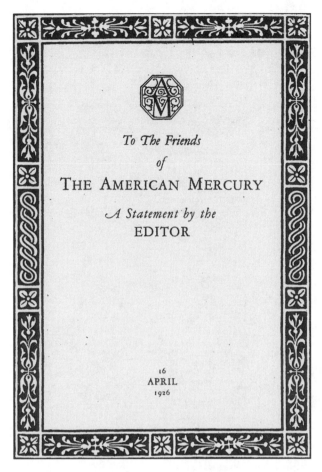

Cover of Mencken's report on the "Hatrack" proceedings

ton Twilight," in the issue for December, 1925. This article was written by my assistant on the <u>American Mercury</u>, Charles Angoff, himself a Bostonian, and in the course of its description of the intellectual decay of the town Chase's activities were again mentioned. Nor was he pleased when he appeared a third time in the issue for April, 1926--in this case in an article entitled "The Methodists," dealing <u>inter alia</u> with his relations to the Board of Temperance, Prohibition and Public Morals at Washington. It was thus not surprising when, on March 28, word came from Crowley that Chase was prepared to ban the April issue, which had been on the stands since March 25. As usual, there would be no formal action. Chase had simply warned John J. Tracey, of the New England News Company, chairman of the aforesaid Massachusetts Magazine Committee, that the issue contained matter in violation of the law, and Tracey had passed on the word to all the other wholesalers, who had notified the newsdealers. "They are being quietly told," wrote Crowley to our circulation manager, Mrs. Dorothea Brande, "to take the April number off their counters." On March 30 the fact was

reported in a brief United Press dispatch from Boston. Chase, following his invariable practise, did not communicate with us, and we were of course offered no opportunity to oppose his fiat. But he was departing from precedent by appearing in the matter openly, and even specifying the precise ground of his complaint. His objection, he said, was to an article called "Hatrack," by Herbert Asbury, which he described, in a statement given to the Boston papers, as "immoral" and "unfit to be read." He went on:

> [It] viciously intimates that the preaching against immorality by the clergy acts as a boomerang, and that by warning their congregations against existing evils the ministers of God thereby indirectly suggest visits to these places of sin. Word pictures of alleged conditions are painted in filthy and degrading descriptions. [. . .]

Arthur Garfield Hays, a veteran of the Scopes trial the year before, picks up the story (excerpts from Hays, Let Freedom Ring *[New York: Boni & Liveright, 1928], pp. 160–162, 166–169).*

[. . .] On April 5, 1926, a milling, enthusiastic and hilarious mob of thousands gathered at the corner of Park and Tremont streets in Boston, the crowd running over onto the Boston Common. Word had leaked out that at two o'clock in the afternoon the April number of *The American Mercury* was to be sold. There was a huge demand for the magazine and at almost any price. People were wildly waving one, five and ten dollar bills. One might imagine mobs of people gathered in a large American city to buy *Jim Jam Jems* or *Snappy Stories*. Be it known that *The American Mercury* is not ordinarily regarded as a thrilling or sensational publication. It is not illustrated. It is quiet in dress, dignified at times, and thoughtful in spots. The demand for *The American Mercury* was not due to any uprising of the intelligentsia in Boston. Quite to the contrary.

A few days before H. L. Mencken, editor of *The American Mercury,* and Alfred Knopf, the publisher, had visited my office. Mencken did not waste time in coming to the point:

> "Those dogs in Boston have banned *The American Mercury.* The swine don't read it. They read 'Hot Dog.' And these wowsers aren't even in the cow country."

Mencken's words were characteristic, but not illuminating. On inquiry it appeared that the April number of his magazine contained an article entitled "Hatrack," a chapter from "Up from Methodism," a book by Herbert Asbury. The claim was made that this article violated the obscenity laws. The real basis of the objection

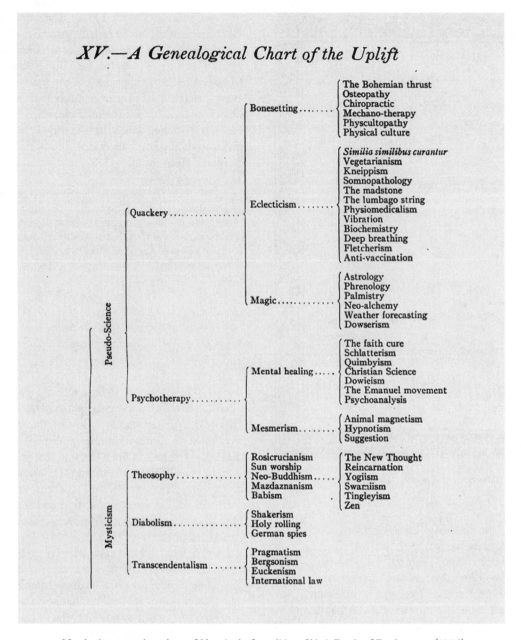

XV.—A Genealogical Chart of the Uplift

Pseudo-Science

Quackery

Bonesetting
- The Bohemian thrust
- Osteopathy
- Chiropractic
- Mechano-therapy
- Physcultopathy
- Physical culture

Eclecticism
- *Similia similibus curantur*
- Vegetarianism
- Kneippism
- Somnopathology
- The madstone
- The lumbago string
- Physiomedicalism
- Vibration
- Biochemistry
- Deep breathing
- Fletcherism
- Anti-vaccination

Magic
- Astrology
- Phrenology
- Palmistry
- Neo-alchemy
- Weather forecasting
- Dowserism

Psychotherapy

Mental healing
- The faith cure
- Schlatterism
- Quimbyism
- Christian Science
- Dowieism
- The Emanuel movement
- Psychoanalysis

Mesmerism
- Animal magnetism
- Hypnotism
- Suggestion

Mysticism

Theosophy
- Rosicrucianism
- Sun worship
- Neo-Buddhism
- Mazdaznanism
- Babism
  - The New Thought
  - Reincarnation
  - Yogiism
  - Swarniism
  - Tingleyism
  - Zen

Diabolism
- Shakerism
- Holy rolling
- German spies

Transcendentalism
- Pragmatism
- Bergsonism
- Euckenism
- International law

Mencken's targets, charted on a foldout in the first edition of his A Book of Burlesques *(1916)*

was that it attacked a widely held religious concept, to wit, the power for "good" of revivalist meetings. In his piece, Asbury had told of such meetings in the small town of Farmington, Missouri, where professional devil-chasers imported for the purpose, "proclaimed loudly and incessantly" that the morals of the town "were compounded of a slice of Sodom and a cut of Gomorrah, with an extract of Babylon to flavor the stew." Particularly, the pious brethren worried over the amorous activities of the inhabitants. They would point out that men were constantly engaged in attacking vir-

gins and advised the young women "to go armed to the teeth prepared to do battle in defense of their chastity." They would add that the town permitted dens of vice, full of alluring women whose devices were aided by trappings of luxury—red carpets, draped walls, settees largely proportioned, all in a background appealing to the senses. The effect of such information was to create an unusual eagerness in the audience. Asbury suggested that all this is more or less of a dream of fevered senses; that in most of our small towns there is no such thing as commercialized prostitution. He illustrated the actual situation with a woman descriptively called "Hatrack"—the occasional prostitute who plied her trade in Farmington. Hatrack was a household drudge, but on Sundays she would go to church to offer "her soul to the Lord." The respectable citizens of the town shunned her. So she went to the devil. [. . .]

There was only one way squarely to raise the issue. Would Mencken go to Boston, sell the *Mercury* and submit to arrest? He would. I went along.

Arrived in Boston we found that no one could sell magazines without a peddler's license. Mencken made the necessary application. He had a choice of two licenses, one permitting the sale of bones, grease and refuse matter; the second giving leave to hawk anything one chose except fish, fruit or vegetables. We took the latter, although it did occur to us that possibly he should take the one applying to "refuse" matter.

Armed with the license, we approached the Reverend J. Franklin Chase and invited him to buy a copy of the *Mercury* on the Boston Common. Chase swallowed the bait. He did not realize that a smut-hunter's business is greatly prejudiced unless attended with due solemnity, nor did he anticipate that his action would provide such hilarious entertainment for the populace. Into the crowd on the Common we made our way carrying handfuls of *American Mercuries*. Oblivious to a demand that would cheer the heart of any publisher, we refused to sell except to Jason Franklin Chase, secretary of the New England Watch and Ward Society, and then at the fixed price of fifty cents. Chase bought and paid. Mencken is said to have bit the coin, although it seemed to me an unnecessary precaution. He should have had confidence that this eminent custodian of Boston morals would not offer a counterfeit piece. A bundle of magazines was passed to W. A. S. Douglas, Baltimore *Sun* reporter who, much to his astonishment, was promptly arrested for possessing indecent literature. Then began the parade of Mencken and his cohorts, followed by a joyous crowd, to the Police Station. Bail was fixed and the hearing set. [. . .]

Mr. Justice Parmenter acquitted Mencken, saying:

> "I cannot imagine any one reading the article in question and finding himself or herself attracted towards vice." [. . .]

As late as 20 April 1945 the combative Mencken was defending free speech in the case of Esquire v. the Postmaster General *(excerpts from* Esquire Incorporated, Appellant, v. Frank C. Walker as Postmaster General of the United States, Appellee; Appeal from the District Court of the United States for the District of Columbia, *pp. 7–9).*

[. . .] We think the Government is clearly right in its contention once the power claimed by the Post Office is assumed to exist. There is a practical reason, apart from respect for the testimony of clergymen, why the administrative imposition of literary and artistic standards cannot be reviewed by a court on it merits. Opinions on such matters differ so widely that if the evidence in the record before the Post Office were to be weighed each side would have to continue calling witnesses indefinitely in order not to be outweighed by the other. We have no doubt that thousands of reputable experts on the public good could have been obtained by each side in this case. We know of no way a court can evaluate the comparative expert qualifications of persons who hold opinions on what the public should read. Once we admit the power claimed here we see no room for effective judicial review of its exercise. And so in practical effect it amounts to a power in the Postmaster General to impose the standards of any reputable minority group on the whole nation.

In addition, the record suggests that the power claimed here would be used by sincere and conscientious officials to bind modern periodical literature to the standards of a former generation. This is dramatically illustrated by the cross examination of H. L. Mencken, who appeared as a witness for Esquire. No one today would question either Mr. Mencken's eminence or his complete respectability. Yet counsel for the Post Office attempts to impeach his testimony because about twenty years ago an issue of the American Mercury was refused all mailing privileges. It would be difficult to find anyone today who could with reason object to this issue of the magazine. The attempt to impeach Mr. Mencken on this account reads as follows:

> Q. Mr. Mencken, you are the author of a story called "Hat-Rack", aren't you? A. I am not, sir.
>
> Q. You published it in your magazine? A. I did, sir.
>
> Q. That story had to deal with some sexual activity in a box car or freight car? A. Not specifically. It dealt with people who engaged in sexual activity, but there was no scene of sexual activity in the story.
>
> Q. Was "Hat-Rack" the name of the woman who did that? A. Nickname. Did you ask who wrote it?
>
> Q. No, sir; I did not. A. I will tell you if you want to know. It was written by Herbert Asbury, the great grand-nephew of Bishop Asbury, the first American Methodist bishop. [. . .]
>
> Q. Mr. Mencken, was the issue of your magazine containing that story declared non-mailable by the Post

Office Department? A. Yes, sir. I think you ought to let me explain what happened, if you care to.

Q. Yes, sir; go right ahead. A. The Post Office entered that case rather late. An effort was made in Boston to suppress the magazine as a measure of revenge by the Boston Watch and Ward Society, which we had been denouncing. They proceeded by threatening a newsdealer. The poor newsdealer had no stake in the thing and was willing to subside and withdraw the magazine, so I went to Boston and sold the magazine myself on Boston Common and insisted on the Watch and Ward Society arresting me.

I was arrested, tried and acquitted.

Meanwhile, subsequent to my arrest, and four or five weeks subsequent to the time the magazine had gone through the mails, the Post Office Department issued an order barring it from the mails. It was a purely imaginary order. There were no more to be mailed.

So I went to court on that and I had injunctions against the Post Office by two Federal judges, both of whom denounced the Post Office as obscene, indecent, unfair and ignominious.

I agreed with the verdict thoroughly and believe it was just to this minute.

The Post Office tried to hit me in the back when I was fighting with the filthy Comstocks in Boston. I fought the Comstocks and I fought the Post Office, and I put my magazine back in the mails and they have never molested me since.

Q. Didn't the Federal Court in New York refuse to issue an injunction as the case was moot? A. That is not precisely what happened. I had my injunction in the district courts of Boston and New York, and the Post Office, pursuing its filthy course of trying to persecute me, appealed to the Circuit and the Circuit after two years decided that the case was completely moot because we were in point of fact through the mails. They decided I could not get relief because the Post Office barring me from the mails was completely dishonest—I wasn't an applicant to the mails. [. . .]

Mencken had thrown up his hands in 1918 at the beginning of Damn! A Book of Calumny, *concluding that George Wash-*

ington would no longer be welcome in the oppressively puritan United States. In the age of political correctness his words have even greater force ("Pater Patriæ," pp. 7–8).

If George Washington were alive today, what a shining mark he would be for the whole camorra of uplifters, forward-lookers and professional patriots! He was the Rockefeller of his time, the richest man in the United States, a promoter of stock companies, a land-grabber, an exploiter of mines and timber. He was a bitter opponent of foreign alliances, and denounced their evils in harsh, specific terms. He had a liking for all forthright and pugnacious men, and a contempt for lawyers, schoolmasters and all other such obscurantists. He was not pious. He drank whisky whenever he felt chilly, and kept a jug of it handy. He knew far more profanity than Scripture, and used and enjoyed it more. He had no belief in the infallible wisdom of the common people, but regarded them as inflammatory dolts, and tried to save the republic from them. He advocated no sure cure for all the sorrows of the world, and doubted that such a panacea existed. He took no interest in the private morals of his neighbors.

Inhabiting These States today, George would be ineligible for any office of honor or profit. The Senate would never dare confirm him; the President would not think of nominating him. He would be on trial in all the yellow journals for belonging to the Invisible Government, the Hell Hounds of Plutocracy, the Money Power, the Interests. The Sherman Act would have him in its toils; he would be under indictment by every grand jury south of the Potomac; the triumphant prohibitionists of his native state would be denouncing him (he had a still at Mount Vernon) as a debaucher of youth, a recruiting officer for insane asylums, a poisoner of the home. The suffragettes would be on his trail, with sentinels posted all along the Accotink road. The initiators and referendors would be bawling for his blood. The young college men of the *Nation* and the *New Republic* would be lecturing him weekly. He would be used to scare children in Kansas and Arkansas. The chautauquas would shiver whenever his name was mentioned. . . .

And what a chance there would be for that ambitious young district attorney who thought to shadow him on his peregrinations—and grab him under the Mann Act!

The Posthumous Career: "Stirring Up the Animals"

Mencken asked the editors of the Sun *not to overdo the notice of his death. Nonetheless, when he died on 29 January 1956, he rated both an obituary and a long reminiscence by his old friend Hamilton Owens, the editor in chief, on the front page the next day. Owens says that Mencken's "The Sahara of the Bozart" was printed in the* Sun; *actually, it was first published in the* New York Evening Mail *in 1917 (excerpts from "H. L.'s Pungent Pen a Challenge to Orthodoxy,"* Baltimore Sun, *30 January 1956, pp. 1, 4).*

Henry Louis Mencken was born in 1880. He was first in a family of three boys and a girl. His father, August Mencken, Sr., manufactured cigars and, like most of the successful men of the time, not only enjoyed life himself but saw to it that his family had a reasonably good time of it. [. . .]

In such a family, schooling presented no complex problem. The head of the Mencken household held to the idea that boys should be trained not by school-marms but under the strict ferrule of a real taskmaster. It was such training that the older Mencken boys received at Professor Knapp's school on Lexington street, opposite the City Hall. During this period, under much the same kind of discipline, H. L. was taught to play the piano, an accomplishment which probably gave him more undiluted pleasure in later life than any other. Mencken was a good scholar from the beginning. He was, in fact, avid for learning, but it was neither his plan, nor that of his father, that he should linger over-long in school. He was graduated from the Baltimore Polytechnic Institute at 16 and then went into his father's business. It is in the record that he actually learned it.[. . .]

Yearned For Newspaper Work

In "Newspaper Days" (1941), the second volume of his informal autobiography, he tells how the itch to write made him yearn to leave his father and go into newspaper work. The shift was not easy. For months he toiled at the cigar business all day and did newspaper work most of the night. His teacher was the late Max Ways, then city editor of the Baltimore *Morning Herald.*

He demonstrated a special capacity in his new calling, for he became city editor of the *Herald* in 1903. In that exciting job he wrote, with the assistance of his reporters, perhaps the best contemporary description of the Baltimore fire, a spectacle which gratified his youthful sense of the dramatic.

But he had already written and privately published his "Ventures Into Verse," a boyish production plainly derivative from Rudyard Kipling, to whom it is dedicated. "Ventures Into Verse" is now such a rarity that it has been sold for as much as $300. His growing abilities, proved in many a magazine article and short story, so impressed the owners of the *Herald* that, when it became an afternoon paper in 1905, Mencken, then less then 25, was made its managing editor, a promotion he did not seek and really did not want.

He came to *The Sun* in 1906 at the suggestion of the late Walter W. Abell to manage the newly created Sunday edition. Baltimoreans with long memories will recall the impact of the boisterous youngster on the staid columns of the paper. Already he was concerned with his discovery of the American Language and *The Sunday Sun* soon bristled with such words as *kaif* for café and *bozart* for *beaux arts.*

The Venerable Suffer

There was also a new and more pungent description of the local scene, especially on the homelier levels. The politicians, the policemen, the magistrates, the judges and all such worthies were depicted with more robustness and much less veneration than had hitherto been accorded them.

The humors of the corner saloon, the free-lunch counter and the crab feast emerged and there were frequent references to a group called the Honorary Pall-bearers. The Mencken battle against frauds and stuffed shirts had begun, and the long debate as to whether he was a "constructive" or "destructive" critic was under way.

During this early period on *The Sun,* his chief literary enthusiasm was for the theater. Every Sunday he wrote an article about the less known of the European dramatists and their plays. In his criticisms of the shows

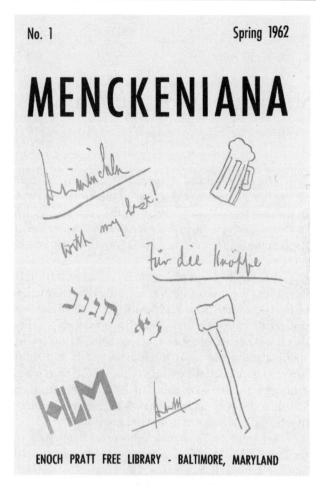

Cover for the first issue of the journal devoted to Mencken, with reproductions of inscriptions in his books

There is a notion abroad that it was the column of an iconoclast, a wrecker. But the truth is that Mencken, as always, upheld in it the ancient virtues, both personal and social. His war was not against men who minded their own business, paid their bills and reared their families. He argued that such men had the right to believe what they pleased. His war was against the frauds and scoundrels in public and quasi-public life who preyed on such citizens.

The politicians who promised, but did not perform, felt the crushing impact of his bludgeon. The business men who would sacrifice the amenities of the town and even its remaining beauties in order to bring in a new and probably smelly factory felt it, too.

"Mencken's Law" Expounded

His deftest and most telling blows were reserved for those members of what he called "the rev. clergy" who forsook their pulpits to engage in dubious ventures in moral reform. In explaining his attitude toward all such, he once propounded "Mencken's law" which went something like this:

"The Sage of Baltimore" in retirement at 1524 Hollins Street (Arlyn Bruccoli Collection)

which came to Baltimore he applied the lessons he had learned by his voracious study of the drama elsewhere, to the great distress of the managers of the local theaters. When he finally concluded that there was something to be said for their point of view he formally eschewed theatergoing and dramatic criticism. [. . .]

His Column Was Famous

Even the newcomers among Baltimoreans—those who have come here from other parts of the country and those generated on the scene—know about his Free Lance column. There is a general impression that this column endured for many years on the editorial page of *The Evening Sun*. In fact, he began it in 1912 and the last one appeared in 1917. Its influence, locally as well as nationally, is now proverbial, but it was all exercised in that relatively brief period. The discipline of editorial writing for *The Evening Sun* did not provide a sufficient outlet for Mencken's cerebral exuberance and it spilled over into a column. That is the long and short of it.

Whenever A pretends to help B by some act which is injurious to X, then A is a scoundrel. [. . .]

Results Were Evident

But the Free Lance did produce some remarkable local results. It made the politicians here more wary in their public pronouncements and part of their wariness is still manifest. It immunized Baltimore against the more ridiculous manifestations of boosterism. It silenced and occasionally ostracized the less palatable political parsons. Also, because of its constant outcries against the contaminated drinking water and hardly less contaminated milk which Baltimoreans had to consume, it helped produce a purer flow of both, thereby reducing the amount of typhoid fever and other intestinal diseases.

The national results were almost entirely in the literary field. The column contained whatever Mencken wanted to put in it, and in those days he was tremendously concerned with his "*beautiful letters*." He beat the drum constantly for the writers he admired–Mark Twain at the top of the classical American list perhaps, with Joseph Conrad and Theodore Dreiser, respectively, leading the British and American contingents of the contemporaries. He was quick to denounce the frauds among the newcomers, but even quicker to praise those who had something to say and who knew how to say it.

New American Literature

In *The Evening Sun* and in the *Smart Set* he began that almost single-handed crusade for a new American literature (created according to his specifications) which came to such a triumphant blooming in the 1920's.

He stopped writing the Free Lance in 1917. Save for a brief period in 1938 when he took over the editorial page of *The Evening Sun* during an interregnum, he never accepted another desk position on a newspaper.

He continued, however, his association with the *Sunpapers*. The general public knew of the connection mainly through his Monday articles on the editorial page of the evening paper. These carried on more or less in the tradition of the Free Lance column. That is, he laid about him with the same old fervor, whether his victim for the week was a president, a mayor, a parson or a professor.

Flowering Of The South

Now and then he would take on the literary folk for a change. His famous article, "The Sahara of the Bozart," an all-too-realistic description of the paucity of Southern writers of talent, was printed in this space. Later on, when a few southerners began to write more to his liking and the Richmond *Reviewer* was created to afford them an outlet, he printed "Violets in the Sahara," a sensitive and understanding appraisal of their efforts. Now and then, he would write one of his nostalgic pieces about the Baltimore of his boyhood days, to the delight of the local citizenry. [. . .]

Covered The Conventions

In addition to this regular work for *The Evening Sun,* Mencken accepted special assignments at intervals. Every four years he "covered" the Republican and Democratic national conventions. These significant affairs he insisted upon regarding as circuses and his judgments of them were based not on the issues formulated but on the quality of entertainment provided. During much of this period both parties were trying to dodge the prohibition issue and nothing delighted Mencken more than to watch and describe the fearful turnings and twistings of the so-called political leaders.

He was on the attack on other fronts as well. The Ku Klux Klan, the would-be censors of newspapers, books and *mores* (to him they were all Comstocks and their avocation Comstockery) and, especially, the obscurantists who were responsible for the anti-evolution laws which some states had passed were his butts.

He delighted the whole country when, in 1925, he went to Dayton, Tenn., and reported the famous trial of John T. Scopes for the *Sunpapers*. For many years he claimed that this trial and especially the long theological duel between W. J. Bryan and Clarence Darrow, Scopes's lawyer, had provided the finest spectacle of the century.

Kept His Eye On The Paper

In this period, inside *The Sun* organization, Mencken exerted an immeasurable influence. His hatred of pusillanimity and sham was not exhausted by his attacks on outsiders; he insisted that the paper to which he had given his allegiance live up to the standards of forthrightness, courage and, above all, vitality, which he had set for himself.

None was quicker than he to detect any potential deviation from the straight path, any danger of yielding to undesirable outside pressure, any lapse into dullness or any taking of an untenable political position. He did not win all the arguments which he started, for he was human and capable, therefore, of being mistaken. But his influence was 90 per cent good and it remained on that side of the ledger until the end of his days. With

Mencken as a critic, craftsmen found it painful to skimp their work. [. . .]

New Writers Welcomed

In 1914 Mencken became, with Nathan, coeditor of the *Smart Set* and could himself select what appeared in it. In a little while it was the recognized outlet for a new generation of American writers. They were not all geniuses, of course. Perhaps some of them aped Mencken's style as assiduously and as arrantly as the "polite" authors of the more formal magazines aped second-rate English models. Nevertheless, a new regiment of American story writers was born and a whole generation of youngsters sought to enroll in it.

From almost the beginning, Mencken's publisher had been Alfred Knopf. In 1924, with Knopf as publisher and Mencken and Nathan as coeditors, the *American Mercury* made its appearance. The *Smart Set* had been a something less than satisfactory outlet for them. The new magazine, in the green cover that was to become a special kind of intellectual *cachet,* was entirely their own. They had lined up their contributors, all champing at the bit.

"To Keep Common Sense"

[. . .] It is probable that even Mencken had underestimated the effect the magazine was destined to have. It became the rage of the college campuses. The bright

Mencken in 1934, the year he sold The American Mercury; *photograph by Ilse Hoffman (courtesy of the Enoch Pratt Free Library)*

PROGRAM

9 a.m.–5 p.m.	Mencken Room open to the public (Third Floor)
10:30 a.m.	Annual Meeting of the Mencken Society (Wheeler Auditorium, Third Floor)
1 p.m.	Screening of *Mencken's America,* a WJZ-TV film written by Gwinn Owens and produced by Jack Hunter (Wheeler Auditorium)
3 p.m.	Annual Mencken Memorial Lecture **MARION RODGERS** Author of *Mencken & Sara: A Life in Letters* will speak on **MENCKEN, THE YOUNG PROFESSIONAL** (Wheeler Auditorium)
4:15 p.m.	Informal reception honoring the speaker

The Board and the Director
of the Enoch Pratt Free Library
cordially invite you to celebrate

MENCKEN DAY

Saturday, September 9, 1989
at the Central Library
400 Cathedral Street in Baltimore

Program for one of the annual meetings of the Mencken Society

young men who had been Wilsonian idealists during World War I now became the passionate cynics of the Twenties. Not many of them managed to break into the highly selective pages of the *Mercury,* but thousands tried. All of them read Mencken, quoted Mencken and did their best not only to write like him but to talk like him.

Much of the movement was froth, of course. The new literary creed produced its share of poseurs and frauds. But it produced, also, a magnificent list of writers.

Naturally, some of those who received the Mencken accolade were established novelists, such as Theodore Dreiser, Joseph Hergesheimer and Branch Cabell. Mencken's support had helped them over the lean years and now it did its part in bringing them their full reward. Others—say, for two extremes, Sinclair Lewis and Scott Fitzgerald—candidly and even fulsomely expressed their debt to H.L.M. On one occasion Lewis announced, with characteristic irreverence, that he favored the election of his hero as pope.

He's A Philosopher

However, it is important to note that Mencken's prime interest at this time was not literary expression for its own sake but rather the use of that expression for social criticism. In Europe, where his writings were almost always available in translation, his role was accepted as that of social philosopher, which was precisely what Baltimoreans had known him to be all the time.

He proclaimed, on every fitting occasion, that he regarded man, the social animal, as wholly incompetent to cope with his problems and that he therefore had no hope whatever of ameliorating the fate of the race. Hence, he was opposed to reform, as such.

He Would Disagree

By this device he maintained his role of the detached, always amused and occasionally compassionate observer of human foibles. But it is a fact that his efforts contributed to the disappearance or at least the reduction of some of the worst of the national hypocrisies. His comment on this remark would have been that the old hypocrisies were succeeded by new and more grotesque ones.

This concern for the social and political scene gradually won out over his literary interest. The *Mercury* became more and more a sociological journal (in the Mencken sense, of course). Nathan had withdrawn as coeditor fairly early. Finally, when the burden of reading the endless flow of manuscripts became a bore and

the routine of editing kept him more and more away from his beloved Baltimore, he and his associates sold the magazine to new owners. That was in 1934. [. . .]

A Precise Routine

The word routine fits precisely. No man in the community ordered his day more carefully, nor imposed upon himself more rigid disciplines. Mencken got up at the same hour every day. He opened his voluminous mail—and it remained voluminous despite his best efforts to control it—and instantly replied to every personal communication in it. The Baltimorean who wrote Mencken a letter on Monday had an answer on Wednesday, if not on Tuesday afternoon.

He lunched at home, save when he had a visitor or a significant engagement, spent about half an hour in *The Sun* office, went back to work on whatever book he was writing, knocked off a short while for dinner and then worked again until about 9. On two or three evenings a week he then repaired to some restaurant where the beer was good, sat for an hour or two with some friends whose conversation was stimulating and went home to bed.

Making Music, The Thing

Saturday evening was special. Then he met at 8 with the members of the Saturday Night Club, which was really a small orchestra. In the club he played the treble part of a four-handed piano arrangement of whatever noble music happened to be chosen. He knew, almost to the last note, the symphonies of Haydn, Mozart, Beethoven, Brahms, Mendelssohn, Schubert, Schumann and a lot more besides. [. . .]

Paying visits to elderly friends who were hospitalized was another expression of the Mencken sense of orderly responsibility. No friend ever felt neglected while he was convalescing from an illness, nor was there ever a more cheerful and engaging caller. The Mencken wit coruscated under this stimulus; doctors and nurses invariably made excuses to come into the room while he was there. There was some kind of special affinity between the high-minded practitioners of healing and the social critic. [. . .]

Was Generally Accepted

By the time the fourth revision [*of* The American Language] was put out in 1936, Mencken's dictum that our spoken language had so far deviated from its English parent as to justify his title was generally accepted—in sorrow by the emotional Anglophiles in this country, but with increasing delight by others. [. . .]

The wide acclaim received by "The American Language" in its several editions and revisions made thoughtful people all over the country anxious to contribute to the author's store of information on the subject. The correspondence which Mencken carried on with reference to this one phase of his activity was enormous. It involved, also, the keeping of careful files in which the constantly increasing mass of material could be got at when needed. Some of it was disposed of with the publication (1945) of "Supplement I" of the original work. Still the material piled in and in 1948 he issued another volume, "Supplement II," which most critics found to be as rich, as engaging and as learned as its predecessors.

He Collected Phrases

The extent of his philological output was another example of the orderliness of his mind. No such works could have been produced by a man who was not in unusual control of the details of his life. A related example of the good order in which his affairs were kept was shown to the world in 1942, when he published his monumental "Dictionary of Quotations." [. . .]

Books Of Many Kinds

There were many other books. Some of them, such as the "Prefaces" and the long series of "Prejudices," were more or less byproducts of his newspaper and magazine work. Some ("In Defense of Women" is a characteristic example) were the expression of the natural exuberance of the man and were so contagious in their good humor that they continue to go through edition after edition.

Others were so much the result of painstaking study and research that they may be ranked not far behind "The American Language." In this category are found "Notes on Democracy" (1926), "Treatise on the Gods" (1930) and "Treatise on Right and Wrong" (1936) [sic; actually 1934]. They all emphasize the basic characteristic of the author: a wholly unfettered mind, so far as dogma of any kind is concerned, together with a profound understanding of the basic human virtues and an almost puritanical devotion to them.

This is not the place or the time for any final appraisal of H. L. Mencken's contribution to the culture of the United States. But whatever the conclusion of the students of such things, his colleagues on *The Sun* had the benefit, over many years, of associa-

tion with one of the most stimulating personalities of their time.

* * *

("From One Friend to Another," Baltimore Sun, *30 January 1956, p. 1).*

New York, Jan. 29 (AP)–George Jean Nathan said today he received a last letter just two days ago from his old friend H. L. Mencken "in which he told me he was in despair."

The two authors and critics were for years an inseparable literary team.

Nathan said he was "deeply distressed" to learn of his friend's passing.

"Mencken and I spent glorious years together editing magazines and putting books together," he said of their joint work between 1908 and 1930.

Mencken's final letter to him, Nathan said, had been dictated and declared that he "was feeling very badly."

Reminded of their old reputation as disturbers of the literary peace, Nathan said: "America needed a couple of bad boys in letters then."

Their final meeting was nine months ago when Nathan visited Baltimore for an afternoon, found Mencken in a cheerful mood "but greatly concerned because he was no longer able to read."

* * *

("Mayor And Governor Express Regret Of City And State," Baltimore Sun, *30 January 1956, p. 4).*

Mayor D'Alesandro and Governor McKeldin expressed the city's and State's sorrow yesterday on the occasion of the death of H. L. Mencken.

"The death of Henry L. Mencken is a great loss to Baltimore and to the world of literature," the Mayor said.

"His pen was sharper than any sword in his life-long duel with the self-righteous."

"Merciless in puncturing the pretentious, he nevertheless was a kindly man who enjoyed life hugely. His love for Baltimore, its people and their ways was well known."

"With his passing we have lost our most distinguished writer and commentator on world affairs."

Governor McKeldin said Mencken's death "removes from our midst a Maryland institution–a name that immediately was connected with that of Maryland wherever it was mentioned, anywhere in the civilized world."

"He enriched our language, and those riches were shared generously with all who cared to read," the Governor said.

"His passing creates a great loss to Maryland and to all who knew him, but his works will live on and his recognition will grow through the years and decades wherever great writing is valued."

Students of Mencken have been appraising his contribution to American culture since long before he died. Their job was made easier when Mencken left most of his books and papers to the Enoch Pratt Free Library in Baltimore. These materials continue to be mined; they have prolonged his publishing career to the end of the twentieth century and will no doubt extend it into the twenty-first. The contents and opening of the Pratt's Mencken Room, one of the nation's great literary treasure troves, were described in two articles in the Sun *(John C. Schmidt, "The Library's Mencken Room,"* Baltimore Sun, *15 April 1956, p. A3).*

"The King is an idiot," commented Henry L. Mencken in 1936 when Edward VIII gave up the British crown to marry Wally Simpson.

This observation from the "Sage of Baltimore" was quoted in newspapers throughout the world, and 79 printed versions of it were collected and saved by Mencken himself. Most of these versions are short headlines. The related stories fill 158 pages in a thick volume of personal newspaper clippings and magazine articles preserved by the author—one of a hundred such volumes. They make up what Richard Hart, of the Pratt Library, calls the core of the collection in the new Mencken Room which will be opened on Tuesday evening.

The idea for such a room is not one that was conceived after Mencken's death. For ten years the library has been receiving material from the author's home, in line with his intention to leave most of his possessions of literary value to the Pratt. His correspondence with people outside the State he left to the New York Public Library.

Dominated By Portrait

Plans for the room have been developing for several years, and actual work was in progress at the time of Mencken's death. When it is finished, library officials believe they will have the most complete store of information about Mencken in existence, as well as copies of every edition of every major book written or edited by him.

The room is located on the third floor of the library's main building, and since it was not intended for general use, it is fairly well isolated from the frequently visited sections.

It is a room of medium size. Bookshelves line three walls, and a large work table sits in the center of the floor. Dominating the room is Nikol Schattenstein's portrait of Mencken at the age of 47 when he was at the height of his career. He is shown in a pose familiar to his friends: open collar, colored suspenders, shirtsleeves. The decor of the room is based largely on the coloring in the portrait.

On the opposite wall are three color photographs of Mr. Mencken with several friends. Directly above the door hangs the insignia of the Saturday Night Music Club which Mencken helped found in 1905. The articles depicted on the insignia are a clear indication of the club's purpose: the enjoyment of music in an atmosphere of informality. The figure of a musical instrument occupies one of four sections. The others contain a beer stein, a cooked lobster, and a grouping of onions and pretzels. The sections are divided by fat sausage links.

Foreign Language Editions

Apart from these items, the room is given over to printed or written material by or about Mencken.

Two tiers of shelves hold all the editions and copies—233 altogether—of the author's 30 principal works. There are, for example, 32 editions and copies of "The American Language" and 19 of "In Defense of Women." Foreign language versions of Mencken's books are included in the overall count.

The 100 volumes of clippings occupy two additional sections of shelf space. Mencken evidently saved every article and clipping he received in which his name was even mentioned. Mr. Hart, head of the library's literature and language department, says that few authors have kept such complete records and the file should be a boon to Mencken scholars and biographers for years to come. There are clippings from all parts of the world where English is read, and some from places where it is not.

The first entry in Volume I is a review of Mencken's first book, "Venture [sic] Into Verse," and is dated July 19, 1903. This reviewer found evidence of "a brave spirit" in the author, "game from start to finish."

Drew Mixed Reaction

Mencken saved the bad reviews, too, as well as stories which concerned him only remotely. A recent example is a Manchester *Guardian* story dealing primarily with Senator McCarthy. The *American Mercury*

Mencken's bookplate

is mentioned briefly, and identified as once having been "ennobled by the genius of H. L. Mencken."

His comments on the 1936 abdication in Britain achieved wide publicity and prompted strong, mixed reaction. Both his chiding of the King and his statement that this was the best news story since the Resurrection made headlines in practically every important newspaper of the day.

Much of Mencken's wit and humor is preserved in these clippings. A profile in the Milwaukee *Journal* tells of the trip he took to Chicago in 1937, when a newspaper photographer snapped Mencken and asked him to write his home and occupation on a caption slip. He identified himself: "H. L. Mencken, retired six-day bicycle rider."

The last entry in Volume C is an *Evening Sun* article from October 28, 1954, on the marriage of his friend and former colleague on the *American Mercury*, George Jean Nathan, to Actress Julie Haydon.

Dedicated To Mencken

The remainder of the shelf space in the room is filled with 2,500 presentation copies of books of other authors of Mencken's time, many of whom were his close friends. Most of the volumes contain inscriptions written in by their authors, and many contain personal letters to Mencken.

One such close friend was Theodore Dreiser, who is represented by 51 books. Another, Joseph Hergesheimer, by 34.

Other important writers who knew Mencken and whose books are on these shelves include Carl Sandburg, William Saroyan, James Branch Cabell and James T. Farrell. Sinclair Lewis, another close friend, formally dedicated his "Elmer Gantry" to Mencken. Wendell Willkie sent a copy of "One World" which he urged Mencken to read as a labor of love.

Taken as a whole, Hart says, these presentation copies form a cross-section of important American writing in the first half of this century. The letters, personal comments, and asides written in by the various authors may well form the basis for new critical studies.

Inscription by Trotsky

Mencken had admirers abroad, among them Aldous Huxley and Leo Trotsky. In his *Geschichte Der Russischen Revolution*, Trotsky wrote an inscription in French, except for part of the last apologetic sentence, which explains, ". . . . because my English is very pitiful."

Adjoining the Mencken Room is a smaller one containing a collection of books, magazines, and other research materials used by Mencken in preparation of "The American Language." This includes some 1,200 separate books and 4,000 pamphlets and periodicals.

Because of its highly specialized and valuable nature, the material in the Mencken room will be available only to scholars, research workers, critics, biographers and other writers doing work on Mencken or his time. For three days following the opening on Tuesday, the public will be permitted to visit the room, but after that, it will be open only to the specialists.

There are other Mencken collections similar to this, notably at Dartmouth and Harvard universities, but here in the city where the man lived and died will be what is believed the most valuable.

* * *

(*Marjorie Mathis, "With Rites 'Rich in Irony,' Pratt Opens Mencken Room," Baltimore Sun, 18 April 1956, pp. 42, 25*).

Laughter was deep and full-bodied in the Enoch Pratt Free Library last night where men and women rejoiced in memories of Henry L. Mencken.

They came by the hundreds to the dedication of the H. L. Mencken room and they stayed to hear his own words read, his philosophies interpreted, his spirit honored.

It was anything but a solemn occasion, but it was touched with a deeply human nostalgia that produced a sort of camaraderie among the hundreds who overflowed the auditorium, and sat or stood in corridors to catch the words of men who knew Mencken.

Arrive Early

Scores of the audience arrived 90 minutes ahead of the time scheduled for the start of the program. Walls of the auditorium were lined with standing listeners after all the seats were filled, and the full length of the corridors outside was massed with others who listened without being able to see the speakers.

In responsively good humor they took delight in every interpretation and every reminiscent anecdote about the great wit and critic, the insistent iconoclast, the incurably human H. L. Mencken who was one of Baltimore's most distinguished men of letters.

It was Alistair Cooke, British author and journalist, radio and television personality and compiler of "The Vintage Mencken," who accented the irony of the occasion.

"Ironic" Ceremony

Mr. Cooke called his remarks "A Funeral Oration for H. L. Mencken," and after an extemporaneous introduction, he said:

"We are gathered together here to perform a truly blasphemous ceremony, one so ironic, so perverse, so Gilbertian that Gilbert wouldn't have touched it.

"We are about to commemorate the professional gifts of a man who held all commemorations nauseous; we are here going through the solemn motions of trying to arrange a little immortality for a man who constantly reminded his pious friends that the human body is 'no more than an unstable congeries of compounds of carbon'; that a man's talent, no matter how fiery, would be reduced in the end to ashes, and that the dust he kicked up as rebel and bad boy would return to dust."

The speaker speculated that Mencken might even at the moment "be flapping his wings in outrage over our efforts to bestow on him the sort of honor he would associate with college men, honorary degree recipients and other such riff-raff."

Then Mr. Cooke gave his own interpretation of another facet of the Mencken nature.

"H. L. Mencken insisted all through his life that he was unholier than thou," he said. "But we have got him now and I think our instinct is sound.

"Mencken in private was most of the time the antithesis of the public war horse. . . . It is not so much, as we might suspect, that Mencken's bark was worse than his bite; but that in such people the bark is often a defensive snort against an unnatural fear of having the enemy put the bite on them."

"Punctured Pretensions"

The speaker went on to say he was relieved of any embarrassment on the occasion by his personal knowledge that Mencken enjoyed nothing so much as an event, "like this, rich in irony, as an occasion which publicly punctured the pretensions of any man, great or small: not the least, H. L. Mencken."

Mr. Cooke spoke of the uncompromising integrity of H. L. Mencken, "a man who would not work for all the gold in Hollywood or the Riviera at anything he did not respect and anything he would not have wished to do."

The importance of the right to disbelieve as well as to believe was underscored by Mr. Cooke in a quotation from the late Associate Justice Robert H. Jackson, who said:

"'The day that this country ceases to be free for irreligion, it will cease to be free for religion, except for the sect that can win political power.'"

"Source of Integrity"

Still in a serious vein, Mr. Cooke said he brought up the matter of Mencken's agnosticism because "it was the source of his integrity" and since some people "may assume we are forgiving him in the usual neighborly way by agreeing, at the end, not to take him seriously."

He said last night's dedication was an effort "to keep the grave from burying the bright sword of his scorn, with which in an earlier prosperity he used to jab and dismay the people of the United States."

Mr. Cooke insisted that visitors to the Mencken room come there for "entertainment when life is gray and baffling, for a dose of precision and skepticism in a world of newspaper men, for a bath of lucidity and humor in a nation of sociologists, for a snicker of disbelief in a country of believers."

It would be "supreme blasphemy," the speaker said, "if anyone came to the Mencken room solemnly, timidly, pedantically, or reverently."

Declares Room Open

Whereupon he declared the room open "for the comfort of sinners and the astonishment of the virtuous."

given to the
ENOCH PRATT FREE LIBRARY
by
HENRY LOUIS MENCKEN

Bookplate used by Mencken for his donations to the library

Hamilton Owens, friend and colleague of H. L. Mencken for decades, opened the door of reminiscence to the delight of an audience which all but whooped as one story followed another.

Mr. Owens, former editor in chief of the *Sunpapers,* was associated with Mr. Mencken professionally and personally and last night he shared his memories with all.

He told of the writer's deep joy of life, his tireless energy, his sardonic glee in barbs at those he thought to be hypocritical or pompous.

Made Up Hoaxes

In his younger days it was Mencken's amusement to perpetrate monstrous hoaxes on individuals who drew his scorn, Mr. Owens said, and the young writer concocted elaborate letters and testimonials to baffle the unfortunate victims of his penetrating wit.

Especially effective was an uproarious leaflet he distributed during the Scopes trial in Tennessee when that young teacher was under attack for giving instruction in the theory of evolution. H. L. Mencken covered

the trial and the issues were a challenge that inspired his most biting satire.

Mr. Owens told, too, of Mencken's profound love of music—of making it as well as listening to it, and recalled meetings of the famous Saturday Night Club where music-makers gathered, sometimes to play most of the night away.

Near the conclusion of his remarks, Mr. Owens used Mencken's own words in a self-description in which he found himself "full of steam and malicious animal magnetism."

Mencken wrote those words in telling how he labored as a young newspaper man to cover the great Baltimore fire and how it was "grand beyond compare" so to labor.

In the summer of 1896 the sixteen-year-old Mencken published "Ode to the Pennant on the Centerfield Pole" in the Baltimore American; *it was his first appearance in print.* Do You Remember?, *a reconstruction of his humorous correspondence with Philip Goodman, was published in 1996. It may be the last work that he planned but did not allow to appear during his lifetime. His diary and memoirs did not need reconstruction, but publication of them was delayed by the terms of his will. He knew that they would have the same effect that his previous works had had, and he wanted to spare the feelings of persons mentioned in them who were still alive. He had seeded the future with writings that would prolong for the rest of the century the commotion begun at* The Smart Set. *The publication of a different kind of posthumous work,* Minority Report: H. L. Mencken's Notebooks, *coincided with the opening of the Mencken Room. It was reviewed by Julian P. Boyd (excerpt from "Prejudices According to Mencken,"* New York Times Book Review, *20 May 1956, pp. 1, 24).*

[. . .] In the fall of 1948, when Mencken suffered a stroke, the flow came to a halt. He recovered most of his physical vigor, but there was no new writing under the famous signature. A few months before his death, however, Mencken's secretary discovered the notebooks which are now published in "Minority Report." Mencken meant them to be published. He wrote in the preface:

"Ever since my earliest attempts as an author I have followed the somewhat banal practice of setting down notions as they came to me * * * and then throwing these notes into a bin. Out of that bin have come a couple of dozen books and pamphlets and an almost innumerable swarm of magazine and newspaper articles, but still the raw materials kept mounting faster than I could work them up, so I am printing herewith some select samples of them * * *."

In the Twenties, with so many asserting their individuality that the idea of revolt became itself a sort of cult of conformity, Mencken's *American Mercury* was the bible of the undergraduate and his word the alpha and omega of the emancipated. His scorn of the Uplifters, the Yahoos, the Wowsers, the Booboisie—the very words need explanation today—was repeated endlessly by many who did not realize that his fulminations proceeded from a solid foundation of self-discipline, learning and an inborn passion for the decencies embedded in the Bill of Rights. This more or less blind adulation filled him with something akin to contempt, for he knew that, at best, on another day his followers would pant after different gods and, at worst, he himself would occupy the role of one of the "jitney Messiahs" upon whom he directed his withering blasts. Yet in a measure he was trapped and forced to permit the follies and aberrations of humanity to employ his superb gifts. He was producing brilliant pyrotechnics against stupidity long before the Twenties, and continued to do so long afterward, but, as the event seems to have proved, this is likely to be the most ephemeral part of his work. His more enduring monuments seem to be promised in the incomparable autobiographical and linguistic volumes.

Yet, all of his belaboring of theologians, politicians and pedagogues was in truth a defense of religion, democracy and learning. He was affronted by attempts to explain the unknowable in terms of the not worth knowing. His blast against democracy was aimed at the detractors of the free man and the cheapeners of free institutions. His ridicule of jargon, pedantry, and obscurantism in education was a blow in behalf of the seeker after truth. He was born without envy and, by his own confession, "with no more public spirit than a cat," yet his blows against the reigning potentates in religion, in politics, and in education would scarcely have been delivered with such fury if he had not felt his own beliefs profaned by their actions. His doubts rested on certainty, his pessimism on an ultimate optimism, even when he hid his sensitive nature behind a cosmic guffaw.

The nature of those beliefs is once more made apparent in "Minority Report," whose title is more painfully apt today than it would have been in the Twenties. This volume of selected observations culled during "long years devoted to the pursuit, anatomizing and embalming of ideas," contains more than 400 items, running from a line or so to several pages. They cover theology, capitalism, communism, education, philosophy, the Negro, the Jew, love, poetry, universal suffrage, democracy, altruism, fashion, adultery, the clergy, Haeckel's recapitulation theory, ethics, canon law, the female moron, life in Mississippi, and a great many other topics familiar to the seasoned Mencken reader, arranged in no more systematic order.

Some of the familiar landmarks still stand out boldly—that belief in immortality is a vestige of childish egoism; that the scientist "who yields anything to theology, however slight, is yielding to ignorance and false pretenses"; that the United States has not only failed to produce a genuine aristocracy but has also failed to produce an indigenous intelligentsia; that in a democracy "the man who is barely human is treated as if he were the peer of Aristotle"; that human life is basically a comedy; that God made a bungling job of the human body, forcing man "to lug around a frame packed with defects, from imperfectly centered eyes to weakly arched feet"; that no other religious system has such troubles with the sex question as Christianity does, and that it is "indeed, the most unhealthy of religions"; that it is impossible for a metaphysician to state his ideas in plain English, most of those ideas being basically nonsensical; that the only part of the Bill of Rights still effective is that prohibiting the quartering of troops on citizens in time of peace.

Further, that democracy, by encouraging the incompetent and envious man, throws its weight against every rational concept of honor, honesty, and common decency; that the proverbial wisdom of the East is "even more blowsy and senseless than the metaphysics of the West"; that the "existence of most human beings is of absolutely no significance to history or to human progress"; that there are some people, "the bibliobibuli," who read too much and are constantly drunk on books, as other men are drunk on whisky or religion; that it "is impossible to imagine the universe run by a wise, just and omnipotent God, but it is quite easy to imagine it run by a board of gods," and if such a board "actually exists it operates precisely like the board of a corporation that is losing money." And so on.

There is no question but that this reflects the minority view, and the faithful Mencken followers will be saddened to consider that it is also a final report. But they will be heartened to know that the Old Master went down with the flag still flying, even snapping more saucily than ever, and they will refuse to believe that the vast bin from which these thoughts were culled has become empty.

The bin was not empty. But prior to the publication of Mencken's controversial memoirs, two other moments in the years after his death were occasions for reassessment: the opening of his correspondence held by the New York Public Library in 1971 and the centennial events of 1980 (George Gent, "Mencken's Letters

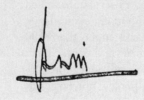

H.L.MENCKEN
1524 HOLLINS ST.
BALTIMORE.

December 16th

Dear Sir:-

      I replied to your inquiry a week ago.   It is answered more fully in " A Book of Prefaces".   [The position of Mr. Dreiser among contemporary American authors could not be higher.   As for his personal character, it is of course difficult to discuss it.   So far as I know, he has never been convicted of an infamous crime.   I would trust him with my money, but not in my wine cellar.]

            Sincerely yours,

H.L.MENCKEN
1524 HOLLINS ST.
BALTIMORE.   December 23, 1940.

Dear Theodor:

      Thanks very much for your Christmas greeting. I hope that you and Mrs. Hemberger are in the best of health. As for me, I begin to break up, but I am still able to do more or less work.

      The death of Pearl, following so soon after that of Sam Dorman, has given the Club a dreadful blow.   It still survives, but it is more or less subdued.

           Yours,

Four of Mencken's letters. His brother, August, estimated that he wrote 100,000 of them. His correspondence held by the New York Public Library was unsealed in 1971 (Collections of Richard J. Schrader and George H. Thompson).

H. L. MENCKEN
1524 HOLLINS ST.
BALTIMORE-23   January 7, 1953.

Dear Mr. Koch:

        Mr. Mencken sends his very best thanks for your pleasant
letter.   Unfortunately, he is still ill and unable to write to
you.   He has done no writing whatsoever for four years past and
it is highly improbable that he will do so in the future.   He
is naturally delighted to hear that you have enjoyed his writings
and he appreciates your writing in to say so.

                              Sincerely yours,

                              Rosalind Lohrfinck
                              Secretary to Mr. Mencken

H.L.MENCKEN
1524 HOLLINS ST.
BALTIMORE.

                              May 31st

Dear Mrs. DePuy:-

        I surely hope the lameness is passing.   It gave me a
shock to see you hobbling in like Julia Ward Howe.
        Our old dog Tessie died on Sunday. A tooth abcess
developed gangrene and the horse-doctor gave her a sniff of prussic acid.
She went out instantly.   Tessie was 16 years old, a great age for a dog.
She never married.   We miss her enormously.   Sunday afternoon my brothers
and I buried her in the garden, and today I ordered a small tablet to be
set in the wall, thus " 1905-Tessie-1921".   Tessie was a Presbyterian.
        I hope you let me know of it when you come back to New York.

        Yours,

Displayed Today," New York Times, *29 January 1971, p. 20C).*

The correspondence of H. L. Mencken, the satirist, wit, iconoclast and confirmed enemy of what he called "boobus Americanus," will be made available to scholars for the first time today when the New York Public Library lifts the seal binding the material since his death 15 years ago.

Believed to be the largest of his correspondence, the collection contains an estimated total of 30,000 letters, notes, postcards, memorandums and other material relating to Mencken's long years as one of America's most influential writers, editors and journalists.

"The great bulk of the material are letters to Mencken from some two thousand correspondents, many of them the most prominent people in the literary, artistic and political worlds of the day," said Paul Rugen, the library's keeper of manuscripts. "But we also have many of Mencken's own letters, even though he rarely kept carbons. The copies were made later from stenographic notes by his secretary."

List of Correspondents

The list of persons who wrote Mencken during his most influential years as editor of Smart Set and The American Mercury, and later, include:

Arnold Bennett, W. Somerset Maugham, George Jean Nathan, Willa Cather, F. Scott and Zelda Fitzgerald, William Faulkner, Henry Miller, John Dos Passos, Theodore Dreiser, Robert Frost, Ellen Glasgow, Sinclair Lewis, Franklin D. Roosevelt, Clarence Darrow, Felix Frankfurter, Alma Gluck, Helen Keller, Drew Pearson, James Thurber and Kaiser Wilhelm II.

The library received the letters, quite unexpectedly, within months after Mencken's death at the age of 75 on Jan. 29, 1956. In an agreement worked out with his literary executors—his brother, August, who has since died, and the Mercantile-Safe Deposit and Trust Company in Baltimore—the library agreed to keep the letters from public scrutiny for 15 years from the date of the author's death.

In willing the letters to the library, Mencken had suggested that some time elapse before making them available. But he stipulated 15 years in an accompanying memorandum to his executors, Mr. Rugen said.

Diary Available in '81

The author's diary is now in the Enoch Pratt Free Library of Baltimore, but will not become available until 1981. In the meantime, scholars who have known

of the existence of the Mencken letters have been trying without avail to tap their treasures. To all requests that they be allowed to look at the collection, the library would do no more than confirm that it possessed some Mencken material.

The letters throw considerable light on many of Mencken's prejudices and enthusiasms, as well as on his generosity to generations of young American writers.

A lifelong debunker and enemy of religion, Mencken wrote to Alfred A. Knopf in 1932 to recommend an author for a book on skepticism. After asserting that it should contain essays by Paine and Ingersoll, among others, he went on to recommend that it include sections on "the contradictions and absurdities in the Bible" and summaries "of the butcheries during the Inquisition."

Later, in a letter to Charles Angoff, an editor of The American Mercury and future Mencken biographer, on his visit to Palestine, he wrote:

"If you ever want any Jordan water for baptizing children, let me know. I have a large supply of it. It is very powerful and one drop on the tongue of a dog is sufficient to convert him to Christianity."

The same letter commends the Palestinian Jews for their realism, asserting that "A rabbi who went among them would have his whiskers pulled out for his pains."

Mencken was an early supporter of Henry Miller, author of "Tropic of Cancer" and "Tropic of Capricorn," and the two men kept up a warm correspondence. On the publication of the latter book in French, Mencken wrote Miller:

"I am only sorry that the country is not yet civilized enough to read and appreciate the book. You achieve with ease all the effects that [James] Joyce tries to get by puffing and fluttering and you make such performers as Hemingway look merely silly. My most sincere congratulations."

Earlier Miller had written about a new magazine, The Booster, with which he was associated, and sent along a prospectus. Mencken replied:

"On my return from the South I find your circular letter. I refuse absolutely to subscribe to the new magazine. Years ago I took a blood oath to spend no money on magazine subscriptions. My belief, indeed, is that anyone who reads magazines is insane. I deplore your decision to go into so evil a trade.

"Very few magazine editors survive more than a few years. The business of reading manuscripts quickly explodes the corpuscles of their cerebra and they have to be slowed up. If I hear that you are actually going on with the project, I shall suggest to the

American consul general at Paris that he have you incarcerated."

Invited Frankfurter

Supreme Court Justice Felix Frankfurter first began corresponding with Mencken in 1939, after reading an article by him on the Sacco-Vanzetti case. Mencken's return letter invited Justice Frankfurter to visit him in Baltimore, where "the cooks in this town have enlightened ideas, and some of the bartenders are talented."

They met many times over the years, drawn by a shared interest in documents and good food. On the day before Mencken's 75th birthday on Sept. 12, 1955, when Mencken was seriously ill and bedridden, Justice Frankfurter wrote him:

"From that first meeting of ours, at the Ritz in Boston, through those happy parties of ours in Baltimore and the messages since and to this day, you have replenished life for me, by confirming my zest for it and adding yours. I hail thee!"

The library will have a small display of the correspondence today on the third floor of its Fifth Avenue building. A larger exhibition will be held in the fall.

* * *

(Anonymous, "A Scout for the Scholars: H. L. Mencken," Bulletin of the New York Public Library, 75 [February 1971]: 63–65).

With a bow to the mercurial ghost of H. L. Mencken, the Library is happy to announce the unsealing of an important repository for the study of twentieth-century history and literature, what is believed to be the largest collection in existence of the correspondence of H. L. Mencken: about 30,000 letters, notes, postcards, and memoranda to and from the great American writer and editor whom the New York *Times* recently described as the "satirist, wit, iconoclast and confirmed enemy of what he called 'boobus Americanus.'" Soon after Mencken's death in 1956, the correspondence came to the Library's Manuscript Division, but in accordance with the terms of a memorandum accompanying his will, it was not made public for fifteen years. Mencken was a long-time friend of The New York Public Library, and of Harry Miller Lydenberg, its director from 1934 to 1941. In addition to his letters, Mencken gave the Library other works, including a manuscript copy of Theodore Dreiser's *Sister Carrie* which had been given him by Dreiser himself, after Mencken had encouraged his early writing efforts. Dreiser wrote to Mencken in 1911, after the initial success of *Sister Carrie*,

saying "I expect to try out this book game for about four or five books after which unless I am enjoying a good income from them I will quit."

The two thousand correspondents represented in the collection came from all over the world and many walks of life: writers, editors, artists, politicians, actors and actresses, musicians, and many unfamous (or is it in-famous) persons who contributed words and phrases to his collection in *The American Language.* There are letters from contributors and would-be contributors to *Smart Set* and *The American Mercury,* the magazines Mencken and George Jean Nathan edited from 1914 to 1923 and from 1924 to 1933 respectively. Mencken exchanged letters with librarians, publishers, prison inmates, and many members of his family, even those living near him in Baltimore. To name a few of the correspondents: Joseph Conrad, Gordon Craig, Douglas Fairbanks, Felix Frankfurter, Alma Gluck, Helen Keller, Joseph Wood Krutch, Fiorello La Guardia, John L. Lewis, Edgar Lee Masters, Margaret Mead, Henry Miller, Gertrude Stein, Norman Thomas, Kaiser Wilhelm II, Frank Lloyd Wright, and Richard Wright. The letters were kept in neat files, often with cross-references and Mencken's comments and observations. Many of Mencken's own letters are in the form of copies made later from stenographic notes by his secretary.

Clarence Darrow was a frequent correspondent, although the two men met only a few times. Even in 1925, when Mencken was reporting to the Baltimore *Sun* on the famous "Monkey Trial" in Dayton, Tennessee and Darrow's defense of John Scopes, they were both too occupied with the trial to meet socially. For many years, Darrow's handwritten letters are addressed to "Dear Menkin," while his secretary typed "Mencken." In 1924, Darrow said he had read almost all of Mencken's writing, and found "little of your stuff I do not believe is true. This of course will show you that your views are logical and correct."

Most of Mencken's correspondents were friendly (Lillian Gish, having just read a new Mencken work in 1927, wrote that she had "again decided that you are a gorgeous man"), and most were inspired to be as witty as the man to whom they wrote (empressario Texas Guinan congratulated him on his marriage but wondered whether that wasn't carrying love too far). Other people occasionally invented feuds between Mencken and his friends. Drew Pearson wrote to Mencken in May 1947 that he had heard they were mortal enemies. Mencken replied "I never deny rumors . . . especially when they are preposterous. . . . This will expunge me of the suspicion that I have fallen for the New Deal and . . . you of the suspicion that you have fallen for Holy Church or Atheism." This is followed by various amicable remarks about his desire to see Pearson very soon.

Mencken was an enemy of the New Deal, and was later criticized for what some people thought to be German sympathies. But, in 1928, when Franklin Roosevelt had just been elected governor of New York, he wrote in a postscript to Mencken "I want to see you soon, to swap yarns." Other "swaps" mentioned in various letters were Frank Harris' request to be put in touch with Mencken's bootlegger (a request repeated by Scott Fitzgerald), and Robert Benchley's thanks for the name of Mencken's hay-fever doctor. He said "We boys must stick together, because no one else takes hay-fever seriously."

Mencken often received compliments for his writing, which he just as often dismissed gruffly. In 1948 William Faulkner compared Mencken's writing in *The American Language* to Laurence Sterne's and Jonathan Swift's: "There are just too goddamn many of the human race and they talk too much." Back in 1920, in the early days of his success, Scott Fitzgerald had written: "how hard it is not to imitate your style at times." These two remarks, a generation apart in time and style, help to indicate the very important contribution Mencken made to writing, and especially to American writing. He denied being a scholar, but preferred to think of himself as "a scout for scholars."

Later this year a major Mencken exhibit will be announced by the Library. A few letters are now on display in the third floor corridor outside the Manuscript Division.

* * *

(From Menckeniana, *75 (Fall 1980): 4–5).*

PROCLAMATION
BY
MAYOR WILLIAM DONALD SCHAEFER
Designating September 7–13, 1980
AS
"H. L. MENCKEN WEEK" IN BALTIMORE

WHEREAS, September 12, 1980, will mark the one hundredth anniversary of the birth of Henry Louis Mencken, newspaperman, editor, and social critic—"the Sage of Baltimore"; and

WHEREAS, through his essays and criticism, H. L. Mencken exerted a powerful influence on American intellectuals during the decade following World War I; and

WHEREAS, a graduate of the Baltimore Polytechnic School, this literary and social critic helped liberate American literature from academic and moralistic restraints and issued bristling attacks on America's vaunted traditions, in particular the imperfections of democracy; and

WHEREAS, upon his death in Baltimore on January 29, 1956, he left his extensive and valuable collection of books and manuscripts to the Enoch Pratt Free Library, Baltimore's public library, for the use of scholars, authors, and journalists; and

WHEREAS, to mark the anniversary of the birth of our most celebrated native citizen, scores of programs have been planned locally and nationally.

NOW, THEREFORE, I, WILLIAM DONALD SCHAEFER, MAYOR OF THE CITY OF BALTIMORE, do hereby proclaim September 7–13, 1980, as "H. L. MENCKEN WEEK" IN BALTIMORE, and do urge all citizens to give the recognition truly deserved by an essayist and critic of the stature of Henry Louis Mencken.

IN WITNESS WHEREOF, I have hereunto set my hand and caused the Great Seal of the City of Baltimore to be affixed this seventh day of September, in the year of Our Lord, one thousand nine hundred and eighty.

William Donald Schaefer
Mayor

Among those "scores of programs" was the Mencken Centennial Banquet, held on 12 September at the Belvedere Hotel in Baltimore. The featured speaker was Mencken's colleague Alistair Cooke, who edited The Vintage Mencken *for Knopf in 1955 (excerpts from* Menckeniana, *77 [Spring 1981]: 5–9).*

Governor and Mrs. Hughes, Mr. Siegel, (*clears throat*), excuse me, I've become the George Jessel of the Mencken circuit. (*Laughter.*) I do all his eulogies. This is the second today. . . . Well, the time is late. Everything that could be said about Mencken has been said. In conclusion—(*Laughter.*)

I was going to apologize for my presence here until I realized this was a typical Mencken absurdity—that you should choose as your spokesman a man who incorporates in one person five human types that Mencken couldn't abide: (*laughter*) an Englishman—he distrusted all Englishmen, and he shared the deep American belief that Englishmen are born talking American and then put on the dog; a Methodist—he abominated Methodists, I was lapsed, but I don't believe he was ever convinced of it, because I was an admirer of Franklin Roosevelt, and he knew there must be something religiously wrong with such a man; a broadcaster—which came to be my trade. Forty-six years ago I started—I was a child prodigy of course. (*Laughter.*) He said all broadcasters, whom he detested, suffered from perfumed tonsils. (*Laughter.*) You've heard tonight the same could not be said of Mr. Mencken. I wrote for a liberal newspaper and he used to say he couldn't remember the times that he staggered out of an editorial meeting wondering dizzily how God had managed for so many years without the *New Republic* and the *Manchester Guardian.* (*Laughter.*) And, a golfer—you've heard him already, almost inarticulate on the subject. But he said the first time he saw a newspaper reporter wearing what was then called plus-fours, it was "as if I had encountered a stud horse with his head done up in frizzies" (*laughter*) and you may recall, he said, "If I had my way, any man guilty of golf would be ineligible for any office of trust under these United States." You may have noticed that the press, especially the superior press (I'm talking geographically now), has made a great point that this occasion and similar celebrations, especially that of the National Press Club today, are basically ludicrous occasions, given Mencken's character, because he took a very dim view of all public ceremonies and held in deep suspicion all public honors. The *New York Times* said this morning that Mencken's most outrageous opinions would not today raise an eyebrow in Peoria. I haven't been in Peoria for sometime, but I began to think if it is the consensus of the population of Peoria that "adultery is the application of democracy to love"; that "a man remembers with a special tenderness his first girl and after that bunches them"; (*laughter*) and, if they also go around the streets chanting that "democracy is the theory that the common people know what they want and deserve to get it good and hard," I can only say that Peoria must be a very rousing place to live in. (*Laughter and applause.*) But, it is true that he regarded honors suspiciously. I remember once asking him what was going on in some large hotel and he said, "I expect they are honoring some dishonorable crook." (*Laughter.*) It may not raise an eyebrow in Peoria, but it might in Harvard if I remind you that he said, "No decent man ever accepts a university degree that he didn't earn with his own labors. Honorary degrees are fit only for realtors, chiropractors, presidents of the United States, and other such riff raff." (*Applause and laughter.*)

I don't think Baltimoreans need the vital statistics—you've had them filled in by the papers almost interminably this week—and you all know that today is The Day. But, I couldn't help noticing in the little excerpts we had from him that though he said psychologists and other frauds said it was impossible to remember anything from the age of three, I'd like to remind you what it was, if I can ever find it, that he remembered.

Nobody, no autobiographer that I know, has ever started so succinctly by telling you how the world first struck you and it's the very first page of *Happy Days:* "At the instant I first became aware of the cosmos we all infest, I was sitting in my mother's lap and blinking at a great burst of lights, some of them red and other green,

The British journalist and author Alistair Cooke, editor of The Vintage Mencken (1955), *who spoke at the Mencken Centennial Banquet*

but most of them only the bright yellow of flaring gas. The time: the evening of Thursday, September 13, 1883, the day after my third birthday. The place: a ledge outside the second-story front windows of my father's cigar factory at 368 Baltimore Street, Baltimore, Maryland, U.S.A., fenced off from space and disaster by a sign bearing the majestic legend: AUG. MENCKEN AND BRO. The occasion: the third and last annual Summer Nights' Carnival of the Order of Orioles, a society that adjourned with a thumping deficit the next morning and has since been forgotten by the whole human race. [. . .]"

[. . .] Well, you all know that the day after his eighteenth birthday, after his father died, he put on his best suit, went to the Baltimore *Morning Herald,* hung around for five weeks waiting for an assignment, got one, which was to track down, in a blizzard, the rumor of a horse stealing out of town. He covered it in two very short, very bald sentences. He framed them. He stood and looked at this little, first printed piece, bedazzled, and he knew absolutely what he wanted to be: a newspaper reporter. [. . .]

Well, I would like to say very briefly, first of all, because I want to speak as a newspaperman, what to me made him a great reporter. But first to mention his serious contribution as a literary dictator—the fact that he, more than anybody, in the late '10's and the early

Ticket to the Mencken Centennial Banquet (courtesy of the Enoch Pratt Free Library)

Postcard with the Mencken centennial postmark (Richard J. Schrader Collection)

The

requests the pleasure
of your company at
a two-day festival

MENCKEN 100

offering a series of
special events
planned in honor of the
One Hundredth Anniversary
of the birth of

H. L. MENCKEN

September 12 & 13, 1980

Cover for the program of the library's Mencken centennial celebration

1920's, destroyed what he called "the marshmallow gentility of American letters" and against great public outcry and the scorn of the practicing literary critics of the time, championed the new realists, beginning with Frank Norris, publishing Dreiser, James M. Cain, James T. Farrell, O'Neill, and many others. Twenty-five years ago in a preface to an anthology—which I hope Alfred put out two million copies of today—I advanced the thesis that Mencken in his heyday—when he was deified as a great thinker, and an enormous rebel and, as he said, a critic of ideas—my thesis was that this reputation did not stand up, that he was primarily an American humorist out of Mark Twain and a superb journalist out of nowhere. I was deeply flattered last Sunday to read that the *New York Times,* after twenty-five years, with its customary circumspection, announced that this thesis is true. (*Laughter.*)

What made him a great journalist? Well, first, of course, that he was an original. His style—nobody in English or American has written like it before or since, though I regret to say that thousands have tried. His ideas, I believe, were very simple. Many, many people have disliked democracy; many people don't like rich men. But Mencken put the two ideas together. Who else could have written, "My distaste for democracy is rooted in a flaw of character. I am devoid of envy. When I contemplate John D. Rockefeller, I am as inert as a stockbroker before Johann Sebastian Bach." (*Laughter.*)

I don't think that the style alone would have done it, but his style, especially when he covered events—I covered many, especially conventions, with him—was disciplined by the rules that he'd learned from his first city editor who, I regret to say to the Patterson family, was on the Baltimore *Morning Herald.* The rules he learned from Max Ways and the principles he worked out for himself. The rules were quite simple. 1. Always get age, addresses, names, dates, all figures accurate; 2. Never trust a cop; verify his report; 3. Get your copy in early; 4. Always be aware of the law of libel. Now, as for the principles he worked out for himself—they, of course, stem from his character. And, I think the first was his prejudice. As he said later, "Reporters seem to have become homunculi at the end of a telephone. The great thing is to go out and feel the wind of the world in your face and cover the story and stay with it till it's finished." And he just told you it took him a week to cover the Baltimore Fire, he had about seven hours sleep, and what he didn't tell you was that between February 7th and February 14th, 1904, he didn't have a bath or a change of linen for precisely one week. I think that explains his prejudice, when the American Newspaper Guild was organized, of saying that "It makes no more sense to have a forty-hour week for a reporter than to have a forty-hour week for an archbishop." (*Laughter.*)

The principles he told me about when I was a starting newspaperman have never left me, and today, I must say, they look like shining virtues, though in my day they were taken for granted. I'm afraid they are violated today by the nicest people, because of the extreme seductions of airlines, inaugural flights, and the like. He said, "Never accept a free ticket from a theatre manager, a free ride from the Chamber of Commerce, or a favor from a politician. That way, Cooke," he said, "you will find that shaving in the morning can be a relatively agreeable pastime." (*Applause and laughter.*) And, I think in the end, even his enemies—these people who came pounding on the door at Hollins Street, enflamed with theological or political grievances, and then found this mild man with the gas jet eyes, this little man who was courteous and mild—even they, I think, came to

Program for the event , mentioned by Cooke, during which the three-year-old Mencken "first became aware of the cosmos we all infest" (George H. Thompson Collection)

instincts, the same deadly, sensible eye to distinguish the discrepancy between the way human beings really thought and acted and the way they pretended they acted, their beliefs. And, as in all great humor, there is a cutting element of almost semi-tragedy in this, because I think Mencken's humor, like that of Twain, is that of a disappointed idealist. It's what I have called elsewhere, from Mark Twain to Woody Allen, the humor of the soured immigrant, who discovers that the American dream can be sometimes a hilarious circus and sometimes a nightmare. [. . .]

Cooke's assessment is borne out by the fact that Mencken appeared in more than 150 anthologies between 1956 and 1989, keeping him on the margin of canonicity. The publication of his diary in the latter year, however, caused an uproar that nearly resulted in banishment. Many reviewers, it seems, got no further than the introduction, where the editor charged Mencken with bigotry and cited examples that were quoted across the country. Mencken was thus restored to the national stage in the way he would have liked best. On Mencken's side were many who had known him or were members of the groups he supposedly disliked; but he did not need defending then any more than he had needed it seventy-five years earlier. The controversy actually pivoted on another national debate: about the inability to read. The same might be said of the parallel and perennial argument over Mencken's favorite novel, Huckleberry Finn *(Jonathan Yardley, "Mencken's Unsurprising Prejudices,"* Washington Post, *11 December 1989, p. B2).*

realize that his great strength was the strength of character. He could not be bought. He was offered fortunes, as you know, to go first to New York, which he dismissed as a third-rate Babylon; to be syndicated; to go on the radio; to write, for very fat fees, speeches for politicians, going, I hate to say in the presence of your Chief Executive, all the way up to a Governor and even a United States Senator. He turned everything down. He was not interested in money. He was not only himself incorruptible, but he had a nostril very finely tuned to the odor of corruption. He could smell it a mile away and he pointed it out, irrespective of party or person, and this, of course, got him a great name in the republic as a nuisance, but it also brought him floods of obscene mail and actual threats to his life (especially when he went south) and the passage through two state legislatures of bills for his deportation.

Well, that's what made him a great journalist. I believe, however, that his permanent reputation will be that—as it was not of Mark Twain's in the beginning—but it will be that of Mark Twain as a great American humorist, and I don't mean just a literary clown. I think he's a direct descendant of Mark Twain, not by way of conscious parody, but because he recognized in Twain not only a kindred spirit, but a man with the same

For the first three years of this column's life—from the fall of 1981 until the fall of 1984, when a change in The Washington Post style replaced column titles with bylines—it was called "Prejudices." As I wrote in my inaugural piece, this was "an act of homage, not of imitation," in memory of Henry Louis Mencken, "the greatest and most widely imitated prose stylist ever to grace the pages of an American newspaper."

Well. Now it is the late autumn of 1989, and if you believe what you read in the newspapers—especially those published in Baltimore—the man to whom this homage was paid turns out to have been an antisemite, a racist, a Nazi and an all-around ingrate. How lucky I am that, even if through no action of my own, Mencken's title no longer sits atop these weekly words. Whew!

Truth to tell, though, I feel no sense of relief at having thus escaped opprobrium-by-association. From where I sit, Mencken looks to be getting a bad rap. You would never know, from the howls of indignation issuing forth from erstwhile Mencken partisans and others bearing complaints, that the remarks around which this new controversy swirls occupy only a minuscule por-

—✗   ⑪

they sufficed to turn away all of the men who came to work at
6 P.M.   In the ~~course of the evening~~ *late afternoon* one of the pickets came
to the Sun composing-room and tried to persuade the men already
at work to stop work at once and go to the union hall, but when
he was detected he was put out.   At the request of the Sunpapers
policemen were detailed to keep order at the entrances to the
Sun Building.   The strikers gathered there were in groups
numbering from as few as two to as many as ten men.   They carried
no banners.   They accosted all men coming to work, and tried to
persuade them to join the illegal strike.   There was no disorder,
but some of the men on picket had been drinking, and the police
were instructed to keep them moving.   They greeted politely all
executives who passed through their lines.

          The first news of the rump meeting had reached the Sun
office at about 4 P.M.   It came from one of the Sun printers who
had been present, but had managed to escape.   Some time elapsed
before any detailed information about the proceedings was obtainable.
Efforts were made during the evening to reach Mr. Brannock at union
headquarters, at the hall, and at his home, but they were unsuccessful
until late in the evening.   Efforts were made at the same time to
reach Mr. Baker in Washington, but he had left for Indianapolis by
air, and he was not reached until he arrived at his home there,
shortly after 9 P.M.   Meanwhile, the following telegram had been
sent to him, signed by Mr. Schmick for the Sunpapers and C. Dorsey
Warfield for the Hearst papers:

          A considerable number of printers on the Sunpapers failed
to cover their situations tonight.   Seven printers are now working
at the Sun instead of twenty-six.   The Sunpapers have only a
skeleton force.   The News-Post anticipates a similar situation
at 11.20 P.M., when their production starts for Monday's paper.
          We have information that a faction Baltimore Typographical
Union has taken illegal stand.
          You have underwritten our contract on behalf of International

Page from the typescript for a 1942 entry in Mencken's diary, which was published posthumously in 1989 (courtesy of the Enoch Pratt Free Library)

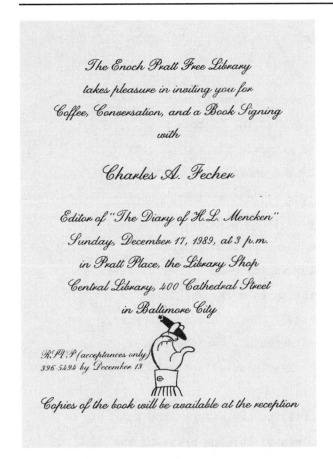

Invitation to a signing of the posthumously published work that led to charges that Mencken was an anti-Semite

know astonishingly little about him. Anyone with a reasonably thorough, but by no means expert, knowledge of his life and work is well aware that: (a) his attitude toward Jews was complex, ambiguous and perhaps, in the end, unknowable; (b) he had an affection for Germany and Teutonic culture that clouded his vision during both world wars; and (c) he could be patronizing if not condescending toward blacks.

All of that has been on the record for years: in Mencken's published work, in his letters and papers, in the several biographies of him. The diaries may supply a bit of especially malodorous icing for this unappetizing cake, but it was baked decades ago and has been in the shop window ever since. Anyone who believes otherwise, who thinks that the contents of the diaries really are "news," was born yesterday or has maintained a blissful ignorance of American literary and journalistic history.

Beyond that, in their eagerness to outdo each other as exemplars of religious and racial piety, Mencken's new critics have done a fairly dandy job of misrepresenting the man who wrote the diaries. The truth is—to the extent any truths can be identified in this business—considerably more complex than any of these people seems willing to acknowledge.

At this point a personal note may be in order. A decade ago I signed a contract to write a biography of Mencken, a project I subsequently abandoned for a number of reasons, one of the most important being that I didn't think I could write sympathetically about him because of what I saw as his antisemitism and racism. But for whatever it may be worth, after reading the diaries I am far from sure that I made the right decision; this is because the diaries show us that, yes, Mencken did have his disagreeable prejudices, but he was able to rise above them in ways no true bigot possibly could.

It is true, for example, that in these diaries Mencken occasionally refers to "a brisk clever Jew" or "a Jew" or "a highly dubious Jew," yet it is also true that he bearded the notorious Gerald L. K. Smith on the subject of antisemitism: "I asked him this morning if he were inclining that way and he denied it. His wife expressed horror of the thought. Nevertheless, I am convinced that Gerald is preparing to get aboard the great antisemitic movement now rolling up in New York." Not merely was Mencken's judgment correct; those are not the words of a man who welcomed the idea of an antisemitic popular movement.

It is true, too, that Mencken said of "colored" women, "they are all essentially child-like, and even hard experience does not teach them anything." It is also true, though, that he wrote of George S. Schuyler, of the Pittsburgh Courier: "He is unquestionably the most competent Negro journalist ever heard of. Unlike

tion of the newly published "Diaries of H. L. Mencken"; nor would you know that the man who wrote these offensive words was merely speaking, albeit with excessive pungency, the language of his time and place.

It's a pity the old boy isn't around to see how he's being pilloried in his beloved Baltimore, because the show would amuse him greatly. For half a century that city's venerable Sunpapers have traded on their association with Mencken ad infinitum and ad nauseam, but now they've turned on him with a viciousness that, in light of past adulation, borders on the incomprehensible. Until the morning Sun finally weighed in with a temperate, balanced and sensible editorial last Friday, it looked for all the world as if writers for the morning and evening papers were in a competition to see who could distance himself or herself the farthest from the "Sage of Baltimore."

If these people are indeed "shocked" by what they found in the Mencken diaries, as most of them are at pains to tell us, it says more about them than it does about Mencken: It says that, for people who have taken it upon themselves to pass judgment on Mencken, they

nearly all the rest, he has no itch for public office, and is completely devoid of the usual cant. When I compare him to any of the dunderheads now roaring on the *Sun*, I am sharply conscious of his enormous superiority. He is not only much more intelligent than they are; he is vastly more honest." Of the same man Mencken wrote elsewhere: "There are few white columnists, in fact, who can match him for information, intelligence, independence and courage."

If Mencken were in fact an antisemite, why is it that—yes—so many of his closest friends were Jewish? If he were an antisemite, why is it that his publisher, business associate and friend, Alfred A. Knopf, himself Jewish, could turn positively apoplectic at any suggestion that Mencken was prejudiced against Jews? If he were anti-black, why is it that he was widely admired by the black intelligentsia during the 1920s for his support of the Harlem Renaissance, many participants in which he published in the *American Mercury*? If he were anti-black, why was he the only writer to testify in person, in 1935, for the Costigan-Wagner anti-lynching bill, saying, "No government pretending to be civilized can go on condoning such atrocities"?

Why did Mencken write what he did in the diaries? No one can say for certain, but a likely explanation is that in the privacy of his study he indulged himself in his penchant for idle invective and excessive language. The time being the 1930s and '40s, the place being conservative old Baltimore, the writer being a man steeped in the Teutonic tradition—all this being so, it's most improbable that he thought twice about what he was writing in these midnight jottings, much less that he imagined any of it to be offensive. Indeed I suspect that he thought much of it to be not merely inoffensive, but humorous.

Those were different times, hard though it may be for today's (pardon the Menckenism) illuminati to believe it. Racial and religious prejudice was everywhere, and the educated were no less prone to it than their alleged inferiors. Mencken was a man of his times, and to judge him by the standards of our own is as unfair as it is self-righteous.

* * *

(Russell Baker, *"Prejudices Without the Mask,"* New York Times, *13 December 1989, p. A31).*

I am profoundly unshocked to learn that the night thoughts H. L. Mencken confided to his diary were sometimes tainted with racism and anti-Semitism. To have been utterly free of such stuff in Mencken's time and place would have been astonishing. I speak with authority here, for I was growing up just a block away from Mencken while he was keeping his diary.

In that setting, southwest Baltimore in the 1930's and 1940's, we were all racists and anti-Semites, and much more that now seems just as unsavory. Oh, there may have been a saint huddled somewhere in one of Union Square's big, decaying row houses, a person as broad-minded as a 1989 editorial writer, but if so he kept mighty quiet.

The neighborhood language bristled with words now considered so barbaric that using one would disqualify the user for public office or television millions. Mencken's diary avoids most of these dreary words, but it is startling indeed to find him writing "kikes," a word that even the street-corner crowd considered too vile to be spoken without the strongest justification.

No need here to run through the full book of southwest Baltimore's synonyms for "black people." Though even barbarians now decline to speak them, I suspect they are still all too well known. Ironically, though, "black" was considered a peculiarly vicious word for a civilized white to use. The proper word was "colored."

Blacks and Jews were not the only people freely subjected to verbal abuse in the neighborhood. Poles were mocked with the word "bohunks," which contains the root of "honky," the word that became the blacks' popular abusive term for whites in the 1960's.

The many Lithuanians in the neighborhood were called, for some unfathomable reason, "flatheads." They, like the Poles and many neighborhood Germans, were Catholic. Protestants, as seen from my inside observer's post, seemed in some ways more anti-Catholic than anti-Semitic.

For instance, Jews were admired and even secretly envied because they were suspected of being unnaturally smart. ("A smart Jew" and "a dumb bohunk" were expressions I often heard.)

Among Protestants it was highly desirable to have a Jewish doctor (smart, highly competent), whereas Catholic doctors were to be avoided. It was suspected that their medical treatments might be corrupted by slavish devotion to antiquated papal doctrines.

There was much amusement among Protestants about the Catholics eating fish every Friday, but the term of abuse around Union Square—"fish eaters"—seemed toothless enough. It wasn't until I met a youth from suburban Catonsville, three miles to the west and much snootier than our inner-city neighborhood, that I heard the term "mackerel snappers."

Italians got off lightly in the neighborhood, because there weren't any. Near Newark, N.J., where I spent my early childhood, Italians were plentiful and the abusive vocabulary rich. "Wop," the most popular slur among non-Italians, was known in southwest Baltimore, however, as "dago." This last was said to be far more insulting to an Italian than "wop," and in Jersey I understood that it should be left unsaid unless you wanted a punch in the nose.

In New Jersey, Protestants and Irish Catholics alike suspected Italians of enjoying life too much. Being in short supply in southwest Baltimore, however, Italians did not bedevil the neighborhood mind, and so there was no firm misconception about them as there was about Poles (dumb), Jews (smart) and Catholics (sinister). The same was true of the Irish, who seemed not to have found Baltimore as hospitable as cities farther north.

Protestants who came of Appalachian stock were called "hillbillies," and the term connoted ignorance, poverty, vile habits and, in general, low-lifers perfectly at home in the pigpen. These, of course, were my people, and they were considered singularly loathsome when they flocked to Baltimore for war jobs in the 1940's.

Mencken's diary laments the decay of the neighborhood, noting that a house just two doors from his has been sold to Jews and filled with "ratty looking" tenants. Two of those tenants were an aunt I loved and her husband, and I went there often.

It pains me a little to realize that to Mencken we were "ratty looking" people, but then, in those times we hadn't yet learned to mask our thoughts with pseudo-civilized cunning. We all spoke meanly of each other back there, and it wasn't quite as monstrous as it now seems, believe it or not. You had to be there.

* * *

(Letter to the editor, New York Times Book Review, *4 February 1990, p. 33).*

To the Editor:

Henry Mencken brought me to The Baltimore Evening Sun in 1947, and for the next eight years—except when I was representing The Sun abroad—we met regularly, in his home at 1524 Hollins Street, at the paper, in the Enoch Pratt Free Library, where he gave me access to his private papers, and for lunch at the Maryland Club or his favorite restaurants, Miller's and Schellhase's, both long gone.

Long afternoons were spent walking the streets of Baltimore while he reminisced about his 50-year career there, his views of literature and society and how he had introduced America to Bernard Shaw, Friedrich Nietzsche, Joseph Conrad, Ruth Suckow, Theodore Dreiser and Mike Gold's "Jews Without Money."

Then he fell ill. Twice, his younger brother August and I brought him home in a wheelchair from the Johns Hopkins Hospital. During the last year of his life I left the Sunpapers to be with him. Each morning after a hospital orderly had given him his morning rubdown we retired to his backyard. There, beneath an awning August had erected, I read him the morning newspapers, the complete works of Conrad and Twain—"Huckleberry Finn" twice—and the prefaces of Shaw.

When he felt fit, we talked, or gardened, or roamed nearby alleys for firewood, which, when we returned, August and I would saw into suitable lengths on a bench by their old pony shed. Once Mencken told me, with considerable relish, of his vasectomy and three fertile New York women who had volunteered to test its efficacy. They left him, he said, childless.

Two or three times a week I would return for an evening with him. Sometimes we passionately disagreed. He had detested Franklin Roosevelt, whom I admired extravagantly. But we were always civil, and before I would leave we always turned to music. Alfred Knopf had sent him a record player. Among the albums I brought him were three of Gilbert and Sullivan—"geniuses," he sighed.

In all our thousands of hours together I never heard Mencken insult Jews or blacks. Not once did he suggest that they be harmed, embarrassed or victimized by discrimination. Jews, he believed, were brighter, more sensitive and more talented than gentiles. But his affection for them was scarcely surprising, considering the large number of Jews who had been close to him throughout his life, both professionally and socially. "I am," he once said, "quite free of anti-Semitism."

Nor was the word "nigger" in his vocabulary. A black family lived next door; he was on the best of terms with them, and frequently produced surprise gifts for the two small sons. It is true that his attitude toward them was paternalistic. It is equally true that it would have been extremely difficult to find more than a few Baltimoreans at that time—including black Baltimoreans—who would have found that paternalism objectionable.

Now the diary of his later years (review, Dec. 24) is being published—he had expressly prohibited publication, but the lawyers found a way to thwart his instruction—and in it one finds several slurs that are taboo, even shocking, *today.* But they were not written today. They were set down, in private, at a time when racial epithets and jokes were commonly heard in polite society.

Once Mencken even referred in the diary to "two dreadful kikes." My father was a social worker who crusaded for birth control and fought housing discrimi-

Mencken leaving the Johns Hopkins Hospital on 20 March 1951. His biographer William Manchester, who defended Mencken against posthumous charges of racism and anti-Semitism, holds the door (courtesy of the Enoch Pratt Free Library).

nation against Jews. Yet I once heard him describe an objectionable Jew as a "kike." All this, it must be remembered, occurred before the Holocaust revealed to the world where such ugliness ultimately led. At the time such slurs were usually as lacking in malice as the Polish and Italian jokes told today.

Those who argue otherwise, I suggest, are practicing what might be described as generational chauvinism—judging past eras by the standards of the present. The passing of such ex post facto judgments seems to be increasingly popular. A recent headline in a Connecticut newspaper read: "Old West Was Sexist"—though neither the word nor the concept of sexism existed on the frontier. Soon, perhaps, it will be disclosed that "Alamo Defenders Were Homophobes." It is sobering to reflect on the consequences were the tables turned. How would past generations judge American sexual behavior in 1990 and the abandonment of the traditional family?

If we are going to adopt generational chauvinism as dogma, many past heroes will be diminished, including liberal heroes. The kind of anti-Semitism that appears in Mencken's private diary may be found elsewhere: for example, in the early letters of Eleanor

Roosevelt and Adlai Stevenson. And after F.D.R.'s crutches collapsed during a 1936 political rally in Philadelphia, he said, "I was the maddest white man you ever saw"—a remark that, in 1990, could lose an election.

Perhaps the most outrageous twisting of the Mencken diary is the charge that he was pro-Nazi. So widely has this libel been published that a Dec. 31 letter to The New York Times, describing him as "a supporter of Hitler," passed almost unnoticed.

Henry Mencken was a third-generation German-American, and his view of his grandfather's homeland was hopelessly sentimental. It was a dream of pre-Wilhelmine Germany, of whimsical pipe-smoking eccentrics like Jo's beloved in "Little Women," of Hegel and Kant, of Beethoven, Bach and, yes, Mendelssohn.

Little would have come of it had not Mencken, then the country's most controversial literary critic, been singled out for persecution during this country's anti-German hysteria in World War I. The New York Tribune attacked him under the headline "What H. L. Mencken's 'Kultur' is Doing to American Literature." The New Republic described him as "swine-like." The New York Evening Mail, with which he had a contract, rejected his literary articles as "unpatriotic" and unilaterally declared the contract void. He was shadowed by agents of the Justice Department, whose files included reports that he was in the Kaiser's pay, was scheduled for a high German decoration after the war and was an intimate friend of "Nitsky, the German monster." (Nietzsche had died in 1900, 14 years before Sarajevo.)

As a consequence, Mencken's attitude toward the Second World War was wholly unrealistic. He dismissed it as "Roosevelt's War," took little interest in it and was clearly unenthusiastic at the prospect of another German defeat.

But Mencken a *Nazi?* He despised the Third Reich from the outset. When Hitler became Chancellor, he wrote: "I give up the Germans as substantially hopeless. All sorts of authorities report that they are in an exalted and happy mood. If so, it is the kind of euphoria that goes with acute infections." To Dreiser he wrote: "God knows what the Nazis are up to. They seem to be a gang of lunatics to me. I hear I am on their blacklist. . . . I don't know a single man among them, and all my friends in Germany seem to be in opposition—that is, all save a few damned fools I'd hesitate to approach."

On May 25, 1933, one Col. Edwin Emerson notified him that he had been elected to honorary membership in the Friends of Germany, one of the early societies to spring up in the 1930's among German-Americans sympathetic to the Nazis. Mencken sharply declined on the ground that the "extraordinary imbecility" of the Nazi politicians had "destroyed at one stroke a work of rehabilitation that has been going on since the war, and they have made it quite impossible to set up any rational defense of their course. I can imagine no more stupendous folly. For ten years, thanks to the hard and intelligent work of both Germans and Americans, the American attitude toward Germany has improved steadily, and there was a growing disposition to take the German view of the 'reparation' obscenity, and the whole treaty of Versailles. But now, by talking and acting in a completely lunatic manner, Hitler and his associates have thrown away the German case and given the enemies of their country enough ammunition to last for ten years."

Any defense of Germany was impossible, he concluded, "so long as the chief officer of the German state continues to make speeches worthy of an Imperial Wizard of the Ku Klux Klan, and his followers imitate, plainly with his connivance, the monkey-shines of the American Legion at its worst."

Mencken has been silent for 34 years now. His work stands, and it towers. He was a master polemicist; he always gave better than he got, and he really needs no defense. But as one who cherishes accuracy in literary history, I am appalled by the distortions of his con-

siderable role in it. And I am deeply offended by the smearing of my old friend by ignorant liberal bigots.

William Manchester
Longboat Key, Fla.

Jonathan Yardley edited the second of Mencken's memoirs to be released, My Life as Author and Editor, *and presented it in such a way as to defuse hostility. Those offended by the diary had for the most part either been silenced by the likes of Yardley, Baker, and Manchester or had moved on to other offenders against political correctness (Terry Teachout, "Mencken Unsealed,"* New York Times Book Review, *31 January 1993, pp. 9–10).*

Posthumous self-justification has been the obsession of any number of aging authors, but few have pursued it as aggressively as H. L. Mencken. Not long after his death in 1956, it was revealed that Mencken had left behind two book-length memoirs, "My Life as Author and Editor" and "Thirty-five Years of Newspaper Work." In his diary, Mencken explained that he wished to leave "really honest" accounts of his tenure at The Smart Set, which he edited from 1914 to 1923; The American Mercury, which he founded, with George Jean Nathan, in 1924 and edited until the end of 1933; and The Baltimore Sun, where he served in various

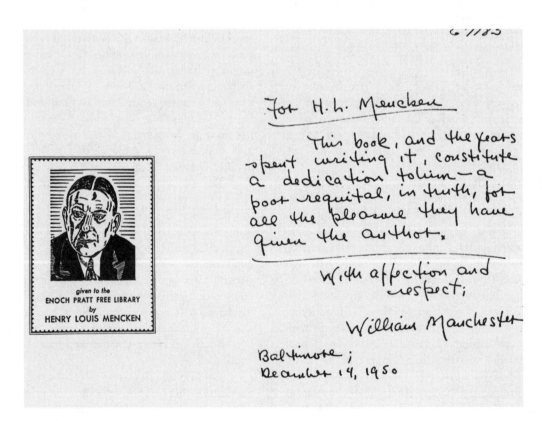

Inscription in Manchester's Disturber of the Peace: The Life of H. L. Mencken, *published in 1950 (courtesy of the Enoch Pratt Free Library and William Manchester)*

Dust jacket for one of Mencken's controversial posthumously published memoirs (1993)

capacities from 1906 to 1948, when he suffered a stroke that left him unable to read or write.

According to the terms of Mencken's will, both memoirs were deposited at Baltimore's Enoch Pratt Free Library "on the explicit and irrevocable understanding that [they were] not to be open to anyone, under any circumstances whatever, until either Jan. 1, 1980, or 35 years after the death of the author, whichever may be the later."

Since 1956, students of Mencken's life and work have labored in the shadow of a tantalizing mystery: what was in the sealed manuscripts? The 1989 publication of Mencken's diary, which contained racist and anti-Semitic language that triggered a nationwide controversy, suggested that his memoirs might well prove equally explosive. The Pratt finally unsealed "My Life as Author and Editor" and "Thirty-five Years of Newspaper Work" on Jan. 29, 1991, right on schedule, and three new Mencken biographers and a host of scholars promptly lined up to read them.

With the publication of a heavily abridged trade version of "My Life as Author and Editor," other interested parties can now see for themselves what the Sage of Baltimore had up his sleeve. ("Thirty-five Years" is being prepared for publication, also in an abridged version, by the Johns Hopkins University Press.)

The first thing they will learn is that the book is a torso. Left incomplete at the time of Mencken's stroke, it ends abruptly in 1923. Fortunately, as Jonathan Yardley explains in his crisp and insightful introduction, "in the first third of his career Mencken met virtually all the people who were important to it; in writing his memoir he set down his impressions of these people as each appeared on the scene, and thus we have almost all of them substantially whole. Dreiser, Nathan, Knopf, Sinclair Lewis, Anita Loos, Scott Fitzgerald: the portrait of each is amply fleshed."

Those familiar with Mencken's diary will find no surprises in "My Life as Author and Editor," which is liberally salted with ethnic slurs, most of them about Jews and a few offensive in the extreme. Prickly readers unwilling to make allowances for the commonly held prejudices of turn-of-the-century authors (it is easy to forget that Mencken was born just 15 years after Appomattox) should therefore stay as far away as possible.

Others will find it engrossing, in large part because it is precisely what Mencken meant it to be: a baldly, at times even shockingly candid account of his magazine career and the people he met in the course of it. Mencken has much to say in "My Life as Author and Editor," little of it unexpected but all of it illuminating, about such close friends and colleagues as Nathan ("I doubt that in his whole career as a dramatic critic he has ever entered a theater with a woman taller, or as tall, as himself") and Theodore Dreiser ("He was, in fact, a polygamist on a really wholesale scale, and during the years of our association I saw almost as much of his women as I did of him"). It is no less illuminating and in some ways perhaps even more interesting to see how he deals with less august acquaintances. Here, for example, is his characteristically pungent verdict on Dorothy Thompson, the newspaper columnist who was Sinclair Lewis's second wife: "She was the true daughter of her Methodist pa—a tinpot messiah with an inflamed egoism that was wholly unameliorated by humor."

Those who have examined the complete 1,742-page typescript of "My Life as Author and Editor" can testify to the editorial skill with which Mr. Yardley, a book critic and columnist at The Washington Post, has turned a massive document of interest mainly to scholars into a rich, absorbing memoir that anyone who cares about modern American literature will want to read, not least because of what it tells us about Mencken himself.

"The goods that a writer produces," Mencken wrote in the preface, "can never be impersonal; his character gets into them as certainly as it gets into the work of any other creative artist, and he must be prepared to endure investigation of it, and speculation upon it, and even gossip about it." Certainly H. L. Mencken's character got into every word he wrote, and it is writ large on every page of this book: witty and abrasive, self-confident and self-contradictory, sometimes maddening, often engaging, always inimitable.

* * *

(Merle Rubin, "Baltimore's Complacent Iconoclast," Christian Science Monitor, *23 February 1993, p. 13).*

A man who relished controversy during his lifetime, launching provocative attacks on American culture (or the paucity thereof), Baltimore-based journalist, critic, and editor Henry Louis Mencken (1880–1956) has continued making waves more than 30 years after his death, first with the publication of his diary in 1990, now with the release of his equally outspoken autobiography, "My Life as Author and Editor."

Mencken had arranged for both these manuscripts to remain sealed in the vaults of Baltimore's Enoch Pratt Library for several decades after his death, when his friends, enemies, and acquaintances would no longer be around to feel insulted by his less-than-glowing accounts of them.

But when his diary was finally published three years ago, the shock came not from Mencken's acid comments or from any personal revelations, but from the sheer extent of his prejudices, most notably his anti-Semitism.

Book critic and columnist Jonathan Yardley, who has edited Mencken's unfinished autobiography (reducing an unwieldy, copiously detailed 1,024-page typescript to a diverting memoir less than half the original length), tries to excuse Mencken's prejudice with a weak sort of historical relativism: ". . . if by the standards of our day Mencken was anti-Semitic, by those of his own he was not. Inasmuch as he lived in his time and not in ours, it is by this we should judge and, I believe, acquit him."

Mencken himself says, "My belief in free speech is so profound that I am seldom tempted to deny it to the other fellow. Nor do I make any effort to differentiate between that other fellow right and that other fellow wrong, for I am convinced that free speech is worth nothing unless it includes a full franchise to be foolish

and even . . . malicious." But neither statement can explain away Mencken's many-faceted bigotry.

The Mencken who cut a figure in the 1910s and '20s as a columnist for the Baltimore Sun, editor of Smart Set and American Mercury, foe of censorship and Puritanism, coiner of such memorable disparaging phrases as "the Bible Belt" and "the booboisie" would seem, at first glance, a far cry from the Mencken who refers in his autobiography to "low-caste Jews," "filthy homos," and "blackamoors." And it was more than just talk. Mencken baldly relates how he once made Carl Van Vechten (a white promoter of the Harlem Renaissance) promise not to have any blacks at his own dinner party lest their presence upset Mencken's Southern-born wife, Sara. But Mencken published black, Jewish, and women writers in his magazines, spoke out against Jim Crow laws, and regularly denounced the racist dogmas of the Ku Klux Klan. And his bigoted generalizations about Jews did not prevent him from becoming close friends with many individual Jews, including his publisher Alfred A. Knopf.

The list of Mencken's strong dislikes is wide-ranging: religious evangelists, sex hygienists, suffragettes, temperance preachers, Christian Scientists, Woodrow Wilson, Greenwich Village "frauds," political reformers, communists, socialists—indeed, anyone who held what he deemed the foolishly misguided view that mankind should and could be "improved."

Mencken characterized himself as a libertarian rather than a liberal. "Under the influence of my father," he recalls in a revealing passage, "who was always the chief figure in his small world and hence inclined toward complacency, I emerged into sentience with an almost instinctive distrust of all schemes of revolution and reform. . . . It always amuses me when I am accused of being a fallen-away Liberal, for I was never anything even remotely resembling what passes for a Liberal in the United States. . . . Even as a boy I never had any belief in religion, and even as a youth I never went through the Socialist green sickness."

The key word, I think, is "complacency," an attitude echoed in Mencken's thumbnail sketch of the "typical reader" he aimed to reach with Smart Set: someone "quite satisfied with the world and himself." Mencken's distrust of reformers included political zealots on the one hand, avant-garde artistic experimenters on the other. (He admired James Joyce's "Dubliners" and "A Portrait of the Artist as Young Man," but suspected "Ulysses" was a "hoax.") Reading his tart, self-assured assessments of his contemporaries, one comes to feel that Mencken's essential conservatism and his celebrated iconoclasm both had roots in an underlying outlook of complacency.

A complacent conservative is understandable, but is there such an animal as a complacent iconoclast? Mencken's iconoclasm proceeded not from the hard-won doubts of a mind stirring to question its own cultural assumptions, but from a ready-made set of ideas that were pretty much in place from the outset of his career. One of the most striking features of his autobiography, which covers his career from 1896 into the 1920s, is how little he seems to change, even though he was writing this account from the perspective of the 1940s.

Yet his voice continues to speak to readers. It is plain-spoken and to the point. Some highlights of his autobiography are Mencken's recollections of such figures as Sinclair Lewis, Theodore Dreiser, F. Scott Fitzgerald, and James Branch Cabell. Mencken was an early champion of Dreiser—not only out of admiration for his work, as he admits, but for the more self-serving reason that Mencken the critic needed to balance his frequent jibes at overrated literary lions with a positive campaign on behalf of talented, underrated newcomers. His efforts to advise the stubborn Dreiser in his fight against censorship, however, were often in vain. Mencken also valued Sinclair Lewis, but felt he ruined his talent by accepting the Nobel Prize. On a more mellow note, Mencken's appreciative portraits of relatively forgotten writers such as Abraham Cahan, Ruth Suckow, and Lilith Benda are unintentionally touching reminders of the vagaries of literary fame.

Mencken made no secret of the fact that he courted controversy to make a splash and establish his position. But he was also expressing his honest reactions with a down-to-earth, witty skepticism that might very well have tickled the fancy of one of his few literary heroes, the great Mark Twain.

Thirty-five Years of Newspaper Work *was published in 1994, and like the diary and* My Life as Author and Editor *it was reprinted as a paperback despite the "shocking" content (Linda Hall, "Mencken Unearthed,"* New York, *28 [23 January 1995]: 90).*

Several years after it came to public attention that H. L. Mencken liked mocking Jews as much as he liked mocking Scots, F.D.R., Greeks, native-born rubes, and William Jennings Bryan, the worrying classes have moved on, and the author's last books—culled from long-sealed manuscripts—are in print.

On the final page of the memoir that became *Thirty-five Years of Newspaper Work* (Johns Hopkins), Mencken expresses doubt that anyone would be interested enough, decades after his death, to read it. He is certain only "that if I am remembered that long it will

be for other and quite different enterprises, and not for my long and vain effort to change the apparently inevitable destiny of the Baltimore *Sunpapers*." Less swashbuckling than his journalism, the memoir nonetheless displays all the qualities that made Mencken one of America's best essayists: the unmistakable voice, the vast learning, the impatience with cant and hypocrisy and pretension. There is also evidence of a fairly generous spirit; it suffused most of his work, but usually in the guise of gruff realism. Mencken notes that the attempt to make the *Sun* exceptional turned even him a little romantic, and when, in his eyes, it failed, he was surprisingly gentle on his publishing peers. "They did their level damndest," he writes, "and angels could have done no more." Mencken thought his memoir could be a contribution toward the history of the country as well as that of journalism, and, reading sections on Harding's inaugural, the Scopes trial, and Prohibition, one agrees.

Reading *My Life as Author and Editor* (new in paperback from Vintage), one realizes that he was right, too, about how history would remember him. The *Sun* is famous because of Mencken, but Mencken is famous because he put much of his considerable energy into writing and promoting literature. The book's back cover promises morsels so tantalizing they might have provoked "a storm of libel suits" when he was alive. But the most interesting material, such as his championing of Theodore Dreiser, is far from extraliterary. Although both memoirs are splendid, only this one can be finished without a terrific sense of gloom. Harding is gone, and we wish we had Mencken on Clinton; newspapers are going, and we wish we had Mencken to sustain them. *Sister Carrie,* as well as Mencken's own prodigious body of work, will always be with us, and we'll always have Mencken on all of it.

* * *

(Chilton Williamson Jr., review of Thirty-five Years of Newspaper Work, Chronicles, *19 [September 1995]: 36).*

This volume is the last substantial legacy provided by the author's will which, operating on the principle of time-release, has already resulted in the publication of the *Diary of H. L. Mencken* and the availability of many useful letters and papers. While *Thirty-five Years* adds little if anything to what was already known of Mencken's life, it does fill out stories and episodes, and in general makes a superior period-piece, less formalized but more informative than the *Days* trilogy. A case may be made, indeed, that period-work, apart from philology, was what Mencken did best, as well as being the most lasting

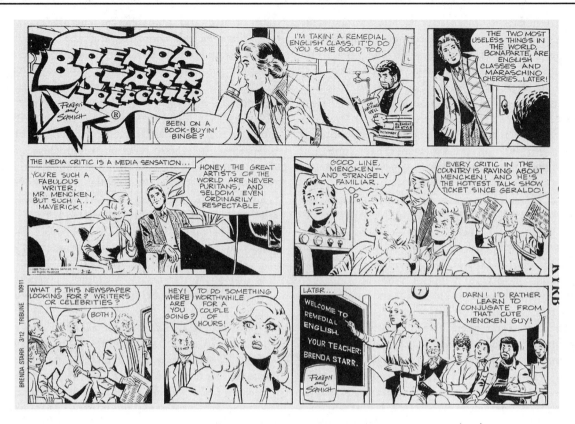

Comic strip featuring a character partly based on Mencken. "W. Faulkner Mencken" is later exposed as a plagiarist (© Tribune Media Services, Inc. All Rights Reserved. Reprinted with permission).

of his accomplishments. He wrote beautifully, with the smoothness of hawser-rope coming off a winch; and his prose, when freed from the rhetorical horsing-around of the essays, columns and other opinion-pieces, is all the more supple, at the same time muscular and smooth as silk. Although the book held no surprises for this reader, I found myself reading on, and on, without skipping, held to the text as if on rails and powered by the terrific momentum generated by the writer himself. *Thirty-five Years* is vastly more interesting than the undeservedly notorious *Diary,* and provides a fitting supplement to *My Life as Author and Editor,* edited by Jonathan Yardley. Contrary to contemporary opinion, Mencken's most baleful influence on the several generations of writers that followed him stemmed not from his bluntness on various tender topics, but rather from the apparent imitability of his absolutely inimitable style. In this regard, the message of the last of his great projects to all young authors, and many mature ones, is invaluable: *Write well,* and you will be read forever.

* * *

(Excerpt from H. Allen Smith, "A Friend in Baltimore," in his A Short History of Fingers [and Other State Papers] *[Boston & Toronto: Little, Brown, 1963], pp. 82–89).*

[. . .] I used to interview him so often that it became an office scandal. "Good God!" they'd exclaim at the United Press, "Here comes Smith with another Mencken interview!" Actually there was never any objection, for the reason that no Mencken interview could ever possibly be dull. Newspaper editors all over the country were always eager for more copy about the salty sage of Baltimore.

It often confused and irritated me that such a courteous and kindly man as Mencken should have such a fierce reputation. Back in 1912 he was writing a daily column in the Baltimore *Sun,* a column in which he first established himself as a spike-tailed monster spitting sulphur and cinders over the Maryland landscape. One day a *Sun* artist named McKee Barclay turned out a hideous caricature of "The Subconscious Mencken." The man he pictured was the Mencken visualized by the multitudes of good souls whom he outraged with his writings. The portrait was that of a mean, bulbous-nosed, white-mustached, malevolent old man—the most unpleasant looking character imaginable, with a puss so sour it would clabber spring water. As a joke Mencken occasionally would run this picture in connection with his column, and before long the portrait was being printed in other cities, and everywhere people assumed that it was a true likeness. I'm told that

H. Allen Smith, who frequently interviewed Mencken for
the United Press

to this day there are people in Baltimore who believe Mencken actually looked like Barclay's fusty old curmudgeon.

Mencken often described the intent of his work as "stirring up the animals" and stir them up he did, with the consequence that he in turn was almost constantly under bitter attack. He was abused and reviled in print so much that he once gleefully put together a book containing the printable invective that had been fired at him (*Menckeniana: a Schimpflexicon* [*sic*]). He was called a dirty buzzard, a maggot, a ghoul of new-made graves, a polecat, a howling hyena, and "a cheap blatherskite of a pen-pusher." Clergymen and editors and politicians had at him alike. He was called "a disappointed, dishonest, distrustful, disgraceful, degraded, degenerate evolute of a species fifty-seven varieties lower than a turkey buzzard." A minister said that Mencken had "a dilated brain impregnated with ego, indigo and gangrene." And another said, "If he ever had a real idea, his skull would pop like a rotten pumpkin."

One reason his reputation suffered was the fact that he employed a stylistic device common to the American humorous writer, namely, gross exaggeration. During the period of his marriage to Sara Haardt when he lived in Cathedral Street, I was walking with him in that neighborhood and he poked a thumb

toward one of Baltimore's landmarks—a statue of George Washington standing on a high pillar. "The first American gentleman," said Mencken, "and the last." He didn't really mean that there have been no American gentlemen since the time of Washington. It was his way of saying that there is an acute shortage of gentlemen in America, that there are not nearly as many gentlemen in this country as there ought to be.

There remain, to this day, many people who for want of better information believe that Mencken was a gross and evil man, satanical and anti-social. Yet the plain truth is, Henry L. Mencken was one of the most polite and considerate gentlemen this country ever produced. He was a good man. He was a prime example of the philosopher who abominates the human race for its congenital and incurable foolishness, yet loves and respects individual members of that race. Mark Twain was of the same breed and it is worth noting that the writings of Mark Twain were largely responsible for Mencken's decision to become a writer rather than a tobacco merchant. It is further worth noting that he wrote blistering, bruising things about people and they hated him deeply until they met him, and then invariably they succumbed to his warmth and his personal charm.

He was famous for the amount of hard work he got through each day, hence time was valuable to him.

The Subconscious Mencken (1912), by McKee Barclay (courtesy
of the Enoch Pratt Free Library)

THE SAGE OF BALTIMORE

H. L. Mencken

The House of Type
Baltimore
1984

Title page for one of the many keepsakes reprinting Mencken's commentary on the American scene

best such expressions as George Jean Nathan's, "He is above the malice and envy of little men." Or Alfred Knopf's, "The private man was . . . sentimental, generous, and unwavering—sometimes almost blind—in his devotion to people he liked." Or Jim Tully's, "His comrades for years have never known him to do a small thing." Or Walter Lippmann's, "He denounces life and makes you want to live."

Lippmann, incidentally, once described Mencken as "the most powerful personal influence on this whole generation of educated people." There is no estimating the number of younger writers who were not only influenced but given active aid by Mencken. He was a major factor in the careers of such literary whales as Sinclair Lewis, Theodore Dreiser, F. Scott Fitzgerald, James T. Farrell and James Branch Cabell. Yet there is many a lesser author or journalist obligated beyond measure to the Baltimore iconoclast. Thumbing through the thick reference work *Twentieth Century Authors,* mentioned in the introduction to this book, it is amazing to find so many writers who say such things as, "With the active assistance of H. L. Mencken . . ." and, "Then H. L. Mencken persuaded me to . . ." and, "At the urging of H. L. Mencken I wrote . . ." Speaking of Mencken's relations with younger writers, Gerald W. Johnson, the Baltimore historian and scholar, has remarked, "To say that he was generous, even lavish with sympathy and assistance for them is true enough, but not the whole truth; he also gave them the rare gift of genuine admiration, and this to some who, as writers, did not deserve it."

Newspapermen idolized Mencken. At the political conventions and other major news-producing carnivals he was often a greater attraction than the main show, and he knew it, but he never held himself aloof from his fellow reporters, no matter how undistinguished they might be. As a magazine editor he never retained a manuscript longer than three days. He knew that most writers urgently needed money and he felt they were entitled to a quick decision on their work. He was equally and famously punctilious in his correspondence. It was his practice to answer every letter on the same day he received it. He never abused people by mail. Much of his incoming correspondence was scurrilous in the extreme, yet he answered the most abusive letters with politeness and tact. He had a delightful method of dealing with people who were in violent disagreement with him. He would write: "Dear sir (or madam): You may be right. Very truly yours, H. L. Mencken." He carried on a running dispute with Upton Sinclair for years, but the quarrel was over principles. Once Mencken wrote to Sinclair: "I find your note on my return from Europe. As always you are right—save in matters of politics, sociology, religion,

Still, he gave of it freely to almost anyone who came along. He was a man who appeared to thrive and prosper by doing things for other people. He usually spent two afternoons of each week visiting people in hospitals. He was almost a landmark at Johns Hopkins Hospital in Baltimore. He would arrive bearing gifts—bottles of wine and boxes of candy and armloads of books—and the word would travel through the long corridors. Immediately there would be a sort of mass movement in his direction; doctors and interns and nurses hurried to greet him and when he entered the rooms of various patients they would follow along because they knew he always put on a good show, delivering mock lectures on medical topics, spouting the old-time religion in the accents of Billy Sunday, or simply littering the premises with quips and drolleries. If a top editor of the *Sun* were in hospital, Mencken would be at his bedside regularly; but he also visited the *Sun's* Negro elevator operator, or his wife or his children, if they were sick.

This man so long regarded as the embodiment of churlish evil could evoke from those who knew him

Title page for a 1988 novel

finance, economics, literature and the exact sciences." They remained warm personal friends to the end.

Julian P. Boyd, former head of the Princeton University Library, considers Mencken to have been one of the great letter-writers of this or any other age, and Boyd once launched an ambitious project for the collection of Mencken letters. Before he resigned to edit the papers of Thomas Jefferson, he managed to gather up eleven thousand letters written by Mencken to about five hundred individuals. Boyd tells me that, even then, he had only scratched the surface—that there were many thousands of additional Mencken letters in the possession of people all over the globe. [. . .]

Mencken has been called the American Swift, the American Voltaire, and "one of the great comic spirits of world literature." He was a man of almost wildly unorthodox views, yet he was not a forward-looking man. He was old-fashioned, bitterly opposed to many material things which we have come to associate with progress. He was reactionary in almost everything except affairs of health and matters of beauty. I have been told that he, more than anyone else, was responsi-

ble for the purification of Baltimore's water supply and the control of diphtheria, typhoid and intestinal sickness in his home city.

He was a train man, and refused to fly. He hated to use the telephone and instead wrote one-line notes to his Baltimore cronies, proposing meetings for lunch or dinner. It was his opinion that the telephone was a contrivance designed specifically for bores, and he avoided it as much as possible.

He rode trolley cars and taxis. "Back in 1918," he once told me, "I owned an automobile. One morning I drove it up in front of the *Sun* building and stopped at the curb. A cop came up and said, 'Hey, you can't stop here.' I said, 'The hell I can't.' He said, 'The hell you can!' So I said, 'Why the hell can't I?' And he said, "We got new rules. We got a parking law." Well, I looked at him a minute and then I said, 'Nuts to that,' and got in the car and drove it around the corner and sold it and invested the proceeds in booze. I've never owned a car since that day."

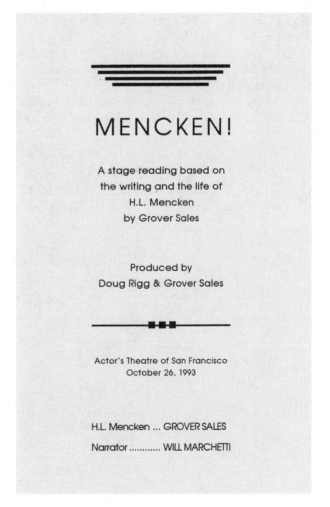

Playbill for a reading from Mencken's works

A few years ago I went back to Baltimore to prowl his old haunts and talk to some of his old friends and visit with his brother August. I went to lunch with Philip M. Wagner, editor of the *Sun*. Wagner's hobby is winegrowing and he is an authority on American winemaking. He had a tank of his own vintage in his car and we delivered it to Haussner's, a famous Baltimore restaurant. In the car Wagner mentioned the fact that Henry Mencken was largely responsible for his interest in wines and the growing of grapes. And at Haussner's he remarked that the restaurant had been no more than a lunch counter until Henry Mencken started whooping for it.

Later I dined with Robert P. Harriss, a columnist who was once associated with Mencken at the *Sun*. For some years Harriss was the editor of a successful Maryland magazine called *Gardens, Houses and People*. "The magazine's success," he said, "was due mainly to suggestions that Henry gave me."

The next day I was at the home of Gerald Johnson. "I was just a smalltown newspaperman in North Carolina," he said, "when a man named H. L. Mencken got in touch with me about something I had written. We carried on a correspondence for a while and then he recommended me for a job as editorial writer on the *Sun*. So here I am."

I went to a famous restaurant operated by an Italian woman. She said that Henry Mencken had been responsible for her success. When she first opened he came in and told her that she should take down the big *Spaghetti* sign out front, that she should de-emphasize spaghetti and go in for more esoteric Italian dishes; otherwise the public would regard her place as just another spaghetti joint. He gave her other suggestions, she followed his advice, and she prospered. And so it went: he influenced every life he touched, often profoundly.

He was inconsistent in many directions. He scoffed at joiners, yet for forty years he was the moving spirit behind the Saturday Night Club, an organization of amateur musicians and beer-drinkers (he was a pianist). And toward the end of his life he joined the sedate Maryland Club because, he said, he had grown tired of saloons and wanted a quiet and dignified place to entertain visiting whales. He ridiculed churches, yet he was married in one by his own arrangement. He spoke of religion as pure superstition, yet he hung horseshoes around his house and refused to do a lick of work on any Friday the thirteenth. Of the many contradictions between his writings and his personal life George Jean Nathan once said, "Consistency is unimportant. Mencken and I both used to believe in Santa Claus and the wisdom of the President of the United States, but the passing years have changed all that." My own way of excusing him is to quote the lines of Walt Whitman: "Do I contradict myself? Very well, then, I contradict myself; (I am large—I contain multitudes)."

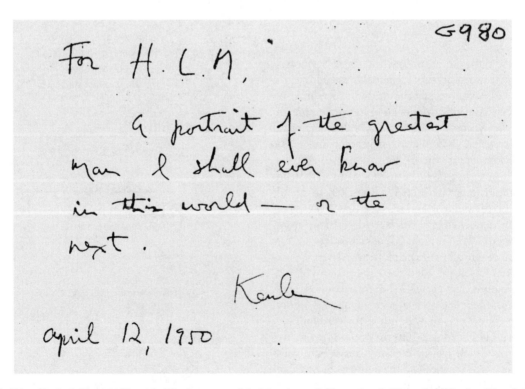

Inscription by Edgar Kemler in his 1950 biography, The Irreverent Mr. Mencken, *alluding to the afterlife in which Mencken did not believe. Smith, however, quotes Kemler as saying that toward the end of his life Mencken began to hedge his bets. (courtesy of the Enoch Pratt Free Library)*

Mencken was a confirmed agnostic, as his father was before him. Yet in his later years, according to Edgar Kemler, he undertook to copper his bet and rehearsed himself for his first day in Heaven just in case he should wake up and find himself there. He pictured himself arriving before the judgment seat, surrounded by the Twelve Apostles, and in this setting he planned to say, simply, "Gentlemen, I was wrong." [. . .]

* * *

(Baron Wormser, "A Satirist," New Republic, *189 [10 October 1983]: 30).*

The world, word-struck,
Revealed a seeping, indignant wound
That was always better in the morning.
Too recuperative,
The human race did not learn.
He lit another cigar or sucked on a sugar cube.
In that it was irresistible,

Life was, to a thinking person, hateful.
"Among our greatest failings is
Our lack of a prehensile tail," he told Clarence Darrow.
Three governors offered him jobs
In other states.
He replied, through intermediaries,
"Thanks, but I must stay near Mother."
Back at his office which featured
A lacquered oak desk and a bottle of
Old Crow, he shivered, swore, half-raved,
Cackled and spat,
As if he was what he was imagined to be,
As if his brazen hurt were some
Elected congruency.
Unlucky in love, the women said.
Dogs, warblers and squirrels came to him.
Children in parks pestered him to play ball.
One misdeed or gaffe became another;
The grafting mayor and the grammar of
Ballplayers were forever.
He spun in his chair like a dial,
Helpless and shrewd,
Responsive as a smile.

Bibliography

1. H. L. Mencken's Works

BOOKS AND PAMPHLETS: *Ventures into Verse* (Baltimore: Marshall, Beek & Gordon, 1903);

George Bernard Shaw: His Plays (Boston & London: Luce, 1905);

The Philosophy of Friedrich Nietzsche (Boston: Luce, 1908; London: Unwin, 1908);

The Gist of Nietzsche (Boston: Luce, 1910);

Men versus the Man: A Correspondence between Robert Rives La Monte, Socialist, and H. L. Mencken, Individualist (New York: Holt, 1910);

What You Ought to Know about Your Baby, by Mencken and Leonard K. Hirshberg (New York: Butterick, 1910);

The Artist: A Drama without Words (Boston: Luce, 1912);

Europe after 8:15, by Mencken, George Jean Nathan, and Willard Huntington Wright (New York: John Lane / Toronto: Bell & Cockburn, 1914);

A Note to Authors (New York: Smart Set, 1915?);

The Editors Regret, by Mencken and Nathan (New York: Smart Set, 1915?);

A Little Book in C Major (New York: John Lane, 1916);

A Book of Burlesques (New York: John Lane, 1916; revised edition, New York: Knopf, 1920; London: Cape, 1923);

A Book of Prefaces (New York: Knopf, 1917; London: Cape, 1922);

Pistols for Two, by Mencken and Nathan, as Owen Hatteras (New York: Knopf, 1917);

Damn! A Book of Calumny (New York: Philip Goodman, 1918); republished as *A Book of Calumny* (New York: Knopf, 1918);

In Defense of Women (New York: Philip Goodman, 1918; revised edition, New York: Knopf, 1922; London: Cape, 1923);

The American Language: A Preliminary Inquiry into the Development of English in the United States (New York: Knopf, 1919; revised and enlarged, 1921; London: Cape, 1922; revised and enlarged edition, New York: Knopf, 1923; corrected, enlarged, and rewritten edition, New York: Knopf, 1936; London: Kegan Paul, Trench, Trubner, 1936);

Prejudices: First Series (New York: Knopf, 1919; London: Cape, 1921);

Heliogabalus: A Buffoonery in Three Acts, by Mencken and Nathan (New York: Knopf, 1920);

The American Credo: A Contribution toward the Interpretation of the National Mind, by Mencken and Nathan (New York: Knopf, 1920);

Prejudices: Second Series (New York: Knopf, 1920; London: Cape, 1921);

A Personal Word (New York: Smart Set, 1921);

Suggestions to Our Visitors, by Mencken and Nathan (New York: Smart Set, 1922);

Prejudices: Third Series (New York: Knopf, 1922; London: Cape, 1923);

The Undersigned Announce, by Mencken and Nathan (New York: Smart Set, 1923);

Prejudices: Fourth Series (New York: Knopf, 1924; London: Cape, 1925);

To the Friends of the American Mercury (New York: American Mercury, 1926);

Notes on Democracy (New York: Knopf, 1926; London: Cape, 1927);

Prejudices: Fifth Series (New York: Knopf, 1926; London: Cape, 1927);

Prejudices: Sixth Series (New York: Knopf, 1927; London: Cape, 1928);

James Branch Cabell (New York: McBride, 1927);

Mr. Mencken to the Book Publishers (New York: American Mercury, 1929);

The 10,000 Best American Books in Print, by Mencken and H. E. Buchholz (Baltimore: Books-Baltimore, 1930);

A Literary History of the American People, by Charles Angoff (New York: Knopf, 1930?);

Treatise on the Gods (New York & London: Knopf, 1930; revised edition, New York: Knopf, 1946);

Making a President: A Footnote to the Saga of Democracy (New York: Knopf, 1932);

Treatise on Right and Wrong (New York: Knopf, 1934; London: Kegan Paul, Trench, Trubner, 1934);

Erez Israel (New York: B. P. Safran, 1935);

The Sunpapers of Baltimore, 1837–1937, by Mencken, Gerald W. Johnson, Frank R. Kent, and Hamilton Owens (New York: Knopf, 1937);

Happy Days, 1880–1892 (New York: Knopf, 1940; London: Kegan Paul, Trench, Trubner, 1940);

An American Editor Speaks (Mt. Vernon, Wash.: Concord Press, 1940?);

"Generally Political" (New York: Columbia University Press, 1940);

Newspaper Days, 1899–1906 (New York: Knopf, 1941; London: Kegan Paul, Trench, Trubner, 1942);

Heathen Days, 1890–1936 (New York: Knopf, 1943);

Stylebook: The Sunpapers of Baltimore (Baltimore: Sunpapers, 1944);

Supplement I: The American Language (New York: Knopf, 1945; London: Routledge & Kegan Paul, 1948);

Christmas Story (New York: Knopf, 1946);

Vachel Lindsay (Washington, D.C.: Published by the Keystone Press for John S. Mayfield, 1947);

Of, By, and About Henry Miller: A Collection of Pieces, by Mencken, Henry Miller, and others (Yonkers, N.Y.: Printed by Leo Porgie for the Alicat Bookshop Press, 1947);

Supplement II: The American Language (New York: Knopf, 1948; London: Routledge & Kegan Paul, 1948);

A Mencken Chrestomathy, Edited and Annotated by the Author (New York: Knopf, 1949);

The Vintage Mencken, edited by Alistair Cooke (New York: Vintage, 1955);

Minority Report: H. L. Mencken's Notebooks (New York: Knopf, 1956);

A Carnival of Buncombe, edited by Malcolm Moos (Baltimore: Johns Hopkins University Press / London: Oxford University Press, 1956);

The Bathtub Hoax, and Other Blasts & Bravos from the Chicago Tribune, edited by Robert McHugh (New York: Knopf, 1958);

H. L. Mencken on Music, edited by Louis Cheslock (New York: Knopf, 1961);

The American Scene: A Reader, edited by Huntington Cairns (New York: Knopf, 1965);

H. L. Mencken's Smart Set Criticism, edited by William H. Nolte (Ithaca, N.Y.: Cornell University Press, 1968);

The Young Mencken: The Best of His Work, edited by Carl Bode (New York: Dial, 1973);

Quotations from Chairman Mencken or Poor Henry's Almanac, edited by Fenwick Anderson (Urbana: University of Illinois Institute of Communications Research, 1974);

A Gang of Pecksniffs, and Other Comments on Newspaper Publishers, Editors and Reporters, edited by Theo

Lippman Jr. (New Rochelle, N.Y.: Arlington House, 1975);

Mencken's Last Campaign: H. L. Mencken on the 1948 Election, edited by Joseph C. Goulden (Washington, D.C.: New Republic Book Co., 1976);

The Editor, the Bluenose, and the Prostitute: H. L. Mencken's History of the "Hatrack" Censorship Case, edited by Carl Bode (Boulder, Colo.: Roberts Rinehart, 1988);

The Diary of H. L. Mencken, edited by Charles A. Fecher (New York: Knopf, 1989);

Tall Tales and Hoaxes of H. L. Mencken: Mencken's Baltimore Sunday Sun Hoaxes, 1908–1910, edited by John W. Baer (Annapolis, Md.: Franklin Printing, 1990);

The Gist of Mencken: Quotations from America's Critic Gleaned from Newspapers, Magazines, Books, Letters, and Manuscripts, edited by Mayo DuBasky (Metuchen, N.J. & London: Scarecrow Press, 1990);

The Impossible H. L. Mencken: A Selection of His Best Newspaper Stories, edited by Marion Elizabeth Rodgers, foreword by Gore Vidal (New York & London: Doubleday, 1991);

My Life as Author and Editor: H. L. Mencken, edited by Jonathan Yardley (New York: Knopf, 1993);

Thirty-five Years of Newspaper Work: A Memoir, edited by Fred Hobson, Vincent Fitzpatrick, and Bradford Jacobs (Baltimore & London: Johns Hopkins University Press, 1994);

A Second Mencken Chrestomathy, Selected, Revised, and Annotated by the Author, edited by Terry Teachout (New York: Knopf, 1995);

Do You Remember? The Whimsical Letters of H. L. Mencken and Philip Goodman, edited by Jack Sanders (Baltimore: Maryland Historical Society, 1996).

Edition: *A One-Volume Abridged Edition of The American Language: An Inquiry into the Development of English in the United States,* edited by Raven I. McDavid Jr. and David W. Maurer (New York: Knopf, 1963; London: Routledge & Kegan Paul, 1963).

RECORDING: *H. L. Mencken Interviewed by Donald Howe Kirkley, Sr.,* U.S. Library of Congress Recording Laboratory, PL18–PL19, 30 June 1948; also released as *H. L. Mencken Speaks,* Caedmon Records, TC-1082; Audio-Forum Sound Seminar AFO175.

OTHER: Henrik Ibsen, *The Player's Ibsen: A Doll's House,* translated by Mencken and Holger A. Koppel (Boston & London: Luce, 1909);

Ibsen, *The Player's Ibsen: Little Eyolf,* translated by Mencken and Koppel (Boston & London: Luce, 1909);

Ibsen, *The Master Builder, Pillars of Society, Hedda Gabler,* introduction by Mencken (New York: Boni & Liveright, 1917);

Friedrich Nietzsche, *The Antichrist,* translated by Mencken (New York: Knopf, 1920);

Americana 1925, edited by Mencken (New York: Knopf, 1925; London: Hopkinson, 1925);

Jonathan Swift, *Gulliver's Travels,* introduction by Mencken (New York: Knopf, 1925);

Americana 1926, edited by Mencken (New York: Knopf, 1926; London: Hopkinson, 1926);

Menckeniana: A Schimpflexikon, edited by Mencken and Sara Powell Haardt (New York: Knopf, 1928);

August Mencken, ed., *By the Neck: A Book of Hangings Selected from Contemporary Accounts,* foreword by H. L. Mencken (New York: Hastings House, 1942);

A New Dictionary of Quotations on Historical Principles from Ancient and Modern Sources, edited by Mencken (New York: Knopf, 1942; London & Glasgow: Collins, 1982).

SELECTED PERIODICAL PUBLICATION–
UNCOLLECTED: "Mencken's Baltimore," edited by John Dorsey, *Baltimore Sunday Sun,* 8 September 1974, supplement.

Letters:

Letters of H. L. Mencken, edited by Guy J. Forgue (New York: Knopf, 1961);

The New Mencken Letters, edited by Carl Bode (New York: Dial, 1977);

Letters from Baltimore: The Mencken-Cleator Correspondence, edited by P. E. Cleator (Rutherford, Madison & Teaneck, N.J.: Fairleigh Dickinson University Press / London & Toronto: Associated University Presses, 1982);

"Ich Kuss die Hand": The Letters of H. L. Mencken to Gretchen Hood, edited by Peter W. Dowell (University: University of Alabama Press, 1986);

Dreiser-Mencken Letters: The Correspondence of Theodore Dreiser & H. L. Mencken 1907–1945, edited by Thomas P. Riggio (Philadelphia: University of Pennsylvania Press, 1986);

Mencken and Sara: A Life in Letters. The Private Correspondence of H. L. Mencken and Sara Haardt, edited by Marion E. Rodgers (New York: McGraw-Hill, 1987);

Fante/Mencken: John Fante & H. L. Mencken. A Personal Correspondence 1930–1952, edited by Michael Moreau and Joyce Fante (Santa Rosa, Cal.: Black Sparrow, 1989).

2. Secondary Sources

Bibliographies:

Betty Adler, *H. L. M.: The Mencken Bibliography* (Baltimore: Johns Hopkins University Press, 1961);

Adler, *Man of Letters: A Census of the Correspondence of H. L. Mencken* (Baltimore: Enoch Pratt Free Library, 1969);

Adler, *The Mencken Bibliography: A Ten-Year Supplement 1962–1971* (Baltimore: Enoch Pratt Free Library, 1971);

Vincent Fitzpatrick, *The Mencken Bibliography: A Second Ten-Year Supplement 1972–1981* (Baltimore: Enoch Pratt Free Library, 1986);

Allison Bulsterbaum, *H. L. Mencken: A Research Guide* (New York & London: Garland, 1988);

Richard J. Schrader, *H. L. Mencken: A Descriptive Bibliography* (Pittsburgh: University of Pittsburgh Press, 1998).

Biographies:

Isaac Goldberg, *The Man Mencken: A Biographical and Critical Survey* (New York: Simon & Schuster, 1925);

Edgar Kemler, *The Irreverent Mr. Mencken* (Boston: Little, Brown, 1950);

William Manchester, *Disturber of the Peace: The Life of H. L. Mencken* (New York: Harper, 1950);

Sara Mayfield, *The Constant Circle: H. L. Mencken and His Friends* (New York: Delacorte, 1968);

Carl Bode, *Mencken* (Carbondale: Southern Illinois University Press, 1969);

Fred C. Hobson Jr., *Mencken: A Life* (New York: Random House, 1994);

Edward A. Martin, *In Defense of Marion: The Love of Marion Bloom and H. L. Mencken* (Athens & London: University of Georgia Press, 1996).

References:

William E. Cain, "A Lost Voice of Dissent: H. L. Mencken in Our Time," *Sewanee Review,* 104 (Spring 1996): 229–247;

John Dorsey, ed., *On Mencken* (New York: Knopf, 1980);

Charles A. Fecher, *Mencken: A Study of His Thought* (New York: Knopf, 1978);

Vincent Fitzpatrick, *H. L. Mencken* (New York: Continuum, 1989);

Fred C. Hobson Jr., *Serpent in Eden: H. L. Mencken and the South* (Chapel Hill: University of North Carolina Press, 1974);

Edward A. Martin, *H. L. Mencken and the Debunkers* (Athens: University of Georgia Press, 1984);

William H. Nolte, *H. L. Mencken, Literary Critic* (Middleton, Conn.: Wesleyan University Press, 1966);

Sheldon L. Richman, "Mr. Mencken and the Jews," *American Scholar,* 59 (Summer 1990): 407–411;

Thomas P. Riggio, "Dreiser and Mencken in the Literary Trenches," *American Scholar,* 54 (Spring 1985): 227–238;

Melita Schaum, "H. L. Mencken and American Cultural Masculinism," *Journal of American Studies,* 29 (December 1995): 379–398;

Charles Scruggs, *The Sage in Harlem: H. L. Mencken and the Black Writers of the 1920s* (Baltimore & London: Johns Hopkins University Press, 1984);

M. K. Singleton, *H. L. Mencken and the American Mercury Adventure* (Durham, N.C.: Duke University Press, 1962);

Douglas C. Stenerson, *H. L. Mencken: Iconoclast from Baltimore* (Chicago & London: University of Chicago Press, 1971);

Stenerson, ed., *Critical Essays on H. L. Mencken* (Boston: G. K. Hall, 1987);

William H. A. Williams, *H. L. Mencken Revisited* (New York: Twayne, 1998).

Journal:
Menckeniana: A Quarterly Review, 1– (Spring 1962–).

Website:
The Mencken Society Home Page: <http://www.mencken.org>.

Papers:
Principal collections of H. L. Mencken's papers are in The Mencken Room, Enoch Pratt Free Library, Baltimore; the Manuscripts and Archives Division, New York Public Library; and the Rare Books and Special Collections, Princeton University Library.

Cumulative Index

Dictionary of Literary Biography, Volumes 1-222
Dictionary of Literary Biography Yearbook, 1980-1998
Dictionary of Literary Biography Documentary Series, Volumes 1-19

Cumulative Index

DLB before number: *Dictionary of Literary Biography,* Volumes 1-222
Y before number: *Dictionary of Literary Biography Yearbook,* 1980-1998
DS before number: *Dictionary of Literary Biography Documentary Series,* Volumes 1-19

D

E

G

O

ISBN 0-7876-3131-0